PHILIP'S

DRIVER'S [ATLAS] Britain

G000107934

Contents

www.philips-maps.co.uk

First published in 2006 by Philip's
a division of Octopus Publishing Group Ltd,
2–4 Heron Quays, London E14 4JP
www.octopus-publishing.co.uk
An Hachette Livre UK company
www.hachettelivre.co.uk

Fourth edition 2009
First impression 2009

Cartography by Philip's

Data for the speed cameras provided by **PocketGPSWorld.com** Ltd.

Information for National Parks, Areas of Outstanding Natural Beauty, National Trails and Country Parks in Wales supplied by the Countryside Council for Wales.

Information for National Parks, Areas of Outstanding Natural Beauty, National Trails and Country Parks in England supplied by Natural England. Data for Regional Parks, Long Distance Footpaths and Country Parks in Scotland provided by Scottish Natural Heritage.

Gaelic name forms used in the Western Isles provided by Comhairle nan Eilean.

Data for the National Nature Reserves in England provided by Natural England. Data for the National Nature Reserves in Wales provided by Countryside Council for Wales. Darparwyd data'n ymwneud â Gwarchodfeydd Natur Cenedlaethol Cymru gan Gyngor Cefn Gwlad Cymru.

Information on the location of National Nature Reserves in Scotland was provided by Scottish Natural Heritage.

Data for National Scenic Areas in Scotland provided by the Scottish Executive Office.

Printed in India

Route-finding system

Town names printed in yellow on a green background are those used on Britain's signposts to indicate primary destinations. To find your route quickly and easily, simply follow the signs to the primary destination immediately beyond the place you require.

Below Driving from St Ives to Camborne, follow the signs to Redruth, the first primary destination beyond Camborne. These will indicate the most direct main route to the side turning for Camborne.

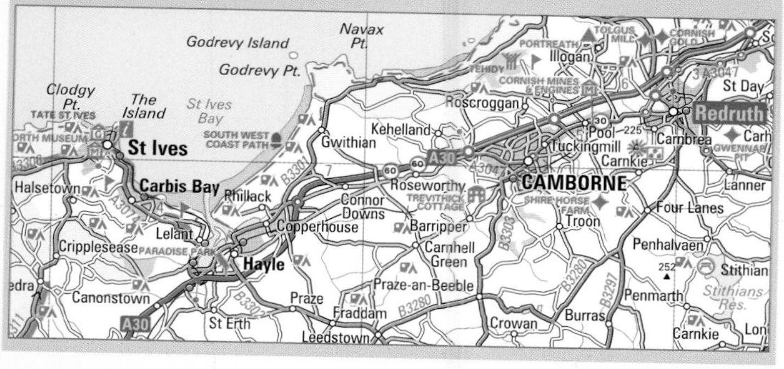

Speed Cameras

Fixed camera locations are shown using the ⓸⓪ symbol.

In congested areas the ⓸⓪ symbol is used to show that there are two or more cameras on the road indicated.

Due to the restrictions of scale the camera locations are only approximate and cannot indicate the operating direction of the camera.

Mobile camera sites, and cameras located on roads not included on the mapping are not shown. Where two or more cameras are shown on the same road, drivers are warned that this may indicate that a SPEC system is in operation. These cameras use the time taken to drive between the two camera positions to calculate the speed of the vehicle.

Road map symbols

- **Motorway, toll motorway**
- **Motorway junction** – full, restricted access
- **Motorway service area** – full, restricted access
- **Motorway under construction**
- **Primary route** – dual, single carriageway
- **Service area, roundabout, multi-level junction**
- **Numbered junction** – full, restricted access
- **Primary route under construction**
- **Narrow primary route**
- **Primary destination** (Derby)
- **A road** – dual, single carriageway (A34)
- **A road under construction, narrow A road**
- **B road** – dual, single carriageway (B2135)
- **B road under construction, narrow B road**
- **Minor road** – over 4 metres, under 4 metres wide
- **Minor road with restricted access**
- **Distance in miles**
- **Scenic route**
- **Speed camera** – single, multiple
- **Toll, steep gradient** – arrow points downhill
- **Tunnel**
- **National trail** – England and Wales
- **Long distance footpath** – Scotland
- **Railway with station**
- **Level crossing, tunnel**
- **Preserved railway with station**
- **National boundary**
- **County / unitary authority boundary**
- **Car ferry, catamaran**
- **Passenger ferry, catamaran**
- **Hovercraft**
- **Ferry destination, journey time** – hrs : mins (CALAIS 1:30)
- **Car ferry** – river crossing
- **Principal airport, other airport**
- **National park**
- **Area of Outstanding Natural Beauty** – England and Wales
  National Scenic Area – Scotland
  forest park / regional park / national forest
- **Woodland**
- **Beach**
- **Linear antiquity**
- **Roman road**
- **Hillfort, battlefield** – with date (1066)
- **Viewpoint, nature reserve, spot height** – in metres (795)
- **Golf course, youth hostel, sporting venue**
- **Camp site, caravan site, camping and caravan site**
- **Shopping village, park and ride** (P&R)
- **Adjoining page number** – road maps (29)

Tourist information

- **Abbey/cathedral/priory**
- **Ancient monument**
- **Aquarium**
- **Art gallery**
- **Bird collection / aviary**
- **Castle**
- **Church**
- **Country park** – England and Wales
- **Country park** – Scotland
- **Farm park**
- **Garden**
- **Historic ship**
- **House**
- **House and garden**
- **Motor racing circuit**
- **Museum**
- **Picnic area**
- **Preserved railway**
- **Race course**
- **Roman antiquity**
- **Safari park**
- **Theme park**
- **Tourist information centre** – open all year
- **Tourist information centre** – open seasonally
- **Zoo**
- **Other place of interest**

Relief

Feet	metres
3000	914
2600	792
2200	671
1800	549
1400	427
1000	305
0	0

Road map scale: 1: 265 320, 4·2 miles to 1 inch

0 1 2 3 4 5 6 7 8 9 miles

0 1 2 3 4 5 6 7 8 9 10 11 12 13 14 15km

NORTH SEA
ATLANTIC OCEAN
SCOTLAND
NORTHERN
Orkney Islands
Outer Hebrides
Lewis
Harris
North Uist
South Uist
Skye
Inner Hebrides
Mull
Jura
Islay
Arran
North Minch
Moray Firth
Firth of Forth
Firth of Clyde
North Channel
Thurso
Wick
Durness
Ledmore
Ullapool
Kincardine
Gairloch
Invergordon
Elgin
Fraserburgh
Peterhead
Uig
Achnasheen
Inverness
Kyle of Lochalsh
Aberdeen
Newtonmore
Braemar
Mallaig
Fort William
Montrose
Forfar
Arbroath
Dundee
Oban
Crianlarich
Perth
St. Andrews
Glenrothes
Stirling
Kirkcaldy
Dunfermline
Falkirk
Edinburgh
Greenock
Clydebank
Cumbernauld
Airdrie
Glasgow
Paisley
Coatbridge
Livingston
Largs
East Kilbride
Motherwell
Peebles
Berwick-upon-Tweed
Coldstream
Galashiels
Irvine
Kilmarnock
Jedburgh
Hawick
Ayr
Sanquhar
Moffat
Alnwick
Campbeltown
Girvan
Ashington
Morpeth
Tynemouth
Newcastle upon Tyne
South Shields
Dumfries
Gretna
Carlisle
Hexham
Gateshead
Sunderland
Washington
Cairnryan
Stranraer
Newton Stewart
Castle Douglas
Durham
Hartlepool
Penrith
Redcar
Dunfanaghy
Londonderry
Limavady
Coleraine
Ballymoney
Dunglow
Letterkenny
Strabane
Ballymena
Larne
Stranorlar
Newtownstewart
Cookstown
Antrim
Newtownabbey
Carrickfergus
Bangor
Killybegs
Donegal
A9
A99
A836
A838
A894
A835
A832
A890
A87
A887
A82
A830
A86
A96
A98
A90
A920
A95
A941
A944
A97
A939
A93
A924
A827
A828
A85
A816
A84
A83
A811
A91
A92
M90
M9
M80
M8
A1
A68
A7
A6112
A697
A71
A702
A703
A72
A736
A78
A77
A76
M74
A708
A712
A713
A714
A75
A74(M)
A696
A69
A686
A689
A692
A19
A1(M)
M6
A595
A596
N56
N13
N14
N15
A5
A2
A37
A29
A26
A6
A36
M2
A8
A505

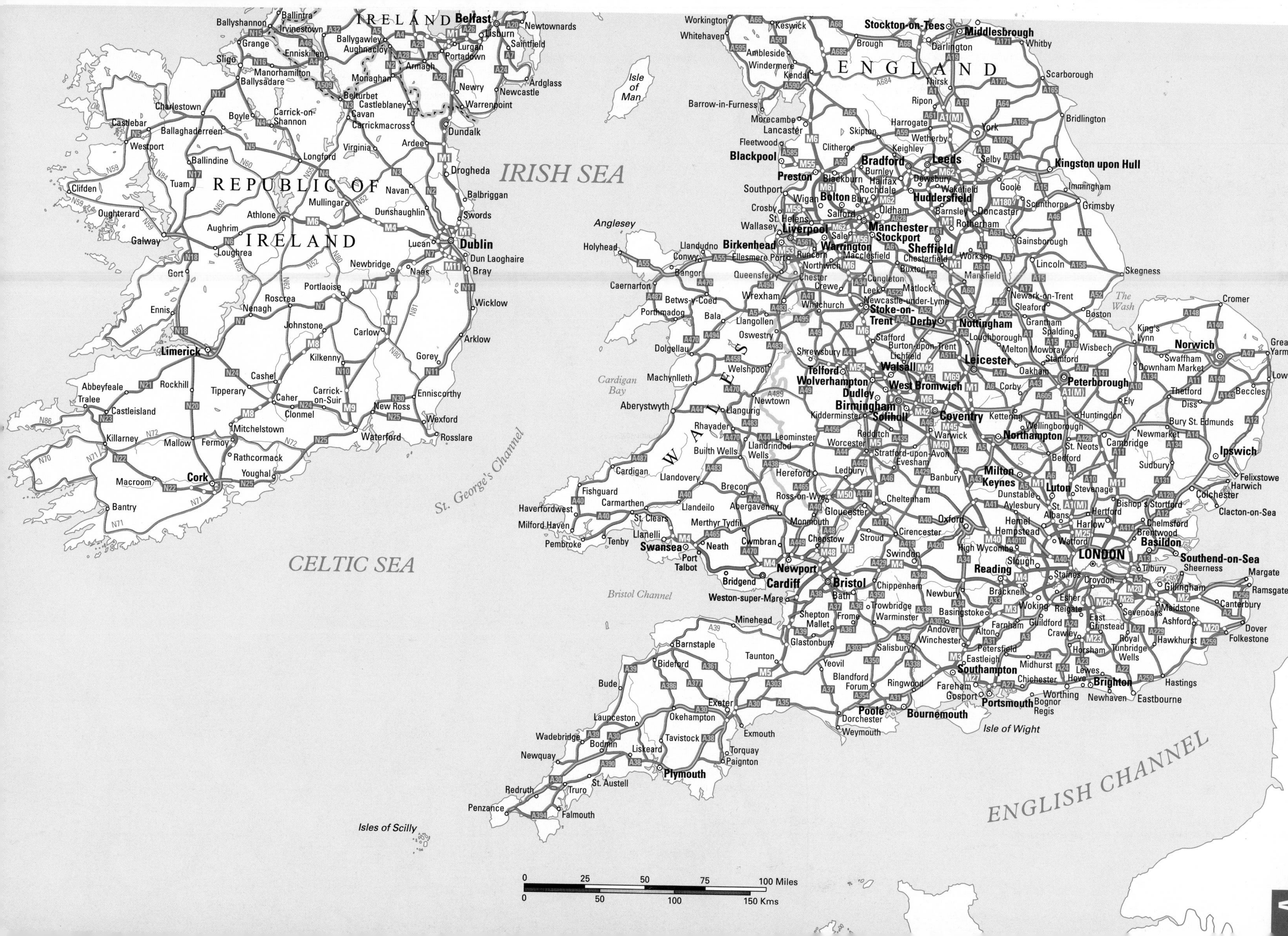
ENGLAND
WALES
IRELAND
REPUBLIC OF IRELAND
IRISH SEA
CELTIC SEA
ENGLISH CHANNEL
St. George's Channel
Bristol Channel
Cardigan Bay
The Wash
Isle of Man
Anglesey
Isle of Wight
Isles of Scilly
LONDON
Birmingham
Manchester
Liverpool
Leeds
Sheffield
Bradford
Kingston upon Hull
Middlesbrough
Stockton-on-Tees
Nottingham
Leicester
Derby
Coventry
Wolverhampton
Stoke-on-Trent
Norwich
Ipswich
Peterborough
Northampton
Milton Keynes
Luton
Reading
Southampton
Portsmouth
Bournemouth
Poole
Brighton
Bristol
Cardiff
Newport
Swansea
Plymouth
Exeter
Cambridge
Oxford
Belfast
Dublin
Cork
Limerick
Galway
Waterford
Wexford
Sligo
Dundalk
0 25 50 75 100 Miles
0 50 100 150 Kms

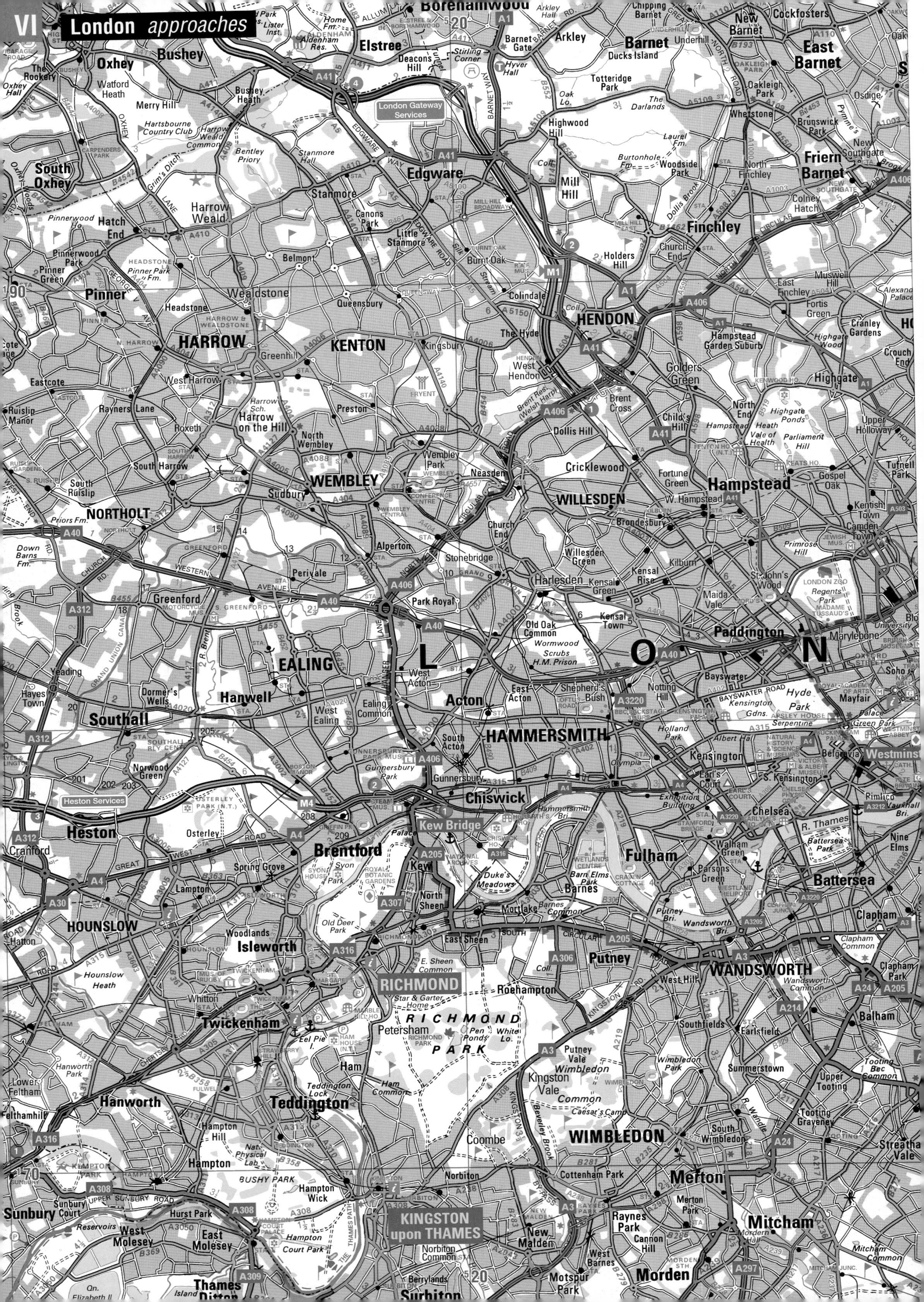
Borehamwood
Elstree
Bushey
Oxhey
Arkley
Barnet
New Barnet
Cockfosters
East Barnet
Edgware
Stanmore
Mill Hill
Finchley
Friern Barnet
Whetstone
Harrow Weald
Hatch End
Pinner
HARROW
KENTON
Kingsbury
Colindale
HENDON
Golders Green
Highgate
Hampstead
Eastcote
Ruislip Manor
Rayners Lane
Wembley
WEMBLEY
Neasden
Cricklewood
WILLESDEN
NORTHOLT
Sudbury
Alperton
Perivale
Greenford
Harlesden
Kilburn
Kensal Green
Maida Vale
Paddington
Marylebone
EALING
Hanwell
Southall
Acton
HAMMERSMITH
Shepherd's Bush
Notting Hill
Bayswater
Mayfair
Kensington
Chelsea
Belgravia
Westminster
Hyde Park
L O N
Heston
Heston Services
Brentford
Chiswick
Kew Bridge
Kew
Fulham
Battersea
Barnes
Mortlake
HOUNSLOW
Isleworth
RICHMOND
East Sheen
Putney
WANDSWORTH
Clapham
Roehampton
Twickenham
RICHMOND PARK
Petersham
Ham
Teddington
Hanworth
Balham
Earlsfield
Tooting
WIMBLEDON
Kingston Vale
Coombe
Hampton
Hampton Wick
Norbiton
KINGSTON upon THAMES
Merton
Mitcham
Morden
New Malden
Sunbury
West Molesey
East Molesey
Thames Ditton
Surbiton
London Gateway Services
M1
M4
A1
A3
A4
A40
A41
A406

Loughton
Chigwell
Hainault
Chingford
Edmonton
Tottenham
Wood Green
Walthamstow
Woodford
South Woodford
Wanstead
Redbridge
Leytonstone
Leyton
Stoke Newington
Islington
Hackney
Stratford
West Ham
East Ham
ILFORD
BARKING
Dagenham
Goodmayes
Becontree
Seven Kings
Southgate
Finsbury
Holborn
City
Southwark
Lambeth
Bermondsey
Rotherhithe
Poplar
Blackwall Tunnel
Millwall
Greenwich
Deptford
CAMBERWELL
Brixton
Peckham
Lewisham
Blackheath
Charlton
WOOLWICH
Woolwich Ferry
Thamesmead
Plumstead
Abbey Wood
Welling
Bexleyheath
BEXLEY
Eltham
Sidcup
Catford
Hither Green
Lee
Forest Hill
Sydenham
Penge
Beckenham
BROMLEY
Chislehurst
Streatham
Norbury
Thornton Heath
South Norwood
Selhurst
Dulwich Village
Thames
Royal Victoria Dock
Royal Albert Dock
Thames Barrier
D
O
N
Scale 1:100 000
0
1
2
3
4
5km

Distance table

Supporting

THINK!

Travel safe – Don't drive tired

How to use this table

Distances are shown in miles and, in *italics*, kilometres.
For example, the distance between Aberdeen and Bournemouth is 564 miles or *908* kilometres.

Place	Swansea	Stranraer	Southampton	Shrewsbury	Sheffield	Portsmouth	Plymouth	Oxford	Oban	Nottingham	Norwich	Newcastle upon Tyne	Manchester	Liverpool	Lincoln	Leicester	Leeds	Land's End	Kyle of Lochalsh	Kingston upon Hull	John o' Groats	Inverness	Holyhead	Harwich	Great Yarmouth	Gloucester	Glasgow	Fort William	Fishguard	Exeter	Edinburgh	Dundee	Dover	Doncaster	Carlisle	Cardiff	Cambridge	Bristol	Brighton	Braemar	Bournemouth	Blackpool	Birmingham	Berwick-upon-Tweed	Ayr	Aberystwyth	Aberdeen	London
Aberdeen																																																517 / 832
Aberystwyth																																															445 / 716	211 / 340
Ayr																																														317 / 510	183 / 295	394 / 634
Berwick-upon-Tweed																																													134 / 216	311 / 501	182 / 293	352 / 567
Birmingham																																												274 / 441	289 / 465	114 / 183	420 / 676	117 / 188
Blackpool																																											123 / 198	181 / 291	180 / 290	153 / 246	308 / 496	226 / 364
Bournemouth																																										270 / 435	147 / 237	412 / 663	436 / 702	207 / 333	564 / 908	107 / 172
Braemar																																									524 / 843	281 / 452	385 / 620	148 / 238	143 / 230	405 / 652	59 / 95	482 / 776
Brighton																																								534 / 859	92 / 148	286 / 460	163 / 262	409 / 658	446 / 718	253 / 407	573 / 922	52 / 84
Bristol																																							147 / 237	477 / 768	82 / 132	204 / 328	81 / 130	362 / 583	370 / 595	125 / 201	493 / 793	122 / 196
Cambridge																																						169 / 272	116 / 187	438 / 705	154 / 248	208 / 335	100 / 161	306 / 493	357 / 575	214 / 344	471 / 758	54 / 87
Cardiff																																					190 / 306	45 / 72	182 / 293	483 / 778	117 / 188	209 / 336	103 / 166	368 / 592	382 / 615	105 / 169	505 / 813	157 / 253
Carlisle																																				289 / 465	264 / 425	277 / 446	370 / 596	196 / 316	343 / 552	87 / 140	196 / 315	87 / 140	93 / 150	224 / 360	221 / 356	301 / 484
Doncaster																																			142 / 229	209 / 336	116 / 187	175 / 282	236 / 380	310 / 499	235 / 378	94 / 151	94 / 151	184 / 296	235 / 378	176 / 283	344 / 554	171 / 275
Dover																																		242 / 390	389 / 626	238 / 383	125 / 201	202 / 325	82 / 132	553 / 890	174 / 280	312 / 502	194 / 312	424 / 683	478 / 769	297 / 478	588 / 947	71 / 114
Dundee																																	523 / 842	275 / 443	152 / 245	441 / 710	406 / 654	430 / 692	517 / 832	52 / 84	495 / 797	239 / 385	349 / 562	113 / 182	117 / 188	376 / 605	67 / 108	448 / 721
Edinburgh																																56 / 90	462 / 744	219 / 352	96 / 154	385 / 620	345 / 555	373 / 600	456 / 734	91 / 146	439 / 707	183 / 295	292 / 470	57 / 92	73 / 117	320 / 515	125 / 201	390 / 628
Exeter																															450 / 724	518 / 834	248 / 399	251 / 404	353 / 568	121 / 195	249 / 401	76 / 122	184 / 296	550 / 885	82 / 132	282 / 454	157 / 253	428 / 689	446 / 718	201 / 323	569 / 916	181 / 291
Fishguard																														230 / 370	399 / 642	460 / 740	331 / 533	247 / 398	297 / 478	112 / 180	270 / 435	154 / 248	291 / 468	493 / 794	222 / 357	209 / 336	170 / 274	371 / 597	373 / 600	56 / 90	504 / 811	260 / 418
Fort William																													486 / 782	560 / 901	144 / 232	127 / 204	596 / 959	357 / 575	206 / 332	485 / 781	479 / 771	486 / 782	575 / 926	125 / 201	539 / 867	296 / 476	392 / 631	190 / 306	133 / 214	430 / 692	149 / 240	510 / 821
Glasgow																												101 / 163	376 / 605	449 / 723	44 / 71	83 / 134	488 / 786	249 / 401	96 / 154	385 / 620	372 / 599	373 / 600	468 / 753	110 / 177	439 / 707	183 / 295	292 / 470	101 / 163	33 / 53	320 / 515	145 / 233	397 / 639
Gloucester																											346 / 557	454 / 731	153 / 246	111 / 179	349 / 562	410 / 660	191 / 307	150 / 241	247 / 398	56 / 90	123 / 198	35 / 56	159 / 256	443 / 713	99 / 159	174 / 280	56 / 90	318 / 512	330 / 531	102 / 164	468 / 753	109 / 175
Great Yarmouth																										225 / 362	419 / 674	527 / 848	366 / 589	335 / 539	386 / 621	484 / 779	185 / 298	167 / 269	320 / 515	284 / 457	82 / 132	275 / 443	180 / 290	477 / 768	240 / 386	252 / 406	180 / 290	345 / 555	402 / 647	294 / 473	517 / 832	128 / 206
Harwich																									82 / 132	196 / 316	432 / 695	543 / 874	337 / 542	279 / 449	413 / 665	469 / 755	125 / 201	194 / 312	336 / 541	246 / 396	67 / 108	217 / 349	128 / 206	504 / 811	187 / 301	275 / 443	167 / 269	372 / 599	425 / 684	281 / 452	535 / 861	76 / 122
Holyhead																								349 / 562	334 / 538	191 / 307	330 / 531	438 / 705	167 / 269	282 / 454	333 / 536	394 / 634	360 / 580	181 / 291	231 / 372	216 / 348	270 / 435	206 / 332	334 / 538	426 / 686	288 / 463	141 / 227	148 / 238	311 / 501	305 / 491	111 / 179	439 / 707	269 / 433
Inverness																							474 / 763	569 / 916	553 / 890	504 / 811	166 / 267	66 / 106	542 / 872	618 / 995	158 / 254	132 / 212	622 / 1001	383 / 617	262 / 422	549 / 884	505 / 813	539 / 867	617 / 993	75 / 121	597 / 961	348 / 560	458 / 737	215 / 346	199 / 320	486 / 782	105 / 169	550 / 885
John o' Groats																						129 / 208	603 / 970	693 / 1116	677 / 1090	628 / 1011	295 / 475	195 / 314	671 / 1080	744 / 1197	285 / 459	259 / 417	746 / 1201	507 / 816	391 / 629	680 / 1094	630 / 1014	668 / 1075	741 / 1193	202 / 325	724 / 1165	478 / 769	574 / 924	342 / 550	328 / 528	601 / 967	232 / 373	663 / 1067
Kingston upon Hull																					518 / 834	394 / 634	231 / 372	196 / 316	207 / 333	169 / 272	254 / 409	369 / 594	280 / 451	309 / 497	234 / 377	295 / 475	256 / 412	47 / 76	158 / 254	244 / 393	139 / 224	233 / 375	245 / 394	327 / 526	264 / 425	127 / 204	134 / 216	185 / 298	251 / 404	223 / 359	364 / 586	184 / 296
Kyle of Lochalsh																				445 / 716	189 / 304	84 / 135	514 / 827	611 / 983	602 / 969	528 / 850	179 / 288	79 / 127	567 / 913	628 / 1011	216 / 348	186 / 299	671 / 1080	432 / 695	275 / 443	564 / 908	555 / 893	552 / 888	651 / 1048	159 / 256	618 / 995	372 / 599	471 / 758	263 / 423	212 / 341	499 / 803	189 / 304	586 / 943
Land's End																			763 / 1228	421 / 678	868 / 1397	741 / 1193	405 / 652	390 / 628	446 / 718	235 / 378	573 / 922	686 / 1104	353 / 568	123 / 198	574 / 924	642 / 1033	381 / 613	374 / 602	477 / 768	245 / 394	374 / 602	200 / 322	308 / 496	665 / 1070	205 / 330	405 / 652	281 / 452	552 / 888	570 / 917	313 / 504	692 / 1114	297 / 478
Leeds																		405 / 652	394 / 634	55 / 89	487 / 784	360 / 579	176 / 283	223 / 359	196 / 315	174 / 280	215 / 346	329 / 530	237 / 381	270 / 435	202 / 325	258 / 415	260 / 418	29 / 47	119 / 192	232 / 373	145 / 233	194 / 312	260 / 419	293 / 472	255 / 410	72 / 116	113 / 182	156 / 251	212 / 341	169 / 272	327 / 526	189 / 304
Leicester																	95 / 153	320 / 515	500 / 805	102 / 164	588 / 947	461 / 742	190 / 306	147 / 237	140 / 225	85 / 137	314 / 505	422 / 679	209 / 336	196 / 315	296 / 476	349 / 562	185 / 298	74 / 119	206 / 332	154 / 248	68 / 109	120 / 193	166 / 267	389 / 626	158 / 254	140 / 225	39 / 63	252 / 406	299 / 481	153 / 246	414 / 666	97 / 156
Lincoln																51 / 82	68 / 109	371 / 597	476 / 766	44 / 71	554 / 892	427 / 687	216 / 348	155 / 249	128 / 206	159 / 256	291 / 468	399 / 642	272 / 438	247 / 398	258 / 415	314 / 505	202 / 325	39 / 63	191 / 307	208 / 335	85 / 137	183 / 295	197 / 317	357 / 575	209 / 336	128 / 206	90 / 145	224 / 360	274 / 441	199 / 320	383 / 616	131 / 211
Liverpool															129 / 208	130 / 209	75 / 121	361 / 581	407 / 655	130 / 209	511 / 822	382 / 615	102 / 164	265 / 427	240 / 386	140 / 225	216 / 348	329 / 530	160 / 257	237 / 381	216 / 348	286 / 460	299 / 481	86 / 138	120 / 193	169 / 272	194 / 312	161 / 259	272 / 438	318 / 512	234 / 377	49 / 79	93 / 150	219 / 352	213 / 343	104 / 167	341 / 549	202 / 325
Manchester														35 / 56	84 / 135	92 / 148	40 / 64	361 / 581	406 / 654	95 / 153	500 / 805	373 / 600	124 / 200	228 / 367	212 / 341	126 / 203	215 / 346	329 / 530	197 / 317	236 / 380	215 / 346	285 / 459	276 / 444	61 / 98	119 / 192	183 / 295	165 / 266	161 / 259	257 / 414	318 / 512	227 / 365	48 / 77	80 / 129	196 / 315	212 / 341	129 / 208	340 / 547	185 / 298
Newcastle upon Tyne													132 / 212	168 / 270	159 / 256	187 / 301	92 / 148	498 / 802	318 / 512	132 / 212	395 / 636	268 / 431	272 / 438	308 / 496	281 / 452	266 / 428	148 / 238	253 / 407	329 / 529	364 / 586	110 / 177	166 / 267	358 / 576	114 / 183	57 / 92	325 / 523	241 / 388	299 / 481	352 / 567	201 / 323	347 / 558	129 / 208	207 / 333	64 / 103	149 / 240	257 / 414	235 / 378	286 / 460
Norwich												264 / 425	185 / 298	220 / 354	105 / 169	119 / 192	176 / 283	421 / 678	582 / 937	149 / 240	654 / 1053	529 / 852	311 / 501	73 / 117	20 / 32	204 / 328	385 / 620	504 / 811	343 / 552	308 / 496	366 / 589	422 / 679	174 / 280	147 / 237	289 / 465	262 / 422	62 / 100	252 / 406	175 / 282	457 / 735	214 / 344	232 / 373	166 / 267	328 / 528	382 / 615	276 / 444	496 / 798	114 / 183
Nottingham											130 / 209	157 / 253	73 / 118	98 / 158	35 / 56	25 / 40	70 / 113	345 / 555	479 / 771	90 / 145	557 / 896	430 / 692	185 / 298	150 / 241	153 / 246	110 / 177	293 / 472	401 / 646	220 / 354	221 / 356	262 / 422	328 / 528	205 / 330	43 / 69	194 / 312	172 / 277	83 / 134	145 / 233	193 / 311	353 / 568	183 / 295	111 / 179	50 / 80	221 / 356	274 / 441	164 / 264	393 / 633	122 / 196
Oban										390 / 628	492 / 792	233 / 375	307 / 494	308 / 496	387 / 623	419 / 674	307 / 494	665 / 1070	128 / 206	346 / 557	244 / 393	117 / 188	427 / 687	524 / 843	515 / 829	441 / 710	92 / 148	49 / 79	481 / 774	549 / 884	123 / 198	117 / 188	585 / 942	346 / 557	188 / 303	477 / 768	468 / 753	465 / 748	565 / 910	141 / 227	530 / 853	285 / 459	384 / 618	180 / 290	94 / 151	412 / 663	178 / 286	499 / 803
Oxford									462 / 744	109 / 175	145 / 233	260 / 418	144 / 232	172 / 277	137 / 221	73 / 117	168 / 270	274 / 441	550 / 885	192 / 309	656 / 1056	532 / 856	238 / 383	145 / 233	200 / 322	52 / 84	356 / 573	472 / 760	205 / 330	156 / 251	372 / 599	433 / 697	141 / 227	145 / 233	260 / 418	108 / 174	83 / 134	74 / 119	108 / 174	465 / 749	90 / 145	187 / 301	64 / 103	324 / 521	353 / 568	154 / 248	483 / 777	57 / 92
Plymouth								199 / 320	587 / 945	267 / 430	343 / 552	410 / 660	283 / 455	283 / 455	293 / 472	242 / 389	316 / 509	89 / 143	674 / 1085	355 / 571	790 / 1271	664 / 1069	328 / 528	309 / 497	365 / 588	157 / 253	495 / 797	595 / 958	264 / 425	46 / 74	496 / 798	552 / 888	300 / 483	297 / 478	399 / 642	167 / 269	293 / 472	122 / 196	224 / 361	587 / 945	128 / 206	328 / 528	203 / 327	474 / 763	492 / 792	237 / 382	615 / 990	218 / 351
Portsmouth							176 / 283	77 / 124	545 / 877	191 / 307	207 / 333	337 / 542	236 / 380	254 / 409	201 / 323	162 / 261	257 / 414	259 / 417	633 / 1019	269 / 433	737 / 1186	613 / 987	311 / 501	166 / 267	221 / 356	119 / 192	448 / 721	555 / 893	251 / 404	135 / 217	453 / 729	514 / 827	130 / 209	234 / 377	348 / 560	142 / 229	144 / 232	97 / 156	48 / 77	547 / 881	52 / 84	264 / 425	141 / 227	401 / 645	430 / 692	222 / 357	560 / 901	70 / 113
Sheffield						230 / 370	283 / 455	135 / 217	339 / 546	37 / 60	146 / 235	125 / 201	38 / 61	72 / 116	46 / 74	62 / 100	33 / 53	361 / 581	427 / 687	65 / 105	520 / 837	393 / 632	168 / 270	187 / 301	166 / 267	126 / 203	248 / 399	348 / 560	215 / 346	237 / 381	235 / 378	291 / 468	245 / 394	18 / 29	152 / 245	194 / 312	120 / 193	161 / 259	226 / 364	320 / 515	216 / 348	86 / 138	76 / 122	190 / 306	245 / 394	159 / 256	360 / 579	159 / 256
Shrewsbury					82 / 132	207 / 333	225 / 362	106 / 171	364 / 586	93 / 150	205 / 330	201 / 323	69 / 111	58 / 93	133 / 214	84 / 135	109 / 175	303 / 488	451 / 726	169 / 272	567 / 912	438 / 705	113 / 182	240 / 386	225 / 362	77 / 124	272 / 438	382 / 615	145 / 233	179 / 288	274 / 441	330 / 531	251 / 404	109 / 175	176 / 283	111 / 179	159 / 256	103 / 166	226 / 364	371 / 597	185 / 298	98 / 158	45 / 72	265 / 426	269 / 433	77 / 124	399 / 642	160 / 258
Southampton				185 / 298	199 / 320	21 / 34	151 / 243	64 / 103	530 / 853	176 / 283	206 / 332	324 / 521	221 / 356	239 / 385	204 / 328	137 / 220	232 / 373	228 / 367	618 / 995	256 / 412	723 / 1164	598 / 963	293 / 472	164 / 264	220 / 354	105 / 169	433 / 697	541 / 871	233 / 375	105 / 169	438 / 705	500 / 805	143 / 230	209 / 336	324 / 521	121 / 195	148 / 238	76 / 122	61 / 98	532 / 856	31 / 50	251 / 404	128 / 206	388 / 624	417 / 671	201 / 323	547 / 880	77 / 124
Stranraer			445 / 716	277 / 446	263 / 423	461 / 742	500 / 805	379 / 610	148 / 238	290 / 467	403 / 649	158 / 254	220 / 354	221 / 356	298 / 480	330 / 531	220 / 354	585 / 942	263 / 423	259 / 417	379 / 610	262 / 422	338 / 544	410 / 660	426 / 686	343 / 552	84 / 135	195 / 314	392 / 631	454 / 731	124 / 200	167 / 269	496 / 798	257 / 414	101 / 163	390 / 628	379 / 610	378 / 608	475 / 765	194 / 312	444 / 715	188 / 303	297 / 478	170 / 274	51 / 82	325 / 523	228 / 367	402 / 647
Swansea		417 / 671	161 / 259	118 / 190	217 / 349	182 / 293	206 / 332	141 / 227	506 / 815	192 / 309	301 / 485	347 / 559	187 / 301	195 / 314	233 / 375	177 / 285	248 / 399	285 / 459	594 / 956	264 / 425	696 / 1120	572 / 921	184 / 296	267 / 430	329 / 530	89 / 143	409 / 658	496 / 798	67 / 108	161 / 259	412 / 663	473 / 761	274 / 441	232 / 373	309 / 497	41 / 66	227 / 365	85 / 137	222 / 357	505 / 813	167 / 269	216 / 348	119 / 192	383 / 616	379 / 610	73 / 117	507 / 816	194 / 312
York	272 / 438	222 / 357	258 / 415	133 / 214	52 / 84	278 / 448	333 / 536	181 / 291	309 / 497	77 / 124	181 / 291	84 / 135	64 / 103	99 / 159	75 / 121	108 / 174	24 / 39	411 / 661	407 / 655	37 / 60	479 / 771	352 / 566	204 / 328	228 / 367	201 / 323	189 / 304	217 / 349	330 / 531	261 / 420	287 / 462	194 / 312	250 / 402	282 / 454	34 / 55	121 / 195	244 / 393	165 / 266	222 / 357	275 / 443	285 / 459	269 / 433	96 / 154	130 / 209	148 / 238	214 / 344	195 / 314	319 / 513	207 / 333

Key to road map pages

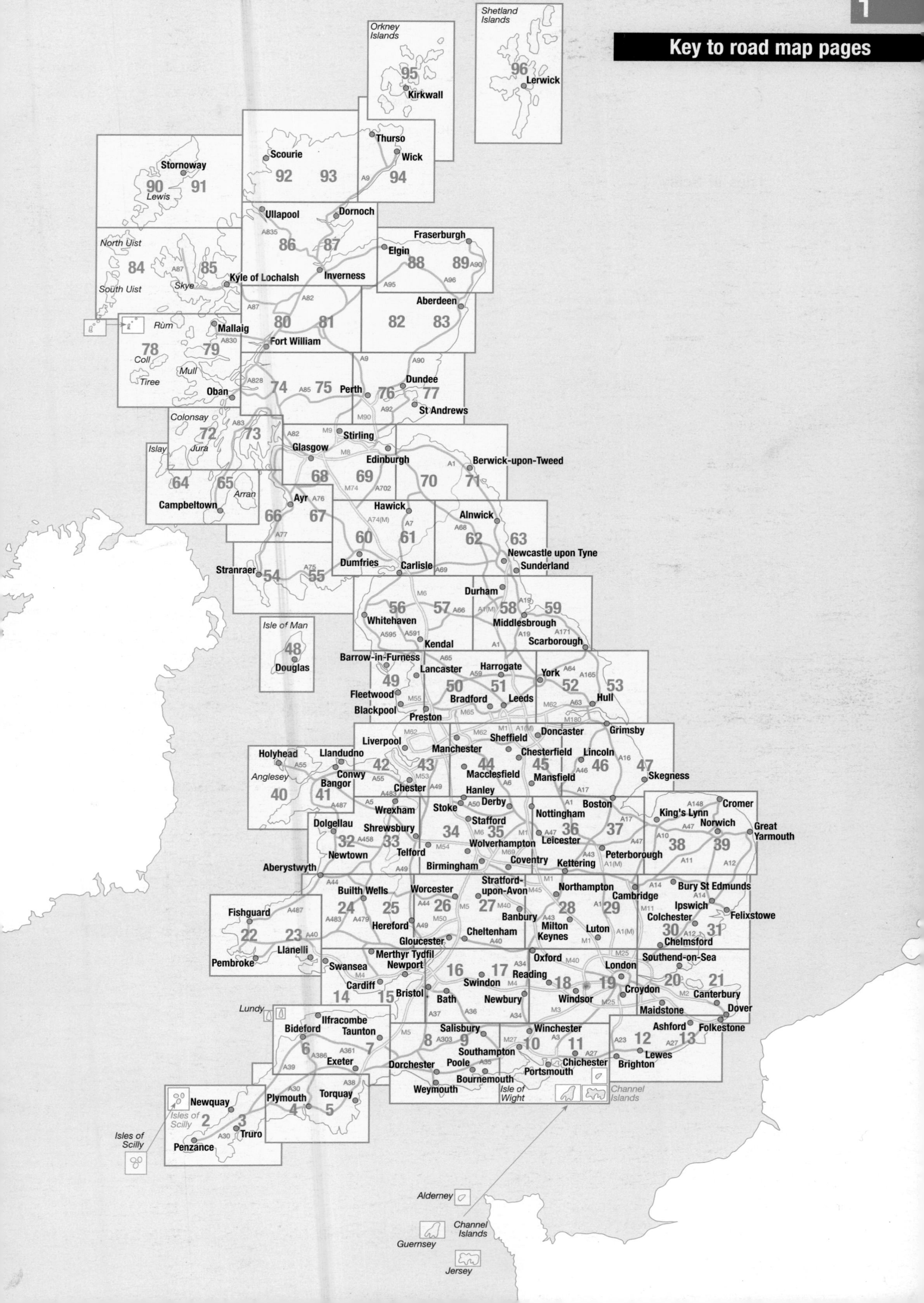

Isles of Scilly
SV
White Island
St Helens
St Martin's
King Charles Castle
Bryher
Cromwell's Castle
New Grimsby
Higher Town
Tresco
Tresco Abbey Gardens
Eastern Isles
Samson
Crow Sound
Bant's Carn
Innisidgen Cairns
Newford
Maypole
Longstone Heritage Cen
St Mary's
North West Passage
Crim Rocks
Hugh Town
Old Town
Garrison Walls
Broad Sound
Annet
Smith Sound
St Mary's Sound
Gugh
St Agnes
Penzance 2:40 (Apr-Nov)
Bishop Rock
SW
CORNWALL
MOUNT'S BAY
St Agnes Hd.
St Agnes
Perranporth
South West Coast Path
Trevellas
Porthtowan
Mount Hawke
Three Burrows
Blackwater
Portreath
Mawla
Illogan
Scorrier
Navax Pt.
Godrevy Island
Godrevy Pt.
St Day
Redruth
Carharrack
Roscroggan
Pool
Tuckingmill
Carnkie
Camborne
Cambrea
Gwithian
Kehelland
The Carracks
Clodgy Pt.
The Island
St Ives Bay
Tate St Ives
Barbara Hepworth Museum
St Ives
Carbis Bay
Lelant
Gurnard's Head
Zennor
Towednack
Halsetown
Phillack
Connor Downs
Copperhouse
Roseworthy
Barripper
Troon
Four Lanes
Lanner
Porthmeor
Wayside Folk Museum
Cripplesease
Paradise Park
Hayle
Carnhell Green
Praze-an-Beeble
Penhalvaen
Stithians
Morvah
Bojewyan
Nancledra
Canonstown
Praze
Erdaddam
Penmarth
Pendeen
Geevor Tin Mine Museum
Chysauster Ancient Village
St Erth
Leedstown
Crowan
Burras
Carnkie
Longdowns
Higher Boscaswell
Trewellard
Newmill
Carnyorth
Botallack
Drym
Releath
Porkellis
Rame
Cape Cornwall
St Just
Madron
Ludgvan
Gulval
Crowlas
Townshend
Relubbus
Nancegollan
Wendron
Seworgan
Penzance Heliport
Trengwainton
Newbridge
Heamoor
Chyandour
St Hilary
Godolphin Cross
Trescowe
The Bisons
Ballowall Barrow
Bosavern
Marazion
Goldsithney
Crowntown
Kelynack
Sancreed
Penzance
St Michael's Mount
Perranuthnoe
Germoe
Ashton
Sithney
Breage
Constantine
Carn Euny Ancient Village
Lower Drift
Tredavoe
Trinity House National Lighthouse Centre
Praa Sands
Trewennack
Whitesand Bay
Brane
Catchall
Newlyn
Newlyn Art Gallery
Cudden Pt.
Rinsey
Helston
Sennen Cove
Crows-an-wra
Kerris
Paul
Mousehole
Gweek
Longships
Sennen
St Buryan
Trewoofe
St Clement's Island
Trewavas Hd.
Porthleven
Flambards Experience
Mawgan
Land's End
Polgigga
Lamorna
The Loe
Porthcurno
Treen
Boskenna
Tregiffian Burial Chamber
Lamorna Cove
Porthleven Sands
Garras
St Martin
Gunwalloe
Berepper
Newtown
St Levan
Minack Open Air Theatre
Cury
Cross Lanes
Gwennap Hd.
Runnel Stone
Goonhilly
Mullion
Penhale
Goonhilly Downs
Mullion Cove
Mullion Island
Isles of Scilly 2:40 (Apr-Nov)
Predannack Wollas
Kuggar
Vellan Hd.
St Ruan
Ruan Minor
Grade
Cadgwith
Kynance Cove
Lizard
Landewednack
Hot Pt.
Lizard Point
0 1 2 3 4 5 6 miles
0 1 2 3 4 5 6 7 8 9 10 km

6
7
8
9
10
11
Camelford
Delabole
Valley Truckle
Helstone
Port Isaac Bay
Port Isaac
Port Quin
Port Gaverne
Pentire Pt.
New Polzeath
Padstow Bay
Polzeath
Trebetherick
Gulland Rock
TREVOSE HEAD
Gunver Hd.
St Minver
Pityme
Trewethern
Chapel Amble
St Endellion
Trelights
Pendoggett
St Teath
Treveighan
Trelill
Michaelstow
St Tudy
St Kew
St Kew Highway
St Breward
Row
High Moor
ROUGH TOR
BROWN WILLY
GARROW TOR
MUSEUM OF SMUGGLING
Codda
Bolventor
Altarnun
Trewint
St Clether
Laneast
Polyphant
Lewannick
Congdon's Shop
Trebartha
North Hill
Constantine Bay
Treyarnon
Trevone
Padstow
St Merryn
Shop
Porthcothan
Rock
Little Petherick
Bodieve
Trevanson
Whitecross
Wadebridge
Egloshayle
St Breock
Burlawn
St Mabyn
Wenfordbridge
Bradford
Blisland
Helland
BODMIN MOOR
Temple
Dozmary Pool
Colliford Lake
KILMAR TOR
Henwood
Upton Cross
Rilla Mill
Minions
THE HURLERS STONE CIRCLES
Siblyback Lake
CARADON HILL
Darite
Commonmoor
Park Hd.
Penrose
St Ervan
Rumford
Tredinnick
St Issey
St Jidgey
Washaway
Bodmin Forest
Millpool
Maidenwell
Warleggan
Cardinham
Mount
St Neot
St Cleer
Tremar
Trenance
St Eval
Berryl's Pt.
Trevarrian
St Mawgan
Talskiddy
WATERGATE BAY
Tregurrian
Rosenannon
Rutherbridge
Withiel
Nanstallon
Bodmin
St Lawrence
Ley
Dobwalls
Liskeard
Merrymeet
St Columb Major
St Wenn
Tregonetha
Lanivet
Lanhydrock House
West Taphouse
East Taphouse
Doublebois
St Pinnock
Towan Hd.
Newquay Bay
Fistral Bay
Porth
St Columb Minor
Kelsey Hd.
Pentire
Crantock
West Pentire
Newquay
Quintrell Downs
Trebudannon
Colan
Mountjoy
Belowda
Victoria
Lockengate
Trebyan
Sweetshouse
Redmoor
Braddock
Herodsfoot
St Keyne
Trewidland
Duloe
Holywell
Cubert
Carines
Lane
Kestle Mill
St Columb Road
Fraddon
Penhale
Trevarren
Indian Queens
Ruthvoes
Tregoss
Roche
Bilberry
Bugle
Trezaise
Lostwithiel
Lanlivery
Couch's Mill
Milltown
Bocaddon
St Newlyn East
Gummow's Shop
St Enoder
St Dennis
Whitemoor
Hensbarrow Downs
Stenalees
Luxulyan
Penhale Sands
Mount
Rejerrah
Rose
Retew
Treviscoe
Nanpean
Carthew
Penwithick
Penpillick
Lerryn
Lanreath
Muchlarnick
Sandplace
Morval
Summercourt
Brighton
Trethosa
Foxhole
Trethurgy
St Blazey
Golant
St Veep
Penpoll
Pelynt
Cornwall
St Martin
Perranporth
Goonhavern
Bolingey
Newlyn Downs
Mitchell
Carland Cross
Trelassick
High Street
St Stephen
Carclaze
Boscoppa
St Austell
Par
Tywardreath
Lanteglos Highway
Trenewan
Looe
East Looe
West Looe
Zelah
Perranzabuloe
St Allen
Callestick
Trispen
St Erme
Ladock
New Mills
Coombe
Trewoon
St Mewan
Holmbush
Charlestown
Polkerris
Menabilly
Fowey
Bodinnick
Polruan
Lansallos
Polperro
Portballow
Looe Bay
Talland Bay
St George's or Looe I.
Marazanvose
Allet
Grampound Road
Sticker
Polgooth
Porthpean
ST. AUSTELL BAY
Gribbin Hd.
Pencarrow Hd.
Hewas Water
Probus
Grampound
Trenarren
Black Hd.
Shortlanesend
Tresillian
Creed
St Ewe
Pentewan
Mevagissey Bay
Truro
Kenwyn
Threemilestone
Chacewater
Tresawle
Merther
Polmassick
Kestle
Mevagissey
SX
Baldhu
Kea
St Clement
Tregony
Portmellon
Chapel Pt.
Trevarrick
Gorran Churchtown
Gorran Haven
St Michael Caerhays
Twelve Heads
Bissoe
Malpas
Ruan Lanihorne
Playing Place
Old Kea
St Michael Penkevil
Lamorran
Carnon Downs
Portholland
Boswinger
Penare
Dodman Pt.
Perranarworthal
Penpol
Trelissick
Philleigh
Treworga
Veryan
Portloe
Veryan Bay
Devoran
Feock
Treworlas
Carne
Gerrans Bay
Nare Hd.
Ponsanooth
Burnthouse
Mylor Bridge
St Just in Roseland
Trewithian
Gerrans
Portscatho
Carrick Roads
Penryn
Flushing
Mabe Burnthouse
Falmouth
St Mawes
Bohortha
Greeb Pt.
Budock Water
Pendennis Pt.
Zone Pt.
Penjerrick
Falmouth Bay
Mawnan Smith
Rosemullion Hd.
Mawnan
Helford River
Helford
St Anthony-in-Meneage
Nare Pt.
Manaccan
Porthallow
Porthoustock
Manacle Pt.
The Manacles
St Keverne
Lowland Pt.
Coverack
Chynhalls Pt.
Black Hd.
C O R N W A L L
E
F
G
H

BUDE BAY
Widemouth Bay
Widemouth Sand
Upton
Marhamchurch
Bridgerule
Derril
Pyworthy
Derriton
Holsworthy
Chasty
Whimble
Hollacombe
Brandis Corner
Highampton
Graddon Moor
Chilla
Winsford Walled Garden
Halwill Junction
CORNWALL
Dizzard Pt.
Millook
Poundstock
Coppathorne
Budd's Titson
Lewworthy
Halwill
Beaworthy
Northlew
Oak Cross
South West Coast Path
Tregole
Treskinnick Cross
Week St Mary
Whitstone
North Tamerton
Clawton
Quoditch
Patchacott
Ashbury
Broadbury
St Gennys
Trewint
Penhallam
Cambeak
Crackington Haven
Rosecare
Jacobstow
Tetcott
Lana
Luffincott
Ashwater
Henford
Eworthy
Wainhouse Corner
Germansweek
Boasley Cross
Thorndon Cross
Tresparrett Posts
West Curry
Chapmans Well
Virginstow
Fire Beacon Pt.
Beeny
Marshgate
South Wheatley
Maxworthy
Bennacott
Northcott
East Panson
Grinacombe Moor
Roadford Res.
Bratton Clovelly
Sourton Cross Services
Boscastle
Tresparrett
Otterham
Canworthy Water
Brazacott
Boyton
St Giles on the Hth.
Lesnewth
Trelash
Warbstow
Tamar Otter & Wildlife Centre
Langdon
Gridley Corner
Sourton
Tintagel Hd.
Castle
Old Post Office
Trevalga
Bossiney
Tintagel
Tremaine
Treneglos
North Petherwin
Bridgetown
Broadwoodwidger
Bridestowe
Trekn ow
Trewarmett
Davidstow
Hallworthy
Tresmeer
Yeolmbridge
Werrington
Cross Green
Thrushelton
Stowford
Shortacombe
Start Pt.
Trebarwith
The Arthurian Centre
Trewassa
Tremail
Tregeare
Egloskerry
Langore
Dingle's Fairground Heritage Centre
Lewdown
Lewtrenchard
Treligga
British Cycling Mus
Cold Northcott
Hidden Valley Discovery Park
Dutson
Launceston Steam Railway
Liftondown
Portgate
Lydford
Delabole
South West Coast Path
Camelford
Davidstow Moor
St Clether
Laneast
Piper's Pool
Trethorne Leisure Farm
Tregadillett
St Stephen's
Launceston
Lifton
Tinhay
Coryton
Lydford Gorge
Port Isaac Bay
Valley Truckle
Crowdy Res.
Trewen
Daw's House
Lawhitton
Kelly
Chillaton
North Brentor
Willsworthy
Helstone
Polyphant
Inny
South Petherwin
Bradstone
Black Down
Port Gaverne
St Teath
Treveighan
High Moor
400 Rough Tor
420 Brown Willy
Altarnun
Trewint
Lewannick
Dunterton
Milton Abbot
Mary Tavy
Horndon
Michaelstow
369
Codda
Congdon's Shop
Lezant
Trekenner
Rezare
Cudliptown
Trelill
St Kew
St Breward
331 Garrow Tor
Museum of Smuggling
Bolventor
Trebartha
Trebullett
Treburley
Sydenham Damerel
Lamerton
Peter Tavy
Wilminstone
St Tudy
Row
North Hill
Coad's Green
Merrivale
St Kew Highway
Bradford
Wenfordbridge
BODMIN MOOR
Dozmary Pool
396 Kilmar Tor
Bathpool
Bray Shop
Stoke Climsland
Horsebridge
Tavistock
Blisland
Colliford Lake
Henwood
Linkinhorne
Luckett
Latchley
St Mabyn
Temple
342
Rilla Mill
South Hill
Downgate
Chilsworthy
Gulworthy
Whitchurch
Camel
Upton Cross
The Hurlers Stone Circles
Minions
369 Caradon Hill
Kelly Bray
Kit Hill
Toll
St Ann's Chapel
Gunnislake
Grenofen
Sampford Spiney
Egloshayle
Pencarrow House
Helland
268
Millpool
Maidenwell
Siblyback Lake
Darite
Golberdon
Haye
Trevigro
Pensilva
Callington
Harrowbarrow
Albaston
Drakewalls
Higher Walreddon
Horrabridge
Walkhampton
Washaway
Bodmin Forest
Bodmin
Warleggan
Commonmoor
Golitha Falls
King Doniert's Stone
Trethevy Quoit
Tremar
Dupath Well House
Morwellham Quay
Buckland
The Garden House
Paperweight Centre
Dousland
Cardinham
St Neot
St Cleer
Gang
St Ive
Newbridge
Cotehele
St Dominick
Calstock
Monachorum
TAMAR VALLEY
Crapstone
Yelverton
Nanstallon
Mount
Carnglaze Slate Caverns
Ley
Merrymeet
Bere Alston
Buckland Abbey
Milton Combe
St Lawrence
Bodmin and Wenford Railway
Fowey
Dobwalls
Doublebois
Pengover Green
162
St Mellion
Weir Quay
Lopwell
Clearbrook
Lanhydrock House
West Taphouse
East Taphouse
St Pinnock
Liskeard
Quethiock
Pillaton
Cornwall
Lanivet
Trebyan
Restormel Castle
Braddock
Menheniot
Blunts
Hatt
Cargreen
Bere Ferrers
Shaugh Prior
Bickleigh
Lockengate
Sweetshouse
Redmoor
Herodsfoot
St Keyne
Music Machines
Tideford Cross
Landrake
Botusfleming
Landulph
Saltash Services
Tamerton Foliot
Roborough
Bilberry
Lostwithiel
Trewidland
Tideford
Trematon
Saltash
Toll
Crownhill Fort
Plymouth City
Plym
Fores
Bugle
Lanlivery
Couch's Mill
208
Duloe
Trerulefoot
Hessenford
St Erney
St Stephens
Crownhill
Eggbuckland
Luxulyan
Milltown
Bocaddon
Lanreath Folk & Farm Museum
Widegates
St Germans
Mary Newman's Cottage
St Budeaux
Plymouth
Stenalees
Penwithick
Penpillick
Lerryn
Lanreath
Sandplace
Morval
Polbathic
Sheviock
Antony House
P&R
Plympton
Treverbyn
Trethurgy
Eden Project
St Blazey
Golant
St Veep
Penpoll
Muchlarnick
Pelynt
St Martin
Monkey Sanctuary
Seaton
Downderry
Crafthole
Torpoint
Antony
Devonport
Merchant's House
Plymouth
Carclaze
Boscoppa
Tywardreath
Looe
East Looe
Looe Museum
Portwrinkle
Cremyll
Royal Citadel
Plymstock
Elburton
St. Austell
Par
Lanteglos Highway
Trenewan
West Looe
Looe Bay
South West Coast Path
Freathy
St John
Mount Edgcumbe
Drake's I.
Hooe
Holmbush
Shipwreck & Heritage Centre
Charlestown
St Austell Brewery
Polkerris
Menabilly
Bodinnick
Fowey
Polruan
St Catherine's Castle
Porthallow
Lansallos
Polperro
Heritage Museum
Talland Bay
St George's or Looe I.
Whitsand Bay
Millbrook
Kingsand
The Sound
Staddiscombe
Polgooth
Porthpean
ST. AUSTELL BAY
Pencarrow Hd.
Cawsand
Bovisand Bay
Down Thomas
Knighton
Trenarren
Gribbin Hd.
Rame
Heybrook Bay
Wembury
Black Hd.
Rame Hd.
Penlee Pt.
Wembury Bay
Pentewan
Great Mew Stone
Worswell
World of Model Railways
Mevagissey
Chapel Pt.
Gorran Churchtown
Gorran Haven
Roscoff 6:00
Santander 20:00
(Mar-Nov)
Penare
A39
A30
A395
A388
A386
A390
A38
A374
A387
A3072
A3079
A3082
A389
A391
B3254
B3262
B3263
B3266
B3314
B3257
B3362
B3268
B3269
B3253
B3359
B3247
B3252
B3254
B3357
B3413
B3273
B3374
0 1 2 3 4 5 6 miles
0 1 2 3 4 5 6 7 8 9 10 km

5
EXETER
Crediton
Okehampton
DARTMOOR
DARTMOOR NATIONAL FOREST PARK
DEVON
Moretonhampstead
Chagford
Bovey Tracey
Chudleigh
Topsham
Exmouth
Budleigh Salterton
Dawlish
Teignmouth
Kingsteignton
NEWTON ABBOT
Torquay
Paignton
TORBAY
Brixham
Tor Bay
Torbay
Ashburton
Buckfastleigh
Totnes
Dartmouth
Kingswear
Ivybridge
Kingsbridge
Salcombe
Modbury
Princetown
Two Bridges
Postbridge
Widecombe in the Moor
Berry Head
Start Point
Bolt Tail
Bolt Hd.
Prawle Pt.
Start Bay
Bigbury Bay
Slapton Sands
Babbacombe Bay
Hope's Nose
Straight Pt.
Scabbacombe Hd.
Mew Stone
Stoke Pt.
Burgh I.
Bigbury on Sea
SOUTH DEVON
A30
A38
A380
A385
A381
A379
A377
A3052
A376
A382
A386
M5
6
7
8
9
10
11
B
C
D
E
F
G
H

LUNDY
North West Point
North East Point
LUNDY MARINE NATURE RESERVE
South West Point
Surf Point
ILFRACOMBE 2:00
BIDEFORD 2:00
LUNDY 2:00
Highveer Pt.
Woody Bay
CLIFF RAILWAY
Lynton
Martinhoe
Trentishoe
Heale
Barbrook
Rillage Pt.
OLD CORN MILL
Combe Martin Bay
Ilfracombe
ILFRACOMBE MUSEUM
WATERMOUTH CASTLE
Hele
Berrynarbor
Combe Martin
Girt Down
Sterridge
Bull Pt.
Rockham Bay
Lee
Whitestone
Slade
Morte Point
Mortehoe
Woolacombe
MORTE BAY
Woolacombe Sand
SOUTH WEST COAST PATH
Trimstone
Cheglinch
Berry Down
Bittadon
Berry Down Cross
Patchole
Kentisbury
Kentisbury Ford
Blackmoor Gate
Parracombe
Martinhoe Cross
Shallowford
Challacombe Common
Challacombe
Shoulsbarrow Common
EXM
Pickwell
Baggy Pt.
Putsborough
North Buckland
Dean
West Down
East Down
Churchill
Arlington
EXMOOR ZOO
Croyde Bay
Georgeham
Croyde
Nethercott
Darracott
Halsinger
Milltown
Muddiford
Loxhore
Knightacott
Lobb
Knowle
Marwood
Guineaford
Kingsheanton
Shirwell
Shirwell Cross
Bratton Fleming
Lewworthy
Saunton
Braunton
Pippacott
ELLIOTT GALLERY
MARWOOD HILL GARDENS
Prixford
Stoke Rivers
Benton
Lydcott
Saunton Sands
Heanton Punchardon
Wrafton
TOLL
Ashford
Burridge
Braunton Burrows
Chivenor
Barnstaple
Goodleigh
Brayford
High Bray
Taw
Pilton
Gunn
MUSEUM OF NORTH DEVON
Charles
Fremington
Westacott
Yelland
Bickington
Bickleton
P&R
Newport
Landkey
West Buckland
East Buckland
NORTH DEVON MARITIME MUSEUM
Instow
Bishops Tawton
Swimbridge Newland
NORTH DEVON FARM PARK
Swimbridge
NORTHAM BURROWS
Appledore
BIDEFORD BAY
NORTH DEVON
Westward Ho!
TAPELEY PARK GDNS
Westleigh
Tawstock
Northam
Filleigh
HARTLAND POINT
Windbury Pt.
Orchard Hill
Eastleigh
Horwood
Newton Tracey
Cobbaton
Titchberry
THE BIG SHEEP
Bideford
Herner
East Stowford
QUINCE HONEY FARM
HARTLAND ABBEY
Abbotsham
BURTON ART GALL & MUS
East-the-Water
Woodtown
Hiscott
Ensis
Chapelton
COBBATON COMBAT COLL
Chittlehampton
South Molton
Stoke
CLOVELLY VILLAGE
Clovelly
Handy Cross
Alverdiscott
Fishleigh Barton
artland Quay
Hartland
Fairy Cross
Ford
ATLANTIC VILLAGE
Landcross
Umberleigh
Clapworthy
Buck's Mills
Horns Cross
Woodtown
Yarnscombe
Atherington
SOUTH WEST COAST PATH
DOCTON MILL
Philham
Higher Clovelly
Littleham
Warkleigh
George Nympton
Milford
Eddistone
THE MILKY WAY ADVENTURE PARK
Buck's Cross
Goldsworthy
Langridge Ford
Satterleigh
ELMSCOTT
Elmscott
Tosberry
Weare Giffard
Sherwood Green
Chittlehamholt
Parkham
Buckland Brewer
Monkleigh
High Bullen
High Bickington
Woolfardisworthy
Parkham Ash
DARTINGTON CRYSTAL
Hartland Forest
Alminstone Cross
Frithelstock
St Giles in the Wood
King's Nympton
South Hole
Great Torrington
Frithelstock Stone
Welcombe
Meddon
Ashmansworthy
Tythecott
Taddiport
R.H.S. GARDEN ROSEMOOR
Kingscott
Roborough
Cadbury Barton
Knaps
Woolley
Gooseham
Eastcott
West Putford
East Putford
Little Torrington
Burrington
Elstone
Morwenstow
Youlstone
GNOME RESERVE & GARDEN
Langtree
Dinworthy
Beaford
Shop
Bulkworthy
Stibb Cross
Riddlecombe
Chulmleigh
Woodford
BROCKLANDS ADVENTURE PARK
Bradworthy
Peters Marland
Ashreigney
Bradworthy Cross
Abbots Bickington
Newton St Petrock
Woollaton
Winswell
Chawleigh
Coombe
Kilkhampton
Alfardisworthy
Sutcombe
Venn Green
Merton
Huish
Dolton
Ashley
Stibb
Milton Damerel
Buckland Filleigh
Hollocombe
Soldon Cross
Dowland
Wembworthy
Petrockstow
Shebbear
Holsworthy Beacon
Thornbury
Meeth
Iddesleigh
Winkleigh
Coldridge
Nymet Rowland
Flexbury
Poughill
Hersham
DUNSDON
Brushford
Bude
Stratton
Grimscott
Bradford
Woodacott
Chilsworthy
Sheepwash
Broadwood Kelly
West Leigh
Black Torrington
Monkokehampton
Launcells
Pancrasweek
Cookbury
Holemoor
Bondleigh
East Leigh
Upton
Derril
Derriton
Holsworthy
Brandis Corner
Highampton
Hatherleigh
Zeal Monachorum
Marhamchurch
Bridgerule
Pyworthy
Chasty
Whimble
Hollacombe
Graddon Moor
WINSFORD WALLED GARDEN
Honeychurch
Bow
Widemouth Bay
Chilla
Exbourne
Jacobstowe
North Tawton
Coppathorne
Leworthy
Halwill Junction
Sampford Courtenay
Halwill
Beaworthy
Northlew
Inwardleigh
Itton
Treskinnick Cross
Clawton
Oak Cross
DARTMOOR RAILWAY
Whitstone
Week St Mary
North Tamerton
Quoditch
Patchacott
Ashbury
Folly Gate
Taw Green
PENHALLAM
BROADBURY
Spreyton
Jacobstow
Tetcott
Lana
Okehampton
Ashwater
Eworthy
Luffincott
Henford
Germansweek
Boasley Cross
Thorndon Cross
Sticklepath
FINCH FOUNDRY
South Tawton
South Zeal
South Wheatley
West Curry
Chapmans Well
Virginstow
SOURTON CROSS SERVICES
CASTLE
OKEHAMPTON (Dartmoor)
Okehampton Camp
Belstone
Whiddon Down
Maxworthy
Northcott
East Panson
Roadford Res.
Grinacombe Moor
Meldon
BRACKEN TOR
Okehampton Common
COSDON HILL
Throwleigh
Canworthy Water
Bennacott
Brazacott
Boyton
Bratton Clovelly
St Giles on the Hth.
YES TOR
Sandypark
Warbstow
TAMAR OTTER & WILDLIFE CENTRE
Langdon
Gridley Corner
Sourton
Wonson
Broadwoodwidger
Bridestowe
BLACK-A-TOR COPSE
HIGH WILLHAYS
Gidleigh
Easton
Tremaine
North Petherwin
Bridgetown
Thrushel
Bridestowe and Sourton Common
Murchington
Hallworthy
Treneglos
Werrington
Cross Green
Thrushelton
Chagford
Tresmeer
Yeolmbridge
DINGLE'S FAIRGROUND HERITAGE CENTRE
Stowford
Lewdown
Shortacombe
OKEMENT HILL
Teigncombe
Egloskerry
Langore
HANGINGSTONE HILL
Frenchbeer
Tregeare
St Stephens
Dutson
Liftondown
Portgate
Lewtrenchard
Cold Northcott
HIDDEN VALLEY DISCOVERY PARK
LAUNCESTON STEAM RAILWAY
Lydford
THE MINIATURE PONY CENTRE
Piper's Pool
Launceston
Lifton
Tinhay
DARTMOOR
DARTMOOR FOREST
Lettaford
TRETHORNE LEISURE FARM
Tregadillett
CASTLE
St Clether
Laneast
Coryton
LYDFORD GORGE
SITTAFORD TOR
CUT HILL
Lawhitton
North Brentor
Black Down
Willsworthy
Kelly
Chillaton
South Petherwin
Bradstone
Altarnun
Lewannick
GRIMSPOUND
0 1 2 3 4 5 6 miles
0 1 2 3 4 5 6 7 8 9 10 km

Foreland Pt.
Lynmouth Bay
Countisbury
Lynmouth
Brendon
Malmsmead
Porlock Weir
Porlock Bay
Porlock
Hurlstone Pt.
Bossington
Allerford
Selworthy
Minehead
Woodcombe
Alcombe
Dunster
Blue Anchor Bay
BRIDGWATER BAY
Watchet
Williton
East Quantoxhead
Kilve
Stolford
Stogursey
Nether Stowey
EXMOOR
EXMOOR FOREST
NATIONAL PARK
Simonsbath
Exford
Withypool
Winsford
Somerset
BRENDON HILLS
BRENDON FOREST
QUANTOCK FOREST
QUANTOCK HILLS
Dulverton
Bampton
Wiveliscombe
VALE OF TAUNTON DEANE
Taunton
Wellington
BLACKDOWN HILLS
Tiverton
Cullompton
Crediton
Devon
EXETER
Topsham
Exmouth
Budleigh Salterton
Sidmouth
Ottery St Mary
Honiton
Seaton
Beer
Seaton Bay
Beer Hd.
Ladram Bay
EAST DEVON
Moretonhampstead
Danger Pt.

Bridgwater
Glastonbury
Street
Somerton
Taunton
Chard
Ilminster
Crewkerne
Yeovil
Sherborne
Castle Cary
Bruton
Wincanton
Evercreech
Milborne Port
Axminster
Lyme Regis
Seaton
Beer
Bridport
Beaminster
Dorchester
Weymouth
Fortuneswell
Easton
PORTLAND
Bill of Portland
Somerset
Dorset
Devon
Blackdown Hills
Blackmoor
Polden Hills
King's Sedge Moor
West Sedge Moor
Lyme Bay
Chesil Beach
Portland Harbour
Charlton Bay
Seaton Bay
West Bay
South Petherton
Merriott
Martock
Langport
Ilchester
Mudford
Maiden Newton
Cerne Abbas
Abbotsbury
Charmouth
Eggardon Down
Black Down
SY
ST
15
16
7
0 1 2 3 4 5 6 miles
0 1 2 3 4 5 6 7 8 9 10 km

Otham
Harrietsham
Stalisfield Green
Leaveland
Chilham
Street End
Adisham
Leeds
Leeds Castle
Broomfield
Warren Street
Molash
Garlinge Green
Lower Hardres
Bishopsbourne
Aylesham
Nonington
Boughton Monchelsea
Langley
Langley Heath
Lenham
Sandway
Petham
Kingston
Snowdown
Kingswood
Warmlake
Linton
Chart Corner
Sutton Valence
Grafty Green
Boughton Malherbe
Lenham Heath
Charing
Charing Heath
Challock
Godmersham
Sole Street
Upper Hardres Court
Bossingham
Barham
Derringstone
Womenswold
Barfrestone
Chart Sutton
Ulcombe
Westwell Leacon
Westwell
Boughton Aluph
Bilting
Crundale
Waltham
Woolage Green
Eythorne
Rabbit's Cross
Egerton
Egerton Forstal
Little Chart
Ram Lane
Boughton Lees
Goat Lees
Wye
Hassell Street
Stelling Minnis
Denton
Wingmore
Coxhill
Shepherdswell
Coldred
Milebush
Cross-at-Hand
Southernden
Hothfield
Kennington
Brook
Hastingleigh
Bodsham
Elmsted
Lyminge Forest
Wootton
Lydden
Selsted
Hawkenbury
Headcorn
Pluckley
Pluckley Thorne
Godinton House
Elham
Ewell Minnis
Staplehurst
Sinkhurst Green
Smarden Bell
Maltman's Hill
Great Chart
Ashford
Hinxhill
Lymbridge Green
Rhodes Minnis
Ottinge
Swingfield Street
Swingfield Minnis
Marden Thorn
Smarden
Haffenden Quarter
Wissenden
Willesborough
Willesborough Lees
Brabourne
Stowting
Densole
Alkham
Drellingore
Knox Bridge
Frittenden
Lashenden
Bethersden
Sevington
Brabourne Lees
Lyminge
Paddlesworth
Hawkinge
West Hougham
Farthingloe
Cranbrook Common
Three Chimneys
Standen
Stubbs Cross
Kingsnorth
Mersham
Smeeth
Sellindge
Sellindge Lees
Postling
Etchinghill
Channel Tunnel
Capel le Ferne
Biddenden
Tanden
Shadoxhurst
Cheeseman's Green
Beachborough
Stanford
Newington
East Cliff & Warren
East Wear Bay
Sissinghurst
Union Mill
High Halden
Henghurst
Bromley Green
Aldington Frith
Clap Hill
Aldington
Newingreen
Pedlinge
Cheriton
Folkestone
Cranbrook
East End
St Michael's
Shirkoak
Orlestone
Bonnington
Court-at-Street
Lympne
Saltwood
Sandgate
Rotunda
Hartley
Parkgate
Woodchurch
South of England Rare Breeds Cen
Ham Street Woods
Ruckinge
Bilsington
Port Lympne Wild Animal Park and Gardens
Brockhill
Hythe
Tenterden
Benenden
Leigh Green
Brook Street
Kenardington
Warehorne
Hamstreet
Royal Military Canal
West Hythe
Palmarsh
Gill's Green
Iden Green
Dingleden
Rolvenden
Colonel Stephens Railway Museum
Small Hythe
Reading Street
Appledore Heath
Newchurch
Burmarsh
Hawkhurst
Four Throws
Rolvenden Layne
Smallhythe Place
Horne's Place Chapel
Snave
Romney, Hythe and Dymchurch Light Railway
The Moor
Isle of Oxney
Peening Quarter
Appledore
Romney Marsh
Dymchurch
Martello Tower
Sandhurst
Linkhill
Stone
Snargate
St Mary in the Marsh
Sandhurst Cross
Newenden
Wittersham
Brenzett
Ivychurch
Aeronautical Museum
St Mary's Bay
Bodiam
Great Dixter
Rother Levels
Ham Green
The Stocks
Brookland
Old Romney
Littlestone on Sea
TR
Northiam
Ewhurst Green
Beckley
Four Oaks
New Romney
Romney Sands
Millcorner
Clayhill
Iden
Houghton Green
Walland Marsh
Staple Cross
Peasmarsh
Horns Cross
Rye Foreign
Playden
East Guldeford
Greatstone on Sea
Cripp's Corner
Tillingham
Rye
Lydd
Lydd on Sea
Vinehall Street
Broad Oak
Broadland Row
Udimore
Rye Heritage Centre
Camber
Denge Marsh
Sedlescombe
Rye Harbour
Brede
Sedlescombe Street
Denge Beach
Whatlington
Winchelsea
Camber Castle
Rye Bay
Dungeness
Dungeness Power Station & Information Centre
The Old Lighthouse
Guestling Thorn
Winchelsea Court Hall Museum
Winchelsea Beach
Icklesham
Three Oaks
Kent Street
Westfield
Pett
Baldslow
Guestling Green
Cliff End
Crowhurst
Hollington
St Helen's
Ore
Fairlight
Fairlight Cove
Silverhill
St Clement's Caves
St Leonards
Underwater World
West Marina
Bulverhythe
Hastings
Kent
North Downs
Kent Downs
ENGLISH CHANNEL
A229
A274
M20
A20
A252
A28
A2
A262
A268
A21
A259
A2070
B2067
B2080
B2082
B2086
B2165
B2089
20
21
6
7
8
9
10
11
C
D
E
F
G
H

SN
SS
Swansea
Neath
Port Talbot
(Castell-Nedd Port Talbot)
Rhondda Cynon Taff
(Rhondda Cynon Taf)
Bridgend
(Pen-y-bont ar Ogwr)
Vale of Glamorgan
(Bro Morgannwg)
SWANSEA BAY
BAE ABERTAWE
BRISTOL CHANNEL
MÔR HAFREN
EXMOOR
EXMOOR FOREST
NATIONAL PARK
BRENDON HILLS
Ystalyfera
Pontardawe
Pontarddulais
Gorseinon
Clydach
Morriston
Swansea (Abertawe)
The Mumbles (Y Mwmbwls)
Mumbles Hd.
Trwyn yr Mwmbwls
Skewen
Neath (Castell-Nedd)
Baglan
Aberavon
Port Talbot
Margam
Glyn-neath (Glynedd)
Resolven
Hirwaun
Aberdare (Aberdâr)
Merthyr Tydfil (Merthyr Tudful)
Mountain Ash (Aberpennar)
Treorchy (Treorci)
Rhondda
Tonypandy
Porth
Pontypridd
Treharris
Abercynon
Maesteg
Pontycymer
Blaengarw
Cymer
Tonyrefail
Llantrisant
Pencoed
Bridgend (Pen-y-bont ar Ogwr)
Pyle (Y Pîl)
Porthcawl
Kenfig
Ogmore-by-Sea
Southerndown
Tusker Rock
Cowbridge (Y Bont-Faen)
Llantwit Major (Llanilltud Fawr)
Nash Pt.
Trwyn yr As
St Athan
Rhoose (Y Rhws)
Breaksea Pt.
Trwyn Breaksea
Foreland Pt.
Highveer Pt.
Lynmouth
Lynton
Countisbury
Hurlstone Pt.
Porlock Bay
Porlock
Minehead
Blue Anchor Bay
Dunster
Watchet
Williton
Combe Martin
Parracombe
Simonsbath
Exford
Withypool
Dulverton
Wheddon Cross
Barnstaple
M4
A465
A48
0 1 2 3 4 5 6 miles
0 1 2 3 4 5 6 7 8 9 10 km

Monmouthshire
(Sir Fynwy)
Torfaen
(Tor-faen)
Caerphilly
(Caerffili)
Cardiff
(Caerdydd)
Newport
(Casnewydd)
North Somerset
Bristol
Somerset
ABER HAFREN
MOUTH OF THE SEVERN
ST
SO
Rhymney
Blaina
Abertillery
Abersychan
Tredegar
Bargoed
Blackwood
Crumlin
Pontypool
Cwmbran
Usk
Caerleon
Risca
Caerphilly
Chepstow
Caldicot
Newport
CARDIFF
Penarth
Barry
Flat Holm
Steep Holm
Avonmouth
Portishead
Clevedon
Nailsea
Long Ashton
Filton
Patchway
Thornbury
Lydney
Weston-super-Mare
Worle
Wrington
Yatton
Congresbury
Cheddar
Axbridge
Wells
Wedmore
Burnham-on-Sea
Highbridge
Bridgwater
Glastonbury
Street
Shepton Mallet
Blagdon
Keynsham
QUANTOCK FOREST
POLDEN HILLS
King's Sedge Moor
BRIDGWATER BAY
STERT FLATS
BERROW FLATS
M4
M5
M48
M49
A48
A38
A39
A37
A371
25
16
7
8

Gloucestershire
South Gloucestershire
Bristol
Bath and N.E. Somerset
Wiltshire
Chepstow (Cas-gwent)
Lydney
Stroud
Stonehouse
Nailsworth
Dursley
Tetbury
Malmesbury
Wotton-under-Edge
Thornbury
Yate
Chipping Sodbury
Filton
Patchway
Avonmouth
Portishead
Mangotsfield
Kingswood
Hanham
Keynsham
Nailsea
Long Ashton
Bath
Chippenham
Corsham
Melksham
Bradford-on-Avon
Trowbridge
Westbury
Warminster
Frome
Radstock
Midsomer Norton
Paulton
Peasedown St John
Wells
Shepton Mallet
Glastonbury
Street
Cheddar
Wrington
Evercreech
Bruton
Castle Cary
Mere
Caldicot
Frampton on Severn
Berkeley
Sharpness
Chalford
Minchinhampton
Severn Beach
Portbury
Pill
Whitchurch
Saltford
Box
Holt
Chew Magna
Blagdon
Cranborne Chase
Salisbury Plain
Longleat
Tidenham Chase
Oakley Wood
Bruton Forest
0 1 2 3 4 5 6 miles
0 1 2 3 4 5 6 7 8 9 10 km

Cirencester
Fairford
Lechlade-on-Thames
Carterton
South Cerney
Cricklade
Highworth
Faringdon
ABINGDON
Didcot
Wantage
Swindon
Stratton St Margaret
Wootton Bassett
Purton
VALE OF WHITE HORSE
LAMBOURN DOWNS
Lambourn
MARLBOROUGH DOWNS
Marlborough
Hungerford
Newbury
Thatcham
Calne
Devizes
Pewsey
VALE OF PEWSEY
Savernake Forest
Tidworth
Ludgershall
Andover
Whitchurch
Overton
Amesbury
Durrington
Wilton
Stockbridge
Kings Worthy
Berkshire
West
Hampshire
Swindon
NORTH WESSEX DOWNS
SALISBURY PLAIN
Wiltshire

28
17
10
11
West Berkshire
Hampshire
Windsor and Maidenhead
Wokingham
Bracknell Forest
Reading
Slough
North Downs
Surrey
SU
SP
Chiltern Hills
Oxford
ABINGDON
Didcot
Wallingford
Thame
High Wycombe
Princes Risborough
Chesham
Amersham
Beaconsfield
Marlow
Maidenhead
Henley-on-Thames
Newbury
Thatcham
WOKINGHAM
Bracknell
CAMBERLEY
FARNBOROUGH
ALDERSHOT
Farnham
Fleet
Basingstoke
Alton
Haslemere
Guildford
Whitchurch
Overton
Tadley
Hook
Bordon
Grayshott
WINDSOR
Berkhamsted
Wendover
0 1 2 3 4 5 6 miles
0 1 2 3 4 5 6 7 8 9 10 km

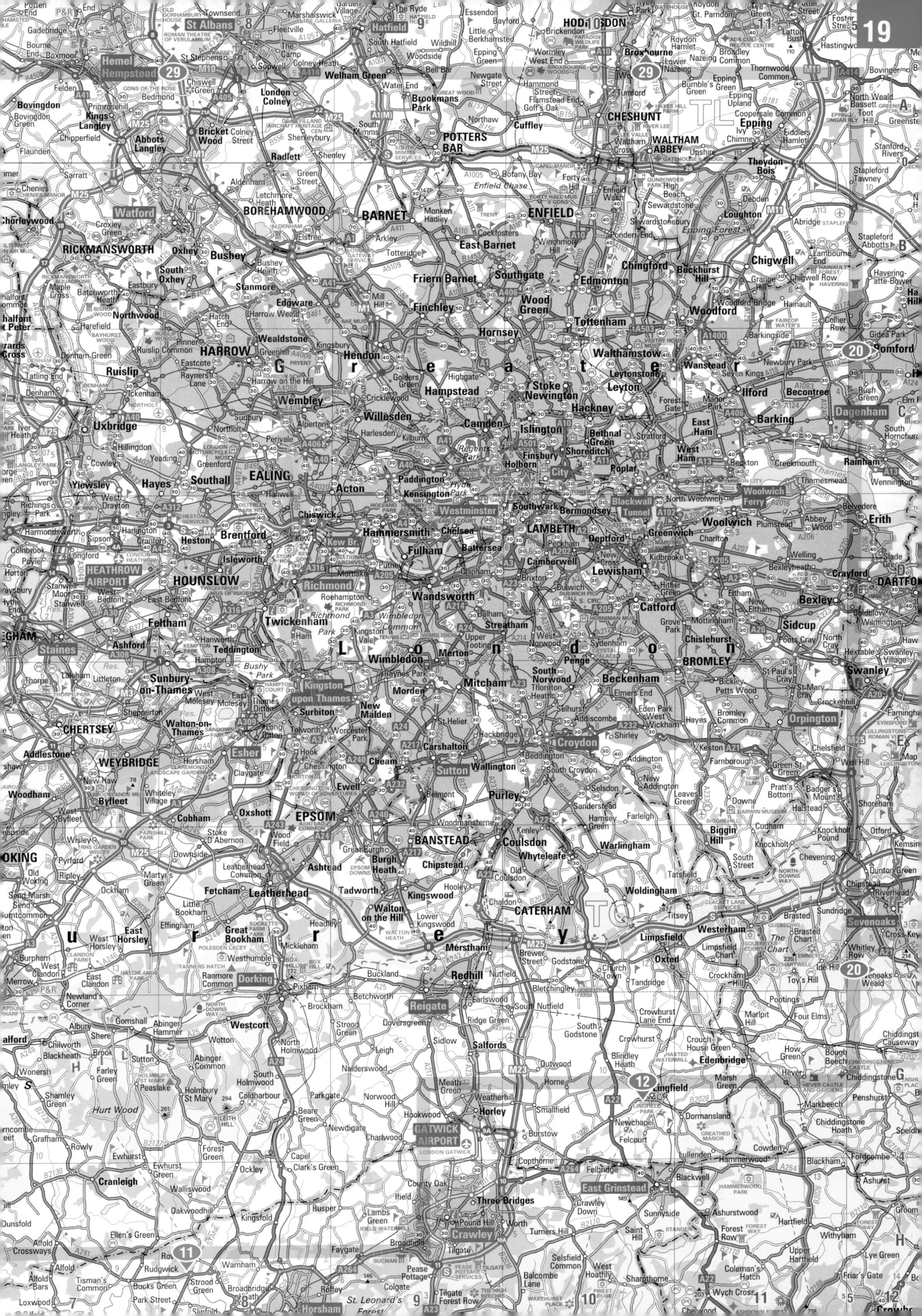
St Albans
Hatfield
Hemel Hempstead
HODDESDON
Broxbourne
CHESHUNT
WALTHAM ABBEY
Epping
POTTERS BAR
Watford
RICKMANSWORTH
BOREHAMWOOD
BARNET
ENFIELD
Chingford
Loughton
Chigwell
HARROW
Wembley
Hampstead
Walthamstow
Ilford
Barking
Dagenham
Romford
Uxbridge
EALING
Southall
Hayes
Acton
Camden
Islington
Hackney
Paddington
Kensington
Westminster
City
Hammersmith
Chelsea
Fulham
Battersea
Southwark
LAMBETH
Bermondsey
Greenwich
Woolwich
Erith
Lewisham
Catford
Bexley
Sidcup
DARTFORD
HEATHROW AIRPORT
HOUNSLOW
Richmond
Wandsworth
Twickenham
Feltham
Staines
Kingston upon Thames
Wimbledon
Merton
Mitcham
Streatham
Beckenham
BROMLEY
Orpington
Swanley
Croydon
Sutton
Purley
EPSOM
Surbiton
Esher
WEYBRIDGE
CHERTSEY
Woodham
Cobham
Leatherhead
BANSTEAD
Coulsdon
CATERHAM
Oxted
Westerham
Sevenoaks
Redhill
Reigate
Dorking
Edenbridge
Lingfield
Horley
GATWICK AIRPORT
Crawley
East Grinstead
Cranleigh
Horsham
Greater London
Surrey

Chelmsford
Maldon
Heybridge
Great Baddow
Danbury
Chipping Ongar
Ingatestone
Billericay
BRENTWOOD
Wickford
Runwell
RAYLEIGH
Hockley
Rochford
Southminster
Burnham-on-Crouch
South Woodham Ferrers
Basildon
Laindon
Pitsea
Thundersley
Hadleigh
Southend-on-Sea
Leigh on Sea
Westcliff-on-Sea
Shoeburyness
CANVEY ISLAND
Romford
Hornchurch
Upminster
Dagenham
Rainham
Thurrock
Stanford-le-Hope
Corringham
Grays
Tilbury
Purfleet
Erith
Dartford Crossing
DARTFORD
Bexley
Sidcup
Crayford
NORTHFLEET
GRAVESEND
Swanscombe
Greenhithe
THAMES ESTUARY
Medway
Sheerness
Minster
ISLE OF SHEPPEY
Strood
ROCHESTER
CHATHAM
Gillingham
Rainham
Walderslade
SITTINGBOURNE
Swanley
Orpington
Sevenoaks
Borough Green
Snodland
Ditton
Maidstone
Bearsted
Kent
Tonbridge
Hildenborough
Paddock Wood
Southborough
ROYAL TUNBRIDGE WELLS
Pembury
Staplehurst
Headcorn
Cranbrook
Tenterden
Charing
Wadhurst
Essex
Kent
0 1 2 3 4 5 6 miles
0 1 2 3 4 5 6 7 8 9 10 km

TM
TR
Bradwell on Sea
Ray Sand
Montsale
Deal Hall
Foulness Sand
Foulness Pt.
Courtsend
Churchend
MAPLIN SANDS
Warden Pt.
Warden
Leysdown-on-Sea
Shell Ness
Isle of Harty
THE SWALE
WHITSTABLE
Tankerton
Swalecliffe
HERNE BAY
Seasalter
Chestfield
Greenhill
Herne
Beltinge
Hillborough
Reculver
RECULVER
RECULVER TOWERS AND ROMAN FORT
Minnis Bay
Birchington
Westgate on Sea
Margate
THE SHELL GROTTO
Cliftonville
Foreness Pt.
Kingsgate
NORTH FORELAND
Northdown
St Peter's
BROADSTAIRS
BLEAK HOUSE
DICKENS HOUSE MUSEUM
Dumpton
Newington
Ramsgate
MARITIME MUSEUM
OOSTENDE 4:00
BOULOGNE 1:15
Isle of Thanet
QUEX HOUSE
SPITFIRE AND HURRICANE MEM
Northwood
Acol
St Nicholas at Wade
Sarre
Broomfield
Boyden Gate
Chislet
Hoath
Monkton
Minster
Manston
Cliffsend
Pegwell
Pegwell Bay
SANDWICH & PEGWELL BAY
ST AUGUSTINE'S CROSS
Upstreet
West Stourmouth
East Stourmouth
Westmarsh
Ware
RICHBOROUGH CASTLE
Stour
Calcott
Hersden
Grove
Preston
Westbere
Sturry
Fordwich
Stodmarsh
Elmstone
Hoaden
Great Stonar
Sandwich
Sandwich Bay
ROYAL ST. GEORGE'S
Wickhambreux
Ickham
Littlebourne
Wingham
Guilton
Ash
Marshborough
Woodnesborough
Stone Cross
Staple
Bramling
HOWLETTS WILD ANIMAL PARK
Bekesbourne
Gore
Worth
Eastry
Ham
Finglesham
Patrixbourne
Goodnestone
GOODNESTONE PARK
Adisham
Knowlton
Chillenden
Betteshanger
Sholden
MARITIME AND LOCAL HISTORY MUSEUM
DEAL
DEAL CASTLE
THE DOWNS
Northbourne
Great Mongeham
Walmer
WALMER CASTLE AND GARDENS
Ripple
Aylesham
Nonington
Easole Street
Snowdown
Tilmanstone
Elvington
Womenswold
Barfrestone
Eythorne
East Studdal
Sutton
Ringwould
Kingsdown
Woolage Green
Coxhill
Shepherdswell
West Langdon
Coldred
East Langdon
Martin
Martin Mill
Whitfield
Guston
St Margaret's at Cliffe
THE BAY MUSEUM
St Margaret's Bay
West Cliffe
THE PINES GARDEN
SOUTH FORELAND
WHITE CLIFFS
DOVER
CALAIS 1:30
DUNKERQUE 1:45
BOULOGNE 1:45
DIEPPE 4:15
Aycliff
SAMPHIRE HOE
DE BRADELEI WHARF
CHANNEL TUNNEL
Denton
Wingmore
Wootton
Lydden
Selsted
ST JOHN'S COMMANDERY
Ewell Minnis
Temple Ewell
Swingfield Street
Swingfield Minnis
Buckland
Alkham
Maxton
Farthingloe
Drellingore
West Hougham
Hawkinge
Densole
Capel le Ferne
EAST CLIFF & WARREN
East Wear Bay
Folkestone
ROTUNDA
CLIFF LIFT
Sandgate
Cheriton
Saltwood
Hythe
Palmarsh
Newington
Peene
Etchinghill
Lyminge
Paddlesworth
Postling
Beachborough
Stanford
Pedlinge
Lympne
PORT LYMPNE WILD ANIMAL PARK AND GARDENS
West Hythe
Burmarsh
Newchurch
ROMNEY, HYTHE AND DYMCHURCH LIGHT RAILWAY
Canterbury
Harbledown
Thanington
Hales Place
Tyler Hill
Blean
Rough Common
Honey Hill
Broadoak
Yorkletts
South Street
Dargate
Hernhill
Graveney
Goodnestone
Faversham
Preston
Boughton Street
Dunkirk
South Street
Oversland
Chartham Hatch
Chartham
Shalmsford Street
Old Wives Lees
Selling
Sheldwich
Badlesmere
Shottenden
Chilham
Leaveland
Molash
Godmersham
Bilting
Crundale
Sole Street
Waltham
Garlinge Green
Petham
Street End
Nackington
Lower Hardres
Bridge
Bishopsbourne
Kingston
Upper Hardres Court
Barham
Derringstone
Bossingham
Stelling Minnis
Bodsham
Elmsted
Hassell Street
Wye
Boughton Lees
Boughton Aluph
Kennington
Brook
Hastingleigh
Hinxhill
Willesborough Lees
Willesborough
Sevington
Mersham
Brabourne
Brabourne Lees
Smeeth
Stowting
Lymbridge Green
Rhodes Minnis
Ottinge
Elham
Lyminge Forest
Sellindge
Cheeseman's Green
Aldington Frith
Aldington
Clap Hill
Bonnington
Court-at-Street
Bilsington
Newingreen
NORTH DOWNS WAY
KENT
DOWNS
A2
A28
A299
A256
A258
A20
M20
A259
13
31

SM
SR
PEMBROKESHIRE COAST
ARFORDIR PENFRO
Pembrokeshire
(Sir Benfro)
MYNYDD PRESELI
ST. BRIDES BAY
BAE SAIN FFRAID
ROSSLARE 3:30
ROSSLARE 1:50 (May-Sept)
ROSSLARE 3:45
Cardigan I.
Ynys Aberteifi
Cemaes Head
Pen Cemaes
Cardigan
(Aberteifi)
Gwbert
Ferwig
Cippyn
St Dogmaels
Bridgend
Moylgrove
Monington
Croft
Pen-y-bryn
Cilgerran
Bridell
Llantood
Glanrhyd
Pont-gareg
Nevern
Felindre Farchog
Rhos-hill
Eglwyswrw
Dinas Head
Newport Bay
Bae Trefdraeth
Berry Hill
Parrog
Newport
(Trefdraeth)
Brynhenllan
Dinas Cross
Carningli
Cilgwyn
Crosswell
Pontyglasier
Eglwyswen
Penygroes
Crymych
Brynberian
Pontfaen
Trecwn
Strumble Head
Pen Caer
Tresinwen
Llanwnda
Goodwick
(Wdig)
Lower Town
Fishguard Bay
Bae Abergwaun
Fishguard
(Abergwaun)
Dyffryn
Manorowen
St Nicholas
Llanychaer
Scleddau
Trefasser
Penbwchdy
Ynysduellyn
Abercastle
Granston
Penclegyr
Porthgain
Trefin
Mathry
Newbridge
Abereiddy
Llanrhian
Penparc
Castlemorris
Croes-goch
Pentre-galar
Mynachlog-ddu
New Inn
Rosebush
Puncheston
Castlebythe
Little Newcastle
Letterston
Tredddiog
Treffynnon
Treglemais
Tretio
Carnhedryn
ST. DAVID'S HEAD
PENMAEN DEWI
Treleddyd-fawr
Whitesand Bay
Porth-mawr
Rhodiad
Caerfarchell
Llanreithan
Llandeloy
Welsh Hook
St Dogwells
Tufton
Henry's Moat
Maenclochog
Llangolman
Glandy Cross
Glandwr
Hebron
Rhosson
St David's
(Tyddewi)
Whitchurch
Middle Mill
Nine Wells
Solva
Ramsey Island
Ynys Dewi
Ramsey Sound
Trefgarn Owen
Hayscastle
Pont-yr-hafod
Wolf's Castle
Ambleston
Woodstock
New Moat
Pant-y-Caws
Llanglydwen
Cefn-y-pant
Efailwen
Rinaston
Wallis
Brimaston
Hayscastle Cross
Mountain Water
Triffleton
Treffgarne
Llys-y-frân
Walton East
Llanycefn
Login
Penycwm
Newgale
Leweston
Spittal
Pen-ffordd
Roch
Wolfsdale
Clarbeston
Bletherston
Llandissilio
Hiraeth
Roch Gate
Camrose
Rudbaxton
Clarbeston Road
Llanfallteg
Nolton Haven
Simpson Cross
Keeston
Tangiers
Leechpool
Gelli
Clunderwen
Cwmfelin Boeth
Nolton
Pelcomb Cross
Crundale
Wiston
Bethesda
Druidston
Lambston
Pelcomb Bridge
Slade
Haverfordwest
(Hwlffordd)
Llawhaden
Robeston Wathen
Llanddewi Velfrey
Portfield Gate
Narberth
(Arberth)
Crinow
Lampeter Velfrey
Trevaughan
Haroldston West
Dreenhill
Uzmaston
The Rhos
Blackpool
Broad Haven
Merlin's Bridge
Millin Cross
Boulston
Minwear
Cross Hands
Templeton
Cold Blow
Princes Gate
Tavernspite
Little Haven
Broadway
Walton West
Pope Hill
Landshipping
Talbenny
North Johnston
Freystrop
Walwyn's Castle
Hook
Landshipping Quay
Martletwy
Ludchurch
Llanteg
Tower Point
Trwyn Twr
St Bride's
Wooltack Point
Trwyn Wooltack
Skomer Island
Ynys Skomer
Tiers Cross
Johnston
Llangwm
Black Tar
Yerbeston
Reynalton
Longstone
Marloes
Hasguard
Robeston Cross
Rosemarket
Thornton
Steynton
Hill Mountain
Port Lion
Houghton
Loveston
Thomas Chapel
Begelly
Stepaside
Amroth
Broad Sound
Gateholm Island
Ynys Gateholm
St Ishmael's
Sandy Haven
Herbrandston
Milford Haven
(Aberdaugleddau)
Honeyborough
Lawrenny
Cresswell Quay
Cresselly
Jeffreyston
Kilgetty
Dale
Hakin
Waterston
Llanstadwell
Neyland
Burton
West Williamston
Broadmoor
Hill
Saundersfoot
Skokholm Island
Ynys Skokholm
MILFORD HAVEN
ABERDAUGLEDDYF
Pembroke Dock
(Doc Penfro)
Pennar
Cosheston
Carew Newton
East Williamston
Redberth
Carew
Milton
Sageston
Broadfield
Angle
Angle Bay
Bae Angle
Pwllcrochan
Rhoscrowther
Carew Cheriton
New Hedges
St Ann's Hd.
Pentir St. Ann
Sheep Island
Ynys y Defaid
Monkton
Pembroke
(Penfro)
Hundleton
St Florence
Gumfreston
Tenby
(Dinbych-y-Pysgod)
Freshwater West
Maiden Wells
Lamphey
Hodgeston
Jameston
Penally
Freshwater East
Lydstep
Giltar Pt.
Caldey Sound
Caldey Island
Ynys Bŷr
Castlemartin
St Twynnells
Warren
Merrion
St Petrox
Cheriton or Stackpole Elidor
Stackpole
Trewent Pt.
Trwyn Trewent
Manorbier
Old Castle Hd.
Chapel Pt.
Trwyn Capel
Linney Hd.
Pentir Linney
The Wash
Bosherston
Stackpole Hd.
Pen Stackpole
St Govan's Hd.
Pen St Gofan
0 1 2 3 4 5 6 miles
0 1 2 3 4 5 6 7 8 9 10 km

Ceredigion
Carmarthenshire
(Sir Gaerfyrddin)
Swansea
(Abertawe)
New Quay
(Ceinewydd)
Aberaeron
Lampeter
(Llanbedr Pont Steffan)
Tregaron
Newcastle Emlyn
(Castell Newydd Emlyn)
Llandysul
Carmarthen
(Caerfyrddin)
St Clears
(Sanclêr)
Llandeilo
Ammanford
(Rhydaman)
Kidwelly
(Cydweli)
Burry Port
(Porth Tywyn)
Llanelli
Pontarddulais
Gorseinon
Pontardawe
Clydach
Brynamman
The Mumbles
(Y Mwmbwls)
Laugharne
Pendine
Cardigan Bay
Ynys-Lochtyn
Aberporth
Brechfa Forest
Pembrey Forest
Carmarthen Bay
Bae Caerfyrddin
Swansea Bay
Bae Abertawe
Black Mountain
Y Mynydd Du
Gower
Worms Head
Penrhyn-Gŵyr
Rhossili Bay
Bae Rhossili
Burry Holms
Whiteford Pt.
Trwyn Whiteford
Mumbles Hd.
Trwyn yr Mwmbwls
Pendine Sands
Traeth Pentywyn
East Marsh
SN
SS
7
8
9
10
11
12
A
B
C
D
E
G
H
24
14
A40
A48
A483
A485
A487
A477
A484
A475
A4138

Ceredigion
(Sir Ceredigion)
Carmarthenshire
(Sir Gaerfyrddin)
SN
P
Rhydyfelin
Moriah
Capel Seion
Ystumtuen
Ysbyty-Cynfyn
Llanfarian
Pisgah
Llanfihangel-y-Creuddyn
Mynydd Bach
Devil's Bridge
Chancery
Gors
New Cross
Trisant
Blaenplwyf
Llanilar
Cnwch-coch
Blaenycwm
Cwmystwyth
Nantgwyn
Pant-y-dwr
St Harmon
Pentre-llyn
Abermagwr
New Row
Hafod Estate
Pont-rhyd-y-groes
Rhos-y-garth
Crosswood
Llanafan
Wenallt
Ysbyty Ystwyth
Llanddeiniol
Llangwyryfon
Lledrod
Mynydd Bach
Tynygraig
Tanyrhydiau
Trawsallt
Geifas
Llanrhystud
Trefenter
Ystradmeurig
Ffair-Rhos
Claerwen
Llansantffraed
Rhyd-Rosser
Rhydfudr
Llanon
Fantasy Farm Park
Bronnant
Swydd-ffynnon
Pontrhydfendigaid
Strata Florida Abbey
Rhayader
(Rhaeadr Gwy)
Llansantffraed Cwmdeuddwr
Elan Village
Penygarreg Res.
Craig-goch Res.
Garreg-ddu Res.
Claerwen Reservoir
Caban-coch Res.
Nebo
Bontnewydd
Dibyn Du
Llanwrthwl
Argoed Mill
Aberarth
Aberaeron
Monachty
Pennant
Cross Inn
Bethania
Blaenpennal
Tyncelyn
Cors Caron
Penuwch
Ty'n-yr-eithin
Afon Claerwen
Crynfryn
Tywi Forest
Cilcennin
Llangeitho
Welsh Gold Centre
Tregaron
Drum-ddu
Drygarn Fawr
Bryn Crwn
Y Drum
Dolgoch
Esgair Cerrig
Tyncornel
Nant Irfon
Llanafan-fawr
Ciliau Aeron
Bwlch-Llan
Capel Betws Lleucu
Trefilan
Llundain-fach
Ystrad Aeron
Tal-sarn
Gartheli
Commins Capel Betws
Dihewyd
Abermeurig
Llwyn-y-groes
Felinfach
Olmarch
Llanddewi-Brefi
Pentre-rhew
Temple Bar
Felindre
Ffynnon-oer
Llangybi
Soar-y-Mynydd
Llyn Brianne Res.
Abergwesyn
Pentre-llwyn-llwyd
Troed-rhiwdalar
Beulah
Llanfechan
Garth
Gorsgoch
Cribyn
Silian
Betws Bledrws
Llanfair Clydogau
Bryn Brawd
Maestir
Lampeter
(Llanbedr Pont Steffan)
Olwen
Cellan
Pentrefelin
Allt Rhyd y Groes
Mynydd Trawsnant
Cwm Irfon
Cambrian Woollen Mill
Llanwrtyd
Aber
Cwrt-newydd
Llanwnnen
Cwmsychpant
Cwmann
Pentre-bach
Ystradffin
Llanwrtyd Wells
(Llanwrtud)
Llangammarch Wells
Drum-ddu
Llanwenog
Dre-fach
Alltyblaca
Pencarreg
Llanybydder
Ram
Parc-y-rhôs
Llanycrwys
Ffarmers
Ffaldybrenin
Afon Cothi
Mynydd Mallaen
Nant-y-Bai
Cefn-gorwydd
Brynteg
Rhuddlan
Glan-Duar
Ty Mawr
Mynydd Pencarreg
Harford
Cwrt-y-cadno
Rhandirmwyn
Mynydd Epynt
Pentre
Dolau-Honddu
Aber-Giâr
Esgairdawe
Llandre
Caeo Forest
Esgair Ferchon
Pumsaint
Dolaucothi Gold Mines
Cilycwm
Cynghordy
Crychan Forest
Tirabad
Bryn Du
Llanllwni
Caio
Llanfair-ar-y-bryn
Rhydcymerau
Crugybar
Porthyrhyd
Siloh
Divlyn
Merthyr Cynog
Lliliad Nenog
New Inn
Llansawel
Blaendyryn
Gwyddgrug
Llandovery
(Llanymddyfri)
Pentre-ty-gwyn
Babel
Mynydd Bwlch-y-groes
Brechfa Forest
Gwernogle
Edwinsford
Llandeilo'r Fan
Llanfihangel Nant Bran
Abergorlech
Talley Abbey
Cynros
Talley
Mynydd Rhos-wen
Nant-y-ffin
Cwm-byr
Waunclunda
Cwmdwr
Halfway
Pentre-bach
Pen-y-garn
Llansadwrn
Llanwrda
Myrtle Hill
Cwmdu
Halfway
Llywel
Pentre'r-felin
Trallong
Llanllawddog
Brechfa
Felindre
Cilgwyn
Myddfai
Horeb
Ashfield
Trecastle
Sennybridge
(Pont Senni)
Soar
Hermon
Llangadog
Usk Reservoir
Cwmwysg
Pont ar Hydfer
Defynnog
Penpont
Llanfynydd
Capel Isaac
Felindre
Pant-glas
Salem
Cwmifor
Manordeilo
Talsarn
Glas Fynydd Forest
Mynydd Illtyd
Mountain Centre
Libanus
Pantgwyn
Dyffryn Ceidrych
Twynllanan
Llanddeusant
Crai
Felingwm uchaf
Felingwm isaf
Pen-y-banc
Rhosmaen
Bethlehem
Pont-ar-llechau
Felin-Crai
Heol Senni
Llanfihangel-uwch-Gwili
Broad Oak
Pentrefelin
Vale of Tywi
Dyffryn Tywi
Pontbren Araeth
Llwyn y Celyn
Court Henry
Dinefwr Park
Llangathen
Trichrug
Capel Gwynfe
Pont Aber
Fan Brycheiniog
Cray Res.
Craig Cerrig Gleisiad a Fan Frynych
Pont-ar-gothi
Llandeilo
Cilsan
Aberglasney
Nantgaredig
Llanegwad
Felindre
Dryslwyn
Ffairfach
Neuadd
Brecon Beacons
Llanarthne
Afon Tywi
Gelli Aur
Golden Grove
Capel Dewi
Trapp
Carreg Cennen Castle & Farm
Foel Fraith
Black Mountain
Y Mynydd Du
Fan Gihirych
Fan Fawr
Ystradfellte Res.
Nantycaws
The National Botanic Garden of Wales
Penrhiw-goch
Temple Bar
Milo
Llandyfan
Fforest Fawr
Llanddarog
Maesybont
Carmel
Pentre-Gwenlais
Dre-fach
The National Showcaves for Wales
Dan-yr-Ogof
Glyntawe
Ogof Ffynnon Ddu
Cantref Res.
Cwmisfael
Porthyrhyd
Llyn Llech Owain
Foel-gastell
Llandybie
Craig-y-nos
Penwyllt
Gwendraeth Fach
Cefneithin
Gorslas
Caer-bryn
Twynmynydd
Brynamman
Rhosaman
Pen-y-cae
Ystradfellte
Crwbin
Drefach
Cwm-y-glo
Pen-y-groes
Glanaman
Tir-y-dail
Afon Amman
Cwmllynfell
Ystradowen
Abercraf
Cefn-yr-erw
Bancffosfelen
Cwm-mawr
Cross Hands
Saron
Pontamman
Garnant
Gwaun-Leision
Tairgwaith
Upper Cwm-twrch
Cwmgiedd
Caehopkin
Coelbren
Pontyberem
Pentre
Tumble
Penybanc
Ammanford
(Rhydaman)
Gwaun-Cae-Gurwen
Penrhos
Meinciau
Cwmgwili
Capel Hendre
Betws
Pantyffynnon
Tycroes
Cwmgors
Lower Cwm-twrch
Ystradgynlais
Onllwyn
Dyffryn Cellwen
Penderyn
Pont Henri
Gurnos
Pontyates
Greynor
Garnswllt
Ystalyfera
Seven Sisters
Llannon
Cynheidre
Sylen
Llwyn-têg
Pont Abraham Services
Mynydd y Gwair
Godre'r-graig
Nant-y-cafn
Glyn-neath
(Glynedd)
Pontneddfechan
Pontbren Llwyd
Carway
Ffos Las
Four Roads
Horeb
Lliedi Resrs.
Llanedi
Sardis
Fforest
Graig Fawr
Pentrebach
Climaen gwyn
Ynys-meudwy
Swansea Valley
Cwm Abertawe
Mynydd March-Hywel
Rheola Forest
Vale of Neath
Cwm Nedd
Morfa Glas
Rhigos
Cwm-hwnt
Hirwaun
Tre-Gibbon
Rhyd-y-fro
Pontardawe
Cilybebyll
Crynant
Blaengwrach
Cwmgwrach
Penywaun
Llwydcoed
Pontarddulais
Rhyd-y-gwin
Craig-cefn-parc
Glantawe Riverside Park
Trebanos
Gellinudd
Rhôs
Cefn Coed Colliery Mus
Resolven
Resolven Mtn.
Cwmdare
Dare Valley
Aberdare
(Aberdâr)
Cwm-Dulais
Rhyd-y-pandy
Felindre
Clydach
Alltwen
Faerdre
Pontlliw
Melincourt
Wye (Gwy)
Usk (Wysg)
Irfon
Neath
Helen
Sarn
0 1 2 3 4 5 6 miles
0 1 2 3 4 5 6 7 8 9 10 km

Herefordshire
Monmouthshire
(Sir Fynwy)
Torfaen
(Tor-faen)
RADNOR FOREST
BLACK MOUNTAINS
Y MYNYDDOEDD DUON
BRECON BEACONS
Llandrindod Wells
(Llandrindod)
Builth Wells
(Llanfair-ym-Muallt)
Brecon
(Aberhonddu)
Knighton
(Tref-y-Clawdd)
Presteigne
(Llanandras)
Kington
Hay-on-Wye
(Y Gelli Gandryll)
Ludlow
Leominster
Hereford
Abergavenny
(Y Fenni)
Monmouth
(Trefynwy)
Merthyr Tydfil
(Merthyr Tudful)
Tredegar
EBBW VALE
(GLYN EBWY)
Brynmawr
Nantyglo
Blaenavon
Blaina
Rhymney
(Rhymni)
New Tredegar
(Tredegar Newydd)
Abertillery
(Abertyleri)
Abersychan
Crickhowell
Talgarth
Usk
Weobley
Kingsland
Wigmore
Bucknell
Clun
Radnor
Llanbister
Crossgates
Penybont
Newchurch
Clyro
Painscastle
Llanigon
Glasbury
Bronllys
Llangorse Lake
Pandy
Grosmont
Skenfrith
Raglan
Longtown
Llanthony
Peterchurch
Madley
Kingstone
Ewyas Harold
Pontrilas
Golden Valley
Wye
Usk
Teme
Lugg
Arrow
A44
A49
A438
A470
A479
A465
A40
A4112
A483
33
26
15

Herefordshire
Worcestershire
Gloucestershire
Ludlow
Kidderminster
Bewdley
Stourport on Severn
Tenbury Wells
Cleobury Mortimer
Leominster
Bromyard
Worcester
Droitwich Spa
Bromsgrove
Catshill
Aston Fields
Great Malvern
Malvern Link
West Malvern
Upton upon Severn
Pershore
Hereford
Ledbury
Newent
Tewkesbury
Bishop's Cleeve
Ross-on-Wye
Cheltenham
Charlton Kings
Gloucester
Hucclecote
Churchdown
Cinderford
Coleford
Monmouth (Trefynwy)
Lydney
Stonehouse
Stroud
Chalford
Frampton on Severn
Forest of Dean
The Noose
River Severn
Wyre Forest
Malvern Hills
Abberley Hill
Teme
Wye
Severn
Avon
Leadon
Lugg
Frome
Oakley Wood
M5
M50
A44
A49
A417
A438
A449
A40
A48
A38
A456
A4103
A4137
A46
A435
A419
25
34
16
SO
0 1 2 3 4 5 6 miles
0 1 2 3 4 5 6 7 8 9 10 km

Coventry
Kenilworth
Royal Leamington Spa
Warwick
Rugby
Redditch
Studley
Alcester
Stratford-upon-Avon
Southam
Shipston-on-Stour
Banbury
Middleton Cheney
Evesham
Broadway
Moreton-in-Marsh
Stow-on-the-Wold
Chipping Norton
Charlbury
Woodstock
Kidlington
Burford
Witney
Carterton
Warwick
Oxford
VALE OF EVESHAM
Dorridge
Henley-in-Arden
Chipping Campden
Shirley

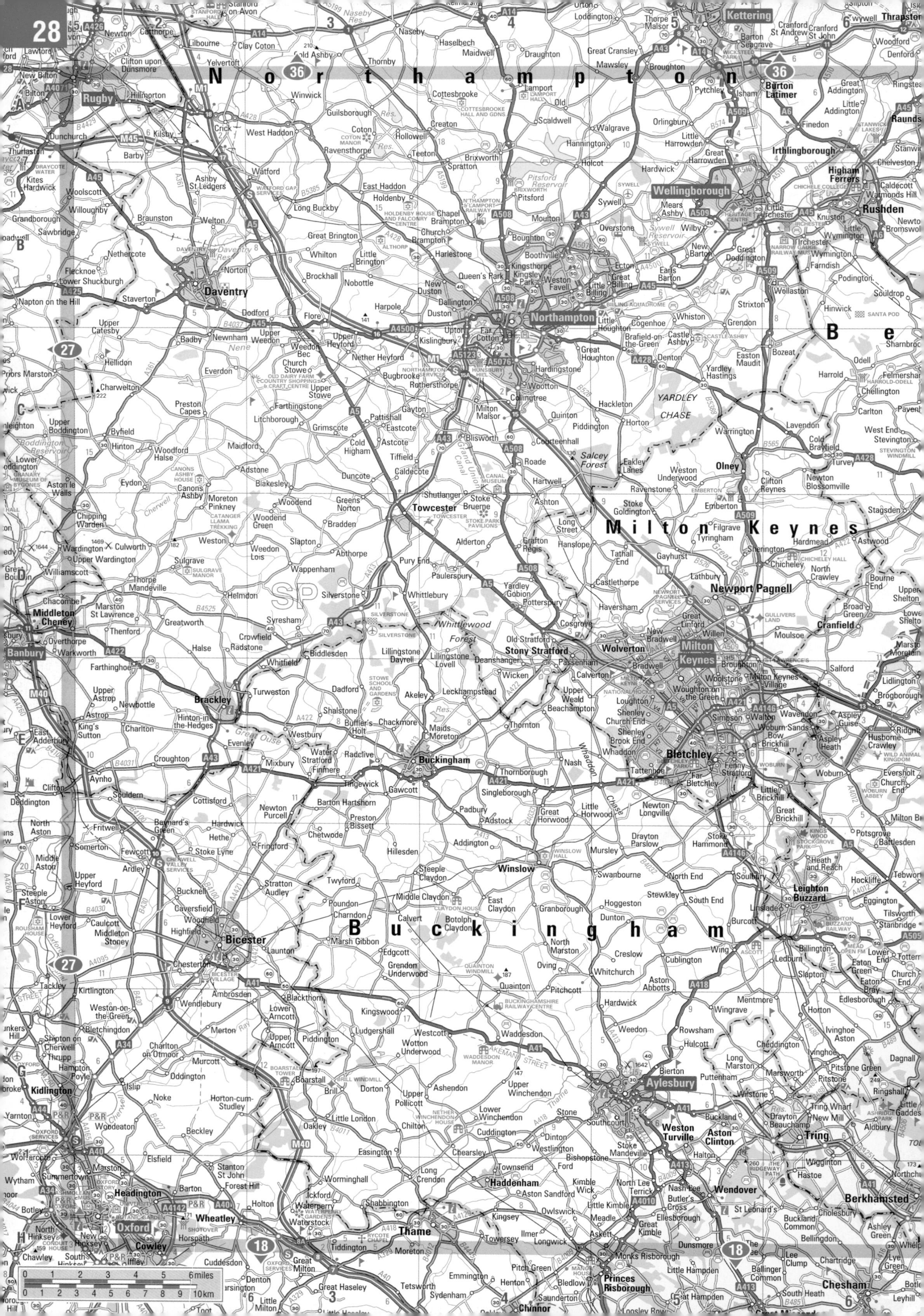
Northampton
Milton Keynes
Buckingham
Be
Rugby
Daventry
Northampton
Kettering
Wellingborough
Rushden
Higham Ferrers
Irthlingborough
Burton Latimer
Towcester
Olney
Newport Pagnell
Milton Keynes
Bletchley
Brackley
Buckingham
Banbury
Middleton Cheney
Winslow
Bicester
Leighton Buzzard
Aylesbury
Tring
Berkhamsted
Wendover
Princes Risborough
Thame
Haddenham
Oxford
Kidlington
Headington
Cowley
Wheatley
Chesham
Stony Stratford
Wolverton
Cranfield
YARDLEY CHASE
Salcey Forest
Whittlewood Forest
SP
27
36
18
M1
M40
M45
A5
A43
A41
A421
0 1 2 3 4 5 6 miles
0 1 2 3 4 5 6 7 8 9 10 km

Cambridgeshire
Bedfordshire
Central Bedfordshire
Hertford
Huntingdon
Godmanchester
St Ives
St Neots
Eynesbury
Eaton Socon
Bedford
Kempston
Sandy
Biggleswade
Cambourne
Cambridge
Histon
Cottenham
Royston
Baldock
LETCHWORTH
HITCHIN
Stevenage
Luton
Dunstable
HARPENDEN
WELWYN GARDEN CITY
Hatfield
St Albans
Hemel Hempstead
Hertford
Ware
HODDESDON
Harlow
BISHOP'S STORTFORD
Sawbridgeworth
CHESHUNT
WALTHAM ABBEY
POTTERS BAR
Epping
Buntingford
Shefford
Ampthill
Flitwick
Stotfold
Sawston
Great Shelford
Stansted Mountfitchet
STANSTED AIRPORT
37
30
19
TL

Middle Fen
Stuntney
Great Fen
Mildenhall Fen
Eriswell
Holywell Row
4
East of England Tank Museum
5
Barnham
Euston
Euston Hall
6
Coney Weston
Hopton
Market Weston
Littleport
Little Thetford
Broad Hill
Isleham Fen
38
Beck Row
West Row
Thistley Green
Fakenham Magna
Barningham
Haddenham
Barway
Soham Cotes
Windmill
Isleham
Priory Church
Mildenhall
The King's Forest
Honington
Sapiston
Hepworth
Wilburton
Stretham
Soham
Soham Mere
Worlington
Barton Mills
Icklingham
Bardwell
Ixworth Thorpe
Stanton
Upthorpe
A
Freckenham
Cavenham Heath
Troston
Walsham le Willows
Down Field Windmill
Tuddenham
West Stow
West Stow
Ingham
Ampton
Great Livermere
Ixworth
Langham
Chittering
Wicken
Wicken Corn Windmill
Fordham
Kennett
Red Lodge
Herringswell
Lackford
Culford
Upware
Wicken Fen
New River
Chippenham
Cavenham
Flempton
Timworth Green
Abbey (rem)
Badwell Ash
River Bank
Chippenham Fen
Hengrave
Hengrave Hall
Conyers Green
Stowlangtoft
Hunston
Cottenham
Farmland Mus & Denny Abbey
Adventures Fen
Landwade
Snailwell
Kennett
Fornham All Saints
Fornham St Martin
Pakenham
Great Ashfield
Reach
Burwell
Kentford
Higham
Risby
Great Barton
Stanton Street
Waterbeach
Exning
Moulton
Packhorse Bridge
Thurston
Norton
B
Newmarket
Newmarket Heath
Little Saxham
Westley
Bury St Edmunds
Elmswell
Lode Mill
Commercial End
Swaffham Prior
Gazeley
Barrow
Cathedral and Abbey Ruins
Tostock
Milton
Lode
Horningsea
National Horseracing Museum
Great Saxham
Blackthorpe
Beyton
Rougham
Woolpit
Swaffham Bulbeck
Anglesey Abbey
National Stud
Dalham
Denham
Horringer
Ickworth House
Rushbrooke
Hessett
Drinkstone
Woolpit Bygones Museum
Stow cum Quy
Cheveley
Ashley
Dunstall Green
Hargrave
Chevington
Sicklesmere
Rougham Green
Drinkstone Green
Bottisham
Fen Ditton
S
u
f
Teversham
Little Wilbraham
Saxon Street
Ousden
Little Welnetham
Bradfield St George
Rattlesden
Museum of Technology
Cambridge
Great Wilbraham
Stetchworth
Woodditton
Hawstead
Whepstead
Great Welnetham
Bradfield St Clare
Gedding
Poystreet Green
Romsey Town
Dullingham
Ditton Green
Upend
Lidgate
TL
Depden Green
Rede Hall
Bradfield Combust
Bradfield Woods
Felsham
29
Six Mile Bottom
Kirtling
Chedburgh
Depden
Hightown Green
Cherry Hinton
Fulbourn
Westley Waterless
Kirtling Green
Thorns
Rede
Hoggard's Green
Cross Green
Burrough Green
Wickhambrook
Clopton Green
Lawshall
Cockfield
Great Green
Thorpe Green
Brinkley
Cowlinge
Brockley Green
Wandlebury
Weston Colville
Great Bradley
Wickham Street
Hawkedon
Brettenham
Great Shelford
Stapleford
Carlton
Denston
Stansfield
Thorpe Morieux
Weston Green
Hartest
Shimpling Street
Cross Green
Little Bradley
Stradishall
Hitcham
Granta
West Wratting
Little Thurlow
Boxted
Shimpling
Alpheton
Preston St Mary
Kettlebaston
Babraham
Balsham
Great Thurlow
Stanstead
Lavenham
Bildeston
Little Abington
Fourwentways Services
Sawston
Great Abington
West Wickham
Barnardiston
Hundon
Guildhall
Kentwell Hall
Bridge Street
Monks Eleigh
Chelsworth
Hildersham
Great Wratting
Poslingford
Glemsford
Whittlesford
Pampisford
Streetly End
Brent Eleigh
Duxford Chapel
Horseheath
Withersfield
High Street
Linton
Little Wratting
Kedington
Chilton Street
Cavendish
Sue Ryder Foundation Museum
Melford Hall
Semer
Linton Zoo
Haverhill
Clare
Pentlow
Long Melford
Little Waldingfield
Milden
Duxford
Imperial War Museum
Bartlow
Boyton End
Clare Castle
Acton
Lindsey
St James Chapel
Hinxton
Hadstock
Shudy Camps
Stoke by Clare
Clare Ancient House
Foxearth
Great Waldingfield
Ickleton
Stump Cross
Castle Camps
Sturmer
Borley
D
Great Chesterford
Wixoe
Baythorn End
Belchamp St Paul
Mill Green
Edwardstone
Little Chesterford
Ashdon
Helions Bumpstead
Birdbrook
Ashen
Ovington
Sudbury
Groton
Little Walden
Church End
Steeple Bumpstead
Ridgewell
Tilbury Juxta Clare
Belchamp Otten
Ballingdon
Great Cornard
Newton
Boxford
Strethall
M11
Littlebury
Saffron Walden
Little Yeldham
Belchamp Walter
Bulmer
Gainsborough's Ho
Stone Street
Calais Street
Elmdon
Sewards End
Stambourne
Bulmer Tye
Middleton
Little Cornard
Whitestreet Green
Littlebury Green
Audley End House
Radwinter
Hempstead
Stambourne Green
Toppesfield
Great Yeldham
Gestingthorpe
Henny Street
Assington
Polstead
Wendens Ambo
Wimbish
Cornish Hall End
Audley End
Great Henny
Twinstead
Harrow Street
Bridge Green
Tye Green
Great Sampford
Gainsford End
Colne Valley Railway
Hedingham Castle
Wickham St Paul
Twinstead Green
Lamarsh
Honey Tye
Stoke-by-Nayland
Arkesden
Wimbish Green
Highstreet Green
Castle Hedingham
Great Maplestead
Alphamstone
Bures Green
E
Newport
Howlett End
Little Sampford
Howe Street
Morris Green
Sible Hedingham
Little Maplestead
Bures
Nayland
Wicken Bonhunt
Debden
Finchingfield
Pebmarsh
Little Horkesley
Rickling
Priors Hall Barn
Widdington
Mole Hall Wildlife Park
Debden Cross
Mount Bures
Stour
Starlings Green
Thaxted
Little Bardfield
Wethersfield
Halstead
Wormingford
Quendon
Hamperden End
Cutlers Green
Blackmore End
Colne Engaine
Wakes Colne
East Anglian Railway Museum
Great Horkesley
Great Bardfield
Shalford
Gosfield
Horkesley Heath
St Mary's Church
Ugley
Henham
Glendale Forge
Monk Street
Church End
Beazley End
Earls Colne
Chappel
Fordham
West Bergholt
Ugley Green
Lindsell
Shalford Green
Greenstead Green
Manuden
House on the Hill Toy Mus
Broxted
Duton Hill
Bardfield Saling
Jasper's Green
Bocking Churchstreet
High Garrett
Fordstreet
Eight Ash Green
Farnham Green
Elsenham
Molehill Green
Brick End
Great Easton
Bran End
Great Saling
Panfield
Stisted
Great Tey
Aldham
F
Stansted Mountfitchet
Butcher's Pasture
Stebbing
Stebbing Green
Bocking
Braintree
Pattiswick Green
Broad Green
Marks Tey
Lexden
Stanway
Beacon End
Stansted Airport
London Stansted
Little Easton
Churchend
Flitch Way
Freeport Braintree
Bradwell
Coggeshall
Copford Green
Shrub End
Birchanger
Bambers Green
Great Dunmow
Maltings
Little Dunmow
Rayne
Bishop's Stortford
Takeley
Birchanger Green Services
Takeley Street
Smith's Green
Dunmow Services
Bannister Green
Great Notley
Black Notley
Tye Green
Cressing
Grange Barn
Paycockes
Coggeshall Hamlet
Easthorpe
Heckfordbridge
Layer de la Haye
Hatfield Forest
Hope End Green
Felsted
Willows Grn
Great Leighs
Feering
Gore Pit
Hardy's Green
Thorley Street
Gt. Hallingbury
Barnston
Young's End
Silver End
Kelvedon
Birch
Thorley
Southern
Bacon End
Cressing Temple
White Notley
Local History Museum
Smythe's Green
Malting Green
Spellbrook
Lit. Hallingbury
Bishop's Green
Hounslow Green
North End
Hartford End
A131
Faulkbourne
Inworth
Messing
Birch Green
Layer Marney
Layer Breton
Abberton Reservoir
Great Canfield
High Roding
Little Leighs
Great Leighs
Rivenhall End
Layer Marney Tower
Tiptree
Ford End
Fairstead
Peldon
Hatfield Heath
Hatfield Broad Oak
Fuller Street
Terling
Great Braxted
Sawbridgeworth
High Easter
Howe Street
Flack's Green
Chipping Hill
Oxley Green
Paternoster Heath
Great Wigborough
G
High Wych
Aythorpe Roding
Pleshey
Witham
Sheering
Leaden Roding
Great Waltham
Little Waltham
Wickham Bishops
Great Totham
Salcott
Copt Hall Marshes
Gibberd Garden
White Roding
Margaret Roding
Good Easter
Little Totham
Tolleshunt D'Arcy
Blackwater Estuary
Matching Tye
Matching
Abbess Roding
Chignall Smealy
Hatfield Peverel
Churchgate Street
E
s
s
e
x
Harlow
Matching Green
Mashbury
Chignall St James
Broomfield
Nounsley
Great Totham
Tolleshunt Major
Beauchamp Roding
Boreham
Broad Street Green
Tollesbury
Potter Street
High Laver
Little Laver
Boyton Cross
Parsonage Green
Springfield
Chelmer Village
Langford
Heybridge
Goldhanger
Foster Street
Shellow Bowells
Chelmer and Blackwater Navigation
Little Baddow
Combined Military Services Museum
Latton Bush
Magdalen Laver
Roxwell
Woodham Walter
Maldon
Hythe Quay
Heybridge Basin
Blackwater
Bradwell Waterside
Hastingwood
Fyfield
Willingale
Great Oxney Green
Writtle
Chelmsford
Moulsham Mill
Osea I.
Northey I.
Moreton
Cooksmill Green
Widford
P&R
Russell Green
Ramsey Island
Bovinger
Bobbingworth
Norton Mandeville
Great Baddow
Sandon
Danbury
Woodham Mortimer
St Lawrence
H
Shelley
20
North Weald Bassett
Norton Heath
Loves Green
Galleyend
Galleywood
Howe Green
Cock Clarks
Rudley Green
Mundon
Tillingham
Steeple
Blackmore
Mill Green
Margaretting
Bicknacre
Purleigh
Cold Norton
Latchingdon
Lower Mayland
Mayland
Dengie
Stondon
East Hanningfield
0 1 2 3 4 5 6 miles
0 1 2 3 4 5 6 7 8 9 10 km

Thelnetham
Redgrave
Hinderclay
Wortham
Palgrave
Scole
Brockdish
Syleham
Fressingfield
Wissett
Chediston
Linstead Parva
Halesworth
Broadway
Holton
Blyford
Wangford
Southwold
Botesdale
Rickinghall
Burgate
Mellis
Yaxley
Brome
Eye
Oakley
Hoxne
Wingfield
Cross Street
Heckfield Green
Denham
Stradbroke
Battlesea Green
Pixey Green
Chippenhall Green
Little Whittingham Green
Silverley's Green
Cratfield
Cookley
Walpole
Wenhaston
Blackheath
Blythburgh
Thorington
Walberswick
Wattisfield
Allwood Green
Cranmer Green
Gislingham
Thornham Parva
Thornham Magna
Braiseworth
Cranley
Denham Street
Horham
Wilby
Wootten Green
Russel's Green
Swan Green
Ashfield Green
Banyard's Green
Huntingfield
Heveningham
Sibton Green
Bramfield
Dunwich
Dunwich Forest
Laxfield
Ubbeston Green
High Street
Darsham
Sibton
Hemp Green
Peasenhall
Yoxford
Westleton
Middleton Moor
Middleton
Theberton
Eastbridge
Wickham Street
Stoke Ash
Occold
Redlingfield
Athelington
Fingal Street
Stanway Green
Brundish
Brundish Street
Crown Corner
Owl's Green
Badingham
Finningham
Wickham Skeith
Thorndon
Rishangles
Southolt
Bedingfield
Worlingworth
Tannington
Maypole Green
Dennington
Bruisyard
Rotten End
North Green
Westhorpe
Wyverstone
Bacton
Cotton
Thwaite
Brockford Street
Wetheringsett
Blacksmith's Green
Kenton
Bedfield
Saxtead
Monk Soham
Brabling Green
Cransford
Rendham
Curlew Green
Kelsale
Carlton
Saxmundham
Leiston
Sizewell
Bacton Green
Ford's Green
Mendlesham
Mendlesham Green
Canham's Green
Haughley Green
Ward Green
Gipping
Wetherup Street
Debenham
Ashfield
Earl Soham
Saxtead Green
Framlingham
Great Glemham
Sweffling
Knodishall
Aldringham
Wetherden
Haughley
Saxham Street
Middlewood Green
Mickfield
Winston
Winston Green
Lampardbrook
Cole's Green
Benhall Street
Sternfield
Benhall Green
Coldfair Green
Stratford St Andrew
Friston
Thorpeness
Harleston
Thorney Green
Stowupland
Forward Green
Little Stonham
Stonham Aspal
Peats Corner
Framsden
Cretingham
Brandeston
Kettleburgh
Parham
Hacheston
Farnham
Gromford
Stowmarket
Earl Stonham
Creeting St Mary
Creeting Bottoms
Pettaugh
Helmingham
Monewden
Easton
Marlesford
Letheringham
Little Glemham
Snape
Aldeburgh
Great Finborough
Combs Ford
Combs
High Street Green
Moats Tye
Needham Market
Crowfield
Gosbeck
Coddenham
Ashbocking
Otley
Charsfield
Clopton Corner
Dallinghoo
Debach
Wickham Market
Pettistree
Lower Hacheston
Campsey Ash
Blaxhall
Tunstall
Iken
High Street
Aldeburgh Bay
Battisford
Battisford Tye
Ringshall
Barking
Barking Tye
Baylham
Hemingstone
Swilland
Clopton
Bredfield
Ufford
Rendlesham
Tunstall Forest
Sudbourne
Chillesford
Wattisham
Ringshall Stocks
Willisham Tye
Great Blakenham
Barham
Claydon
Henley
Witnesham
Grundisburgh
Burgh
Hasketon
Melton
Bromeswell
Eyke
Butley
Orford
Orford Ness
Great Bricett
Nedging Tye
Offton
Little Blakenham
Akenham
Tuddenham St Martin
Culpho
Boot Street
Great Bealings
Woodbridge
Rendlesham Forest
Butley High Corner
Naughton
Somersham
Whitton
Westerfield
Playford
Little Bealings
Maidensgrave
Capel St Andrew
Elmsett
Flowton
Rushmere St Andrew
Martlesham
Boyton
Whatfield
Aldham
Bramford
Sproughton
Westbourne
Ipswich
Kesgrave
Martlesham Heath
Waldringfield Heath
Waldringfield
Sutton
Shottisham
Duck Corner
Stores Corner
Hollesley
Hollesley Bay
TM
Burstall
Hintlesham
Chantry
Rose Hill
Stoke
Warren Heath
Brightwell
Newbourne
Hemley
Shingle Street
Hadleigh
Chattisham
Copdock
Maidenhall
Gainsborough
Bucklesham
Alderton
Layham
Coles Green
Mace Green
Belstead
Wherstead
Nacton
Kirton
Bawdsey
Falkenham
Raydon
Great Wenham
Capel St Mary
Freston
Woolverstone
Levington
Pin Mill
Chelmondiston
Thorpe Common
Trimley St Martin
Shelley
Holton St Mary
Bentley
Tattingstone
Holbrook
Trimley Lower Street
Trimley St Mary
Felixstowe Ferry
Higham
The Heath
Alton Water Reservoir
Lower Holbrook
Stutton
Erwarton
Shotley
Walton
Old Felixstowe
East Bergholt
Brantham
Upper Street
Harkstead
Shotley Gate
Shop Corner
FELIXSTOWE
Dedham
Cattawade
Holbrook Bay
Stour
HARWICH
Boxted Cross
Dedham Heath
Lawford
Mistley
Parkeston
Langham
Manningtree
Bradfield
Wrabness
Ramsey
Upper Dovercourt
Dovercourt
Ardleigh
Bradfield Heath
Little Bromley
Horsleycross Street
Horsley Cross
Wix
Little Oakley
Great Oakley
Fox Street
Crockleford Heath
Great Bromley
Little Bentley
Tendring Green
Stone's Green
ESBJERG 18:00
HOEK VAN HOLLAND 6:15
Colchester
Elmstead Market
Hare Green
Balls Green
Beaumont
Horsey Island
The Naze
Old Heath
Wivenhoe Cross
Tendring
Thorpe Green
Thorpe-le-Soken
Kirby-le-Soken
Wivenhoe
Frating Green
Great Bentley
Weeley
Weeley Heath
Walton-on-the-Naze
Rowhedge
Alresford
Aingers Green
Kirby Cross
Frinton-on-Sea
Fingringhoe
Thorrington
Row Heath
Little Clacton
Great Holland
Abberton
Langenhoe
St Osyth Heath
Holland-on-Sea
Brightlingsea
River Colne
Mersea Island
East Mersea
St Osyth
Point Clear
Great Clacton
Clacton-on-Sea
Blue Row
Jaywick
West Mersea
Colne Pt.
Virley Channel
Sales Pt.
7
8
9
10
11
12
A
B
C
D
E
F
G
H
39
21

Beddgelert
Pass of Aberglaslyn
782 MOEL HEBOG
Nantmor
SYGUN COPPER MINE
WELSH HIGHLAND RLY
Llanfihangel-y-pennant
Tyddyn-mawr
Golan
BRYNKIR WOOLLEN MILL
Prenteg
Penmorfa
Tremadog
Pentrefelin
Porthmadog
MARITIME MUSEUM
Morfa Bychan
Borth-y-Gest
Croesor
770 MOELWYN MAWR
FFESTINIOG POWER STATION
Tan-y-lan
Garreg
Rhyd
Llanfrothen
Tan-y-bwlch
Maentwrog
Gellilydan
Penrhyndeudraeth
Minffordd
Portmeirion
Cilfor
Caerwych
Glan-y-wern
Talsarnau
Eisingrug
Llanfihangel-y-traethau
Glyn-cywarch
623 MOEL YSGYFARNOGOD
Traeth Bach
TREMADOG BAY
BAE TREMADOG
Morfa Harlech
Harlech
Llanfair
Llandanwg
Pen-sarn
Pen-y-bont
Pentre Gwynfryn
Llanbedr
Morfa Dyffryn
Coed Ystumgwern
Llanenddwyn
Dyffryn Ardudwy
Cors-y-Gedol
Llanddwywe
Tal-y-bont
Plas-canol
Llanaber
Caerdeon
Bontddu
Cutiau
Barmouth (Abermaw)
BARMOUTH BAY The Bar
BAE BERMO
Arthog
Ynysgyfflog
Fairbourne
Friog
Llwyngwril
Llangelynin
Rhoslefain
Llanfendigaid
Llanegryn
Peniarth
Tonfanau
Bryncrug
Pandy
Rhyd-yr-onen
TALYLLYN RAILWAY
Tywyn
Caethle
Aberdovey
Aberdovey Bar
Bae Aberdyfi
Ynyslas
Llancynfelyn
Borth
Upper Borth
Tal-y-bont
Dol-y-Bont
Llandre
Pen-y-garn
Bow Street
Clarach
Aberystwyth
Llanbadarn Fawr
Comins Coch
Capel Dewi
Penparcau
Rhydyfelin
Southgate
Moriah
Capel Seion
Llanfarian
Gors
Chancery
New Cross
Blaenplwyf
Llanilar
Pentre-llyn
Abermagwr
Crosswood
Llanafan
Wenallt
Blaenau Ffestiniog
Rhiwbryfdir
Tanygrisiau
Bethania
Congl-y-wal
Rhyd-y-sarn
Llan Ffestiniog
Bont Newydd
Cwm Penmachno
Carrog
623 MOEL PENAMNEN
Pont yr Afon-Gam
Migneint
Llyn Conwy
556 CRAIG WEN
TRAWSFYNYDD NUCLEAR POWER STATION
Llyn Trawsfynydd
Pont Dolydd Prysor
Trawsfynydd
Cwm Prysor
Bronaber
Mynydd Bach
720 RHINOG FAWR
Bed-y-coedwr
Coed y Brenin Forest
Ganllwyd
Capel Hermon
734 RHOBELL FAWR
Llanfachreth
Blaen-y-cwm
Nannau
Rhydymain
Llanelltyd
CYMER ABBEY
Pen-y-bryn
Penmaenpool
Abergwynant
Dolgellau
Rhyd-wen
Bont Newydd
Brithdir
893 CADAIR IDRIS
Minffordd
Tal-y-llyn
Llanfihangel-y-pennant
CASTELL Y BERE
Abergynolwyn
Corris Uchaf
Aberllefenni
Corris
CORRIS RAILWAY AND MUSEUM
Esgairgeiliog
KING ARTHUR'S LABYRINTH & CRAFT CENTRE
Plas Llwyngwern
CENTRE FOR ALTERNATIVE TECHNOLOGY
Pantperthog
633 TARRENHENDRE
Pen-y-bont
Pennal
Machynlleth
Cwrt
DOVEY DYFFRYN
Forge
Penegoes
Derwenlas
Glandyfi
Glaspwll
Pant-glâs
Eglwys Fach
YNYS HIR RESERVE
DYFI FURNACE
Tre'r-ddôl
Tre-Taliesin
521 MOEL-Y-LLYN
Nant-y-Moch Reservoir
PLYNLIMON PUMLUMON FAWR 752
Source of R. Severn Blaen Hafren
Source of R. Wye Blaen Gwy
Bont-goch
Salem
Penrhyn-coch
Pen-bont Rhydybeddau
Plas Gogerddan
Capel Bangor
Dollwen
Goginan
LLYWERNOG SILVER LEAD MINE
Dyffryn Castell
Ponterwyd
Cwmbrwyno
VALE OF RHEIDOL RAILWAY
Aberffrwd
Ystumtuen
Ysbyty-Cynfyn
Pisgah
Llanfihangel-y-Creuddyn
Mynydd Bach
Trisant
Devil's Bridge
Cnwch-coch
New Row
Pont-rhyd-y-groes
HAFOD ESTATE
Cwmystwyth
571 GEIFAS
Ysbyty Ystwyth
Mynydd Bach
Ysbyty Ifan
539 GARN PRYS
Cerrigydrudion
Afon Ceirw
Ty Mawr Cwm
Pen-y-gop
669 CARNEDD Y FILIAST
689 ARENIG FACH
Llyn Celyn
Llyn Arenig fawr
ARENIG FAWR 854
Llidiardau
Ciltalgarth
Frongoch
Glan-yr-afon
Llangwm
Tai-mawr
Wenallt
611 FOEL GOCH
Ty-nant
Dinmael
Maerdy
Glan-yr-afon
Melin-y-Wig
Sarnau
Bethel
Cefn-ddwysarn
Rhiwlas
Bala (Y Bala)
Llanfor
Llandderfel
Llanycil
Rhyd-uchaf
Rhos-y-gwaliau
Pale
Cefn Coch
Parc
750 MOEL LLYFRANT
Buarthmeini
Mynydd Bryn-llech
Llangower
Llyn Tegid or Bala Lake
BALA LAKE RAILWAY
Aber-Hirnant
Aberhirnant Forest
Pont Cwm Pydew
Blaen-y-Cwm
Llanuwchllyn
Pont-Rhyd-sarn
Cwm-hesgen
Pont Aber-Geirw
Pont Fronwydd
Talardd
Ty-nant
Cwm Cynllwyd
626 FOEL Y GEIFR
884
907 ARAN FAWDDWY
Gwynedd
Pennant Melangell
Pencraig
Alltforgan
Y BERWYN
Lake Vyrnwy
Ty-uchaf
Aber-Rhiwlech
Pont y Pennant
Hen Gerrig
Llanwddyn
Cywarch
Llanymawddwy
Y Gribin
Bryn Sion
Afon Cerist
670 WAUN-OER
Dinas-Mawddwy
Aber Cowarch
Minllyn
Cwm-Cewydd
Mallwyd
MEIRION MILL
Mynydd Ceiswyn
Mynydd Dolgoed
Dyfi Forest
TIR RHIWIOG 545
Moel y Llyn
Ddôl-Cownwy
Dyfnant Forest
Pont-Llogel
Mynydd y Gadfa
Wern
Foel
Llangadfan
Ffridd Goch
Llanerfyl
Pen Coed
GLYNDWR'S WAY
Aberangell
Cwm-Llinau
Mynydd y Cemaes
Dol-fôr
Cemmaes
Pentre-Celyn
Clegyrnant
Dolwen
Neinthirion
Sychtyn
Cwmderwen
Pandy
Mynydd Waun Fawr
Powys
Llanwrin
Cemmaes Road
Waun
Abercegir
Commins Coch
Darowen
Tal-y-wern
Tafolwern
Llanbrynmair
Dolfach
Llan
Bont-Dolgadfan
Talerddig
Rhyd
Melinbyrhedyn
468 MOELFRE
Pennant
Aberhosan
Carno
Glaslyn
Dylife
Clatter
Llanwnog
Staylittle
GLYNDWR'S WAY
Llawryglyn
Gleiniant
Trefeglwys
Caersws
Llyn Clywedog
482 FAN HILL
Van
Oakley Park
Llandinam
Severn (Hafren)
Tan Hinon
Old Hall
Glan-y-nant
Llanidloes
Hafren Forest
Glynbrochan
Newchapel
Cwmbelan
Pant Mawr
Llanifyny
Llangurig
Tylwch
Nantgwyn
Pant-y-dwr
610 PEN Y GARN
Blaenycwm
Bwlch-y-sarnau
St Harmon
Wye (Gwy)
SH
SN
41
42
24
A
B
C
D
E
F
G
H
1
2
3
4
5
6
0 1 2 3 4 5 6 miles
0 1 2 3 4 5 6 7 8 9 10 km

Wrexham
(Wrecsam)
Shropshire
Llangollen
Corwen
Ruabon
(Rhiwabon)
Chirk
(Y Waun)
Oswestry
Ellesmere
Whitchurch
Wem
Shrewsbury
Baschurch
Shawbury
Welshpool
(Y Trallwng)
Llanfyllin
Llanfair
Caereinion
Newtown
(Y Drenewydd)
Montgomery
(Trefaldwyn)
Bishop's
Castle
Church
Stretton
Craven
Arms
Clun
Ludlow
Knighton
(Tref-y-Clawdd)
Overton
(Owrtyn)
Malpas
Bayston
Hill
Llangynog
Meifod
Welshampton
Cynwyd
Forest
Clun Forest
Black Mountain
THE LONG MYND
WENLOCK EDGE
Stiperstones
Corve Dale
Severn
A5
A483
A458
A49
A41
A495
A528
A488
A489
A4113
42
43
34
25

Stoke
-on-
Trent
Newcastle-under-Lyme
Stoke-on-Trent
Hanley
Fenton
Longton
Whitchurch
Audlem
Madeley
Market Drayton
Stone
Eccleshall
Stafford
Staffor
Newport
Telford
and
Wrekin
Shrewsbury
Wellington
Hadley
Oakengates
Donnington
Telford
Dawley
Shifnal
Albrighton
Penkridge
Rugeley
Cannock
Hednesford
Brewood
Codsall
Tettenhall
Wolverhampton
Wednesfield
Willenhall
Walsall
Bilston
Darlaston
Wednesbury
Sedgley
Coseley
Tipton
Dudley
Oldbury
Rowley Regis
SMETHWICK
Kingswinford
Brierley Hill
Stourbridge
HALESOWEN
W e s t
M
Wombourne
Shawbury
Much Wenlock
Broseley
S h r o p s h i r e
Bridgnorth
Kinver
Kidderminster
Bewdley
Stourport on Severn
Bromsgrove
Catshill
Wyre Forest
Cannock Chase
M6
M54
M5
A5
A41
A442
A449
A458
A518
A34
A51
A53
Keele Services
Stafford Services
Telford Services
Frankley Services
43
44
33
26
0 1 2 3 4 5 6 miles
0 1 2 3 4 5 6 7 8 9 10km

Derby City
Nottingham City
Leicester
Ashbourne
Uttoxeter
Burton upon Trent
Lichfield
Tamworth
Nuneaton
Hinckley
Coventry
Rugby
Loughborough
BIRMINGHAM
Solihull
SUTTON COLDFIELD
Ashby-de-la-Zouch
COALVILLE
Swadlincote
Shepshed
Belper
HEANOR
ILKESTON
LONG EATON
BEESTON
Stapleford
Bedworth
Atherstone
Kenilworth
Lutterworth
NATIONAL FOREST
NEEDWOOD FOREST
CHARNWOOD FOREST
M1
M6
M42
M69
A38
A42
A50
A5
A444
44
45
36
27

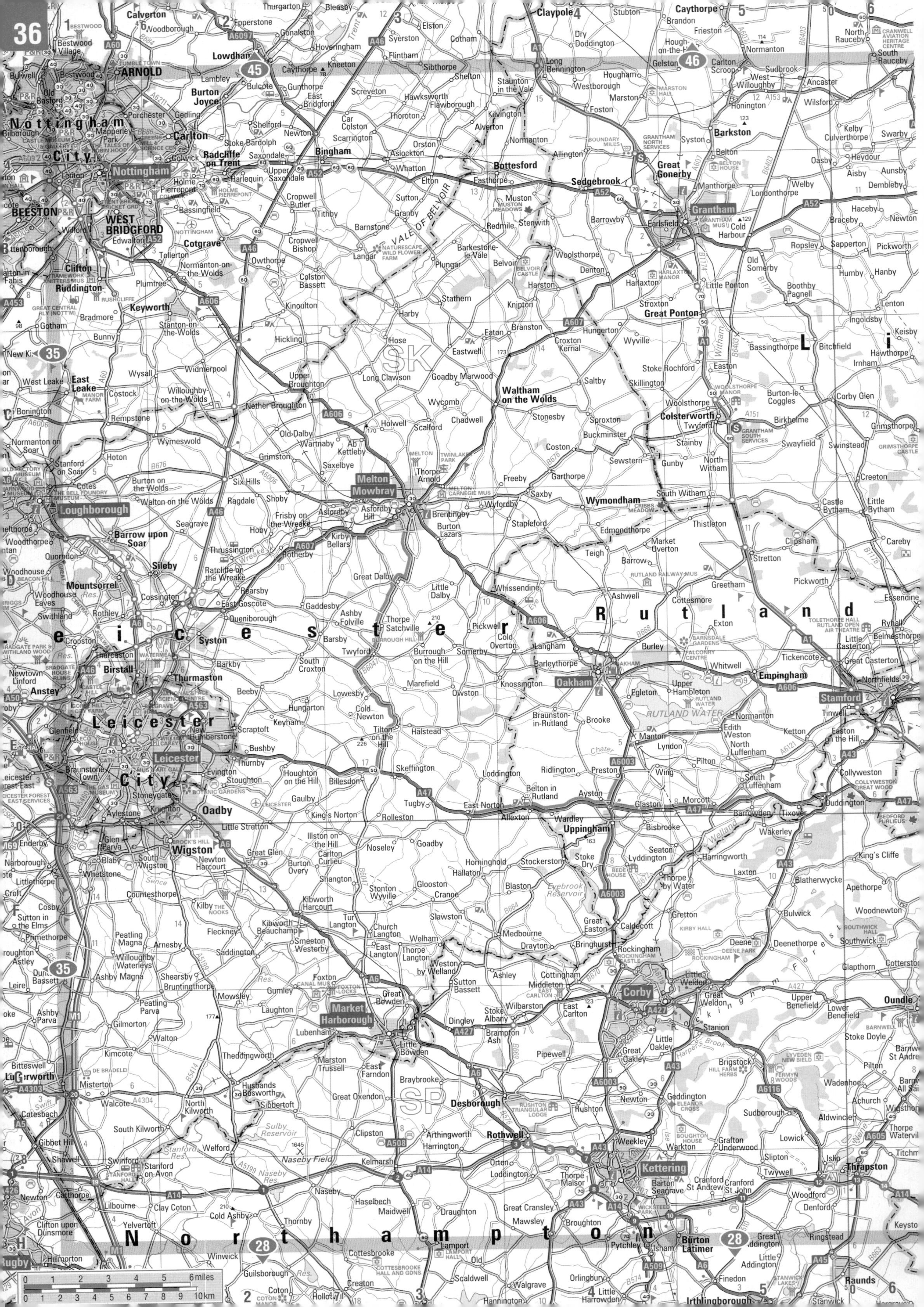

Calverton
Woodborough
Epperstone
Thurgarton
Bleasby
Elston
Claypole
Stubton
Caythorpe
Brandon
Frieston
North Rauceby
CRANWELL AVIATION HERITAGE CENTRE
South Rauceby
Bestwood Village
Lowdham
Gonalston
Hoveringham
Syerston
Cotham
Dry Doddington
Hough-on-the-Hill
Normanton
ARNOLD
Lambley
Caythorpe
Kneeton
Flintham
Long Bennington
Gelston
Carlton Scroop
Bulwell
Bestwood
Burton Joyce
Bulcote
Gunthorpe
East Bridgford
Sibthorpe
Shelton
Staunton in the Vale
Houghham
Westborough
Marston
Sudbrook
West Willoughby
Ancaster
Wilsford
Old Basford
Gedling
Screveton
Hawksworth
Flawborough
Honington
Porchester
Mapperley
Shelford
Car Colston
Thoroton
Kilvington
Foston
Barkston
Kelby
Culverthorpe
Swarby
Nottingham
Carlton
Newton
Scarrington
Alverton
Normanton
Syston
Stoke Bardolph
Orston
Bingham
Aslockton
Allington
Belton
Heydour
City
Radcliffe on Trent
Saxondale
Upper Saxondale
Whatton
Bottesford
Sedgebrook
Great Gonerby
Oasby
Aisby
Aunsby
Dembleby
Nottingham
Holme Pierrepont
Harlequin
Elton
Easthorpe
Manthorpe
Welby
Londonthorpe
Lenton
Cropwell Butler
Sutton
Muston
BEESTON
Bassingfield
Tithby
Granby
Stenwith
Barrowby
Earlsfield
Grantham
Haceby
Braceby
Newton
WEST BRIDGFORD
Wilford
Barnstone
VALE OF BELVOIR
Redmile
Cold Harbour
Sapperton
Ropsley
Pickworth
Attenborough
Edwalton
Cotgrave
Cropwell Bishop
Langar
Barkestone-le-Vale
Woolsthorpe
Old Somerby
Humby
Hanby
Clifton
Tollerton
Normanton-on-the-Wolds
Owthorpe
Plungar
Belvoir
Denton
Harlaxton
Little Ponton
Boothby Pagnell
Barton in Fabis
Ruddington
Plumtree
Colston Bassett
Harston
Stroxton
Keyworth
Kinoulton
Stathern
Knipton
Great Ponton
Lenton
Bradmore
Gotham
Stanton-on-the-Wolds
Harby
Branston
Hungerton
Ingoldsby
Keisby
Bunny
Hickling
Hose
Eaton
Croxton Kerrial
Wyville
Bassingthorpe
Bitchfield
Hawthorpe
Irnham
New Kingston
SK
Eastwell
Stoke Rochford
Easton
Widmerpool
Upper Broughton
Long Clawson
Goadby Marwood
Saltby
Skillington
Corby Glen
West Leake
East Leake
Wysall
Costock
Willoughby-on-the-Wolds
Waltham on the Wolds
Burton-le-Coggles
Bonington
Nether Broughton
Wycomb
Stonesby
Woolsthorpe
Colsterworth
Twyford
Birkholme
Grimsthorpe
Rempstone
Holwell
Chadwell
Sproxton
Normanton on Soar
Wymeswold
Old Dalby
Wartnaby
Ab Kettleby
Scalford
Buckminster
Coston
Stainby
Swayfield
Swinstead
Hoton
Grimston
Saxelbye
Thorpe Arnold
Sewstern
Gunby
North Witham
Stanford on Soar
Burton on the Wolds
Six Hills
Melton Mowbray
Freeby
Garthorpe
Creeton
Cotes
Loughborough
Walton on the Wolds
Ragdale
Shoby
Asfordby
Asfordby Hill
Brentingby
Wyfordby
Saxby
Wymondham
South Witham
Castle Bytham
Little Bytham
Seagrave
Frisby on the Wreake
Burton Lazars
Stapleford
Thistleton
Barrow upon Soar
Hoby
Kirby Bellars
Edmondthorpe
Clipsham
Carby
Woodthorpe
Quorndon
Thrussington
Rotherby
Market Overton
Teigh
Barrow
Stretton
Sileby
Ratcliffe on the Wreake
Great Dalby
Greetham
Pickworth
Woodhouse
Mountsorrel
Rearsby
Little Dalby
Whissendine
Ashwell
Cottesmore
Essendine
Woodhouse Eaves
Cossington
East Goscote
Gaddesby
Swithland
Rothley
Queniborough
Ashby Folville
Thorpe Satchville
Pickwell
Rutland
Exton
Ryhall
Belmesthorpe
Cropston
Syston
Barsby
Cold Overton
Langham
Burley
Little Casterton
Great Casterton
Tickencote
Leicester
Thurcaston
Birstall
Barkby
Twyford
Burrough on the Hill
Somerby
Barleythorpe
Oakham
Whitwell
Empingham
Newtown Linford
Thurmaston
South Croxton
Marefield
Knossington
Upper Hambleton
Northfields
Stamford
Anstey
Beeby
Lowesby
Owston
Egleton
RUTLAND WATER
Normanton
Tinwell
Glenfield
Leicester
Hungarton
Cold Newton
Braunston-in-Rutland
Brooke
Edith Weston
Ketton
Easton on the Hill
Keyham
Halstead
Manton
North Luffenham
Scraptoft
New Humberstone
Tilton on the Hill
Lyndon
Bushby
Thurnby
Skeffington
Loddington
Ridlington
Preston
Pilton
Collyweston
Braunstone Town
City
Evington
Stoughton
Houghton on the Hill
Billesdon
Wing
South Luffenham
Stoneygate
Knighton
Aylestone
Oadby
Gaulby
Tugby
East Norton
Belton in Rutland
Ayston
Glaston
Morcott
Barrowden
Tixover
Duddington
King's Norton
Rolleston
Allexton
Wardley
Uppingham
Bisbrooke
Little Stretton
Enderby
Glen Parva
Wigston
Illston on the Hill
Goadby
Seaton
Wakerley
Narborough
Blaby
South Wigston
Newton Harcourt
Great Glen
Noseley
Carlton Curlieu
Horninghold
Stockerston
Stoke Dry
Lyddington
Harringworth
King's Cliffe
Whetstone
Burton Overy
Shangton
Hallaton
Thorpe by Water
Laxton
Blatherwycke
Apethorpe
Littlethorpe
Croft
Countesthorpe
Stonton Wyville
Glooston
Cranoe
Blaston
Eyebrook Reservoir
Kibworth Harcourt
Woodnewton
Cosby
Kilby
Kibworth Beauchamp
Slawston
Great Easton
Caldecott
Gretton
Bulwick
Sutton in the Elms
Fleckney
Tur Langton
Church Langton
Medbourne
Deene
Deenethorpe
Southwick
Primethorpe
Peatling Magna
Arnesby
Saddington
Smeeton Westerby
East Langton
Welham
Thorpe Langton
Drayton
Bringhurst
Rockingham
Astley
Dunton Bassett
Willoughby Waterleys
Ashby Magna
Shearsby
Bruntingthorpe
Foxton
Weston by Welland
Ashley
Sutton Bassett
Cottingham
Middleton
Corby
Little Weldon
Great Weldon
Glapthorn
Cotterstock
Leire
Peatling Parva
Mowsley
Gumley
Great Bowden
Stoke Albany
Wilbarston
East Carlton
Upper Benefield
Lower Benefield
Oundle
Ashby Parva
Gilmorton
Laughton
Market Harborough
Lubenham
Dingley
Brampton Ash
Stanion
Stoke Doyle
Walton
Little Bowden
Little Oakley
Great Oakley
Kimcote
Theddingworth
Pipewell
Brigstock
Pilton
Barnwell
Bitteswell
Lutterworth
Misterton
Husbands Bosworth
Marston Trussell
East Farndon
Braybrooke
Wadenhoe
Walcote
North Kilworth
Sibbertoft
Great Oxendon
SP
Desborough
Rushton
Newton
Geddington
Achurch
Cotesbach
South Kilworth
Sulby Reservoir
Clipston
Arthingworth
Rothwell
Sudborough
Aldwincle
Gibbet Hill
Welford
Naseby Field
Harrington
Weekley
Warkton
Grafton Underwood
Lowick
Thorpe Waterville
Shawell
Swinford
Stanford on Avon
Kelmarsh
Orton
Slipton
Islip
Thrapston
Loddington
Kettering
Twywell
Titchmarsh
Naseby
Thorpe Malsor
Barton Seagrave
Cranford St Andrew
Cranford St John
Woodford
Denford
Newton
Catthorpe
Lilbourne
Clay Coton
Haselbech
Maidwell
Draughton
Great Cransley
Mawsley
Broughton
Keyston
Clifton upon Dunsmore
Yelvertoft
Cold Ashby
Thornby
Northampton
Lamport
Pytchley
Isham
Burton Latimer
Great Addington
Ringstead
Rugby
Hillmorton
Winwick
Cottesbrooke
Old
Little Addington
Guilsborough
Scaldwell
Walgrave
Orlingbury
Finedon
Raunds
Coton
Creaton
Hollowell
Hannington
Little Harrowden
Irthlingborough
Stanwick
0 1 2 3 4 5 6 miles
0 1 2 3 4 5 6 7 8 9 10 km

Sleaford
Heckington
Helpringham
Swineshead
Boston
HOLLAND FEN
Kirton
Donington
Horbling
Billingborough
Folkingham
Gosberton
Surfleet
Pinchbeck
Spalding
Moulton
Whaplode
Holbeach
Long Sutton
Sutton Bridge
Bourne
Rippingale
Morton
Market Deeping
Deeping St James
Crowland
Wisbech
Peterborough
Whittlesey
March
Chatteris
Ramsey
Yaxley
Sawtry
Huntingdon
St Ives
Somersham
Sutton
Ely
Littleport
Soham
Upwell
Outwell
Terrington St Clement
THE WASH
BOSTON DEEPS
LYNN DEEPS
HOLBEACH MARSH
Gedney Marsh
Terrington Marsh
Deeping Fen
North Fen
Morris Fen
BEDFORD LEVEL (MIDDLE)
BEDFORD LEVEL (SOUTH)
Whittlesey Mere
Tydd St Giles Fen
Marshland Fen
ISLE OF ELY
TF
TL
Lincoln
Peterborough
Cambridge
46
47
38
29

BRANCASTER ROADS
NORFOLK COAST
LYNN DEEPS
THE WASH
Lynn Channel
NORFOLK
Blakeney Point
Holkham Bay
Brancaster Bay
Hunstanton
Old Hunstanton
Holme next the Sea
Titchwell
Thornham
Brancaster
Brancaster Staithe
Burnham Deepdale
Burnham Norton
Burnham Market
Burnham Overy Staithe
Burnham Overy Town
Burnham Thorpe
Holkham
Wells-Next-The-Sea
Stiffkey
Morston
Blakeney
Cley next the Sea
Wiveton
Warham
Cockthorpe
Langham
Glandford
Saxlingham
Ringstead
Heacham
Sedgeford
Docking
Stanhoe
Summerfield
North Creake
South Creake
New Holkham
Waterden
Wighton
Binham
Copy's Green
Field Dalling
Great Walsingham
Little Walsingham
Houghton St Giles
North Barsham
West Barsham
East Barsham
Snettisham
Ingoldisthorpe
Shepherd's Port
Fring
Bircham Newton
Great Bircham
Bircham Tofts
Shernborne
Barmer
Syderstone
Bagthorpe
Blenheim Park
Wicken Green Village
Sculthorpe
Great Snoring
Little Snoring
Thursford
Hindringham
Sharrington
Brinton
Gunthorpe
Briningham
Barney
Swanton Novers
Melton Constable
Kettlestone
Fulmodestone
Dersingham
Sandringham
Wolferton
Anmer
West Newton
Flitcham
Houghton Hall
New Houghton
West Rudham
East Rudham
Tattersett
Coxford
Dunton
Shereford
Tatterford
Hempton
Fakenham
Little Ryburgh
Great Ryburgh
Stibbard
Hindolveston
Wood Norton
Toftrees
Helhoughton
Colkirk
Oxwick
Castle Rising
North Wootton
South Wootton
Terrington Marsh
Ongar Hill
King's Lynn
Gaywood
Hillington
Harpley
Little Massingham
Great Massingham
Congham
Roydon
Grimston
Pott Row
West Raynham
East Raynham
South Raynham
Weasenham St Peter
Weasenham All Saints
Whissonsett
Horningtoft
Twyford
Foulsham
Gateley
Guist
Bintree
Wellingham
Tittleshall
Brisley
North Elmham
Billingford
Bawdeswell
Foxley
Clenchwarton
Terrington St Clement
Walpole Cross Keys
West Lynn
Fairstead
Hardwick
Tilney All Saints
Tilney High End
Hay Green
Gayton
Leziate
Ashwicken
Massingham Heath
Rougham
Fair Green
Tower End
Gayton Thorpe
Middleton
Litcham
Mileham
Bittering
Beetley
Worthing
Stanfield
East Bilney
Swanton Morley
West Winch
North Runcton
East Winch
East Walton
West Lexham
East Lexham
Saddle Bow
Wiggenhall St Germans
Terrington St John
Tilney St Lawrence
Walpole Highway
Wiggenhall St Mary the Virgin
Setchey
Blackborough End
West Bilney
Pentney
West Acre
Castle Acre
South Acre
Newton
Great Dunham
Little Dunham
Drury Square
Beeston
Longham
Gressenhall
Sparrow Green
Crane's Corner
Hoe
Woodgate
Etling Green
North Tuddenham
Dereham
St John's Fen End
Marshland
Wiggenhall St Mary Magdalen
Tottenhill Row
Watlington
Tottenhill
Wormegay
Narborough
Great Fransham
Great Palgrave
Sporle
Little Fransham
Wendling
Scarning
Toftwood
Clint Green
Yaxham
Marshland St James
Marshland Fen
Runcton Holme
South Runcton
Shouldham
Marham
Shouldham Thorpe
Beachamwell Warren
Swaffham
Necton
West End
Bradenham
Westfield
Whinbury
Emneth Hungate
Stowbridge
Stow Bardolph
West Head
Wimbotsham
Downham Market
Fincham
Barton Bendish
Beachamwell
Shingham
Cockley Cley
North Pickenham
Holme Hale
Crowshill
Shipdham
Letton Green
Garvestone
Reymerston
Southburgh
Hardingham
Outwell
Stow Bardolph Fen
Barroway Drove
Broomhill
Stradsett
Crimplesham
Bexwell
Eastmoor
South Pickenham
Ashill
Saham Hills
Saham Toney
Ovington
Cranworth
Woodrising
Carbrooke
Nordelph
Denver
Wereham
Boughton
Oxborough
Gooderstone
Great Cressingham
Caudlesprings
Hingham
Three Holes
West Dereham
Fordham
Wretton
Stoke Ferry
Whittington
Foulden
Hilborough
Bodney
Little Cressingham
Watton
Griston
Scoulton
Upwell Fen
Hilgay
Ten Mile Bank
Wissey
Northwold
Brookville
The Arms
Merton
Northacre
Caston
Rockland St Peter
Little Ellingham
Great Ellingham
Deopham Green
Stow Bedon
Rockland All Saints
Thompson
Lakesend
Hilgay Fen
Southery
Methwold Hythe
Methwold
Cranwich
Ickburgh
Mundford
Lower Stow Bedon
Shropham
Welney
Gold Hill
Southery Fens
Methwold Fens
Queen's Ground
West Tofts
THETFORD FOREST PARK
BRECKLAND
Great Hockham
Apes Hall
Brandon Creek
Feltwell
Wretham
Eccles Road
Brandon Bank
Feltwell Fens
Hockwold cum Wilton
Weeting
Larling
Quidenham
Mare Fen
Fodder Fen
Burnt Fen
Hockwold Fens
Little Ouse
Brandon
Santon Downham
Croxton
Bridgham
Kenninghall
East Harling
Littleport
BEDFORD LEVEL (SOUTH)
Little Downham
Shippea Hill Sta.
Brandon Park
Kenninghall Heath
Chettisham
West Fen
Prickwillow
Lakenheath
Wangford Warren
Thetford Warren
Thetford
Brettenham
Shadwell
North Lopham
Queen Adelaide
Ely
Kenny Hill
Lakenheath Warren
Rushford
Gasthorpe
Garboldisham
Middle Fen
Stuntney
Great Fen
Mildenhall Fen
Eriswell
Elveden
Barnham
Euston
Knettishall
Coney Weston
Hopton
Market Weston
Blo' Norton
Thelnetham
Redgrave
Little Thetford
Broad Hill
Beck Row
Holywell Row
Barningham
Hinderclay
Isleham Fen
Thistley Green
West Row
Fakenham Magna
Sapiston
Hepworth
Rickinghall
Barway
Soham Cotes
Isleham
Mildenhall
The King's Forest
Honington
Soham
Worlington
Barton Mills
Icklingham
Bardwell
Wattisfield
Freckenham
Tuddenham
West Stow
Ingham
Troston
Ixworth Thorpe
Stanton
Upthorpe
Walsham le Willows
Cranmer Green
Ampton
Great Livermere
Four Ashes
0 1 2 3 4 5 6 miles
0 1 2 3 4 5 6 7 8 9 10 km

Sheringham
Cromer
Overstrand
Mundesley
Holt
North Walsham
Aylsham
Reepham
Coltishall
Hoveton
Wroxham
Drayton
Sprowston
NORWICH
Thorpe St Andrew
Brundall
Acle
Great Yarmouth
Gorleston-on-Sea
Caister-on-Sea
Hemsby
Belton
Loddon
Lowestoft
Beccles
Bungay
Harleston
Diss
Eye
Halesworth
Southwold
Wymondham
Cringleford
Kessingland
NORFOLK COAST
THE BROADS
TG
TM
A140
A47
A146
A143
A12
A149
A1074
A11
A148
31
6
7
8
9
10
11
A
B
C
D
E
F
G
H

Isle of Anglesey
(Sir Ynys Môn)
Holyhead
(Caergybi)
Holy Island
Ynys Gybi
The Skerries
Ynysoedd y
Moelrhoniaid
Carmel Head
Pen Carmel
Wilfa
Head
Pen Wilfa
Cemaes
Bay
Bae
Cemaes
Cemlyn Bay
Bae Cemlyn
WYLFA POWER STATION
AND OBSERVATION TOWER
Llanbadrig
Porthllechog
Bull Bay
Porth
Llechog
Burwen
Amlwch
Port
Amlwch
Point Lynas
Llaneilian
Pengorffwysfa
Penysarn
Nebo
Dulas
Tregele
Cemaes
Rhosbeirio
Bodewryd
Llanfechell
Llanfairynghornwy
Church Bay
Porth Swtan
Rhydwyn
Llanrhyddlad
Llanfflewyn
Rhosgoch
Carreglefn
Rhosybol
Tyn-
y-pwll
City
Dulas
Brynrefail
Ty-mawr
Llanallgo
Llanbabo
Alaw
Res.
Gwredog
LLYNON
WINDMILL
Llanddeusant
Llandyfrydog
Mynydd
Bodafon
Hebron
Elim
Llanerchymedd
Bachau
Maenaddwyn
Llanfaethlu
Llanfwrog
Llantrisant
Carmel
Capel Coch
Brynteg
Llanfachraeth
Pen-llyn
Res.
Llechcynfarwy
CORS
ERDDREINIOG
HOLYHEAD BAY
BAE
CAERGYBI
DUBLIN 1:49
DUN LAOGHAIRE 1:59
DUBLIN 3:15
North Stack
BREAKWATER
HOLYHEAD MOUNTAIN
220
Llaingoch
Goferydd
South Stack
ELLINS TOWER RSPB RESERVE
PENRHOS FEILW
STANDING STONES
Kingsland
Penrhosfeilw
ANGLESEY
Penrhyn Mawr
Newlands
Park
Llanynghenedl
Valley
Bodedern
Trefor
Tregaian
Llangwyllog
Trearddur
Glan-traeth
Four Mile
Bridge
Caergeiliog
A55
Bryngwran
Llynfaes
Llanfihangel
yn Nhowyn
Gwalchmai
Bodffordd
Rhosmeirch
ORIEL
YNYS MÔN
Heneglwys
Llangefni
Llanfairyneubwll
Rhoscolyn
Cymyran
Bay
Bae Cymyran
Capel-
gwyn
Ddrydwy
Llanfaelog
Pencarnisiog
Bryn Du
Rhosneigr
Cerrigceinwen
Llangristiolus
HENBLAS COUNTRY
PARK
Soar
Capel Mawr
Pentre
Berw
Gaerwen
Bethel
Trefdraeth
Afon Cefni
Llangwyfan-isaf
Aberffraw
Llangadwaladr
Hermon
Malltraeth
Llangaffo
Brynsiencyn
Bodorgan
NEWBOROUGH WARREN
AND YNYS LLANDDWYN
Newborough
Dwyran
SEA ZOO
Pen-lon
Newborough
Forest
BIRD
WORLD
MODEL
VILLAGE
FOEL
FARM
PARK
Malltraeth Bay
Bae Malltraeth
SEIONT II MARITIME MUSEUM
CASTLE &
REGIMENTAL MUS
MENAI STRAIT
Llanddwyn I.
Ynys Llanddwyn
The Bar
Caernarfon
Abermenai
Pt.
Trwyn
Abermenai
WELSH
HIGHLAND
RAILWAY
Llanfaglan
Bontnewydd
CAERNARFON
AIR MUSEUM
Saron
Morfa Dinlle
Glan-rhyd
Llanwnda
Rhostryfan
Dinas Dinlle
Ffrwd
Llandwrog
GLYNLLIFON
Groeslon
Carmel
Cilgwyn
Penygroes
Talysarn
Tan-yr-allt
Pontllyfni
Llanllyfni
Nebo
Aberdesach
Clynnog-fawr
WELSH LIFE
Tainlon
Nasareth
Capel Uchaf
A487
Gyrn-goch
Pant-glas
Bryn-yr-eryr
509
BWLCH
MAWR
Upper
Clynnog
Dafarn Faig
Trefor
522
GYRN DDU
564
YR EIFL
Llanaelhaearn
Cenin
Pen-sarn
Garndolbenmaen
Llecheiddior
Dwyfan
Llithfaen
Pistyll
Pencaenewydd
Carreg Ddu
Porth
Dinllaen
Llwyndyrys
Llangybi
Morfa Nefyn
Nefyn
LLEYN HISTORICAL
MARITIME MUSEUM
Edern
Fron
Llanarmon
Tan-y-
graig
Rhos-fawr
Y Ffôr
Chwilog
Llanystumdwy
PENARTH FAWR
MEDIEVAL HOUSE
LLOYD
GEORGE
MEMORIAL
MUSEUM
Criccieth
Porth Ysgadan
Glanrhyd
Rhos-y-llan
Boduan
Llannor
Abererch
CORS
GEIRCH
BODVEL HALL
ADVENTURE PARK
Efailnewydd
HAVEN
Tudweiliog
Dinas
Rhyd-y-
clafdy
Denio
Pwllheli
Carreg yr Imbill
South Beach
Porth Golmon
Garnfadryn
Bryn-mawr
Llaniestyn
Penrhos
Pen-y-graig
Llangwnnadl
Rhedyn
Penrhyn Mawr
Pen-y-
groeslon
Sarn
Meyllteyrn
Llanbedrog
Ty-hen
Bryncroes
Botwnnog
Nanhoron
Mynytho
Trwyn Llanbedrog
Methlem
Rhydlios
Llandegwning
304
MYNYDD
RHIW
PLAS-YN-
RHIW
Capel Carmel
Rhoshirwaun
Llawr
Dref
Llangian
St Tudwal's
Road
Angorfa St Tudwal
Rhiw
Abersoch
191
Porth Neigwl or
Hell's Mouth
Llanengan
St Tudwal's Island East
Ynys St Tudwal Dwyrain
Uwchmynydd
Aberdaron
Llanfaelrhys
Sarn Bach
Bwlchtocyn
Marchroes
Bodermid
St Tudwal's Island West
Ynys St Tudwal Gorllewin
Pen-y-cil
Bardsey Sound
Swnt Enlli
Cilan Uchaf
Trwyn
Cilan
YNYS ENLLI
167
Bardsey
Island
Ynys Enlli
PENRHYN LLŶN
YNYS MÔN
ANGLESEY
CAERNARFON
BAY
BAE
CAERNARFON
LLEYN
LLŶN
SH
0 1 2 3 4 5 6 miles
0 1 2 3 4 5 6 7 8 9 10km

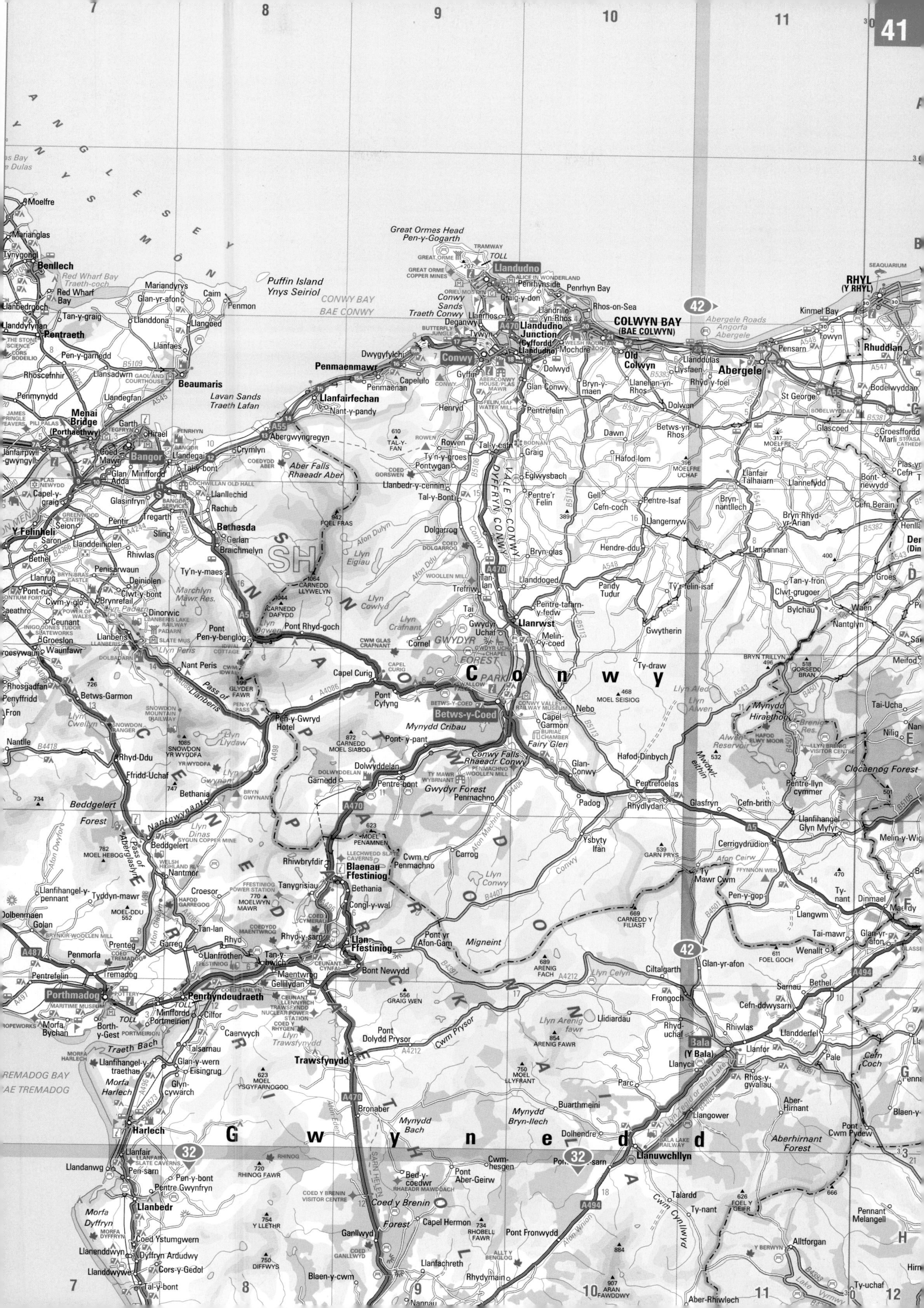

7
8
9
10
11
Great Ormes Head
Pen-y-Gogarth
Llandudno
Puffin Island
Ynys Seiriol
CONWY BAY
BAE CONWY
Red Wharf Bay
Traeth-coch
Moelfre
Marianglas
Benllech
Pentraeth
Beaumaris
Menai Bridge
(Porthaethwy)
Bangor
Penmaenmawr
Llanfairfechan
Conwy
Llandudno Junction
(Cyffordd Llandudno)
COLWYN BAY
(BAE COLWYN)
Old Colwyn
Abergele
RHYL
(Y RHYL)
Rhuddlan
Kinmel Bay
Towyn
Penmon
Lavan Sands
Traeth Lafan
Aber Falls
Rhaeadr Aber
Bethesda
Y Felinheli
Llanberis
Pass of Llanberis
Capel Curig
Betws-y-Coed
Llanrwst
Conwy Falls
Rhaeadr Conwy
Gwydyr Forest
Mynydd Cribau
Dolwyddelan
Blaenau Ffestiniog
Llan Ffestiniog
Tanygrisiau
Migneint
Beddgelert Forest
Beddgelert
Porthmadog
Penrhyndeudraeth
Maentwrog
Trawsfynydd
Harlech
Morfa Harlech
Llanbedr
Coed y Brenin Forest
Llyn Celyn
Bala
(Y Bala)
Llanuwchllyn
Cerrigydrudion
Pentrefoelas
Clocaenog Forest
Mynydd Hiraethog
Alwen Reservoir
Llyn Brenig
Abergele Roads
Angorfa Abergele
Vale of Conwy
Dyffryn Conwy
Snowdon
Yr Wyddfa
1085
SH
Conwy
Gwynedd
SNOWDONIA NATIONAL PARK
PARC CENEDLAETHOL ERYRI
TREMADOG BAY
BAE TREMADOG
Traeth Bach
Aberhirnant Forest
42
32
A5
A55
A470
A494
A487
A4086
A4212

SC
IRISH SEA
LIVERPOOL BAY
SH
Southport
49
41
32
33
Formby
Formby Pt.
Ainsdale
Hightown
Little Crosby
Crosby Channel
BELFAST 8:00
DOUGLAS 4:15 (Winter only)
DUBLIN 7:00
DOUGLAS 2:30 (March-Nov)
Bootle
LITHERLAND
Wallasey
Mockbeggar Wharf
New Brighton
Birkenhead
HOYLAKE
West Kirby
Hilbre I.
West Hoyle Bank
Welsh Channel
Point of Ayr
Yr Parlwr Du
River Dee
Afon Dyfrdwy
BEBINGTON
Heswall
Dawpool Bank
Neston
Holywell Bank
Gayton Sands
Willaston
Talacre
Gwespyr
Ffynnongroyw
Mostyn
Mostyn Quay
RHYL
(Y RHYL)
Prestatyn
Kinmel Bay
Towyn
Rhuddlan
Dyserth
Abergele Roads
Angorfa Abergele
Rhos-on-Sea
COLWYN BAY
(BAE COLWYN)
Old Colwyn
Abergele
Pensarn
St George
Bodelwyddan
St Asaph
(Llanelwy)
Holywell
(Treffynnon)
Greenfield
Flint (Y Fflint)
Connah's Quay
Shotton
Queensferry
Hawarden
(Penarlâg)
Flintshire
(Sir Y Fflint)
Mold
(Yr Wyddgrug)
Buckley
(Bwcle)
VALE OF CLWYD
DYFFRYN CLWYD
Denbigh
(Dinbych)
Conwy
Denbighshire
(Sir Ddinbych)
Ruthin
(Rhuthun)
Clocaenog Forest
Llyn Brenig
Alwen Reservoir
Mynydd Hiraethog
Hope
(Yr Hôb)
Caergwrle
Wrexham
(Wrecsam)
Rhosllanerchrugog
Ruabon
(Rhiwabon)
Llangollen
Corwen
Cynwyd Forest
Llantysilio Mountain
Eglwyseg Mountain
Pandy Tudur
Llanfihangel Glyn Myfyr
Cerrigydrudion
Glasfryn
Pentrefoelas
Rhydlydan
Druid
Carrog
Glyndyfrdwy
Cefn-mawr
0 1 2 3 4 5 6 miles
0 1 2 3 4 5 6 7 8 9 10km

CHORLEY
Ramsbottom
Edgworth
Turton Moor
White Coppice
Anglezarke Moor
Holmeswood
Rufford
Mawdesley
Eccleston
Burscough
Scarisbrick
ORMSKIRK
Skelmersdale
Wigan
Coppull
Adlington
Standish
Blackrod
Horwich
Bolton
Bury
HEYWOOD
Rochdale
Greater Manchester
WESTHOUGHTON
FARNWORTH
Radcliffe
Whitefield
Middleton
PRESTWICH
Chadderton
Hindley
ATHERTON
Tyldesley
Leigh
Worsley
Swinton
Pendlebury
SALFORD
MANCHESTER
Eccles
Trafford Park
URMSTON
Stretford
SALE
Altrincham
GATLEY
Cheadle
Manchester Airport
WILMSLOW
Knutsford
Maghull
Kirkby
Knowsley
St Helens
Haydock
ASHTON-IN-MAKERFIELD
Golborne
Newton-le-Willows
Merseyside
Prescot
Huyton
Warrington
Widnes
Runcorn
Halton
Speke
Garston
Liverpool John Lennon Airport
Ellesmere Port
Frodsham
Helsby
Lymm
Northwich
Weaverham
Cheshire West and Chester
Cheshire East
Chester
WINSFORD
Middlewich
Holmes Chapel
Sandbach
Congleton
Macclesfield
Alsager
Kidsgrove
Crewe
Nantwich
Tarporley
Farndon
Malpas
Whitchurch
Audlem
Madeley
Newcastle-under-Lyme
Stoke-on-Trent
Tunstall
Burslem
Hanley
Biddulph
Prestbury
Alderley Edge
M6
M56
M62
M60
M61
M58
M57
M53
A49
A50
A51
A54
A34
A41
A533
A556
A580
44
49
50
33
34

Rochdale
Littleborough
Milnrow
HEYWOOD
Bury
Radcliffe
Whitefield
Middleton
ROYTON
Shaw
Chadderton
Oldham
PRESTWICH
Swinton
Pendlebury
Failsworth
Ashton-under-Lyne
STALYBRIDGE
MANCHESTER
SALFORD
Eccles
Trafford Park
Stretford
Droylsden
Dukinfield
Denton
Hyde
SALE
Stockport
Cheadle
GATLEY
Altrincham
Hale
Manchester Airport
HAZEL GROVE
Bramhall
Marple
Romiley
Bredbury
Poynton
WILMSLOW
Alderley Edge
Prestbury
Bollington
Macclesfield
Hurdsfield
Congleton
Biddulph
Kidsgrove
Alsager
Tunstall
Burslem
Stoke-on-Trent
Hanley
Newcastle-under-Lyme
Fenton
Longton
Leek
Cheddleton
Endon
Cheadle
Alton
Huddersfield
Slaithwaite
Marsden
Meltham
HOLMFIRTH
Honley
Skelmanthorpe
Denby Dale
Clayton West
Penistone
Stocksbridge
GLOSSOP
Hadfield
Hollingworth
Mossley
New Mills
Low Leighton
Hayfield
Whaley Bridge
Chapel-en-le-Frith
Buxton
Burbage
Castleton
Hope
Hathersage
Bamford
Edale
Tideswell
Eyam
Baslow
Bakewell
Ashford in the Water
Youlgreave
Matlock
Wirksworth
Cromford
Ashbourne
Hartington
PEAK DISTRICT NATIONAL PARK
HIGH PEAK
HOPE FOREST
Saddleworth Moor
Howden Moors
Derwent Res.
Ladybower Res.
Greater Manchester
Cheshire East
Stafford
Derbyshire
Yorkshire
43
50
51
34
35
0 1 2 3 4 5 6 miles
0 1 2 3 4 5 6 7 8 9 10 km

Barnsley
Doncaster
Rotherham
Sheffield
Chesterfield
Worksop
Mansfield
RETFORD
Gainsborough
Newark-on-Trent
Nottingham City
Hemsworth
Thorne
Hatfield
Bentley
Armthorpe
Bessacarr
Adwick le Street
Mexborough
Conisbrough
Wath upon Dearne
Swinton
Rawmarsh
Maltby
Tickhill
Harworth
Bawtry
Dinnington
Langold
Blyth
Staveley
Bolsover
Shirebrook
Market Warsop
Edwinstowe
Ollerton
Tuxford
MANSFIELD WOODHOUSE
SUTTON IN ASHFIELD
KIRKBY IN ASHFIELD
ALFRETON
RIPLEY
HEANOR
HUCKNALL
ARNOLD
Eastwood
ILKESTON
Belper
Dronfield
ECKINGTON
Southwell
Carlton
Epworth
ISLE OF AXHOLME
SHERWOOD PINES FOREST PARK
Hatfield Moors
Thorne Waste or Moors
South Yorkshire
Derbyshire
Nottinghamshire

North Lincolnshire
North East Lincolnshire
Lincolnshire
SE
SK
52
53
45
36
37
Winterton
Scunthorpe
Immingham
Grimsby
Brigg
Broughton
Messingham
Epworth
ISLE OF AXHOLME
Kirton in Lindsey
Scotter
Hibaldstow
Caistor
Laceby
Healing
Keelby
Waltham
Binbrook
Market Rasen
Gainsborough
Laughton Forest
Saxilby
Lincoln
Nettleham
Washingborough
Wragby
Horncastle
Bardney
North Hykeham
Boultham
Bracebridge
Waddington
Metheringham
Woodhall Spa
Coningsby
Billinghay
Collingham
Bassingham
Navenby
Leadenham
Ruskington
Leasingham
Sleaford
Heckington
Helpringham
Caythorpe
Claypole
Newark-on-Trent
Balderton
Sutton on Trent
Faldingworth
Ermine Street
Holland Fen
South Kyme Fen
Wildmore Fen
0 1 2 3 4 5 6 miles
0 1 2 3 4 5 6 7 8 9 10 km

Kilnsea
53
TA
SPURN
SPURN HEAD
ROTTERDAM 10:25
ZEEBRUGGE 10:25
CLEETHORPES
MOUTH OF THE HUMBER
CLEETHORPES COAST LIGHT RAILWAY
PLEASURE ISLAND THEME PARK
Humberston
Tetney Lock
North Cotes
Tetney
N O R T H
S E A
Donna Nook
Marshchapel
Eskham
Wragholme
Grainthorpe
Fulstow
LINCOLNSHIRE WOLDS RLY.
North Somercotes
DONNA NOOK
Skidbrooke North End
Covenham St Bartholomew
Conisholme
South Somercotes
Saltfleet
Utterby
Covenham St Mary
Yarburgh
Skidbrooke
ALVINGHAM MILL
Alvingham
Fotherby
Little Grimsby
North Cockerington
Saltfleetby St Clements
SALTFLEETBY THEDDLETHORPE
RUSHMOOR
Saltfleetby All Saints
Theddlethorpe St Helen
South Cockerington
Keddington
Louth
Grimoldby
Saltfleetby St Peter
Theddlethorpe All Saints
Stewton
Manby
SEAL SANCTUARY & NATURE CENTRE
Hallington
Little Carlton
Great Carlton
Meers Bridge
Mablethorpe
Legbourne
South Reston
Little Cawthorpe
Gayton le Marsh
Trusthorpe
North Reston
Tathwell
Strubby
Haugham
Muckton
Tothill
Withern
Thorpe
Sutton on Sea
Maltby le Marsh
Authorpe
Sandilands
Maidenwell
Burwell
Woodthorpe
Beesby
WOODY'S TOP
Belleau
CLAYTHORPE WATER MILL AND WILDFOWL GARDENS
Saleby
Hannah
Farforth
Ruckland
White Pit
Aby
Markby
Swaby
Asserby
ALFORD WINDMILL
South Thoresby
Ketsby
ALFORD MANOR HOUSE
Bilsby
Huttoft
South Ormsby
Haugh
Rigsby
Alford
Calceby
Anderby
Tetford
Farlesthorpe
ON YOUR MARQUES
Mumby
Authorpe Row
Brinkhill
Driby
Well
Salmonby
Cumberworth
Somersby
Ulceby
TF
Helsey
Chapel St Leonards
Sutterby
Bonthorpe
Hogsthorpe
Bag Enderby
Harrington
Ashby Puerorum
Willoughby
Claxby
Greetham
Langton
Sloothby
Aswardby
HARDY'S ANIMAL FARM
Skendleby
Hagworthingham
Sausthorpe
Ingoldmells
SNIPE DALES
Partney
Addlethorpe
FANTASY ISLAND CHILDREN'S PLAYDROME & THE MILLENNIUM ROLLERCOASTER
Lusby
Welton le Marsh
Hameringham
Mavis Enderby
Raithby
Scremby
FUNCOAST WORLD
Asgarby
Candlesby
Orby Marsh
Spilsby
Ashby by Partney
Orby
Old Bolingbroke
GUNBY HALL
Hareby
Hundleby
Bratoft
Burgh le Marsh
Winthorpe
Seathorne
NORTHCOTE HEAVY HORSE CENTRE
BOLINGBROKE
Great Steeping
Halton Holegate
NATURELAND SEAL SANCTUARY
West Keal
Toynton All Saints
Irby in the Marsh
BURGH LE MARSH WINDMILL
CHURCH FARM MUS
Skegness
East Keal
East Kirkby
Toynton St Peter
THE LIFEBOAT STATION
Toynton Fen Side
Firsby
Little Steeping
LINCOLNSHIRE AVIATION HERITAGE CENTRE
Keal Cotes
Thorpe Culvert
Thorpe St Peter
Croft
Revesby Bridge
Thorpe Fendykes
Seacroft
Croft Marsh
Stickford
Wainfleet All Saints
New Bolingbroke
Fen Side
Wainfleet Bank
MAGDALEN MUSEUM
New Leake
Midville
Wainfleet Tofts
Wainfleet St Mary
GIBRALTAR POINT
Stickney
Eastville
Medlam
Friskney Eaudike
Wainfleet Sand
East Fen
Carrington
Friskney
Lade Bank
Wrangle Bank
Fen
Northlands
Friskney Tofts
Leake Commonside
SIBSEY TRADER MILL
Sibsey
Wrangle Lowgate
Friskney Flats
Frithville
Old Leake
Wrangle
Hurn's End
38
BRANCASTER ROADS
Hill Dyke
Leverton Outgate
Frith Bank
Boston
Long Hedges
Leverton Highgate
BOSTON DEEPS
Cowbridge
Leverton
Leverton Lucasgate
LYNN DEEPS
Benington
Brancaster Bay
SCOLT HEAD ISLAND
HOLME DUNES
Haltoft End
GUILDHALL
Butterwick
37
Freiston
Brancaster Staithe
Burnham Deepdale
HOLME BIRD OBSERVATORY
Holme next the Sea
Titchwell
Brancaster
Burnham Norton
Westgate
Skirbeck
THE WASH
Old Hunstanton
Thornham
Fishtoft
Wyberton
Scrane End
Hunstanton
A B C D E F G H
7 8 9 10 11

NX
IRISH SEA
Isle of Man
SC
POINT OF AYRE
Rue Pt.
The Ayres
Glentruan
Cranstal
The Lhen
Dhowin
Bride
Andreas
MANX CROSSES
Jurby Head
JURBY SOUTH
Jurby East
Sandygate
Jurby West
Ballasalla
Regaby
The Cronk
St Judes
Dhoor
CURRAGHS WILDLIFE PARK
Sulby
GROVE MUSEUM
RAMSEY BAY
Ramsey
MANX ELECTRIC RAILWAY
Port e Vullen
Orrisdale
Ballaugh
T.T.Course
Churchtown
Glen Auldyn
Maughold
Maughold Head
Ravensdale
Dreemskerry
Rhencullen
565 NORTH BARRULE
Ballajora
Kirk Michael
CELTIC CRAFT CENTRE
Corrany
Cornaa
Ballaleigh
SNAEFELL 621
Glen Mona
Barregarrow
Druidale
Dhoon
MURRAYS MOTORCYCLE MUSEUM
Agneash
LAXEY WHEEL AND MINES
Bulgham Bay
MANX TRANSPORT MUSEUM
Knocksharry
Cronk-y-Voddy
544
SNAEFELL MOUNTAIN RAILWAY
Ballaquine
Laxey
St Patrick's I.
PEEL
487 COLDEN
LAXEY WOOLLEN MILLS
Old Laxey
Laxey Head
Peel
HOUSE OF MANANNAN
BALLALHEANNAGH GARDENS
Fairy Cottage
Laxey Bay
Contrary Head
KIPPER MUSEUM
TYNWALD CRAFT CENTRE
TYNWALD HILL
Patrick
St John's
Greeba
Baldwin
Creg-ny-Baa
Ballacannel
Baldrine
Clay Head
Glenmaye
333
Lower Foxdale
Crosby
MANX CROSSES
Dalby Pt.
Glen Vine
Strang
Onchan
HEYSHAM 3:30
GROUDLE GLEN RAILWAY
Dalby
Niarbyl
Foxdale
Union Mills
Tromode
ONCHAN PLEASURE PARK
HEYSHAM 2:00
(TT race period only)
Eairy
Braaid
Spring Valley
Douglas
Niarbyl Bay
483 SOUTH BARRULE
222
Cooil
Douglas Bay
Close Clark
Ellenbrook
Douglas Head
CAMERA OBSCURA
St Mark's
Ballaveare
LIVERPOOL 2:30
(March-Nov)
Ballamodha
Newtown
Little Ness
Lingague
Ronague
ISLE OF MAN STEAM RAILWAY
LIVERPOOL 4:15
(Winter only)
Fleshwick Bay
Grenaby
Surby
Ballabeg
RUSHEN ABBEY
Santon Head
Bradda Head
Bradda
Colby
Ballasalla
Port Greenaugh
Port Erin
BILLOWN
ISLE OF MAN
RAILWAY MUS
Four Roads
Derbyhaven
The Howe
Castletown
CASTLE RUSHEN
NAUTICAL MUS
St Michael's I.
Cregneash
SCARLETT VISITOR CENTRE
OLD HOUSE OF KEYS
Port St Mary
CREGNEASH VILLAGE FOLK MUSEUM
128
Scarlett Point
Calf of Man
Spanish Head
Dreswick Pt.
BELFAST 2:55
DUBLIN 2:55
(April-Sept)
Chicken Rock
0 1 2 3 4 5 6 miles
0 1 2 3 4 5 6 7 8 9 10km

Cumbria
Lancashire
MORECAMBE
BAY
IRISH
SEA
SD
Bootle
Broughton in Furness
Lower Hawthwaite
Blawith
Nibthwaite
Rusland
Finsthwaite
Lakeside
FURNESS FELLS
Oxen Park
Bouth
Cartmel Fell
Bowland Bridge
Row
The Howe
Cotes
Levens
Sedgwick
Barrow Green
Middleshaw
Black Combe
Hallthwaites
Foxfield
Grizebeck
Gawthwaite
Lowick Bridge
Lowick Green
Colton
Spark Bridge
Newby Bridge
Staveley
Backbarrow
Haverthwaite
Ayside
Witherslack
High Newton
Low Newton
Town End
Mill Side
Sampool Bridge
Hincaster
Stainton
Endmoor
Gatebeck
Crooklands
Leasgill
Heversham
Whitbeck
The Green
The Hill
Whicham
Silecroft
Kirksanton
Millom
Haverigg
Kirkby-in-Furness
Beck Side
Penny Bridge
Broughton Beck
Greenodd
Arrad Foot
Mansriggs
Soutergate
Field Broughton
Lindale
Meathop
Milnthorpe
Lupton
Farleton
DUDDON SANDS
Askam in Furness
Ireleth
Lindal in Furness
Ulverston
Pennington
Swarthmoor
Cartmel
Holker
Allithwaite
Grange-over-Sands
Arnside
Storth
Beetham
Holme
Hutton Roof
Clawthorpe
Burton-in-Kendal
Yealand Redmayne
Yealand Conyers
Silverdale
Kents Bank
Flookburgh
Cark
Ravenstown
Humphrey Head Pt.
Warton Sands
Warton
Priest Hutton
Borwick
Capernwray
Arkholme
Millhead
Carnforth
Over Kellet
Gressingham
Hornby
Nether Kellet
Bolton-le-Sands
Hest Bank
Slyne
Bolton Town End
Aughton
Halton
Caton Green
Caton
Brookhouse
Claughton
Bardsea
Great Urswick
Little Urswick
Dalton-in-Furness
Stainton with Adgarley
Scales
Baycliff
Aldingham
Hawcoat
Newton
Ormsgill
Newbarns
Dendron
Gleaston
Barrow-in-Furness
North Scale
Vickerstown
Barrow Island
Yarlside
Leece
Newbiggin
Roosebeck
Biggar
Rampside
Roa Island
Foulney Island
Piel Island
South End
Isle of Walney
South End Point
South Channel
Morecambe
Bare
Sandylands
Torrisholme
Skerton
White Lund
Heysham
Lancaster
Heaton
Aldcliffe
Scotforth
Crossgill
Clougha
Quernmore
Middleton
Overton
Sunderland Pt.
Shoulder of Lune
Glasson
Conder Green
Galgate
Thurnham
Smith Green
Lee Fell
Ortner
Lee
Abbeystead
Dolphinholme
Cockerham Sands
Cockerham
Forton
Hollins Lane
Street
Hawthornthwaite Fell
Braides
DOUGLAS 3:30
DOUGLAS 2:00 (TT race period only)
LARNE 8:00
Knott End-on-Sea
Fleetwood
Rossall Point
Preesall
Pilling Lane
Pilling
Dam Side
Stake Pool
Winmarleigh
Scorton
Cabus
Bleasdale Moors
Oakenclough
Eagland Hill
Garstang
Calder Vale
Bleasdale
Stalmine
Staynall
Nateby
Bowgreave
Cleveleys
Anchorsholme
Norbreck
Thornton
Trunnah
Hambleton
Out Rawcliffe
Little Eccleston
Moss Edge
Ratten Row
Churchtown
Catterall
Claughton
Whitechapel
St Michael's on Wyre
Bispham
Carleton
Skippool
Little Singleton
Great Eccleston
Bilsborrow
Inglewhite
Blackpool
Warbreck
North Shore
Poulton-le-Fylde
Singleton
Elswick
Crossmoor
Myerscough
Inskip
Thistleton
Roseacre
Cuddy Hill
Barton
Goosnargh
Queenstown
Layton
Normoss
Staining
Esprick
Catforth
Great Marton
Weeton
Corner Row
Wharles
Woodplumpton
Broughton
Haighton Green
South Shore
Hawes Side
Mereside
Common Edge
Little Plumpton
Great Plumpton
Wesham
Treales
Lower Bartle
Higher Bartle
Cottam
Sharoe Green
Squires Gate
Westby
Kirkham
Dowbridge
Lea Town
Ingol
Fulwood
Cadley
Ribbleton
Moss Side
Wrea Green
Newton
Scales
Clifton
Preston
Higher Ballam
St Annes
Lytham St Anne's
Ansdell
Lytham
Fairhaven
Salters Bank
Warton
Freckleton
Bottom of Hutton
Penwortham
Walton-le-Dale
Bamber Bridge
Ribble
Hutton
Middleforth Green
Lostock Hall
Longton
New Longton
Farington
Banks Sands
Great Bank
Hesketh Bank
Walmer Bridge
Midge Hall
Much Hoole
Becconsall
Hundred End
LEYLAND
Broadfield
Clayton Green
Clayton-le-Woods
Horse Bank
Banks
Tarleton
Crossens
Bretherton
Euxton
Marshside
Sollom
Croston
Ulnes Walton
Shaw Green
Mere Brow
Churchtown
Southport
Holmeswood
Eccleston
CHORLEY
Blowick
Rufford
Charnock Richard
Birkdale
Brown Edge
Tarlscough
Mawdesley
Heskin Green
Hillside
Snape Green
Bescar
Scarisbrick
New Lane
Bispham Green
Wrightington Bar
Coppull
Ainsdale-on-Sea
Ainsdale
Shirdley Hill
Burscough
Hill Dale
Mossy Lea
Woodvale
Pinfold
Burscough Bridge
Parbold
Dangerous Corner
Heskin
6 miles
10km

57
49
43
44
Y O R K S H I R E
D A L E S
N A T I O N A L
P A R K
F O R E S T
O F
B O W L A N D
L a n c a s h i r e
SD
Kirkby Lonsdale
Ingleton
High Bentham
Settle
Skipton
Clitheroe
Preston
Blackburn
Burnley
Keighley
Rochdale
Bury
ACCRINGTON
RAWTENSTALL
COLNE
NELSON
CHORLEY
LEYLAND
HEYWOOD
Blackburn with Darwen
Todmorden
Hebden Bridge
Bacup
Haslingden
Oswaldtwistle
Padiham
Barnoldswick
Earby
Gargrave
Grassington
Hellifield
Long Preston
Gisburn
Slaidburn
Chatburn
Whalley
Great Harwood
Clayton-le-Moors
Longridge
Ribchester
Fulwood
Littleborough
Whitworth
Ramsbottom
Edgworth
Darwen
Horwich
Tottington
Milnrow
Wardle
Dent
Sedbergh
Clapham
Austwick
Horton in Ribblesdale
Malham
Kettlewell
Buckden
Kilnsey
Conistone
Ribblehead
Langstrothdale Chase
Ingleborough
Pen-y-ghent
Whernside
Gisburn Forest
Stocks Reservoir
Trough of Bowland
Pendle Hill
The Forest of Pendle
The Forest of Trawden
Forest of Rossendale
Longridge Fell
Anglezarke Moor
Keighley Moor
0 1 2 3 4 5 6 miles
0 1 2 3 4 5 6 7 8 9 10km

Bedale
Masham
Thirsk
Sowerby
Ripon
Easingwold
Boroughbridge
NIDDERDALE
Pateley Bridge
Knaresborough
Harrogate
Wetherby
Spofforth
York
ILKLEY
Otley
Burley in Wharfedale
Addingham
Menston
Guiseley
Yeadon
Baildon
BINGLEY
SHIPLEY
Bradford
Horsforth
LEEDS
PUDSEY
Garforth
Tadcaster
Bramham
Boston Spa
Collingham
Copmanthorpe
Sherburn in Elmet
Queensbury
Halifax
BRIGHOUSE
Elland
Cleckheaton
BATLEY
MORLEY
Rothwell
Middleton
Dewsbury
OSSETT
Wakefield
Normanton
CASTLEFORD
Pontefract
Knottingley
Ferrybridge
Featherstone
Mirfield
Horbury
Huddersfield
Hemsworth
Kippax
MARSTON MOOR
HAMBLETON HILLS
Sowerby Bridge

North Yorkshire
City of York
East Riding of Yorkshire
North Lincolnshire
Rievaulx Moor
Hutton-le-Hole
Spaunton
Cropton
Appleton-le-Moors
Fadmoor
Kirkbymoorside
Keldholme
Sinnington
Wrelton
Aislaby
Middleton
Pickering
Kirkby Mills
Carlton
Old Byland
Rievaulx
Pockley
Beadlam
Nawton
Wombleton
Welburn
Helmsley
Rye Dale
Duncombe Park
Cold Kirby
Scawton
Great Edstone
Marton
Normanby
Harome
Sproxton
Muscoates
Little Barugh
Nunnington
Nunnington Hall
Salton
West Ness
East Ness
Great Barugh
Kirby Misperton
Flamingo Land
Oldstead
Wass
High Kilburn
Byland Abbey
Ampleforth
Oswaldkirk
Stonegrave
South Holme
Butterwick
Brawby
Coxwold
Gilling East
Cawton
Little Habton
Great Habton
Ryton
Hovingham
Husthwaite
Oulston
Yearsley
Wath
Fryton
Coulston
Slingsby
Barton-le-Street
Amotherby
Eden Camp Modern History Theme Museum
Appleton-le-Street
Swinton
Broughton
Howardian Hills
Brandsby
Scackleton
Stearsby
Dalby
Skewsby
Terrington
Ganthorpe
Coneysthorpe
Castle Howard
Yorkshire Lavender
Malton
Old Malton
Norton-on-Derwent
Crayke
Easingwold
Whenby
Whitewall Corner
High Hutton
Stillington
Farlington
Bulmer
Welburn
Low Hutton
Langton
Firby
Sheriff Hutton
Thornton-le-Clay
Whitwell-on-the-Hill
Kirkham
Kirkham Priory
Huby
Sutton-on-the-Forest
Sutton Park
Cross Lanes
West Lilling
Foston
Crambe
Westow
Kennythorpe
Burythorpe
Birdsall
Leavening
Barton-le-Willows
Harton
Howsham
Acklam
Flaxton
Leppington
Bossall
Strensall
Claxton
Scrayingham
Sand Hutton
Towthorpe
Newton on Ouse
Beningbrough Hall
Shipton
Beningbrough
Wigginton
Haxby
Earswick
Moor End
Upper Helmsley
Buttercrambe
Skirpenbeck
Bugthorpe
Stamford Bridge
Gate Helmsley
Stockton on the Forest
Warthill
Holtby
Moor Monkton
Skelton
Overton
Nether Poppleton
Upper Poppleton
Huntington
New Earswick
Rawcliffe
Clifton
York
Murton
Dunnington
Yorkshire Museum of Farming
Low Catton
High Catton
Full Sutton
Youlthorpe
Gowthorpe
Fangfoss
Bolton
Hessay
Knapton
Rufforth
Acomb
Holgate
Heworth
Osbaldwick
National Railway Museum
York Minster
Jorvik Viking Centre
Castle Museum
Grimston
Kexby
Wilberfoss
Hutton Wandesley
Nunthorpe
Heslington
Fulford
Askham Bryan
Askham Richard
Woodthorpe
Bishopthorpe
York Designer Outlet
Crockey Hill
Elvington
Yorkshire Air Museum
Newton upon Derwent
Barmby Moor
Bilbrough
Copmanthorpe
York West Services
Acaster Malbis
Naburn
Deighton
Wheldrake
Sutton upon Derwent
Allerthorpe
Pocklington
Colton
Appleton Roebuck
Acaster Selby
Escrick
Storwood
Melbourne
Thornton
Bielby
Lower Derwent Valley
Bolton Percy
Ulleskelf
Holme Green
Stillingfleet
Thorganby
East Cottingwith
Seaton Ross
Harswell
Everingham
Ryther
Kelfield
Ellerton
Laytham
Aughton
Water End
Moor End
Holme-on-Spalding-Moor
Church Fenton
Cawood
Skipwith
North Duffield
Riccall
Harlthorpe
Foggathorpe
Sand Hole
Rascal Moor
Bubwith
Highfield
Gribthorpe
Willitoft
Wistow
Biggin
Little Fenton
Barlby
Selby Abbey
Osgodby
Menthorpe
South Duffield
Gunby
Breighton
Spaldington
Bursea
Selby
Thorpe Willoughby
Lund
Cliffe
Wressle
Brind
North Howden
Portington
Hive
Hambleton
Brayton
East Common
Hemingbrough
Cavil
Sandholme
Monk Fryston
Newsholme
Howden Minster
Eastrington
Scalby
Gilberdyke
Newport
Hillam
Barlow
Long Drax
Barmby on the Marsh
Howden
Asselby
Knedlington
Kilpin Pike
Kilpin
Balkholme
Staddlethorpe
Broomfleet
Gateforth
West Haddlesey
Burn
Yorkshire Garden World
Birkin
Chapel Haddlesey
Drax
Boothferry
Temple Hirst
Hirst Courtney
Camblesforth
Newland
Airmyn
Hook
Skelton
Laxton
Saltmarshe
Yokefleet
Blacktoft
Faxfleet
Whitton
Beal
Kellington
Kellingley
Eggborough
Hensall
Carlton
Goole
The Yorkshire Waterways Museum
Reedness
Swinefleet
Whitgift
Ousefleet
Blacktoft Sands RSPB
Julian's Bower Turf Maze
Little Reedness
Snaith
East Cowick
West Cowick
Rawcliffe
Rawcliffe Bridge
Old Goole
Gowdall
High Eggborough
Cridling Stubbs
Whitley
Great Heck
Pollington
Southfield Reservoir
Dutch River
Goole Fields
Adlingfleet
Alkborough
Walcot
West Halton
Womersley
Balne
Aire and Calder Navigation
Fockerby
Garthorpe
Coleby
Winterton
Little Smeaton
Walden Stubbs
Sykehouse
Pincheon Green
Goole Moors
Eastoft
Luddington
Burton Stather
Burton upon Stather
Normanby
Normanby Hall
Thealby
Roxby
Kirk Smeaton
Fenwick
Barnsdale Bar Services
Norton
Moorends
Humberhead Peatlands
Thorne Waste or Moors
Flixborough
Appleby
Campsall
Moss
Fosterhouses
Fishlake
Amcotts
Flixborough Stather
Dragonby
Thorne
Crowle
Doncaster North Services
Canal Side
Wike Well End
Stainforth & Keadby Canal
Windsor
Ealand
Keadby
Gunness
Crosby
Scunthorpe
Santon
Stainforth
Bramwith
North Riding Forest Park
Low Dalby
Dalby Forest
Dalby Forest Visitor Centre
North Yorkshire Moors Railway
St Peter and St Paul Church
Pickering Castle
Thornton-le-Dale
Ellerburn
Wilton
Allerston
Ebberston
Snainton
Trouts Dale
Wrench Green
Everley
Barrowcliff
Wykeham Forest
Forge Valley Woodlands
Falsgrave
East Ayton
West Ayton
Sawdon
Wordsworth Gallery
Hutton Buscel
Ruston
Irton
Seamer
Eastfield
Wykeham
Brompton
Flixton
Yedingham
The Carrs
Willerby
Staxton
High Marishes
Low Marishes
Derwent
East Heslerton
West Knapton
East Knapton
Sherburn
Ganton
Yorkshire Wolds Way
Scampston
Scampston Hall
Wolds Way Lavender
West Heslerton
Potter Brompton
Fordon
Wykeham
Rillington
Thorpe Bassett
Wintringham
Wold Newton
Foxholes
Scagglethorpe
Place Newton
Butterwick
Settrington
Helperthorpe
Weaverthorpe
Octon
East Lutton
West Lutton
Octon Cross Roads
North Grimston
Duggleby
Kirby Grindalythe
Langtoft
Wharram le Street
Wharram Percy Medieval Village
Sledmere
Sledmere House
Cottam
The Wolds
Thixendale
Fimber
Garton-on-the-Wolds
Kirby Underdale
Painsthorpe
Fridaythorpe
Wetwang
Driffield
Elmswell
Little Driffield
Kelleythorpe
Yorkshire Wolds Way
Huggate
Tibthorpe
Kirkburn
Southburn
Bishop Wilton
Great Givendale
Meltonby
Yapham
Millington
North Dalton
Bainton
Hutton Cranswick
Kilnwick Percy
Warter
Middleton-on-the-Wolds
Watton
Kilnwick
Nunburnholme
Stewart's Burnby Hall Gardens & Museum
Burnby
Lund
Beswick
Holme on the Wolds
Lockington
Thorpe
Hayton
Londesborough
South Dalton
Scorborough
Thorpe le Street
Shiptonthorpe
Goodmanham
Market Weighton
Etton
Leconfield
Gardham
Cherry Burton
Molescroft
Beverley
Bishop Burton
Sancton
North Cliffe
North Newbald
South Newbald
Walkington
South Cliffe
Bentley
Hotham
High Hunsley
Skidby
Skidby Windmill
Little Weighton
Rowley
Cottingham
North Cave
Everthorpe
South Cave
West End
Riplingham
Eppleworth
Kirk Ella
Willerby
Brantingham
Ellerker
Swanland
West Ella
Elloughton
Welton
North Ferriby
Brough
Humber Bridge
Hessle
Redcliff Channel
Read's Island
Barton-upon-Humber
Winteringham
South Ferriby
Horkstow
Saxby All Saints
Bonby
Worlaby
Elsham Hall
Kings
Market Weighton Canal
River Trent
New River Ancholme
0 1 2 3 4 5 6 miles
0 1 2 3 4 5 6 7 8 9 10km

6
7
8
9
10
11
A
B
C
D
E
F
G
H
NORTH
SEA
TA
Filey Brigg
Filey
Filey Bay
Yons Nab
CLEVELAND WAY
Cayton Bay
Gristhorpe
Muston
Primrose Valley
Hunmanby
Hunmanby Moor
Reighton Sands
Reighton Gap
Reighton
Speeton
Burton Fleming
Buckton
Bempton
FLAMBOROUGH HEAD
Flamborough
Grindale
SEWERBY HALL AND GARDENS
Sewerby
BONDVILLE MODEL VILLAGE
Boynton
Rudston
BAYLE MUSEUM
Bridlington
OLD PENNY MEMORIES
West Hill
Bessingby
Carnaby
Hilderthorpe
BRIDLINGTON BAY
Haisthorpe
Thornholme
BURTON AGNES HALL
BURTON AGNES MANOR HOUSE
PARK ROSE BIRD OF PREY CENTRE
Kilham
Burton Agnes
Harpham
Fraisthorpe
Lowthorpe
Nafferton
Gransmoor
Barmston
Great Kelk
Lissett
Gembling
Ulrome
Wansford
Foston on the Wolds
SKIPSEA CASTLE
CRUCKLEY ANIMAL FARM
Church End
Beeford
Skipsea
Skipsea Brough
North Frodingham
Rotsea
Dunnington
Hempholme
Bewholme
Atwick
North Cliff
Burshill
Hornsea
Hornsea Mere
HORNSEA MUSEUM
Brandesburton
Baswick Steer
Seaton
FREEPORT HORNSEA
Hornsea Bridge
Leven
Leven Canal
Catwick
Sigglesthorne
Rolston
Goxhill
Mappleton
Little Hatfield
Routh
Tickton
Long Riston
Rise
Great Hatfield
Great Cowden
Arnold
Withernwick
Weel
Meaux
Skirlaugh
New Ellerby
Marton
West Newton
Aldbrough
East Newton
Woodmansey
Wawne
Old Ellerby
BURTON CONSTABLE HALL
Flinton
Thearne
Swine
Coniston
Garton
Grimston
Dunswell
Bransholme
Thirtleby
Sproatley
Humbleton
Fitling
Hilston
Sutton on Hull
Ganstead
Kingston-upon-Hull
Lelley
Owstwick
Tunstall
Bilton
Sutton Ings
Elstronwick
Newland
Stoneferry
Burton Pidsea
North End
Roos
Sculcoates
Summergangs
Preston
WILBERFORCE HOUSE
West End
Waxholme
Ella
P&R
Marfleet
Salt End
Owthorne
THE DEEP
STREETLIFE
Haven Side
Hedon
Rimswell
Withernsea
KINGSTON UPON HULL
FERENS ART GALLERY
Burstwick
Halsham
East End
Paull
Thorngumbald
Camerton
FORT PAULL
Ryehill
Keyingham
HUMBER
Hollym
Goxhill Haven
Ottringham
New Holland
Little Humber
Winestead
Holmpton
Thorney Crofts
Patrington
Cherry Cob Sands
Out Newton
Goxhill
Welwick
Weeton
Barrow upon Humber
South End
East Halton
Skeffling
Sunk Island
Easington
THORNTON ABBEY
Thornton Curtis
North Killingholme
Wootton
Immingham
Ulceby Skitter
South Killingholme
Ulceby
Kilnsea
MUSEUM
Habrough
SPURN
Croxton
Kirmington
Brocklesby
Stallingborough
Keelby
ROTTERDAM 10:25
ZEEBRUGGE 10:25
A165
A1039
A614
A1035
A1033
A1165
A63
A160
A180
B1229
B1255
B1259
B1253
B1249
B1242
B1244
B1243
B1238
B1240
B1239
B1237
B1233
A1105
B1362
B1445
B1211
46
47

CARLETON CASTLE
260
Poundland
Pinwherry
Bellamore
335 PINDONNAN
Bennane Hd.
Colmonell
B734
Knockdolian
Ballochmorrie
Black Clauchrie
Loch Moan
Palgowan
Ballantrae Bay
Heronsford
Glen Tig
Water of Tig
Ballantrae
Balkissock
Barrhill
Laggan
Eldrick
A714
Glentrool
Downan Pt.
Auchencrosh
Arecleoch Forest
Glentrool Village
GLENTROOL VISITOR CENTRE
LARNE 1:00 (Mar-Oct)
LARNE 1:45
BELFAST 3:15
BELFAST 2:20
439 BENERAIRD
Drumlamford Loch
Dornal
Chirmorrie
A77
B7027
Bargrennan
Mark
Loch Dornal
Loch Ochiltree
Clachaneasy
Loch Maberry
Milleur Pt.
Miltonise
Glen App
Craig Airie Fell
Loch Derry
Polbae
Kirroughtree Forest
Corsewall Pt.
287
257
Barnhills
Portencalzie
LAGGANGAIRN STANDING STONES
Knowe
North Cairn
South Cairn
Corsewall
B738
Loch Connell
Kirkcolm
Dounan Bay
Cairnryan
Penwhirn Res.
Main Water of Luce
Cross Water of Luce
B7027
Mains of Airies
Ervie
244
Artfield Fell
Penninghame Forest
Carseriggan
Braid Fell
Challoch
Low Salchrie
The Wig
B798
LOCH RYAN
Black Loch
213
Knocknain
New Luce
Benfield
Slouchnawen Bay
Leswalt
A77
Innermessan
Auchmantle
SOUTHERN UPLAND WAY
Loch Heron
Loch Ronald
Craigencross
Shennanton
B7043
Drumphail
205
A75
A718
A751
Black Loch
CASTLE KENNEDY GARDENS
Tarf Water
B733
B735
123
Glenstockadale
White Loch
14
Kirkcowan
Stranraer
Aird
Castle Kennedy
Whitecairn
Carscreugh
Craighlaw Mains
Broadsea Bay
CASTLE OF ST JOHN VISITOR CENTRE
THE RHINS
WIGTOWN DISTRICT MUSEUM
Knockglass
Soulseat Loch
A75
GLENWHAN GARDENS
Dunragit
GLENLUCE ABBEY
Glenluce
Dernaglar Loch
High Mindork
Knock Moss
Spittal
CASTLE OF PARK
Mark
Black Hd.
Lochans
B738
182
B7077
A747
Whitefield Loch
131
Bladnoch
B7052
Dunskey Ho.
NW
A77
Torrs Warren
Fell Loch
LITTLE WHEELS
Portpatrick
Awhirk
B7084
Luce Sands
Milton
Stairhaven
Castle Loch
Culmazie
Stoneykirk
A716
Auchenmalg
Mochrum Loch
THE MACHARS
Port of Spittal Bay
B7042
Culshabbin
Auchenmalg Bay
Alticry
B7005
197
Barrachan
Cairngarroch
Sandhead
Loch Head
Cairngarroch Bay
KIRKMADRINE STONES
Sandhead Bay
CHAPEL FINIAN
Money Hd.
Elrig
MOTE OF DRUCHTAG
A747
B7085
Clachanmore
Mochrum
Airyhass
Hole Stone Bay
Milton Pt.
ARDWELL GDNS
Ardwell
Ardwell Mains
Chapel Rossan Bay
Drumtroddan
Drummod
DRUMTRODDAN
Ardwell Pt.
Logan Mains
Port William
Monreith Mains
LOGAN BOTANIC GARDEN
Balgowan Pt.
LUCE BAY
Mull of Logan
LOGAN FISH POND MARINE LIFE CENTRE
BARSALLOCH FORT
Moor Ravenstone
Barsalloch Pt.
Monreith
Port Nessock or Port Logan Bay
MONREITH ANIMAL WORLD, SHORE CENTRE AND MUSEUM
Port Logan
Cairnywellan Hd.
Monreith Bay
B7065
A716
Clanyard Bay
Low Clanyard
Laggantalluch Hd.
Kirkmaiden
Drummore
164
Cailliness Pt.
Damnaglaur
B7041
Crammag Hd.
Maryport
Cairngaan
Port Kemin
MULL OF GALLOWAY
1 2 3 4 5 6
A B C D E F G H
0 1 2 3 4 5 6 miles
0 1 2 3 4 5 6 7 8 9 10 km

Castlemaddy
Dundeugh
Kendoon
Glenhoul
Glencrosh
Castlefairn
Holmhead
Dalmacallan Forest
Wallaceton
Glenmidge
Auldgirth
Forrest Lodge
Loch Harrow
MULLWHARCHAR
MERRICK
Loch Enoch
Loch Dungeon
RHINNS OF KELLS
Loch Neldricken
Loch Valley
SILVER FLOWE
BRUCE'S STONE
Loch Trool
Clatteringshaws Forest
Clatteringshaws Loch
Loch Dee
LAMACHAN HILL
Drumbuie
St John's Town of Dalry
Earlstoun Loch
Millquarter
Bogue
Garroch
Glenlee
New Galloway
Balmaclellan
BLOWPLAIN OPEN FARM
Corriedoo Forest
Lochurr
BOGRIE HILL
Loch Urr
Sundaywell
Dunscore
Milton
Cairn Water
Newtonairds
Drumpark
Glenkiln Res.
Glenkiln
Irongray
Terregles Banks
Shawhead
Blackcraig
Knocklearn
Gibbshill
Corsock
Ironmacannie
Craig
Merkland
Urr Water
Brooklands
Brae
Lochfoot
Lochrutton Loch
Crocketford or Ninemile Bar
Milton Loch
Auchenreoch Loch
Kirkpatrick Durham
Springholm
Milton
Beeswing
Loch Arthur
Lochaber Loch
DRUMCOLTRAN TOWER
CLATTERINGSHAWS FOREST WILDLIFE CENTRE
RAIDERS ROAD FOREST DRIVE
Bennan Forest
Cairn Edward Hill
Loch Grannoch
FELL OF FLEET
WILD GOAT PARK
Mossdale
Stroan Loch
Drumrash
Parton
Loch Ken
Loch Skerrow
Woodhall Loch
Craig
Crossmichael
Old Bridge of Urr
Clarebrand
Haugh of Urr
Kirkgunzeon
Dumfries and Galloway
Minnigaff
Creebridge
Newton Stewart
Palnure
CAINSMORE OF FLEET
CAIRNSMORE OF FLEET
Fleet Forest
Lochenbreck Loch
Laurieston
Townhead of Greenlaw
MOTE OF URR
Clints of Dromore
Laurieston Forest
Loch Glentoo
THREAVE CASTLE
Castle Douglas
Carlingwark Loch
KELTON MAINS OPEN FARM
THREAVE GARDENS
Rhonehouse or Kelton Hill
Bridge of Dee
Loch Bargatton
Loch Whinyeon
Loch Mannoch
Glengap Forest
BENGRAY
Glengap
OLD BUITTLE TOWER
Barhill
Dalbeattie
LONG FELL
Baltersan
Big Water of Fleet
Cree
Causeway End
Carsegowan
GEM ROCK MUSEUM
Creetown
Wigtown Sands
Wigtown
SCOTLAND'S BOOK TOWN
Glen
NX
FLEET VALLEY
Anwoth
CARDONESS CASTLE
MILL ON THE FLEET
Gatehouse of Fleet
Valleyfield
Ringford
Gelston
Airieland
Palnackie
Dalbeattie Forest
Drumstinchall
Barnbarroch
Caulkerbush
Mainsriddle
Sandyhills
Colvend
Rockcliffe
Portling
Mersehead Sands
ORCHARDTON TOWER
Kippford or Scaur
MOTE OF MARK
ROUGH ISLAND
Rough I.
Castlehill Pt.
CAIRNHARROW
CARSLUITH CASTLE
Carsluith
CAIRNHOLY CAIRNS
Girthon
Twynholm
GALLOWAY HYDRO VISITOR CENTRE
Tongland
BROUGHTON HOUSE AND GARDEN
BENGAIRN
EAST STEWARTRY COAST
Braehead
Kirkinner
Baldoon Sands
Ravenshall Pt.
Ringdoo Pt.
Fleet Bay
Sandgreen
Barharrow
MACLELLAN'S CASTLE
STEWARTRY MUSEUM
Kirkcudbright
Whinnieliggate
Auchencairn
Auchencairn Bay
Hestan I.
Whauphill
Islands of Fleet
Knockbrex
Kirkandrews
Borgue
St Mary's Island
Mutehill
Kirkcarswell
Dundrennan
Rascarrel
Balcary Pt.
Rascarrel Bay
Sorbie
Garlieston
Eggerness Pt.
WIGTOWN BAY
Kirkcudbright Bay
Townhead
Orroland
DUNDRENNAN ABBEY
GALLOWAY HOUSE GARDENS
Borness
Ross
Borness Pt.
Balmae
Netherlaw
Port Mary
Abbey Hd.
Little Ross
Cults
CRUGGLETON CHURCH AND CASTLE
Bishopton
PRIORY AND MUSEUM
Whithorn
Port Allen
Portyerrock Bay
Cairn Hd.
ST NINIAN'S CHAPEL
ST NINIAN'S CAVE
Isle of Whithorn
Cutcloy
BURROW HEAD
SOLWAY FIRTH
ST BEES HEAD
A712
A713
A762
A75
A711
A745
A746
A714
A755
B727
B795
B794
B736
B793
B7004
B7052
B7063
B7005
B729
B7000
A702
A76
60
67
56
7
8
9
10
11
12
A
B
C
D
E
F
G
H

SOLWAY FIRTH
SOLWAY COAST
Southerness Pt.
Dubmill Pt.
Allonby Bay
Saltom Bay
Selker Bay
NX
SC
60
61
49
Kirkbean
Southerness
Cardurnock
Anthorn
Easton
Boustead Hill
Kirkandrews upon Eden
Kingstown
Houghton
Linstock
Grinsdale
Stanwix
Carlisle
Warwick on Eden
Whitrigg
Kirkbride
Finglandrigg Woods
Drumburgh Moss
Thurstonfield
Kirkbampton
Moorhouse
Newton Arlosh
Skinburness
Silloth
Greenrow
Calvo
Seaville
Wedholme Flow
South Solway Mosses
Little Bampton
Aikton
Great Orton
Little Orton
Newby West
Morton
Harraby
Botcherby
Scotby
Wetheral
Upperby
Cummersdale
Carleton
Cumwhinton
Wiggonby
Baldwinholme
Durdar
Brisco
Causewayhead
Blitterlees
Kingside Hill
Abbey Town
Oulton
Dalston
Cotehill
Beckfoot
Highlaws
Pelutho
Kelsick
Dundraw
Lessonhall
Waverbridge
Thursby
Buckabank
Wreay
Newtown
Blencogo
Wigton
West Curthwaite
East Curthwaite
Holme St Cuthbert
Bromfield
Waverton
Waterside
Brackenthwaite
Gaitsgill
Mawbray
Langrigg
Red Dial
Westward
Rosley
Raughton Head
Stockdalewath
Low Hesket
Southwaite
Edderside
New Cowper
Westnewton
Bolton Low Houses
Welton
Ivegill
Allonby
Aspatria
Watchhill
Fletchertown
Brocklebank
Sebergham
Low Braithwaite
Hayton
Mealsgate
Prospect
Oughterside
Blennerhasset
Boltongate
Thomas Close
Calthwaite
Allerby
Threapland
Torpenhow
Sandale
Caldbeck
Hesket Newmarket
Sowerby Row
Hutton End
Crosscanonby
Crosby Villa
Parsonby
Plumbland
Bothel
Whitrigg
Ireby
Crosby
Bullgill
Gilcrux
Uldale
Fell Side
Branthwaite
Millhouse
New Rent
Maryport Maritime Museum
Maryport
Dearham
High Ireby
Binsey
Over Water
Low Row
Lamonby
Unthank
Skelton
Tallentire
Blindcrake
Sunderland
High Pike
High Row
Ellonby
Flimby
Dovenby
Bridekirk
Bewaldeth
Orthwaite
Hutton Roof
Broughton Moor
Standingstone
Johnby
Little Blencow
Siddick
Great Broughton
Little Broughton
Papcastle
Bassenthwaite
Knott
Mosedale
Great Blencow
Camerton
Cockermouth
Embleton
Great Calva
Mungrisdale
Greystoke
Seaton
Great Clifton
Brigham
Skiddaw Forest
Wythop Mill
Berrier
North Side
Workington
Stainburn
Bridgefoot
Greysouthen
Little Clifton
Skiddaw
Saddleback or Blencathra
Motherby
Penruddock
Newbiggin
Helena Thompson Mus
Westfield
Eaglesfield
Thornthwaite Forest
Scales
Mossbay
Deanscales
Sandybeck Meadow
Millbeck
Applethwaite
Troutbeck
Hutton
Dacre
Winscales
Low Lorton
Thornthwaite
Threlkeld
Harrington
High Harrington
Dean
Mosser
High Lorton
Whinlatter Pass
Braithwaite
Cumberland Pencil Museum
Branthwaite
Pardshaw
Wreay
Distington
Ullock
Mockerkin
Thackthwaite
Whinlatter Forest Park
Grisedale Pike
Portinscale
Keswick
Castlerigg Stone Circle
Matterdale End
Lowca
Pica
Longthwaite
Watermillock
Moresby
Loweswater
Lamplugh
Brackenthwaite Fell
Stair
Derwent Water
Dockray
Knotts
Parton
Asby
Dowthwaitehead
Bransty
Moresby Parks
Arlecdon
Loweswater Fell
Little Town
Stanah
Fisher Place
Howtown
Sandwich
The Rum Story
Whitehaven
Haig Colliery Mining Museum
Walk Mill
Rowrah
High Leys
Kirkland
Croasdale
Rannerdale
Crummock Water
Buttermere
Derwent Fells
Grange
High Seat
Thirlmere
Glenridding
Patterdale
Martindale Common
Dale Head
Hensingham
Frizington
Great Borne
Watendlath
Helvellyn
Mirehouse
Cleator Moor
Ennerdale Bridge
Ennerdale Forest
High Stile
Buttermere Fell
Borrowdale
Rosthwaite
Bridgend
Sandwith
Moor Row
Wath Brow
Ennerdale Water
Ennerdale Fell
Black Sail
Honister Hause
Seatoller
Stonethwaite
Wythburn
Hartsop
Brothers Water
Rottington
Cleator
Longlands Lake
Pillar
Ullscarf
Wythburn Fells
Grisedale Tarn
St Bees
Egremont
Wilton
Seathwaite
LAKE DISTRICT NATIONAL PARK
CUMBRIAN MOUNTAINS
Cumbria
Great Gable
High Street
Kirkstone Pass
Harter Fell
Coulderton
Middletown
Nethertown
Thornhill
Haile
Seatallan
Wasdale Head
High White Stones
Easedale Tarn
Stickle Tarn
Grasmere
Dove Cottage and Wordsworth Museum
Inn
Beckermet
Copeland Forest
Scafell Pike
Bow Fell
Langdale Pikes
Chapel Stile
Rydal
Rydal Mount
Rydal Water
Braystones
Calder Bridge
Wastwater
Wast Water
Burnmoor Tarn
Elterwater
Langdale
Ambleside
Kentmere
High Sellafield
Sellafield Visitors Centre
Calder Hall
Wellington
Nether Wasdale
The Screes
Little Langdale
Clappersgate
Waterhead
Troutbeck
Gosforth
Hardknott Fort
Hard Knott Pass
Wrynose Pass
Skelwith Bridge
Townend
Seascale
Santon Bridge
Boot
Eskdale
Cockley Beck
Holmrook
Eskdale Green
Beckfoot
Furness Fells
Troutbeck Bridge
Elfhowe
Low Wray
Harter Fell
Seathwaite Tarn
Outgate
High Wray
Ings
Staveley
Drigg
Birker Fell
Coniston
Hawkshead Hill
Colthouse
Hawkshead
Windermere
Bowness-on-Windermere
Saltcoats
Ravenglass
Devoke Water
The Old Man of Coniston
Bowmanstead
Woodend
Hall Dunnerdale
Ulpha Fell
Near Sawrey
Far Sawrey
Ferney Green
Broad Oak
Grizedale
Grizedale Forest
Grizedale Forest Park
Newbiggin
Caw
Torver
Storrs
Winster
Whitfell
Lane End
Ulpha
Hoses
Satterthwaite
Force Mills
Underbarrow
Crosthwaite
Corney Fell
Stub Place
Corney
Broughton Mills
Hycemoor
Water Yeat
Blawith
High Nibthwaite
Rusland
Finsthwaite
Bowland Bridge
Bootle
Duddon Bridge
Lower Hawthwaite
Broughton in Furness
Oxen Park
Cartmel Fell
Lakeside
The Howe
Black Combe
Lowick Bridge
Colton
Bouth
Lowick Green
Hallthwaites
Grizebeck
Newby Bridge
Sampool Bridge
Whitbeck
The Green
Foxfield
Gawthwaite
Spark Bridge
Backbarrow
Mill Side
Witherslack
The Hill
Penny Bridge
High Newton
Ayside
Town End
Whicham
Kirkby-in-Furness
Beck Side
Broughton Beck
Greenodd
Haverthwaite
Low Newton
Silecroft
Field Broughton
Arrad Foot
Meathop
Millom
Soutergate
miles
km

Hayton
Talkin
Tindale Fells
Forest Head
Halton Lea Gate
Lambley
Stonehouse
Whitfield
Bearsbridge
Catton
Dye House
Dalton
Whitley Chapel
Warwick Bridge
How
Heads Nook
Faugh
Castle Carrock
Cold Fell
Glendue Fell
Eals
Allendale Town
Slaley Forest
Great Corby
King's Forest of Geltsdale
Knarsdale
Whitfield Moor
Hexhamshire Common
Broadwell House
Slaggyford
Cumwhitton
Geltsdale Middle
Ninebanks
Sinderhope
Blanchland Moor
Cumrew
Allendale Common
Hornsby
Newbiggin
Ayle
Blanchland
Edmundbyers
Holmwrangle
Spartylea
Hunstanworth
Croglin
Nookton Fell
Aiketgate
Ainstable
South Tynedale Railway
Blagill
Carrshield
Armathwaite
Scale Houses
Watch Hill
Raise
Alston
Nenthall
Dirt Pot
High Hesket
Ruckcroft
Gilderdale Forest
Bayles
Middle Fell
Coalcleugh
Allenheads
Bolt's Law
Old Town
Renwick
Leadgate
Nenthead
Staffield
Haresceugh
High Bankhill
Nenthead Mines Heritage Centre
North of England Lead Mining Museum
Rookhope
Lanehead
Middlehope Moor
Stanhope Common
Kirkoswald
Unthank
Garrigill
Rookhope Nurseries
NORTH PENNINES
Cowshill
Crawleyside
Lazonby Fell
Townhead
Lazonby
Gamblesby
Alston Moor
Burnhope Reservoir
Wearhead
WEARDALE
Eastgate
Glassonby
Ireshopeburn
Westgate
Stanhope
Plumpton
Brockleymoor
Great Salkeld
Melmerby
Melmerby Fell
Little Salkeld
Pennine Way
Burnhope Seat
St John's Chapel
Daddry Shield
Plumpton Head
Hunsonby
Round Hill
Ireshope Moor
Winskill
Cross Fell
Ousby
Harwood
Westernhope Moor
Bollihope Common
Catterlen
Langwathby
Skirwith
Milburn Forest
Viewing Hill
Langdon Common
Chapelfell Top
Fair Hill
Newton Reigny
Edenhall
Kirkland
Tees
Trout Beck
Moor House-Upper Teesdale
Langdon Beck
Newbiggin Common
Middleton Common
Pawlaw
Penrith
Carleton
Blencarn
Crowdundle Beck
Mayburgh Henge
Brougham Castle
Culgaith
Milburn
Widdybank Fell
Forest
Ettersgill
Eamont Bridge
Acorn Bank
Newbiggin
Cow Green Reservoir
Dufton Fell
Cauldron Snout
High Force
Bowlees Visitor Centre
Stainton
Sockbridge
Clifton Hall
Temple Sowerby
Cronkley Fell
TEESDALE
Tirril
Lilliput Lane
Clifton
Wetheriggs Country Pottery
Lowmoor Row
Knock
Holwick
Middleton-in-Teesdale
Lakeland Bird of Prey Centre
Cliburn Moss
Kirkby Thore
Dufton
Murton Fell
Mickle Fell
Hill Top
Eggleston Hall
Askham
Lowther
Melkinthorpe
Cliburn
Long Marton
Brampton
LUNE FOREST
Lune Moor
Bowbank
Helton
Hackthorpe
Great Strickland
Morland
Bolton
Crackenthorpe
Thringarth
Mickleton
Romaldkirk
Whale
King's Meaburn
Murton
Grassholme Reservoir
Grassholme
Little Strickland
Newby
Colby
Hilton
Warcop Fell
Hunderthwaite
Bampton Grange
Sleagill
Appleby-in-Westmorland
Selset Reservoir
Hury
Bampton
Burrells
Dow Crag
Hunderthwaite Moor
Reagill
Hoff
Eden Valley Railway
Great Ormside
Hury Reservoir
Rosgill
Maulds Meaburn
Stainmore Common
Balderhead Reservoir
Clove Lodge
Baldersdale
Cotherstone Moor
Lartington
Shap Abbey
Shap
Sandford
Drybeck
Warcop
Hillbeck
North Stainmore
Deep Dale
Deepdale Beck
Keld
Crosby Ravensworth
Bowes
Oddendale
Great Asby
Bleatarn
Brough Castle
Brough
South Stainmore
Ralfland Forest
Great Musgrave
Little Musgrave
Brough Sowerby
Kaber
Barras
Moudy Mea
Bowes Moor
Gilmonby
Crosby Ravensworth Fell
Soulby
Winton
Heggerscales
STAINMORE FOREST
Sleightholme
Great Asby Scar
Shap Fells
Little Asby
Crosby Garrett
Hartley
Scargill High Moor
Orton
Kirkby Stephen
Smardale
Waitby
Winton Fell
Sleightholme Moor
Raisbeck
Smardale Gill
Nateby
Cleasby Hill
Tebay Services
Sadgill
Greenholme
Gaisgill
Kelleth
Newbiggin-on-Lune
Ash Fell
Arkengarthdale Moor
Bretherdale Head
Tebay
Bowderdale
Coldbeck
Ravenstonedale
Stonesdale Moor
Whaw
Weasdale
Borrowdale
Ravenseat
Rogan's Seat
Sleddale
Lowbridge House
Forest Hall
Langdale Fell
Ravenstonedale Common
Outhgill
Birkdale Common
West Stonesdale
Great Pinseat
Keld
Melbecks Moor
Garnett Bridge
Angram
Watchgate
Howgill Fell
Mallerstang
Angram Common
Gunnerside
Kearton
Healaugh
Bowston
Patton Bridge
Lowgill
Common
Thwaite
Muker
Satron
Feetham
Garth Row
Grayrigg
The Calf
Great Shunner Fell
Buttertubs Pass
Low Row
SWALE DALE
Burneside
Meal Bank
Beck Foot
Brant Fell
YORKSHIRE DALES NATIONAL PARK
Crackpot
Lakeland Climbing Centre
Lambrigg Fell
Abbotside Common
Cotterdale
East Bolton Moor
Cautley
Kendal
Sedbergh
Farfield Mill Arts & Heritage Centre
Baugh Fell
Garsdale Head
Askrigg Common
New Hutton
K Village Heritage Centre
Killington Services (Southbound Only)
High Shaw
Askrigg
Millholme
Millthrop
Hardrow
Sedbusk
Low Mill Outdoor Centre
Newbiggin
Castle Bolton
Oxenholme
Garsdale
Mossdale Moor
Appersett
Dales Countryside Museum
Bainbridge
Worton
Woodhall
Natland
Killington
Wensleydale Pottery
Hawes
Cubeck
Middleshaw
Garsdale
Widdale Fell
Gayle
Burtersett
Thornton Rust
Barrows Green
Old Hutton
Rise Hill
Wensleydale Creamery
WENSLEYDALE
Aysgarth
Cotes
Sedgwick
Gawthrop
Cowgill
Countersett
Semer Water
Thoralby
Stainton
Dent
Dentdale
Wether Fell
Carpley Green
Bishopdale Valley
Gatebeck
Middleton
Dodd Fell
Marsett
Newbiggin
Hincaster
Endmoor
Calf Top
Stone House
Wold Fell
Stalling Busk
Crooklands
Deepdale
Leasgill
Heversham
Old Town
Pennine Way
Cragdale Moor
Bishopdale Beck
Barbon
Crag Hill
Gayle Moor
Milnthorpe
Mansergh
Lupton
Whernside
Blea Moor
Cam Fell
Oughtershaw
Kidstones
NY
SD
A6
A66
A686
A689
A683
A684
A685
A65
M6
B6413
B6412
B6277
B6276
B6278
B6270
B6259
B6260
B6261
B6255
B6295
B6303
B6306
B6542
B6282
B6281
B6257
B6254
B6160
B5305
B5320
61
62
58
50

Durham
York
North
Washington
Sunderland
Stanley
Chester-le-Street
Houghton-le-Spring
Seaham
Consett
Lanchester
Sacriston
Peterlee
Easington Colliery
Spennymoor
Ferryhill
Crook
Willington
Wolsingham
Stanhope
Bishop Auckland
Shildon
Newton Aycliffe
Sedgefield
Hartlepool
Billingham
Stockton-on-Tees
Thornaby-on-Tees
Middlesbrough
Eaglescliffe
Egglescliffe
Yarm
Darlington
Barnard Castle
Staindrop
Richmond
Scotch Corner
Catterick
Catterick Garrison
Leyburn
Bedale
Northallerton
Thirsk
Hamsterley Forest
Wensleydale
Swale Dale

NZ
SE
ST HILDA'S PARISH CHURCH
artlepool Bay
rtlepool
Seaton Carew
Tees Bay
ENERGY INFORMATION CENTRE
Salt Scar
REDCAR
Coatham
Dormanstown
Marske-by-the-Sea
KIRKLEATHAM OLD HALL MUSEUM
MINIATURE RAILWAY
SALTBURN SMUGGLERS HERITAGE CENTRE
Saltburn-by-the-Sea
CHRIS BIRKBECK INTERNATIONAL RALLY SCHOOL
South Bank
Grangetown
Kirkleatham
Yearby
New Marske
Lazenby
Wilton
Upleatham
Brotton
Skinningrove
Boulby
Eston
Dunsdale
Skelton
Carlin How
Loftus
Staithes
TOCKETTS WATER MILL
North Skelton
Kilton Thorpe
Easington
Port Mulgrave
Ormesby
FLATTS LANE WOODLAND
Redcar and Cleveland
Guisborough
Boosbeck
Margrove Park
Stanghow
Liverton
Roxby
Hinderwell
Runswick Bay
Kettleness
Goldsborough
Hutton Gate
Charltons
Newton Mulgrave
Nunthorpe
Hutton Village
Gisborough Moor
Moorsholm
Scaling
Ellerby
Newton under Roseberry
Lythe
Sandsend
THE DRACULA EXPERIENCE
Sandsend Wyke
SUTCLIFFE GALLERY
Commondale Moor
Scaling Dam Res.
Mickleby
East Barnby
West Barnby
East Row
Dunsley
Whitby
Saltwick Bay
WHITBY ABBEY
Great Ayton
Little Ayton
New Row
Commondale
Danby Low Moor
Lealholm Moor
Ugthorpe
Newholm
CAPTAIN COOK MEMORIAL MUSEUM
Easby
Kildale
Danby
THE MOORS CENTRE
Stonegate
Ruswarp
Stokesley
Kildale Moor
Castleton
Ainthorpe
Houlsyke
Lealholm
Aislaby
Stainsacre
Battersby
Sleights
Briggswath
Sneaton
High Hawsker
Great Broughton
Ingleby Greenhow
Ugglebarnby
Westerdale
Low Garth
Street
Glaisdale
Egton
Grosmont
Sneatonthorpe
Raw
Ness Pt.
CLEVELAND WAY
Robin Hood's Bay
MUSEUM OF VICTORIAN SCIENCE
Egton Bridge
GROSMONT GALLERY
Esk Valley
Littlebeck
Fylingthorpe
OLD COASTGUARD STATION
BOGGLE HOLE
Robin Hood's Bay
Westerdale Moor
Glaisdale Moor
Egton High Moor
Beck Hole
Goathland
Old Peak
Ravenscar
Urra
Seave Green
Farndale Moor
Rosedale Moor
Flask Inn
Chop Gate
COCKAYNE RIDGE
Wake Lady Green
Cockayne
WHEELDALE MOOR ROMAN ROAD
Fylingdales Moor
Staintondale
STAINTONDALE SHIRE HORSE FARM
NORTH YORK MOORS
Bilsdale West Moor
Bilsdale East Moor
Church Houses
Wheeldale Moor
Harwood Dale Forest
Thorgill
Rosedale Abbey
Goathland Moor
Harwood Dale
Cloughton Newlands
Cloughton Wyke
Cloughton
Fangdale Beck
Low Mill
Bransdale
Rudland Rigg
Blakey Ridge
ROSEDALE
PICKERING MOOR
Pickering Forest
Saltergate
Langdale Forest
Broxa Forest
Burniston
Cromer Pt.
Scalby Ness Rocks
NATIONAL PARK
East Moors
Spaunton Moor
Cropton Hartoft End Forest
Stape
Helmsley Moor
Skiplam Moor
RYEDALE FOLK MUSEUM
Lastingham
Newton Dale
Levisham
LOCKTON
MOORLAND EXPERIENCE
Langdale End
Broxa
Silpho
Suffield
Scalby
SEA LIFE CENTRE
KINDERLAND
North Bay
Gillamoor
Fadmoor
Hutton-le-Hole
Spaunton
Newton-on-Rawcliffe
Lockton
Hackness
Staindale Forest
Wrench Green
Everley
Barrowcliff
Newby
Rievaulx Moor
NORTH RIDING FOREST PARK
Trouts Dale
Wykeham Forest
Cropton
Appleton-le-Moors
Scarborough
SCARBOROUGH CASTLE
ROTUNDA MUS.
NORTH YORKSHIRE MOORS RAILWAY
Low Dalby
Falsgrave
Carlton
Kirkbymoorside
Keldholme
Sinnington
Wrelton
Aislaby
DALBY FOREST VISITOR CENTRE
Dalby Forest
FORGE VALLEY WOODLANDS
East Ayton
Byland
Rievaulx
Pockley
Beadlam
Kirkby Mills
ST PETER AND ST PAUL CHURCH
West Ayton
CLEVELAND WAY
RIEVAULX ABBEY
HELMSLEY
Welburn
Middleton
PICKERING CASTLE
Sawdon
Hutton Buscel
THE HONEY FARM
Osgodby
Helmsley
Scawton
Wombleton
Great Edstone
Pickering
Ellerburn
WORDSWORTH GALLERY
Ruston
Irton
Seamer
Eastfield
Rye Dale
DUNCOMBE PARK
Marton
Thornton-le-Dale
Wilton
Ebberston
Snainton
Wykeham
Cayton
Sproxton
Harome
Normanby
Allerston
Lebberston
52

East Ayrshire
Dumfries and
NS
NX
68
69
67
55
56
Muirkirk
Kames
Smallburn
Netherwood
Glespin
Auchensaugh Hill
Middle Muir
Robertson
Abington
Abington Services
Glentaggart
Crawfordjohn
Cairn Table
Airds Moss
Cronberry
Lugar
Logan
Glenmuir
Wardlaw Hill
Glenmuirshaw
Keir Hardie Statue
Cumnock
Netherthird
Craigens
Dalblair
Glenmuir Water
Mount Stuart
Fingland
Duneaton Water
Drake Law
Tewsgill Hill
Camps Water
Camps Reservoir
Kirkton
Crawford
Upper Reservoir
Culter Waterhead Reservoir
Glenwhappen Rig
Tweedsmuir
Glenbreck
Lowther Hills
Rake Law
Wellgrain Dod
Elvanfoot
Craigmaid
Clyde Law
Source of River Tweed
Kirkland Hill
Kirkland
Leadhills
Leadhills & Wanlockhead Rly
Museum of Lead Mining
Wanlockhead Beam Engine
Wanlockhead
Conrig Hill
Lotus Lodge
Green Lowther
Lowther Hill
Mennock Pass
Elvan Water
Watermeetings
March
Devil's Beef Tub
Nether Howecleuch
Ericstane
Granton
Howslack
Pathhead
Mansfield
Connel Park
Bankglen
New Cumnock
Burnside
Dalleagles
The Knipe
Kirkconnel
Kelloholm
Nith
Crawick
Sanquhar
Tolbooth Museum
Sanquhar Post Office
Mennock
Afton Water
Kello Water
Euchan Water
Blackcraig Hill
Afton Reservoir
Southern Upland Way
Daer Reservoir
Potrail Water
Cairn Hill
Enterkinfoot
Durisdeermill
Durisdeer
Durisdeer Parish Church
Ballencleuch Law
Moffat
Coatsgate
Easter Earshaig
Garpol Water
Beattock
Kinnelhead
Gana Hill
Scar Water
Cairnkinna Hill
Enoch
Carsphairn Forest
Holestane
Morton Castle
Queensberry
Drumlanrig Castle
Carronbridge
Cairnsmore of Carsphairn
Corlae
Benbrack
Benbuie
Auchenbrack
Shinnel Water
Auchenbainzie
Gatelawbridge
Locherben
Lochwood
Burnhead
Penpont
Thornhill
Loch Ettrick
Kinnel Water
Water of Ken
Dalwhat Water
Tynron
Keir Mill
Closeburn
Park
Forest of Ae
St Ann's
Johnstonebridge
Chapelhill
Blackacre
Carsphairn
Knowehead
Kendoon Loch
Craigdarroch
Moniaive
James Paterson Museum
Kirkland
Maxwelton House
Courance
Dundeugh
Kendoon
Glenhoul
Glencrosh
Black Water
Straith
Wallaceton
Dalmacallan Forest
Glenmidge
Ae Village
Water of Ae
Nethermill
Parkgate
Templand
Wether Hill
Castlefairn
Holmhead
Carsfad Loch
Lochinvar
Auldgirth
Dalswinton
Auchencairn
Shieldhill
Lochurr
Bogrie Hill
Dunscore
Ellisland Farm
Duncow
Marjoriebanks
Lochmaben
Sundaywell
Milton
Loch Urr
Millquarter
Earlstoun Loch
St John's Town of Dalry
Bogue
Corriedoo Forest
Cairn Water
Gallaberry
Amisfield
Tinwald
Kirkton
Locharbriggs
Lochmaben Castle
Garroch
Glenlee
Blackcraig
Knocklearn
Newtonairds
Holywood
Heathhall
Dumfries and Galloway Aviation Mus
Drumpark
Glenkiln Res.
Irongray
Newbridge
Lincluden College
The Grove
Torthorwald
Hightae
New Galloway
Balmaclellan
Gibbshill
Blowplain Open Farm
Glenkiln
Lincluden
Old Bridge House Mus
Greystone
Rammerscales House
Collin
Terregles Banks
Dumfries
Maxwelltown
Ironmacannie
Craig
Corsock
Glen
Shawhead
Greenlea
Burns House
Robert Burns Centre
Clatteringshaws Forest Wildlife Centre
Raiders Road Forest Drive
Merkland
Urr Water
Brooklands
Brae
Lochfoot
Lochrutton Loch
Cargenbridge
Dumfries Museum & Camera Obscura
Racks
Cleughbrae
Mouswald
Bennan
Forest
Dee
Cairn Edward Hill
Loch Ken
Drumrash
Auchenreoch Loch
Crocketford or Ninemile Bar
Milton Loch
Islesteps
Kingholm Quay
Lochar Water
Lochar Moss
Mossdale
Stroan Loch
Parton
Kirkpatrick Durham
Springholm
Milton
Mabie Forest
Mabie
Kelton
Kirkconnell Flow
Lochaber Loch
Loch Arthur
Beeswing
Mcoltran Tower
Glencaple
Bankend
Clarencefield
Ruthwell
Loch Skerrow
Woodhall Loch
Old Bridge of Urr
Crossmichael
Kirkgunzeon
Kirkconnell
Shambellie House Costume Museum
River Nith
Shearington
Blackshaw
Caerlaverock Castle
Eastpark
Fleet Forest
Lochenbreck Loch
Townhead of Greenlaw
Clarebrand
Haugh of Urr
Mote of Urr
New Abbey
New Abbey Pow
Sweetheart Abbey
New Abbey Corn Mill
Bowhouse
Wildfowl and Wetland Centre
Caerlaverock
Overton
Blackshaw Bank
Nith Estuary
Laurieston
Laurieston Forest
Loch Glentoo
Threave Castle
Long Fell
Loch Kindar
Loch Whinyeon
Loch Mannoch
Kelton Mains Open Farm
Threave Gardens
Castle Douglas
Carlingwark Loch
Old Buittle Tower
Bathill
Dalbeattie
Criffell
Drumburn
Loch Bargatton
Glengap
Glengap Forest
Bengray
Bridge of Dee
Rhonehouse or Kelton Hill
Gelston
Dalbeattie Forest
Carsethorn
Kirkbean
Arbigland Gardens
Drumstinchall
Caulkerbush
Prestonmill
Fleet
Anworth
Mill on the Fleet
Gatehouse of Fleet
Cardoness Castle
Ringford
Valleyfield
Airieland
Palnackie
Orchardton Tower
Barnbarroch
Mainsriddle
Mersehead RSPB Nature Reserve
John Paul Jones Cottage Museum
Sandyhills
Colvend
Southerness
Southerness Pt.
Mersehead Sands
Galloway Hydro Visitor Centre
Tongland
Broughton House and Garden
Twynholm
Girthon
Bengairn
Kippford or Scaur
Mote of Mark
Rockcliffe
Rough I.
Rough Island
Portling
East Stewartry Coast
Castlehill Pt.
Whinnieliggate
Kirkcudbright
Stewartry
Auchencairn
Auchencairn Bay
0 1 2 3 4 5 6 miles
0 1 2 3 4 5 6 7 8 9 10km

Scottish Borders
Galloway
Cumbria
Ettrick Forest
Eskdalemuir Forest
Craik Forest
Kielder Forest Park
Wauchope Forest
Kershope Forest
Newcastleton Forest
Spadeadam Forest
Solway Coast
Teviotdale
Liddesdale
Eskdale
Annandale
NT
NY
Selkirk
Hawick
Langholm
Lockerbie
Annan
Gretna
Longtown
Carlisle
Brampton
Wetheral
Silloth
Newcastleton
Ettrickbridge
Denholm
Bonchester Bridge
Kielder
Newton Arlosh
Kirkbride
Canonbie
Ecclefechan
Eastriggs
Eskdalemuir
Mountbenger
Yarrow
Philiphaugh
Lilliesleaf
Ancrum
Jedburgh
A7
A74(M)
A75
M6
A69
A689
B709
B711
B6357
B6399
B6318
69
70
62
56
57
A698
A708
A68
A6071
A595

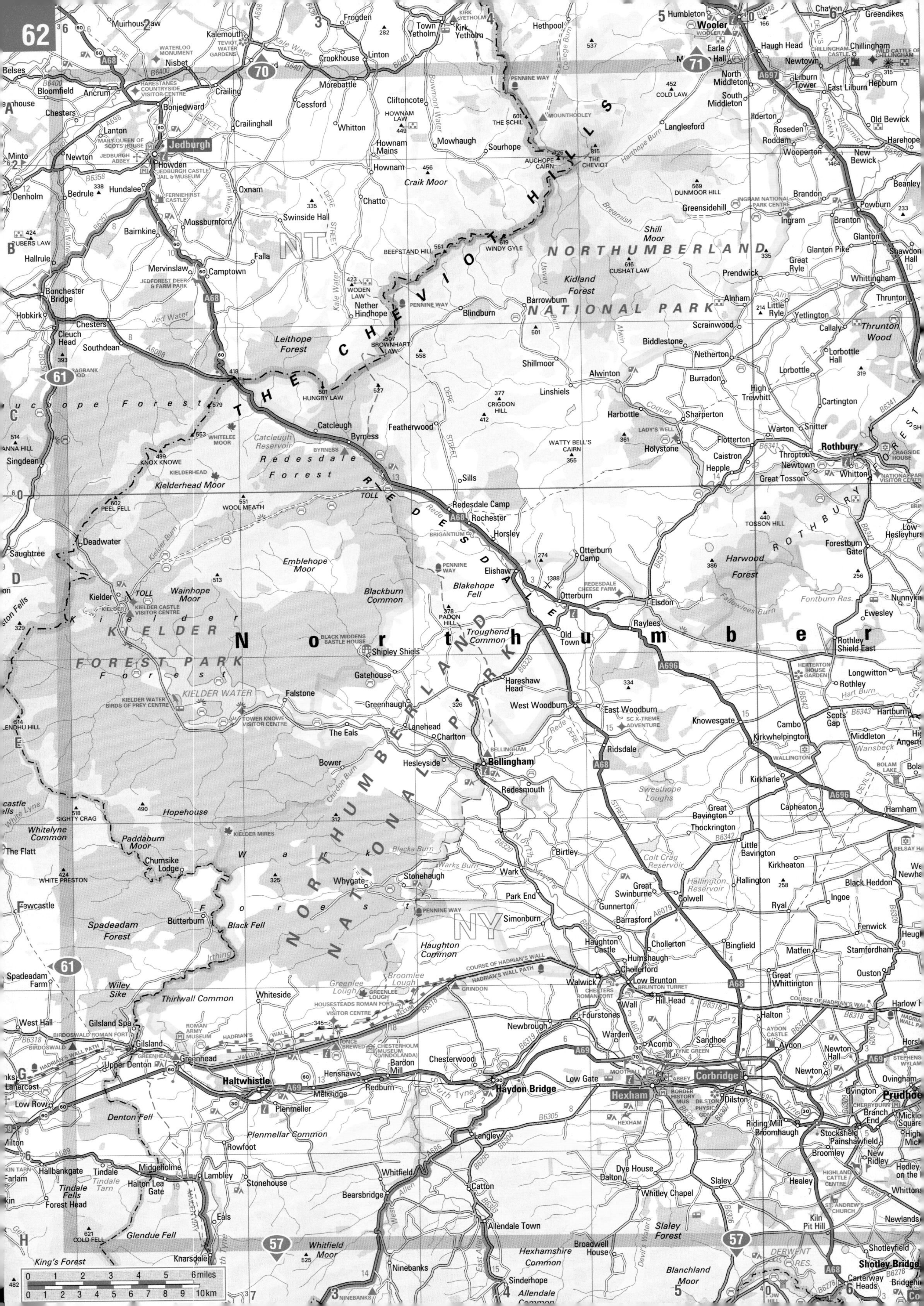
Muirhouselaw
Kalemouth
Frogden
Town Yetholm
Kirk Yetholm
Hethpool
Humbleton
Wooler
Chatton
Greendikes
Waterloo Monument
Teviot Water Gardens
Nisbet
Kale Water
Crookhouse
Linton
Haugh Head
Chillingham
Chillingham Castle
Wild Cattle of Chillingham
Belses
Bloomfield
Ancrum
Harestanes Countryside Visitor Centre
Crailing
Morebattle
Pennine Way
North Middleton
South Middleton
Lilburn Tower
East Lilburn
Newtown
Hepburn
Earle
Hall
Bonjedward
Chesters
Cessford
Cliftoncote
Hownam Law
Cold Law
Crailinghall
Whitton
The Schil
Mounthooley
Langleeford
Ilderton
Roseden
Roddam
Old Bewick
Harehope
Lanton
Mary Queen of Scots' House
Jedburgh Abbey
Jedburgh
Minto
Newton
Howden
Jedburgh Castle Jail & Museum
Hownam Mains
Mowhaugh
Sourhope
Auchope Cairn
The Cheviot
Harthope Burn
Wooperton
New Bewick
Hownam
Craik Moor
Denholm
Bedrule
Hundalee
Oxnam
Ferniehirst Castle
Chatto
Dunmoor Hill
Brandon
Beanley
Greensidehill
Ingram National Park Centre
Ingram
Powburn
Branton
Mossburnford
Swinside Hall
Bairnkine
Rubers Law
Dere Street
Shill Moor
Glanton
Hallrule
Falla
Beefstand Hill
Windy Gyle
Northumberland National Park
Cushat Law
Glanton Pike
Shawdon Hall
Great Ryle
Mervinslaw
Camptown
Jedforest Deer & Farm Park
Kidland Forest
Prendwick
Whittingham
Bonchester Bridge
Woden Law
Nether Hindhope
Blindburn
Barrowburn
Alnham
Little Ryle
Thrunton
Yetlington
Hobkirk
Chesters
Jed Water
Scrainwood
Callaly
Thrunton Wood
Cleuch Head
Southdean
Leithope Forest
Brownhart Law
Biddlestone
Netherton
Lorbottle Hall
Ragbank Wood
Hungry Law
Shillmoor
Burradon
Lorbottle
Alwinton
High Trewhitt
The Cheviot Hills
Crigdon Hill
Linshiels
Cartington
Wauchope Forest
Catcleugh
Byrness
Featherwood
Harbottle
Coquet
Sharperton
Warton
Snitter
Whitelee Moor
Catcleugh Reservoir
Redesdale Forest
Lady's Well
Holystone
Watty Bell's Cairn
Flotterton
Rothbury
Cragside House
Anna Hill
Singdean
Knox Knowe
Kielderhead
Kielderhead Moor
Sills
Caistron
Hepple
Thropton
Newtown
Whitton
National Park Visitor Centre
Great Tosson
Peel Fell
Wool Meath
Toll
Redesdale Camp
Rochester
Tosson Hill
Rothbury Forest
Brigantium
Horsley
Low Hesleyhurst
Deadwater
Saughtree
Kielder Burn
Emblehope Moor
Otterburn Camp
Forestburn Gate
Harwood Forest
Pennine Way
Elishaw
Blakehope Fell
Wainhope Moor
Redesdale Cheese Farm
Otterburn
Elsdon
Kielder
Kielder Castle Visitor Centre
Blackburn Common
Fontburn Res.
Fallowlees Burn
Nunnykirk
Padon Hill
Ewesley
Kielder Forest Park
Raylees
Black Middens Bastle House
Troughend Common
Old Town
Northumberland
Rothley Shield East
Shipley Shiels
Herterton House Garden
Longwitton
Rothley
Hart Burn
Gatehouse
Hareshaw Head
Kielder Water
Kielder Water Birds of Prey Centre
Falstone
Greenhaugh
West Woodburn
East Woodburn
SC X-Treme Adventure
Knowesgate
Cambo
Scots' Gap
Hartburn
Tower Knowe Visitor Centre
Lanehead
The Eals
Charlton
Ridsdale
Kirkwhelpington
Middleton
Wansbeck
Wallington
Bolam Lake
Bellingham
Hesleyside
Bower
Chirdon Burn
Redesmouth
Sweethope Loughs
Kirkharle
Capheaton
Harnham
Castle
White Lyne
Sighty Crag
Hopehouse
Great Bavington
Thockrington
Whitelyne Common
Kielder Mires
Little Bavington
Belsay Hall
Paddaburn Moor
Blacka Burn
Birtley
Colt Crag Reservoir
Kirkheaton
The Flatt
Churnsike Lodge
Warks Burn
Wark
Hallington Reservoir
Hallington
Black Heddon
White Preston
Stonehaugh
Whygate
Great Swinburne
North Tyne
Park End
Colwell
Ingoe
Ryal
Fewcastle
Wark Forest
Simonburn
Gunnerton
Barrasford
Fenwick
Spadeadam Forest
Butterburn
Black Fell
Haughton Common
Haughton Castle
Chollerton
Bingfield
Matfen
Stamfordham
Humshaugh
Chollerford
Ouston
Spadeadam Farm
Irthing
Course of Hadrian's Wall
Hadrian's Wall Path
Greenlee Lough
Broomlee Lough
Grindon
Walwick
Chesters Roman Fort
Low Brunton
Brunton Turret
Great Whittington
Wiley Sike
Thirlwall Common
Whiteside
Housesteads Roman Fort
Visitor Centre
Vallum
Wall
Hill Head
Harlow Hill
West Hall
Gilsland Spa
Birdoswald Roman Fort
Roman Army Museum
Hadrian's Wall
Once Brewed
Chesterholm Museum (Vindolanda)
Fourstones
Newbrough
Warden
Halton
Aydon Castle
Aydon
Gilsland
Greenhead
Upper Denton
Bardon Mill
Henshaw
Chesterwood
Acomb
Sandhoe
Tyne Green
Newton Hall
Lanercost
Haltwhistle
Melkridge
Redburn
Haydon Bridge
Low Gate
Moothall
Hexham
Abbey
Corbridge
Newton
Ovingham
Ovington
Prudhoe
Low Row
Plenmeller
South Tyne
Border History Mus
Dilston Physic Gdn
Dilston
Tyne
Denton Fell
Plenmellar Common
Riding Mill
Broomhaugh
Stocksfield
Painshawfield
Cherryburn
Branch End
Rowfoot
Langley
Broomley
Milton
Tindale
Hallbankgate
Midgeholme
Lambley
Whitfield
Dye House
Dalton
New Ridley
Hedley on the Hill
Farlam
Halton Lea Gate
Stonehouse
Tindale Fells
Tindale Tarn
Forest Head
Bearsbridge
West Allen
Catton
Whitley Chapel
Slaley
Healey
Highland Cattle Centre
Whittonstall
St Andrew's Church
Kiln Pit Hill
Newlands
Eals
Cold Fell
Glendue Fell
Maiden Way
Allendale Town
Slaley Forest
Whitfield Moor
Broadwell House
Devil's Water
Hexhamshire Common
Derwent Res.
Shotleyfield
Shotley Bridge
King's Forest
Knarsdale
East Allen
Ninebanks
Sinderhope
Allendale Common
Blanchland Moor
Blanchland
Carterway Heads
Bridgehill
NT
NY
0 1 2 3 4 5 6 miles
0 1 2 3 4 5 6 7 8 9 10 km

NORTHUMBERLAND COAST
NU
NZ
Warenford
Newham
Newstead
Fleetham
Swinhoe
Beadnell
Benthall
Beadnell Bay
Rosebrough
Chathill
Ellingham
Preston
High Newton-by-the-Sea
Low Newton-by-the-Sea
Brockdam
Brownyside
North Charlton
Doxford
Brunton
Christon Bank
Embleton Bay
Embleton
Dunstan Steads
Castle Point
DUNSTANBURGH CASTLE
West Ditchburn
South Charlton
Rock
Dunstan
Craster
Rennington
Littlemill
Howick
Littlehoughton
Shipley
Howick Haven
HULNE PRIORY
Longhoughton
Boulmer
Denwick
ALNWICK ABBEY
Alnwick
Boulmer Haven
Abberwick
Broome Park
Hawkhill
Lesbury
Lemmington Hall
Bilton
Alnmouth
Alnmouth Bay
High Buston
Shilbottle
Low Buston
Birling
Newton-on-the-Moor
Eastfield Hall
Warkworth
Gloster Hill
Amble
Coquet I.
Hazon
Swarland Estate
Guyzance
Hauxley
Brainshaugh
North Togston
Swarland
Acklington
Radcliffe
Togston
Broomhill
South Broomhill
Felton
LONGFRAMLINGTON GARDENS
West Thirston
East Thirston
Red Row
DRURIDGE BAY
Weldon
Eshott
Druridge Bay
West Chevington
Helm
Widdrington
Longhorsley
Stobswood
Causey Park Bridge
Widdrington Station
Cresswell
The Scars
Fenrother
Tritlington
Ellington
Ulgham
Lynemouth
Linton
THE SANCTUARY WILDLIFE CENTRE
Stanton
Hebron
Longhirst
COLLIERY MUSEUM
Beacon Pt.
Woodhorn
QUEEN ELIZABETH II
Pigdon
Pegswood
Ashington
Newbiggin-by-the-Sea
Mitford
NORTHUMBRIA CRAFT CENTRE
Bothal
Hirst
Throphill
Morpeth
Stakeford
North Seaton
Molesden
Guide Post
Scotland Gate
West Sleekburn
Choppington
Cambois
Tranwell
Hepscott
Clifton
Bedlington
Bedlington Station
East Sleekburn
Cowpen
Whalton
BLYTH
Netherton
Shilvington
Bebside
Saltwick
East Hartford
New Delaval
Newsham
Stannington
PLESSEY WOODS
Ogle
Shankhouse
KIRKLEY HALL
Nelson Village
New Hartley
Seaton
Seaton Sluice
NORTHUMBERLAND CHEESE FARM
Cramlington
SEATON DELAVAL HALL
Berwick Hill
Higham Dykes
Southfield
Hartley
East Cramlington
Seaton Delaval
ST MARY'S LIGHTHOUSE
St Mary's or Bait I.
Brenkley
Seaton Burn
Holywell
Seghill
Ponteland
Dinnington
Dudley
Annitsford
Brunswick Village
Wide Open
Burradon
Backworth
Earsdon
WHITLEY BAY
Prestwick
NEWCASTLE INTERNATIONAL
Darras Hall
Hazlerigg
Camperdown
Monkseaton
AMSTERDAM 15:30
Medburn
High Callerton
Killingworth
Shiremoor
Cullercoats
Woolsington
Marden
BLUE REEF AQUARIUM
TYNEMOUTH CASTLE & PRIORY
Black Callerton
Kenton Bankfoot
Longbenton
STEPHENSON RAILWAY MUSEUM
Tynemouth
North Walbottle
Gosforth
THE RISING SUN
North Shields
ARBEIA ROMAN FORT AND MUSEUM
Westerhope
Kenton
Wallsend
Willington
South Shields
Heddon-on-the-Wall
Throckley
Jesmond
WALLSEND
SOUTH SHIELDS MUSEUM
NEWCASTLE UPON TYNE
Walbottle
Heaton
Tyne Tunnel
Jarrow
Westoe
THE LEAS AND MARSDEN ROCK
Newburn
Byker
BEDE'S WORLD
ST PAUL'S MONASTERY
Harton
Marsden Bay
Clara Vale
Scotswood
Walker
Marsden
Wylam
Ryton
Crawcrook
Gateshead
Hebburn
SOUTER LIGHTHOUSE
BLAYDON
Dunston
Bensham
Hedworth
Whiteleas
Cleadon
Whitburn Colliery
Greenside
Winlaton
Felling
Pelaw
Boldon Colliery
Whitburn
Coalburns
Whickham
Carr Hill
Boldon
Barlow
Low Fell
FULWELL WINDMILL
Downhill
Fulwell
High Spen
Highfield
Sunniside
Street Gate
Chowdene
Wrekenton
Hylton Castle
Southwick
Roker
Rowlands Gill
GIBSIDE
Byermoor
Marley Hill
Lamesley
Springwell
Usworth
Castletown
Monkwearmouth
NATIONAL GLASS CENTRE
ST PETER'S CHURCH
SUNDERLAND MINSTER
Blackhall Mill
DERWENTCOTE STEEL FURNACE
Burnopfield
Blackfell
South Hylton
Pallion
Leazes
Kibblesworth
ANGEL OF THE NORTH
Birtley
WASHINGTON
Pennywell
High Barnes
Sunderland
Hobson
TANFIELD RAILWAY
High Westwood
Medomsley
Tanfield
BEAMISH
Ouston
Lambton
THE WILDFOWL & WETLANDS TRUST
Hendon
Tantobie
Urpeth
Barley Mow
Fatfield
East Herrington
New Silksworth
Dipton
Tanfield Lea
Beamish
Perkinsville
Penshaw
STANLEY
Rickleton
Shiney Row
New Herrington
Tunstall
Ryhope
RYHOPE ENGINES MUS
Catchgate
West Pelton
Pelton
The Middles
Grange Villa
CHESTER-
Doxford Park
Leadgate
Annfield
Bournmoor
Newbottle
Burdon
Tyne and Wear
Northumberland
58
71
A B C D E F G H
7 8 9 10 11 12

Rubha Bholsa
COLONSAY 1:10 (Summer only)
Loch an Aircill
JURA
785 PAPS OF JURA
Loch a Chnuic Bhric
JURA FOREST
Corran
Leargybreck
Gleann Astaile
Nave Island
Ardnave Pt.
364 SGARBH BREAC
Gortantaoid
Bunnahabhain
BUNNAHABHAIN DISTILLERY
Carraig Bhan
Ardnave
Killinallan
Loch Gruinart
An Clachan
Sanaigmore
Caol Ila
CAOL ILA DISTILLERY
Port Askaig
Feolin Ferry
FINLAGGAN CENTRE
Keills
Leckgruinart
Braigo
Loch Finlaggan
Loch Cam
Loch Ballygrant
Gleann Ullibh
Craighouse
ISLE OF JURA DISTILLERY
BRAT BHEINN
Ballinaby
Carnduncan
LOCH GRUINART NATURE RESERVE VISITORS CENTRE
Aoradh
Craigens
Ballygrant
Kilmeny
Cabrach
Saligo Bay
Loch Gorm
ISLAY
Coull
Coul Pt.
Sunderland
Blackrock
Redhouses
Daill
267 BEINN DUBH
JURA HOUSE WALLED GARDEN
Rubha na Trà
Machir Bay
Kilchoman
Bridgend
Am Fraoch Eilean
Brosdale I.
Conisby
Bruichladdich
Kilchiaran
Kilchiaran Bay
Bowmore
BOWMORE ROUND CHURCH
Mulindry
McArthur's Hd.
Argyll
ISLAY LIFE MUSEUM
Tormisdale
RHINNS OF ISLAY
Port Charlotte
Kilennan
LOCH INDAAL
Laggan
471 BEINN BHAN
491 BEINN BHEIGEIR
Carraig Mhór
Lossit
Lossit Pt.
Nerabus
Laggan Pt.
Duich
Ardtalla
Loch Beinn Uraraidh
Claggain Bay
Rubha na Faing
Portnahaven
Port Wemyss
Orsay
Rinns Pt.
LAGGAN BAY
Glenegedale
Kintour
Ardmore Pt.
KILDALTON CHURCH AND CROSSES
347 BEINN SHOLUM
Eilean Craobhach
Eilean a'Chuirn
Port Alsaig
Rubha Môr
Kintra
Leorin
Eilean Bhride
ARDBEG DISTILLERY
Cornabus
Lower Cragabus
Imeraval
Port Ellen
Lagavulin
Ardbeg
Eilean Imersay
LAGAVULIN DISTILLERY
LAPHROAIG DISTILLERY
Laphroaig
Texa
Dùn Mór Ghil
THE OA
Risabus
Lower Killeyan
Inerval
AMERICAN MONUMENT
Mull of Oa
Rubha nan Leacan
NR
NORTH CHANNEL
Rathlin Island
0 1 2 3 4 5 6 miles
0 1 2 3 4 5 6 7 8 9 10 km

Argyll and Bute
KNAPDALE
KINTYRE
ISLE OF ARRAN
NORTH ARRAN
ISLAND OF BUTE
KYLES OF BUTE
NS
Lagg
Loch Lesgamaill
Danna
Lochead
Achahoish
St Columba's Cave
Eilean Mòr
St Cormac's Chapel
Kilmory
Kilmory Bay
Ellary
Clachbreck
Erines
Baile Boidheach
Stob Odhar
Ormsary
An Dùnan
Knockrome
Lowlandman's Bay
Pt. of Knap
Loch Caolisport
Loch Chaorain
Druimdrishaig
Loch nan Torran
Miller's Bay
Cretshengan
Cruach Lagain
Coulaghailtro
Kilberry Hd.
Sculptured Stones
Kilberry
Torinturk
Dun
Rhu
Tarbert
West Tarbert
Corranbuie
Barfad
East Loch Tarbert
Glenan Bay
Carse Ho.
Dunmore
Kennacraig
Cnoc a'Bhaileshios
Redhouse
Whitehouse
Kilchamaig
Ardpatrick
Loch Stornoway
West Loch Tarbert
Ardpatrick Ho.
Gartnagrenach
Portachoillan
Ardpatrick Pt.
Eilean Traighe
Ronachan Pt.
Clachan
Cruach nam Fiadh
Glenreasdell Mains
Skipness
Skipness Castle
Skipness Pt.
Skipness Bay
Claonaig
Claonaig Bay
Loch Ciaran
Eilean Garbh
West Tarbert Bay
East Tarbert Bay
Tarbert
Gigha Island
Druimyeon More
Ardminish
Ardminish Bay
Achamore Gardens
Gigalum Island
Cara Island
Sound of Gigha
Balochroy
Crossaig Glen
Crossaig
Loch Garasdale
Cruach Mhic Gougan
Rhunahaorine
Cour Bay
Cour
Beinn Bhreac
Tayinloan
Cnoc nan Craobh
Cruach Mhic-an t-Saoir
Carradale Water
Killean
Beacharr
Grogport
Cruach nan Gabhar
Brackley
Clachaig Water
Muasdale
Glenacardoch Pt.
Amod
Belloch
Barr Water
Glenbarr
Clan Macalister Centre
Carradale
Port Righ
Bridgend
Torrisdale Square
Beinn an Tuirc
Carradale Pt.
Carradale Bay
Cleongart
Saddell Glen
Bellochantuy Bay
Bellochantuy
Saddell
Saddell Abbey
A'Chruach
Saddell Bay
Killocraw
Lussa Loch
Tangy Loch
Sgreadan Hill
Ugadale
Skeroblingarry
Westport
Black Bay
Kilchenzie
Glenlussa Water
Peninver
Ardnacross Bay
West Darlochan
Kilmichael
Machrihanish Bay
Campbeltown
Low Smerby
Campbeltown Heritage Centre
Machrihanish
Trodigal
Campbeltown Loch
Island Davaar
Davaar Island Cave Painting
Drumlemble
Stewarton
Kilkerran
Kildalloig
Earadale Pt.
Knocknaha
Beinn Ghuilean
Achinhoan Hd.
The Slate
Woodbank
Cnoc Moy
Feochaig
Rubh'a' Mharaiche
Glen Breackerie
Cnoc Odhar
Conie Glen
Johnston's Pt.
North Carrine
Kepnigan
Strone Glen
Macharioch
Polliwilline Bay
Carskiey
Southend
Brunerican Bay
Cove Pt.
Mull of Kintyre
Port Mean
Rubha Chlachan
Sheep I.
Sanda Island
Kilfinan Bay
Kilfinan
Drum
Beinn Bhreac
Melldalloch
Auchalick Bay
Ardmarnock Bay
Barmore I.
Port Driseach
Tighnabruaich
Auchenlochan
Kames
Asgog Loch
Millhouse
Portavadie
Blair's Ferry
Kyles of Bute
Asgog Bay
Kilbride Bay
Ardlamont Ho.
Ardlamont Pt.
Rubha Leathan
Ardentraive
Colintraive
Algaltraig
Glen More
Windy Hill
St Colmac
Kames
Rothesay Castle
Rothesay
Ettrick Bay
Straad
Loch Fad
Inchmarnock
Scalpsie
Ardscalpsie Pt.
Scalpsie Bay
Stravanan Bay
Sound of Bute
Cock of Arran
Lochranza Castle
Lochranza
Loch Ranza
Isle of Arran Distillery
Catacol
Catacol Bay
Millstone Pt.
Meall nan Damh
Thundergay
North Sannox Farm Park
Sannox
Sannox Bay
Glen Sannox
Pirnmill
Loch Tanna
Kilbrannan Sound
Whitefarland
Beinn Bharrain
Cir Mhòr
Beinn Tarsuinn
Goat Fell
Corrie
Imachar
Glen Iorsa
Glen Rosa
Brodick Castle
Arran Aromatics Visitor Centre
Brodick Bay
Ardrossan
Dougarie
Isle of Arran Heritage Museum
Brodick
Strathwhillan
Machrie Water
Auchagallon
Glenloig
A'Chruach
Glen Cloy
Machrie Bay
Tormore
Machrie Moor Standing Stones
Clauchlands Pt.
King's Cave
Balmichael Visitor Centre
Balmichael
Blairbeg
Margnaheglish
Lamlash
Lamlash Bay
Holy Island
Cordon
Drumadoon Pt.
Torbeg
Shiskine
Blackwaterfoot
Drumadoon Bay
Kilpatrick
Kilpatrick Dun
Tighvein
Sliddery Water
Auchencairn
Kingscross Pt.
Kingscross
Knockenkelly
Whiting Bay
North Kiscadale
South Kiscadale
Glenree
Brown Hd.
Carn Ban
Corriecravie
Glenashdale Falls
Largymore
Largybeg
Dippen
Dippin Head
Kilmory Water
Sliddery
Lagg
Levencorroch
Kilmory
Torrylinn Cairn
South Bank Farm Park
Bennan
Bennan Hd.
Kildonan
Sound of Pladda
Pladda

Glenreasdell Mains
Skipness
SKIPNESS CASTLE
Skipness Pt.
Skipness Bay
Claonaig
269
CRUACH NAM FIADH
Claonaig Bay
B8001
B842
Inchmarnock
Scalpsie
Ardscalpsie Pt.
Scalpsie Bay
Stravanan Bay
A844
Kingarth
Kilchattan Bay
157
ST BLANE'S CHAPEL
Great Cumbrae Island
CHRISTIAN HERITAGE MUSEUM
Downcraig Ferry
MUSEUM OF THE CUMBRAES
Millport
Fairlie Roads
Fairlie
484
RISH LAW
Ladyland Moor
Muirhead Reservoir
Camphill Reservoir
Kilbirnie
73
SOUND OF BUTE
0:30
Cock of Arran
Garroch Hd.
The Tan
HUNTERSTON POWER STATION VISITOR CENTRE
Little Cumbrae Island
387
KAIM HILL
Knockendon Reservoir
Rye Water
Glengarnock
Longbar
Crossaig
Loch Ranza
LOCHRANZA CASTLE
Lochranza
Millstone Pt.
Thirdpart
Portencross
Farland Hd.
A78
Drakemyre
Highfield
Blairland
Gifford land
Dalry
BLACKSHAW FARM PARK
Catacol Bay
LOCHRANZA
ISLE OF ARRAN DISTILLERY
Catacol
444
Cour Bay
Cour
West Kilbride
Seamill
A737
A841
NORTH SANNOX FARM PARK
570
MEALL NAN DAMH
Thundergay
573
North Ayrshire
Sannox
Sannox Bay
AYRSHIRE MUSEUM OF COUNTRY LIFE & COSTUME
Dalgarven
B780
B714
B778
NORTH
Loch Tanna
859
Glen Sannox
Pirnmill
Grogport
65
Chapelhill
Dykesmains
Kilwinning
Horse Isle
798
CIR MHÒR
Corrie
Whitefarland
721
BEINN BHARRAIN
BEINN TARSUINN
825
874
GOAT FELL
EGLINTON
Ardrossan
NORTH AYRSHIRE MUSEUM
Stevenston
Saltcoats
0:55
Imachar
ISLE OF ARRAN
Carradale
Port Righ
BRODICK
BRODICK CASTLE
Glen Rosa
Glen Iorsa
Irvine
SCOTTISH MARITIME MUSEUM
Fullarton
Dougarie
228
ARRAN AROMATICS VISITOR CENTRE
ISLE OF ARRAN HERITAGE MUSEUM
Brodick Bay
Strathwhillan
Brodick
Irvine Bay
Carradale Pt.
Machrie Water
Auchagallon
Glenloig
A'CHRUACH
512
Glen Cloy
B880
Machrie Bay
FIRTH OF CLYDE
Clauchlands Pt.
Barassie
North Bay
Muirhead
Tormore
MACHRIE MOOR STANDING STONES
503
Blairbeg
Margnaheglish
Lamlash
Lamlash Bay
Cordon
Holy Island
KING'S CAVE
BALMICHAEL VISITOR CENTRE
Balmichael
Troon
Torbeg
Shiskine
314
Lady Isle
Drumadoon Pt.
South Bay
ROYAL TROON
Blackwaterfoot
Drumadoon Bay
Kingscross Pt.
458
TIGHVEIN
Auchencairn
Kingscross
Kilpatrick
KILPATRICK DUN
Sliddery Water
Knockenkelly
Whiting Bay
LARNE 1:50 (March-Oct)
North Kiscadale
South Kiscadale
Whiting Bay
Glenree
GLENASHDALE FALLS
Largymore
Prestwick
NR
Brown Hd.
CARN BAN
Corriecravie
Kilmory Water
Largybeg
Dippen
Woodford
Newton on Ayr
Wallacetown
Sliddery
Lagg
Levencorroch
Dippin Head
Ayr
Seafield
Kilmory
SOUTH BANK FARM PARK
Bennan
Kildonan
TORRYLINN CAIRN
Bennan Hd.
Sound of Pladda
Pladda
BURNS COTTAGE
Heads of Ayr
HEADS OF AYR FARM PARK
A719
Doonfoot
Alloway
BURNS NATIONAL HERITAGE PARK
Fisherton
Dunure
287
B7024
Culroy
ELECTRIC BRAE
Minishant
Culzean Bay
CULZEAN CASTLE
270
B7023
Whitefaulds
Maybole
Kirkmichael
Maidenhead Bay
CULZEAN
COLLEGIATE CHURCH
Maidens
A77
Aitkenhead
TURNBERRY
Kirkoswald
CROSSRAGUEL ABBEY
Crosshill
SOUTER JOHNNIE'S COTTAGE
Turnberry Bay
Turnberry
Brest Rocks
252
Ruglen
Townhead
Wallacetown
Water of Girvan
Dipple
Burnhead
B741
Dailly
BARGANY GARDENS
Old Dailly
Ailsa Craig
338
Girvan
Penkill
South Ayrshire
B734
Houdston
Penwhapple Res.
Glendoune
355
MULL OF MILJOAN
Dalwyne
Woodland Bay
South Balloch
NW
Tormitchell
Pinminnoch
CARRICK
Auchensoul
Barr
Changue Forest
Kennedy's Pass
297
GREY HILL
A714
Pinmore
Stinchar
Merkland
Currarie
Straid
565
CRAIGENREOCH
Lendalfoot
Pinmore Mains
CARLETON CASTLE
260
Poundland
335
PINDONNAN
Bennane Hd.
Pinwherry
Bellamore
Colmonell
Knockdolian
265
Ballochmorrie
Black Clauchrie
54
Heronsford
Ballantrae Bay
B7044
Glen Tig
Water of Tig
Duisk
Ballantrae
Barrhill
Laggan
Balkissock
Eldrick
0 1 2 3 4 5 6 miles
0 1 2 3 4 5 6 7 8 9 10 km

Renfrewshire
East Renfrewshire
South Lanarkshire
East Ayrshire
Dumfries and Galloway
LOWTHER HILLS
NITHSDALE
THE GLENKENS
RHINNS OF KELLS
GALLOWAY FOREST PARK
Barrhead
Neilston
Newton Mearns
Clarkston
East Kilbride
Eaglesham
Bothwell
MOTHERWELL
HAMILTON
WISHAW
Larkhall
Carluke
Stonehouse
Strathaven
Blackwood
Kirkmuirhill
Lanark
Lesmahagow
Coalburn
Douglas
Stewarton
Kilmaurs
Kilmarnock
Galston
Newmilns
Darvel
Greenholm
Riccarton
Hurlford
Crossroads
Mauchline
Tarbolton
Catrine
Sorn
Muirkirk
Auchinleck
Cumnock
Netherthird
Ochiltree
Drongan
Dalrymple
Patna
Dalmellington
New Cumnock
Kirkconnel
Sanquhar
Wanlockhead
Mennock
Moniaive
Carsphairn
St John's Town of Dalry
Flow Moss
Airds Moss
Carsphairn Forest
Tairlaw Forest
CARRICK FOREST
Dundeugh Forest
Dalmacallan Forest
Corriedoo Forest
M77
M74
A71
A70
A76
A713
68
60
55
NS
NX

LOCH LOMOND AND THE TROSSACHS NATIONAL PARK
75
73
67
West
Dunbartonshire
East
Dunbartonshire
Inverclyde
Renfrewshire
East
Renfrewshire
Glasgow
GLASGOW
CUNNINGHAME
North
Lanarkshire
South
Lanark
East
Ayrshire
CLYDE MUIRSHIEL REGIONAL PARK
CAMPSIE FELLS
KILPATRICK HILLS
NS
Helensburgh
Greenock
PORT GLASGOW
DUMBARTON
ALEXANDRIA
Balloch
CLYDEBANK
BEARSDEN
Milngavie
RENFREW
Paisley
JOHNSTONE
Erskine Bridge
KIRKINTILLOCH
Kilsyth
Lennoxtown
COATBRIDGE
AIRDRIE
Rutherglen
Cambuslang
Uddingston
Bothwell
HAMILTON
MOTHERWELL
East Kilbride
Barrhead
Newton Mearns
Eaglesham
Strathaven
Larkhall
Stonehouse
Kilmacolm
Bridge of Weir
Lochwinnoch
Kilbirnie
Beith
Dalry
Kilwinning
Stevenston
Irvine
Kilmarnock
Stewarton
Galston
Newmilns
Darvel
Troon
Prestwick
Tarbolton
Mauchline
Catrine
Auchinleck
Muirkirk
Drymen
Killearn
Balfron
Buchlyvie
Kippen
Fintry
Strathblane
Luss
Balmaha
Irvine Bay
North Bay
South Bay
Lady Isle
LARNE 1:50 (March-Oct)
KILCREGGAN 0:25
SCOTTISH MARITIME MUSEUM
0 1 2 3 4 5 6 miles
0 1 2 3 4 5 6 7 8 9 10 km

Clackmannanshire
Fife
West Lothian
Midlothian
Edinburgh
Scottish Borders
Falkirk
FIRTH OF FORTH
PENTLAND HILLS
REGIONAL PARK
UPPER TWEEDDALE
TINTO HILLS
MOORFOOT HILLS
CLYDESDALE
76
70
61
60
Menstrie
Tillicoultry
Dollar
Alva
Tullibody
Devonside
Coalsnaughton
Alloa
Clackmannan
Sauchie
Forest Mill
Kincardine
Kincardine Bridge
Cowie
Bannockburn
Plean
Airth
Letham
Torwood
Dunipace
Denny
Larbert
Stenhousemuir
Carron
Grangemouth
Bonnybridge
Falkirk
Polmont
Bo'ness
Linlithgow
Blackness
Queensferry
Forth Road Bridge
Rosyth
Inverkeithing
North Queensferry
Dunfermline
Oakley
Saline
Kelty
Lochgelly
Cowdenbeath
Ballingry
Lochore
Cardenden
Kirkcaldy
Dysart
Kinghorn
Burntisland
Aberdour
Dalgety Bay
Inchkeith
Inchcolm
Inchmickery
Cramond I.
Leith
Granton
Newhaven
Musselburgh
Portobello
Joppa
Kirkliston
Winchburgh
Broxburn
Uphall
Livingston
Bathgate
Armadale
Whitburn
Blackburn
West Calder
Fauldhouse
Harthill
Shotts
Ratho
Currie
Balerno
Juniper Green
Colinton
Loanhead
Bonnyrigg and Lasswade
Roslin
Penicuik
Dalkeith
Newmains
Carluke
Forth
Lanark
New Lanark
Carnwath
Carstairs
Biggar
West Linton
Carlops
Leadburn
Peebles
Eddleston
Glentress
Cardrona
Innerleithen
Broughton
Symington
Coulter
Lamington
Abington
Crawford
Crawfordjohn
Douglas
Coalburn
Tweedsmuir
Crookhaugh
Stanhope
Drumelzier
Stobo
Dryhope
Cappercleuch
Mountbenger
Glenbreck
A702
A720
M8
M9
M90
M74
A985

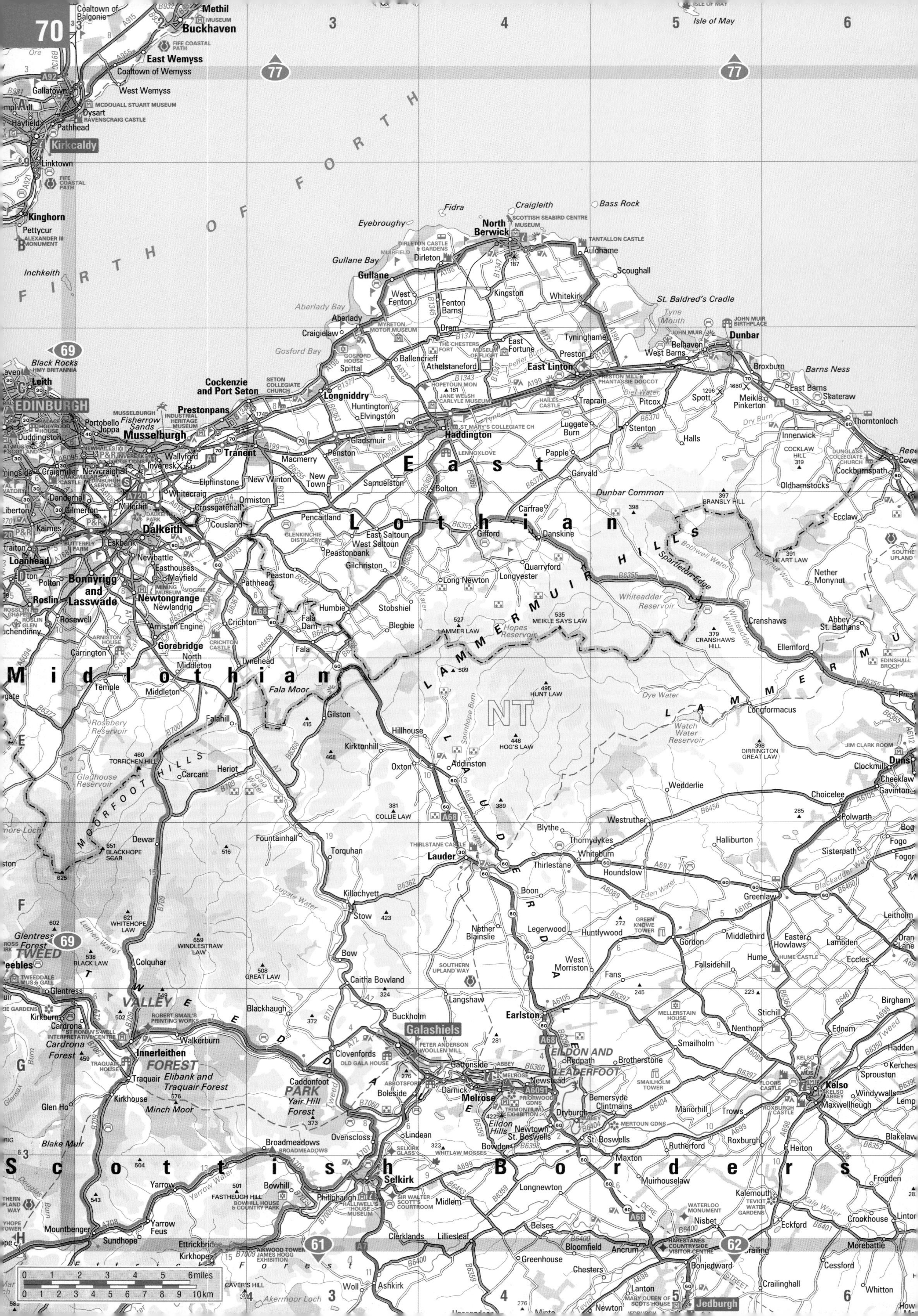
Methil
Buckhaven
Coaltown of Balgonie
East Wemyss
Coaltown of Wemyss
West Wemyss
Gallatown
MCDOUALL STUART MUSEUM
Dysart
RAVENSCRAIG CASTLE
Hayfield
Pathhead
Kirkcaldy
Linktown
FIFE COASTAL PATH
Kinghorn
Pettycur
ALEXANDER III MONUMENT
Inchkeith
FIRTH OF FORTH
Isle of May
77
69
Fidra
Craigleith
Bass Rock
Eyebroughy
North Berwick
SCOTTISH SEABIRD CENTRE
TANTALLON CASTLE
Auldhame
Scoughall
DIRLETON CASTLE & GARDENS
Dirleton
Gullane Bay
Gullane
West Fenton
Fenton Barns
Kingston
Whitekirk
St. Baldred's Cradle
Aberlady Bay
Aberlady
Craigielaw
MYRETON MOTOR MUSEUM
Drem
Tyne Mouth
JOHN MUIR BIRTHPLACE
Dunbar
Belhaven
West Barns
Tyninghame
Gosford Bay
GOSFORD HOUSE
Spittal
Ballencrieff
Athelstaneford
THE CHESTERS FORT
MUSEUM OF FLIGHT
East Fortune
Preston
East Linton
PRESTON MILL & PHANTASSIE DOOCOT
Broxburn
Barns Ness
East Barns
Skateraw
Black Rocks
HMY BRITANNIA
Leith
EDINBURGH
Cockenzie and Port Seton
SETON COLLEGIATE CHURCH
Longniddry
Huntington
Elvingston
HOPETOUN MON
JANE WELSH CARLYLE MUSEUM
HAILES CASTLE
Traprain
Pitcox
Spott
Meikle Pinkerton
Thorntonloch
Prestonpans
MUSSELBURGH
Fisherrow Sands
INDUSTRIAL HERITAGE MUSEUM
Portobello
Joppa
PALACE OF HOLYROOD HOUSE
Duddingston
Musselburgh
Tranent
Gladsmuir
Haddington
ST MARY'S COLLEGIATE CH
Luggate Burn
Stenton
Halls
Innerwick
COCKLAW HILL
DUNGLASS COLLEGIATE CHURCH
Cockburnspath
Wallyford
Inveresk
Macmerry
Penston
LENNOXLOVE
Papple
Garvald
Craigmillar
Newcraighall
Elphinstone
New Winton
New Town
Samuelston
Bolton
East Lothian
Oldhamstocks
Danderhall
Gilmerton
Millerhill
Whitecraig
Crossgatehall
Ormiston
Dunbar Common
BRANSLY HILL
Ecclaw
Liberton
Kaimes
Dalkeith
Cousland
Pencaitland
GLENKINCHIE DISTILLERY
East Saltoun
West Saltoun
Gifford
Carfrae
Danskine
Lammermuir Hills
Spartleton Edge
HEART LAW
Nether Monynut
Loanhead
Eskbank
BUTTERFLY FARM
Newbattle
Easthouses
Mayfield
Peastonbank
Gilchriston
Quarryford
Longyester
Long Newton
Bonnyrigg and Lasswade
Roslin
Newtongrange
Newlandrig
MINING MUSEUM
Pathhead
Peaston
Humbie
Stobshiel
Blegbie
Whiteadder Reservoir
Cranshaws
Abbey St. Bathans
Rosewell
Arniston Engine
Crichton
CRICHTON CASTLE
Fala Dam
LAMMER LAW
Hopes Reservoir
MEIKLE SAYS LAW
CRANSHAWS HILL
Ellemford
EDINSHALL BROCH
ARNISTON HOUSE
Carrington
Gorebridge
North Middleton
Fala
Tynehead
Midlothian
Temple
Middleton
Fala Moor
HUNT LAW
Dye Water
Lammermuir
Rosebery Reservoir
Falahill
Gilston
Hillhouse
NT
Longformacus
Kirktonhill
HOG'S LAW
Watch Water Reservoir
DIRRINGTON GREAT LAW
JIM CLARK ROOM
TORFICHEN HILL
Gladhouse Reservoir
Carcant
Heriot
Moorfoot Hills
Oxton
Addinston
Clockmill
Duns
Cheeklaw
Gavinton
Wedderlie
Choicelee
COLLIE LAW
Polwarth
Westruther
Blythe
Thornydykes
Halliburton
Dewar
Fountainhall
Torquhan
THIRLSTANE CASTLE
Lauder
Whiteburn
Thirlestane
Houndslow
Sisterpath
BLACKHOPE SCAR
Killochyett
Boon
Greenlaw
Stow
Nether Blainslie
Legerwood
Huntlywood
GREEN KNOWE TOWER
Gordon
Middlethird
Easter Howlaws
Lambden
WHITEHOPE LAW
WINDLESTRAW LAW
Leithholm
Glentress Forest
TWEED
BLACK LAW
Colquhar
Bow
SOUTHERN UPLAND WAY
West Morriston
Fans
Fallsidehill
Hume
HUME CASTLE
Eccles
Peebles
TWEEDDALE MUS & GALL
Glentress
GREAT LAW
Caitha Bowland
Langshaw
Stichill
Birgham
Kirkburn
Cardrona
ROBERT SMALL'S PRINTING WORKS
Blackhaugh
Buckholm
Earlston
MELLERSTAIN HOUSE
Nenthorn
Ednam
VALLEY
Walkerburn
Galashiels
PETER ANDERSON WOOLLEN MILL
Smailholm
Cardrona Forest
Innerleithen
TRAQUAIR HOUSE
Traquair
FOREST
Elibank and Traquair Forest
Clovenfords
OLD GALA HOUSE
Gattonside
EILDON AND LEADERFOOT
Redpath
Brotherstone
Kelso
KELSO ABBEY
Hadden
Sprouston
Caddonfoot
PARK
Yair Hill Forest
ABBOTSFORD
Boleside
Darnick
Melrose
MELROSE ABBEY
Newstead
SMAILHOLM TOWER
FLOORS CASTLE
Windywalls
Maxwellheugh
Kirkhouse
Minch Moor
Glen Ho
PRIORWOOD GDNS
TRIMONTIUM EXHIBITION
Eildon Hills
Bemersyde
Clintmains
Dryburgh
DRYBURGH ABBEY
MERTOUN GDNS
Manorhill
Trows
ROXBURGH CASTLE
Blake Muir
Broadmeadows
Ovenscloss
Lindean
SELKIRK GLASS
WHITLAW MOSSES
Newtown St. Boswells
St. Boswells
Bowden
Rutherford
Roxburgh
Heiton
Blakelaw
Scottish Borders
Maxton
Muirhouselaw
Yarrow
FASTHEUGH HILL
Bowhill
BOWHILL HOUSE & COUNTRY PARK
Philiphaugh
HALLIWELL'S HOUSE MUSEUM
Selkirk
SIR WALTER SCOTT'S COURTROOM
Midlem
Longnewton
Kalemouth
TEVIOT WATER GARDENS
Frogden
WATERLOO MONUMENT
Nisbet
Eckford
Crookhouse
Mountbenger
Yarrow Feus
Sundhope
Ettrickbridge
Kirkhope
AIKWOOD TOWER JAMES HOGG EXHIBITION
Clerklands
Lilliesleaf
Belses
Bloomfield
Ancrum
HARESTANES COUNTRYSIDE VISITOR CENTRE
Crailing
Morebattle
Ettrick Forest
61
62
Greenhouse
Chesters
Bonjedward
Cessford
CAVER'S HILL
Akermoor Loch
Woll
Ashkirk
Lanton
MARY QUEEN OF SCOTS HOUSE
Jedburgh
Crailinghall
Whitton
3
4
5
6
0 1 2 3 4 5 6 miles
0 1 2 3 4 5 6 7 8 9 10 km

7
8
9
10
11
12
A
B
C
D
E
F
G
H
N O R T H
S E A
NU
N O R T H U M B E R L A N D C O A S T
Siccar Pt.
Wheat Stack
FAST CASTLE
ST ABB'S HEAD
St. Abb's Head
KITTIWAKE GALLERY
Lumsdaine
Coldingham Moor
Northfield
St Abbs
Coldingham Bay
St. Abb's Haven
Grantshouse
Huxton
Coldingham
COLDINGHAM PRIORY
Ale Water
Houndwood
Eye Water
Cairncross
EYEMOUTH MUSEUM
Eyemouth
AYTON CASTLE
Reston
Auchencrow
Ayton
Burnmouth
Prendergues
Lintlaw
Lamberton Beach
Lamberton
Chirnside
Chirnsidebridge
Edrom
Buxley
MANDERSTON
Foulden
FOULDEN TITHE BARN
Whiteadder Water
Clappers
Allanton
Hutton
Paxton
Highfields
Berwick-upon-Tweed
BARRACKS MUSEUM & RAMPARTS
Tweedmouth
TOWER HOUSE POTTERY
Spittal
CRUMSTANE FARM PARK
Blackadder West
East Ord
PAXTON HOUSE
Tweed
Fishwick
UNION SUSPENSION BRIDGE
Loanend
Prior Park
Sinclair's Hill
Whitsome
Horncliffe
Redshin Cove
Horndean
Thorntonpark
Murton
Scremerston
Leet Water
Ladykirk
Thornton
NORHAM CASTLE
Swinton
SWINTON KIRK
Norham
West Allerdean
Cheswick
Simprim
Shoreswood
Shoresdean
Goswick
DEVIL'S CAUSEWAY
Grindon
Ancroft
North Low
Haggerston
LINDISFARNE
Emmanuel Hd.
Holy Island (Lindisfarne)
Felkington
Berrington
South Low
Beal
Shellacres
Causeway
Holy Island
LINDISFARNE CASTLE
Castle Pt.
Holy Island Sands
LINDISFARNE HERITAGE CENTRE
LINDISFARNE PRIORY
Castle Heaton
Duddo
Bowsden
Fenham
Guile Pt.
Lennel
Coldstream
HIRSEL
Cornhill-on-Tweed
HEATHERSLAW LIGHT RAILWAY
ERROL HUT SMITHY AND WOOD WORKSHOP
Barmoor Castle
Barmoor Lane End
West Kyloe
Fenwick
Etal
HEATHERSLAW CORNMILL
Lowick
Kyloe Hills
East Kyloe
Farne Islands
Wark
LADY WATERFORD HALL
Buckton
East Learmouth
Crookham
West Learmouth
Branxton
Ford
ST CUTHBERT'S WAY
Elwick
Ross
Bude Bay
Staple Sound
BAMBURGH CASTLE
FARNE ISLANDS
Pressen
Holburn
Detchant
Flodden
Middleton
Budle
Bamburgh
Inner Sound
Kimmerston
Hetton Steads
Downham
Howtel
Belford
Easington
Waren Mill
Mindrum
Milfield
Fenton Town
Nesbit
North Hazelrigg
Spindlestone
Glororum
Burton
Seahouses
Pawston
Kilham
Glen
Doddington
South Hazelrigg
Mousen
Bradford
Shotton
Lanton
Newtown
West Horton
East Horton
Bellshill
Elford
North Sunderland
Westnewton
Coupland
Weetwood Hall
Warenton
Adderstone
Lucker
Kirknewton
Akeld
Newham Hall
Beadnell
KIRK YETHOLM
Humbleton
Warenford
Swinhoe
Kirk Yetholm
Hethpool
Wooler
Chatton
Greendikes
Newham
Fleetham
Benthall
WOOLER
Earle
Newstead
Beadnell Bay
College Burn
Haugh Head
CHILLINGHAM CASTLE
Chillingham
WILD CATTLE OF CHILLINGHAM
Rosebrough
Chathill
Middleton Hall
Newtown
Ellingham
Preston
High Newton-by-the-Sea
PENNINE WAY
COLD LAW
North Middleton
Lilburn Tower
Hepburn
Brockdam
PRESTON TOWER
Brunton
Low Newton-by-the-Sea
South Middleton
East Lilburn
Brownyside
Christon Bank
Embleton Bay
Cliftoncote
North Charlton
Doxford
Embleton
Dunstan Steads
MOUNTHOOLEY
Ilderton
Old Bewick
West Ditchburn
Castle Point
THE SCHIL
Langleeford
Roseden
South
DUNSTANBURGH CASTLE
Mowhaugh
Roddam
A1
A697
A698
A6105
A6112
A1107
B6438
B6437
B6355
B6460
B6461
B6470
B6437
B6354
B6525
B6353
B6352
B6351
B6348
B6349
B1342
B1341
B1340
B6347
B1339
B6346
62
63

STAFFA 0:45 (April-Oct)
ARDMEANACH
Killiemore House
Aird of Kinloch
Kilfinichen Bay
Loch Airdeglais
BEN BUIE 717
698 CREACH BEINN
Loch Spelve
Croggan
Rubha nan Sailthean
Bach I.
Eilean Annraidh
Rubha nan Cearc
IONA ABBEY AND CATHEDRAL
Kintra
ST COLUMBA EXHIBITION & WELCOME CENTRE
Baile Mor
Iona
Fionnphort
Aridhglas
A849
Eorabus
LOCH SCRIDAIN
THE BURG
Pennycross
Torrans
Loch Fuaron
503 BEINN NA CROISE
Kinlochspelve
Lochbuie
Barachandroman
Loch Uisg
BROLASS
Leidle
Carsaig
Loch Buie
Laggan Deer Forest
405 DRUIM FADA
LORD LOVAT'S CAVE
Fidden
Tiraghoil
Bunessan
Lee
376 CRUACHAN MIN
Rubha Dubh
Carsaig Bay
Loch Assapol
Erraid
ROSS OF MULL
Ardalanish
Uisken
Scoor
Ardchiavaig
CARSAIG ARCHES
Malcolm's Pt.
Frank Lockwood's Island
Insh I.
Seil
Clachan-Seil
Easdale
AN CALA GARDENS
EASDALE ISLAND FOLK MUSEUM
Balvicar
Eilean a'Chalmain
125
Rubha nam Braithrean
Rubh Ardalanish
78
79
Dubh-fheith
Cuan
Torran Rocks
NM
FIRTH OF LORN
Garbh Eileach
Garvellachs
SCARBA, LUNGA AND THE GARVELLACHS
Eilean Dubh Mor
Eileach an Naoimh
Cullipool
Luing
Achafolla
Toberonochy
Shuna
Shuna Pt.
OBAN 2:20
Lunga
CRUACH SCARBA 449
Scarba
Rubha Aird Luing
Gulf of Corryvreckan
Aird
Rèisa an t-Sruith
Craignish Pt.
Island Macaskin
Rubh'a'Geadha
Balnahard
Kiloran Bay
KILORAN GARDENS
Kiloran
Kilchattan
COLONSAY
Scalasaig
Loch Staosnaig
Garvard
Rubha Dubh
PRIORY
Dubh Eilean
Oronsay
Eilean nan Ron
Kinuachdrachd
Glengarrisdale Bay
296 CRUACH NA SEILCHEIG
Kinuachdrachd Harbour
Glendebadel Bay
365 BEN GARRISDALE
Loch Crinan
Crinan
Kilmahumaig
Bellanoch
Corpach Bay
Lussa
Lealt Burn
Lealt
467 BEINN BHREAC
Gallachoille
Carsaig
Tayvallich
KNAPDALE
Ardlussa
Ardlussa Bay
Inverlussa
Lussagiven
Gleann Aoistail
Shian Bay
453 RAINBERG MOR
Loch Righ Mòr
318
Barrahormid
TAYNISH
Taynish
Achanar
Kilmichael Inverluss
466 CRUACH LUS
Rubh'an t-Sàilein
1:10 (Summer Only)
Tarbert
Loch Tarbert
KEILLS CHAPEL
Keillmore
Dunrostan
New Ulva
Rubha Lang-aoinidh
Rubha a'Mhail
Rubha Bholsa
Lagg
439
Loch an Aircill
Loch Lesgamaill
Island of Danna
CASTLE SWEEN
Lochead
241 ST COLUMBA'S CAVE
Achahoish
364 SGARBH BREAC
Nave Island
Ardnave Pt.
JURA
785 755 PAPS OF JURA
Loch a Chnuic Bhric
JURA FOREST
Eilean Mòr
ST CORMAC'S CHAPEL
Kilmory
Kilmory Bay
Ellary
Clachbreck
Gortantaoid
Bunnahabhain
BUNNAHABHAIN DISTILLERY
316
Ardnave
Killinallan
Corran
Knockrome
An Dùnan
Lowlandman's Bay
Baile Boidheach
Ormsary
Leargybreck
Gleann Astaile
Pt. of Knap
Loch Gruinart
Caol Ila
CAOL ILA DISTILLERY
Port Askaig
Feolin Ferry
561
Loch na Mile
Druimdrishaig
FINLAGGAN CENTRE
LOCH GRUINART NATURE RESERVE VISITORS CENTRE
Aoradh
Craigens
Loch Finlaggan
Keills
Keils
Craighouse
ISLE OF JURA DISTILLERY
Small Isles
Loch nan Torran
305
Miller's Bay
Cretshengan
Loch Cam
Ballygrant
Loch Ballygrant
Gleann Ullibh
342 BRAT BHEINN
NR
CRUACH LAGAIN 264
Coulaghailtro
Kilberry
Kilberry Hd.
SCULPTURED STONES
ISLAY
Kilmeny
64
Cabrach
JURA HOUSE WALLED GARDEN
Blackrock
Redhouses
Daill
267 BEINN DUBH
Bridgend
Am Fraoch Eilean
Brosdale I.
Rubha na Tràille
SOUND OF ISLAY
Carse Ho.
Dunmore
LOCH INDAAL
Bowmore
BOWMORE ROUND CHURCH
Mulindry
McArthur's Hd.
Loch Stornoway
Ardpatrick
Ardpatrick Ho.
Gartnagrenach
Kilennan
2:05
Portachoillan
Ardpatrick Pt.
Eilean Traighe
Laggan
Laggan Pt.
471 BEINN BHAN
491 BEINN BHEIGEIR
Carraig Mhór
Ronachan Pt.
Clachan
A83
Duich
Ardtalla
65
Eilean Garbh
West Tarbert Bay
Loch Beinn Uraraidh
Claggain Bay
East Tarbert Bay
Tarbert
Loch Ciaran
Balochroy
PORT ELLEN 2:20
Gigha Island
Ardmore Pt.
KILDALTON CHURCH
0 1 2 3 4 5 6 miles
0 1 2 3 4 5 6 7 8 9 10 km

Oban
Glenamachrie
Glen Lonan
Pass of Brander
Falls of Cruachan
Kilchurn Castle
Lochawe
tronmilchan
Strath of Orchy
Achnafalnich
Inverlochy
Dalmally
Gallanach
Barran
Kilbride
Kilmore
Am Buth
Glen Feochan
Glenfeochan House Gardens
Beinn Ghlas
Loch Nell
Loch Nant
Loch Tromlee
Cruachan Dam Visitor Centre
Ardanaiseig Gardens
Ardanaiseig
Innis Chonain
Inishail
McIntyre Monument
Teatle Water
Ben Lui
Beinn Dubhchraig
Meall nan Tighearn
Kilchrenan
Annat
North Port
Cladich
Musdale
Sior Loch
A'Chruach
Barochreal
Glen Euchar
Bragleenmore
Portsonachan
South Port
Loch Scamadale
Beinn Chapull
Carn Dearg
Argyll
and
Bute
Inverinan
Ballimeanoch
Tullich
Glen Aray
Beinn Ghlas
Cruach Mhor
Braes of Lorn
Blaran
Loch Tralaig
Lochavich Ho
Drissaig
Kilmun
Loch Avich
Dalavich
Blarghour
Melfort
Kilmelford
Glenmore
Kames
Lagalochan
Portinnisherrich
Ardchonnell Castle
Carn Duchara
Inverliever Forest
Kilmaha
Eredine
Durran
Arichamish
Kintraw
Torran
Cruach an Eachlaich
Eredine Forest
Ford
Ederline
Finchairn
Finchairn Castle
Cruach Mhic Fhionnlaich
Loch Gaineamhach
Kilmartin
Kilmartin House Trust
Slockavullin
Carnassarie Castle
Creag Mhor
Dun Dubh
Gleann Airigh
Kilmichael Glassary
Bridgend
Moine Mhor
Dunadd Fort
Rock Markings
Cup and Ring Marks
Cairnbaan
Lochgilphead
Cam Loch
Kilmory Castle Gardens
Kilmory Woodland Park
Ardrishaig
Loch Gilp
Achabraid
Inverneill
Tarbert
West Tarbert
Corranbuie
Rhu
Kennacraig
Redhouse
Whitehouse
Cnoc a'Bhaileshios
Glenreasdell Mains
Skipness
Skipness Castle
Skipness Pt.
Skipness Bay
Claonaig
Claonaig Bay
Cruach Nam Fiadh
Crossaig
Lochranza
Cock of Arran
Inveraray
Inveraray Castle
Bell Tower
Combined Operations Museum
Inveraray Jail
Maritime Museum
Newtown
Dalchenna
An Suidhe
Douglas Water
Beinn Dearg
Auchindrain
Auchindrain Open Air Museum
Loch Leacann
Furnace
Crarae
Crarae Glen Gardens
Minard
Tullochgorm
Lachlan Bay
Lachlan Castle
Garbhallt
Newton
Strachur Bay
Creggans
Clachan Strachur
Glen Sluain
Strathlachlan Forest
Lephinmore
Caol Ghleann
Dunans
Lephinchapel
Asknish
Lochgair
Loch Glashan
Loch Fyne
Carrick
Port Ann
Largiemore
Achnaba
Otter Ferry
Castleton
Eilean Mòr
Ballimore
Auchnaha
Cruach Chuilceachan
Glendaruel Forest
Glendaruel
Conchra
Clachan of Glendaruel
Kilmodan Sculptured Stones
Balliemore
Cruach nan Cuilean
Craigendive
Auchenbreck
Loch Riddon
Cruach nan Caorach
Kilfinan
Kilfinan Bay
Drum
Melldalloch
Auchalick Bay
Ardmarnock Bay
Barmore I.
Loch Chaorain
Kyles of Bute
Beinn Bhreac
Ardentraive
Colintraive
Algaltraig
Port Driseach
Tighnabruaich
Auchenlochan
Kames
Asgog Loch
Portavadie
Millhouse
Blair's Ferry
Barfad
Glenan Bay
East Loch Tarbert
Asgog Bay
Kilbride Bay
Ardlamont Ho.
Ardlamont Pt.
Rubha Leathan
Inchmarnock
Ardscalpsie Pt.
Sound of Bute
Island of Bute
Glen More
Windy Hill
Ettrick Bay
St Colmac
Kames B.
Port Bannatyne
Ardyne Pt.
Rothesay
Rothesay Castle
Rothesay Bay
Craigmore
Ardencraig Gardens
Montford
Victorian Fernery
Ascog
Kerrycroy
Scoulag
Mount Stuart House and Garden
Straad
Loch Fad
Loch Quien
Scalpsie
Scalpsie Bay
Stravanan Bay
Kingarth
Kilchattan Bay
St Blane's Chapel
Garroch Hd.
Toward
Toward Pt.
Port Lamont
Loch Striven
Glenstriven
Cruach nan Capull
Inverchaolain
Black Craig
Corlarach Hill
Corlarach Forest
Glen Fyne
Wave Whisper Gallery
Innellan
Newton Park
Bullwood
Lunderston Bay
Dunoon
Cloch Pt.
Highland Mary's Statue
St John's Church
Kirn
Hunter's Quay
Ardnadam
Sandbank
Holy Loch
Glen Lean
Clachaig
Glen Kin
Inverneck
Dalinlongart
Ardbeg
Kilmun Arboretum
Blairmore
Kilmun
Strone
Strone Pt.
Benmore Botanic Garden
Benmore
Uig
Glen Massan
Sgorach Mor
Loch Tarsan
Glenmassan
Beinn Mhor
Bernice
Loch Eck
Whistlefield
Beinn Bheag
Glenbranter
Glenbranter Forest
Invernoaden
Beinn Bheula
Argyll Forest Park
Beinn Ruadh
Glenfinart Deer Farm
Glen Finart
Ardentinny
Creachan Mor
Linn Botanic Gardens
St Catherine's
Ardno
Cruach nan Capull
Hell's Glen
Beinn an Lochain
Rest and Be Thankful
Glen Kinglas
Cairndow
Ardkinglas Woodland Garden
Drishaig
Clachan
Dubh Loch
Kilblaan Burn
Glen Shira
Beinn Ghlas
Lochan Shira
Loch Stron Mor
Beinn Bhuidhe
Brannie Burn
Glen Fyne
Glenfyne Lodge
Allt na Lairige
Maol Breac
Monevechadan
Ben Donich
Drimsynie
Lochgoilhead
European Sheep and Wool Centre
Corrow
Beinn Lochain
Blairlomond
Cnoc Coinnich
Ardgoil Forest
The Saddle
Carrick Castle
Loch Goil
Loch Long
Glen Croe
Ardgartan
Arrochar
Tarbet
Succoth
Stuckgowan
Ardmay
Loch Lomond and the Trossachs National Park
Beinn Ime
Inveruglas
Ben Vorlich
Loch Sloy
Inverarnan
Troisgeach
Ardlui
Glen Douglas
Doune Hill
Inverbeg Gallery
Glenmallan
Beinn Eich
Edentaggart
Glen Luss
Portincaple
Beinn Chaorach
Garelochhead
Beinn Ruisg
Faslane Port
Coulport
Rahane
Gare Loch
Shandon
Glen Fruin
Ardpeaton
Clynder
Rosneath
Cove
Rhu
Glenarn Garden
The Hill House
Helensburgh
Craigendoran
Rosneath Pt.
Portkil
Kilcreggan
Gourock
Ashton
Greenock
Greenock West
Midton
McLean Mus & Art Gall
HM Customs & Excise Museum & Exhibition
Newark Castle
Port Glasgow
Levan
Larkfield
Braeside
Ravenscraig
Loch Thom
Gryfe Resrs.
Inverkip
Shielhill
Garvock
Devol
Mid Auchinlech
Inverclyde
Clyde-Muirshiel Regional Park
Wemyss Bay
Upper Skelmorlie
Skelmorlie
Creuch Hill
Duchal Moor
Meigle
Queenside Muir
Hill of Stake
Waterhead Moor
Routenburn
Mistylaw Muir
Largs
Largs Bay
Old Kirk
Tomont End
Great Cumbrae Island
Christian Heritage Museum
Downcraig Ferry
Millport
Museum of the Cumbraes
Irish Law
Ladyland Moor
Lochwinnoch
Muirhead Reservoir
Kelburn Country Centre
Camphill Reservoir
Fairlie
Fairlie Roads
Kilbirnie
Kilbirnie Loch
Glengarnock
Kaim Hill
Knockendon Reservoir
Rye Water
Longbar
The Tan
Little Cumbrae Island
Hunterston Power Station Visitor Centre
Drakemyre
NN
NS

Highland
Argyll and Bute
BEN NEVIS AND GLEN COE
MAMORE FOREST
BLACK MOUNT
LOCH LINNHE
LYNN OF LORN
BENDERLOCH
LOCH ETIVE
LOCH LOMOND
NM
NR
Ardgour
Glen Scaddle
Coruanan Lodge
Blarmachfoldach
Achriabhach
Glen Nevis
Blar a'Chaorainn
Glenrigh Forest
Ardgour
Clovullin
Corran
Inchree
Sallachan
Keppanach
Onich
North Ballachulish
Kinlochmore
Kinlochleven
THE ALUMINIUM STORY
BLACKWATER RESERVOIR
Glen Tarbert
Inversanda
Kentallen
South Ballachulish
Ballachulish
Glencoe
GLENCOE AND NORTH LORN FOLK MUSEUM
HIGHLAND MYSTERYWORLD
GLENCOE VISITOR CENTRE
Glen Coe
Altnafeadh
Black Corries Lodge
Kingshouse Hotel
STOB NA CRUAICHE
Loch Laidon
Kilmalieu
Duror
Rubha Mor
Glenduror Forest
Beinn a'Bheithir
Eilean Balnagowan
Keil
Glen Duror
Camasnacroise
Salachan Glen
BIDEAN NAM BIAN
Royal Forest
GLENCOE SKI CENTRE
MUSEUM OF SCOTTISH SKIING AND MOUNTAINEERING
Dalness
Glen Etive
Alltchaorunn
Shuna I.
Appin House
Glen Stockdale
Elleric
Glen Creran
Fasnacloich
Invercreran
Portnacroish
KINLOCHLAICH HOUSE GARDENS
GLASDRUM WOOD
Glasdrum
Glen Ure
Invercharnan
Glenceitlein
Gualachulain
Appin
Port Appin
Strath of Appin
Creagan
Druimavuic
Port Ramsay
Eriska
North Shian
South Creagan
South Shian
Barcaldine
SCOTTISH SEA LIFE SANCTUARY
Barcaldine Forest
Baravullin
Ferlochan
Kiel Crofts
Benderloch
Ledaig
Achnaba
ARDCHATTAN PRIORY GARDENS
North Connel
Connel
Black Crofts
FALLS OF LORA
Achnacloich
ACHNACLOICH GARDEN
Bonawe
Dunbeg
Brochroy
Fearnoch Forest
Taynuilt
BONAWE IRON FURNACE
INVERAWE FISHERIES AND SMOKERIES EXHIBITION
Ichrachan
Bridge of Awe
Pass of Brander
Oban
OBAN DISTILLERY
OBAN RARE BREEDS FARM PARK
BARGUILLEAN GARDENS
Glenamachrie
Glen Lonan
Glen Nant
Cruachan Reservoir
Falls of Cruachan
KILCHURN CASTLE
Lochawe
Stronmilchan
Strath of Orchy
Dalmally
MCINTYRE MONUMENT
Inverlochy
Achnafalnich
CRUACHAN DAM VISITOR CENTRE
ARDANAISEIG GARDENS
Ardanaiseig
Innis Chonain
Inishail
Barran
Kilmore
Glen Feochan
GLENFEOCHAN HOUSE GARDENS
Kilbride
Kilchrenan
Annat
North Port
Musdale
Cladich
Portsonachan
South Port
Bragleenmore
Glen Kinglass
Glen Liver
Glen Noe
Glen Strae
GLEN ORCHY
Bridge of Orchy
Inveroran Hotel
Forest Lodge
Black Mount
Loch Tulla
Achallader
WEST HIGHLAND WAY
Arichastlich
Glen Lochy
Arrivain
Clifton
Tyndrum
Strath Fillan
Inverherive
Crianlarich
Cononish
BEN LUI
Glen Falloch
Falls of Falloch
Inverarnan
Lochan Shira
Loch Sron Mor
Glen Fyne
Glenfyne Lodge
Ardlui
Loch Sloy
Inveruglas
ROB ROY'S CAVE
Inversnaid Hotel
Tarbet
Arrochar
Succoth
Ardgartan
Glen Croe
Rest and Be Thankful
Glen Kinglas
Cairndow
Clachan
Drishaig
ARDKINGLAS WOODLAND GARDEN
Ardno
St Catherine's
Hell's Glen
Inveraray
INVERARAY CASTLE
BELL TOWER
INVERARAY JAIL
Newtown
Glen Aray
Glen Shira
Tullich
Ballimeanoch
Inverinan
Blarghour
Lochavich Ho
Drissaig
Kilmun
Dalavich
Loch Avich
Lagalochan
Portinnisherrich
ARDCHONNELL CASTLE
Inverliever Forest
Kilmaha
Eredine
Durran
Eredine Forest
Arichamish
Finchairn
FINCHAIRN CASTLE
Ederline
Loch Gaineamhach
Dalchenna
Auchindrain
AUCHINDRAIN OPEN AIR MUSEUM
Creggans
Clachan
Strachur
Strachur Bay
Furnace
Glen Sluain
Newton
Craraе
CRARAE GLEN GARDENS
Minard
Tullochgorm
Garbhallt
LACHLAN CASTLE
Lachlan Bay
Strathlachlan Forest
Glenbranter
Glenbranter Forest
Invernoaden
Loch Eck
Whistlefield
Bernice
Dunans
Lochgair
Asknish
Lephinchapel
Lochgoilhead
Drimsynie
EUROPEAN SHEEP AND WOOL CENTRE
Corrow
Blairlomond
Ardgoil Forest
Carrick Castle
CARRICK CASTLE
Glenmallan
Portincaple
Whistlefield
Garelochhead
Ardmay
Stuckgowan
Ptarmigan Lodge
Glen Douglas
Rowardennan
Inverbeg
INVERBEG GALLERY
Rowardennan Forest
Edentaggart
Glen Luss
Inchlonaig
Luss
Aldochlay
Craig Rostan
BEN LOMOND
0 1 2 3 4 5 6 miles
0 1 2 3 4 5 6 7 8 9 10 km

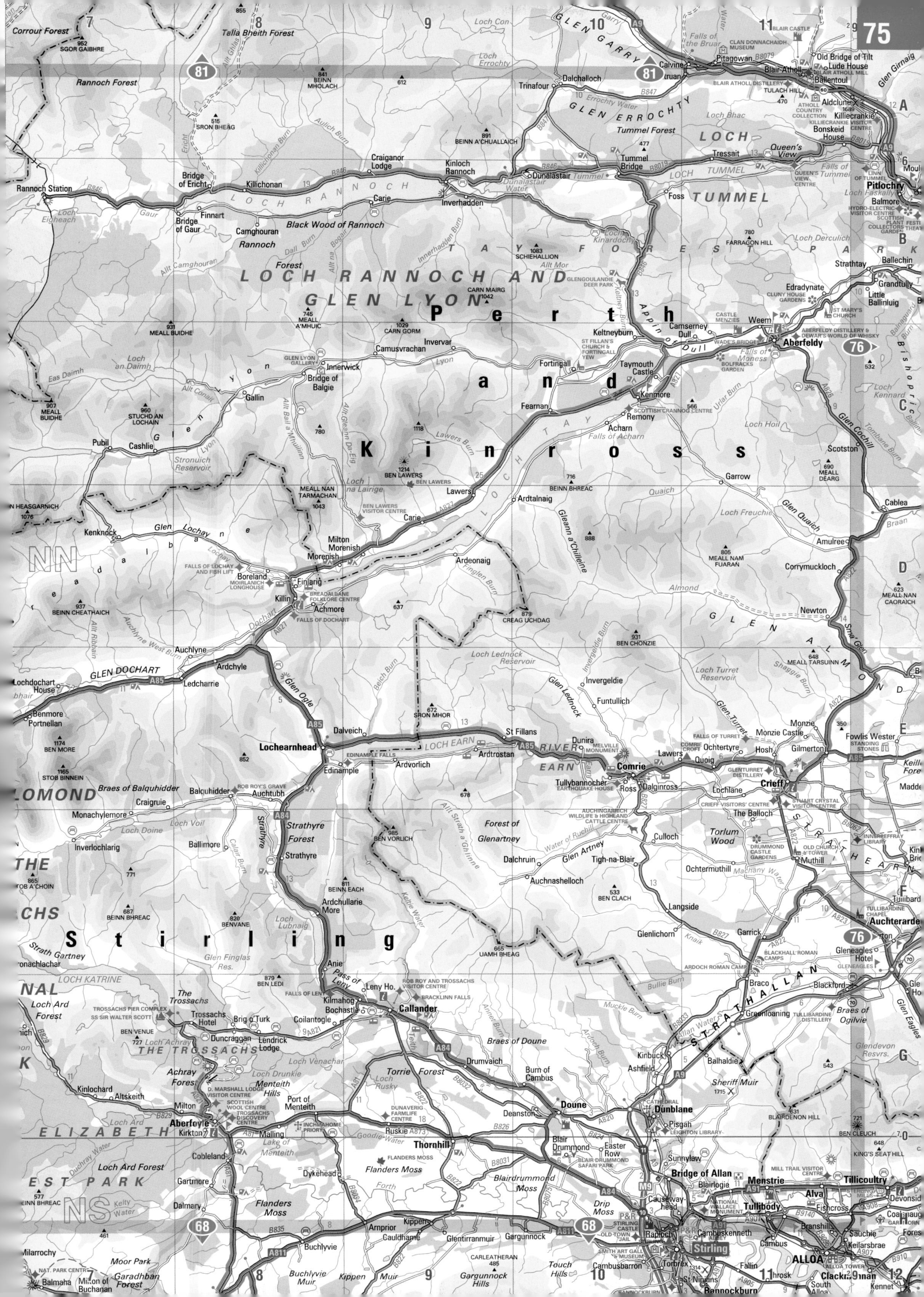

Perth and Kinross
Stirling
LOCH RANNOCH AND GLEN LYON
TAY FOREST PARK
LOCH TUMMEL
GLEN GARRY
GLEN ERROCHTY
Rannoch Forest
Corrour Forest
Talla Bheith Forest
Rannoch Station
Bridge of Ericht
Killichonan
Kinloch Rannoch
Craiganor Lodge
Dunalastair
Tummel Bridge
Trinafour
Dalchalloch
Calvine
Struan
Pitagowan
Blair Atholl
Old Bridge of Tilt
Lude House
Killiecrankie
Pitlochry
Tressait
Queen's View
Foss
Bridge of Gaur
Finnart
Camghouran
Carie
Inverhadden
Black Wood of Rannoch
Schiehallion
Carn Mairg
Keltneyburn
Coshieville
Camserney
Weem
Aberfeldy
Strathtay
Grandtully
Edradynate
Fortingall
Taymouth Castle
Kenmore
Fearnan
Acharn
Scottish Crannog Centre
Innerwick
Bridge of Balgie
Camusvrachan
Invervar
Gallin
Pubil
Cashlie
Stronuich Reservoir
Ben Lawers
Lawers
Carie
Milton Morenish
Morenish
Kenknock
Glen Lochay
Boreland
Finlarig
Killin
Achmore
Falls of Dochart
Ardeonaig
Ardtalnaig
Creag Uchdag
Loch Tay
Amulree
Corrymuckloch
Newton
Glen Almond
Glen Quaich
Garrow
Scotston
Cablea
Ben Chonzie
Glen Dochart
Auchlyne
Ardchyle
Ledcharrie
Lochdochart House
Benmore
Portnellan
Ben More
Stob Binnein
Glen Ogle
Lochearnhead
Dalveich
Loch Earn
St Fillans
Ardtrostan
Edinample
Ardvorlich
Dunira
Invergeldie
Funtullich
Glen Lednock
Loch Lednock Reservoir
Comrie
Tullybannocher
Ross
Dalginross
Lawers
Ochtertyre
Monzie Castle
Fowlis Wester
Gilmerton
Hosh
Crieff
The Balloch
Culloch
Tigh-na-Blair
Dalchruin
Glen Artney
Forest of Glenartney
Auchnashelloch
Ben Clach
Torlum Wood
Ochtermuthill
Muthill
Strathearn
Langside
Glenlichorn
Garrick
Auchterarder
Gleneagles Hotel
Blackford
Braco
Greenloaning
Strathallan
Braes of Ogilvie
Braes of Balquhidder
Balquhidder
Auchtubh
Craigruie
Monachylemore
Loch Voil
Loch Doine
Inverlochlarig
Ballimore
Strathyre
Strathyre Forest
Ben Vorlich
Beinn Each
Ardchullarie More
Benvane
Ben Ledi
Uamh Bheag
Loch Lubnaig
Glen Finglas Res.
Anie
Pass of Leny
Kilmahog
Leny Ho.
Bochastle
Callander
Coilantogle
Loch Katrine
The Trossachs
Trossachs Hotel
Brig o' Turk
Duncraggan
Lendrick Lodge
Loch Venachar
Loch Achray
Achray Forest
Loch Ard Forest
Braes of Doune
Drumvaich
Burn of Cambus
Torrie Forest
Loch Rusky
Menteith Hills
Port of Menteith
Lake of Menteith
Kinlochard
Altskeith
Milton
Aberfoyle
Kirkton
Cobleland
Gartmore
Dalmary
Malling
Ruskie
Thornhill
Deanston
Doune
Dunblane
Kinbuck
Ashfield
Balhaldie
Sheriff Muir
Blair Drummond
Easter Row
Blairdrummond Moss
Flanders Moss
Dykehead
Drip Moss
Bridge of Allan
Blairlogie
Causewayhead
Menstrie
Alva
Tillicoultry
Tullibody
Cambus
Alloa
Stirling
Raploch
Cambuskenneth
Cambusbarron
Bannockburn
Kippen
Arnprior
Cauldhame
Glentirranmuir
Gargunnock
Gargunnock Hills
Touch Hills
Buchlyvie
Buchlyvie Muir
Balmaha
Milton of Buchanan
Garadhban Forest
Moor Park
Milarrochy
Strath Gartney
LOMOND
THE TROSSACHS
ELIZABETH
FOREST PARK
NN
NS

Perth and Kinross
Clackmannanshire
Fife
Pitlochry
Moulin
Killiecrankie
Aldclune
Old Bridge of Tilt
Lude House
Blair Atholl
Ballentoul
Bonskeid House
Ben Vrackie
Tarvie
Straloch
Dalnavaid
Enochdhu
Glen Brerachan
Strathardle
Kirkmichael
Ashintully Castle
Glen Shee
Dalnaglar Castle
Meikle Forter
Cray
Folda
Glenisla Forest
Brewlands Bridge
Freuchies
Backwater Res.
Glenhead Farm
Glenprosen Lodge
Glenprosen Village
Balnaboth
Glen Clova
Clachnabrain
Easter Lednathie
Kilburn
Rottal
Dykehead
Cortachy
Pearsie
Balloch
Balintore
Bellaty
Dykends
Blacklunans
Kirkton of Glenisla
Mount Blair
Cairn Gibbs
Creag Dhubh
Edradour Distillery
Milton of Edradour
Balmore
Loch Faskally
Loch Broom
Meall Reamhar
Knock of Balmyle
Forest of Alyth
Ballintuim
Black Water
Milton of Dalcapon
Loch Derculich
Strathtay
Ballechin
Grandtully
Little Ballinluig
Tulliemet
Ballinluig
Logierait
Balnaguard
Edradynate
Aberfeldy
Balmacneil
Kindallachan
Kincraigie
Guay
Dowally
Dalguise
Craigvinean Forest
Bishopric
Strath Tay
Deuchary Hill
Riemore
Riechip
Loch Ordie
Forest of Clunie
Loch Benachally
Blackcraig Forest
Bridge of Cally
Cochrage Muir
Netherton
Middleton
Lornty
Westfields of Rattray
Blairgowrie
Rattray
Kinloch
Rosemount
Butterstone
Forneth
Achalader
Loch of Lowes
Concraigie
Clunie
Loch of Clunie
Loch of Drumellie
Craigie
Muirton of Ardblair
Kirkton of Lethendy
Snaigow House
Dunkeld
Little Dunkeld
Birnam
Inver
River Tay
Loch Kennard
Glen Cochill
Scotston
Meall Dearg
Ballinlick
Trochry
Spittalfield
Delvine
Caputh
Meikleour
Kinclaven
Gellyburn
Murthly
Muir of Thorn
Ardoch
Obney Hills
Upper Obney
Balquharn
Waterloo
Cargill
Bankfoot
Airntully
Stanley
West Tofts
Woodside
Burrelton
Coupar Angus
Markethill
Campmuir
Kettins
Hallyburton House
Pitcur
Leys
Lundie
Auchterhouse
Whitefield
Saucher
Collace
Kirkton of Collace
King's Seat
Wolfhill
Guildtown
Kinrossie
St Martins
Newmiln
Abernyte
Bandirran
Knapp
Littleton
Sidlaw Hills
Alyth
New Alyth
Balhary
Ruthven
Ruthven House
Meigle
Kinloch
Arthurstone
Ardler
New-bigging
Newtyle
Keillor
Castleton
Balkeerie
Eassie
Kirkinch
Wester Denoon
Ark Hill
Nether Handwick
Glamis
Charleston
Kirriemuir
Westmuir
Kirkton of Airlie
Craigton
Leys of Cossans
Bridgend of Lintrathen
Loch of Lintrathen
Bridge of Craigisla
Auchrannie
Tullymurdoch
Bamff
Shanzie
Tullyfergus
Kirkton of Kingoldrum
Northmuir
Mile Hill
Catlaw
Creigh Hill
Strathbraan
Cablea
Glen Quaich
Amulree
Corrymuckloch
Little Glenshee
Meall nan Caoraich
Tullybelton
Logiealmond Lodge
Loch Logiealmond
Newton
Glen Almond
Harrietfield
Chapelhill
Moneydie
Luncarty
Downhill
Redgorton
Pitcairngreen
Almondbank
Methven
Keillour
Buchanty
Fowlis Wester
Gilmerton
Crieff
Keillour Forest
Braegrum
Tibbermore
Lochty
Huntingtower
Tulloch
Muirton
Scone
Gannochy
Letham
Perth
Cherrybank
Craigie
Friarton
Kinfauns
Kinfauns Forest
Glendoick
Glencarse
St Madoes
Chapelhill
Errol
Carse of Gowrie
Braes of the Carse
Kilspindie
Pole Hill
Rait
Kinnaird
Ballindean
Inchture
Grange
Megginch
Myreside
Rossie Priory
Invergowrie
Longforgan
Castle Huntly
Kingoodie
Dundee
Benvie
Denhead of Gray
Fowlis
Lochee
Muirhead
Birkhill
Downfield
Dronley
Bridgefoot
Kirkton of Auchterhouse
Leoch
Bonnyton
Balkemback
Coldstream
Firth of Tay
Tay Rail Bridge
Newport
Wormit
Balmerino
Kirkton
Bottomcraig
Gauldry
Kilmany
Hazelton Walls
Creich
Brunton
Rathillet
Luthrie
Glenduckie
Newburgh
Mugdrum I.
Carthagena Bank
Moonzie
Dunbog
Lindores
Lindores Loch
Grange of Lindores
Lindifferon
Mount Hill
Kilmaron Castle
Cupar
Fernie
Letham
Monimail
Collessie
Bow of Fife
Cupar Muir
Kinloch
Giffordtown
Springfield
Ladybank
Pitlessie
Kingskettle
Balmalcolm
Kettlebridge
Kettlehill
Montrave
Freuchie
Newton of Falkland
Falkland
Lomond Hills
Regional Park
Glasslie
West Lomond
Ramelldry Mill Bank
Langdyke
Muirhead
Star
Kennoway
Bonnybank
Scoonie
Markinch
Balcurvie
Milton of Balgonie
Coaltown of Balgonie
Windygates
Leven
Methil
Buckhaven
Innerleven
East Wemyss
Coaltown of Wemyss
West Wemyss
Stenton
Thornton
Glenrothes
Leslie
Cadham
Pitkevy
Auchmuirbridge
Kinglassie
Cluny
Auchterderran
Cardenden
Gallatown
Chapel
Templehall
Dysart
Hayfield
Pathhead
Kirkcaldy
Madderty
Clathy
Findo Gask
St David's
Kirkton
Kinkell Bridge
Muthill
Strathearn
Aberuthven
Tullibardine
Auchterarder
Muirton
Milton
Gleneagles Hotel
Gleneagles House
Glen Eagles
Blackford
Braes of Ogilvie
Steel's Knowe
Glendevon Resvrs.
Glen Devon
Glendevon
Burnfoot
Castle Hill Reservoir
Carnbo
Dalqueich
Pool o' Muckhart
Yetts o' Muckhart
Drum
Crook of Devon
Rumbling Bridge
Powmill
Coldrain
Cleish
Cleish Hills
Blairingone
Dollar
Tillicoultry
Alva
Devonside
Coalsnaughton
Fishcross
Sauchie
Forest Mill
Menstrie
Ben Cleuch
King's Seat Hill
Hill End
Balgonar
Knock Hill
Saline
Kennet
Milltown of Aberdalgie
Aberdalgie
Dupplin Castle
Forteviot
Craigend
Tarsappie
Rhynd
Elcho
Inchyra
Easter Rhynd
Bridge of Earn
Forgandenny
Kintillo
Dron
Aberargie
Abernethy
Glenfoot
Pitmedden Forest
Auchtermuchty
Dunshalt
Strathmiglo
Howe of Fife
Gateside
Nether Urquhart
Burnside
Ardargie House Hotel
Dunning
Rossie Ochill
Pathstruie
Path of Condie
Glenfarg Res.
Glenfarg
Arngask
Newton of Balcanquhal
Duncrievie
Common of Dunning
Middle Rigg
Innerdouny Hill
Middleton
Craigow
Upper Tillyrie
Milnathort
Wester Balgedie
Kinnesswood
Scotlandwell
Kinross
Loch Leven
St Serf's Island
Gairney Bank
Ballingry
Lochore
Crosshill
Glencraig
Benarty Hill
Kelty
Lochgelly
Lumphinnans
Cowdenbeath
Lassodie
Loch Fitty
Bowershall
Hill of Beath
Cowstrandburn
0 1 2 3 4 5 6 miles
0 1 2 3 4 5 6 7 8 9 10 km

83
Edzell
Dunlappie
Tillyarblet
Dykelands
Johnshaven
North Water Bridge
Marykirk
Pert
Inchbare
Kirkton of Menmuir
Tigerton
Newtonmill
Craigo
Ecclesgreig
Lochside
Logie
Morphie
St Cyrus
Milton Ness
Pathhead
Glenmoy
Auchnacree
Mains of Balhall
Belliehill
Lochty
Little Brechin
Keithock
Logie Pert
Muirton of Ballochy
Glenogil
Glenquiech
Ogil
Fern
West Muir
Trinity
Hillside
Kirkhill
Hornichaugh
Newmill of Inshewan
Noran Water
Brechin
Caledonian Railway
House of Dun
Dun
Memus
Careston Castle
South Esk
Tannadice
Montrose
Inverquharity
Shielhill
Murthill
Finavon
Oathlaw
Aldbar Castle
Netherton
Mains of Melgund
Middle Drums
Kinnaird Castle
Bridge of Dun
Barnhead
Montrose Basin
Inchbraoch
Museum and Art Gallery
Scurdie Ness
Ferryden
William Lamb Memorial Studio
Aberlemno
Pitkennedy
Montreathmont Forest
Montreathmont Moor
Farnell
Bonnyton
Maryton
Carcary
Kirkton of Craig
Long Craig
Fishtown of Usan
Dunninald
Rossie Moor
Westerton
Boddin Pt.
Carse Gray
Mosside
Lunanhead
Rescobie
Turin
Padanaram
Forfar
Reswallie
Dubton
Bolshan
Braehead of Lunan
Lunan
Lunan Bay
Balgavies
Milldens
Glasterlaw
Kinnell
Drumgley
Burnside
Kingsmuir
Guthrie
Pitmuies
Redcastle
Dunnichen
Letham
Friockheim
Boysack
Inverkeilor
Lunan Water
Caldhame
Lownie Moor
Chapelton
Lang Craig
Ethie Mains
Douglastown
Idvies
Leysmill
Cauldcots
Red Head
Ethie Castle
Craichie
Tulloes
Drunkendub
Mosston
Colliston
Letham Grange
Gateside
Inverarity
Whigstreet
Auchmithie
Greystone
Redford
Marywell
Meg's Craig
Kirkbuddo
St Vigeans
Gallowfauld
Hayhillock
Carmyllie
Denhead of Arbilot
Hayshead
Cliffburn
The Deil's Heid
Arbroath
Arbroath Abbey
Arbirlot
Signal Tower Museum
Balmirmer
Elliot
Newbigging
Monikie
Kirkton of Monikie
Craigton
Salmond's Muir
Inveraldie
East March
Wellbank
Muirdrum
Bucklerheads
Burnside of Duntrune
Drumsturdy
Kellas
East Haven
Panbride
NO
Barry
Carnoustie
Fintry
Baldovie
Mains of Ardestie
Douglas & Angus
Monifieth
Barry Links
Craigie
West Ferry
Broughty Ferry
Stannergate
Barnhill
Broughty Castle Museum
Frigate Unicorn
Buddon Ness
Tay Bridge
Tayport
Scotscraig
Tentsmuir Forest
Pickletillem
Rhynd
Carrick
Lucklawhill
Leuchars
Balmullo
Leuchars Norman Church
Logie
Eden Mouth
Guardbridge
Eden Estuary Centre
St Andrews Bay
Kincaple
St Andrews Aquarium
Dairsie or Osnaburgh
British Golf Mus
St Andrews
Cath & St Rule's Tower
Strathkinness
Newpark
Kemback
Brownhills
Buddo Ness
Blebocraigs
Balone
Boarhills
Babbet Ness
Craigtoun
St Andrews Botanic Garden
Denhead
Pitscottie
Prior Muir
Kingsbarns
Cambo Ness
Cambo Gardens
Carr Brigs
Cameron Res.
Cameron Burn
Stravithie
Dunino
Tullybothy Craigs
Baldinnie
Fife Folk Museum
Balcomie
Craighead
Peat Inn
Fife Ness
Radernie
Kingsmuir
Crail Tolbooth
Lathones
Lochty
Scotland's Secret Bunker
Woodside
New Gilston
Crail
Largoward
Carnbee
Pitcorthie
Crail Museum and Heritage Centre
West Ness
Wester Newburn
Kellie Castle and Garden
Pitkierie
Fife Coastal Path
Arncroach
Kilrenny
Kirkton of Largo
Drumeldrie
Colinsburgh
Anstruther Easter
Scottish Fisheries Museum
Robinson Crusoe Statue
Balchrystie
Abercrombie
Pittenweem
Anstruther Wester
Kilconquhar
St Fillan's Cave
St Monan's Windmill
Lower Largo
Ardross
St Monans
St Monan's Church
Largo Bay
Ruddons Pt.
Elie
Earlsferry
Saucharl Pt.
Chapel Ness
Isle of May
NT
70
A B C D E F G H
7 8 9 10 11 12

NF
NL
84
85
72
Canna
A'Chill
Garrisdale Pt.
Canna Harbour
Sanday
Sound of Canna
Guirdil Bay
Kilmory
Kilmory Glen
Rubha Shamhnan Insir
MALLAIG 2:30
0:55
Kinloch Glen
Rubha na Roinne
A'Bhrideanach
388
571 ORVAL
R Ù M
Kinloch
KINLOCH CASTLE
Loch Scresort
Rubha Port na Caranean
Schooner Pt.
Oigh-sgeir
Harris
Glen Harris
812 ASKIVAL
781 AINSHVAL
Rubha Sgorr an t-Snidhe
THE SMALL ISLES
SOUND OF RÙM
Rubha nam Meirleach
Bay of Laig
Rubha an Fhasaidh
Eigg
393 AN SGURR
Galmisdale
SOUND OF EIGG
Eilean nan Each
Muck
137
Port Mor
0:35
1:10
Bhatarsaigh (Vatersay)
Uidh
Bagh Bhatarsaigh
Bhatarsaigh
Caolas Shanndraigh
Flodaigh (Flodday)
Sanndraigh (Sandray)
207
Lingeigh (Lingay)
Greanamul
Caolas Phabaigh
Theisgeir (Heiskers)
171
Pabaidh (Pabbay)
Caolas Mhiui Laigh
Miùgh Laigh (Mingulay)
273
Bearnaraigh (Berneray)
Caolas Bhearnaraigh
Barra Hd.
Sanna Point
Sanna Bay
Sanna
Portuairk
Achnaha
Point of Ardnamurchan
ARDNAMURCHAN LIGHTHOUSE
Achosnich
B8007
Ormsaigmore
Ormsaigbeg
An Acairseid
Kilchoan Bay
Cairns of Coll
Eilean Mor
Rubha Mor
Bousd
Sorisdale
Cliad Bay
Arnabost
Gallanach
Grishipoll
73
COLL
Ballyhaugh
104
Loch Cliad
Hogh Bay
Totronald
Arinagour
OBAN 2:40
Feall Bay
Arileod
Acha
Loch Eatharna
Eilean Ornsay
Breachacha Castle
Friesland
Calgary Pt.
Gunna
Crossapol Bay
Soa
Loch Breachacha
TIREE
Vaul Bay
Vaul
Salum
Caolas
Rubha Dubh
Balephetrish Bay
Hough Skerries
Balevullin
B8069
Ruaig
Kenovay
Gott Bay
R. Chraiginis
Kilkenneth
Soa
Moss
Scarinish
Middleton
Heylipol
TIREE
Heanish
Port Mor
B8065
Crossapol
Rubha Traigh an Duin
Loch a'Phuill
Barrapol
Hynish Bay
B8068
B8067
Balemartine
Rinn Thorbhais
Balephuil
141
Mannal
Balephuil Bay
Port Snoig
Hynish
Ardmore Bay
Ardmore
Glengorm Castle
Quinish Pt.
MULL MUSEUM
Rubha an Aird
Caliach Pt.
Sunipol
Mishnish
'S AIRDE BEINN
292
Mornish
Penmore Mill
MULL LITTLE THEATRE
Achnadrish
Dervaig
Calgary
Calgary Bay
THE OLD BYRE HERITAGE CENTRE
Treshnish Pt.
Ensay
342 CARN MOR
Lettermore
Haunn
B8073
Achnacraig
Rubh a'Chaoil
Burg
Kilninian
Achleck
Fanmore
390
Treshnish Isles
Fladda
Ballygown
LOCH TUATH
EAS FORS WATERFALL
424 BEINN NA DRISE
Eilean Dioghlum
Lagganulva
Lunga
Gometra
Laggan Bay
Bearnus
313
Oskamull
Ulva
Ulva House
Killiemor
Bac Mor
LOCH NA KEAL
Sound of Ulva
Eorsa
Little Colonsay
Staffa
STAFFA
FINGAL'S CAVE
INCH KENNETH CHAPEL
Inch Kenneth
Derryguaig
Balnahard
MACKINNON'S CAVE
Erisgeir
(April-Oct) 0:45
519 BEINN NA SREINE
Glen Seilisdeir
ARDMEANACH
THE BURG
Eilean Annraidh
MACLEAN'S CROSS
IONA ABBEY AND CATHEDRAL
Rubha nan Cearc
100
IONA HERITAGE CENTRE
Kintra
Loch na Lathaich
LOCH SCRIDAIN
Iona
Baile Mor
ST COLUMBA EXHIBITION & WELCOME CENTRE
Aridhglas
Eorabus
Stac an Aoineidh
Fionnphort
A849
18
Sound of Iona
Fidden
Tiraghoil
Lee
Bunessan
376 CRUACHAN MIN
Erraid
Loch Assapol
ROSS OF MULL
Soa I.
Ardalanish
Uisken
Scoor
Ardchiavaig
125
Rubha nam Braithrean
Malcolm's
Eilean a'Chalmain
Rubh Ardalanish
Torran Rocks
Scale : 1:332 000
(approx 5 miles to 1 inch)
0 1 2 3 4 5 6 miles
0 1 2 3 4 5 6 7 8 9 10 km

NG
NH
NM
NN
Highland
Argyll and Bute
KNOYDART
MOIDART
LOCH SHIEL
SUNART
MORVERN
ISLAND OF MULL
ORAR, MOIDART AND ARDNAMURCHAN
SOUND OF SLEAT
SOUND OF MULL
LYNN OF LORN
FIRTH OF LORN
LOCH MORAR
LOCH LINNHE
LOCH ARKAIG
LOCH QUOICH
LOCH ETIVE
LOCH SUNART
LOCH EIL
Kilbeg
Kilmore
Armadale Castle
Glen Meadhonach
Rubha Charn nan Cearc
Calligarry
Ardvasar
Aird of Sleat
Ard Thurinish
Point of Sleat
Airor
Sandaig
Scottas
Inverie
Rubha Raonuill
Mallaig
Glasnacardoch
Beoraidbeg
Morar
Bracara
Bracorina
Stoul
Tarbet
Kylesknoydart
Kylesmorar
Brinacory
Swordland
Kinlochmorar
Scamadale
Lettermorar
South Morar
Meoble
Bunacaimb
Portnaluchaig
Back of Keppoch
Kinloid
Arisaig
Eilean Ighe
Luinga Bheag
Luinga Mhor
Druimindarroch
Polnish
Lochailort
Inverailort
Ranochan
Glenfinnan
Kinlocheil
Fassfern
Drumsallie
Corpach
Banavie
Fort William
Inverlochy
Claggan
Lochyside
Torlundy
Achintee
Strone
Muirshearlich
Wauchan
Kinlochbeoraid
Ardnish
Laggan
Alisary
Roshven
Glenuig
Smirisary
Samalaman I.
Eilean nan Gobhar
Eilean Shona
Kinlochmoidart
Ardmolich
Brunery
Gaskan
Scamodale
Ardtoe
Newton of Ardtoe
Shielfoot
Kentra
Blain
Moss
Dalnabreck
Dalelia
Acharacle
Ardshealach
Polloch
Glenhurich
Kinlochan
Resipole
Salen
Ariundle
Scotstown
Anaheilt
Strontian
Ardnastang
Glenborrodale
Glenbeg
Ardslignish
Laga
Carna
Oronsay
Glencripesdale
Camuschoirk
Liddesdale
Lochuisge
Beach
Kingairloch
Camasnacroise
Kilmalieu
Inversanda
Sallachan
Clovullin
Ardgour
Corran
Inchree
Onich
North Ballachulish
South Ballachulish
Ballachulish
Glencoe
Kentallen
Duror
Keil
Appin
Portnacroish
Port Appin
Creagan
Druimavuic
Barcaldine
Benderloch
Ledaig
Connel
North Connel
Dunbeg
Ganavan
Dunollie
Oban
Kerrera
Taynuilt
Bonawe
Bridge of Awe
Lochawe
Dalmally
Innis Chonain
Glenamachrie
Kilmore
Kilninver
Barochreal
Glen Euchar
Clachan-Seil
Easdale
Balvicar
Cuan
Cullipool
Kilchoan
Ardanstur
Melfort
Kilmelford
Lochavich
Kilmun
Dalavich
Inverinan
Portsonachan
South Port
North Port
Kilchrenan
Annat
Tullich
Lismore
Port Ramsay
Achnacroish
Clachan
Eriska
Drimnin
Bonnavoulin
Rhemore
Killundine
Ardnacross
Fiunary
Savary
Larachbeg
Achranich
Claggan
Acharn
Lochaline
Aros Mains
Salen
Pennygown
Killiechronan
Gruline
Knock
Garmony
Scallastle
Craignure
Lochdon
Duart Pt.
Strathcoil
Grass Pt.
Lochbuie
Kinlochspelve
Barachandroman
Croggan
Carsaig
Laggan Deer Forest
Rubha Dubh
Frank Lockwood's Island
Garbh Eileach
Garvellachs
Dubh-fheith
Glen More
Glen Coe
Glen Tarbert
Glen Dessarry
Glen Pean
Glen Kingie
Glen Mallie
Glen Loy
Glen Nevis
Glen Creran
Glen Ure
Glen Noe
Glen Kinglass
Glen Liver
Glen Lonan
Glen Nant
Glen Feochan
Pass of Brander
Glenduror Forest
Barcaldine Forest
Fearnoch Forest
Locheil Forest
Glenrigh Forest
Glenquoich Forest
A830
A861
A82
A828
A85
A816
A849
A884
B8043
A848
85
80
74
73
72
8
9
10
11
12
13
14

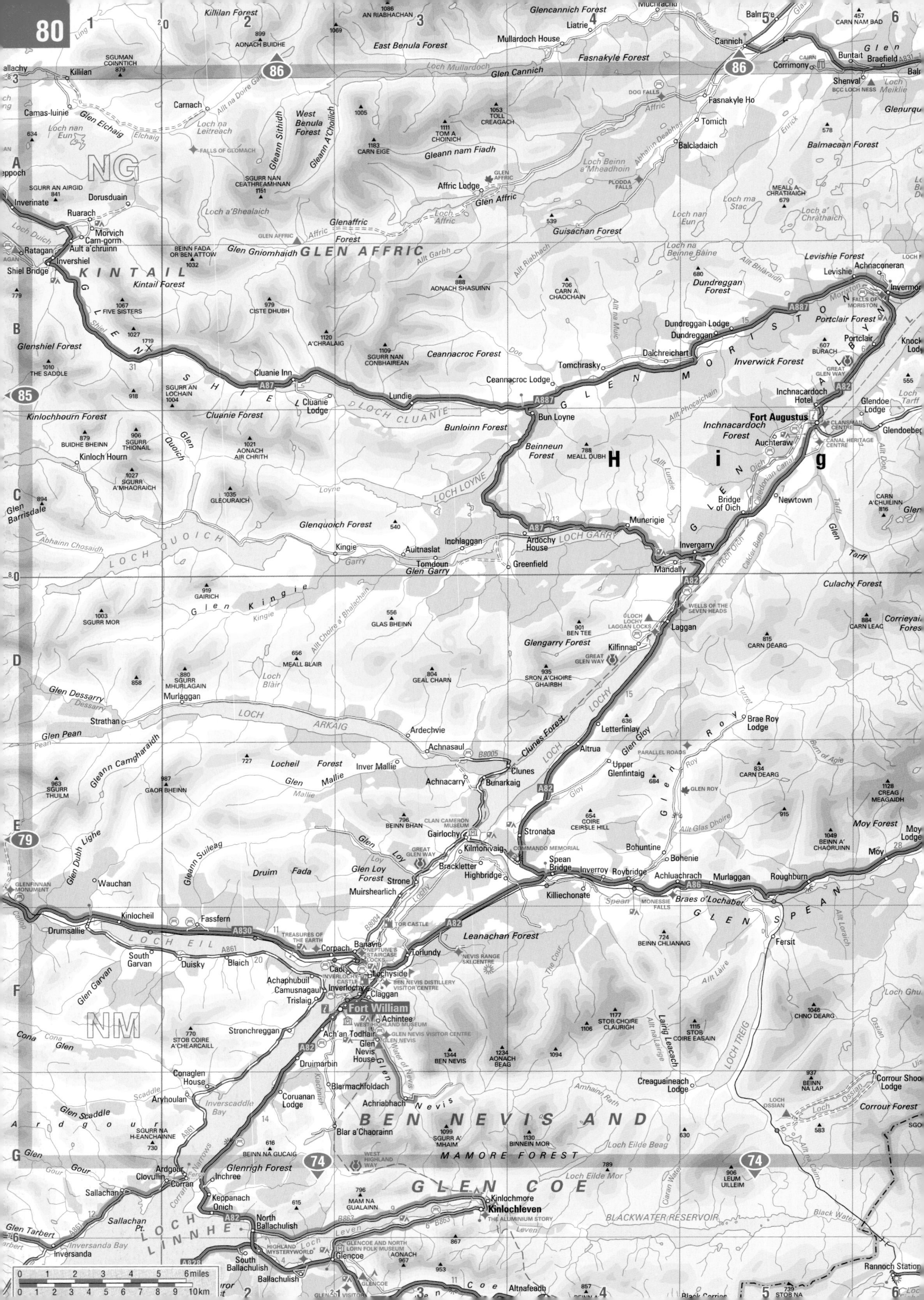

Killilan Forest
Glencannich Forest
East Benula Forest
Mullardoch House
Liatrie
Cannich
Fasnakyle Forest
Corrimony
Buntait
Braefield
Shenval
Glenurquhart
Killilan
Loch Mullardoch
Glen Cannich
86
Camas-luinie
Glen Elchaig
Carnach
West Benula Forest
Gleann Sithidh
Glenn A'Choilich
Dog Falls
Fasnakyle Ho
Tomich
Balcladaich
Balmacaan Forest
Falls of Glomach
Carn Eige
Gleann nam Fiadh
Loch Beinn a'Mheadhoin
Plodda Falls
NG
Sgurr nan Ceathreamhnan
Affric Lodge
Glen Affric
Inverinate
Dorusduain
Ruarach
Morvich
Carn-gorm
Ault a'chruinn
Ratagan
Invershiel
Shiel Bridge
Loch a'Bhealaich
Glenaffric Forest
Guisachan Forest
Loch nan Eun
Glen Gniomhaidh
GLEN AFFRIC
KINTAIL
Kintail Forest
Five Sisters
Glenshiel Forest
Glen Shiel
Levishie Forest
Achnaconeran
Levishie
Invermoriston
Dundreggan Forest
Dundreggan Lodge
Dundreggan
Aonach Shasuinn
Ciste Dhubh
A'Chralaig
Sgurr nan Conbhairean
Ceannacroc Forest
Dalchreichart
Tomchrasky
Portclair Forest
Portclair
Inverwick Forest
Glen Moriston
Cluanie Inn
Ceannacroc Lodge
Inchnacardoch Hotel
85
Cluanie Lodge
Lundie
Loch Cluanie
Bun Loyne
Fort Augustus
Glendoe Lodge
Kinlochhourn Forest
Cluanie Forest
Bunloinn Forest
Inchnacardoch Forest
Auchteraw
Glendoebeg
Glen Quoich
Aonach Air Chrith
Beinneun Forest
Meall Dubh
Highland
Kinloch Hourn
Sgurr a'Mhaoraich
Gleouraich
Loch Loyne
Glen Oich
Caledonian Canal
Bridge of Oich
Newtown
Glen Barrisdale
Glenquoich Forest
Munerigie
Loch Quoich
Inchlaggan
Ardochy House
Loch Garry
Invergarry
Kingie
Aultnaslat
Tomdoun
Glen Garry
Greenfield
Mandally
Loch Oich
Glen Tarff
Gairich
Glen Kingie
Culachy Forest
Sgurr Mor
Glas Bheinn
Wells of the Seven Heads
Laggan Locks
Laggan
Ben Tee
Carn Leac
Corrieyairack Forest
Carn Dearg
Glengarry Forest
Kilfinnan
Great Glen Way
Meall Blair
Geal Charn
Sron a'Choire Ghairbh
Sgurr Mhurlagain
Murlaggan
Loch Blair
Glen Dessarry
Loch Lochy
Strathan
Loch Arkaig
Ardechvie
Letterfinlay
Brae Roy Lodge
Glen Roy
Glen Pean
Achnasaul
Clunes Forest
Altrua
Glen Gloy
Parallel Roads
Gleann Camgharaidh
Locheil Forest
Inver Mallie
Glen Mallie
Upper Glenfintaig
Clunes
Achnacarry
Bunarkaig
Sgurr Thuilm
Gaor Bheinn
Glen Roy
Creag Meagaidh
Clan Cameron Museum
Beinn Bhan
Coire Ceirsle Hill
Stronaba
Moy Forest
Moy Lodge
79
Glen Dubh Lighe
Gleann Suileag
Glen Loy
Gairlochy
Kilmonivaig
Commando Memorial
Bohuntine
Bohenie
Beinn a'Chaorainn
Moy
Drum Fada
Glen Loy Forest
Brackletter
Highbridge
Spean Bridge
Inverroy
Roybridge
Achluachrach
Murlaggan
Roughburn
Glenfinnan Monument
Wauchan
Strone
Muirshearlich
Killiechonate
Braes o'Lochaber
Glen Spean
Monessie Falls
Kinlocheil
Fassfern
Tor Castle
Drumsallie
Loch Eil
Treasures of the Earth
Corpach
Banavie
Neptune's Staircase Locks
Torlundy
Leanachan Forest
Beinn Chlianaig
Fersit
South Garvan
Duisky
Blaich
Caol
Lochyside
Nevis Range Ski Centre
Glen Garvan
Achaphubuil
Camusnagaul
Inverlochy Castle
Ben Nevis Distillery Visitor Centre
Trislaig
Inverlochy
Claggan
Fort William
Achintee
West Highland Museum
Glen Nevis Visitor Centre
NM
Stronchreggan
Stob Coire a'Chearcaill
Ach'an Todhair
Glen Nevis House
Stob Choire Claurigh
Stob Coire Easain
Chno Dearg
Cona Glen
Ben Nevis
Aonach Beag
Loch Treig
Conaglen House
Druimarbin
Creaguaineach Lodge
Corrour Shooting Lodge
Aryhoulan
Blarmachfoldach
Coruanan Lodge
Inverscaddle Bay
Achriabhach
Beinn na Lap
Glen Scaddle
Ardgour
Sgurr na h-Eanchainne
Blar a'Chaorainn
BEN NEVIS AND
Sgurr a'Mhaim
Binnein Mor
Loch Eilde Beag
Loch Ossian
Corrour Forest
Beinn na Gucaig
Mamore Forest
74
Glen Gour
Clovullin
Ardgour
Corran
Inchree
Glenrigh Forest
Loch Eilde Mor
Leum Uilleim
Sallachan
Corran Narrows
Keppanach
Onich
GLEN COE
Mam na Gualainn
Kinlochmore
Kinlochleven
The Aluminium Story
Blackwater Reservoir
Glen Tarbert
Sallachan Pt.
Loch Linnhe
North Ballachulish
Inversanda Bay
Inversanda
Highland Mysteryworld
Glencoe and North Lorn Folk Museum
Glencoe
Aonach Eagach
South Ballachulish
Ballachulish
Rannoch Station
Stob na
Altnafeadh
Coe
0 1 2 3 4 5 6 miles
0 1 2 3 4 5 6 7 8 9 10 km

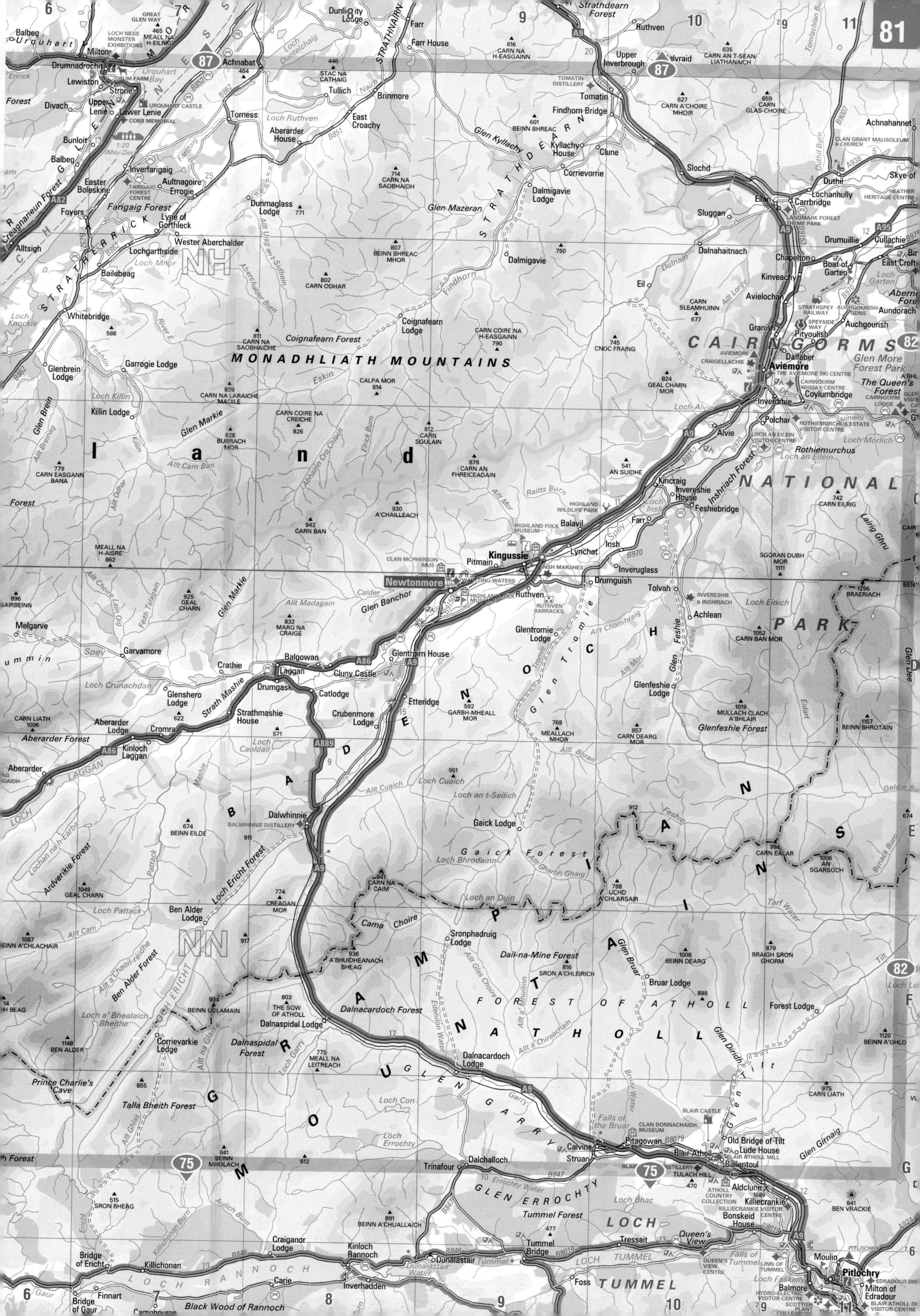

Balbeg
Urquhart
Milton
Drumnadrochit
Lewiston
Strone
Divach
Upper Lenie
Lower Lenie
URQUHART CASTLE
COBB MEMORIAL
Bunloit
Balbeg
LOCH NESS MONSTER EXHIBITIONS
GREAT GLEN WAY
465 MEALL NA H-EILRIG
Achnabat
87
Urquhart Bay
Torness
Loch Ruthven
Aberarder House
Tullich
Brinmore
East Croachy
Dunlichity Lodge
Farr
Farr House
STRATHNAIRN
Loch Duntelchaig
446 STAC NA CATHAIG
616 CARN NA H-EASGAINN
Strathdearn Forest
Ruthven
Upper Inverbrough
Dalvraid
TOMATIN DISTILLERY
Tomatin
Findhorn Bridge
635 CARN AN T-SEAN-LIATHANAICH
627 CARN A'CHOIRE MHOIR
659 CARN GLAS-CHOIRE
Achnahannet
CLAN GRANT MAUSOLEUM & CHURCH
Glen Kyllachy
601 BEINN BHREAC
Kyllachy House
Clune
Corrievorrie
STRATHDEARN
Slochd
Duthil
Skye of Curr
Carrbridge
Lochanhully
HEATHER HERITAGE CENTRE
LANDMARK FOREST THEME PARK
Ellan
Sluggan
Inverfarigaig
Aultnagoire
Errogie
Easter Boleskine
FARIGAIG FOREST CENTRE
Farigaig Forest
Foyers
Lyne of Gorthleck
Wester Aberchalder
Lochgarthside
Loch Mhor
Alltsigh
Bailebeag
STRATHERRICK
Creagnaneun Forest
Dunmaglass Lodge
771
714 CARN NA SAOBHAIDH
Glen Mazeran
Dalmigavie Lodge
807 BEINN BHREAC MHOR
Dalmigavie
750
Dalnahaitnach
Drumuillie
Cullachie
Chapelton
Boat of Garten
Loch Garten
Kinveachy
Avielochan
Aundorach
Auchgourish
STRATHSPEY RAILWAY
SPEYSIDE WAY
Pityoulish
Granish
Dalfaber
Eil
NH
Whitebridge
588
Loch Knockie
802 CARN ODHAR
Coignafearn Lodge
Coignafearn Forest
811 CARN NA SAOBHAIDHE
CARN COIRE NA H-EASGAINN 790
745 CNOC FRAING
CARN SLEAMHUINN 677
CAIRNGORMS
AVIEMORE
CRAIGELLACHIE
Aviemore
THE AVIEMORE SKI CENTRE
CAIRNGORM WHISKY CENTRE
Glen More Forest Park
The Queen's Forest
Coylumbridge
Inverdruie
Glenbrein Lodge
Garrogie Lodge
MONADHLIATH MOUNTAINS
Loch Killin
Killin Lodge
809 CARN NA LARAICHE MAOILE
CALPA MOR 814
824 GEAL CHARN MOR
Loch Alvie
Alvie
Polchar
ROTHIEMURCHUS ESTATE VISITOR CENTRE
Loch Morlich
Rothiemurchus
Loch an Eilein
LOCH AN EILEIN VISITOR CENTRE
Glen Markie
828 BURRACH MOR
CARN COIRE NA CREICHE 826
812 CARN SGULAIN
Glen Brein
779 CARN EASGANN BANA
Allt Cam Ban
I a n d
878 CARN AN FHREICEADAIN
541 AN SUIDHE
Kincraig
Invereshie House
Feshiebridge
Inshriach Forest
NATIONAL
742 CARN EILRIG
Forest
930 A'CHAILLEACH
942 CARN BAN
HIGHLAND WILDLIFE PARK
Balavil
HIGHLAND FOLK MUSEUM
Farr
Insh
Lynchat
Kingussie
Pitmain
CLAN MCPHERSON MUS
Newtonmore
WALTZING WATERS
INSH MARSHES
Inveruglass
Drumguish
Ruthven
RUTHVEN BARRACKS
Tolvah
INVERESHIE & INSHRIACH
SGORAN DUBH MOR 1111
1296 BRAERIACH
Lairig Ghru
MEALL NA H-AISRE 862
896
925 GEAL CHARN
Glen Markie
832 MARG NA CRAIGE
Allt Madagain
Glen Banchor
Calder
Glentromie Lodge
Glen Tromie
Achlean
Loch Einich
1052 CARN BAN MOR
PARK
Melgarve
Garvamore
Spey
Crathie
Laggan
Balgowan
Glentruim House
Cluny Castle
A86
A9
Drumgask
Catlodge
Etteridge
592 GARBH-MHEALL MOR
Glenfeshie Lodge
Glen Feshie
1019 MULLACH CLACH A'BHLAIR
Glenfeshie Forest
1157 BEINN BHROTAIN
Loch Crunachdan
Glenshero Lodge
Strath Mashie
Strathmashie House
622
CARN LIATH 1006
Aberarder Lodge
Cromra
Aberarder Forest
Kinloch Laggan
Crubenmore Lodge
571
Loch Caoldair
A889
768 MEALLACH MHOR
857 CARN DEARG MOR
Aberarder
LAGGAN
951
Loch Cuaich
Loch an t-Seilich
Allt Cuaich
BADENOCH
Dalwhinnie
DALWHINNIE DISTILLERY
674 BEINN EILDE
911
Gaick Lodge
Gaick Forest
Loch Bhrodainn
912
994 CARN EALAR
1006 AN SGARSOCH
Ardverikie Forest
1049 GEAL CHARN
Loch Ericht Forest
774 CREAGAN MOR
941 CARN NA CAIM
Loch an Duin
788 UCHD A'CHLARSAIR
Tarf Water
Loch Pattack
Ben Alder Lodge
1087 BEINN A'CHLACHAIR
NN
917
Cama Choire
936 A'BHUIDHEANACH BHEAG
Sronphadruig Lodge
Dail-na-Mine Forest
816 SRON A'CHLEIRICH
Glen Bruar
1008 BEINN DEARG
879 BRAIGH SRON GHORM
82
Ben Alder Forest
LOCH ERICHT
934 BEINN UDLAMAIN
803 THE SOW OF ATHOLL
Dalnaspidal Lodge
Dalnacardoch Forest
FOREST OF ATHOLL
Bruar Lodge
899
Forest Lodge
Loch a' Bhealaich Bheithe
1148 BEN ALDER
Corrievarkie Lodge
Dalnaspidal Forest
775 MEALL NA LEITREACH
Loch Garry
Dalnacardoch Lodge
Glen Diridh
1120 BEINN A'GHLO
Prince Charlie's Cave
855
Talla Bheith Forest
GRAMPIAN MOUNTAINS
GLEN GARRY
Loch Con
975 CARN LIATH
Falls of the Bruar
CLAN DONNACHAIDH MUSEUM
BLAIR CASTLE
Glen Tilt
Old Bridge of Tilt
Lude House
Glen Girnaig
Loch Errochty
841 BEINN MHOLACH
612
Calvine
Pitagowan
Blair Atholl
BLAIR ATHOLL MILL
Struan
Bridge of Tilt
Ballentoul
Trinafour
Dalchalloch
75
TULACH HILL
Aldclune
Killiecrankie
KILLIECRANKIE VISITOR CENTRE
ATHOLL COUNTRY COLLECTION
841 BEN VRACKIE
515 SRON BHEAG
GLEN ERROCHTY
Errochty Water
Loch Bhac
Bonskeid House
Tummel Forest
LOCH
891 BEINN A'CHUALLAICH
477
Tressait
Queen's View
Falls of Tummel
QUEEN'S VIEW CENTRE
LINN OF TUMMEL
PITLOCHRY
Moulin
Pitlochry
EDRADOUR DISTILLERY
Milton of Edradour
Bridge of Ericht
Killichonan
Craiganor Lodge
Kinloch Rannoch
Tummel Bridge
Dunalastair
Dunalastair Water
LOCH TUMMEL
LOCH RANNOCH
Carie
Inverhadden
Foss
TUMMEL
Loch Faskally
Balmore
HYDRO-ELECTRIC VISITOR CENTRE
SCOTTISH PLANT
Gaur
Finnart
Bridge of Gaur
Camghouran
Black Wood of Rannoch
6
7
8
9
10
11

Moray
CAIRNGORMS
NATIONAL
CAIRNGORM
MOUNTAINS
THE CAIRNGORM MOUNTAINS
PARK
GRAMPIAN
BRAEMAR
DEESIDE AND
LOCHNAGAR
BALMORAL FOREST
Angus
HILLS OF CROMDALE
LADDER HILLS
GLEN AVON
Forest of Glenavon
Forest of Mar
Forest of Glen Tanar
Glenfiddich Forest
Blackwater Forest
Glenlivet Forest
Clashindarroch Forest
Abernethy Forest
Braes of Abernethy
Ballochbuie Forest
Glendoll Forest
Caenlochan Forest
Glenisla Forest
Forest of Alyth
Tornashean Forest
Glen Muick
Glen Clova
Glen Prosen
Glen Shee
Glen Doll
Glen Callater
Glen Gelder
Glen Gairn
Glen Fenzie
Glen Ernan
Glen Tanar
Glen Mark
Glen Lee
Glen Effock
Glen Brerachan
Gleann Fearnach
Glen Dee
Glen Ey
Glen Lui
STRATHARDLE
Strath Avon
Grantown-on-Spey
Nethy Bridge
Boat of Garten
Tomintoul
Glenlivet
Tomnavoulin
Braemar
Crathie
Ballater
Bridge of Gairn
Strathdon
Cock Bridge
Corgarff
Inverey
Spittal of Glenshee
Kirkmichael
Clova
Glenprosen Village
Kirkton of Glenisla
Dykends
Dykehead
Cortachy
Memus
Inverquharity
Dinnet
Logie Coldstone
Kildrummy
Lumsden
Rhynie
Mossat
Auchallater
Glas-allt Shiel
Spittal of Glenmuick
Invermark Lodge
Tarfside
Lochnagar 1150
Ben Macdui 1309
Cairn Gorm 1245
Ben Avon 1171
Beinn a' Bhuird
Glas Maol 1068
The Cairnwell 933
Mount Keen 939
Morven 871
Devil's Elbow
76
81
88
NJ
NO
0 1 2 3 4 5 6 miles
0 1 2 3 4 5 6 7 8 9 10 km

Aberdeenshire
Aberdeen City
Gairioch
Formartine
Mearns
Angus
Aberdeen
Inverurie
Oldmeldrum
Ellon
Insch
Alford
Kemnay
Kintore
Dyce
Westhill
Peterculter
Cults
Banchory
Stonehaven
Newtonhill
Portlethen
Cove Bay
Inverbervie
Laurencekirk
Montrose
Brechin
Edzell
St Cyrus
Johnshaven
Newmachar
Balmedie
Newburgh
Udny Station
Pitmedden
Tarves
Meldrum Ho.
Fyvie
Rothmaise
Kirkton of Rayne
Old Rayne
Oyne
Chapel of Garioch
Pitcaple
Monymusk
Cluny
Echt
Skene
Kincardine O'Neil
Aboyne
Lumphanan
Torphins
Crathes
Drumoak
Durris Forest
Fetteresso Forest
Drumtochty Forest
Glen Dye
Cairn o' Mount
Fettercairn
Auchenblae
Fordoun
Arbuthnott
Kinneff
Gourdon
Marykirk
Craigo
Logie Pert
Hillside
Ferryden
Scurdie Ness
Montrose Basin
Girdle Ness
Nigg Bay
Greg Ness
Hare Ness
Findon Ness
Garron Pt.
Todhead Point
Milton Ness
Bervie Bay
Little John's Haven
Crawton Bay
Thornyhive Bay
Castle Haven
Sands of Forvie
Hackley Hd.
Newburgh Bar
KIRKWALL 6:00
LERWICK 12:30
NK
NP
89
77
A
B
C
D
E
F
G
7
8
9
10
11
12

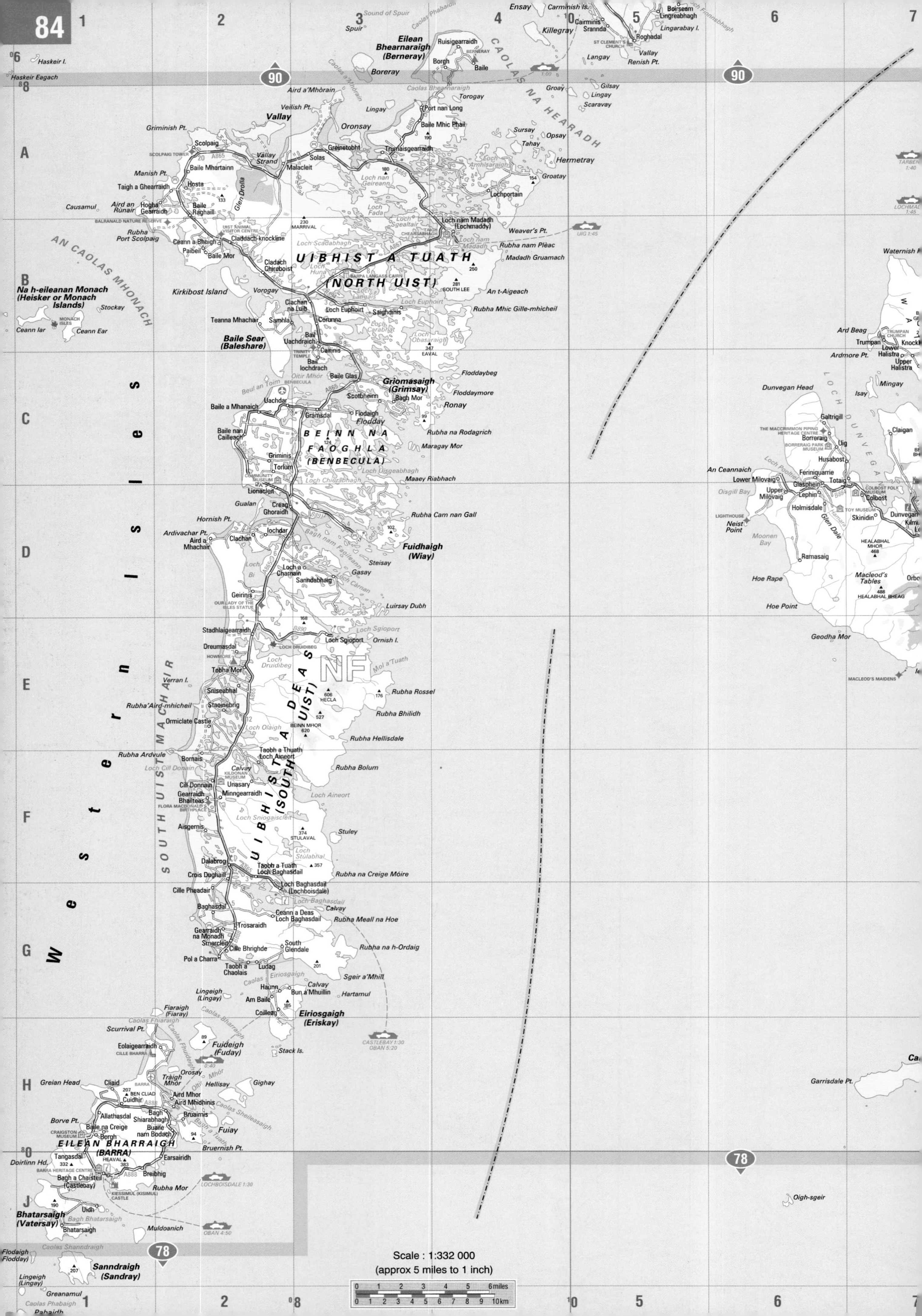

Western Isles
UIBHIST A TUATH (NORTH UIST)
BEINN NA FAOGHLA (BENBECULA)
UIBHIST A DEAS (SOUTH UIST)
EILEAN BHARRAIGH (BARRA)
SOUTH UIST MACHAIR
AN CAOLAS MHONACH
CAOLAS NA HEARADH
LOCH DUNVEGAN
NF
Eilean Bhearnaraigh (Berneray)
Boreray
Vallay
Oronsay
Lingay
Pabbay
Haskeir I.
Haskeir Eagach
Na h-eileanan Monach (Heisker or Monach Islands)
Stockay
Ceann Iar
Ceann Ear
Kirkibost Island
Baile Sear (Baleshare)
Griomasaigh (Grimsay)
Ronay
Fuidhaigh (Wiay)
Eiriosgaigh (Eriskay)
Fuideigh (Fuday)
Bhatarsaigh (Vatersay)
Sanndraigh (Sandray)
Lingeigh (Lingay)
Greanamul
Caolas Phabaigh
Pabaidh
Flodaigh (Floday)
Muldoanich
Gighay
Hellisay
Fiaraigh (Fiaray)
Stack Is.
Lochmaddy
Loch nam Madadh (Lochmaddy)
Lochportain
Baile
Borgh
Ruisigearraidh
Port nan Long
Baile Mhic Phail
Trumaisgearraidh
Greinetobht
Solas
Malacleit
Scolpaig
Baile Mhartainn
Hosta
Taigh a Ghearraidh
Hogha Gearraidh
Baile Raghaill
Ceann a Bhaigh
Paibeil
Baile Mor
Claddach-knockline
Cladach Chireboist
Vorogay
Clachan na Luib
Loch Euphoirt
Saighdinis
Corunna
Samhla
Teanna Mhachair
Bail Uachdraich
Cairinis
Bail Iochdrach
Baile Glas
Scotbheinn
Bagh Mor
Uachdar
Baile a Mhanaich
Gramsdal
Flodaigh
Flodday
Baile nan Cailleach
Griminis
Torlum
Lionacleit
Creag Ghoraidh
Iochdar
Clachan
Aird a Mhachair
Loch a Charnain
Sanndabhaig
Geirinis
Stadhlaigearraidh
Dreumasdal
Tobha Mor
Sniseabhal
Staoinebrig
Ormiclate Castle
Bornais
Taobh a Tuath Loch Aineort
Calvay
Cill Donnain
Unasary
Gearraidh Bhailteas
Minngearraidh
Aisgernis
Dalabrog
Crois Dughaill
Taobh a Tuath Loch Baghasdail
Loch Baghasdail (Lochboisdale)
Cille Pheadair
Baghasdal
Ceann a Deas Loch Baghasdail
Trosaraidh
Gearraidh na Monadh
Smercleit
Cille Bhrighde
South Glendale
Pol a Charra
Taobh a Chaolais
Ludag
Haunn
Bun a'Mhuillin
Am Baile
Coilleag
Eolaigearraidh
Cille Bharra
Traigh Mhor
Orosay
Aird Mhor
Aird Mhidhinis
Cliaid
Cuidhir
Allathasdal
Bagh Shiarabhagh
Bruairnis
Baile na Creige
Borgh
Buaile nam Bodach
Tangasdal
Bagh a Chaisteil (Castlebay)
Earsairidh
Breibhig
Uidh
Bhatarsaigh
Ben Cliad
Heaval
Griminish Pt.
Manish Pt.
Aird an Runair
Causamul
Rubha Port Scolpaig
Veilish Pt.
Aird a'Mhòrain
Hornish Pt.
Ardivachar Pt.
Gualan
Verran I.
Rubha'Aird-mhicheil
Rubha Ardvule
Rubha Mor
Borve Pt.
Greian Head
Scurrival Pt.
Doirlinn Hd.
Bruernish Pt.
Fuiay
Sgeir a'Mhill
Hartamul
Calvay
Rubha na h-Ordaig
Rubha Meall na Hoe
Rubha na Creige Móire
Stuley
Loch Aineort
Rubha Bolum
Rubha Hellisdale
Rubha Bhilidh
Rubha Rossel
Mol a'Tuath
Loch Sgioport
Ornish I.
Luirsay Dubh
Gasay
Steisay
Rubha Cam nan Gall
Maaey Riabhach
Maragay Mor
Rubha na Rodagrich
Floddaymore
Floddaybeg
Rubha Mhic Gille-mhicheil
An t-Aigeach
Madadh Gruamach
Rubha nam Plèac
Weaver's Pt.
Groatay
Hermetray
Opsay
Tahay
Sursay
Torogay
Groay
Lingay
Scaravay
Gilsay
Langay
Killegray
Ensay
Carminish Is.
Cairminis
Srannda
St Clement's Church
Roghadal
Boirseam
Lingreabhagh
Lingarabay I.
Renish Pt.
Valley
Sound of Spuir
Spuir
Caolas Bhearnaraigh
Beul an Toim
Oitir Mhòr
Loch Scadabhagh
Loch Hunn
Loch Obasaraigh
Loch Carabhat
Loch Uisgeabhagh
Loch Chiurabhagh
Loch Bi
Loch Druidibeg
Loch Olaigh
Loch Cill Donnain
Loch Sniogaisclett
Loch Stùlabhal
Loch Baghasdail
Caolas Eiriosgaigh
Caolas Fhiaraigh
Caolas Shanndraigh
Bagh Bhatarsaigh
Glen Drolla
Eaval
South Lee
Marrival
Hecla
Beinn Mhor
Stulaval
Balranald Nature Reserve
Scolpaig Tower
Barpa Langass Cairn
Trinity Temple
Our Lady of the Isles Statue
Howmore
Kildonan Museum
Flora MacDonald's Birthplace
Barra Heritage Centre
Kiessimul (Kisimul) Castle
Craigston Museum
Castlebay 1:30 Oban 5:20
Lochboisdale 1:30
Oban 4:50
Uig 1:45
Tarbert 1:40
Lochmaddy 1:45
Waternish Pt.
Ard Beag
Trumpan
Trumpan Church
Lower Halistra
Upper Halistra
Ardmore Pt.
Mingay
Isay
Dunvegan Head
Galtrigill
The MacCrimmon Piping Heritage Centre
Borreraig
Borreraig Park Museum
Uig
Claigan
Husabost
An Ceannaich
Lower Milovaig
Feriniquarrie
Totaig
Upper Milovaig
Glasphein
Lephin
Colbost Folk Museum
Colbost
Oisgill Bay
Holmisdale
Toy Museum
Lighthouse
Neist Point
Skinidin
Dunvegan
Glen Dale
Moonen Bay
Healabhal Mhor
Ramasaig
Hoe Rape
Macleod's Tables
Healabhal Bheag
Hoe Point
Geodha Mor
Macleod's Maidens
Garrisdale Pt.
Oigh-sgeir
Scale : 1:332 000
(approx 5 miles to 1 inch)
6 miles
10 km

8
9
10
11
12
13
91
Fladda-chùain
Eilean Trodday
Rubha Hunish
Rubha na h-Aiseig
Duntulm Castle
Duntulm
Balmacqueen
Kilmaluag
Lub Score
Hungladder
Museum of Island Life
Borneskettaig
Eilean Flodigarry
Flodigarry
Kilmuir
Flora MacDonald's Memorial
Meall na Suiramach
543
Kilvaxter
Digg
Staffin I.
Balgown
The Quiraing
Glashvin
Staffin Bay
Brogaig
Stenscholl
Staffin
Trotternish
Linicro
Totscore
Kilbride Point
Kilt Rock
Kilt Rock & Mealt Falls
466
Biod Buidhe
Maligar
Elishader
Loch Mealt
Valtos
Ascrib Islands
Idrigill
Uig
Uig Bay
Conon
Marishader
Garros
Rubha nam Brathairean
Ru Chorachan
Balnaknock
611
Beinn Edra
Breckrey
Culnaknock
Earlish
Lealt Falls
Lealt
Loch Snizort
Lower Tote
Upper Tote
A87
Peinlich
Hinnisdal
607
Creag a'Lain
Greshornish Pt.
Lyndale Pt.
Island of Rona
125
Eilean Garbh
Lyndale Ho.
Kingsburgh
Greshornish
Loch Greshornish
Loch Snizort Beag
Romesdal
719
The Storr
Old Man of Storr
Eilean Tigh
Garbh Eilean
Treaslane
Flashader
Suladale
Eyre
The Aird
Trotternish
Bearreraig Bay
Holm I.
Loch a' Sguirr
An Caol
Edinbane
Kensaleyre
Bernisdale
Haultin
Loch Leathan
Blackhill
Eilean Fladday
254
Sound of Raasay
Tote
Borve
Glen Bernisdale
Skeabost
Carbost
Loch Fada
Manish Pt.
Torran
Arnish
Loch Arnish
Prince Charles's Cave
Cruachan Beinn A'Chearcaill
266
Uigshader
Drumuie
Achachork
392
Brochel Castle
Brochel
Rubha na h Airde Glaise
Roskhill
Glengrasco
An Tuireann Arts Centre
Torvaig
Island of Skye
Shulishadermor
Portree
Loch Connan
The Aros Experience
Vatten
Ose
Heatherfield
Glame
385
Island of Raasay
Balmore
Ullinish
Glenmore
Penifiler
413
Ben Tianavaig
Balmeanach
Balachuirn
Loch Duagrich
Mugeary
Bracadale
Camastianavaig
Tianavaig Bay
Holoman Bay
443
Dun Caan
Rubha na'Leac
Tarner I.
Struan
Coillore
A863
A87
Conordan
Lower Ollach
Oskaig
Raasay
Loch Bracadale
Raasay Ho.
Clachan
Raasay Outdoor Centre
Oronsay
Upper Ollach
Inner Sound
NG
Portnalong
Glen Varragill
The Braes
Gedintailor
Battle of the Braes Monument
Inverarish
North Fearns
Fiskavaig
439
Roineval
East Suisnish
Eyre Point
Eyre
Caol Mòr
Crowlin Islands
Rubha nan Clach
Arnaval
369
Fernilea
Talisker Distillery
Loch Harport
444
Ben Lee
Peinchorran
Loch Sligachan
Eilean Mòr
Drynoch
Crossal
Carbost
Gleann Oraid
Merkadale
Sconser
Longay
Talisker Bay
Talisker
Glamaig
775
Moll
Scalpay
Sligachan Hotel
Loch Ainort
Scalpay Ho.
Eynort
Glen Brittle Forest
Grula
459
Sgurr nan Gillean
964
Glen Sligachan
Luib
Dunan
Old Skye Crofter's House
Guillamon I.
Pabay
445
Beinn Bhreac
Loch Eynort
570
Glas Bheinn Mhor
736
Marsco
Caolas Scalpay
Minginish
Sgurr a'Ghreadaidh
973
Red Hills
Skye Serpentarium
The Cuillin Hills
Broadford
Glen Brittle
Glenbrittle
Bla Bheinn
928
732
Corry
Broadford Bay
Waterloo
Cuillin Hills
Glenbrittle House
Harrapool
Upper Breakish
Lower Breakish
Bualintur
992
Sgurr Alasdair
Loch Coruisk
Loch na Creitheach
Torrin
Suardal
World of Wood
Skye Environmental Centre
Skulamus
924
Sgurr nan Eag
Camasunary
Strathaird
Kilbride
Strath
Loch Brittle
Kirkibost
Loch Slapin
Rubh an Dunain
Ben Meabost
346
Kilmarie
301
Heast
Kinloch
Soay Sound
Loch Scavaig
Soay
Rubha Suisnish
Loch Eishort
Drumfearn
Mol-chlach
Elgol
Boat Trips
Glasnakille
Ord
Duisdalemore
Dunsgaith Castle
Prince Charles's Cave
Eilean na h-Airde
Rubha na h-Easgainne
Tokavaig
Camuscross
Isleornsay
Ornsay
Sleat
Tarskavaig
Tarskavaig Pt.
Achnacloich
Teangue
Knock Castle
Knock Bay
Ferindonald
Kilbeg
Kilmore
Rubha Shamhnan Insir
Canna Harbour
Glen Meadhonach
Armadale Castle
Clan Donald Centre
Armadale Gardens
Armadale Bay
Kilmory
Sound of Canna
Rubha Charn nan Cearc
Gildill Bay
280
Calligarry
Ardvasar
0:55
Mallaig 2:30
388
Kilmory Glen
Kinloch Glen
Rubha na Roinne
Aird of Sleat
Ard Thurinish
Sound of Sleat
78
571
Orval
Kinloch
Kinloch Castle
Loch Scresort
Rubha Port na Caranean
Point of Sleat
0:30
79
Rùm
Rùm
Sound of Rùm
Mallaig
Mallaig Heritage Centre
0:45
Harris
Glen Harris
812
Askival
781
Ainshval
1:15
Eigg 1:00
Rubha Sgorr an t-Snidhe
Muck 1:30
Eigg 1:20
Isles
Rubha nam Meirleach
Bay of Laig
Cleadale
Glasnacardoch
A830
Beoraidbeg
Morar
Portnaluchaig
Bracara
Bracorina
North Morar
Brinacory
Scamadale
Stoul
Tarbet
Swordland
Loch Morar
Kylesknoydart
Kylesmorar
Kinlochmorar
Loch Nevis
Inverie
Inverie Bay
Scottas
Sandaig
Sandaig Bay
Knoydart
Gleann na Guiserein
Gleann an Dubh-Lochain
Airor
Inverguseran
Rubha Ard Slisneach
785
Beinn na Caillich
1020
Ladhar Bheinn
Luinne Bheinn
939
946
Meall Buidhe
Beinn Bhuidhe
855
Camusrory
Carnach
1040
Sgurr na Ciche
522
Glen Barrisdale
Barrisdale Bay
Loch Hourn
Corran
Arnisdale
Glen Arnisdale
713
Druim Fada
Kinlochhourn Forest
974
Beinn Sgritheall
Beinn nan Caorach
774
742
Beinn a'Chapaill
Upper Sandaig
Sandaig Is.
Balvraid
Glen More
Glenelg Brochs
Eilanreach
Bernera Barracks
Glenelg
Glenelg Bay
Galltair
Bernera
Kylerhea
Kyle Rhea
Kylerhea Otter Haven
Glen Arroch
Allt Mòr
610
Ben Aslak
Sgurr na Coinnich
739
603
Beinn a'Chuirn
Letterfearn
Ratagan
Shiel Bridge
779
80
Glenshiel Forest
1010
The Saddle
Loch Duich
Inverinate
Keppoch
Eilean Donan Castle
Dornie
Totaig
Ardelve
Nostie
Auchertyre
Kirkton
Reraig
Balmacara
Balmacara Square
Lochalsh Woodland Garden
Kyleakin
Castle Moil
Brightwater Visitor Centre
Kyle of Lochalsh
Badicaul
Erbusaig
Black Is.
Drumbuie
Duirinish
Port Cam
Plockton
Craig Highland Farm
Achmore
Glas Eilean
Ardintoul Pt.
Loch Alsh
Bundalloch
Loch Long
Camas-luinie
Allt-nan-sùgh
Sallachy
Gleann Udalain
An Dubh-aird
Stromeferry
Loch Carron
Ardaneaskan
Stromemore
Strome Castle
Ardnarff
486
Carn nan Iomairean
Uags
Kishorn I.
Loch Kishorn
Achintraid
Ardarroch
Slumbay
Lochcarron
Sanachan
Kirkton
A896
Eilean na Bà
Toscaig
Ard-dhubh
Culduie
Camusteel
Camusterrach
Bealach na Bà
710
Meall Gorm
Rassal Ashwood
Applecross
Applecross Bay
Applecross Ho.
Chapel of St Maelrubha
896
Beinn Bhan
Loch Coultrie
Applecross Forest
626
Beinn a'Chlachain
Loch nan Eun
Loch Lundie
Glenshieldaig Forest
513
Ben Shieldaig
439
902
Beinn Damh
993
Maol Chean-dearg
Loch Gaineamhach
493
Croic-bheinn
Abhainn Dubh
Callakille
Lonbain
Allt na h-Eirigh
Abhainn Chuaig
Shieldaig
Loch Shieldaig
Balgy
A896
Annat
Ben-damph Forest
Loch an Eoin
Torridon
Torridon Visitor Centre
Torridon Ho.
Inveralligin
Upper Loch Torridon
Rechullin
Fasag
86
Glen
Torridon Forest
Alligin Shuas
Cuaig
Kenmore
Loch a' Chracaich
Ardheslaig
Arinacrinachd
Fearnbeg
Fearnmore
Rubha na Fearn
Loch Torridon
Lower Diabaig
985
Beinn Alligin
624
Beinn Bhreac
Shieldaig Forest
Baosbheinn
875
Flowerdale Forest
Wester Ross
Loch Gaineamhach
Loch a'Bhealaich
Loch na h-Oidhche
Dubh Loch
Craig
Abhainn Braigh-horrisdale
Erradale
Redpoint
South Erradale
Opinan
Loch Clàir
Shieldaig
Port Henderson
B8056
Aird
Badachro
Kerrysdale
Charlestown
Loch Gairloch
Gairloch
Gairloch Heritage Museum
Smithstown
Strath
Carn Dearg
Caolas Beag
Longa Island
Rubha Bàn
Big Sand
North Erradale
Port Erradale
Meall an Doirean
420
Loch Tollaidh
Poolewe
Londubh
Inverewe Garden
Naast
Loch Bad a'Chreamh
Rubha 'Ard na Bà
Tournaig
Brae
Midtown
Aultgrishan
Peterburn
Seana Chamas
Kerry
Loch Bad an Sgalaig
Victoria Falls
Eilean Subhainn
Talladale
Loch Maree Islands
Loch Maree

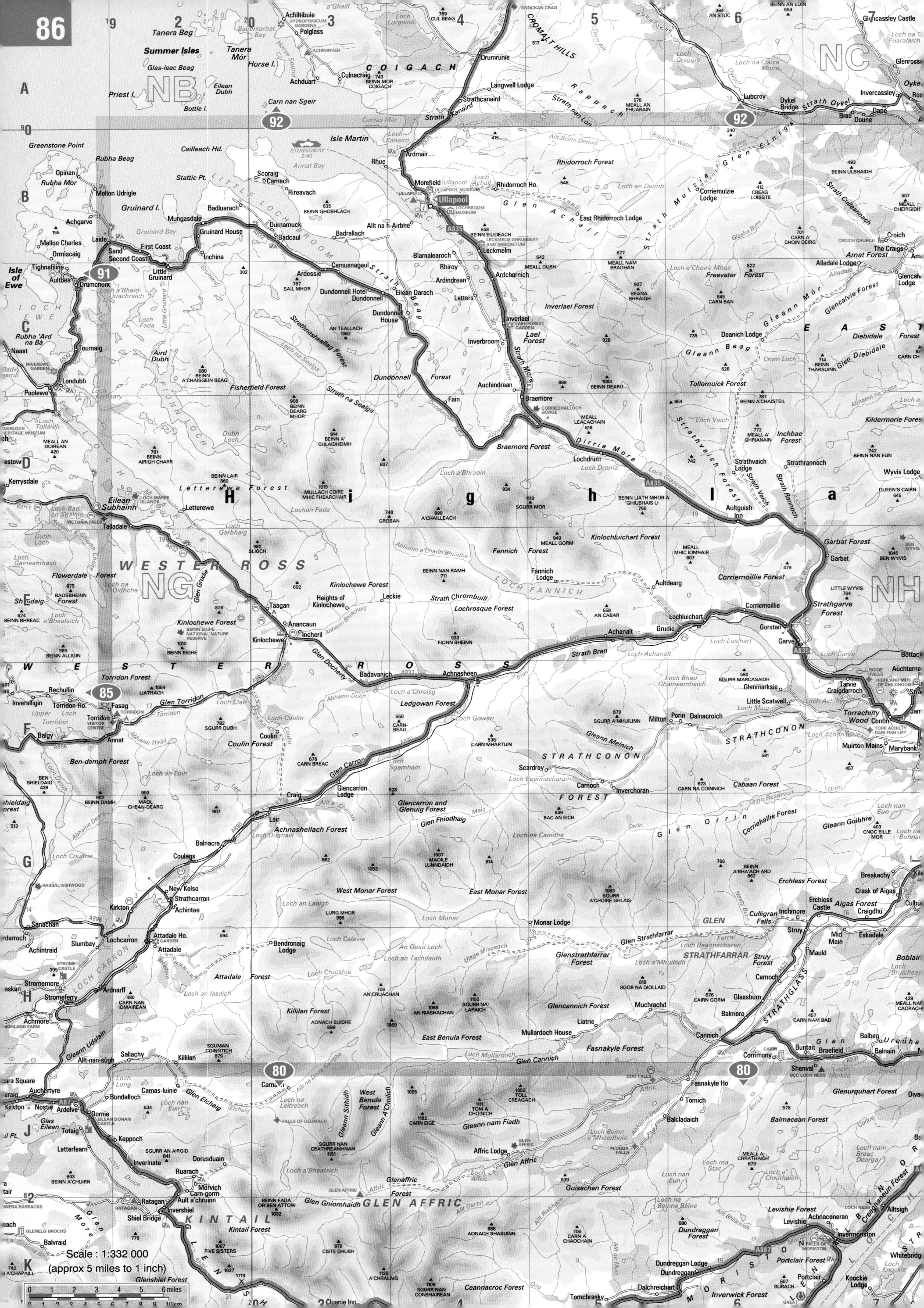
Summer Isles
Tanera Beg
Tanera Mór
Glas-leac Beag
Horse I.
Priest I.
Eilean Dubh
Bottle I.
NB
NC
NG
NH
Achiltibuie
Polglass
Achduart
Culnacraig
COIGACH
Drumrunie
CUL BEAG
CROMALT HILLS
KNOCKAN CRAG
Langwell Lodge
Strathcanaird
Strath Kanaird
Rappach
Strath nan Lon
Lubcroy
Oykel Bridge
Strath Oykel
Invercassley
Glencassley Castle
Glenrossal
Doune
Carn nan Sgeir
92
Isle Martin
Greenstone Point
Rubha Beag
Cailleach Hd.
Opinan
Rubha Mor
Stattic Pt.
Scoraig
Carnach
Rireavach
Mellon Udrigle
Ardmair
Rhue
Morefield
Ullapool
Rhidorroch Forest
Rhidorroch Ho.
Glen Achall
East Rhidorroch Lodge
Corriemulzie Lodge
Strath Mulzie
Glen Einig
BEINN ULBHAIDH
Gruinard I.
Badluarach
Mungasdale
Dundonnell
Achgarve
Laide
Mellon Charles
Ormiscaig
Sand
Second Coast
First Coast
Gruinard House
Little Gruinard
Inchina
Badcaul
Badrallach
Allt na h-Airbhe
Leckmelm
Ardcharnich
Croick
The Craigs
Amat Forest
Alladale Lodge
Isle of Ewe
Tighnafiline
Aultbea
Drumchork
91
Camusnagaul
Ardessie
Dundonnell Hotel
Eilean Darach
Dundonnell House
Blarnalearoch
Rhiroy
Ardindrean
Letters
MEALL DUBH
Inverlael Forest
Freevater
Gleann Mór
Glencalvie Forest
LOCH EWE
Rubha 'Ard na Bà
Naast
Tournaig
INVEREWE GARDEN
Londubh
Poolewe
AN TEALLACH
Strathnasheallag Forest
Aird Dubh
BEINN A'CHAISGEIN BEAG
Fisherfield Forest
Inverlael
Lael Forest
Inverbroom
Strath More
Auchindrean
Braemore
CORRIESHALLOCH GORGE
BEINN DEARG
Deanich Lodge
Gleann Beag
Tollomuick Forest
Diebidale
Strath na Sealga
BEINN DEARG MHOR
BEINN A' CHLAIDHEIMH
Fain
Braemore Forest
Dirrie More
Lochdrum
Loch Droma
Loch Vaich
Strathvaich Forest
Strathvaich Lodge
Strathrannoch
Inchbae Forest
Kildermorie Forest
Wyvis Lodge
Kerrysdale
BEINN LAIR
Letterewe Forest
Highland
MULLACH COIRE MHIC FHEARCHAIR
A' CHAILLEACH
SGURR MOR
BEINN LIATH MHOR A 'GHIUBHAIS LI
Aultguish Inn
Strath Rannoch
Eilean Subhainn
LOCH MAREE ISLANDS
Letterewe
Talladale
VICTORIA FALLS
GROBAN
Kinlochluichart Forest
Fannich Forest
MEALL GORM
Garbat Forest
Garbat
BEN WYVIS
SLIOCH
WESTER ROSS
Flowerdale Forest
BAOSBHEINN
Kinlochewe Forest
Heights of Kinlochewe
Leckie
Strath Chrombuill
LOCH FANNICH
Fannich Lodge
Aultdearg
Corriemoillie Forest
LITTLE WYVIS
Strathgarve Forest
Shieldaig
BEINN ALLIGIN
Taagan
Anancaun
Incheril
Kinlochewe
Lochrosque Forest
FIONN BHEINN
AN CABAR
Achanalt
Grudie
Lochluichart
Corriemoillie
Gorstan
Garve
Loch Garve
Strath Bran
Glen Docherty
WESTER ROSS
Torridon Forest
LIATHACH
Badavanich
Achnasheen
SGURR MARCASAIDH
Glenmarksie
Little Scatwell
Tarvie
Craigdarroch
Rechullin
Inveralligin
Torridon Ho.
Torridon
Fasag
85
Glen Torridon
Loch Clair
Ledgowan Forest
Loch Gowan
Loch Coulin
Coulin
SGURR DUBH
Coulin Forest
Annat
Balgy
CARN BEAG
CARN MHARTUIN
SGURR A'MHUILINN
Milton
Porin
Dalnacroich
STRATHCONON
Torrachilty Wood
Contin
Muirton Mains
Marybank
Gleann Meinich
Ben-damph Forest
Loch an Eoin
CARN BREAC
Glen Carron
Scardroy
Loch Beannacharain
Carnoch
Inverchoran
CARN NA COINNICH
Cabaan Forest
BEN SHIELDAIG
BEINN DAMH
MAOL CHEAN-DEARG
Craig
Glencarron Lodge
Glencarron and Glenuig Forest
Glen Fhiodhaig
BAC AN EICH
Orrin Reservoir
Corriehallie Forest
Glen Orrin
Gleann Goibhre
CNOC EILLE MOR
Lair
Achnashellach Forest
Loch Dughaill
Balnacra
Coulags
Loch Coultrie
MAOILE LUNNDAIDH
Loch na Caoidhe
BEINN A'BHA'ACH ARD
Breakachy
Crask of Aigas
Erchless Forest
RASSAL ASHWOOD
New Kelso
Strathcarron
Achintee
Kirkton
Sanachan
West Monar Forest
East Monar Forest
SGURR A'CHOIRE GHLAIS
Loch an Laoigh
LURG MHOR
Loch Monar
Monar Lodge
Erchless Castle
Aigas Forest
Inchmore
Culligran Falls
Craigdhu
GLEN
Lochcarron
Slumbay
Attadale Ho.
Attadale
Achintraid
Bendronaig Lodge
Loch Calavie
An Gead Loch
Loch an Tachdaidh
Glen Strathfarrar
Glenstrathfarrar Forest
STRATHFARRAR
Struy
Mid Main
Eskadale
Mauld
Boblair
LOCH CARRON
STROME CASTLE
Stromemore
Ardnarff
Stromeferry
Attadale Forest
Loch Cruoshie
AN CRUACHAN
SGOR NA DIOLLAID
Struy Forest
Carnoch
CARN NAN IOMAIREAN
Achmore
Loch an Iasaich
Killilan Forest
AONACH BUIDHE
AN RIABHACHAN
SGURR NA LAPAICH
Glencannich Forest
Muchrachd
CAIRN GORM
Glassburn
STRATHGLASS
Balmore
CARN NAM BAD
East Benula Forest
Mullardoch House
Liatrie
Cannich
Gleann Udalain
SGUMAN COINNTICH
Allt-nan-sùgh
Sallachy
Killilan
Loch Mullardoch
Glen Cannich
Fasnakyle Forest
Corrimony
Buntait
Glen Urquhart
Braefield
Balbeg
Balnain
80
Camas-luinie
Carnach
West Benula Forest
Gleann Sithidh
Gleann A'Choilich
TOLL CREAGACH
TOM A' CHOINICH
DOG FALLS
Fasnakyle Ho
Shenval
BCC LOCH NESS
Glenurquhart Forest
Auchertyre
Nostie
Ardelve
Dornie
EILEAN DONAN CASTLE
Bundalloch
Glen Elchaig
Kirkton
Glas Eilean
Totaig
Keppoch
Letterfearn
FALLS OF GLOMACH
CARN EIGE
Gleann nam Fiadh
Tomich
Balcladaich
Balmacaan Forest
SGURR AN AIRGID
Inverinate
Dorusduain
SGURR NAN CEATHREAMHNAN
Affric Lodge
Glen Affric
PLODDA FALLS
MEALL A' CHRATHAICH
BEINN A'CHUIRN
Ruarach
Morvich
Carn-gorm
Ault a'chruinn
Ratagan
Inversheil
Shiel Bridge
Glenaffric Forest
Guisachan Forest
GLEN AFFRIC
Glen Gniomhaidh
BEINN FADA OR BEN ATTOW
KINTAIL
Kintail Forest
Glen More
GLENELG BROCHS
Balvraid
FIVE SISTERS
CISTE DHUBH
AONACH SHASUINN
CARN A' CHAOCHAIN
Dundreggan Forest
Levishie Forest
Levishie
Achnaconeran
Invermoriston
Alltsigh
Creag nan Eun Forest
Portclair Forest
Portclair
Whitebridge
Knockie Lodge
Scale : 1:332 000
(approx 5 miles to 1 inch)
Glenshiel Forest
A'CHRALAIG
SGURR NAN CONBHAIREAN
Ceannacroc Forest
Tomchrasky
Dalchreichart
Dundreggan Lodge
Dundreggan
GLEN MORISTON
Inverwick Forest
BURACH
Cluanie Inn
6 miles
10km

ND
NJ
93
81
88
Lairg
Brora
Golspie
Dornoch
Bonar Bridge
DORNOCH FIRTH
Tarbat Ness
Portmahomack
Tain
Morangie Forest
ROSS
Strath Rory
Balintore
Alness
Invergordon
Cromarty
CROMARTY FIRTH
MORAY FIRTH
BLACK ISLE
Dingwall
Conon Bridge
Fortrose
Rosemarkie
Ardersier
Nairn
Auldearn
Forres
Findhorn
Burghead
BURGHEAD BAY
Kinloss
Culbin Forest
Darnaway Forest
Moray
Dallas
Muir of Ord
Beauly
BEAULY FIRTH
INVERNESS
Culloden
Cawdor
Croy
Strathdearn Forest
Moy
Tomatin
DRUMMOSSIE MUIR
Strathnairn
Dores
Lochindorb
Dava
Grantown-on-Spey
STRATH SPEY
HILLS OF CROMDALE
Carrbridge
Boat of Garten
Nethy Bridge
Aviemore
Abernethy Forest
Glen More Forest Park
CAIRNGORMS NATIONAL PARK
MONADHLIATH MOUNTAINS
Coignafearn Forest
Strathdearn
Glen Mazeran
Whitebridge
Foyers
Errogie
Glenlivet Forest
Tomintoul

1
2
3
4
5
A
B
C
D
E
F
G
H
Halliman Skerries
Covesea Skerries
LOSSIEMOUTH FISHERIES & COMMUNITY MUSEUM
Stotfield
Branderburgh
Lossiemouth
Covesea
BURGHEAD MUSEUM
Burghead
Hopeman
Duffus
Gordonstoun
Cummingston
Roseisle
Roseisle Forest
DUFFUS CASTLE
PALACE OF SPYNIE
Loch Spynie
Lossie Forest
Spynie
Quarrywood
Bishopmill
Elgin
ELGIN MUSEUM
CATHEDRAL
CASHMERE VISITOR CENTRE
OLD MILLS
MOTOR MUSEUM
New Elgin
Newton
Coltfield
Alves
Miltonhill
Pittendreich
Miltonduff
Mains of Burgie
Monaughty Forest
PLUSCARDEN ABBEY
Auchtertyre
Barnhill
Foresterseat
Paddockhaugh
BIRNIE CHURCH
Thornshill
Longmorn
Moss of Barmuckity
COXTON TOWER
Lhanbryde
Urquhart
Leuchars Ho.
Lochhill
Garmouth
Lochs Crofts
Mosstodloch
Blackhills
MILLBUIES
Dallas Forest
Kellas
Glenlatterach
Dallas
Branchill
Craigroy
CAIRN UISH
Moray
Glen of Rothes
Auchinroath
Newlands
Rothes
GLEN GRANT DISTILLERY
Burn of Rothes
Elchies Forest
CARN NA CAILLICHE
Whiteacen
LADYCROFT AGRICULTURAL MUSEUM
Archiestown
CARDHU DISTILLERY
Cardow
Upper Knockando
Knockando
Knockando Ho.
Carron
Daugh of Kinermony
SPEYSIDE WAY VISITOR CENTRE
Speyview
Charlestown of Aberlour
Milltown of Edinvillie
Ringorm
Craigellachie
SPEYSIDE COOPERAGE VISITOR CENTRE
Dandaleith
Maggieknockater
Kininvie Ho.
Midtown of Buchromb
BALVENIE CASTLE
GLENFIDDICH DISTILLERY
Dufftown
Kirktown of Mortlach
MEIKLE CONVAL
Milltown of Auchindoun
AUCHINDOUN CASTLE
THE SCALP
SPEY BAY
Kingston
TUGNET ICE HOUSE
Spey Bay
DOLPHIN CENTRE
Porttanachy
Nether Dallachy
Upper Dallachy
Bogmoor
SPEYSIDE WAY
Auchenhalrig
Newlands of Tynet
BAXTERS HIGHLAND VILLAGE
FOCHABERS FOLK MUSEUM
Fochabers
Braes of Enzie
Speymouth Forest
Dipple
Orbliston
Teindland Forest
Ordiequish
Wood of Ordiequish
Inchberry
Mulben
Rosarie Forest
BEN AIGAN
KEITH AND DUFFTOWN RLY
Towiemore
Drummuir Castle
Drummuir
THE BUCKIE DRIFTER
Findochty
Portknockie
Gordonsburgh
Buckie
Buckpool
Portessie
Rathven
Portgordon
Slackhead
Cairnfield Ho.
Drybridge
Broadley
ST. GREGORY'S CHAPEL
Clochan
Shiel Muir
MILLSTONE HILL
Forgie
Broadrashes
Aultmore
Newmill
Keith
STRATHISLA DISTILLERY
ISLA
STRATH
Balloch Wood
Edintore
Little Pitlurg
Coachford
Glen of Coachford
NJ
Daugh of Cairnborrow
Cairnborrow
Torry
Haugh of Glass
Deveron
STRATHBOGIE
Bailiesward
Bridgend
Succoth
Tillathrowie
Tomnaven
Clashindarroch Forest
Clashindarroch
Coynachie
Kirkney
Gartly
Cullen Bay
Logie Hd.
Cullen
FINDLATER CASTLE
Sandend Bay
Sandend
Redhythe Pt.
Portsoy
Seatown
Lintmill
JOINER'S WORKSHOP
Fordyce
Milton
Kirktown of Deskford
DESKFORD CHURCH
Ardiecow
Berryhillock
Craibstone
Little Toux
Newmills of Boyne
Cornhill
Mains of Edingight
Gordonstown
Deerhill
Grange Crossroads
Edingight Ho.
KNOCK HILL
Crannoch
Sillyearn
Bracobrae
Knock
Davoch of Grange
Drumnagorrach
Glen Barry
Farmtown
Knowes of Elrick
Aberchirder
Old Crombie
Knauchland
Marnoch
Milltown of Rothiemay
Mains of Mayen
Ruthven
Yonder Bognie
Bogniebrae
FOURMAN HILL
Cairnie
THE BIN
The Bin Forest
NORDIC SKI CENTRE
Corse of Kinnoir
HUNTLY CASTLE
Huntly
BRANDER MUSEUM
Lessendrum
Drumblade
Brideswell
Slioch
Thomastown
Hillhead
Kirkstile
Shanquhar
Blackburn
Culdrain
Clashindarroch Forest
Glens of Foudland
HILL OF FOUDLAND
Cults
KNOCKANDY HILL
LEITH HALL
Kennethmont
Milton of Noth
Oldtown
Ardlair
Cottown
Rhynie
The Shevock
Clatt
Duncanstone
Leslie
Knockespock Ho.
Coldwells Croft
Whitehaugh Forest
Muckletown
Tullynessle
Bridge of Alford
Montgarrie
ALFORD VALLEY RAILWAY
HAUGHTON
GRAMPIAN TRANSPORT MUS
Alford
HERITAGE CENTRE
Whitehouse
Gateside
Keig
Asloun
Little Lynturk
Muir of Fowlis
Bridgend
Tillyfour
Kintocher
BENAQUHALLIE
Findrach Ho.
Lumphanan
PEEL RING OF LUMPHANAN
Milton of Auchinhove
Auchlossan
Milton of Lesmore
Belhinnie
Wheedlemont
Craig Castle
ST MARY'S CHURCH
Clova
SCOTTISH SCULPTURE WORKSHOP
Lumsden
CORREEN HILLS
Aber
Mossat
LORD ARTHUR'S CAIRN
Kildrummy
Milltown of Kildrummy
KILDRUMMY CASTLE & GARDEN
Rinmore
Auchintoul
Sinnahard
Hillockhead
Ley
Milton of Cushnie
Leochel-Cushnie
CRAIGIEVAR CASTLE
Towie
Milltown of Towie
Glenkindie
Boultenstone
Easter Davoch
Migvie
Coynach
Douneside
Craskins
CULSH SOUTERRAIN
Logie Coldstone
Tarland
CROMAR
TOMNAVERIE STONE CIRCLE
Coull
Milton of Logie
Glendavan Ho.
Ordie
Kinnitty
Advie
Bridge of Avon
Dalchirach
CRAGGANMORE DISTILLERY
Marypark
GLENFARCLAS DISTILLERY
Bellehiglash
SPEYSIDE WAY
Mains of Dalvey
Drumin
GLENLIVET DISTILLERY
Glenlivet
Shenval
Auchbreck
BEN RINNES
Favillar
Kirkhill
Glen Rinnes
Dullan Water
Glen Fiddich
Fiddich
Ballochford
Bridgend
Inverharroch
Glenfiddich Forest
Black Water
Auchmair
Cabrach
Aldunie
ROUND HILL
Blackwater Forest
CARN AN T-SUIDHE
Ballcorach
HILLS OF CROMDALE
Tomnavoulin
Strath Avon
CARN DAIMH
Glenlivet Forest
Knockandhu
Livet
Clashnoir
Braes of Glenlivet
Chapeltown
HILL OF THREE STONES
THE BUCK
CREGGAN A'CHAISE
Bridge of Brown
Fodderletter
TOMINTOUL MUSEUM
Tomintoul
Delnabo
GLENLIVET ESTATE VISITOR CENTRE
CARN MEADHONACH
Conglass Water
Blairnamarrow
LADDER HILLS
CARN MOR
Glenbuchat Lodge
Badenyon
Water of Buchat
Belnacraig
Kirkton of Glenbuchat
THE SOCACH
LECHT SKI CENTRE
CAIRNGORMS
NATIONAL PARK
CARN EALASAID
Glen Ernan
Ernan Water
Bellabeg
Forbestown
Strathdon
Inverernan Ho.
Candacraig Ho.
Heugh-head
Tornashean Forest
Hillockhead
CRAIG OF BUNZEACH
Colnabaichin
Allt Tuileach
Cock Bridge
Corgarff
CORGARFF CASTLE
Tornahaish
Delnadamph
BIG GARVOUN
GLEN AVON
THE BRUACH
Forest of Glenavon
BROWN COW HILL
MORVEN
Glen Fenzie
Gairnshiel
Water of Ailnack
Burn of Loin
Water of Caiplich
Deskry Water
Dorback Lodge
ALL CHARN
0 1 2 3 4 5 6 miles
0 1 2 3 4 5 6 7 8 9 10 km
87
82
A96
A95
A941
A920
A97
A939
A944
A98
A942
A980

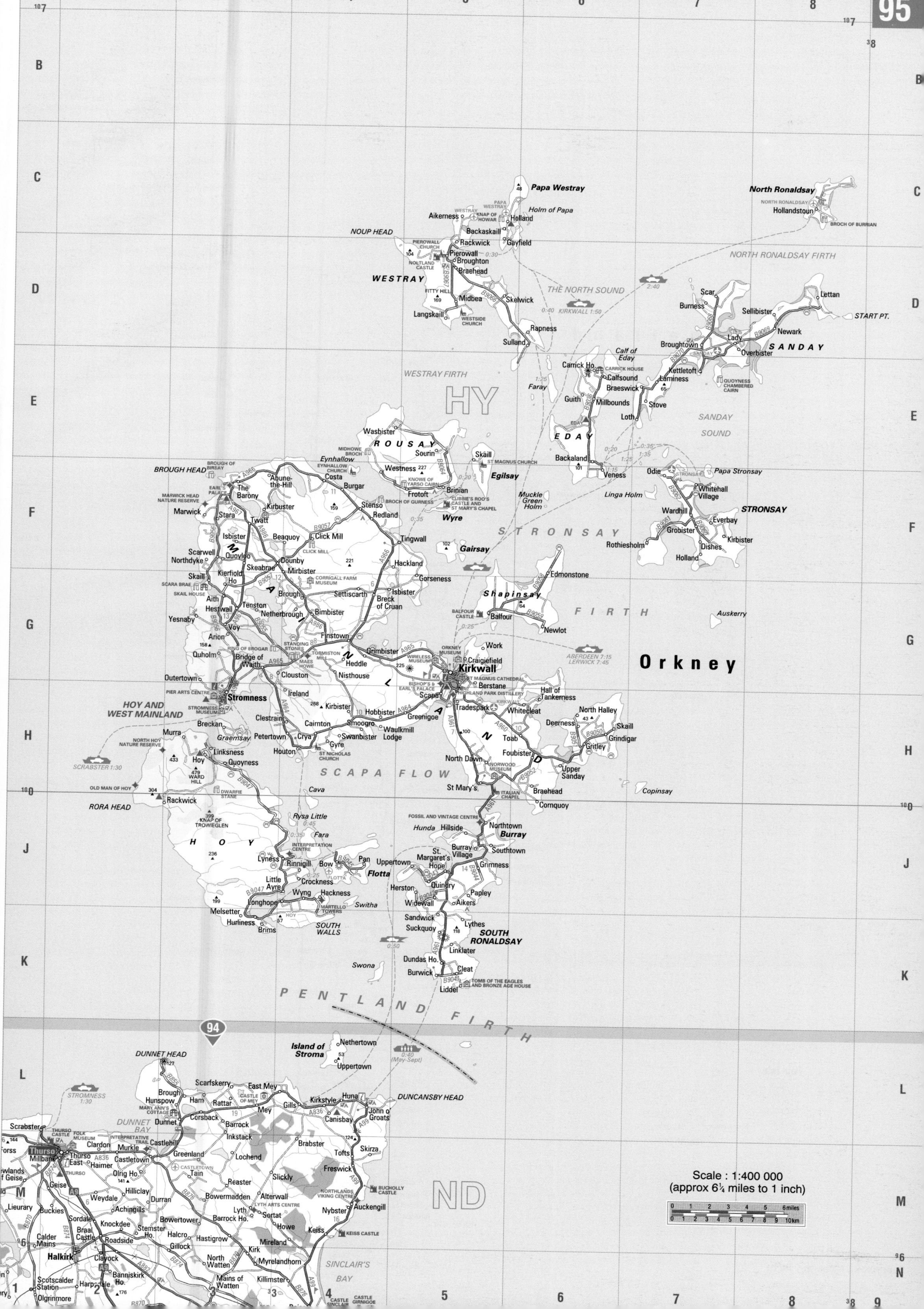
Orkney
Papa Westray
North Ronaldsay
Hollandstoun
BROCH OF BURRIAN
NORTH RONALDSAY FIRTH
Holm of Papa
Aikerness
Holland
Backaskaill
NOUP HEAD
Rackwick
Gayfield
PIEROWALL CHURCH
Pierowall
Broughton
NOLTLAND CASTLE
Braehead
WESTRAY
FITTY HILL
Midbea
Skelwick
Langskaill
WESTSIDE CHURCH
THE NORTH SOUND
KIRKWALL 1:50
Rapness
Sulland
Scar
Burness
Sellibister
Lettan
START PT.
Newark
Lady
Broughtown
Overbister
SANDAY
Calf of Eday
Carrick Ho.
CARRICK HOUSE
Calfsound
Kettletoft
Laminess
QUOYNESS CHAMBERED CAIRN
WESTRAY FIRTH
Faray
Braeswick
Guith
Millbounds
Stove
Loth
HY
SANDAY SOUND
Wasbister
EDAY
ROUSAY
Sourin
MIDHOWE BROCH
Skaill
Eynhallow
ST MAGNUS CHURCH
Backaland
Westness
Veness
Odie
Papa Stronsay
BROUGH HEAD
BROUGH OF BIRSAY
KNOWE OF YARSO CAIRN
Egilsay
Whitehall Village
Costa
Abune-the-Hill
Burgar
Linga Holm
The Barony
Frotoft
Brinian
Muckle Green Holm
MARWICK HEAD NATURE RESERVE
BROCH OF GURNESS
Marwick
Stara
Kirbuster
Stenso
Redland
Wyre
Wardhill
STRONSAY
Twatt
Everbay
Grobister
Isbister
Beaquoy
Click Mill
Tingwall
STRONSAY
Kirbister
Rothiesholm
Dishes
Scarwell
Northdyke
Quoylee
Gairsay
Holland
Skeabrae
Dounby
Hackland
Skaill
Kierfield Ho
Mirbister
CORRIGALL FARM MUSEUM
Gorseness
Edmonstone
SCARA BRAE
SKAIL HOUSE
Settiscarth
Isbister
Shapinsay
Aith
Brough
Breck of Cruan
Hestwall
Tenston
Bimbister
Netherbrough
BALFOUR CASTLE
Balfour
FIRTH
Auskerry
Yesnaby
Voy
Newlot
Arion
Finstown
Quholm
RING OF BRODGAR
STANDING STONES
MAES HOWE
Work
ORKNEY MUSEUM
Craigiefield
Bridge of Waith
Grimbister
WIRELESS MUSEUM
Heddle
Kirkwall
ABERDEEN 7:15
LERWICK 7:45
Outertown
Clouston
Nisthouse
ST MAGNUS CATHEDRAL
Berstane
PIER ARTS CENTRE
Ireland
BISHOP'S & EARL'S PALACE
HIGHLAND PARK DISTILLERY
Hall of Tankerness
Stromness
Scapa
HOY AND WEST MAINLAND
STROMNESS MUSEUM
Kirbister
Hobbister
Tradespark
Whitecleat
North Halley
Greenigoe
Deerness
Skaill
Breckan
Clestrain
Cairnton
Smoogro
Waulkmill Lodge
Grindigar
Murra
Graemsay
Petertown
Crya
Swanbister
Toab
NORTH HOY NATURE RESERVE
Houton
Gyre
Foubister
Gritley
Linksness
Hoy
ST NICHOLAS CHURCH
SCRABSTER 1:30
Quoyness
WARD HILL
SCAPA FLOW
North Dawn
NORWOOD MUSEUM
Upper Sanday
OLD MAN OF HOY
DWARFIE STANE
Cava
St Mary's
Braehead
Copinsay
RORA HEAD
Rackwick
ITALIAN CHAPEL
Cornquoy
KNAP OF TROWIEGLEN
Rysa Little
FOSSIL AND VINTAGE CENTRE
Northtown
Hunda
Hillside
Burray
Fara
HOY
INTERPRETATION CENTRE
Burray Village
Southtown
Lyness
Rinnigill
Bow
Pan
Uppertown
St. Margaret's Hope
Grimness
Flotta
Little Ayre
Crockness
Herston
Quindry
Papley
Longhope
Wyng
Hackness
Widewall
Aikers
Swithа
Melsetter
MARTELLO TOWERS
Sandwick
Lythes
Hurliness
Brims
SOUTH WALLS
Suckquoy
SOUTH RONALDSAY
Linklater
Swona
Dundas Ho.
Cleat
Burwick
TOMB OF THE EAGLES AND BRONZE AGE HOUSE
Liddel
PENTLAND FIRTH
94
Island of Stroma
Nethertown
Uppertown
(May-Sept)
DUNNET HEAD
STROMNESS 1:30
Scarfskerry
East Mey
Brough
Hunspow
Ham
CASTLE OF MEY
Rattar
Gills
Kirkstyle
Huna
DUNCANSBY HEAD
MARY ANN'S COTTAGE
Mey
Canisbay
John o' Groats
Scrabster
DUNNET BAY
Dunnet
Corsback
Barrock
THURSO CASTLE
FOLK MUSEUM
INTERPRETATIVE TRAIL
Castlehill
Inkstack
Brabster
Clardon
Murkle
Thurso
Millbank
East
Castletown
Greenland
Lochend
Tofts
Skirza
Haimer
Olrig Ho.
Tain
Freswick
Geise
Hilliclay
Reaster
Slickly
BUCHOLLY CASTLE
ND
Weydale
Bowermadden
Alterwall
NORTHLANDS VIKING CENTRE
Auckengill
Achingills
Durran
Lyth
LYTH ARTS CENTRE
Buckies
Nybster
Knockdee
Stemster Ho.
Bowertower
Barrock Ho.
Sortat
Howe
Calder Mains
Braal Castle
Roadside
Halcro
Hastigrow
Mireland
Keiss
KEISS CASTLE
Halkirk
Clayock
Gillock
Kirk
North Watten
Myrelandhorn
SINCLAIR'S BAY
Scotscalder Station
Harpsdale
Banniskirk Ho.
Mains of Watten
Killimster
Olgrinmore
CASTLE SINCLAIR
CASTLE GIRNIGOE
Scale : 1:400 000
(approx 6¼ miles to 1 inch)
6 miles
10km

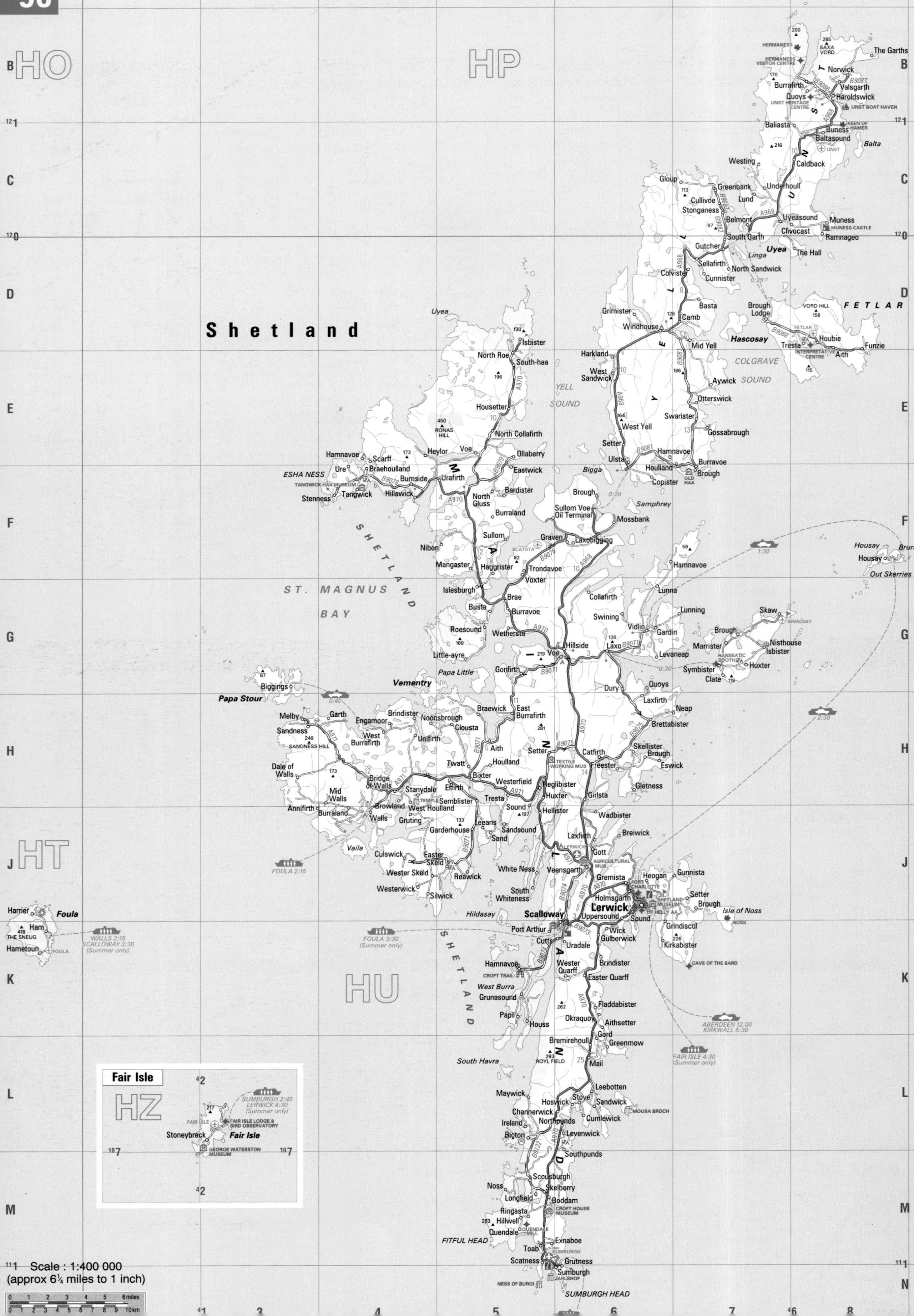
Shetland
HO
HP
HT
HU
Hermaness
Hermaness Visitor Centre
Saxa Vord
The Garths
Norwick
Burrafirth
Valsgarth
Haroldswick
Quoys
Unst Heritage Centre
Unst Boat Haven
Baliasta
Keen of Hamer
Buness
Baltasound
Balta
Unst
Westing
Caldback
Gloup
Greenbank
Underhoull
Cullivoe
Lund
Stonganess
Belmont
Uyeasound
Muness
Muness Castle
Clivocast
Ramnageo
South Garth
Gutcher
Linga
Uyea
The Hall
Sellafirth
North Sandwick
Colvister
Cunnister
Basta
Grimister
Camb
Brough Lodge
Vord Hill
Fetlar
Windhouse
Hascosay
Tresta
Houbie
Funzie
Fetlar Interpretative Centre
Aith
Mid Yell
Harkland
West Sandwick
Colgrave Sound
Aywick
Yell Sound
Yell
Otterswick
Swarister
West Yell
Gossabrough
Setter
Ulsta
Hamnavoe
Burravoe
Houlland
Brough
Copister
Old Haa
Uyea
Isbister
North Roe
South-haa
Housetter
Ronas Hill
North Collafirth
Hamnavoe
Scarff
Heylor
Voe
Ollaberry
Esha Ness
Ure
Braehoulland
Eastwick
Tangwick Haa Museum
Burnside
Urafirth
Bigga
Stenness
Tangwick
Hillswick
Bardister
North Gluss
Brough
Samphrey
Sullom Voe Oil Terminal
Mossbank
Burraland
Sullom
Graven
Laxobigging
Nibon
Scatsta
Mangaster
Haggrister
Trondavoe
Hamnavoe
Housay
Bruray
Out Skerries
Voxter
St. Magnus Bay
Islesburgh
Collafirth
Lunna
Busta
Brae
Burravoe
Swining
Lunning
Skaw
Whalsay
Roesound
Wethersta
Vidlin
Gardin
Brough
Hillside
Laxo
Marrister
Symbister
Isbister
Nisthouse
Hanseatic Booth
Huxter
Little-ayre
Voe
Levaneap
Clate
Papa Little
Gonfirth
Biggings
Vementry
Papa Stour
Dury
Quoys
Laxfirth
Braewick
East Burrafirth
Neap
Brettabister
Melby
Garth
Brindister
Noonsbrough
Engamoor
Clousta
Sandness
West Burrafirth
Uniirth
Sandness Hill
Aith
Setter
Catfirth
Skellister
Brough
Eswick
Dale of Walls
Twatt
Houlland
Textile Working Mus
Freester
Bridge of Walls
Stanydale
Effirth
Bixter
Westerfield
Weisdale
Gletness
Mid Walls
Brownland
Semblister
Tresta
Huxter
Girlsta
Annifirth
Burraland
Walls
West Houlland
Sound
Hellister
Wadbister
Gruting
Garderhouse
Sandsound
Laxfirth
Breiwick
Vaila
Sand
Culswick
Easter Skeld
Gott
Wester Skeld
Reawick
White Ness
Veensgarth
Agricultural Mus
Gremista
Heogan
Gunnista
Foula 2:15
Westerwick
Silwick
South Whiteness
Holmsgarth
Fort Charlotte
Shetland Museum
Up Helly Aa
Setter
Brough
Harrier
Foula
Hildasay
Scalloway
Lerwick
Uppersound
Sound
Isle of Noss
Noss
Ham
The Sneug
Walls 2:15
Scalloway 3:30
(Summer only)
Port Arthur
Wick
Grindiscol
Hametoun
Foula 3:30
(Summer only)
Cutts
Gulberwick
Kirkabister
Uradale
Hamnavoe
Wester Quarff
Brindister
Cave of the Bard
Croft Trail
Easter Quarff
West Burra
Grunasound
Fladdabister
Papil
Okraquoy
Aithsetter
Aberdeen 12:00
Kirkwall 5:30
Houss
Gord
Bremirehoull
Greenmow
Royl Field
Fair Isle 4:30
(Summer only)
South Havra
Mail
Fair Isle
Leebotten
Maywick
Hoswick
Stove
Sandwick
Sumburgh 2:40
Lerwick 4:30
(Summer only)
Channerwick
Cumlewick
Mousa Broch
Fair Isle Lodge & Bird Observatory
Ireland
Northpunds
Stoneybreck
Fair Isle
Bigton
Levenwick
George Waterston Museum
Southpunds
Scousburgh
Noss
Skelberry
Longfield
Boddam
Ringasta
Croft House Museum
Hillwell
Quendale
Quendale Mill
Fitful Head
Exnaboe
Toab
Sumburgh
Scatness
Grutness
Jarlshof
Ness of Burgi
Sumburgh Head
Scale : 1:400 000
(approx 6¼ miles to 1 inch)
6 miles
10 km

Town plan symbols

- Motorway
- Primary route – dual, single carriageway
- A road – dual, single carriageway
- B road – dual, single carriageway
- Minor through road
- One-way street
- Pedestrian roads
- Shopping streets
- Railway with station
- Tramway with station (City Hall)
- Underground or Metro station (Bank, West St)
- Hospital
- Parking
- Police, Post Office
- Shopmobility
- Youth hostel
- Bus or railway station building
- Shopping precinct or retail park
- Park
- Congestion charge zone
- Abbey or cathedral
- Ancient monument
- Aquarium
- Art gallery
- Bird collection or aviary
- Building of interest
- Castle
- Church of interest
- Cinema
- Garden
- Historic ship
- House
- House and garden
- Museum
- Preserved railway
- Roman antiquity
- Safari park
- Theatre
- Tourist information centre
- Zoo
- Other place of interest

Aberdeen

0 Miles ¼

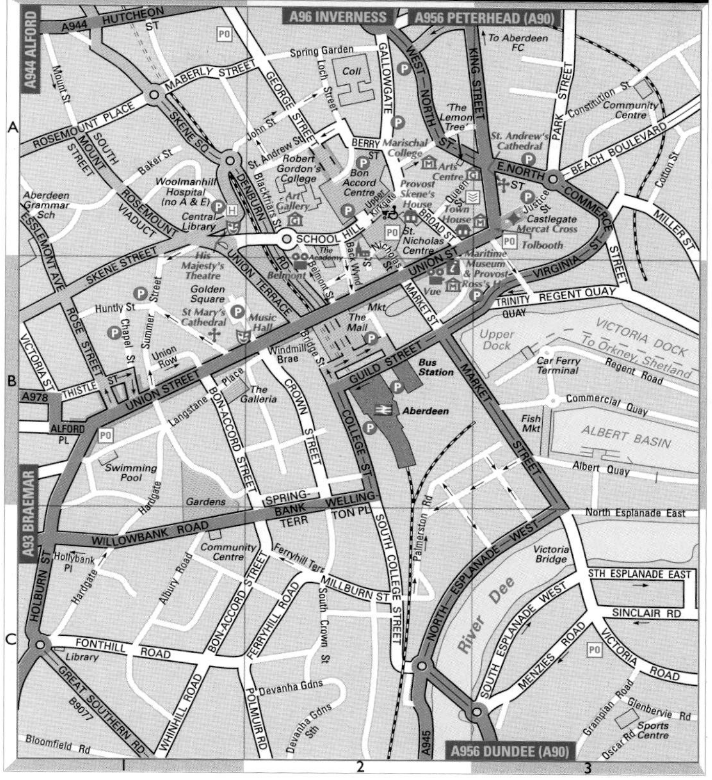

Bath

0 Miles ¼

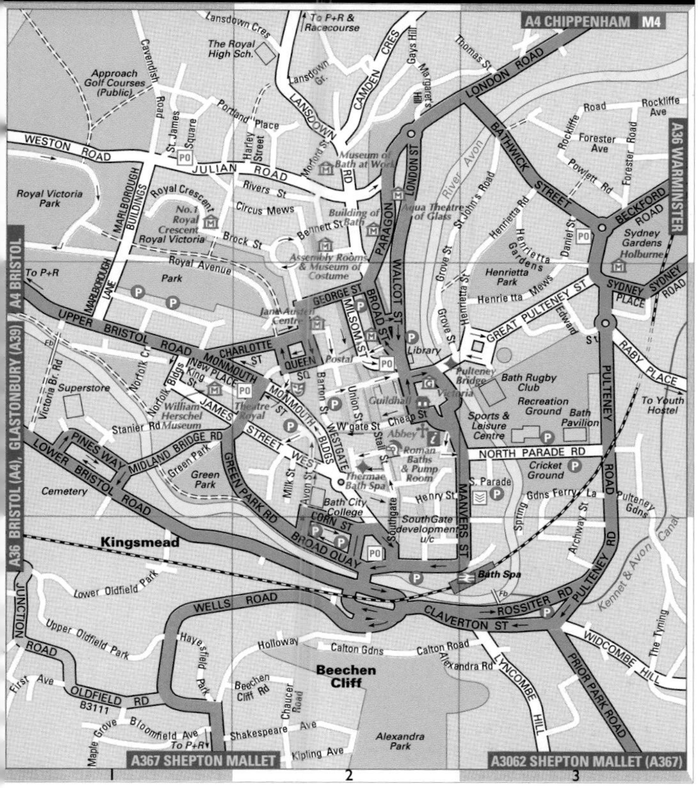

Blackpool

0 Miles ¼

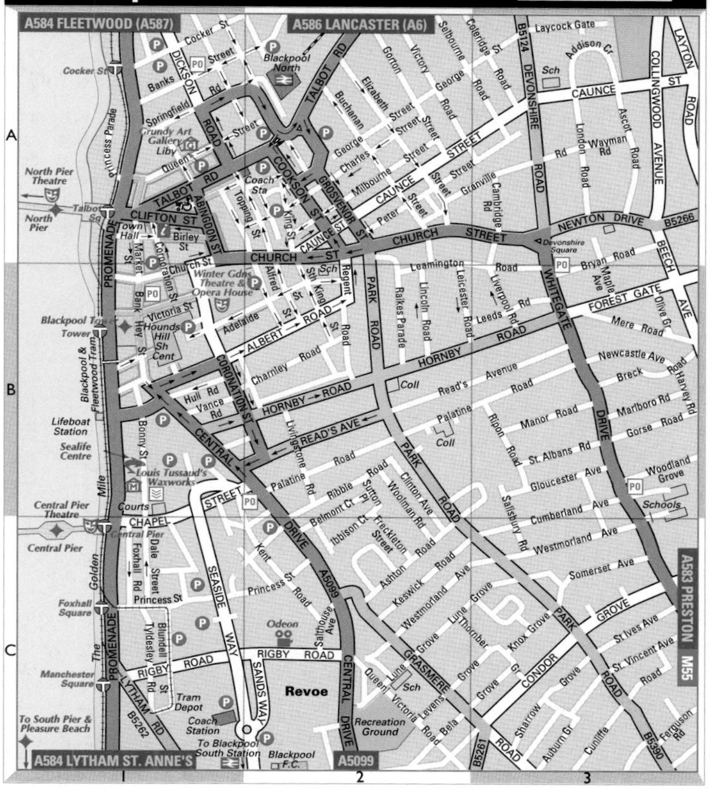

Birmingham

0 Miles ¼

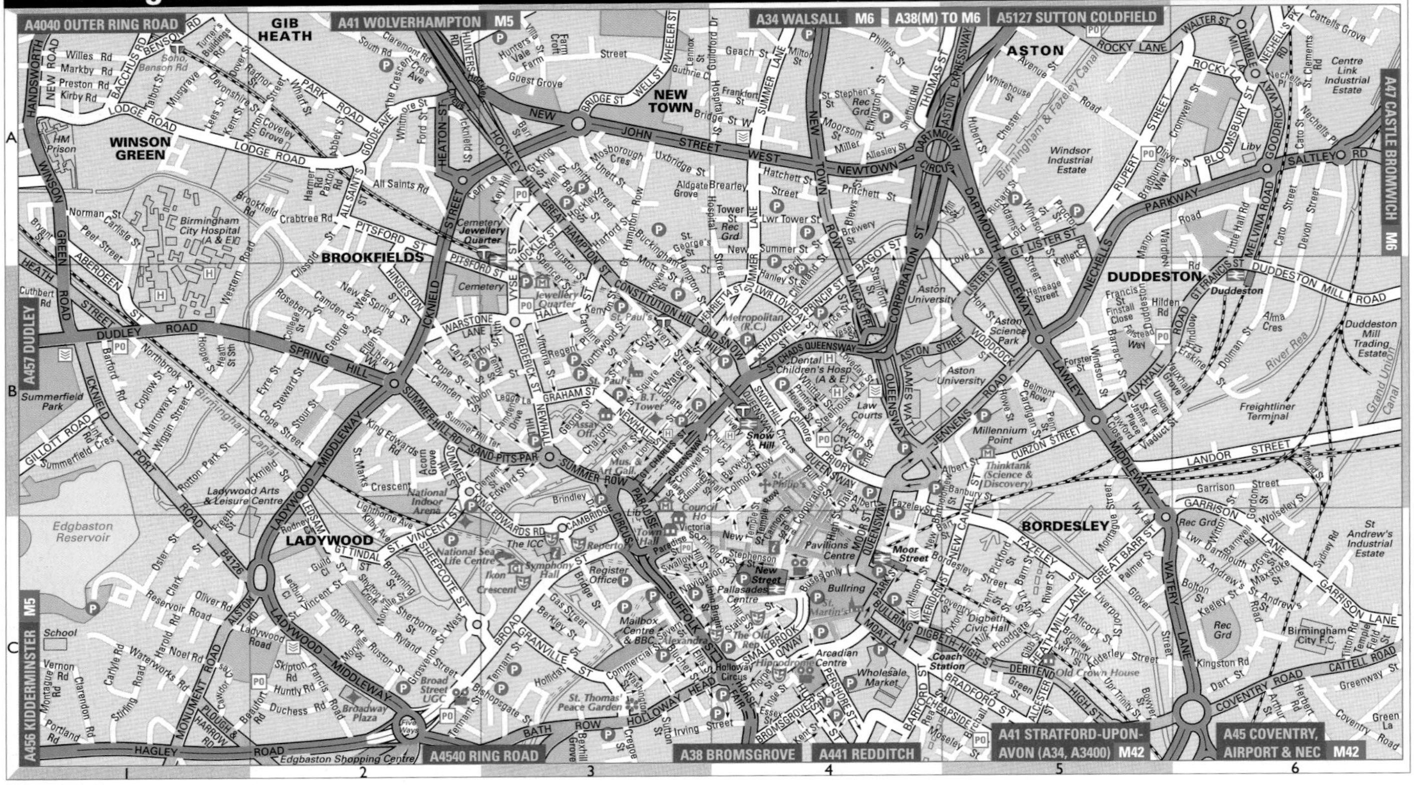

Bournemouth

0 Miles ¼

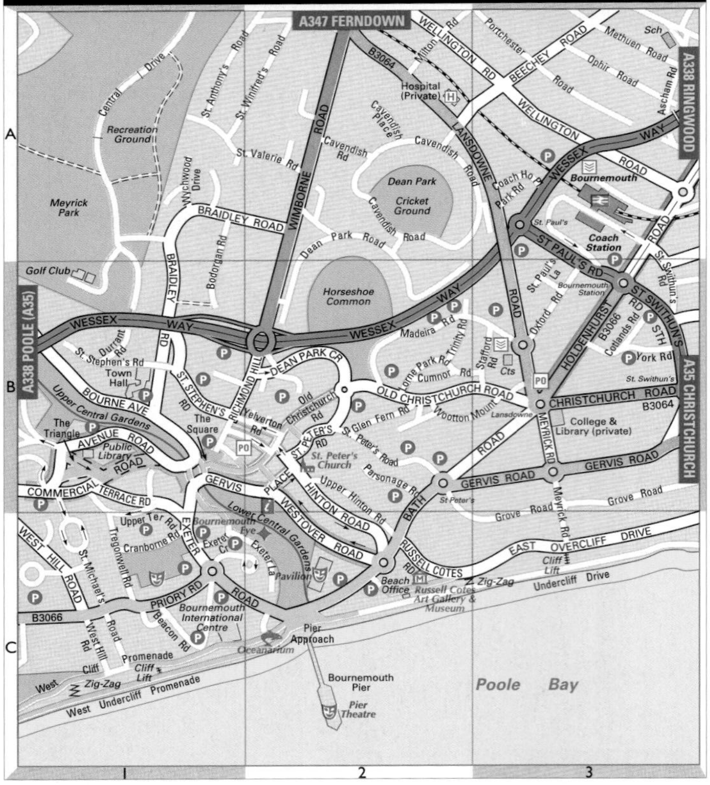

Bradford

0 Miles ¼

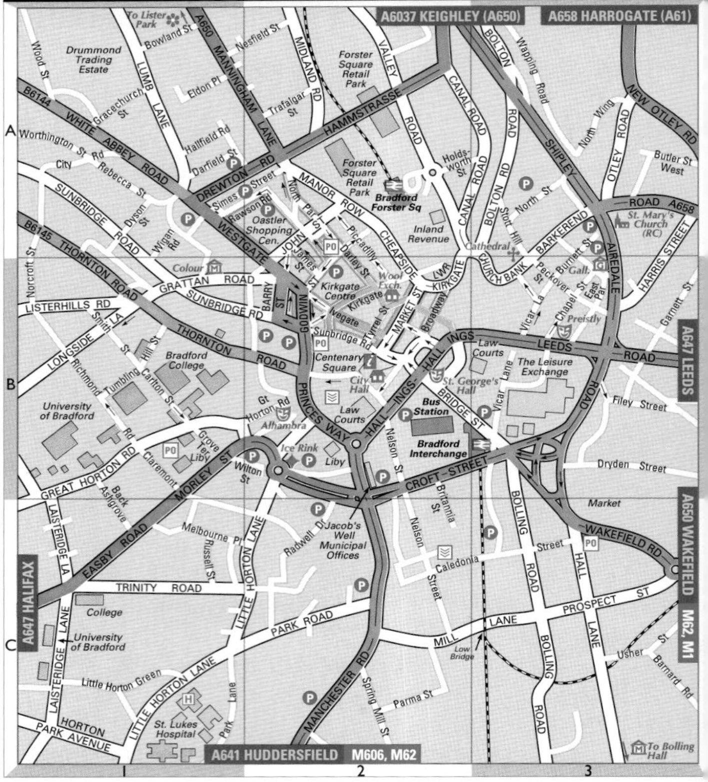

Bristol

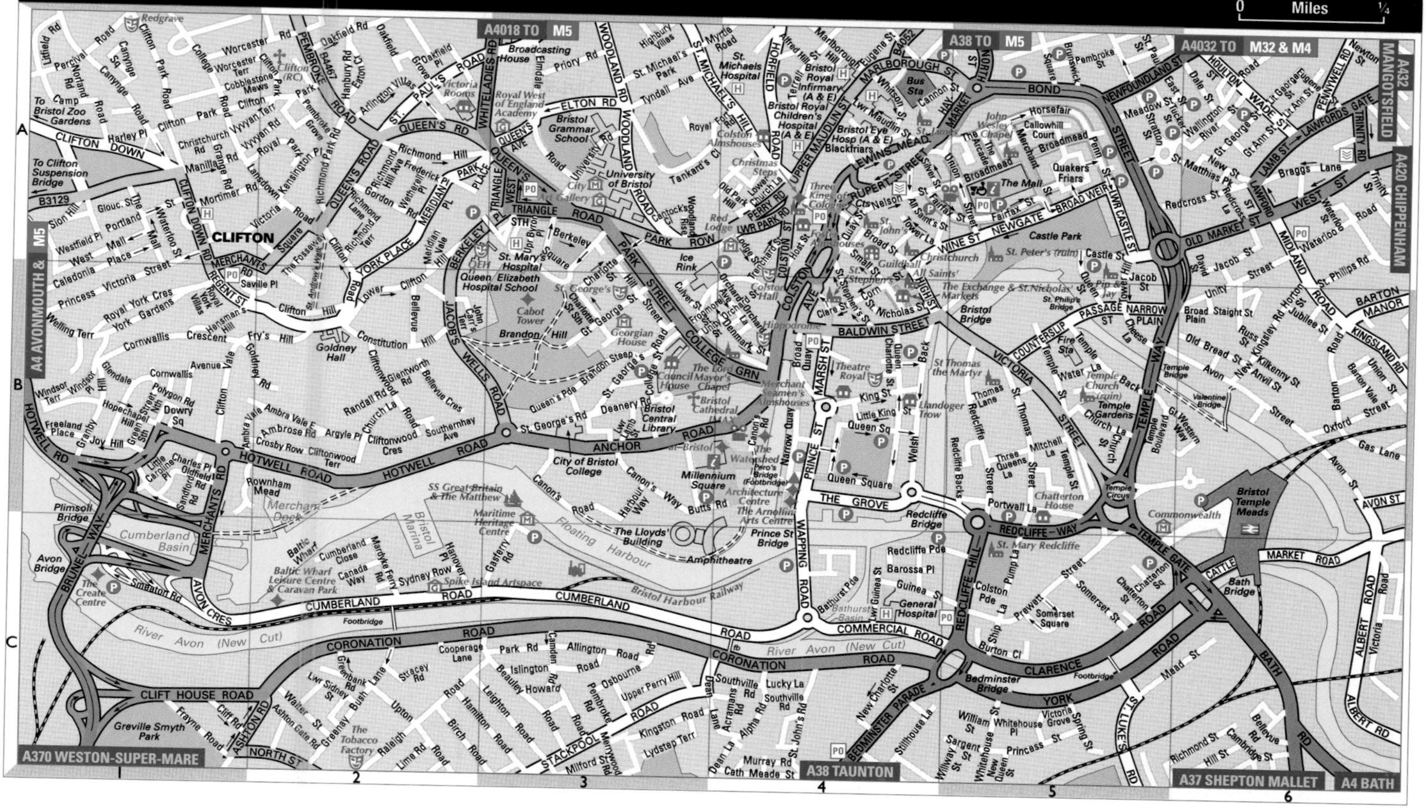

Brighton

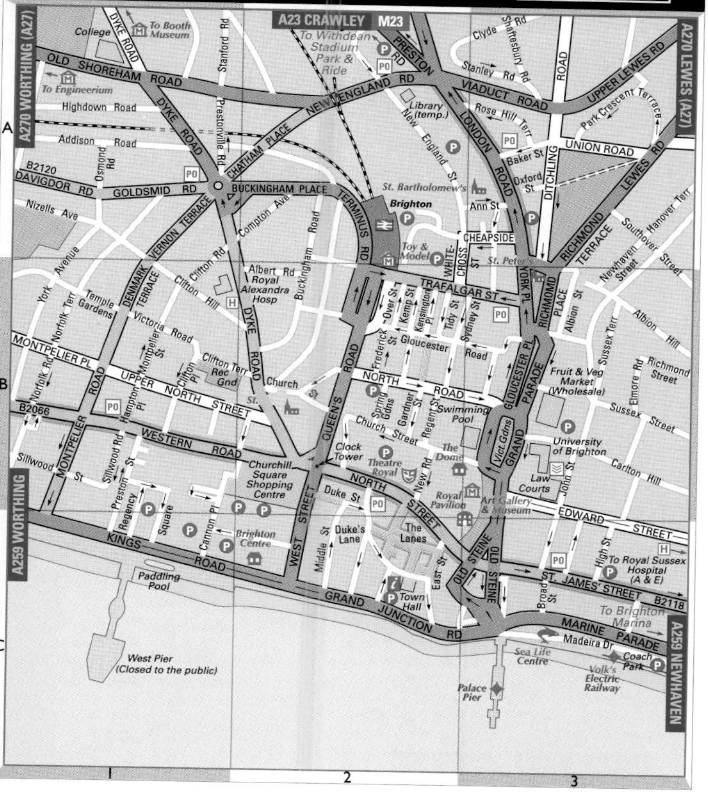

Cambridge

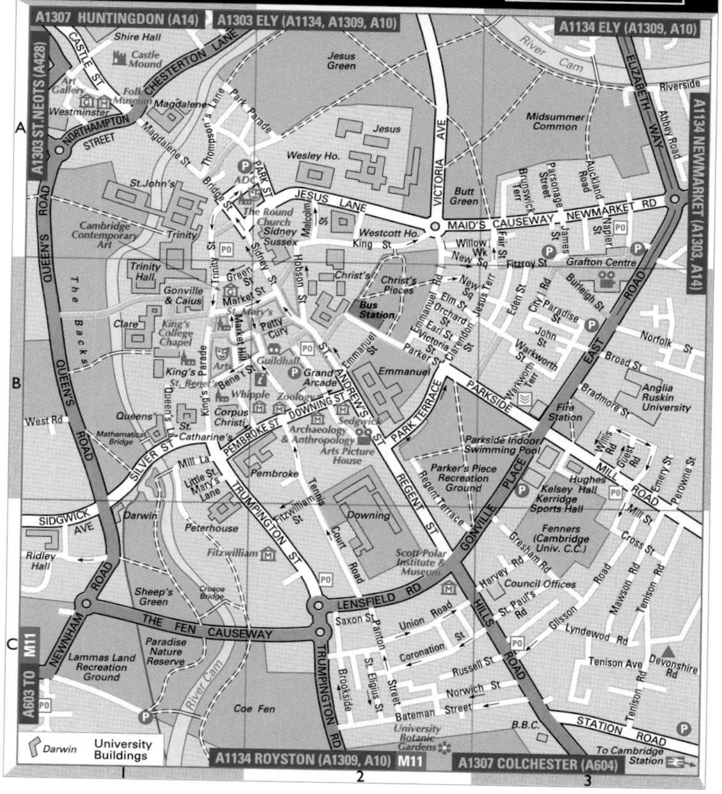

Canterbury

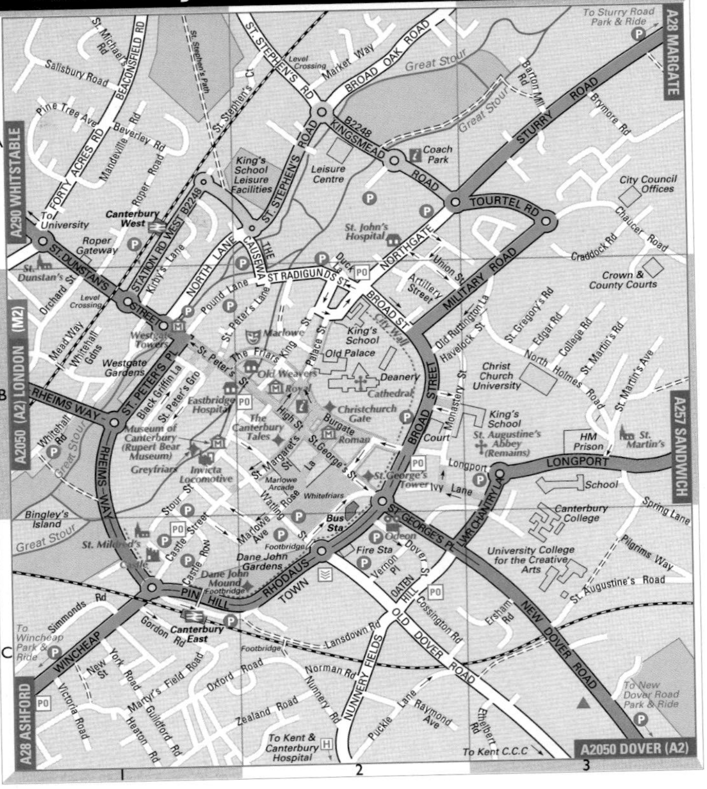

Cardiff / Caerdydd

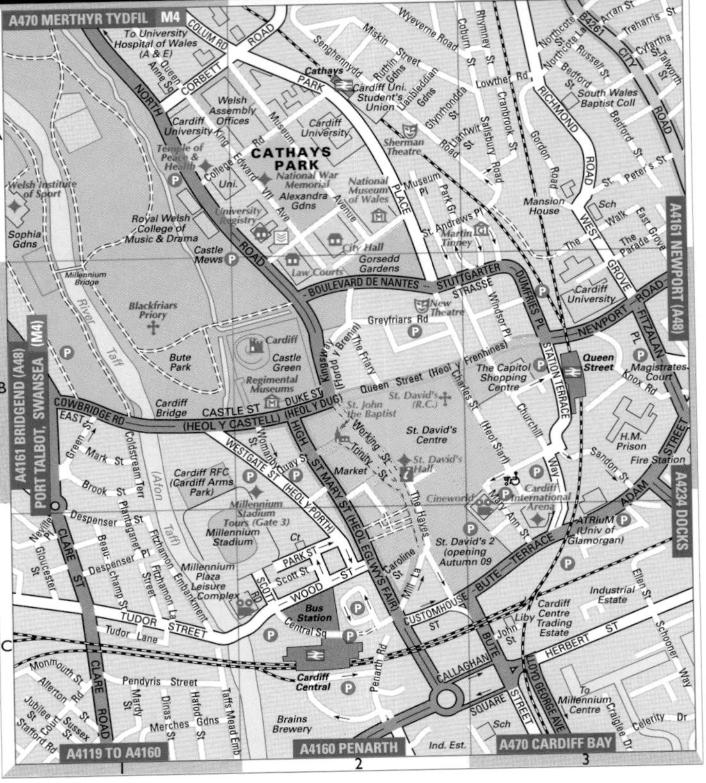

Cheltenham

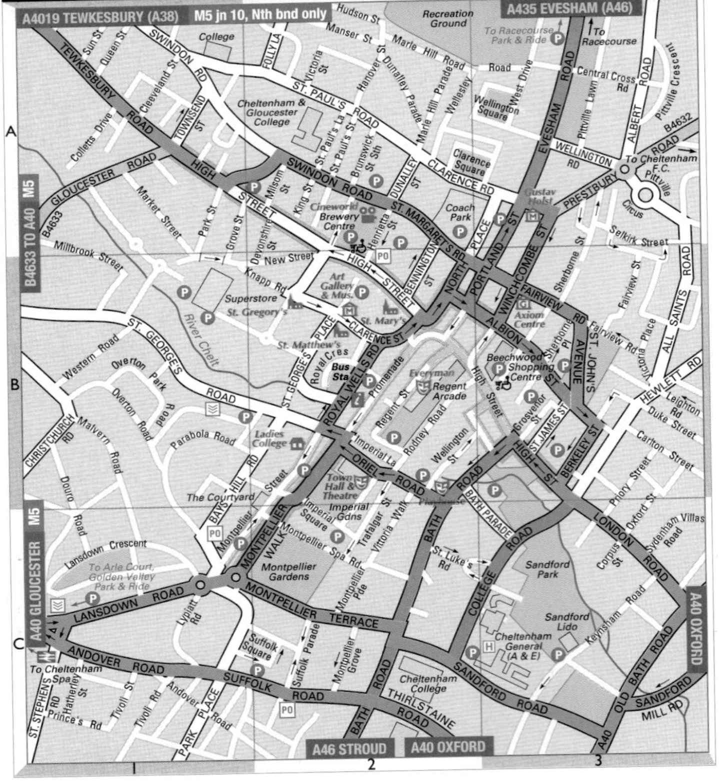

Chester

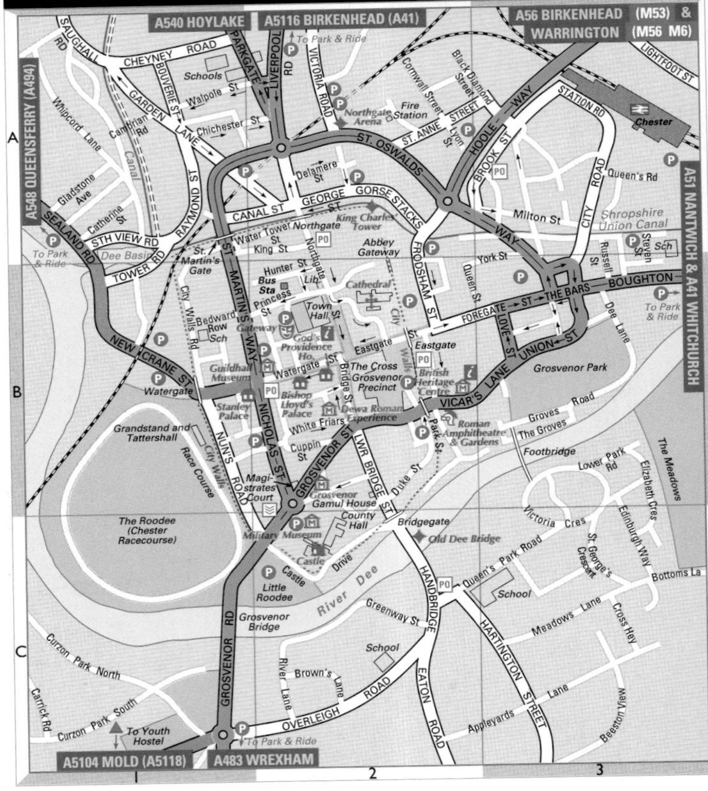

Colchester

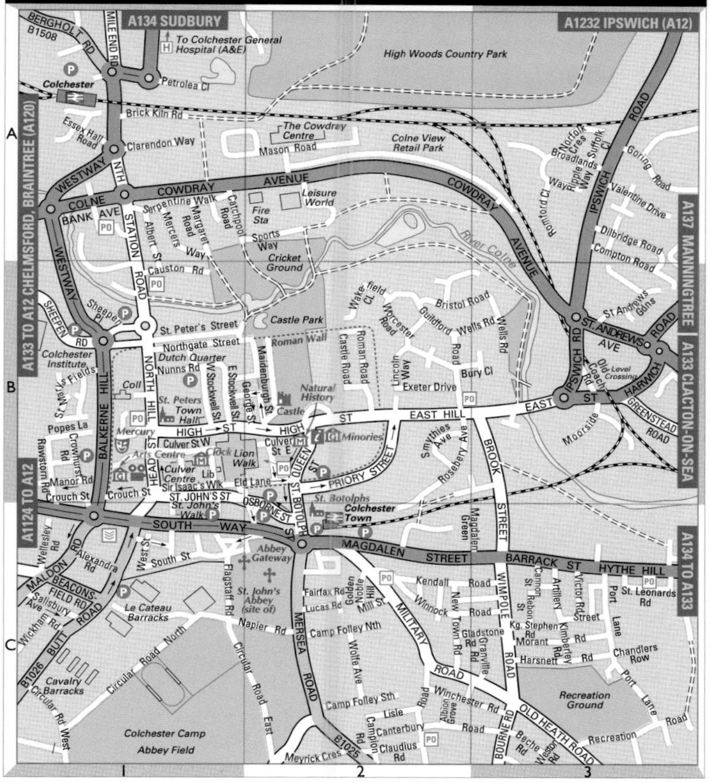

Coventry

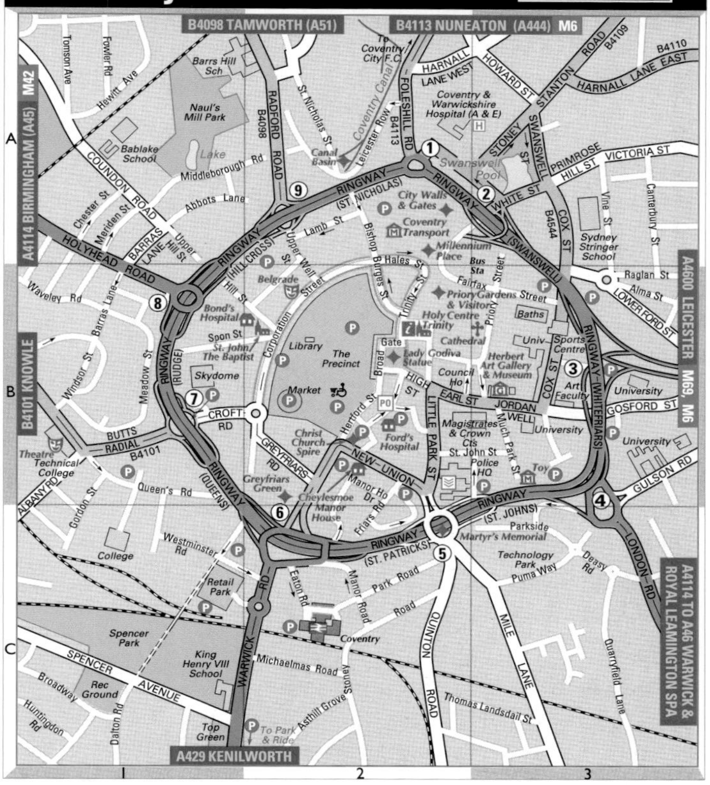

Derby

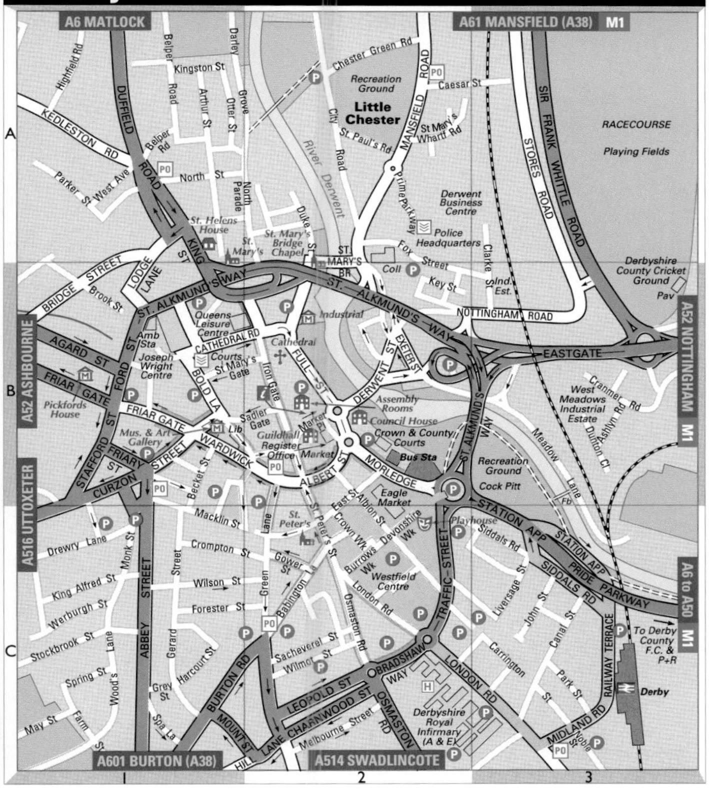

Durham

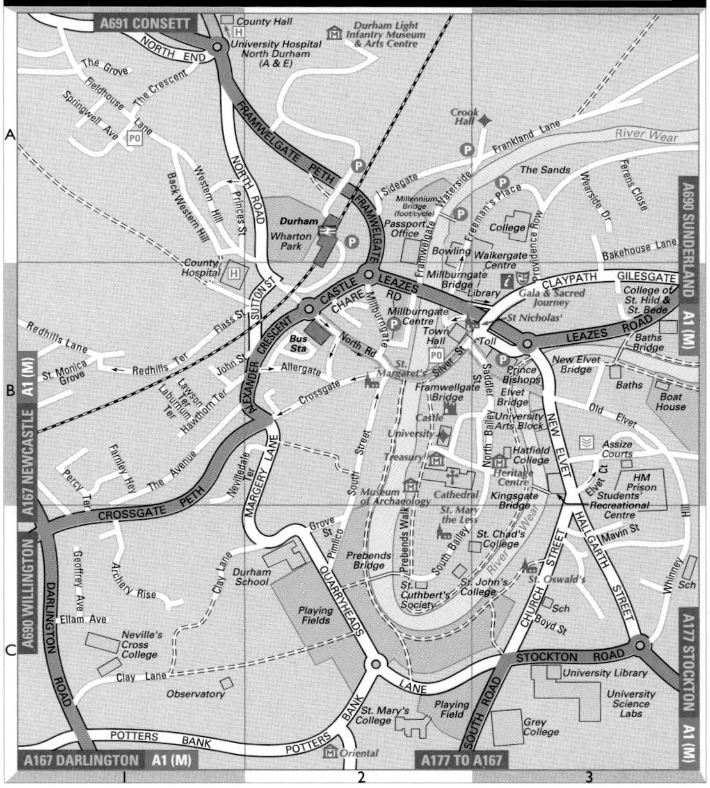

Edinburgh

0 Miles ¼

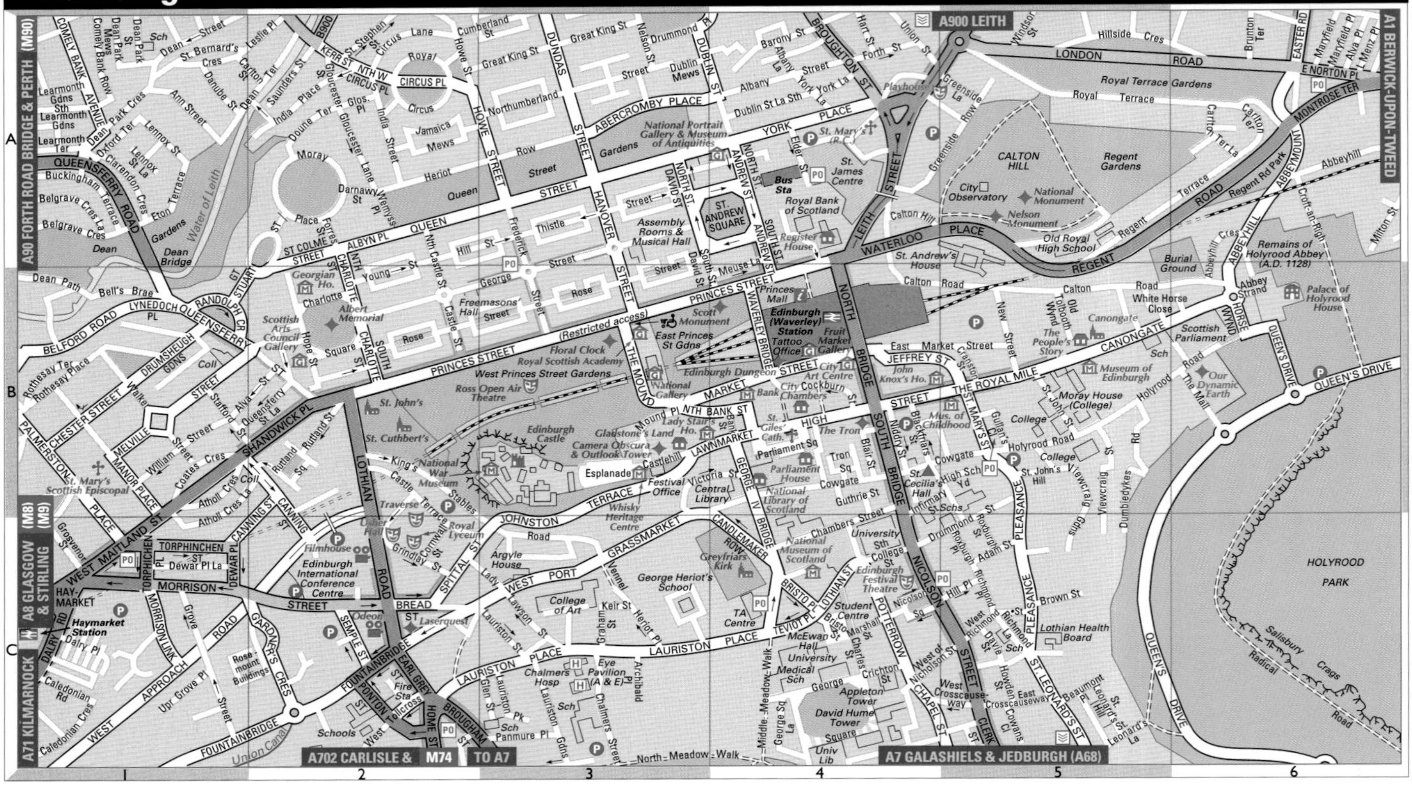

Exeter

0 Miles ¼

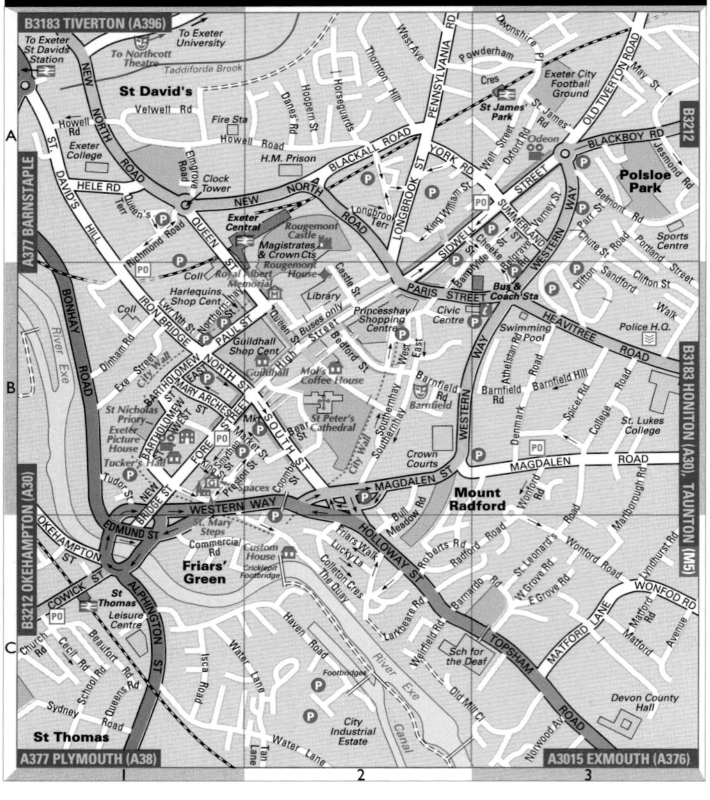

Gloucester

0 Miles ¼

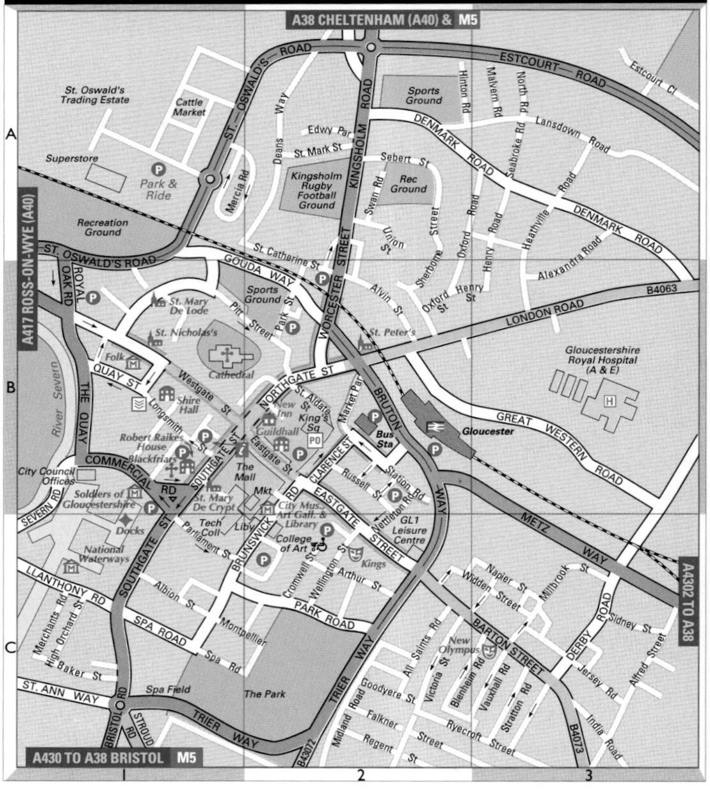

Glasgow

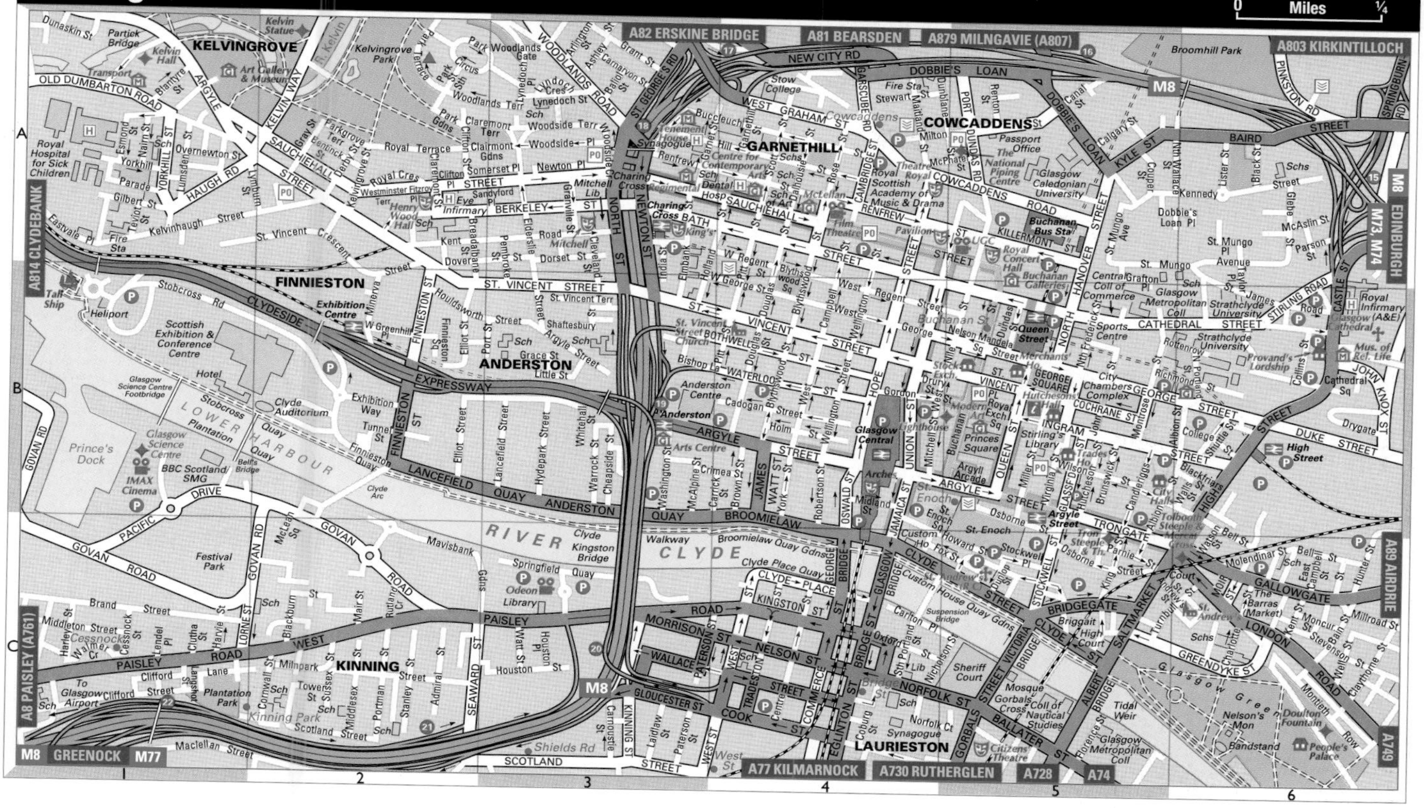

Hull

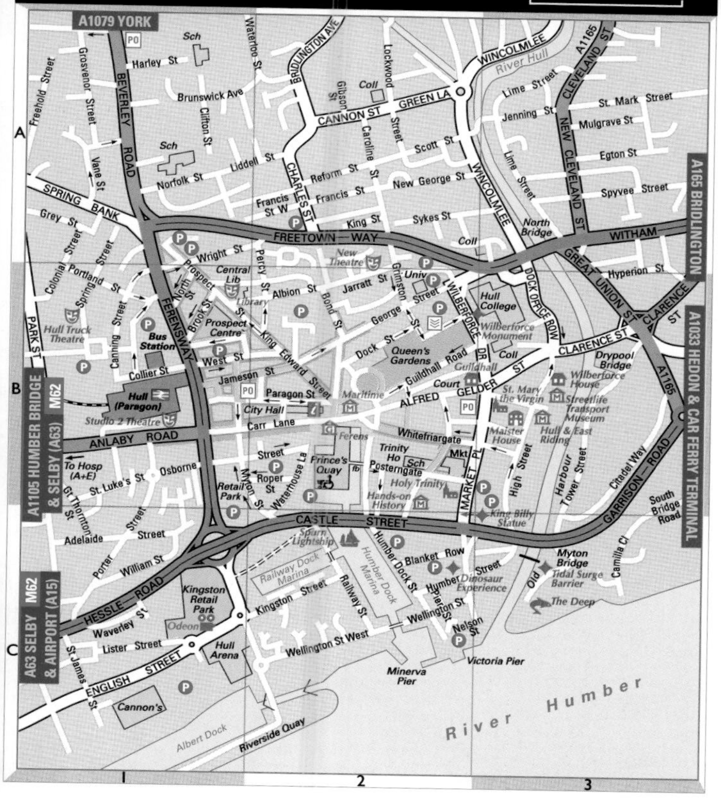

Ipswich

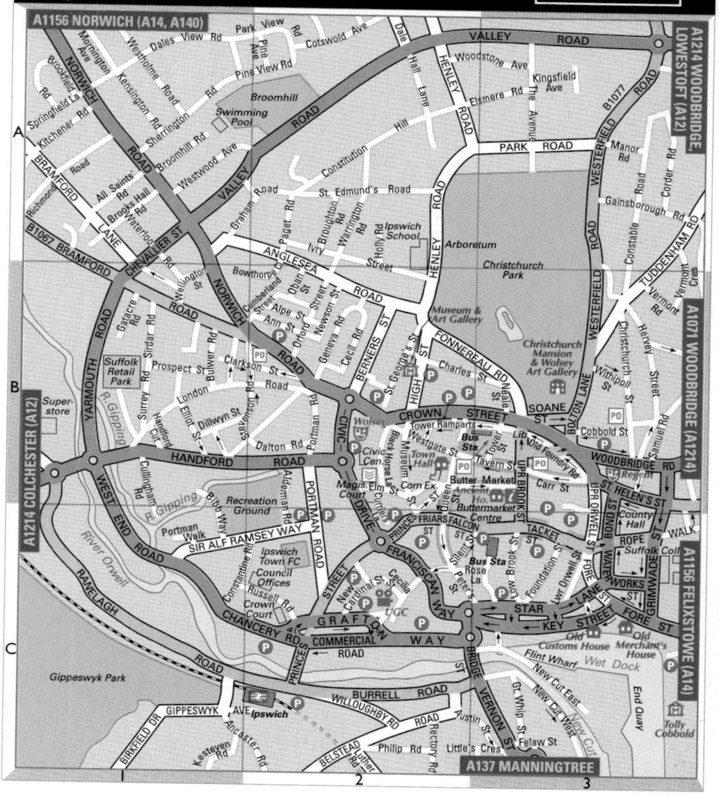

REGENT'S PARK
Queen Mary's Gardens
Open Air Theatre
Regent's Park Boating Lake
London Business School
Regents College
Royal Academy of Music
Madame Tussaud's
MARYLEBONE ROAD
EUSTON ROAD
SOMERS TOWN
Euston
St. Pancras International
King's Cross
British Library
University College
FITZROVIA
BLOOMSBURY
British Museum
University of London
Coram's Fields (Children's Playground)
The Foundling Museum
Wallace Collection
OXFORD STREET
Oxford Circus
Marble Arch
SOHO
MAYFAIR
Roosevelt Memorial
American Embassy
Piccadilly Circus
Trafalgar Square
Nelson's Column
National Gallery
National Portrait Gall
Charing Cross
Covent Garden
Royal Opera Ho
London Transport Mus
ST. JAMES'S
PICCADILLY
GREEN PARK
HYDE PARK
Speakers Corner
Wellington Arch
Apsley House Wellington Museum
Hyde Park Corner
KNIGHTSBRIDGE
Buckingham Palace Gardens
Buckingham Palace
Queen Victoria Memorial
ST. JAMES'S PARK
Duck Island
St. James's Palace
Clarence House
Lancaster House
Horse Guards' Parade
The Admiralty
Admiralty Arch
Banqueting Ho
Downing St
Home, Commonwealth & Foreign Offices
Cabinet War Rooms & Churchill Museum
Cenotaph
Westminster Abbey
Houses of Parliament
WESTMINSTER BRIDGE
London Aquarium
Dali Universe
Waterloo Pier
Embankment Pier
Hungerford Bridges (Footbridge)
Cleopatra's Needle
St. Thomas' Hospital
Lambeth Pier
LAMBETH BRIDGE
WESTMINSTER
Westminster Cathedral (RC)
Victoria
Royal Mews
Belgrave Square
Westminster City Hall
New Scotland Yard
Victoria Place Shopping Centre
Dept of Transport & Environment
Fire Brigade

FINSBURY
CLERKENWELL
HOLBORN
HOXTON
SHOREDITCH
THE CITY
SOUTHWARK
LAMBETH
RIVER THAMES
London Docklands
STEPNEY
POPLAR
CANNING TOWN
WAPPING
ROTHERHITHE
BERMONDSEY
MILLWALL
ISLE OF DOGS
DEPTFORD
GREENWICH
Congestion Charging Zone
Uncharged Roads
0 Miles 1

Leeds

0 Miles ¼

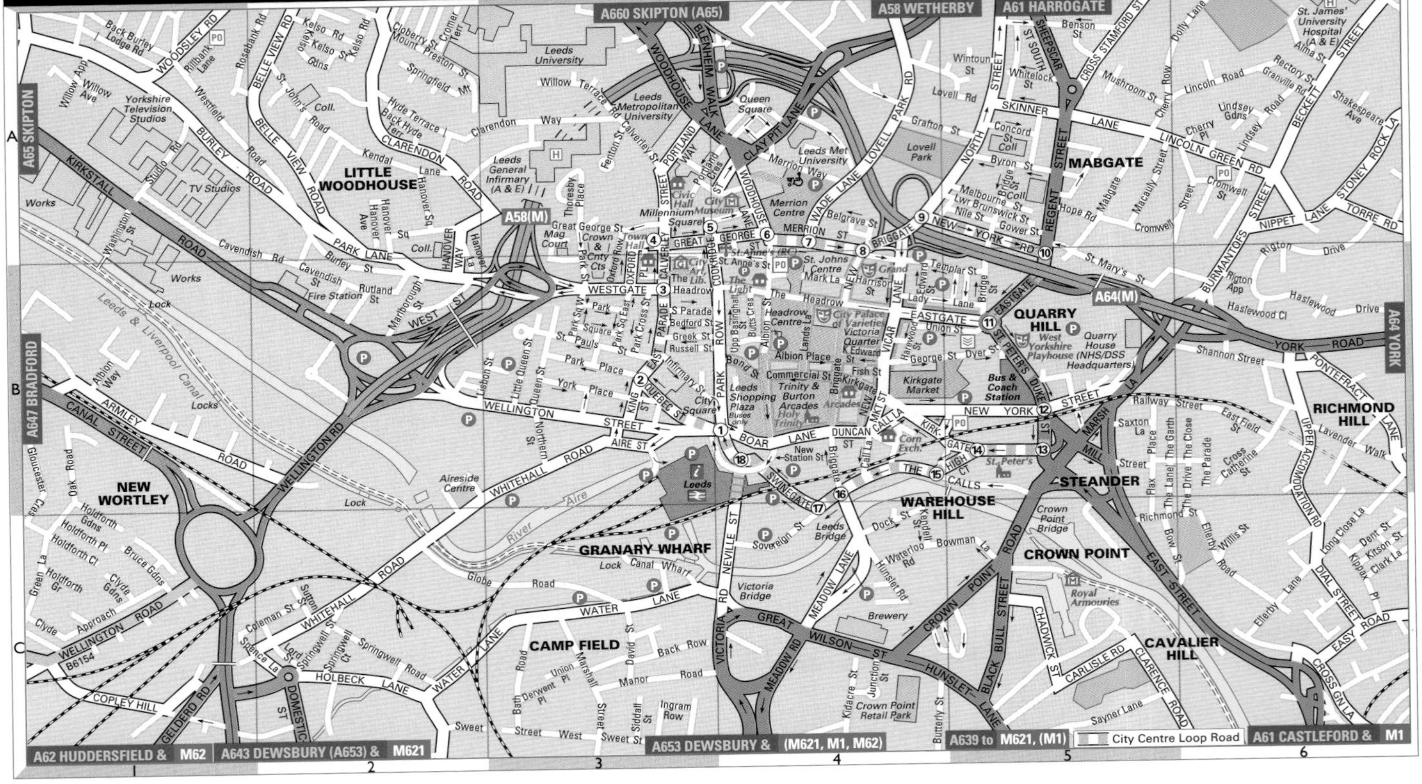

Leicester

0 Miles ¼

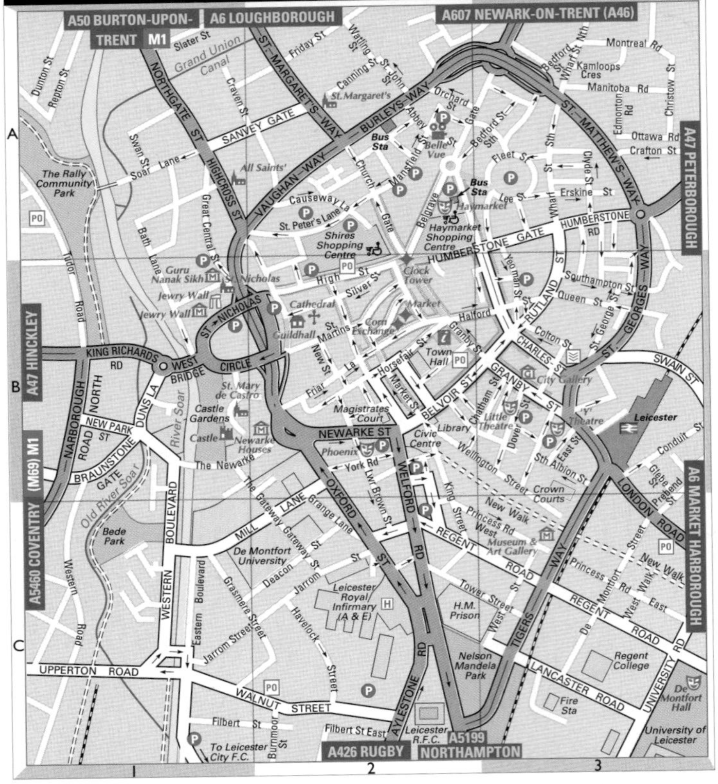

Lincoln

0 Miles ¼

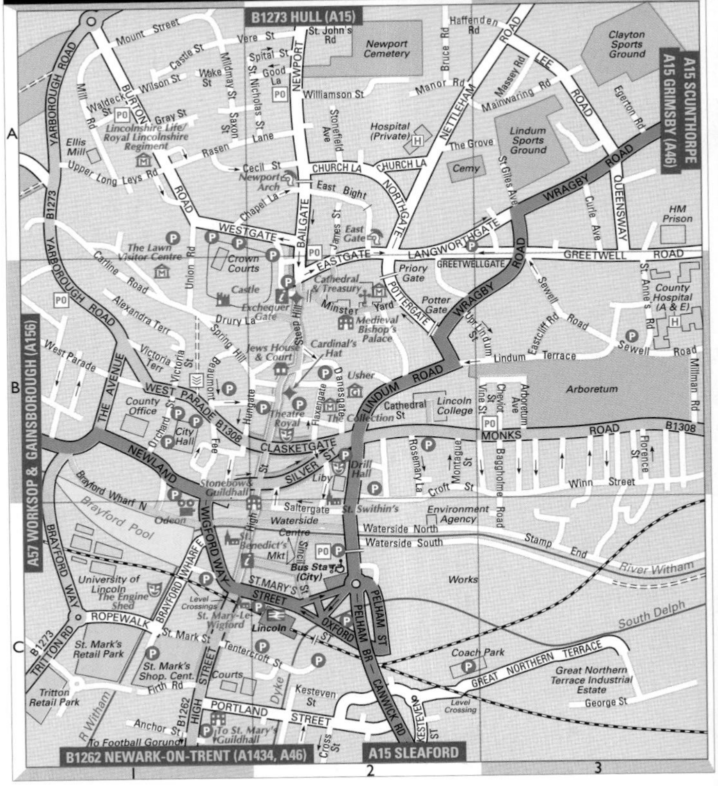

Liverpool

Manchester

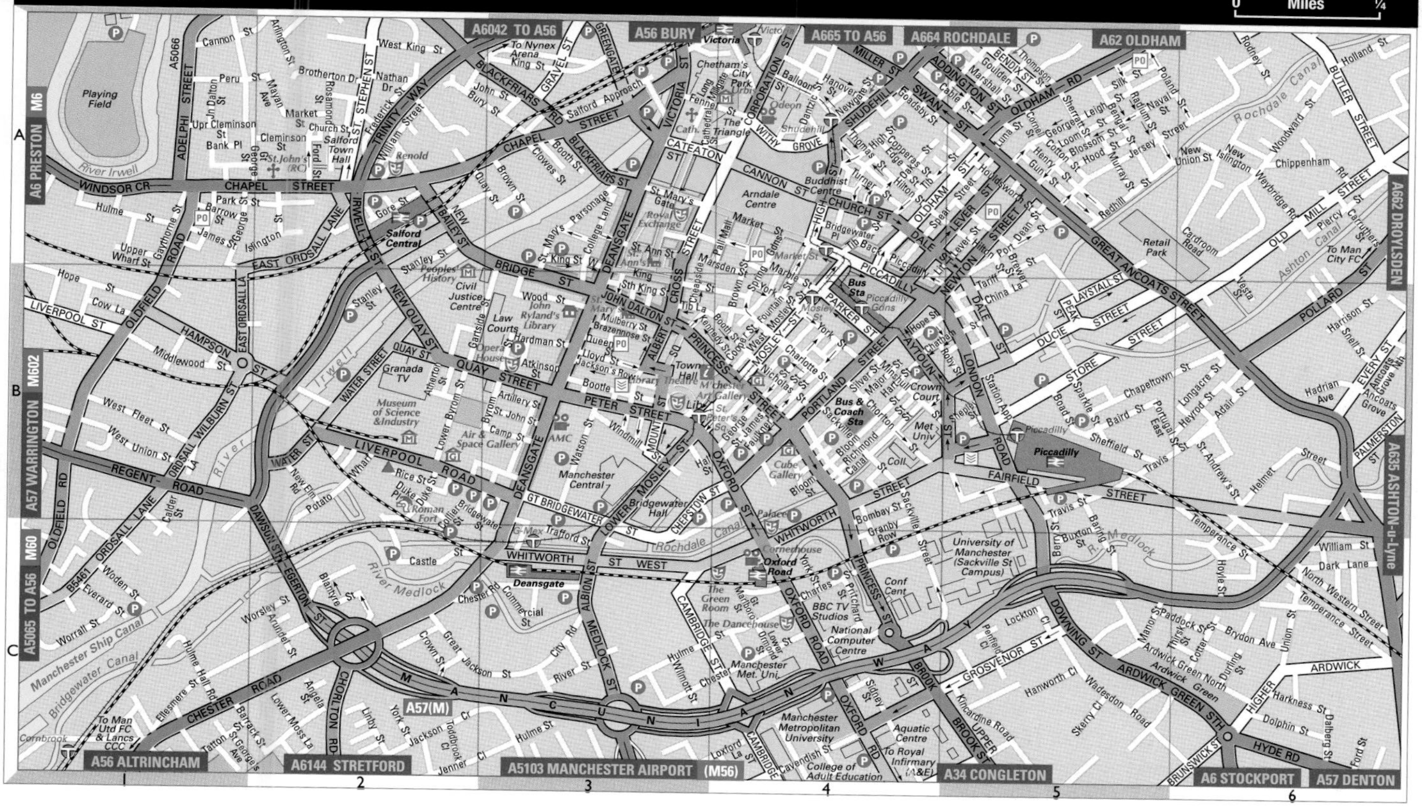

Middlesbrough

0 Miles ¼

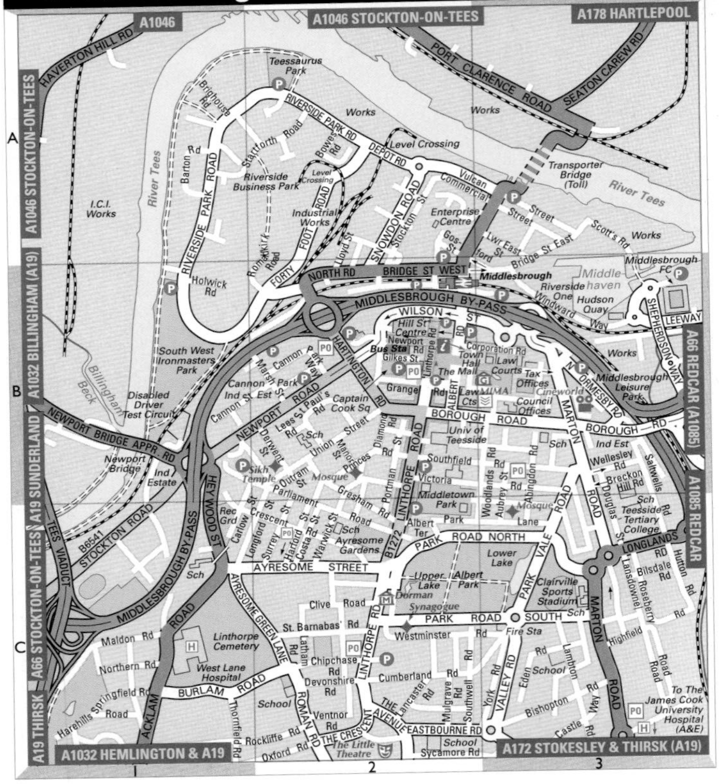

Newcastle upon Tyne

0 Miles ¼

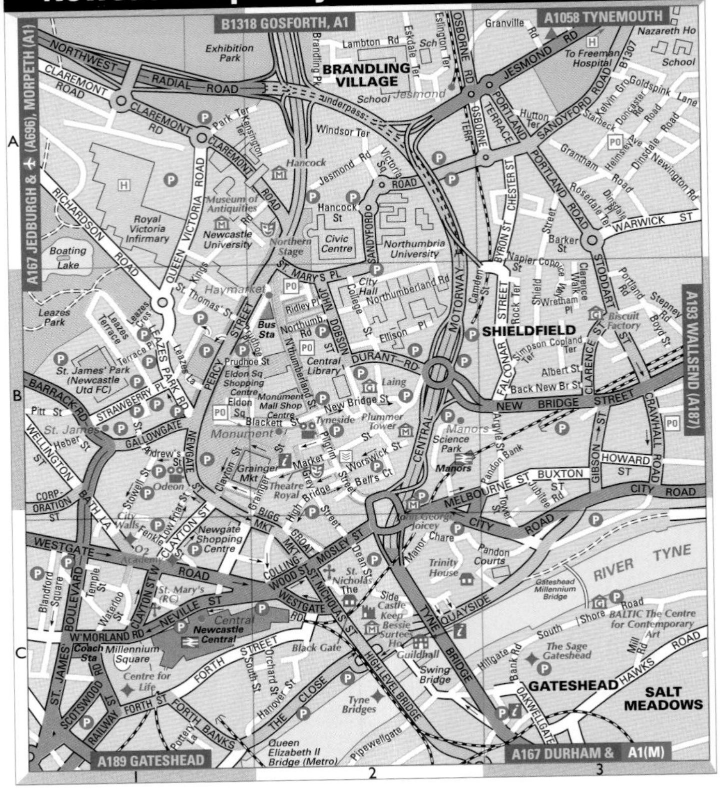

Northampton

0 Miles ¼

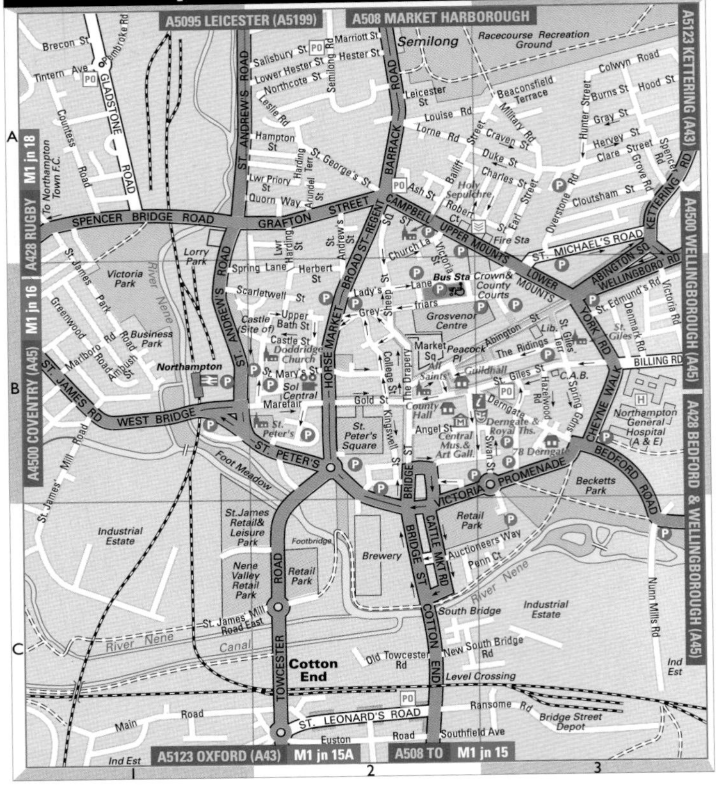

Norwich

0 Miles ¼

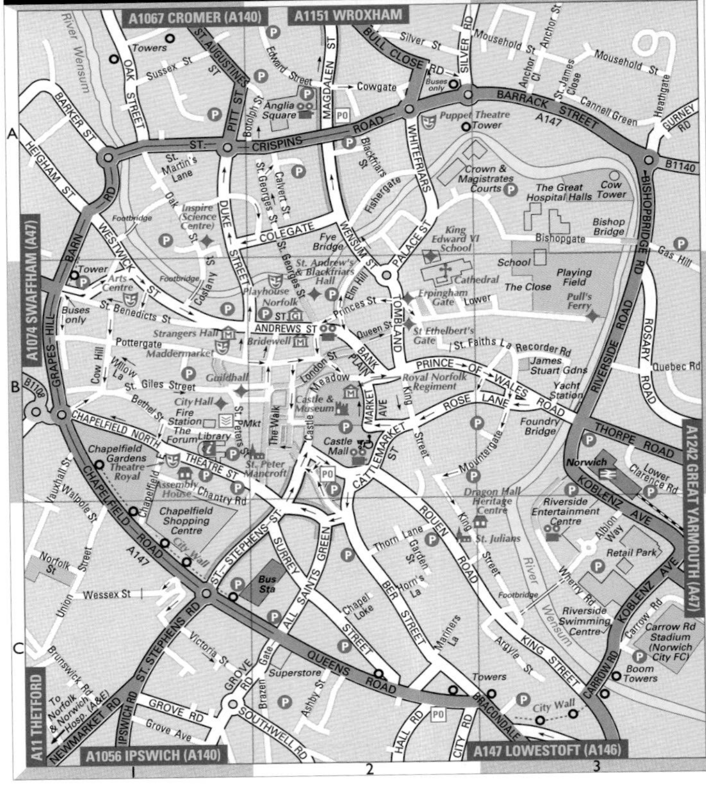

Index to road maps of Britain

Abbreviations used in the index

berdeen **Aberdeen City**
Aberds **Aberdeenshire**
Ald **Alderney**
nglesey **Isle of Anglesey**
Angus **Angus**
Argyll **Argyll and Bute**
Bath **Bath and North East Somerset**
Bedford **Bedford**
Bl Gwent **Blaenau Gwent**
ackburn **Blackburn with Darwen**
ackpool **Blackpool**
Bmouth **Bournemouth**
Borders **Scottish Borders**
Brack **Bracknell**
ridgend **Bridgend**
Brighton **City of Brighton and Hove**
Bristol **City and County of Bristol**
Bucks **Buckinghamshire**
C Beds **Central Bedfordshire**
Caerph **Caerphilly**
Cambs **Cambridgeshire**
Cardiff **Cardiff**
Carms **Carmarthenshire**
Ceredig **Ceredigion**
Ches E **Cheshire East**
Ches W **Cheshire West and Chester**
Clack **Clackmannanshire**
Conwy **Conwy**
Corn **Cornwall**
Cumb **Cumbria**
Darl **Darlington**
Denb **Denbighshire**
Derby **City of Derby**
Derbys **Derbyshire**
Devon **Devon**
Dorset **Dorset**
umfries **Dumfries and Galloway**
Dundee **Dundee City**
Durham **Durham**
E Ayrs **East Ayrshire**
E Dunb **East Dunbartonshire**

E Loth **East Lothian**
E Renf **East Renfrewshire**
E Sus **East Sussex**
E Yorks **East Riding of Yorkshire**
Edin **City of Edinburgh**
Essex **Essex**
Falk **Falkirk**
Fife **Fife**
Flint **Flintshire**
Glasgow **City of Glasgow**
Glos **Gloucestershire**
Gtr Man **Greater Manchester**
Guern **Guernsey**
Gwyn **Gwynedd**
Halton **Halton**
Hants **Hampshire**
Hereford **Herefordshire**
Herts **Hertfordshire**
Highld **Highland**
Hrtlpl **Hartlepool**
Hull **Hull**
IoM **Isle of Man**
IoW **Isle of Wight**
Invclyd **Inverclyde**
Jersey **Jersey**
Kent **Kent**
Lancs **Lancashire**
Leicester **City of Leicester**
Leics **Leicestershire**
Lincs **Lincolnshire**
London **Greater London**
Luton **Luton**
M Keynes **Milton Keynes**
M Tydf **Merthyr Tydfil**
Mbro **Middlesbrough**
Medway **Medway**
Mers **Merseyside**
Midloth **Midlothian**
Mon **Monmouthshire**
Moray **Moray**
N Ayrs **North Ayrshire**
N Lincs **North Lincolnshire**
N Lanark **North Lanarkshire**
N Som **North Somerset**
N Yorks **North Yorkshire**

How to use the index

Example

Trudoxhill Som **16** G4

- grid square
- page number
- county or unitary authority

NE Lincs **North East Lincolnshire**
Neath **Neath Port Talbot**
Newport **City and County of Newport**
Norf **Norfolk**
Northants **Northamptonshire**
Northumb **Northumberland**
Nottingham **City of Nottingham**
Notts **Nottinghamshire**
Orkney **Orkney**
Oxon **Oxfordshire**
Pboro **Peterborough**
Pembs **Pembrokeshire**
Perth **Perth and Kinross**
Plym **Plymouth**
Poole **Poole**
Powys **Powys**
Ptsmth **Portsmouth**
Reading **Reading**
Redcar **Redcar and Cleveland**
Renfs **Renfrewshire**
Rhondda **Rhondda Cynon Taff**
Rutland **Rutland**
S Ayrs **South Ayrshire**
S Glos **South Gloucestershire**
S Lanark **South Lanarkshire**
S Yorks **South Yorkshire**
Scilly **Scilly**
Shetland **Shetland**
Shrops **Shropshire**
Slough **Slough**
Som **Somerset**

Soton **Southampton**
Staffs **Staffordshire**
Southend **Southend-on-Sea**
Stirling **Stirling**
Stockton **Stockton-on-Tees**
Stoke **Stoke-on-Trent**
Suff **Suffolk**
Sur **Surrey**
Swansea **Swansea**
Swindon **Swindon**
T&W **Tyne and Wear**
Telford **Telford and Wrekin**
Thurrock **Thurrock**
Torbay **Torbay**
Torf **Torfaen**
V Glam **The Vale of Glamorgan**
W Berks **West Berkshire**
W Dunb **West Dunbartonshire**
W Isles **Western Isles**
W Loth **West Lothian**
W Mid **West Midlands**
W Sus **West Sussex**
W Yorks **West Yorkshire**
Warks **Warwickshire**
Warr **Warrington**
Wilts **Wiltshire**
Windsor **Windsor and Maidenhead**
Wokingham **Wokingham**
Worcs **Worcestershire**
Wrex **Wrexham**
York **City of York**

Anstruther Wester Fife 77 G8
Ansty Hants 18 G4
Ansty W Sus 12 D1
Ansty Warks 35 G9
Ansty Wilts 9 B8
Anthill Common Hants 10 C5
Anthorn Cumb 61 H7
Antingham Norf 39 B8
Anton's Gowt Lincs 46 H6
Antonshill Falk 69 B7
Antony Corn 4 F4
Anwick Lincs 46 G5
Anwoth Dumfries 55 D8
Aoradh Argyll 64 B3
Apes Hall Cambs 38 F1
Apethorpe Northants 36 F6
Apeton Staffs 34 D4
Apley Lincs 46 E5
Apperknowle Derbys 45 E7
Apperley Glos 26 F5
Apperley Bridge W Yorks 51 F7
Appersett N Yorks 57 G10
Appin Argyll 74 C2
Appin House Argyll 74 C2
Appleby N Lincs 46 A3
Appleby-in-Westmorland Cumb 57 D8
Appleby Magna Leics 35 E9
Appleby Parva Leics 35 E9
Applecross Highld 85 D12
Applecross Ho. Highld 85 D12
Appledore Devon 6 C3
Appledore Devon 7 E9
Appledore Kent 13 D8
Appledore Heath Kent 13 C8
Appleford Oxon 18 B2
Applegarthtown Dumfries 61 E7
Appleshaw Hants 17 G10
Applethwaite Cumb 56 D4
Appleton Halton 43 D8
Appleton Oxon 17 A11
Appleton-le-Moors N Yorks 59 H8
Appleton-le-Street N Yorks 52 B3
Appleton Roebuck N Yorks 52 E1
Appleton Thorn Warr 43 D9
Appleton Wiske N Yorks 58 F4
Appletreehall Borders 61 B11
Appletreewick N Yorks 51 C6
Appley Som 7 D9
Appley Bridge Lancs 43 B8
Apse Heath IoW 10 F4
Apsley End C Beds 29 E8
Apuldram W Sus 11 D7
Aquhythie Aberds 83 B9
Arabella Highld 87 D11
Arbeadie Aberds 83 D8
Arberth = Narberth Pembs 22 E6
Arbirlot Angus 77 C9
Arboll Highld 87 C11
Arborfield Wokingham 18 E4
Arborfield Cross Wokingham 18 E4
Arborfield Garrison Wokingham 18 E4
Arbour-thorne S Yorks 45 D7
Arbroath Angus 77 C9
Arbuthnott Aberds 83 F9
Archiestown Moray 88 D2
Arclid Ches E 43 F10
Ard-dhubh Highld 85 D12
Ardachu Highld 93 J9
Ardalanish Argyll 78 K6
Ardanaiseig Argyll 74 E3
Ardaneaskan Highld 85 E13
Ardanstur Argyll 73 B7
Ardargie House Hotel Perth 76 F3
Ardarroch Highld 85 E13
Ardbeg Argyll 64 D5
Ardbeg Argyll 73 E10
Ardcharnich Highld 86 C4
Ardchiavaig Argyll 78 K6
Ardchullarie More Stirling 75 F8
Ardchyle Stirling 75 E8
Arddleen Powys 33 D8
Ardechvie Highld 80 D3
Ardeley Herts 29 F10
Ardelve Highld 85 F13
Arden Argyll 68 B2
Ardens Grafton Warks 27 C8
Ardentinny Argyll 73 E10
Ardentraive Argyll 73 F9
Ardeonaig Stirling 75 D9
Ardersier Highld 87 F10
Ardessie Highld 86 C3
Ardfern Argyll 73 C7
Ardgartan Argyll 74 G5
Ardgay Highld 87 B8
Ardgour Highld 74 A3
Ardheslaig Highld 85 C12
Ardiecow Moray 88 B5
Ardindrean Highld 86 C4
Ardingly W Sus 12 D2
Ardington Oxon 17 C11
Ardlair Aberds 83 A7
Ardlamont Ho. Argyll 73 G8
Ardleigh Essex 31 F7
Ardler Perth 76 C5
Ardley Oxon 28 F2
Ardlui Argyll 74 F6
Ardlussa Argyll 72 E5
Ardmair Highld 86 B4
Ardmay Argyll 74 G5
Ardminish Argyll 65 D7
Ardmolich Highld 79 D10
Ardmore Argyll 79 J10
Ardmore Highld 87 C10
Ardmore Highld 92 D5
Ardnacross Argyll 79 G8
Ardnadam Argyll 73 F10
Ardnagrask Highld 87 G8
Ardnarff Highld 85 E13
Ardnastang Highld 79 E11
Ardnave Argyll 64 A3
Ardno Argyll 73 C10
Ardo Aberds 89 E8
Ardo Ho. Aberds 89 F9
Ardoch Perth 76 D3
Ardochy House Highld 80 C4
Ardoyne Aberds 83 A8
Ardpatrick Argyll 72 G6
Ardpatrick Ho. Argyll 72 H6
Ardpeaton Argyll 73 E11
Ardrishaig Argyll 73 E7
Ardross Fife 77 G8
Ardross Highld 87 D9
Ardross Castle Highld 87 D9
Ardrossan N Ayrs 66 B5
Ardshealach Highld 79 E9
Ardsley S Yorks 45 B7
Ardslignish Highld 79 E8
Ardtalla Argyll 64 C5
Ardtalnaig Perth 75 D10
Ardtoe Highld 79 D9
Ardtrostan Perth 75 E9
Arduaine Argyll 72 B6
Ardullie Highld 87 E8
Ardvasar Highld 85 H11
Ardvorlich Perth 75 E9
Ardwell Dumfries 54 E4
Ardwell Mains Dumfries 54 E4
Ardwick Gtr Man 44 C2
Areley Kings Worcs 26 A5
Arford Hants 18 H5
Argoed Caerph 15 B7
Argoed Mill Powys 24 B6
Arichamish Argyll 73 C8
Arichastlich Argyll 74 D5
Aridhglas Argyll 78 J6
Arileod Argyll 78 F4
Arinacrinachd Highld 85 C12
Arinagour Argyll 78 F5
Arion Orkney 95 G3
Arisaig Highld 79 C9
Ariundle Highld 79 E11
Arkendale N Yorks 51 C9
Arkesden Essex 29 E11
Arkholme Lancs 50 B1
Arkle Town N Yorks 58 F1
Arkleton Dumfries 61 D9
Arkley London 19 B9
Arksey S Yorks 45 B9
Arkwright Town Derbys 45 E8
Arle Glos 26 F6
Arlecdon Cumb 56 E2
Arlesey C Beds 29 E8
Arleston Telford 34 D2
Arley Ches E 43 D9
Arlingham Glos 26 G4
Arlington Devon 6 B5
Arlington E Sus 12 F4
Arlington Glos 27 H8
Armadale Highld 93 C10
Armadale W Loth 69 D8
Armadale Castle Highld 85 H11
Armathwaite Cumb 57 B7
Arminghall Norf 39 E8
Armitage Staffs 35 D6
Armley W Yorks 51 F8
Armscote Warks 27 D9
Armthorpe S Yorks 45 B10
Arnabost Argyll 78 F5
Arncliffe N Yorks 50 B5
Arncroach Fife 77 G8
Arne Dorset 9 F8
Arnesby Leics 36 F2
Arngask Perth 76 F4
Arnisdale Highld 85 G13
Arnish Highld 85 D10
Arniston Engine Midloth 70 D2
Arnol W Isles 91 C8
Arnold E Yorks 53 E7
Arnold Notts 45 H9
Arnprior Stirling 68 A5
Arnside Cumb 49 B4
Aros Mains Argyll 79 G8
Arowry Wrex 33 B10
Arpafeelie Highld 87 F9
Arrad Foot Cumb 49 A3
Arram E Yorks 52 E6
Arrathorne N Yorks 58 G3
Arreton IoW 10 F4
Arrington Cambs 29 C10
Arrivain Argyll 74 D5
Arrochar Argyll 74 G5
Arrow Warks 27 C7
Arthington W Yorks 51 E8
Arthingworth Northants 36 G3
Arthog Gwyn 32 D2
Arthrath Aberds 89 E9
Arthurstone Perth 76 C5
Artrochie Aberds 89 E10
Arundel W Sus 11 D9
Aryhoulan Highld 80 G2
Asby Cumb 56 D2
Ascog Argyll 73 G10
Ascot Windsor 18 E6
Ascott Warks 27 E10
Ascott-under-Wychwood Oxon 27 G10
Asenby N Yorks 51 B9
Asfordby Leics 36 D3
Asfordby Hill Leics 36 D3
Asgarby Lincs 46 H5
Asgarby Lincs 47 F7
Ash Kent 20 E2
Ash Kent 21 F9
Ash Som 8 B3
Ash Sur 18 F5
Ash Bullayne Devon 7 F6
Ash Green Warks 35 G9
Ash Magna Shrops 34 B1
Ash Mill Devon 7 D6
Ash Priors Som 7 D10
Ash Street Suff 31 D7
Ash Thomas Devon 7 E9
Ash Vale Sur 18 F5
Ashampstead W Berks 18 D2
Ashbocking Suff 31 C8
Ashbourne Derbys 44 H5
Ashbrittle Som 7 D9
Ashburton Devon 5 E8
Ashbury Devon 6 G4
Ashbury Oxon 17 C9
Ashby N Lincs 46 B3
Ashby by Partney Lincs 47 F8
Ashby cum Fenby NE Lincs 46 B6
Ashby de la Launde Lincs 46 G4
Ashby-de-la-Zouch Leics 35 D9
Ashby Folville Leics 36 D3
Ashby Magna Leics 36 F1
Ashby Parva Leics 35 G11
Ashby Puerorum Lincs 47 E7
Ashby St Ledgers Northants 28 B2
Ashby St Mary Norf 39 E9
Ashchurch Glos 26 E6
Ashcombe Devon 5 D10
Ashcott Som 15 H10
Ashdon Essex 30 D2
Ashe Hants 18 G2
Asheldham Essex 20 A6
Ashen Essex 30 D4
Ashendon Bucks 28 G4
Ashfield Carms 24 F3
Ashfield Stirling 75 G10
Ashfield Suff 31 B9
Ashfield Green Suff 31 A9
Ashfold Crossways W Sus 11 B11
Ashford Devon 6 C4
Ashford Hants 9 C10
Ashford Kent 13 B9
Ashford Sur 19 D7
Ashford Bowdler Shrops 26 A2
Ashford Carbonell Shrops 26 A2
Ashford Hill Hants 18 E2
Ashford in the Water Derbys 44 F5
Ashgill S Lanark 68 F6
Ashill Devon 7 E9
Ashill Norf 38 E4
Ashill Som 8 C2
Ashingdon Essex 20 B5
Ashington Northumb 63 E8
Ashington Som 8 B4
Ashington W Sus 11 C10
Ashintully Castle Perth 76 A4
Ashkirk Borders 61 A10
Ashlett Hants 10 D3
Ashleworth Glos 26 F5
Ashley Cambs 30 B3
Ashley Ches E 43 D10
Ashley Devon 6 E5
Ashley Dorset 9 D10
Ashley Glos 16 B6
Ashley Hants 10 E2
Ashley Hants 10 A2
Ashley Northants 36 F3
Ashley Staffs 34 B3
Ashley Green Bucks 28 H6
Ashley Heath Dorset 9 D10
Ashley Heath Staffs 34 B3
Ashmanhaugh Norf 39 C9
Ashmansworth Hants 17 F11
Ashmansworthy Devon 6 E2
Ashmore Dorset 9 C8
Ashorne Warks 27 C10
Ashover Derbys 45 F7
Ashow Warks 27 A10
Ashprington Devon 5 F9
Ashreigney Devon 6 E5
Ashtead Sur 19 F8
Ashton Ches W 43 F8
Ashton Corn 2 G5
Ashton Hants 10 C4
Ashton Hereford 26 B2
Ashton Invclyd 73 F11
Ashton Northants 28 D4
Ashton Northants 37 G6
Ashton Common Wilts 16 F5
Ashton-In-Makerfield Gtr Man 43 C8
Ashton Keynes Wilts 17 B7
Ashton under Hill Worcs 26 E6
Ashton-under-Lyne Gtr Man 44 C3
Ashton upon Mersey Gtr Man 43 C10
Ashurst Hants 10 C2
Ashurst Kent 12 C4
Ashurst W Sus 11 C10
Ashurstwood W Sus 12 C3
Ashwater Devon 6 G2
Ashwell Herts 29 E9
Ashwell Rutland 36 D4
Ashwell Som 8 C2
Ashwellthorpe Norf 39 F7
Ashwick Som 16 G3
Ashwicken Norf 38 D3
Ashybank Borders 61 B11
Askam in Furness Cumb 49 B2
Askern S Yorks 45 A9
Askerswell Dorset 8 E4
Askett Bucks 28 H5
Askham Cumb 57 D7
Askham Notts 45 E11
Askham Bryan York 52 E1
Askham Richard York 51 E11
Asknish Argyll 73 D8
Askrigg N Yorks 57 G11
Askwith N Yorks 51 E7
Aslackby Lincs 37 B6
Aslacton Norf 39 F7
Aslockton Notts 36 B3
Asloun Aberds 83 B7
Aspatria Cumb 56 B3
Aspenden Herts 29 F10
Asperton Lincs 37 B8
Aspley Guise C Beds 28 E6
Aspley Heath C Beds 28 E6
Aspull Gtr Man 43 B9
Asselby E Yorks 52 G3
Asserby Lincs 47 E8
Assington Suff 30 E6
Assynt Ho. Highld 87 E8
Astbury Ches E 44 F2
Astcote Northants 28 C3
Asterley Shrops 33 E9
Asterton Shrops 33 F9
Asthall Oxon 27 G9
Asthall Leigh Oxon 27 G10
Astley Shrops 33 D11
Astley Warks 35 G9
Astley Worcs 26 B4
Astley Abbotts Shrops 34 F3
Astley Bridge Gtr Man 43 A10
Astley Cross Worcs 26 B5
Astley Green Gtr Man 43 C10
Aston Ches E 43 H9
Aston Ches W 43 E8
Aston Derbys 44 D5
Aston Hereford 25 A11
Aston Herts 29 F9
Aston Oxon 17 A10
Aston S Yorks 45 D8
Aston Shrops 33 C11
Aston Staffs 34 A3
Aston Telford 34 E2
Aston W Mid 35 G6
Aston Wokingham 18 C4
Aston Abbotts Bucks 28 F5
Aston Botterell Shrops 34 G2
Aston-By-Stone Staffs 34 B5
Aston Cantlow Warks 27 C8
Aston Clinton Bucks 28 G5
Aston Crews Hereford 26 F3
Aston Cross Glos 26 E6
Aston End Herts 29 F9
Aston Eyre Shrops 34 F2
Aston Fields Worcs 26 B6
Aston Flamville Leics 35 F10
Aston Ingham Hereford 26 F3
Aston juxta Mondrum Ches E 43 G9
Aston le Walls Northants 27 C11
Aston Magna Glos 27 E8
Aston Munslow Shrops 33 G11
Aston on Clun Shrops 33 G9
Aston-on-Trent Derbys 35 C10
Aston Rogers Shrops 33 E9
Aston Rowant Oxon 18 B4
Aston Sandford Bucks 28 H4
Aston Somerville Worcs 27 E7
Aston Subedge Glos 27 D8
Aston Tirrold Oxon 18 C2
Aston Upthorpe Oxon 18 C2
Astrop Northants 28 E2
Astwick C Beds 29 E9
Astwood M Keynes 28 D6
Astwood Worcs 26 C5
Astwood Bank Worcs 27 B7
Aswarby Lincs 37 B6
Aswardby Lincs 47 E7
Atch Lench Worcs 27 C7
Atcham Shrops 33 E11
Athelhampton Dorset 9 E6
Athelington Suff 31 A9
Athelney Som 8 B2
Athelstaneford E Loth 70 C4
Atherington Devon 6 D4
Atherstone Warks 35 F9
Atherstone on Stour Warks 27 C9
Atherton Gtr Man 43 B9
Atley Hill N Yorks 58 F3
Atlow Derbys 44 H6
Attadale Highld 86 H2
Attadale Ho. Highld 86 H2
Attenborough Notts 35 B11
Atterby Lincs 46 C3
Attercliffe S Yorks 45 D7
Attleborough Norf 38 F6
Attleborough Warks 35 F9
Attlebridge Norf 39 D7
Atwick E Yorks 53 D7
Atworth Wilts 16 E5
Aubourn Lincs 46 F3
Auchagallon N Ayrs 66 C1
Auchallater Aberds 82 E3
Aucharnie Aberds 89 D6
Auchattie Aberds 83 D8
Auchavan Angus 82 G3
Auchbreck Moray 82 A4
Auchenback E Renf 68 E4
Auchenbainzie Dumfries 60 D4
Auchenblae Aberds 83 F9
Auchenbrack Dumfries 60 D3
Auchenbreck Argyll 73 E9
Auchencairn Dumfries 55 D10
Auchencairn Dumfries 60 E5
Auchencairn N Ayrs 66 D3
Auchencrosh S Ayrs 54 B4
Auchencrow Borders 71 D7
Auchendinny Midloth 69 D11
Auchengray S Lanark 69 E8
Auchenhalrig Moray 88 B3
Auchenheath S Lanark 69 F7
Auchenlochan Argyll 73 F8
Auchenmalg Dumfries 54 D5
Auchensoul S Ayrs 66 G5
Auchentiber N Ayrs 67 B6
Auchertyre Highld 85 F13
Auchgourish Highld 81 B11
Auchincarroch W Dunb 68 B3
Auchindrain Argyll 73 C9
Auchindrean Highld 86 C4
Auchininna Aberds 89 D6
Auchinleck E Ayrs 67 D8
Auchinloch N Lanark 68 C5
Auchinroath Moray 88 C2
Auchintoul Aberds 83 B7
Auchiries Aberds 89 E10
Auchlee Aberds 83 D10
Auchleven Aberds 83 A8
Auchlochan S Lanark 69 G7
Auchlossan Aberds 83 C7
Auchlunies Aberds 83 D10
Auchlyne Stirling 75 E8
Auchmacoy Aberds 89 E9
Auchmair Moray 82 A5
Auchmantle Dumfries 54 C4
Auchmillan E Ayrs 67 D8
Auchmithie Angus 77 C9
Auchmuirbridge Fife 76 G5
Auchmull Angus 83 F7
Auchnacree Angus 77 A7
Auchnagallin Highld 87 H13
Auchnagatt Aberds 89 D9
Auchnaha Argyll 73 E8
Auchnashelloch Perth 75 F10
Aucholzie Aberds 82 D5
Auchrannie Angus 76 B5
Auchroisk Highld 82 A2
Auchronie Angus 82 E6
Auchterarder Perth 76 F2
Auchteraw Highld 80 C5
Auchterderran Fife 76 H5
Auchterhouse Angus 76 D6
Auchtermuchty Fife 76 F5
Auchterneed Highld 86 F7
Auchtertool Fife 69 A11
Auchtertyre Moray 88 C1
Auchtubh Stirling 75 E8
Auckengill Highld 94 D5
Auckley S Yorks 45 B10
Audenshaw Gtr Man 44 C3
Audlem Ches E 34 A2
Audley Staffs 43 G10
Audley End Essex 30 E5
Auds Aberds 89 B6
Aughton E Yorks 52 F3
Aughton Lancs 43 B6
Aughton Lancs 50 C1
Aughton S Yorks 45 D8
Aughton Wilts 17 F9
Aughton Park Lancs 43 B7
Auldearn Highld 87 F12
Aulden Hereford 25 C11
Auldgirth Dumfries 60 E5
Auldhame E Loth 70 B4
Auldhouse S Lanark 68 E5
Ault a'chruinn Highld 80 A1
Aultanrynie Highld 92 F6
Aultbea Highld 91 J13
Aultdearg Highld 86 E5
Aultgrishan Highld 91 J12
Aultguish Inn Highld 86 D6
Aultibea Highld 93 G13
Aultiphurst Highld 93 C11
Aultmore Moray 88 C4
Aultnagoire Highld 81 A7
Aultnamain Inn Highld 87 C9
Aultnaslat Highld 80 C3
Aulton Aberds 83 A8
Aundorach Highld 82 B1
Aunsby Lincs 36 B6
Auquhorthies Aberds 89 F8
Aust S Glos 16 C2
Austendike Lincs 37 C8
Austerfield S Yorks 45 C10
Austrey Warks 35 E8
Austwick N Yorks 50 C3
Authorpe Lincs 47 D8
Authorpe Row Lincs 47 E9
Avebury Wilts 17 E8
Aveley Thurrock 20 C2
Avening Glos 16 B5
Averham Notts 45 G11
Aveton Gifford Devon 5 G7
Avielochan Highld 81 B11
Aviemore Highld 81 B10
Avington Hants 10 A4
Avington W Berks 17 E10
Avoch Highld 87 F10
Avon Hants 9 E10
Avon Dassett Warks 27 D11
Avonbridge Falk 69 C8
Avonmouth Bristol 15 D11
Avonwick Devon 5 F8
Awbridge Hants 10 B2
Awhirk Dumfries 54 D3
Awkley S Glos 16 C2
Awliscombe Devon 7 F10
Awre Glos 26 H4
Awsworth Notts 35 A10
Axbridge Som 15 F10
Axford Hants 18 G3
Axford Wilts 17 D9
Axminster Devon 8 E1
Axmouth Devon 8 E1
Axton Flint 42 D4
Aycliff Kent 21 G10
Aycliffe Durham 58 D3
Aydon Northumb 62 G6
Aylburton Glos 16 A3
Ayle Northumb 57 B9
Aylesbeare Devon 7 G9
Aylesbury Bucks 28 G5
Aylesby NE Lincs 46 B6
Aylesford Kent 20 F4
Aylesham Kent 21 F9
Aylestone Leicester 36 E1
Aylmerton Norf 39 B7
Aylsham Norf 39 C7
Aylton Hereford 26 E3
Aymestrey Hereford 25 B11
Aynho Northants 28 E2
Ayot St Lawrence Herts 29 G8
Ayot St Peter Herts 29 G9
Ayr S Ayrs 66 D6
Aysgarth N Yorks 58 H1
Ayside Cumb 49 A3
Ayston Rutland 36 E4
Aythorpe Roding Essex 30 G2
Ayton Borders 71 D8
Aywick Shetland 96 E7
Azerley N Yorks 51 B8

B

Babbacombe Torbay 5 E10
Babbinswood Shrops 33 B9
Babcary Som 8 B4
Babel Carms 24 E5
Babell Flint 42 E4
Babraham Cambs 30 C2
Babworth Notts 45 D10
Bac W Isles 91 C9
Bachau Anglesey 40 B6
Back of Keppoch Highld 79 C9
Back Rogerton E Ayrs 67 D8
Backaland Orkney 95 E6
Backaskaill Orkney 95 C5
Backbarrow Cumb 49 A3
Backe Carms 23 E7
Backfolds Aberds 89 C10
Backford Ches W 43 E7
Backford Cross Ches W 43 E6
Backhill Aberds 89 E10
Backhill Aberds 89 E7
Backhill of Clackriach Aberds 89 D9
Backhill of Fortree Aberds 89 D9
Backhill of Trustach Aberds 83 D8
Backies Highld 93 J11
Backlass Highld 94 E4
Backwell N Som 15 E10
Backworth T&W 63 F9
Bacon End Essex 30 G3
Baconsthorpe Norf 39 B7
Bacton Hereford 25 E10
Bacton Norf 39 B9
Bacton Suff 31 B7
Bacton Green Suff 31 B7
Bacup Lancs 50 G4
Badachro Highld 85 A12
Badanloch Lodge Highld 93 F10
Badavanich Highld 86 F4
Badbury Swindon 17 C8
Badby Northants 28 C2
Badcall Highld 92 D5
Badcaul Highld 86 B3
Baddeley Green Stoke 44 G3
Baddesley Clinton Warks 27 A9
Baddesley Ensor Warks 35 F8
Baddidarach Highld 92 G3
Baddoch Aberds 82 E3
Baddock Highld 87 F10
Badenscoth Aberds 89 E7
Badenyon Aberds 82 B5
Badger Shrops 34 F3
Badger's Mount Kent 19 E11
Badgeworth Glos 26 G6
Badgworth Som 15 F9
Badicaul Highld 85 F12
Badingham Suff 31 B10
Badlesmere Kent 21 F7
Badlipster Highld 94 F4
Badluarach Highld 86 B2
Badminton S Glos 16 C5
Badnaban Highld 92 G3
Badninish Highld 87 B10
Badrallach Highld 86 B3
Badsey Worcs 27 D7
Badshot Lea Sur 18 G5
Badsworth W Yorks 45 A8
Badwell Ash Suff 30 B6
Bae Colwyn = Colwyn Bay Conwy 41 C10
Bag Enderby Lincs 47 E7
Bagby N Yorks 51 A10
Bagendon Glos 27 H7
Bagh a Chaisteil = Castlebay W Isles 84 J1
Bagh Mor W Isles 84 C3
Bagh Shiarabhagh W Isles 84 H2
Baghasdal W Isles 84 G2
Bagillt Flint 42 E5
Baginton Warks 27 A10
Baglan Neath 14 B3
Bagley Shrops 33 C10
Bagnall Staffs 44 G3
Bagnor W Berks 17 E11
Bagshot Sur 18 E6
Bagshot Wilts 17 E10
Bagthorpe Norf 38 B3
Bagthorpe Notts 45 G8
Bagworth Leics 35 E10
Bagwy Llydiart Hereford 25 F11
Bail Àrd Bhuirgh W Isles 91 B9
Bail' Iochdrach W Isles 84 C3
Bail Uachdraich W Isles 84 B3
Bail' Ur Tholastaidh W Isles 91 C10
Baildon W Yorks 51 F7
Baile W Isles 90 J4
Baile a Mhanaich W Isles 84 C2
Baile Ailein W Isles 91 E7
Baile an Truiseil W Isles 91 B8
Baile Boidheach Argyll 72 F6
Baile Glas W Isles 84 C3
Baile Mhartainn W Isles 84 A2
Baile Mhic Phail W Isles 84 A3
Baile Mor Argyll 78 J5
Baile Mor W Isles 84 B2
Baile na Creige W Isles 84 H1
Baile nan Cailleach W Isles 84 C2
Baile Raghaill W Isles 84 A2
Bailebeag Highld 81 B7
Baileyhead Cumb 61 F11
Bailiesward Aberds 88 E4
Baillieston Glasgow 68 D5
Bainbridge N Yorks 57 G11
Bainsford Falk 69 B7
Bainshole Aberds 88 E6
Bainton E Yorks 52 D5
Bainton Pboro 37 E6
Bairnkine Borders 62 B2
Baker Street Thurrock 20 C3
Baker's End Herts 29 G10
Bakewell Derbys 44 F6
Bala = Y Bala Gwyn 32 B5
Balachuirn Highld 85 D10
Balavil Highld 81 C9
Balbeg Highld 81 A6
Balbeg Highld 86 H7
Balbeggie Perth 76 E4
Balbithan Aberds 83 B9
Balbithan Ho. Aberds 83 B10
Balblair Highld 87 B8
Balblair Highld 87 E10
Balby S Yorks 45 B9
Balchladich Highld 92 F3
Balchraggan Highld 87 G8
Balchraggan Highld 87 H8
Balchrick Highld 92 D4
Balchrystie Fife 77 G7
Balcladaich Highld 80 A4
Balcombe W Sus 12 C2
Balcombe Lane W Sus 12 C2
Balcomie Fife 77 F9
Balcurvie Fife 76 G6
Baldersby N Yorks 51 B9
Baldersby St James N Yorks 51 B9
Balderstone Lancs 50 F2
Balderton Ches W 42 F6
Balderton Notts 46 G2
Baldhu Corn 3 E6
Baldinnie Fife 77 F7
Baldock Herts 29 E9
Baldovie Dundee 77 D7
Baldrine IoM 48 D4
Baldslow E Sus 13 E6
Baldwin IoM 48 D3
Baldwinholme Cumb 56 A5
Baldwin's Gate Staffs 34 A3
Bale Norf 38 B6
Balearn Aberds 89 C10
Balemartine Argyll 78 G2
Balephuil Argyll 78 G2
Balerno Edin 69 D10
Balevullin Argyll 78 G2
Balfield Angus 83 G7
Balfour Orkney 95 G5
Balfron Stirling 68 B4
Balfron Station Stirling 68 B4
Balgaveny Aberds 89 D6
Balgavies Angus 77 B8
Balgonar Fife 69 A9
Balgove Aberds 89 E8
Balgowan Highld 81 D8
Balgown Highld 85 B8
Balgrochan E Dunb 68 C5
Balgy Highld 85 C13
Balhaldie Stirling 75 G11
Balhalgardy Aberds 83 A9
Balham London 19 D9
Balhary Perth 76 C5
Baliasta Shetland 96 C8
Baligill Highld 93 C11
Balintore Angus 76 B5
Balintore Highld 87 D11
Balintraid Highld 87 D10
Balk N Yorks 51 A10
Balkeerie Angus 76 C6
Balkemback Angus 76 D6
Balkholme E Yorks 52 G3
Balkissock S Ayrs 54 A4
Ball Shrops 33 C9
Ball Haye Green Staffs 44 G3
Ball Hill Hants 17 E11
Ballabeg IoM 48 E2
Ballacannel IoM 48 D4
Ballachulish Highld 74 B3
Ballajora IoM 48 C4
Ballaleigh IoM 48 D3
Ballamodha IoM 48 E2
Ballantrae S Ayrs 54 A3
Ballaquine IoM 48 D4
Ballards Gore Essex 20 B6
Ballasalla IoM 48 C3
Ballasalla IoM 48 E2
Ballater Aberds 82 D5
Ballaugh IoM 48 C3
Ballaveare IoM 48 E3
Ballcorach Moray 82 A3
Ballechin Perth 76 B2
Balleigh Highld 87 C10
Ballencrieff E Loth 70 C3
Ballentoul Perth 81 G10
Ballidon Derbys 44 G6
Balliemore Argyll 73 E9
Balliemore Argyll 79 J11
Ballikinrain Stirling 68 B4
Ballimeanoch Argyll 73 B9
Ballimore Argyll 73 E8
Ballimore Stirling 75 F8
Ballinaby Argyll 64 B3
Ballindean Perth 76 E5
Ballingdon Suff 30 D5
Ballinger Common Bucks 18 A6
Ballingham Hereford 26 E2
Ballingry Fife 76 H4
Ballinlick Perth 76 C2
Ballinluig Perth 76 B2
Ballintuim Perth 76 B4
Balloch Angus 76 B6
Balloch Highld 87 G10
Balloch N Lanark 68 C6
Balloch W Dunb 68 B2
Ballochan Aberds 83 D7
Ballochford Moray 88 E3
Ballochmorrie S Ayrs 54 A5
Balls Cross W Sus 11 B8
Balls Green Essex 31 F7
Ballygown Argyll 78 G7
Ballygrant Argyll 64 B4
Ballyhaugh Argyll 78 F4
Balmacara Highld 85 F13
Balmacara Square Highld 85 F13
Balmaclellan Dumfries 55 B9
Balmacneil Perth 76 B2
Balmacqueen Highld 85 A9
Balmae Dumfries 55 E9
Balmaha Stirling 68 A3
Balmalcolm Fife 76 G6
Balmeanach Highld 85 D10
Balmedie Aberds 83 B11
Balmer Heath Shrops 33 B10
Balmerino Fife 76 E6
Balmerlawn Hants 10 D2
Balmichael N Ayrs 66 C2
Balmirmer Angus 77 D8
Balmore Highld 85 D7
Balmore Highld 86 H6
Balmore Highld 87 G11
Balmore Perth 76 B2
Balmule Fife 69 B11
Balmullo Fife 77 E7
Balmungie Highld 87 F10
Balnaboth Angus 82 G5
Balnabruaich Highld 87 E10
Balnabruich Highld 94 H3
Balnacoil Highld 93 H11
Balnacra Highld 86 G2
Balnafoich Highld 87 H9
Balnagall Highld 87 C11
Balnaguard Perth 76 B2
Balnahard Argyll 72 D3
Balnahard Argyll 78 H7
Balnain Highld 86 H7
Balnakeil Highld 92 C6
Balnaknock Highld 85 B9
Balnapaling Highld 87 E10
Balne N Yorks 52 H1
Balochroy Argyll 65 C8
Balone Fife 77 F7
Balornock Glasgow 68 D5
Balquharn Perth 76 D3
Balquhidder Stirling 75 E8
Balsall W Mid 35 H8
Balsall Common W Mid 35 H8
Balsall Hth. W Mid 35 G6
Balscott Oxon 27 D10
Balsham Cambs 30 C2
Baltasound Shetland 96 C8
Balterley Staffs 43 G10
Baltersan Dumfries 55 C7
Balthangie Aberds 89 C8
Baltonsborough Som 8 A4
Balvaird Highld 87 F8
Balvicar Argyll 72 B6
Balvraid Highld 85 G13
Balvraid Highld 87 H11
Bamber Bridge Lancs 50 G1
Bambers Green Essex 30 F2
Bamburgh Northumb 71 G10
Bamff Perth 76 B5
Bamford Derbys 44 D6
Bamford Gtr Man 44 A2
Bampton Cumb 57 E7
Bampton Devon 7 D8
Bampton Oxon 17 A10
Bampton Grange Cumb 57 E7
Banavie Highld 80 F3
Banbury Oxon 27 D11
Bancffosfelen Carms 23 E9
Banchory Aberds 83 D8
Banchory-Devenick Aberds 83 C11
Bancycapel Carms 23 E9
Bancyfelin Carms 23 E8
Bancyffordd Carms 23 C9
Bandirran Perth 76 D5
Banff Aberds 89 B6
Bangor Gwyn 41 C7
Bangor-is-y-coed Wrex 43 H6
Banham Norf 39 G6
Bank Hants 10 D1
Bank Newton N Yorks 50 D5
Bank Street Worcs 26 B3
Bankend Dumfries 60 G6
Bankfoot Perth 76 D3
Bankglen E Ayrs 67 E9
Bankhead Aberdeen 83 B10
Bankhead Aberds 83 C8
Banknock Falk 68 C6
Banks Cumb 61 G11
Banks Lancs 49 G3
Bankshill Dumfries 61 E7
Banningham Norf 39 C8
Banniskirk Ho. Highld 94 E3
Bannister Green Essex 30 F3
Bannockburn Stirling 69 A7
Banstead Sur 19 F9
Bantham Devon 5 G7
Banton N Lanark 68 C6
Banwell N Som 15 F9
Banyard's Green Suff 31 A9
Bapchild Kent 20 E6
Bar Hill Cambs 29 B10
Barabhas W Isles 91 C8
Barabhas Iarach W Isles 91 C8
Barabhas Uarach W Isles 91 B8
Barachandroman Argyll 79 J9
Barassie S Ayrs 66 C6
Baravullin Argyll 79 H11
Barbaraville Highld 87 D10
Barber Booth Derbys 44 D5
Barbieston S Ayrs 67 E7
Barbon Cumb 50 A2
Barbridge Ches E 43 G9
Barbrook Devon 6 B6
Barby Northants 28 A2
Barcaldine Argyll 74 C2
Barcheston Warks 27 E9
Barcombe E Sus 12 E3
Barcombe Cross E Sus 12 E3
Barden N Yorks 58 G2
Barden Scale N Yorks 51 D6
Bardennoch Dumfries 67 G8
Bardfield Saling Essex 30 F3
Bardister Shetland 96 F5
Bardney Lincs 46 F5
Bardon Leics 35 D10
Bardon Mill Northumb 62 G3
Bardowie E Dunb 68 C4
Bardrainney Invclyd 68 C2
Bardsea Cumb 49 B3
Bardsey W Yorks 51 E9
Bardwell Suff 30 A6
Bare Lancs 49 C4
Barfad Argyll 73 G7
Barford Norf 39 E7
Barford Warks 27 B9
Barford St John Oxon 27 E11
Barford St Martin Wilts 9 A9
Barford St Michael Oxon 27 E11
Barfrestone Kent 21 F9
Bargod = Bargoed Caerph 15 B7
Bargoed = Bargod Caerph 15 B7
Bargrennan Dumfries 54 B6
Barham Cambs 37 H7
Barham Kent 21 F9
Barham Suff 31 C8
Barharrow Dumfries 55 D9
Barhill Dumfries 55 C11
Barholm Lincs 37 D6
Barkby Leics 36 E2
Barkestone-le-Vale Leics 36 B3
Barkham Wokingham 18 E4
Barking London 19 C11
Barking Suff 31 C7
Barking Tye Suff 31 C7
Barkingside London 19 C11
Barkisland W Yorks 51 H6
Barkston Lincs 36 A5
Barkston N Yorks 51 F10
Barkway Herts 29 E10
Barlaston Staffs 34 B4
Barlavington W Sus 11 C8
Barlborough Derbys 45 E8
Barlby N Yorks 52 F2
Barlestone Leics 35 E10
Barley Herts 29 E10
Barley Lancs 50 E4
Barley Mow T&W 58 A3
Barleythorpe Rutland 36 E4
Barling Essex 20 C6
Barlow Derbys 45 E7
Barlow N Yorks 52 G2
Barlow T&W 63 G7
Barmby Moor E Yorks 52 E3
Barmby on the Marsh E Yorks 52 G2
Barmer Norf 38 B4
Barmoor Castle Northumb 71 G8
Barmoor Lane End Northumb 71 G9
Barmouth = Abermaw Gwyn 32 D2
Barmpton Darl 58 E4
Barmston E Yorks 53 D7
Barnack Pboro 37 E6
Barnacle Warks 35 G9
Barnard Castle Durham 58 E1
Barnard Gate Oxon 27 G11
Barnardiston Suff 30 D4
Barnbarroch Dumfries 55 D11
Barnburgh S Yorks 45 B8
Barnby Suff 39 G10
Barnby Dun S Yorks 45 B10
Barnby in the Willows Notts 46 G2
Barnby Moor Notts 45 D10
Barnes Street Kent 20 G3
Barnet London 19 B9
Barnetby le Wold N Lincs 46 B4
Barney Norf 38 B5
Barnham Suff 38 H4
Barnham W Sus 11 D8
Barnham Broom Norf 39 E6
Barnhead Angus 77 B9
Barnhill Ches W 43 G7
Barnhill Dundee 77 D7
Barnhill Moray 88 C1
Barnhills Dumfries 54 B2
Barningham Durham 58 E1
Barningham Suff 38 H5
Barnoldby le Beck NE Lincs 46 B6
Barnoldswick Lancs 50 E4
Barns Green W Sus 11 B10
Barnsley Glos 27 H7
Barnsley S Yorks 45 B7
Barnstaple Devon 6 C4
Barnston Essex 30 G3
Barnston Mers 42 D5
Barnstone Notts 36 B3
Barnt Green Worcs 27 A7
Barnton Ches W 43 E9
Barnton Edin 69 C10
Barnwell All Saints Northants 36 G6
Barnwell St Andrew Northants 36 G6
Barnwood Glos 26 G5
Barochreal Argyll 79 J11
Barons Cross Hereford 25 C11
Barr S Ayrs 66 G5
Barra Castle Aberds 83 A9
Barrachan Dumfries 54 E6
Barrack Aberds 89 D8
Barraglom W Isles 90 D6
Barrahormid Argyll 72 E6
Barran Argyll 79 J11
Barrapol Argyll 78 G2
Barras Aberds 83 E10
Barras Cumb 57 E10
Barrasford Northumb 62 F5
Barravullin Argyll 73 C7
Barregarrow IoM 48 D3
Barrhead E Renf 68 E3
Barrhill S Ayrs 54 A5
Barrington Cambs 29 D10
Barrington Som 8 C2
Barripper Corn 2 F5
Barrmill N Ayrs 67 A6
Barrock Highld 94 C4
Barrock Ho. Highld 94 D4
Barrow Lancs 50 F3
Barrow Rutland 36 D4
Barrow Suff 30 B4
Barrow Green Kent 20 E6
Barrow Gurney N Som 15 E11
Barrow Haven N Lincs 53 G
Barrow-in-Furness Cumb 49 C
Barrow Island Cumb 49 C
Barrow Nook Lancs 43 B
Barrow Street Wilts 9 A
Barrow upon Humber N Lincs 53 G
Barrow upon Soar Leics 36 D
Barrow upon Trent Derbys 35 C
Barroway Drove Norf 38 E
Barrowburn Northumb 62 B
Barrowby Lincs 36 B
Barrowcliff N Yorks 59 H1
Barrowden Rutland 36 E
Barrowford Lancs 50 F
Barrows Green Ches E 43 G
Barrows Green Cumb 57 H
Barrow's Green Mers 43 D
Barry Angus 77 D
Barry = Y Barri V Glam 15 E
Barry Island V Glam 15 E
Barsby Leics 36 D
Barsham Suff 39 G
Barston W Mid 35 H
Bartestree Hereford 26 D
Barthol Chapel Aberds 89 E
Barthomley Ches E 43 G1
Bartley Hants 10 C
Bartley Green W Mid 34 G
Bartlow Cambs 30 D
Barton Cambs 29 C1
Barton Ches W 43 G
Barton Glos 27 F
Barton Lancs 42 B
Barton Lancs 49 F
Barton N Yorks 58 F
Barton Oxon 28 H
Barton Torbay 5 E
Barton Warks 27 C
Barton Bendish Norf 38 E
Barton Hartshorn Bucks 28 E
Barton in Fabis Notts 35 B
Barton in the Beans Leics 35 E
Barton-le-Clay C Beds 29 E
Barton-le-Street N Yorks 52 B
Barton-le-Willows N Yorks 52 C
Barton Mills Suff 30
Barton on Sea Hants 9 E
Barton on the Heath Warks 27
Barton St David Som 8
Barton Seagrave Northants 36 H
Barton Stacey Hants 17 G
Barton Turf Norf 39 C
Barton-under-Needwood Staffs 35
Barton-upon-Humber N Lincs 52
Barton Waterside N Lincs 52 G
Barugh S Yorks 45
Barway Cambs 37 H
Barwell Leics 35 F
Barwick Herts 29 G
Barwick Som 8
Barwick in Elmet W Yorks 51
Baschurch Shrops 33 C
Bascote Warks 27 B
Basford Green Staffs 44
Bashall Eaves Lancs 50
Bashley Hants 9 E
Basildon Essex 20
Basingstoke Hants 18
Baslow Derbys 44
Bason Bridge Som 15
Bassaleg Newport 15
Bassenthwaite Cumb 56
Bassett Soton 10
Bassingbourn Cambs 29 D
Bassingfield Notts 36
Bassingham Lincs 46
Bassingthorpe Lincs 36
Basta Shetland 96
Baston Lincs 37
Bastwick Norf 39 D
Baswick Steer E Yorks 53
Batchworth Heath Herts 19
Batcombe Dorset 8
Batcombe Som 16
Bate Heath Ches E 43
Batford Herts 29
Bath Bath 16
Bathampton Bath 16
Bathealton Som 7
Batheaston Bath 16
Bathford Bath 16
Bathgate W Loth 69
Bathley Notts 45 G
Bathpool Corn 4
Bathpool Som 8
Bathville W Loth 69
Batley W Yorks 51
Batsford Glos 27
Battersby N Yorks 59
Battersea London 19
Battisborough Cross Devon 5
Battisford Suff 31
Battisford Tye Suff 31
Battle E Sus 12
Battle Powys 25
Battledown Glos 26
Battlefield Shrops 33
Battlesbridge Essex 20
Battlesden C Beds 28
Battlesea Green Suff 39
Battleton Som 7
Battram Leics 35
Battramsley Hants 10
Baughton Worcs 26
Baughurst Hants 18
Baulking Oxon 17
Baumber Lincs 46
Baunton Glos 17
Baverstock Wilts 9
Bawburgh Norf 39
Bawdeswell Norf 38
Bawdrip Som 15
Bawdsey Suff 31
Bawtry S Yorks 45
Baxenden Lancs 50
Baxterley Warks 35
Baybridge Hants 10

aycliff Cumb 49 B2
aydon Wilts 17 D9
ayford Herts 29 H10
ayford Som 8 B6
ayles Cumb 57 B9
aylham Suff 31 C8
aynard's Green Oxon 28 F2
ayston Hill Shrops 33 E10
aythorn End Essex 30 D4
ayton Worcs 26 A3
each Highld 79 F10
eachampton Bucks 28 E4
eachamwell Norf 38 E3
eachans Moray 87 G13
eacharr Argyll 65 D7
eachborough Kent 21 H8
eachley Glos 16 B2
eacon Devon 7 F10
eacon End Essex 30 F6
eacon Hill Sur 18 H5
eacon's Bottom Bucks 18 B4
eaconsfield Bucks 18 C6
eacrabhaic W Isles 90 H6
eadlam N Yorks 52 A2
eadlow C Beds 29 E8
eadnell Northumb 71 H11
eaford Devon 6 E4
eal N Yorks 51 G11
eal Northumb 71 F9
eamhurst Staffs 35 B6
eaminster Dorset 8 D3
eamish Durham 58 A3
eamsley N Yorks 51 D6
ean Kent 20 D2
eanacre Wilts 16 E6
eanley Northumb 62 B6
eaquoy Orkney 95 F4
ear Cross Bmouth 9 E9
eardwood Blackburn 50 G2
eare Green Sur 19 G8
earley Warks 27 B8
earnus Argyll 78 G6
earpark Durham 58 B3
earsbridge Northumb 62 H3
earsden E Dunb 68 C4
earsted Kent 20 F4
earstone Shrops 34 B3
earwood Hereford 25 C10
earwood Poole 9 E9
earwood W Mid 34 G6
eattock Dumfries 60 C6
eauchamp Roding Essex 30 G2
eauchief S Yorks 45 D7
eaufort Bl Gwent 25 G8
eaufort Castle Highld 87 G8
eaulieu Hants 10 D2
eauly Highld 87 G8
eaumaris Anglesey 41 C8
eaumont Cumb 61 H9
eaumont Essex 31 F8
eaumont Hill Darl 58 E3
eausale Warks 27 A9
eauworth Hants 10 B4
eaworthy Devon 6 G3
eazley End Essex 30 F4
ebington Mers 42 D6
ebside Northumb 63 E8
eccles Suff 39 F10
ecconsall Lancs 49 G4
eck Foot Cumb 57 G8
eck Hole N Yorks 59 F9
eck Row Suff 38 H2
eck Side Cumb 49 A2
eckbury Shrops 34 E3
eckenham London 19 E10
eckermet Cumb 56 F2
eckfoot Cumb 56 B2
eckfoot Cumb 56 F3
eckford Worcs 26 E6
eckhampton Wilts 17 E7
eckingham Lincs 46 G2
eckingham Notts 45 D11
eckington Som 16 F5
eckley E Sus 13 D7
eckley Hants 9 E11
eckley Oxon 28 G2
eckton London 19 C11
eckwithshaw N Yorks 51 D8
econtree London 19 C11
ed-y-coedwr Gwyn 32 C3
edale N Yorks 58 H3
edburn Durham 58 C2
edchester Dorset 9 C7
eddau Rhondda 14 C6
eddgelert Gwyn 41 F7
eddingham E Sus 12 F3
eddington London 19 E10
eddington Corner London 19 E10
edfield Suff 31 B9
edford Bedford 29 C7
edham W Sus 11 B9
edhampton Hants 10 D6
edingfield Suff 31 B8
edlam N Yorks 51 C8
edlington Northumb 63 E8
edlington Station Northumb 63 E8
edlinog M Tydf 14 A6
edminster Bristol 16 D2
edmond Herts 19 A7
ednall Staffs 34 D5
edrule Borders 62 B2
edstone Shrops 33 H9
edwas Caerph 15 C7
edworth Warks 35 G9
edworth Heath Warks 35 G9
eeby Leics 36 E2
eech Hants 18 H3
eech Staffs 34 B4
eech Hill Gtr Man 43 B8
eech Hill W Berks 18 E3
eechingstoke Wilts 17 F7
eedon W Berks 17 D11
eeford E Yorks 53 D7
eeley Derbys 44 F6
eelsby NE Lincs 46 B6
eenham W Berks 18 E2
eeny Corn 4 B2
eer Devon 7 H11
eer Hackett Dorset 8 C4
eercrocombe Som 8 B2
eesands Devon 5 G9
eesby Lincs 47 D8
eeson Devon 5 G9
eeston C Beds 29 D8
eeston Ches W 43 G8
eeston Norf 38 D5
eeston Notts 35 B11
eeston W Yorks 51 F8
eeston Regis Norf 39 A7
eeswing Dumfries 55 C11
eetham Cumb 49 B4
eetley Norf 38 D5
egbroke Oxon 27 G11
egelly Pembs 22 F6
eggar's Bush Powys 25 B9
eguildy Powys 33 H7
eighton Norf 39 E9
eighton S Yorks 45 D8
eighton Hill Derbys 44 G6
eith N Ayrs 66 A6
Bekesbourne Kent 21 F8
Belaugh Norf 39 D8
Belbroughton Worcs 34 H5
Belchamp Otten Essex 30 D5
Belchamp St Paul Essex 30 D4
Belchamp Walter Essex 30 D5
Belchford Lincs 46 E6
Belford Northumb 71 G10
Belhaven E Loth 70 C5
Belhelvie Aberds 83 B11
Belhinnie Aberds 82 A6
Bell Bar Herts 29 H9
Bell Busk N Yorks 50 D5
Bell End Worcs 34 H5
Bell o' th' Hill Ches W 43 H8
Bellabeg Aberds 82 B5
Bellamore S Ayrs 66 H5
Bellanoch Argyll 72 D6
Bellaty Angus 76 B5
Belleau Lincs 47 E8
Bellehiglash Moray 88 E1
Bellerby N Yorks 58 G2
Bellever Devon 5 D7
Belliehill Angus 77 A8
Bellingdon Bucks 28 H6
Bellingham Northumb 62 E4
Belloch Argyll 65 E7
Bellochantuy Argyll 65 E7
Bells Yew Green E Sus 12 C5
Bellsbank E Ayrs 67 F7
Bellshill N Lanark 68 D6
Bellshill Northumb 71 G10
Bellspool Borders 69 G10
Bellsquarry W Loth 69 D9
Belmaduthy Highld 87 F9
Belmesthorpe Rutland 36 D6
Belmont Blackburn 50 H2
Belmont London 19 E9
Belmont S Ayrs 66 D6
Belmont Shetland 96 C7
Belnacraig Aberds 82 B5
Belowda Corn 3 C8
Belper Derbys 45 H7
Belper Lane End Derbys 45 H7
Belsay Northumb 63 F7
Belses Borders 70 H4
Belsford Devon 5 F8
Belstead Suff 31 D8
Belston S Ayrs 67 D6
Belstone Devon 6 G5
Belthorn Blackburn 50 G3
Beltinge Kent 21 E8
Beltoft N Lincs 46 B2
Belton Leics 35 C10
Belton Lincs 36 B5
Belton N Lincs 45 B11
Belton Norf 39 E10
Belton in Rutland Rutland 36 E4
Beltring Kent 20 G3
Belts of Collonach Aberds 83 D8
Belvedere London 19 D11
Belvoir Leics 36 B4
Bembridge IoW 10 F5
Bemersyde Borders 70 G4
Bemerton Wilts 9 A10
Bempton E Yorks 53 B7
Ben Alder Lodge Highld 81 F7
Ben Armine Lodge Highld 93 H10
Ben Casgro W Isles 91 E9
Benacre Suff 39 G11
Benbuie Dumfries 60 D3
Benderloch Argyll 74 D2
Bendronaig Lodge Highld 86 H3
Benenden Kent 13 C7
Benfield Dumfries 54 C6
Bengate Norf 39 C9
Bengeworth Worcs 27 D7
Benhall Green Suff 31 B10
Benhall Street Suff 31 B10
Benholm Aberds 83 G10
Beningbrough N Yorks 51 D11
Benington Herts 29 F9
Benington Lincs 47 H7
Benllech Anglesey 41 B7
Benmore Argyll 73 E10
Benmore Stirling 75 E7
Benmore Lodge Highld 92 H6
Bennacott Corn 6 G1
Bennan N Ayrs 66 D2
Benniworth Lincs 46 D6
Benover Kent 20 G4
Bensham T&W 63 G8
Benslie N Ayrs 66 B6
Benson Oxon 18 B3
Bent Aberds 83 F8
Bent Gate Lancs 50 G3
Benthall Northumb 71 H11
Benthall Shrops 34 E2
Bentham Glos 26 G6
Benthoul Aberdeen 83 C10
Bentlawnt Shrops 33 E9
Bentley E Yorks 52 F6
Bentley Hants 18 G4
Bentley S Yorks 45 B9
Bentley Suff 31 E8
Bentley Warks 35 F8
Bentley Worcs 26 B6
Bentley Heath W Mid 35 H7
Benton Devon 6 C5
Bentpath Dumfries 61 D9
Bents W Loth 69 D8
Bentworth Hants 18 G3
Benvie Dundee 76 D6
Benwick Cambs 37 F9
Beoley Worcs 27 B7
Beoraidbeg Highld 79 B9
Bepton W Sus 11 C7
Berden Essex 29 F11
Bere Alston Devon 4 E5
Bere Ferrers Devon 4 E5
Bere Regis Dorset 9 E7
Berepper Corn 2 G5
Bergh Apton Norf 39 E9
Berinsfield Oxon 18 B2
Berkeley Glos 16 B3
Berkhamsted Herts 28 H6
Berkley Som 16 G5
Berkswell W Mid 35 H8
Bermondsey London 19 D10
Bernera Highld 85 F13
Bernice Argyll 73 D10
Bernisdale Highld 85 C9
Berrick Salome Oxon 18 B3
Berriedale Highld 94 H3
Berrier Cumb 56 D5
Berriew Powys 33 E7
Berrington Northumb 71 F9
Berrington Shrops 33 E11
Berrow Som 15 F9
Berrow Green Worcs 26 C4
Berry Down Cross Devon 6 B4
Berry Hill Glos 26 G2
Berry Hill Pembs 22 B5
Berry Pomeroy Devon 5 E9
Berryhillock Moray 88 B5
Berrynarbor Devon 6 B4
Bersham Wrex 42 H6
Berstane Orkney 95 G5
Berwick E Sus 12 F4
Berwick Bassett Wilts 17 D7
Berwick Hill Northumb 63 F7
Berwick St James Wilts 17 H7
Berwick St John Wilts 9 B8
Berwick St Leonard Wilts 9 A8
Berwick-upon-Tweed Northumb 71 E8
Bescar Lancs 43 A6
Besford Worcs 26 D6
Bessacarr S Yorks 45 B10
Bessels Leigh Oxon 17 A11
Bessingby E Yorks 53 C7
Bessingham Norf 39 B7
Bestbeech Hill E Sus 12 C5
Besthorpe Norf 39 F6
Besthorpe Notts 46 F2
Bestwood Nottingham 36 A1
Bestwood Village Notts 45 H9
Beswick E Yorks 52 E6
Betchworth Sur 19 G9
Bethania Ceredig 24 B2
Bethania Gwyn 41 E8
Bethania Gwyn 41 F9
Bethel Anglesey 40 C5
Bethel Gwyn 32 B5
Bethel Gwyn 41 D7
Bethersden Kent 13 B8
Bethesda Gwyn 41 D8
Bethesda Pembs 22 E5
Bethlehem Carms 24 F3
Bethnal Green London 19 C10
Betley Staffs 43 H10
Betsham Kent 20 D3
Betteshanger Kent 21 F10
Bettiscombe Dorset 8 E3
Bettisfield Wrex 33 B10
Betton Shrops 33 E9
Betton Shrops 34 B2
Bettws Bridgend 14 C5
Bettws Mon 25 G9
Bettws Newport 15 B8
Bettws Cedewain Powys 33 F7
Bettws Gwerfil Goch Denb 42 H3
Bettws Ifan Ceredig 23 B8
Bettws Newydd Mon 25 H10
Bettws-y-crwyn Shrops 33 G8
Bettyhill Highld 93 C10
Betws Carms 24 G3
Betws Bledrws Ceredig 23 A10
Betws-Garmon Gwyn 41 E7
Betws-y-Coed Conwy 41 E9
Betws-yn-Rhos Conwy 42 E2
Beulah Ceredig 23 B7
Beulah Powys 24 C6
Bevendean Brighton 12 F2
Bevercotes Notts 45 E10
Beverley E Yorks 52 F6
Beverston Glos 16 B5
Bevington Glos 16 B3
Bewaldeth Cumb 56 C4
Bewcastle Cumb 61 F11
Bewdley Worcs 34 H3
Bewerley N Yorks 51 C7
Bewholme E Yorks 53 D7
Bexhill E Sus 12 F6
Bexley London 19 D11
Bexleyheath London 19 D11
Bexwell Norf 38 E2
Beyton Suff 30 B6
Bhaltos W Isles 90 D5
Bhatarsaigh W Isles 84 J1
Bibury Glos 27 H8
Bicester Oxon 28 F2
Bickenhall Som 8 C1
Bickenhill W Mid 35 G7
Bicker Lincs 37 B8
Bickershaw Gtr Man 43 B9
Bickerstaffe Lancs 43 B7
Bickerton Ches E 43 G8
Bickerton N Yorks 51 D10
Bickington Devon 5 D8
Bickington Devon 6 C4
Bickleigh Devon 4 E6
Bickleigh Devon 7 F8
Bickleton Devon 6 C4
Bickley London 19 E11
Bickley Moss Ches W 43 H8
Bicknacre Essex 20 A4
Bicknoller Som 7 C10
Bicknor Kent 20 F5
Bickton Hants 9 C10
Bicton Shrops 33 D10
Bicton Shrops 33 G8
Bidborough Kent 12 B4
Biddenden Kent 13 C7
Biddenham Bedford 29 D7
Biddestone Wilts 16 D5
Biddisham Som 15 F9
Biddlesden Bucks 28 D3
Biddlestone Northumb 62 C5
Biddulph Staffs 44 G2
Biddulph Moor Staffs 44 G3
Bideford Devon 6 D3
Bidford-on-Avon Warks 27 C8
Bidston Mers 42 C5
Bielby E Yorks 52 E3
Bieldside Aberdeen 83 C10
Bierley IoW 10 G4
Bierley W Yorks 51 F7
Bierton Bucks 28 G5
Big Sand Highld 85 A12
Bigbury Devon 5 G7
Bigbury on Sea Devon 5 G7
Bigby Lincs 46 B4
Biggar Cumb 49 C1
Biggar S Lanark 69 G9
Biggin Derbys 44 G5
Biggin Derbys 44 H6
Biggin N Yorks 51 F11
Biggin Hill London 19 F11
Biggings Shetland 96 G3
Biggleswade C Beds 29 D8
Bighouse Highld 93 C11
Bighton Hants 10 A5
Bignor W Sus 11 C8
Bilberry Corn 3 C9
Bilborough Nottingham 35 A11
Bilbrook Som 7 B9
Bilbrough N Yorks 51 E11
Bilbster Highld 94 E4
Bildershaw Durham 58 D3
Bildeston Suff 30 D6
Billericay Essex 20 B3
Billesdon Leics 36 E3
Billesley Warks 27 C8
Billingborough Lincs 37 B7
Billinge Mers 43 B8
Billingford Norf 38 C6
Billingham Stockton 58 D5
Billinghay Lincs 46 G5
Billingley S Yorks 45 B8
Billingshurst W Sus 11 B9
Billingsley Shrops 34 G3
Billington C Beds 28 F6
Billington Lancs 50 F3
Billockby Norf 39 D10
Billy Row Durham 58 C2
Bilsborrow Lancs 49 F5
Bilsby Lincs 47 E8
Bilsham W Sus 11 D8
Bilsington Kent 13 C9
Bilson Green Glos 26 G3
Bilsthorpe Notts 45 F10
Bilsthorpe Moor Notts 45 G10
Bilston Midloth 69 D11
Bilston W Mid 34 F5
Bilstone Leics 35 E9
Bilting Kent 21 G7
Bilton E Yorks 53 F7
Bilton Northumb 63 B8
Bilton Warks 27 A11
Bilton in Ainsty N Yorks 51 E10
Bimbister Orkney 95 G4
Binbrook Lincs 46 C6
Binchester Blocks Durham 58 C3
Bincombe Dorset 8 F5
Bindal Highld 87 C12
Binegar Som 16 G3
Binfield Brack 18 D5
Binfield Hth. Oxon 18 D4
Bingfield Northumb 62 F5
Bingham Notts 36 B3
Bingley W Yorks 51 F7
Bings Heath Shrops 33 D11
Binham Norf 38 B5
Binley Hants 17 F11
Binley W Mid 35 H9
Binley Woods Warks 35 H9
Binniehill Falk 69 C7
Binsoe N Yorks 51 B8
Binstead IoW 10 E4
Binsted Hants 18 G4
Binton Warks 27 C8
Bintree Norf 38 C6
Binweston Shrops 33 E9
Birch Essex 30 G6
Birch Gtr Man 44 B2
Birch Green Essex 30 G6
Birch Heath Ches W 43 F8
Birch Hill Ches W 43 E8
Birch Vale Derbys 44 D4
Bircham Newton Norf 38 B3
Bircham Tofts Norf 38 B3
Birchanger Essex 30 F2
Birchencliffe W Yorks 51 H7
Bircher Hereford 25 B11
Birchgrove Cardiff 15 D7
Birchgrove Swansea 14 B3
Birchington Kent 21 E9
Birchmoor Warks 35 E8
Birchover Derbys 44 F6
Birchwood Lincs 46 F3
Birchwood Warr 43 C9
Bircotes Notts 45 C10
Birdbrook Essex 30 D4
Birdforth N Yorks 51 B10
Birdham W Sus 11 E7
Birdholme Derbys 45 F7
Birdingbury Warks 27 B11
Birdlip Glos 26 G6
Birds Edge W Yorks 44 B6
Birdsall N Yorks 52 C4
Birdsgreen Shrops 34 G3
Birdsmoor Gate Dorset 8 D2
Birdston E Dunb 68 C5
Birdwell S Yorks 45 B7
Birdwood Glos 26 G4
Birgham Borders 70 G6
Birkby N Yorks 58 F4
Birkdale Mers 49 H3
Birkenhead Mers 42 D6
Birkenhills Aberds 89 D7
Birkenshaw N Lanark 68 D5
Birkenshaw W Yorks 51 G8
Birkhall Aberds 82 D5
Birkhill Angus 76 D6
Birkhill Borders 61 B8
Birkholme Lincs 36 C5
Birkin N Yorks 51 G11
Birley Hereford 25 C11
Birling Kent 20 E3
Birling Northumb 63 C8
Birling Gap E Sus 12 G4
Birlingham Worcs 26 D6
Birmingham W Mid 35 G6
Birnam Perth 76 C3
Birse Aberds 83 D7
Birsemore Aberds 83 D7
Birstall Leics 36 E1
Birstall W Yorks 51 G8
Birstwith N Yorks 51 D8
Birthorpe Lincs 37 B7
Birtley Hereford 25 B10
Birtley Northumb 62 F4
Birtley T&W 63 H8
Birts Street Worcs 26 E4
Bisbrooke Rutland 36 F4
Biscathorpe Lincs 46 D6
Biscot Luton 29 F7
Bish Mill Devon 7 D6
Bisham Windsor 18 C5
Bishampton Worcs 26 C6
Bishop Auckland Durham 58 D3
Bishop Burton E Yorks 52 F5
Bishop Middleham Durham 58 C4
Bishop Monkton N Yorks 51 C9
Bishop Norton Lincs 46 C3
Bishop Sutton Bath 16 F2
Bishop Thornton N Yorks 51 C8
Bishop Wilton E Yorks 52 D3
Bishopbridge Lincs 46 C4
Bishopbriggs E Dunb 68 D5
Bishopmill Moray 88 B2
Bishops Cannings Wilts 17 E7
Bishop's Castle Shrops 33 G9
Bishop's Caundle Dorset 8 C5
Bishop's Cleeve Glos 26 F6
Bishops Frome Hereford 26 D3
Bishop's Green Essex 30 G3
Bishop's Hull Som 7 D11
Bishop's Itchington Warks 27 C10
Bishops Lydeard Som 7 D10
Bishops Nympton Devon 7 D6
Bishop's Offley Staffs 34 C3
Bishop'S Stortford Herts 29 F11
Bishop's Sutton Hants 10 A5
Bishop's Tachbrook Warks 27 B10
Bishops Tawton Devon 6 C4
Bishop's Waltham Hants 10 C4
Bishop's Wood Staffs 34 E4
Bishopsbourne Kent 21 F8
Bishopsteignton Devon 5 D10
Bishopstoke Hants 10 C3
Bishopston Swansea 23 H10
Bishopstone Bucks 28 G5
Bishopstone E Sus 12 F3
Bishopstone Hereford 25 D11
Bishopstone Swindon 17 C9
Bishopstone Wilts 9 B9
Bishopstrow Wilts 16 G5
Bishopswood Som 8 C1
Bishopsworth Bristol 16 E2
Bishopthorpe York 52 E1
Bishopton Darl 58 D4
Bishopton Dumfries 55 E7
Bishopton N Yorks 51 B9
Bishopton Renfs 68 C3
Bishopton Warks 27 C8
Bishton Newport 15 C9
Bisley Glos 26 H6
Bisley Sur 18 F6
Bispham Blackpool 49 E3
Bispham Green Lancs 43 A7
Bissoe Corn 3 E6
Bisterne Close Hants 9 D11
Bitchfield Lincs 36 C5
Bittadon Devon 6 B4
Bittaford Devon 5 F7
Bittering Norf 38 D5
Bitterley Shrops 34 H1
Bitterne Soton 10 C3
Bitteswell Leics 35 G11
Bitton S Glos 16 E3
Bix Oxon 18 C4
Bixter Shetland 96 H5
Blaby Leics 36 F1
Black Bourton Oxon 17 A9
Black Callerton T&W 63 G7
Black Clauchrie S Ayrs 54 A5
Black Corries Lodge Highld 74 B5
Black Crofts Argyll 74 D2
Black Dog Devon 7 F7
Black Heddon Northumb 62 F6
Black Lane Gtr Man 43 B10
Black Marsh Shrops 33 F9
Black Mount Argyll 74 C5
Black Notley Essex 30 F4
Black Pill Swansea 14 B2
Black Tar Pembs 22 F4
Black Torrington Devon 6 F3
Blackacre Dumfries 60 D6
Blackadder West Borders 71 E7
Blackawton Devon 5 F9
Blackborough Devon 7 F9
Blackborough End Norf 38 D2
Blackboys E Sus 12 D4
Blackbrook Derbys 45 H7
Blackbrook Mers 43 C8
Blackbrook Staffs 34 B3
Blackburn Aberds 83 B10
Blackburn Aberds 88 E5
Blackburn Blackburn 50 G2
Blackburn W Loth 69 D8
Blackcraig Dumfries 60 E3
Blackden Heath Ches E 43 E10
Blackdog Aberds 83 B11
Blackfell T&W 63 H8
Blackfield Hants 10 D3
Blackford Cumb 61 G9
Blackford Perth 75 G11
Blackford Som 8 B5
Blackford Som 15 G10
Blackfordby Leics 35 D9
Blackgang IoW 10 G3
Blackhall Colliery Durham 58 C5
Blackhall Mill T&W 63 H7
Blackhall Rocks Durham 58 C5
Blackham E Sus 12 C3
Blackhaugh Borders 70 G3
Blackheath Essex 31 F7
Blackheath Suff 31 A11
Blackheath Sur 19 G7
Blackheath W Mid 34 G5
Blackhill Aberds 89 C10
Blackhill Aberds 89 D10
Blackhill Highld 85 C8
Blackhills Highld 87 F12
Blackhills Moray 88 C2
Blackhorse S Glos 16 D3
Blackland Wilts 17 E7
Blacklaw Aberds 89 C6
Blackley Gtr Man 44 B2
Blacklunans Perth 76 A4
Blackmill Bridgend 14 C5
Blackmoor Hants 11 A6
Blackmoor Gate Devon 6 B5
Blackmore Essex 20 A3
Blackmore End Essex 30 E4
Blackmore End Herts 29 G8
Blackness Falk 69 C9
Blacknest Hants 18 G4
Blacko Lancs 50 E4
Blackpool Blackpool 49 F3
Blackpool Devon 5 G9
Blackpool Pembs 22 E5
Blackpool Gate Cumb 61 F11
Blackridge W Loth 69 D7
Blackrock Argyll 64 B4
Blackrock Mon 25 G9
Blackrod Gtr Man 43 A9
Blackshaw Dumfries 60 G6
Blackshaw Head W Yorks 50 G5
Blacksmith's Green Suff 31 B8
Blackstone W Sus 11 C11
Blackthorn Oxon 28 G3
Blackthorpe Suff 30 B6
Blacktoft E Yorks 52 G4
Blacktop Aberdeen 83 C10
Blacktown Newport 15 C8
Blackwall Tunnel London 19 C10
Blackwater Corn 2 E6
Blackwater Hants 18 F5
Blackwater IoW 10 F4
Blackwaterfoot N Ayrs 66 D1
Blackwell Darl 58 E3
Blackwell Derbys 44 E5
Blackwell Derbys 45 G8
Blackwell W Sus 12 C2
Blackwell Warks 27 D9
Blackwell Worcs 26 A6
Blackwood = Coed Duon Caerph 15 B7
Blackwood S Lanark 68 F6
Blackwood Hill Staffs 44 G3
Blacon Ches W 43 F6
Bladnoch Dumfries 55 D7
Bladon Oxon 27 G11
Blaen-gwynfi Neath 14 B4
Blaen-waun Carms 23 D7
Blaen-y-coed Carms 23 D8
Blaen-y-Cwm Denb 32 B6
Blaen-y-cwm Gwyn 32 C3
Blaen-y-cwm Powys 33 C6
Blaenannerch Ceredig 23 B7
Blaenau Ffestiniog Gwyn 41 F9
Blaenavon Torf 25 H9
Blaencelyn Ceredig 23 A8
Blaendyryn Powys 24 E6
Blaenffos Pembs 22 C6
Blaengarw Bridgend 14 B5
Blaengwrach Neath 24 H5
Blaenpennal Ceredig 24 B3
Blaenplwyf Ceredig 32 H1
Blaenporth Ceredig 23 B7
Blaenrhondda Rhondda 14 A5
Blaenycwm Ceredig 32 H4
Blagdon N Som 15 F11
Blagdon Torbay 5 E9
Blagdon Hill Som 7 E11
Blagill Cumb 57 B9
Blaguegate Lancs 43 B7
Blaich Highld 80 F2
Blain Highld 79 E9
Blaina Bl Gwent 25 H9
Blair Atholl Perth 81 G10
Blair Drummond Stirling 75 H10
Blairbeg N Ayrs 66 C3
Blairdaff Aberds 83 B8
Blairglas Argyll 68 B2
Blairgowrie Perth 76 C4
Blairhall Fife 69 B9
Blairingone Perth 76 H2
Blairland N Ayrs 66 B6
Blairlogie Stirling 75 H11
Blairlomond Argyll 74 H4
Blairmore Argyll 73 E10
Blairnamarrow Moray 82 B4
Blairquhosh Stirling 68 B4
Blair's Ferry Argyll 73 G8
Blairskaith E Dunb 68 C4
Blaisdon Glos 26 G4
Blakebrook Worcs 34 H4
Blakedown Worcs 34 H4
Blakelaw Borders 70 G6
Blakeley Staffs 34 F4
Blakeley Lane Staffs 44 H3
Blakemere Hereford 25 D10
Blakeney Glos 26 H3
Blakeney Norf 38 A6
Blakenhall Ches E 43 H10
Blakenhall W Mid 34 F5
Blakeshall Worcs 34 G4
Blakesley Northants 28 C3
Blanchland Northumb 57 A11
Bland Hill N Yorks 51 D8
Blandford Forum Dorset 9 D7
Blandford St Mary Dorset 9 D7
Blanefield Stirling 68 C4
Blankney Lincs 46 F4
Blantyre S Lanark 68 E5
Blar a'Chaorainn Highld 80 G3
Blaran Argyll 73 B7
Blarghour Argyll 73 B8
Blarmachfoldach Highld 80 G2
Blarnalearoch Highld 86 B4
Blashford Hants 9 D10
Blaston Leics 36 F4
Blatherwycke Northants 36 F5
Blawith Cumb 56 H4
Blaxhall Suff 31 C10
Blaxton S Yorks 45 B10
Blaydon T&W 63 G7
Bleadon N Som 15 F9
Bleak Hey Nook Gtr Man 44 B4
Blean Kent 21 E8
Bleasby Lincs 46 D5
Bleasby Notts 45 H11
Bleasdale Lancs 50 E1
Bleatarn Cumb 57 E9
Blebocraigs Fife 77 F7
Bleddfa Powys 25 B9
Bledington Glos 27 F9
Bledlow Bucks 18 A4
Bledlow Ridge Bucks 18 B4
Blegbie E Loth 70 D3
Blencarn Cumb 57 C8
Blencogo Cumb 56 B3
Blendworth Hants 10 C6
Blenheim Park Norf 38 B4
Blennerhasset Cumb 56 B3
Blervie Castle Moray 87 F13
Bletchingdon Oxon 28 G2
Bletchingley Sur 19 F10
Bletchley M Keynes 28 E5
Bletchley Shrops 34 B2
Bletherston Pembs 22 D5
Bletsoe Bedford 29 C7
Blewbury Oxon 18 C2
Blickling Norf 39 C7
Blidworth Notts 45 G9
Blindburn Northumb 62 B4
Blindcrake Cumb 56 C3
Blindley Heath Sur 19 G10
Blisland Corn 4 D2
Bliss Gate Worcs 26 A4
Blissford Hants 9 C10
Blisworth Northants 28 C4
Blithbury Staffs 35 C6
Blitterlees Cumb 56 A3
Blo' Norton Norf 38 H6
Blockley Glos 27 E8
Blofield Norf 39 E9
Blofield Heath Norf 39 D9
Bloomfield Borders 61 A11
Blore Staffs 44 H5
Blount's Green Staffs 35 B6
Blowick Mers 49 H3
Bloxham Oxon 27 E11
Bloxholm Lincs 46 G4
Bloxwich W Mid 34 E5
Bloxworth Dorset 9 E7
Blubberhouses N Yorks 51 D7
Blue Anchor Som 7 B9
Blue Anchor Swansea 23 G10
Blue Row Essex 31 G7
Blundeston Suff 39 F11
Blunham C Beds 29 C8
Blunsdon St Andrew Swindon 17 C8
Bluntington Worcs 26 A5
Bluntisham Cambs 29 A10
Blunts Corn 4 E4
Blyborough Lincs 46 C3
Blyford Suff 39 H10
Blymhill Staffs 34 D4
Blyth Northumb 63 E9
Blyth Notts 45 D10
Blyth Bridge Borders 69 F10
Blythburgh Suff 39 H10
Blythe Borders 70 F4
Blythe Bridge Staffs 34 A5
Blyton Lincs 46 C2
Boarhills Fife 77 F8
Boarhunt Hants 10 D5
Boars Head Gtr Man 43 B8
Boars Hill Oxon 17 A11
Boarshead E Sus 12 C4
Boarstall Bucks 28 G3
Boasley Cross Devon 6 G3
Boat of Garten Highld 81 B11
Boath Highld 87 D8
Bobbing Kent 20 E5
Bobbington Staffs 34 F4
Bobbingworth Essex 30 H2
Bocaddon Corn 4 F2
Bochastle Stirling 75 G9
Bocking Essex 30 F4
Bocking Churchstreet Essex 30 F4
Boddam Aberds 89 D11
Boddam Shetland 96 M5
Boddington Glos 26 F5
Bodedern Anglesey 40 B5
Bodelwyddan Denb 42 E3
Bodenham Hereford 26 C2
Bodenham Wilts 9 B10
Bodenham Moor Hereford 26 C2
Bodermid Gwyn 40 H3
Bodewryd Anglesey 40 A5
Bodfari Denb 42 E3
Bodffordd Anglesey 40 C6
Bodham Norf 39 A7
Bodiam E Sus 13 D6
Bodicote Oxon 27 E11
Bodieve Corn 3 B8
Bodinnick Corn 4 F2
Bodle Street Green E Sus 12 E5
Bodmin Corn 4 E1
Bodney Norf 38 F4
Bodorgan Anglesey 40 D5
Bodsham Kent 21 G8
Boduan Gwyn 40 G5
Bodymoor Heath Warks 35 F7
Bogallan Highld 87 F9
Bogbrae Aberds 89 E10
Bogend Borders 70 F6
Bogend S Ayrs 67 C6
Boghall W Loth 69 D8
Boghead S Lanark 68 F6
Bogmoor Moray 88 B3
Bogniebrae Aberds 88 D5
Bognor Regis W Sus 11 E8
Bograxie Aberds 83 B9
Bogside N Lanark 69 E7
Bogton Aberds 89 C6
Bogue Dumfries 55 A9
Bohenie Highld 80 E4
Bohortha Corn 3 F7
Bohuntine Highld 80 E4
Boirseam W Isles 90 J5
Bojewyan Corn 2 F2
Bolam Durham 58 D2
Bolam Northumb 62 E6
Bolberry Devon 5 H7
Bold Heath Mers 43 D8
Boldon T&W 63 G9
Boldon Colliery T&W 63 G9
Boldre Hants 10 E2
Boldron Durham 58 E1
Bole Notts 45 D11
Bolehill Derbys 44 G6
Boleside Borders 70 G3
Bolham Devon 7 E8
Bolham Water Devon 7 E10
Bolingey Corn 3 D6
Bollington Ches E 44 E3
Bollington Cross Ches E 44 E3
Bolney W Sus 12 D1
Bolnhurst Bedford 29 C7
Bolshan Angus 77 B9
Bolsover Derbys 45 E8
Bolsterstone S Yorks 44 C6
Bolstone Hereford 26 E2
Boltby N Yorks 58 H5
Bolter End Bucks 18 B4
Bolton Cumb 57 D8
Bolton E Loth 70 C4
Bolton E Yorks 52 D3
Bolton Gtr Man 43 B10
Bolton Northumb 63 B7
Bolton Abbey N Yorks 51 D6
Bolton Bridge N Yorks 51 D6
Bolton-by-Bowland Lancs 50 E3
Bolton-le-Sands Lancs 49 C4
Bolton Low Houses Cumb 56 B4
Bolton-on-Swale N Yorks 58 G3
Bolton Percy N Yorks 51 E11
Bolton Town End Lancs 49 C4
Bolton upon Dearne S Yorks 45 B8
Boltonfellend Cumb 61 G10
Boltongate Cumb 56 B4
Bolventor Corn 4 D2
Bomere Heath Shrops 33 D10
Bon-y-maen Swansea 14 B2
Bonar Bridge Highld 87 B9
Bonawe Argyll 74 D3
Bonby N Lincs 46 A4
Boncath Pembs 23 C7
Bonchester Bridge Borders 61 B11
Bonchurch IoW 10 G4
Bondleigh Devon 6 F5
Bonehill Devon 5 D8
Bonehill Staffs 35 E7
Bo'ness Falk 69 B8
Bonhill W Dunb 68 C2
Boningale Shrops 34 E4
Bonjedward Borders 62 A2
Bonkle N Lanark 69 E7
Bonnavoulin Highld 79 F8
Bonnington Edin 69 D10
Bonnington Kent 13 C9
Bonnybank Fife 76 G6
Bonnybridge Falk 69 B7
Bonnykelly Aberds 89 C8
Bonnyrigg and Lasswade Midloth 70 D2
Bonnyton Aberds 89 E6
Bonnyton Angus 76 D6
Bonnyton Angus 77 B9
Bonsall Derbys 44 G6
Bonskeid House Perth 75 A11
Bont Mon 25 G10
Bont-Dolgadfan Powys 32 E4
Bont-goch Ceredig 32 G2
Bont-newydd Conwy 42 E3
Bont Newydd Gwyn 32 C3
Bont Newydd Gwyn 41 F9
Bontddu Gwyn 32 D2
Bonthorpe Lincs 47 E8
Bontnewydd Ceredig 24 B3
Bontnewydd Gwyn 40 E6
Bontuchel Denb 42 G3
Bonvilston V Glam 14 D6
Booker Bucks 18 B5
Boon Borders 70 F4
Boosbeck Redcar 59 E7
Boot Cumb 56 F3
Boot Street Suff 31 D9
Booth W Yorks 50 G6
Booth Wood W Yorks 50 H6
Boothby Graffoe Lincs 46 G3
Boothby Pagnell Lincs 36 B5
Boothen Stoke 34 A4
Boothferry E Yorks 52 G3
Boothville Northants 28 B4
Bootle Cumb 56 H3
Bootle Mers 42 C6
Booton Norf 39 C7
Boquhan Stirling 68 B4
Boraston Shrops 26 A3
Borden Kent 20 E5
Borden W Sus 11 B7
Bordley N Yorks 50 C5
Bordon Hants 18 H5
Bordon Camp Hants 18 H4
Boreham Essex 30 H4
Boreham Wilts 16 G5
Boreham Street E Sus 12 E5
Borehamwood Herts 19 B8
Boreland Dumfries 61 D7
Boreland Stirling 75 D8
Borgh W Isles 84 H1
Borgh W Isles 90 J4
Borghastan W Isles 90 C7
Borgie Highld 93 D9
Borgue Dumfries 55 E9
Borgue Highld 94 H3
Borley Essex 30 D5
Bornais W Isles 84 F2
Bornesketaig Highld 85 A8
Borness Dumfries 55 E9
Borough Green Kent 20 F3
Boroughbridge N Yorks 51 C9
Borras Head Wrex 42 G6
Borreraig Highld 84 C6
Borrobol Lodge Highld 93 G11
Borrowash Derbys 35 B10
Borrowby N Yorks 58 H5
Borrowdale Cumb 56 E4
Borrowfield Aberds 83 D10
Borth Ceredig 32 F2
Borth-y-Gest Gwyn 41 G7
Borthwickbrae Borders 61 B10
Borthwickshiels Borders 61 B10
Borve Highld 85 D9
Borve Lodge W Isles 90 H5
Borwick Lancs 49 B5
Bosavern Corn 2 F2
Bosbury Hereford 26 D3
Boscastle Corn 4 B2
Boscombe Bmouth 9 E10
Boscombe Wilts 17 H9
Boscoppa Corn 3 D9
Bosham W Sus 11 D7
Bosherston Pembs 22 G4
Boskenna Corn 2 G3
Bosley Ches E 44 F3
Bossall N Yorks 52 C3
Bossiney Corn 4 C1
Bossingham Kent 21 G8
Bossington Som 7 B7
Bostock Green Ches W 43 F9
Boston Lincs 37 A9
Boston Long Hedges Lincs 47 H7
Boston Spa W Yorks 51 E10
Boston West Lincs 46 H6
Boswinger Corn 3 E8
Botallack Corn 2 F2
Botany Bay London 19 B9
Botcherby Cumb 61 H10
Botcheston Leics 35 E10
Botesdale Suff 38 H6
Bothal Northumb 63 E8
Bothamsall Notts 45 E10
Bothel Cumb 56 C3
Bothenhampton Dorset 8 E3
Bothwell S Lanark 68 E6
Botley Bucks 18 A6
Botley Hants 10 C4
Botley Oxon 27 H11
Botolph Claydon Bucks 28 F4
Botolphs W Sus 11 D10
Bottacks Highld 86 E7
Bottesford Leics 36 B4
Bottesford N Lincs 46 B2
Bottisham Cambs 30 B2
Bottlesford Wilts 17 F8
Bottom Boat W Yorks 51 G9
Bottom House Staffs 44 G4
Bottom o' th' Moor Gtr Man 43 A9
Bottom of Hutton Lancs 49 G4
Bottomcraig Fife 76 E6
Botusfleming Corn 4 E5
Botwnnog Gwyn 40 G4
Bough Beech Kent 19 G11
Boughrood Powys 25 E8
Boughspring Glos 16 B2
Boughton Norf 38 E2
Boughton Northants 28 B4
Boughton Notts 45 F10
Boughton Aluph Kent 21 G7
Boughton Lees Kent 21 G7
Boughton Malherbe Kent 20 G5
Boughton Monchelsea Kent 20 F4
Boughton Street Kent 21 F7
Boulby Redcar 59 E8
Boulden Shrops 33 G11
Boulmer Northumb 63 B8
Boulston Pembs 22 E4
Boultenstone Aberds 82 B6
Boultham Lincs 46 F3
Bourn Cambs 29 C10
Bourne Lincs 37 C6
Bourne End Bucks 18 C5
Bourne End C Beds 28 D6
Bourne End Herts 29 H7
Bournemouth Bmouth 9 E9
Bournes Green Glos 16 A6
Bournes Green Southend 20 C6
Bournheath Worcs 26 A6
Bournmoor Durham 58 A4
Bournville W Mid 34 G6
Bourton Dorset 9 A6
Bourton N Som 15 E9
Bourton Oxon 17 C9
Bourton Shrops 34 F1
Bourton on Dunsmore Warks 27 A11
Bourton on the Hill Glos 27 E8
Bourton-on-the-Water Glos 27 F8
Bousd Argyll 78 E5
Boustead Hill Cumb 61 H8
Bouth Cumb 56 H5
Bouthwaite N Yorks 51 B7
Boveney Bucks 18 D6
Boverton V Glam 14 E5
Bovey Tracey Devon 5 D9
Bovingdon Herts 19 A7
Bovingdon Green Bucks 18 C5
Bovingdon Green Herts 19 A7
Bovinger Essex 30 H2
Bovington Camp Dorset 9 F7
Bow Borders 70 F3
Bow Devon 7 F6
Bow Orkney 95 J4
Bow Brickhill M Keynes 28 E6
Bow of Fife Fife 76 F6
Bow Street Ceredig 32 G2
Bowbank Durham 57 D11
Bowburn Durham 58 C4
Bowcombe IoW 10 F3
Bowd Devon 7 G10
Bowden Borders 70 G4
Bowden Devon 5 G9
Bowden Hill Wilts 16 E6
Bowderdale Cumb 57 F8
Bowdon Gtr Man 43 D10
Bower Northumb 62 E3
Bower Hinton Som 8 C3
Bowerchalke Wilts 9 B9
Bowerhill Wilts 16 E6
Bowermadden Highld 94 D4
Bowers Gifford Essex 20 C4
Bowershall Fife 69 A9
Bowertower Highld 94 D4
Bowes Durham 57 E11
Bowgreave Lancs 49 E4
Bowgreen Gtr Man 43 D10
Bowhill Borders 70 H3
Bowhouse Dumfries 60 G6
Bowland Bridge Cumb 56 H6
Bowley Hereford 26 C2
Bowlhead Green Sur 18 H6
Bowling W Dunb 68 C3
Bowling W Yorks 51 F7
Bowling Bank Wrex 43 H6
Bowling Green Worcs 26 C5
Bowmanstead Cumb 56 G5
Bowmore Argyll 64 C4
Bowness-on-Solway Cumb 61 G8
Bowness-on-Windermere Cumb 56 G6
Bowsden Northumb 71 F8
Bowside Lodge Highld 93 C11
Bowston Cumb 57 G6
Bowthorpe Norf 39 E7
Box Glos 16 A5
Box Wilts 16 E5
Box End Bedford 29 D7
Boxbush Glos 26 G4
Boxford Suff 30 D6
Boxford W Berks 17 D11
Boxgrove W Sus 11 D8
Boxley Kent 20 F4
Boxmoor Herts 29 H7
Boxted Essex 30 E6
Boxted Suff 30 C5
Boxted Cross Essex 31 E7
Boxted Heath Essex 31 E7
Boxworth Cambs 29 B10
Boxworth End Cambs 29 B10
Boyden Gate Kent 21 E9
Boylestone Derbys 35 B7
Boyndie Aberds 89 B6
Boynton E Yorks 53 C7
Boysack Angus 77 C9
Boyton Corn 6 G2
Boyton Suff 31 D10
Boyton Wilts 16 H6
Boyton Cross Essex 30 H3
Boyton End Suff 30 D4
Bozeat Northants 28 C6
Braaid IoM 48 E3
Braal Castle Highld 94 D3
Brabling Green Suff 31 B9
Brabourne Kent 13 B9
Brabourne Lees Kent 13 B9
Brabster Highld 94 D5
Bracadale Highld 85 E8
Bracara Highld 79 B10
Braceborough Lincs 37 D6
Bracebridge Lincs 46 F3
Bracebridge Heath Lincs 46 F3
Bracebridge Low Fields Lincs 46 F3
Braceby Lincs 36 B6
Bracewell Lancs 50 E4
Brackenfield Derbys 45 G7
Brackenthwaite Cumb 56 B4
Brackenthwaite N Yorks 51 D8
Bracklesham W Sus 11 E7
Brackletter Highld 80 E3
Brackley Argyll 65 D8
Brackley Northants 28 E2
Brackloch Highld 92 G4
Bracknell Brack 18 E5
Braco Perth 75 G11
Bracobrae Moray 88 C5
Bracon Ash Norf 39 E7
Bracorina Highld 79 B10
Bradbourne Derbys 44 G6
Bradbury Durham 58 D4

Bradda IoM 48 F1
Bradden Northants 28 D3
Braddock Corn 4 E2
Bradeley Stoke 44 G2
Bradenham Bucks 18 B5
Bradenham Norf 38 E5
Bradenstoke Wilts 17 D7
Bradfield Essex 31 E8
Bradfield Norf 39 B8
Bradfield W Berks 18 D3
Bradfield Combust Suff 30 C5
Bradfield Green Ches E 43 G9
Bradfield Heath Essex 31 F8
Bradfield St Clare Suff 30 C6
Bradfield St George Suff 30 B6
Bradford Corn 4 D2
Bradford Derbys 44 F6
Bradford Devon 6 F3
Bradford Northumb 71 G10
Bradford W Yorks 51 F7
Bradford Abbas Dorset 8 C4
Bradford Leigh Wilts 16 E5
Bradford-on-Avon Wilts 16 E5
Bradford-on-Tone Som 7 D10
Bradford Peverell Dorset 8 E5
Brading IoW 10 F5
Bradley Derbys 44 H6
Bradley Hants 18 G3
Bradley NE Lincs 46 B6
Bradley Staffs 34 D4
Bradley W Mid 34 F5
Bradley W Yorks 51 G7
Bradley Green Worcs 26 B6
Bradley in the Moors Staffs 35 A6
Bradlow Hereford 26 E4
Bradmore Notts 36 B1
Bradmore W Mid 34 F4
Bradninch Devon 7 F9
Bradnop Staffs 44 G4
Bradpole Dorset 8 E3
Bradshaw Gtr Man 43 A10
Bradshaw W Yorks 44 A4
Bradstone Devon 4 C4
Bradwall Green Ches E 43 F10
Bradway S Yorks 45 D7
Bradwell Derbys 44 D5
Bradwell Essex 30 F5
Bradwell M Keynes 28 E5
Bradwell Norf 39 E11
Bradwell Staffs 44 H2
Bradwell Grove Oxon 27 H9
Bradwell on Sea Essex 31 H7
Bradwell Waterside Essex 30 H6
Bradworthy Devon 6 E2
Bradworthy Cross Devon 6 E2
Brae Dumfries 60 F4
Brae Highld 91 J13
Brae Highld 92 J7
Brae Shetland 96 G5
Brae of Achnahaird Highld 92 H3
Brae Roy Lodge Highld 80 D5
Braeantra Highld 87 D8
Braedownie Angus 82 F4
Braefield Highld 86 H7
Braegrum Perth 76 E3
Braehead Dumfries 55 D7
Braehead Orkney 95 D5
Braehead Orkney 95 H6
Braehead S Lanark 69 E8
Braehead S Lanark 69 G7
Braehead of Lunan Angus 77 B9
Braehoulland Shetland 96 F4
Braehungie Highld 94 G3
Braelangwell Lodge Highld 87 B8
Braemar Aberds 82 D3
Braemore Highld 86 D4
Braemore Highld 94 G2
Braes of Enzie Moray 88 C3
Braeside Invclyd 73 F11
Braeswick Orkney 95 E7
Braewick Shetland 96 H5
Brafferton Darl 58 D3
Brafferton N Yorks 51 B10
Brafield-on-the-Green Northants 28 C5
Bragar W Isles 91 C7
Bragbury End Herts 29 F9
Bragleenmore Argyll 74 E2
Braichmelyn Gwyn 41 D8
Braid Edin 69 D11
Braides Lancs 49 D4
Braidley N Yorks 50 A6
Braidwood S Lanark 69 F7
Braigo Argyll 64 B3
Brailsford Derbys 35 A8
Brainshaugh Northumb 63 C8
Braintree Essex 30 F4
Braiseworth Suff 31 A8
Braishfield Hants 10 B2
Braithwaite Cumb 56 D4
Braithwaite S Yorks 45 A10
Braithwaite W Yorks 50 E6
Braithwell S Yorks 45 C9
Bramber W Sus 11 C10
Bramcote Notts 35 B11
Bramcote Warks 35 G10
Bramdean Hants 10 B5
Bramerton Norf 39 E8
Bramfield Herts 29 G9
Bramfield Suff 31 A10
Bramford Suff 31 D8
Bramhall Gtr Man 44 D2
Bramham W Yorks 51 E10
Bramhope W Yorks 51 E8
Bramley Hants 18 F3
Bramley S Yorks 45 C8
Bramley Sur 19 G7
Bramley W Yorks 51 F8
Bramling Kent 21 F9
Brampford Speke Devon 7 G8
Brampton Cambs 29 A9
Brampton Cumb 57 D8
Brampton Cumb 61 G11
Brampton Derbys 45 E7
Brampton Hereford 25 E11
Brampton Lincs 46 E2
Brampton Norf 39 C8
Brampton S Yorks 45 B8
Brampton Suff 39 G10
Brampton Abbotts Hereford 26 F3
Brampton Ash Northants 36 G3
Brampton Bryan Hereford 25 A10
Brampton en le Morthen S Yorks 45 D8
Bramshall Staffs 35 B6
Bramshaw Hants 10 C1
Bramshill Hants 18 E4
Bramshott Hants 11 A7
Bran End Essex 30 F3
Branault Highld 79 E8
Brancaster Norf 38 A3
Brancaster Staithe Norf 38 A3
Brancepeth Durham 58 C3
Branch End Northumb 62 G6
Branchill Moray 87 F13
Brand Green Glos 26 F4
Branderburgh Moray 88 A2
Brandesburton E Yorks 53 E7
Brandeston Suff 31 B9
Brandhill Shrops 33 H10
Brandis Corner Devon 6 F3
Brandiston Norf 39 C7
Brandon Durham 58 C3
Brandon Lincs 46 H3
Brandon Northumb 62 B6
Brandon Suff 38 G3
Brandon Warks 35 H10
Brandon Bank Cambs 38 G2
Brandon Creek Norf 38 F2
Brandon Parva Norf 39 E6
Brandsby N Yorks 52 B1
Brandy Wharf Lincs 46 C4
Brane Corn 2 G3
Branksome Poole 9 E9
Branksome Park Poole 9 E9
Bransby Lincs 46 E2
Branscombe Devon 7 H10
Bransford Worcs 26 C4
Bransgore Hants 9 E10
Branshill Clack 69 A7
Bransholme Hull 53 F7
Branson's Cross Worcs 27 A7
Branston Leics 36 C4
Branston Lincs 46 F4
Branston Staffs 35 C8
Branston Booths Lincs 46 F4
Branstone IoW 10 F4
Bransty Cumb 56 E1
Brant Broughton Lincs 46 G3
Brantham Suff 31 E8
Branthwaite Cumb 56 C4
Branthwaite Cumb 56 D2
Brantingham E Yorks 52 G5
Branton Northumb 62 B6
Branton S Yorks 45 B10
Branxholm Park Borders 61 B10
Branxholme Borders 61 B10
Branxton Northumb 71 G7
Brassey Green Ches W 43 F8
Brassington Derbys 44 G6
Brasted Kent 19 F11
Brasted Chart Kent 19 F11
Brathens Aberds 83 D8
Bratoft Lincs 47 F8
Brattleby Lincs 46 D3
Bratton Telford 34 D2
Bratton Wilts 16 F6
Bratton Clovelly Devon 6 G3
Bratton Fleming Devon 6 C5
Bratton Seymour Som 8 B5
Braughing Herts 29 F10
Braunston Northants 28 B2
Braunston-in-Rutland Rutland 36 E4
Braunstone Town Leicester 36 E1
Braunton Devon 6 C3
Brawby N Yorks 52 B3
Brawl Highld 93 C11
Brawlbin Highld 94 E2
Bray Windsor 18 D6
Bray Shop Corn 4 D4
Bray Wick Windsor 18 D5
Braybrooke Northants 36 G3
Braye Ald 11
Brayford Devon 6 C5
Braystones Cumb 56 F2
Braythorn N Yorks 51 E8
Brayton N Yorks 52 F2
Brazacott Corn 6 G1
Breach Kent 20 E5
Breachacha Castle Argyll 78 F4
Breachwood Green Herts 29 F8
Breacleit W Isles 90 D6
Breaden Heath Shrops 33 B10
Breadsall Derbys 35 B9
Breadstone Glos 16 A4
Breage Corn 2 G5
Breakachy Highld 86 G7
Bream Glos 26 H3
Breamore Hants 9 C10
Brean Som 15 F8
Breanais W Isles 90 E4
Brearton N Yorks 51 C9
Breascleit W Isles 90 D7
Breaston Derbys 35 B10
Brechfa Carms 23 C10
Brechin Angus 77 A8
Breck of Cruan Orkney 95 G4
Breckan Orkney 95 H3
Breckrey Highld 85 B10
Brecon = Aberhonddu Powys 25 F7
Bredbury Gtr Man 44 C3
Brede E Sus 13 E7
Bredenbury Hereford 26 C3
Bredfield Suff 31 C9
Bredgar Kent 20 E5
Bredhurst Kent 20 E4
Bredicot Worcs 26 C6
Bredon Worcs 26 E6
Bredon's Norton Worcs 26 E6
Bredwardine Hereford 25 D10
Breedon on the Hill Leics 35 C10
Breibhig W Isles 84 J1
Breibhig W Isles 91 D9
Breich W Loth 69 D8
Breightmet Gtr Man 43 B10
Breighton E Yorks 52 F3
Breinton Hereford 25 E11
Breinton Common Hereford 25 D11
Breiwick Shetland 96 J6
Bremhill Wilts 16 D6
Bremirehoull Shetland 96 L6
Brenchley Kent 12 B5
Brendon Devon 7 B6
Brenkley T&W 63 F8
Brent Eleigh Suff 30 D6
Brent Knoll Som 15 F9
Brent Pelham Herts 29 E11
Brentford London 19 D8
Brentingby Leics 36 D3
Brentwood Essex 20 B2
Brenzett Kent 13 D9
Brereton Staffs 35 D6
Brereton Green Ches E 43 F10
Brereton Heath Ches E 44 F2
Bressingham Norf 39 G6
Bretby Derbys 35 C8
Bretford Warks 35 H10
Bretforton Worcs 27 D7
Bretherdale Head Cumb 57 F7
Bretherton Lancs 49 G4
Brettabister Shetland 96 H6
Brettenham Norf 38 G5
Brettenham Suff 30 C6
Bretton Derbys 44 E6
Bretton Flint 42 F6
Brewer Street Sur 19 F10
Brewlands Bridge Angus 76 A4
Brewood Staffs 34 E4
Briach Moray 87 F13
Briants Puddle Dorset 9 E7
Brick End Essex 30 F2
Brickendon Herts 29 H10
Bricket Wood Herts 19 A8
Bricklehampton Worcs 26 D6
Bride IoM 48 B4
Bridekirk Cumb 56 C3
Bridell Pembs 22 B6
Bridestowe Devon 4 C6
Brideswell Aberds 88 E5
Bridford Devon 5 C9
Bridfordmills Devon 5 C9
Bridge Kent 21 F8
Bridge End Lincs 37 B7
Bridge Green Essex 29 E11
Bridge Hewick N Yorks 51 B9
Bridge of Alford Aberds 83 B7
Bridge of Allan Stirling 75 H10
Bridge of Avon Moray 88 E1
Bridge of Awe Argyll 74 E3
Bridge of Balgie Perth 75 C8
Bridge of Cally Perth 76 B4
Bridge of Canny Aberds 83 D8
Bridge of Craigisla Angus 76 B5
Bridge of Dee Dumfries 55 D10
Bridge of Don Aberdeen 83 B11
Bridge of Dun Angus 77 B9
Bridge of Dye Aberds 83 E8
Bridge of Earn Perth 76 F4
Bridge of Ericht Perth 75 B8
Bridge of Feugh Aberds 83 D9
Bridge of Forss Highld 93 C13
Bridge of Gairn Aberds 82 D5
Bridge of Gaur Perth 75 B8
Bridge of Muchalls Aberds 83 D10
Bridge of Oich Highld 80 C5
Bridge of Orchy Argyll 74 D5
Bridge of Waith Orkney 95 G3
Bridge of Walls Shetland 96 H4
Bridge of Weir Renfs 68 D2
Bridge Sollers Hereford 25 D11
Bridge Street Suff 30 D5
Bridge Trafford Ches W 43 E7
Bridge Yate S Glos 16 D3
Bridgefoot Angus 76 D6
Bridgefoot Cumb 56 D2
Bridgehampton Som 8 B4
Bridgehill Durham 58 A1
Bridgemary Hants 10 D4
Bridgemont Derbys 44 D4
Bridgend Aberds 83 B7
Bridgend Aberds 88 E5
Bridgend Angus 83 G7
Bridgend Argyll 64 B4
Bridgend Argyll 65 E8
Bridgend Argyll 73 D7
Bridgend = Pen-y-bont ar Ogwr Bridgend 14 D5
Bridgend Cumb 56 E5
Bridgend Fife 76 F6
Bridgend Moray 88 E3
Bridgend N Lanark 68 C5
Bridgend Pembs 22 B6
Bridgend W Loth 69 C9
Bridgend of Lintrathen Angus 76 B5
Bridgerule Devon 6 F1
Bridges Shrops 33 F9
Bridgeton Glasgow 68 D5
Bridgetown Corn 4 C4
Bridgetown Som 7 C8
Bridgham Norf 38 G5
Bridgnorth Shrops 34 F3
Bridgtown Staffs 34 E5
Bridgwater Som 15 H9
Bridlington E Yorks 53 C7
Bridport Dorset 8 E3
Bridstow Hereford 26 F2
Brierfield Lancs 50 F4
Brierley Glos 26 G3
Brierley Hereford 25 C11
Brierley S Yorks 45 A8
Brierley Hill W Mid 34 G5
Briery Hill Bl Gwent 25 H8
Brig o'Turk Stirling 75 G8
Brigg N Lincs 46 B4
Briggswath N Yorks 59 F9
Brigham Cumb 56 C2
Brigham E Yorks 53 D6
Brighouse W Yorks 51 G7
Brighstone IoW 10 F3
Brightgate Derbys 44 G6
Brighthampton Oxon 17 A10
Brightling E Sus 12 D5
Brightlingsea Essex 31 G7
Brighton Brighton 12 F2
Brighton Corn 3 D8
Brighton Hill Hants 18 G3
Brightons Falk 69 C8
Brightwalton W Berks 17 D11
Brightwell Suff 31 D9
Brightwell Baldwin Oxon 18 B3
Brightwell cum Sotwell Oxon 18 B2
Brignall Durham 58 E1
Brigsley NE Lincs 46 B6
Brigsteer Cumb 57 H6
Brigstock Northants 36 G5
Brill Bucks 28 G3
Brilley Hereford 25 D9
Brimaston Pembs 22 D4
Brimfield Hereford 26 B2
Brimington Derbys 45 E8
Brimley Devon 5 D8
Brimpsfield Glos 26 G6
Brimpton W Berks 18 E2
Brims Orkney 95 K3
Brimscombe Glos 16 A5
Brimstage Mers 42 D6
Brinacory Highld 79 B10
Brind E Yorks 52 F3
Brindister Shetland 96 H4
Brindister Shetland 96 K6
Brindle Lancs 50 G2
Brindley Ford Stoke 44 G2
Brineton Staffs 34 D4
Bringhurst Leics 36 F4
Brington Cambs 37 H6
Brinian Orkney 95 F5
Briningham Norf 38 B6
Brinkhill Lincs 47 E7
Brinkley Cambs 30 C3
Brinklow Warks 35 H10
Brinkworth Wilts 17 C7
Brinmore Highld 81 A8
Brinscall Lancs 50 G2
Brinsea N Som 15 E10
Brinsley Notts 45 H8
Brinsop Hereford 25 D11
Brinsworth S Yorks 45 D8
Brinton Norf 38 B6
Brisco Cumb 56 A6
Brisley Norf 38 C5
Brislington Bristol 16 D3
Bristol Bristol 16 D2
Briston Norf 39 B6
Britannia Lancs 50 G4
Britford Wilts 9 B10
Brithdir Gwyn 32 D3
British Legion Village Kent 20 F4
Briton Ferry Neath 14 B3
Britwell Salome Oxon 18 B3
Brixham Torbay 5 F10
Brixton Devon 5 F6
Brixton London 19 D10
Brixton Deverill Wilts 16 H5
Brixworth Northants 28 A4
Brize Norton Oxon 27 H10
Broad Blunsdon Swindon 17 B8
Broad Campden Glos 27 E8
Broad Chalke Wilts 9 B9
Broad Green C Beds 28 D6
Broad Green Essex 30 F5
Broad Green Worcs 26 C4
Broad Haven Pembs 22 E3
Broad Heath Worcs 26 B3
Broad Hill Cambs 38 H1
Broad Hinton Wilts 17 D8
Broad Laying Hants 17 E11
Broad Marston Worcs 27 D8
Broad Oak Carms 23 D10
Broad Oak Cumb 56 G3
Broad Oak Dorset 8 E3
Broad Oak Dorset 9 C6
Broad Oak E Sus 12 D5
Broad Oak E Sus 13 E7
Broad Oak Hereford 25 F11
Broad Oak Mers 43 C8
Broad Street Kent 20 F5
Broad Street Green Essex 30 H5
Broad Town Wilts 17 D7
Broadbottom Gtr Man 44 C3
Broadbridge W Sus 11 D7
Broadbridge Heath W Sus 11 A10
Broadclyst Devon 7 G8
Broadfield Gtr Man 44 A2
Broadfield Lancs 49 G5
Broadfield Pembs 22 F6
Broadfield W Sus 12 C1
Broadford Highld 85 F11
Broadford Bridge W Sus 11 B9
Broadhaugh Borders 61 C10
Broadhaven Highld 94 E5
Broadheath Gtr Man 43 D10
Broadhembury Devon 7 F10
Broadhempston Devon 5 E9
Broadholme Derbys 45 H7
Broadholme Lincs 46 E2
Broadland Row E Sus 13 E7
Broadlay Carms 23 F8
Broadley Lancs 50 H4
Broadley Moray 88 B3
Broadley Common Essex 29 H11
Broadmayne Dorset 8 F6
Broadmeadows Borders 70 G3
Broadmere Hants 18 G3
Broadmoor Pembs 22 F5
Broadoak Kent 21 E8
Broadrashes Moray 88 C4
Broadsea Aberds 89 B9
Broadstairs Kent 21 E10
Broadstone Poole 9 E9
Broadstone Shrops 33 G11
Broadtown Lane Wilts 17 D7
Broadwas Worcs 26 C4
Broadwater Herts 29 F9
Broadwater W Sus 11 D10
Broadway Carms 23 F7
Broadway Pembs 22 E3
Broadway Som 8 C2
Broadway Suff 39 H9
Broadway Worcs 27 E7
Broadwell Glos 26 G2
Broadwell Glos 27 F9
Broadwell Oxon 17 A9
Broadwell Warks 27 B11
Broadwell House Northumb 57 A11
Broadwey Dorset 8 F5
Broadwindsor Dorset 8 D3
Broadwood Kelly Devon 6 F5
Broadwoodwidger Devon 4 C5
Brobury Hereford 25 D10
Brochel Highld 85 D10
Brochloch Dumfries 67 G8
Brochroy Argyll 74 D3
Brockamin Worcs 26 C4
Brockbridge Hants 10 C5
Brockdam Northumb 63 A7
Brockdish Norf 39 H8
Brockenhurst Hants 10 D2
Brocketsbrae S Lanark 69 G7
Brockford Street Suff 31 B8
Brockhall Northants 28 B3
Brockham Sur 19 G8
Brockhampton Glos 27 F7
Brockhampton Hereford 26 E2
Brockholes W Yorks 44 A5
Brockhurst Derbys 45 F7
Brockhurst Hants 10 D5
Brocklebank Cumb 56 B5
Brocklesby Lincs 46 A5
Brockley N Som 15 E10
Brockley Green Suff 30 C5
Brockleymoor Cumb 57 C6
Brockton Shrops 33 E9
Brockton Shrops 33 G9
Brockton Shrops 34 E3
Brockton Shrops 34 F1
Brockton Telford 34 D3
Brockweir Glos 15 A11
Brockwood Hants 10 B5
Brockworth Glos 26 G5
Brocton Staffs 34 D5
Brodick N Ayrs 66 C3
Brodsworth S Yorks 45 B9
Brogaig Highld 85 B9
Brogborough C Beds 28 E6
Broken Cross Ches E 44 E2
Broken Cross Ches W 43 E9
Brokenborough Wilts 16 C6
Bromborough Mers 42 D6
Brome Suff 39 H7
Brome Street Suff 39 H7
Bromeswell Suff 31 C10
Bromfield Cumb 56 B3
Bromfield Shrops 33 H10
Bromham Bedford 29 C7
Bromham Wilts 16 E6
Bromley London 19 E11
Bromley W Mid 34 G5
Bromley Common London 19 E11
Bromley Green Kent 13 C8
Brompton Medway 20 E4
Brompton N Yorks 52 A5
Brompton N Yorks 58 G4
Brompton-on-Swale N Yorks 58 G3
Brompton Ralph Som 7 C9
Brompton Regis Som 7 C8
Bromsash Hereford 26 F3
Bromsberrow Hth. Glos 26 E4
Bromsgrove Worcs 26 A6
Bromyard Hereford 26 C3
Bromyard Downs Hereford 26 C3
Bronaber Gwyn 41 G9
Brongest Ceredig 23 B8
Bronington Wrex 33 B10
Bronllys Powys 25 E8
Bronnant Ceredig 24 B3
Bronwydd Arms Carms 23 D9
Bronydd Powys 25 D9
Bronygarth Shrops 33 B8
Brook Carms 23 F7
Brook Hants 10 B2
Brook Hants 10 C1
Brook IoW 10 F2
Brook Kent 13 B9
Brook Sur 18 H6
Brook Sur 19 G7
Brook End Bedford 29 B7
Brook Hill Hants 10 C1
Brook Street Kent 13 C8
Brook Street Kent 20 G2
Brook Street W Sus 12 D2
Brooke Norf 39 F8
Brooke Rutland 36 E4
Brookenby Lincs 46 C6
Brookend Glos 16 B2
Brookfield Renfs 68 D3
Brookhouse Lancs 49 C5
Brookhouse Green Ches E 44 F2
Brookland Kent 13 D8
Brooklands Dumfries 60 F4
Brooklands Gtr Man 43 C10
Brooklands Shrops 33 A11
Brookmans Park Herts 19 A9
Brooks Powys 33 F7
Brooks Green W Sus 11 B10
Brookthorpe Glos 26 G5
Brookville Norf 38 F3
Brookwood Sur 18 F6
Broom C Beds 29 D8
Broom S Yorks 45 C8
Broom Warks 27 C7
Broom Worcs 34 H5
Broom Green Norf 38 C5
Broom Hill Dorset 9 D9
Broome Norf 39 F9
Broome Shrops 33 G10
Broome Park Northumb 63 B7
Broomedge Warr 43 D10
Broomer's Corner W Sus 11 B10
Broomfield Aberds 89 E9
Broomfield Essex 30 G4
Broomfield Kent 20 F5
Broomfield Kent 21 E8
Broomfield Som 7 C11
Broomfleet E Yorks 52 G4
Broomhall Ches E 43 H9
Broomhall Windsor 18 E6
Broomhaugh Northumb 62 G6
Broomhill Norf 38 E2
Broomhill Northumb 63 C8
Broomhill S Yorks 45 B8
Broomholm Norf 39 B9
Broomley Northumb 62 G6
Broompark Durham 58 B3
Broom's Green Glos 26 E4
Broomy Lodge Hants 9 C11
Brora Highld 93 J12
Broseley Shrops 34 E2
Brotherhouse Bar Lincs 37 D8
Brotherstone Borders 70 G5
Brothertoft Lincs 46 H6
Brotherton N Yorks 51 G10
Brotton Redcar 59 E7
Broubster Highld 93 C13
Brough Cumb 57 E9
Brough Derbys 44 D5
Brough E Yorks 52 G5
Brough Highld 94 C4
Brough Notts 46 G2
Brough Orkney 95 G4
Brough Shetland 96 F7
Brough Shetland 96 F6
Brough Shetland 96 G7
Brough Shetland 96 H6
Brough Shetland 96 J7
Brough Lodge Shetland 96 D7
Brough Sowerby Cumb 57 E9
Broughall Shrops 34 A1
Broughton Borders 69 G10
Broughton Cambs 37 H8
Broughton Flint 42 F6
Broughton Hants 10 A2
Broughton Lancs 49 F5
Broughton M Keynes 28 D5
Broughton N Lincs 46 B3
Broughton N Yorks 50 D5
Broughton N Yorks 52 B3
Broughton Northants 36 H4
Broughton Orkney 95 D5
Broughton Oxon 27 E11
Broughton V Glam 14 D5
Broughton Astley Leics 35 F11
Broughton Beck Cumb 49 A2
Broughton Common Wilts 16 E5
Broughton Gifford Wilts 16 E5
Broughton Hackett Worcs 26 C6
Broughton in Furness Cumb 56 H4
Broughton Mills Cumb 56 G4
Broughton Moor Cumb 56 C2
Broughton Park Gtr Man 44 B2
Broughton Poggs Oxon 17 A9
Broughtown Orkney 95 D7
Broughty Ferry Dundee 77 D7
Browhouses Dumfries 61 G8
Browland Shetland 96 H4
Brown Candover Hants 18 H2
Brown Edge Lancs 42 A6
Brown Edge Staffs 44 G3
Brown Heath Ches W 43 F7
Brownhill Aberds 89 D8
Brownhill Aberds 89 D6
Brownhill Blackburn 50 F2
Brownhill Shrops 33 C10
Brownhills Fife 77 F8
Brownhills W Mid 34 E6
Brownlow Ches E 44 F2
Brownlow Heath Ches E 44 F2
Brownmuir Aberds 83 F9
Brown's End Glos 26 E4
Brownshill Glos 16 A5
Brownston Devon 5 F7
Brownyside Northumb 63 A7
Broxa N Yorks 59 G10
Broxbourne Herts 29 H10
Broxburn E Loth 70 C5
Broxburn W Loth 69 C9
Broxholme Lincs 46 E3
Broxted Essex 30 F2
Broxton Ches W 43 G7
Broxwood Hereford 25 C10
Broyle Side E Sus 12 E3
Brù W Isles 91 C8
Bruairnis W Isles 84 H2
Bruan Highld 94 G5
Bruar Lodge Perth 81 F10
Brucehill W Dunb 68 C2
Bruera Ches W 43 F7
Bruern Abbey Oxon 27 F9
Bruichladdich Argyll 64 B3
Bruisyard Suff 31 B10
Brumby N Lincs 46 B2
Brund Staffs 44 F5
Brundall Norf 39 E9
Brundish Suff 31 B9
Brundish Street Suff 31 A9
Brunery Highld 79 D10
Brunshaw Lancs 50 F4
Brunswick Village T&W 63 F8
Bruntcliffe W Yorks 51 G8
Bruntingthorpe Leics 36 F2
Brunton Fife 76 E6
Brunton Northumb 63 A8
Brunton Wilts 17 F9
Brushford Devon 6 F5
Brushford Som 7 D8
Bruton Som 8 A5
Bryanston Dorset 9 D7
Brydekirk Dumfries 61 F7
Bryher Scilly 2 C2
Brymbo Wrex 42 G5
Brympton Som 8 C4
Bryn Carms 23 F10
Bryn Gtr Man 43 B8
Bryn Neath 14 B4
Bryn Shrops 33 G8
Bryn-coch Neath 14 B3
Bryn Du Anglesey 40 C5
Bryn Gates Gtr Man 43 B8
Bryn-glas Conwy 41 D10
Bryn Golau Rhondda 14 C5
Bryn-Iwan Carms 23 C8
Bryn-mawr Gwyn 40 G4
Bryn-nantllech Conwy 42 F2
Bryn-penarth Powys 33 E7
Bryn Rhyd-yr-Arian Conwy 42 F2
Bryn Saith Marchog Denb 42 G3
Bryn Sion Gwyn 32 D4
Bryn-y-gwenin Mon 25 G10
Bryn-y-maen Conwy 41 C10
Bryn-yr-eryr Gwyn 40 F5
Brynamman Carms 24 G4
Brynberian Pembs 22 C6
Brynbryddan Neath 14 B3
Brynbuga = Usk Mon 15 A9
Bryncae Rhondda 14 C5
Bryncethin Bridgend 14 C5
Bryncir Gwyn 40 F6
Bryncroes Gwyn 40 G4
Bryncrug Gwyn 32 E2
Bryneglwys Denb 42 H4
Brynford Flint 42 E4
Bryngwran Anglesey 40 C5
Bryngwyn Ceredig 23 B7
Bryngwyn Mon 25 H10
Bryngwyn Powys 25 D8
Brynhenllan Pembs 22 C5
Brynhoffnant Ceredig 23 A8
Brynithel Bl Gwent 15 A8
Brynmawr Bl Gwent 25 G8
Brynmenyn Bridgend 14 C5
Brynmill Swansea 14 B2
Brynna Rhondda 14 C5
Brynrefail Anglesey 40 B6
Brynrefail Gwyn 41 D7
Brynsadler Rhondda 14 C6
Brynsiencyn Anglesey 40 D6
Brynteg Anglesey 40 B6
Brynteg Ceredig 23 B9
Buaile nam Bodach W Isles 84 H2
Bualintur Highld 85 F9
Buarthmeini Gwyn 41 G10
Bubbenhall Warks 27 A10
Bubwith E Yorks 52 F3
Buccleuch Borders 61 B9
Buchanhaven Aberds 89 D11
Buchanty Perth 76 E2
Buchlyvie Stirling 68 A4
Buckabank Cumb 56 B5
Buckden Cambs 29 B8
Buckden N Yorks 50 B5
Buckenham Norf 39 E9
Buckerell Devon 7 F10
Buckfast Devon 5 E8
Buckfastleigh Devon 5 E8
Buckhaven Fife 76 H6
Buckholm Borders 70 G3
Buckholt Mon 26 G2
Buckhorn Weston Dorset 9 B6
Buckhurst Hill Essex 19 B11
Buckie Moray 88 B4
Buckies Highld 94 D3
Buckingham Bucks 28 E3
Buckland Bucks 28 G5
Buckland Devon 5 G7
Buckland Glos 27 E7
Buckland Hants 10 E2
Buckland Herts 29 E10
Buckland Kent 21 G10
Buckland Oxon 17 B10
Buckland Sur 19 F9
Buckland Brewer Devon 6 D3
Buckland Common Bucks 28 H6
Buckland Dinham Som 16 F4
Buckland Filleigh Devon 6 F3
Buckland in the Moor Devon 5 D8
Buckland Monachorum Devon 4 E5
Buckland Newton Dorset 8 D5
Buckland St Mary Som 8 C1
Bucklebury W Berks 18 D2
Bucklegate Lincs 37 B9
Bucklerheads Angus 77 D7
Bucklers Hard Hants 10 E3
Bucklesham Suff 31 D9
Buckley = Bwcle Flint 42 F5
Bucklow Hill Ches E 43 D10
Buckminster Leics 36 C4
Bucknall Lincs 46 F5
Bucknall Stoke 44 H3
Bucknell Oxon 28 F2
Bucknell Shrops 25 A10
Buckpool Moray 88 B4
Buck's Cross Devon 6 D2
Bucks Green W Sus 11 A9
Bucks Horn Oak Hants 18 G5
Buck's Mills Devon 6 D2
Bucksburn Aberdeen 83 C10
Buckskin Hants 18 F3
Buckton E Yorks 53 B7
Buckton Hereford 25 A10
Buckton Northumb 71 G9
Buckworth Cambs 37 H7
Budbrooke Warks 27 B9
Budby Notts 45 F10
Budd's Titson Corn 4 A3
Bude Corn 6 F1
Budlake Devon 7 G8
Budle Northumb 71 G10
Budleigh Salterton Devon 7 H9
Budock Water Corn 3 F6
Buerton Ches E 34 A2
Buffler's Holt Bucks 28 E3
Bugbrooke Northants 28 C3
Buglawton Ches E 44 F2
Bugle Corn 3 D9
Bugley Wilts 16 G5
Bugthorpe E Yorks 52 D3
Buildwas Shrops 34 E2
Builth Road Powys 25 C7
Builth Wells = Llanfair-ym-Muallt Powys 25 C7
Buirgh W Isles 90 H5
Bulby Lincs 37 C6
Bulcote Notts 36 A2
Buldoo Highld 93 C12
Bulford Wilts 17 G8
Bulford Camp Wilts 17 G8
Bulkeley Ches E 43 G8
Bulkington Warks 35 G9
Bulkington Wilts 16 F6
Bulkworthy Devon 6 E2
Bull Hill Hants 10 E2
Bullamoor N Yorks 58 G4
Bullbridge Derbys 45 G7
Bullbrook Brack 18 E5
Bulley Glos 26 G4
Bullgill Cumb 56 C2
Bullington Hants 17 G11
Bullington Lincs 46 E4
Bull's Green Herts 29 G9
Bullwood Argyll 73 F10
Bulmer Essex 30 D5
Bulmer N Yorks 52 C2
Bulmer Tye Essex 30 E5
Bulphan Thurrock 20 C3
Bulverhythe E Sus 13 F6
Bulwark Aberds 89 D9
Bulwell Nottingham 45 H9
Bulwick Northants 36 F5
Bumble's Green Essex 29 H11
Bun Abhainn Eadarra W Isles 90 G6
Bun a'Mhuillin W Isles 84 G2
Bun Loyne Highld 80 C4
Bunacaimb Highld 79 C9
Bunarkaig Highld 80 E3
Bunbury Ches E 43 G8
Bunbury Heath Ches E 43 G8
Bunchrew Highld 87 G9
Bundalloch Highld 85 F13
Buness Shetland 96 C8
Bunessan Argyll 78 J6
Bungay Suff 39 G9
Bunker's Hill Lincs 46 E3
Bunker's Hill Lincs 46 G6
Bunkers Hill Oxon 27 G11
Bunloit Highld 81 A7
Bunnahabhain Argyll 64 A5
Bunny Notts 36 C1
Buntait Highld 86 H6
Buntingford Herts 29 F10
Bunwell Norf 39 F7
Burbage Derbys 44 E4
Burbage Leics 35 F10
Burbage Wilts 17 E9
Burchett's Green Windsor 18 C5
Burcombe Wilts 9 A9
Burcot Oxon 18 B2
Burcott Bucks 28 F5
Burdon T&W 58 A4
Bures Suff 30 E6
Bures Green Suff 30 E6
Burford Ches E 43 G9
Burford Oxon 27 G9
Burford Shrops 26 B2
Burg Argyll 78 G6
Burgar Orkney 95 F4
Burgate Hants 9 C10
Burgate Suff 39 H6
Burgess Hill W Sus 12 E2
Burgh Suff 31 C9
Burgh by Sands Cumb 61 H9
Burgh Castle Norf 39 E10
Burgh Heath Sur 19 F9
Burgh le Marsh Lincs 47 F9
Burgh Muir Aberds 83 A9
Burgh next Aylsham Norf 39 C8
Burgh on Bain Lincs 46 D6
Burgh St Margaret Norf 39 D10
Burgh St Peter Norf 39 F10
Burghclere Hants 17 E11
Burghead Moray 87 E14
Burghfield W Berks 18 E3
Burghfield Common W Berks 18 E3
Burghfield Hill W Berks 18 E3
Burghill Hereford 25 D11
Burghwallis S Yorks 45 A9
Burham Kent 20 E4
Buriton Hants 10 B6
Burland Ches E 43 G9
Burlawn Corn 3 B8
Burleigh Brack 18 E5
Burlescombe Devon 7 E9
Burleston Dorset 9 E6
Burley Hants 9 D11
Burley Rutland 36 D4
Burley W Yorks 51 F8
Burley Gate Hereford 26 D2
Burley in Wharfedale W Yorks 51 E7
Burley Lodge Hants 9 D11
Burley Street Hants 9 D11
Burleydam Ches E 34 A2
Burlingjobb Powys 25 C9
Burlow E Sus 12 E4
Burlton Shrops 33 C10
Burmarsh Kent 13 C9
Burmington Warks 27 E9
Burn N Yorks 52 G1
Burn of Cambus Stirling 75 G10
Burnaston Derbys 35 B8
Burnbank S Lanark 68 E6
Burnby E Yorks 52 E4
Burncross S Yorks 45 C7
Burneside Cumb 57 G7
Burness Orkney 95 D7
Burneston N Yorks 58 H4
Burnett Bath 16 E3
Burnfoot Borders 61 B11
Burnfoot Borders 61 B10
Burnfoot E Ayrs 67 F7
Burnfoot Perth 76 G2
Burnham Bucks 18 C6
Burnham N Lincs 53 H6
Burnham Deepdale Norf 38 A4
Burnham Green Herts 29 G9
Burnham Market Norf 38 A4
Burnham Norton Norf 38 A4
Burnham-on-Crouch Essex 20 B6
Burnham-on-Sea Som 15 G9
Burnham Overy Staithe Norf 38 A4
Burnham Overy Town Norf 38 A4
Burnham Thorpe Norf 38 A4
Burnhead Dumfries 60 D4
Burnhead S Ayrs 66 F5
Burnhervie Aberds 83 B9
Burnhill Green Staffs 34 E3
Burnhope Durham 58 B2
Burnhouse N Ayrs 67 A6
Burniston N Yorks 59 G11
Burnlee W Yorks 44 B5
Burnley Lancs 50 F4
Burnley Lane Lancs 50 F4
Burnmouth Borders 71 D8
Burnopfield Durham 63 H7
Burnsall N Yorks 50 C6
Burnside Angus 77 B8
Burnside E Ayrs 67 E8
Burnside Fife 76 G4
Burnside S Lanark 68 D5
Burnside Shetland 96 F4
Burnside W Loth 69 C9
Burnside of Duntrune Angus 77 D7
Burnswark Dumfries 61 F7
Burnt Heath Derbys 44 E6
Burnt Houses Durham 58 D2
Burnt Yates N Yorks 51 C8
Burntcommon Sur 19 F7
Burnthouse Corn 3 F6
Burntisland Fife 69 B11
Burnton E Ayrs 67 F7
Burntwood Staffs 35 E6
Burnwynd Edin 69 D10
Burpham Sur 19 F7
Burpham W Sus 11 D9
Burradon Northumb 62 C5
Burradon T&W 63 F8
Burrafirth Shetland 96 B8
Burraland Shetland 96 F5
Burraland Shetland 96 J4
Burras Corn 2 F5
Burravoe Shetland 96 F7
Burravoe Shetland 96 G5
Burray Village Orkney 95 J5
Burrells Cumb 57 E8
Burrelton Perth 76 D5
Burridge Devon 6 C4
Burridge Hants 10 C4
Burrill N Yorks 58 H3
Burringham N Lincs 46 B2
Burrington Devon 6 E5
Burrington Hereford 25 A11
Burrington N Som 15 F10
Burrough Green Cambs 30 C3
Burrough on the Hill Leics 36 D3
Burrow-bridge Som 8 B2
Burrowhill Sur 18 E6
Burry Swansea 23 G9
Burry Green Swansea 23
Burry Port = Porth Tywyn Carms 23
Burscough Lancs 43
Burscough Bridge Lancs 43
Bursea E Yorks 52
Burshill E Yorks 53
Bursledon Hants 10
Burslem Stoke 44
Burstall Suff 31
Burstock Dorset 8
Burston Norf 39
Burston Staffs 34
Burstow Sur 12
Burstwick E Yorks 53
Burtersett N Yorks 57
Burtle Som 15
Burton Ches W 42
Burton Ches W 43
Burton Dorset 9
Burton Lincs 46
Burton Northumb 71
Burton Pembs 22
Burton Som 7
Burton Wilts 16
Burton Agnes E Yorks 53
Burton Bradstock Dorset 8
Burton Dassett Warks 27
Burton Fleming E Yorks 53
Burton Green W Mid 35
Burton Green Wrex 42
Burton Hastings Warks 35
Burton-in-Kendal Cumb 49
Burton in Lonsdale N Yorks 50
Burton Joyce Notts 36
Burton Latimer Northants 28
Burton Lazars Leics 36
Burton-le-Coggles Lincs 36
Burton Leonard N Yorks 51
Burton on the Wolds Leics 36
Burton Overy Leics 36
Burton Pedwardine Lincs 37
Burton Pidsea E Yorks 53
Burton Salmon N Yorks 51
Burton Stather N Lincs 52
Burton upon Stather N Lincs 52
Burton upon Trent Staffs 35
Burtonwood Warr 43
Burwardsley Ches W 43
Burwarton Shrops 34
Burwash E Sus 12
Burwash Common E Sus 12
Burwash Weald E Sus 12
Burwell Cambs 30
Burwell Lincs 47
Burwen Anglesey 40
Burwick Orkney 95
Bury Cambs 37
Bury Gtr Man 44
Bury Som 7
Bury W Sus 11
Bury Green Herts 29
Bury St Edmunds Suff 30
Burythorpe N Yorks 52
Busby E Renf 68
Buscot Oxon 17
Bush Bank Hereford 25
Bush Crathie Aberds 82
Bush Green Norf 39
Bushbury W Mid 34
Bushby Leics 36
Bushey Herts 19
Bushey Heath Herts 19
Bushley Worcs 26
Bushton Wilts 17
Buslingthorpe Lincs 46
Busta Shetland 96
Butcher's Cross E Sus 12
Butcher's Pasture Essex 30
Butcombe N Som 15
Butetown Cardiff 15
Butleigh Som 8
Butleigh Wootton Som 15
Butler's Cross Bucks 28
Butler's End Warks 35
Butlers Marston Warks 27
Butley Suff 31
Butley High Corner Suff 31
Butt Green Ches E 43
Butterburn Cumb 62
Buttercrambe N Yorks 52
Butterknowle Durham 58
Butterleigh Devon 7
Buttermere Cumb 56
Buttermere Wilts 17
Buttershaw W Yorks 51
Butterstone Perth 76
Butterton Staffs 44
Butterwick Durham 58
Butterwick Lincs 47
Butterwick N Yorks 52
Butterwick N Yorks 52
Buttington Powys 33
Buttonoak Worcs 34
Butt's Green Hants 10
Buttsash Hants 10
Buxhall Suff 31
Buxhall Fen Street Suff 31
Buxley Borders 71
Buxted E Sus 12
Buxton Derbys 44
Buxton Norf 39
Buxworth Derbys 44
Bwcle = Buckley Flint 42
Bwlch Powys 25
Bwlch-Llan Ceredig 23
Bwlch-y-cibau Powys 33
Bwlch-y-fadfa Ceredig 23
Bwlch-y-ffridd Powys 33
Bwlch-y-sarnau Powys 25
Bwlchgwyn Wrex 42
Bwlchnewydd Carms 23
Bwlchtocyn Gwyn 40

Bwlchyddar Powys 33 C7
Bwlchygroes Pembs 23 C7
Byermoor T&W 63 H7
Byers Green Durham 58 C3
Byfield Northants 28 C2
Byfleet Sur 19 E7
Byford Hereford 25 D10
Bygrave Herts 29 E9
Byker T&W 63 G8
Bylchau Conwy 42 F2
Byley Ches W 43 F10
Bynea Carms 23 G10
Byrness Northumb 62 C3
Bythorn Cambs 37 H6
Byton Hereford 25 B10
Byworth W Sus 11 B8

C

Cabharstadh W Isles 91 E8
Cablea Perth 76 D2
Cabourne Lincs 46 B5
Cabrach Argyll 72 G3
Cabrach Moray 82 A5
Cabrich Highld 87 G8
Cabus Lancs 49 E4
Cackle Street E Sus 12 D3
Cadbury Devon 7 F8
Cadbury Barton Devon 6 E5
Cadder E Dunb 68 C5
Caddington C Beds 29 G7
Caddonfoot Borders 70 G3
Cade Street E Sus 12 D5
Cadeby Leics 35 E10
Cadeby S Yorks 45 B9
Cadeleigh Devon 7 F8
Cadgwith Corn 2 H6
Cadham Fife 76 G5
Cadishead Gtr Man 43 C10
Cadle Swansea 14 B2
Cadley Lancs 49 F5
Cadley Wilts 17 E9
Cadley Wilts 17 F9
Cadmore End Bucks 18 B4
Cadnam Hants 10 C1
Cadney N Lincs 46 B4
Cadole Flint 42 F5
Cadoxton V Glam 15 E7
Cadoxton-Juxta-Neath Neath 14 B3
Cadshaw Blackburn 50 H3
Cadzow S Lanark 68 E6
Caeathro Gwyn 41 D7
Caehopkin Powys 24 G5
Caenby Lincs 46 D4
Caenby Corner Lincs 46 D3
Caér-bryn Carms 23 E10
Caer Llan Mon 25 H11
Caerau Bridgend 14 B4
Caerau Cardiff 15 D7
Caerdeon Gwyn 32 D2
Caerdydd = Cardiff Cardiff 15 D7
Caerfarchell Pembs 22 D2
Caerffili = Caerphilly Caerph 15 C7
Caerfyrddin = Carmarthen Carms 23 D9
Caergeiliog Anglesey 40 C5
Caergwrle Flint 42 G6
Caergybi = Holyhead Anglesey 40 B4
Caerleon = Caerllion Newport 15 B9
Caerllion = Caerleon Newport 15 B9
Caernarfon Gwyn 40 D6
Caerphilly = Caerffili Caerph 15 C7
Caersws Powys 32 F6
Caerwedros Ceredig 23 A8
Caerwent Mon 15 B10
Caerwych Gwyn 41 G8
Caerwys Flint 42 E4
Caethle Gwyn 32 F2
Caim Anglesey 41 B8
Caio Carms 24 E3
Cairinis W Isles 84 B3
Cairisiadar W Isles 90 D5
Cairminis W Isles 90 J5
Cairnbaan Argyll 73 D7
Cairnbanno Ho. Aberds 89 D8
Cairnborrow Aberds 88 D4
Cairnbrogie Aberds 89 F8
Cairnbulg Castle Aberds 89 B10
Cairncross Angus 82 F6
Cairncross Borders 71 D7
Cairndow Argyll 74 F4
Cairness Aberds 89 B10
Cairneyhill Fife 69 B9
Cairnfield Ho. Moray 88 B4
Cairngaan Dumfries 54 F4
Cairngarroch Dumfries 54 E3
Cairnhill Aberds 89 E6
Cairnie Aberds 83 C10
Cairnie Aberds 88 D4
Cairnorrie Aberds 89 D8
Cairnpark Aberds 83 B10
Cairnryan Dumfries 54 C3
Cairnton Orkney 95 H4
Caister-on-Sea Norf 39 D11
Caistor Lincs 46 B5
Caistor St Edmund Norf 39 E8
Caistron Northumb 62 C5
Caitha Bowland Borders 70 F3
Calais Street Suff 30 E6
Calanais W Isles 90 D7
Calbost W Isles 91 F9
Calbourne IoW 10 F3
Calceby Lincs 47 E7
Calcot Row W Berks 18 D3
Calcott Kent 21 E8
Caldback Shetland 96 C8
Caldbeck Cumb 56 C5
Caldbergh N Yorks 58 H1
Caldecote Cambs 29 C10
Caldecote Cambs 37 G7
Caldecote Herts 29 E9
Caldecote Northants 28 C3
Caldecott Northants 28 B6
Caldecott Oxon 17 B11
Caldecott Rutland 36 F4
Calder Bridge Cumb 56 E2
Calder Hall Cumb 56 F2
Calder Mains Highld 94 E2
Calder Vale Lancs 49 E5
Calderbank N Lanark 68 D6
Calderbrook Gtr Man 50 H5
Caldercruix N Lanark 69 D7
Caldermill S Lanark 68 F5
Calderwood S Lanark 68 E5
Caldhame Angus 77 C7
Caldicot Mon 15 C10
Caldwell Derbys 35 D8
Caldwell N Yorks 58 E2
Caldy Mers 42 D5
Caledrhydiau Ceredig 23 A9
Calfsound Orkney 95 E6
Calgary Argyll 78 F6
Califer Moray 87 F13
California Falk 69 C8
California Norf 39 D11
Calke Derbys 35 C9
Callakille Highld 85 C11
Callaly Northumb 62 C6
Callander Stirling 75 G9
Callaughton Shrops 34 F2
Callestick Corn 3 D6
Calligarry Highld 85 H11
Callington Corn 4 E4
Callow Hereford 25 E11
Callow End Worcs 26 D5
Callow Hill Wilts 17 C7
Callow Hill Worcs 26 A4
Callows Grave Worcs 26 B2
Calmore Hants 10 C2
Calmsden Glos 27 H7
Calne Wilts 17 D7
Calow Derbys 45 E8
Calshot Hants 10 D3
Calstock Corn 4 E5
Calstone Wellington Wilts 17 E7
Calthorpe Norf 39 B7
Calthwaite Cumb 56 B6
Calton N Yorks 50 D5
Calton Staffs 44 G5
Calveley Ches E 43 G8
Calver Derbys 44 E6
Calver Hill Hereford 25 D10
Calverhall Shrops 34 B2
Calverleigh Devon 7 E8
Calverley W Yorks 51 F8
Calvert Bucks 28 F3
Calverton M Keynes 28 E4
Calverton Notts 45 H10
Calvine Perth 81 G10
Calvo Cumb 56 A3
Cam Glos 16 B4
Camas-luinie Highld 80 A1
Camasnacroise Highld 79 F11
Camastianavaig Highld 85 E10
Camasunary Highld 85 G10
Camault Muir Highld 87 G8
Camb Shetland 96 D7
Camber E Sus 13 E8
Camberley Sur 18 E5
Camberwell London 19 D10
Camblesforth N Yorks 52 G2
Cambo Northumb 62 E6
Cambois Northumb 63 E9
Camborne Corn 2 E5
Cambourne Cambs 29 C10
Cambridge Cambs 29 C11
Cambridge Glos 16 A4
Cambridge Town Southend 20 C6
Cambus Clack 69 A7
Cambusavie Farm Highld 87 B10
Cambusbarron Stirling 68 A6
Cambuskenneth Stirling 69 A7
Cambuslang S Lanark 68 D5
Cambusmore Lodge Highld 87 B10
Camden London 19 C9
Camelford Corn 4 C2
Camelsdale Sur 11 A7
Camerory Highld 87 H13
Camer's Green Worcs 26 E4
Camerton Bath 16 F3
Camerton Cumb 56 C2
Camerton E Yorks 53 G8
Camghouran Perth 75 B8
Cammachmore Aberds 83 D11
Cammeringham Lincs 46 D3
Camore Highld 87 B10
Camp Hill Warks 35 F9
Campbeltown Argyll 65 F8
Camperdown T&W 63 F8
Campmuir Perth 76 D5
Campsall S Yorks 45 A9
Campsey Ash Suff 31 C10
Campton C Beds 29 E8
Camptown Borders 62 B2
Camrose Pembs 22 D4
Camserney Perth 75 C11
Camster Highld 94 F4
Camuschoirk Highld 79 E10
Camuscross Highld 85 G11
Camusnagaul Highld 80 F2
Camusnagaul Highld 86 C3
Camusrory Highld 79 B11
Camusteel Highld 85 D12
Camusterrach Highld 85 D12
Camusvrachan Perth 75 C9
Canada Hants 10 C1
Canadia E Sus 12 E6
Canal Side S Yorks 45 A10
Candacraig Ho. Aberds 82 B5
Candlesby Lincs 47 F8
Candy Mill S Lanark 69 F9
Cane End Oxon 18 D3
Canewdon Essex 20 B5
Canford Bottom Dorset 9 D9
Canford Cliffs Poole 9 F9
Canford Magna Poole 9 E9
Canham's Green Suff 31 B7
Canholes Derbys 44 E4
Canisbay Highld 94 C5
Cann Dorset 9 B7
Cann Common Dorset 9 B7
Cannard's Grave Som 16 G3
Cannich Highld 86 H6
Cannington Som 15 H8
Cannock Staffs 34 E5
Cannock Wood Staffs 34 D6
Canon Bridge Hereford 25 D11
Canon Frome Hereford 26 D3
Canon Pyon Hereford 25 D11
Canonbie Dumfries 61 F9
Canons Ashby Northants 28 C2
Canonstown Corn 2 F4
Canterbury Kent 21 F8
Cantley Norf 39 E9
Cantley S Yorks 45 B10
Cantlop Shrops 33 E11
Canton Cardiff 15 D7
Cantraybruich Highld 87 G10
Cantraydoune Highld 87 G10
Cantraywood Highld 87 G10
Cantsfield Lancs 50 B2
Canvey Island Essex 20 C4
Canwick Lincs 46 F3
Canworthy Water Corn 4 B3
Caol Highld 80 F3
Caol Ila Argyll 64 A5
Caolas Argyll 78 G3
Caolas Scalpaigh W Isles 90 H7
Caolas Stocinis W Isles 90 H6
Capel Sur 19 G8
Capel Bangor Ceredig 32 G2
Capel Betws Lleucu Ceredig 24 C3
Capel Carmel Gwyn 40 H3
Capel Coch Anglesey 40 B6
Capel Curig Conwy 41 E9
Capel Cynon Ceredig 23 B8
Capel Dewi Carms 23 D9
Capel Dewi Ceredig 23 B9
Capel Dewi Ceredig 32 G2
Capel Garmon Conwy 41 E10
Capel-gwyn Anglesey 40 C5
Capel Gwyn Carms 23 D9
Capel Gwynfe Carms 24 F4
Capel Hendre Carms 23 E10
Capel Hermon Gwyn 32 C3
Capel Isaac Carms 23 D10
Capel Iwan Carms 23 C7
Capel le Ferne Kent 21 H9
Capel Llanilltern Cardiff 14 C6
Capel Mawr Anglesey 40 C6
Capel St Andrew Suff 31 D10
Capel St Mary Suff 31 E7
Capel Seion Ceredig 32 H2
Capel Tygwydd Ceredig 23 B7
Capel Uchaf Gwyn 40 F6
Capel-y-graig Gwyn 41 D7
Capelulo Conwy 41 C9
Capenhurst Ches W 42 E6
Capernwray Lancs 49 B5
Capheaton Northumb 62 E6
Cappercleuch Borders 61 A8
Capplegill Dumfries 61 C7
Capton Devon 5 F9
Caputh Perth 76 D3
Car Colston Notts 36 A3
Carbis Bay Corn 2 F4
Carbost Highld 85 D9
Carbost Highld 85 E8
Carbrook S Yorks 45 D7
Carbrooke Norf 38 E5
Carburton Notts 45 E10
Carcant Borders 70 E2
Carcary Angus 77 B9
Carclaze Corn 3 D9
Carcroft S Yorks 45 A9
Cardenden Fife 69 A11
Cardeston Shrops 33 D9
Cardiff = Caerdydd Cardiff 15 D7
Cardigan = Aberteifi Ceredig 22 B6
Cardington Bedford 29 D7
Cardington Shrops 33 F11
Cardinham Corn 4 E2
Cardonald Glasgow 68 D4
Cardow Moray 88 D1
Cardrona Borders 70 G2
Cardross Argyll 68 C2
Cardurnock Cumb 61 H7
Careby Lincs 36 D6
Careston Castle Angus 77 B8
Carew Pembs 22 F5
Carew Cheriton Pembs 22 F5
Carew Newton Pembs 22 F5
Carey Hereford 26 E2
Carfrae E Loth 70 D4
Cargenbridge Dumfries 60 F5
Cargill Perth 76 D4
Cargo Cumb 61 H9
Cargreen Corn 4 E5
Carham Northumb 71 G7
Carhampton Som 7 B9
Carharrack Corn 2 E6
Carie Perth 75 B9
Carie Perth 75 D9
Carines Corn 3 D6
Carisbrooke IoW 10 F3
Cark Cumb 49 B3
Carlabhagh W Isles 90 C7
Carland Cross Corn 3 D7
Carlby Lincs 37 D6
Carlecotes S Yorks 44 B5
Carlesmoor N Yorks 51 B7
Carleton Cumb 56 A6
Carleton Cumb 57 D7
Carleton Lancs 49 F3
Carleton N Yorks 50 E5
Carleton Forehoe Norf 39 E6
Carleton Rode Norf 39 F7
Carlin How Redcar 59 E8
Carlingcott Bath 16 F3
Carlisle Cumb 61 H10
Carlops Borders 69 E10
Carlton Bedford 28 C6
Carlton Cambs 30 C3
Carlton Leics 35 E9
Carlton N Yorks 51 A6
Carlton N Yorks 52 G2
Carlton N Yorks 58 E2
Carlton N Yorks 59 H7
Carlton Notts 36 A2
Carlton S Yorks 45 A7
Carlton Stockton 58 D4
Carlton Suff 31 B10
Carlton W Yorks 51 G9
Carlton Colville Suff 39 G11
Carlton Curlieu Leics 36 F2
Carlton Husthwaite N Yorks 51 B10
Carlton in Cleveland N Yorks 58 F6
Carlton in Lindrick Notts 45 D9
Carlton le Moorland Lincs 46 G3
Carlton Miniott N Yorks 51 A9
Carlton on Trent Notts 45 F11
Carlton Scroop Lincs 36 A5
Carluke S Lanark 69 E7
Carmarthen = Caerfyrddin Carms 23 D9
Carmel Anglesey 40 B5
Carmel Carms 23 E10
Carmel Flint 42 E4
Carmel Guern 11
Carmel Gwyn 40 E6
Carmont Aberds 83 E10
Carmunnock Glasgow 68 E5
Carmyle Glasgow 68 D5
Carmyllie Angus 77 C8
Carn-gorm Highld 80 A1
Carnaby E Yorks 53 C7
Carnach Highld 80 A2
Carnach Highld 86 B3
Carnach W Isles 90 H7
Carnachy Highld 93 D10
Càrnais W Isles 90 D5
Carnbee Fife 77 G8
Carnbo Perth 76 G3
Carnbrea Corn 2 E5
Carnduff S Lanark 68 F5
Carnduncan Argyll 64 B3
Carne Corn 3 F8
Carnforth Lancs 49 B4
Carnhedryn Pembs 22 D3
Carnhell Green Corn 2 F5
Carnkie Corn 2 F5
Carnkie Corn 2 F6
Carno Powys 32 F5
Carnoch Highld 86 F5
Carnoch Highld 86 H6
Carnock Fife 69 B9
Carnon Downs Corn 3 E6
Carnousie Aberds 89 C6
Carnoustie Angus 77 D8
Carnwath S Lanark 69 F8
Carnyorth Corn 2 F2
Carperby N Yorks 58 H1
Carpley Green N Yorks 57 H11
Carr S Yorks 45 C9
Carr Hill T&W 63 G8
Carradale Argyll 65 E9
Carragraich W Isles 90 H6
Carrbridge Highld 81 A11
Carrefour Selous Jersey 11
Carreg-wen Pembs 23 B7
Carreglefn Anglesey 40 B5
Carrick Argyll 73 E8
Carrick Fife 77 E7
Carrick Castle Argyll 73 D10
Carrick Ho. Orkney 95 E6
Carriden Falk 69 B9
Carrington Gtr Man 43 C10
Carrington Lincs 47 G7
Carrington Midloth 70 D2
Carrog Conwy 41 F9
Carrog Denb 33 A7
Carron Falk 69 B7
Carron Moray 88 D2
Carron Bridge Stirling 68 B6
Carronbridge Dumfries 60 D4
Carrshield Northumb 57 B10
Carrutherstown Dumfries 61 F7
Carrville Durham 58 B4
Carsaig Argyll 72 E6
Carsaig Argyll 79 J8
Carscreugh Dumfries 54 D5
Carse Gray Angus 77 B7
Carse Ho. Argyll 72 G6
Carsegowan Dumfries 55 D7
Carseriggan Dumfries 54 C6
Carsethorn Dumfries 60 H5
Carshalton London 19 E9
Carsington Derbys 44 G6
Carskiey Argyll 65 H7
Carsluith Dumfries 55 D7
Carsphairn Dumfries 67 G8
Carstairs S Lanark 69 F8
Carstairs Junction S Lanark 69 F8
Carswell Marsh Oxon 17 B10
Carter's Clay Hants 10 B2
Carterton Oxon 27 H9
Carterway Heads Northumb 58 A1
Carthew Corn 3 D9
Carthorpe N Yorks 51 A9
Cartington Northumb 62 C6
Cartland S Lanark 69 F7
Cartmel Cumb 49 B3
Cartmel Fell Cumb 56 H6
Carway Carms 23 F9
Cary Fitzpaine Som 8 B4
Cas-gwent = Chepstow Mon 15 B11
Cascob Powys 25 B9
Cashlie Perth 75 C7
Cashmoor Dorset 9 C8
Casnewydd = Newport Newport 15 C9
Cassey Compton Glos 27 G7
Cassington Oxon 27 G11
Cassop Durham 58 C4
Castell Denb 42 F4
Castell-Howell Ceredig 23 B9
Castell-Nedd = Neath Neath 14 B3
Castell Newydd Emlyn = Newcastle Emlyn Carms 23 B8
Castell-y-bwch Torf 15 B8
Castellau Rhondda 14 C6
Casterton Cumb 50 B2
Castle Acre Norf 38 D4
Castle Ashby Northants 28 C5
Castle Bolton N Yorks 58 G1
Castle Bromwich W Mid 35 G7
Castle Bytham Lincs 36 D5
Castle Caereinion Powys 33 E7
Castle Camps Cambs 30 D3
Castle Carrock Cumb 61 H11
Castle Cary Som 8 A5
Castle Combe Wilts 16 D5
Castle Donington Leics 35 C10
Castle Douglas Dumfries 55 C10
Castle Eaton Swindon 17 B8
Castle Eden Durham 58 C5
Castle Forbes Aberds 83 B8
Castle Frome Hereford 26 D3
Castle Green Sur 18 E6
Castle Gresley Derbys 35 D8
Castle Heaton Northumb 71 F8
Castle Hedingham Essex 30 E4
Castle Hill Kent 12 B5
Castle Huntly Perth 76 E6
Castle Kennedy Dumfries 54 D4
Castle O'er Dumfries 61 D8
Castle Pulverbatch Shrops 33 E10
Castle Rising Norf 38 C2
Castle Stuart Highld 87 G10
Castlebay = Bagh a Chaisteil W Isles 84 J1
Castlebythe Pembs 22 D5
Castlecary N Lanark 68 C6
Castlecraig Highld 87 E11
Castlefairn Dumfries 60 E3
Castleford W Yorks 51 G10
Castlehill Borders 69 G11
Castlehill Highld 94 D3
Castlehill W Dunb 68 C2
Castlemaddy Dumfries 67 H8
Castlemartin Pembs 22 G4
Castlemilk Dumfries 61 F7
Castlemilk Glasgow 68 E5
Castlemorris Pembs 22 C4
Castlemorton Worcs 26 E4
Castleside Durham 58 B1
Castlethorpe M Keynes 28 D5
Castleton Angus 76 C6
Castleton Argyll 73 E7
Castleton Derbys 44 D5
Castleton Gtr Man 44 A2
Castleton N Yorks 59 F7
Castleton Newport 15 C8
Castletown Ches W 43 G7
Castletown Highld 87 G10
Castletown Highld 94 D3
Castletown IoM 48 F2
Castletown T&W 63 H9
Castleweary Borders 61 C10
Castley N Yorks 51 E8
Caston Norf 38 F5
Castor Pboro 37 F7
Catacol N Ayrs 66 B2
Catbrain S Glos 16 C2
Catbrook Mon 15 A11
Catchall Corn 2 G3
Catchems Corner W Mid 35 H8
Catchgate Durham 58 A2
Catcleugh Northumb 62 C3
Catcliffe S Yorks 45 D8
Catcott Som 15 H9
Caterham Sur 19 F10
Catfield Norf 39 C9
Catfirth Shetland 96 H6
Catford London 19 D10
Catforth Lancs 49 F4
Cathays Cardiff 15 D7
Cathcart Glasgow 68 D4
Cathedine Powys 25 F8
Catherington Hants 10 C5
Catherton Shrops 34 H2
Catlodge Highld 81 D8
Catlowdy Cumb 61 F10
Catmore W Berks 17 C11
Caton Lancs 49 C5
Caton Green Lancs 49 C5
Catrine E Ayrs 67 D8
Cat's Ash Newport 15 B9
Catsfield E Sus 12 E6
Catshill Worcs 26 A6
Cattal N Yorks 51 D10
Cattawade Suff 31 E8
Catterall Lancs 49 E4
Catterick N Yorks 58 G3
Catterick Bridge N Yorks 58 G3
Catterick Garrison N Yorks 58 G2
Catterlen Cumb 57 C6
Catterline Aberds 83 F10
Catterton N Yorks 51 E11
Catthorpe Leics 36 H1
Cattistock Dorset 8 E4
Catton N Yorks 51 B9
Catton Northumb 62 H4
Catwick E Yorks 53 E7
Catworth Cambs 29 A7
Caudlesprings Norf 38 E5
Caulcott Oxon 28 F2
Cauldcots Angus 77 C9
Cauldhame Stirling 68 A5
Cauldmill Borders 61 B11
Cauldon Staffs 44 H4
Caulkerbush Dumfries 60 H5
Caulside Dumfries 61 E10
Caunsall Worcs 34 G4
Caunton Notts 45 G11
Causeway End Dumfries 55 C7
Causeway Foot W Yorks 51 F6
Causeway-head Stirling 75 H10
Causewayend S Lanark 69 G9
Causewayhead Cumb 56 A3
Causey Park Bridge Northumb 63 D7
Causeyend Aberds 83 B11
Cautley Cumb 57 G8
Cavendish Suff 30 D5
Cavendish Bridge Leics 35 C10
Cavenham Suff 30 A4
Caversfield Oxon 28 F2
Caversham Reading 18 D4
Caverswall Staffs 34 A5
Cavil E Yorks 52 F3
Cawdor Highld 87 F11
Cawkwell Lincs 46 E6
Cawood N Yorks 52 F1
Cawsand Corn 4 F5
Cawston Norf 39 C7
Cawthorne S Yorks 44 B6
Cawthorpe Lincs 37 C6
Cawton N Yorks 52 B2
Caxton Cambs 29 C10
Caynham Shrops 26 A2
Caythorpe Lincs 46 H3
Caythorpe Notts 45 H10
Cayton N Yorks 53 A6
Ceann a Bhaigh W Isles 84 B2
Ceann a Deas Loch Baghasdail W Isles 84 G2
Ceann Shiphoirt W Isles 91 F7
Ceann Tarabhaigh W Isles 90 F7
Ceannacroc Lodge Highld 80 B4
Cearsiadair W Isles 91 E8
Cefn Berain Conwy 42 F2
Cefn-brith Conwy 42 G2
Cefn Canol Powys 33 B8
Cefn-coch Conwy 41 D10
Cefn Coch Powys 33 C7
Cefn-coed-y-cymmer M Tydf 25 H7
Cefn Cribbwr Bridgend 14 C4
Cefn Cross Bridgend 14 C4
Cefn-ddwysarn Gwyn 32 B5
Cefn Einion Shrops 33 G8
Cefn-gorwydd Powys 24 D6
Cefn-mawr Wrex 33 A8
Cefn-y-bedd Flint 42 G6
Cefn-y-pant Carms 22 D6
Cefneithin Carms 23 E10
Cei-bach Ceredig 23 A9
Ceinewydd = New Quay Ceredig 23 A8
Ceint Anglesey 40 C6
Cellan Ceredig 24 D3
Cellarhead Staffs 44 H3
Cemaes Anglesey 40 A5
Cemmaes Powys 32 E4
Cemmaes Road Powys 32 E4
Cenarth Carms 23 B7
Cenin Gwyn 40 F6
Central Invclyd 73 F11
Ceos W Isles 91 E8
Ceres Fife 77 F7
Cerne Abbas Dorset 8 D5
Cerney Wick Glos 17 B7
Cerrigceinwen Anglesey 40 C6
Cerrigydrudion Conwy 42 H2
Cessford Borders 62 A3
Ceunant Gwyn 41 D7
Chaceley Glos 26 E5
Chacewater Corn 3 E6
Chackmore Bucks 28 E3
Chacombe Northants 27 D11
Chad Valley W Mid 34 G6
Chadderton Gtr Man 44 B3
Chadderton Fold Gtr Man 44 B2
Chaddesden Derby 35 B9
Chaddesley Corbett Worcs 26 A5
Chaddleworth W Berks 17 D11
Chadlington Oxon 27 F10
Chadshunt Warks 27 C10
Chadwell Leics 36 C3
Chadwell St Mary Thurrock 20 D3
Chadwick End W Mid 27 A9
Chadwick Green Mers 43 C8
Chaffcombe Som 8 C2
Chagford Devon 5 C8
Chailey E Sus 12 E2
Chain Bridge Lincs 37 A9
Chainbridge Cambs 37 E10
Chainhurst Kent 20 G4
Chalbury Dorset 9 D9
Chalbury Common Dorset 9 D9
Chaldon Sur 19 F10
Chaldon Herring Dorset 9 F6
Chale IoW 10 G3
Chale Green IoW 10 G3
Chalfont Common Bucks 19 B7
Chalfont St Giles Bucks 18 B6
Chalfont St Peter Bucks 19 B7
Chalford Glos 16 A5
Chalgrove Oxon 18 B3
Chalk Kent 20 D3
Challacombe Devon 6 B5
Challoch Dumfries 54 C6
Challock Kent 21 F7
Chalton C Beds 29 F7
Chalton Hants 10 C6
Chalvington E Sus 12 F4
Chancery Ceredig 32 H1
Chandler's Ford Hants 10 B3
Channel Tunnel Kent 21 H8
Channerwick Shetland 96 L6
Chantry Som 16 G4
Chantry Suff 31 D8
Chapel Fife 69 A11
Chapel Allerton Som 15 F10
Chapel Allerton W Yorks 51 F9
Chapel Amble Corn 3 B8
Chapel Brampton Northants 28 B4
Chapel Chorlton Staffs 34 B4
Chapel-en-le-Frith Derbys 44 D4
Chapel End Warks 35 F9
Chapel Green Warks 27 B11
Chapel Green Warks 35 G8
Chapel Haddlesey N Yorks 52 G1
Chapel Head Cambs 37 G9
Chapel Hill Aberds 89 E10
Chapel Hill Lincs 46 G6
Chapel Hill Mon 15 B11
Chapel Hill N Yorks 51 E9
Chapel Lawn Shrops 33 H9
Chapel-le-Dale N Yorks 50 B3
Chapel Milton Derbys 44 D4
Chapel of Garioch Aberds 83 A9
Chapel Row W Berks 18 E2
Chapel St Leonards Lincs 47 E9
Chapel Stile Cumb 56 F5
Chapelgate Lincs 37 C10
Chapelhall N Lanark 68 D6
Chapelhill Dumfries 60 D6
Chapelhill Highld 87 D11
Chapelhill N Ayrs 66 B5
Chapelhill Perth 76 D3
Chapelhill Perth 76 E5
Chapelknowe Dumfries 61 F9
Chapelton Angus 77 C9
Chapelton Devon 6 D4
Chapelton Highld 81 B11
Chapelton S Lanark 68 F5
Chapeltown Blackburn 50 H3
Chapeltown Moray 82 A4
Chapeltown S Yorks 45 C7
Chapmans Well Devon 6 G2
Chapmanslade Wilts 16 G5
Chapmore End Herts 29 G10
Chappel Essex 30 F5
Chard Som 8 D2
Chardstock Devon 8 D2
Charfield S Glos 16 B4
Charford Worcs 26 B6
Charing Kent 20 G6
Charing Cross Dorset 9 C10
Charing Heath Kent 20 G6
Charingworth Glos 27 E9
Charlbury Oxon 27 G10
Charlcombe Bath 16 E4
Charlecote Warks 27 C9
Charles Devon 6 C5
Charles Tye Suff 31 C7
Charlesfield Dumfries 61 G7
Charleston Angus 76 C6
Charleston Renfs 68 D3
Charlestown Aberdeen 83 C11
Charlestown Corn 3 D9
Charlestown Derbys 44 C4
Charlestown Dorset 8 G5
Charlestown Fife 69 B9
Charlestown Gtr Man 44 B2
Charlestown Highld 85 A13
Charlestown Highld 87 G9
Charlestown W Yorks 50 G5
Charlestown of Aberlour Moray 88 D2
Charlesworth Derbys 44 C4
Charleton Devon 5 G8
Charlton Hants 17 G10
Charlton Herts 29 F8
Charlton London 19 D11
Charlton Northants 28 E2
Charlton Northumb 62 E4
Charlton Som 16 F3
Charlton Telford 34 D1
Charlton W Sus 11 C7
Charlton Wilts 9 B8
Charlton Wilts 16 C6
Charlton Wilts 17 F8
Charlton Worcs 27 D7
Charlton Abbots Glos 27 F7
Charlton Adam Som 8 B4
Charlton-All-Saints Wilts 9 B10
Charlton Down Dorset 8 E5
Charlton Horethorne Som 8 B5
Charlton Kings Glos 26 F6
Charlton Mackerell Som 8 B4
Charlton Marshall Dorset 9 D7
Charlton Musgrove Som 8 B6
Charlton on Otmoor Oxon 28 G2
Charltons Redcar 59 E7
Charlwood Sur 19 G9
Charlynch Som 7 C11
Charminster Dorset 8 E5
Charmouth Dorset 8 E2
Charndon Bucks 28 F3
Charney Bassett Oxon 17 B10
Charnock Richard Lancs 50 H1
Charsfield Suff 31 C9
Chart Corner Kent 20 F4
Chart Sutton Kent 20 G5
Charter Alley Hants 18 F2
Charterhouse Som 15 F10
Charterville Allotments Oxon 27 G10
Chartham Kent 21 F8
Chartham Hatch Kent 21 F8
Chartridge Bucks 18 A6
Charvil Wokingham 18 D4
Charwelton Northants 28 C2
Chasetown Staffs 34 E6
Chastleton Oxon 27 F9
Chasty Devon 6 F2
Chatburn Lancs 50 E3
Chatcull Staffs 34 B3
Chatham Medway 20 E4
Chathill Northumb 71 H10
Chattenden Medway 20 D4
Chatteris Cambs 37 G9
Chattisham Suff 31 D7
Chatto Borders 62 B3
Chatton Northumb 71 H9
Chawleigh Devon 7 E6
Chawley Oxon 17 A11
Chawston Bedford 29 C8
Chawton Hants 18 H4
Cheadle Gtr Man 44 D2
Cheadle Staffs 34 A6
Cheadle Heath Gtr Man 44 D2
Cheadle Hulme Gtr Man 44 D2
Cheam London 19 E9
Cheapside Sur 19 F7
Chearsley Bucks 28 G4
Chebsey Staffs 34 C4
Checkendon Oxon 18 C3
Checkley Ches E 43 H10
Checkley Hereford 26 E2
Checkley Staffs 34 B6
Chedburgh Suff 30 C4
Cheddar Som 15 F10
Cheddington Bucks 28 G6
Cheddleton Staffs 44 G3
Cheddon Fitzpaine Som 8 B1
Chedglow Wilts 16 B6
Chedgrave Norf 39 F9
Chedington Dorset 8 D3
Chediston Suff 39 H9
Chedworth Glos 27 G7
Chedzoy Som 15 H9
Cheeklaw Borders 70 E6
Cheeseman's Green Kent 13 C9
Cheglinch Devon 6 B4
Cheldon Devon 7 E6
Chelford Ches E 44 E2
Chell Heath Stoke 44 G2
Chellaston Derby 35 B9
Chellington Bedford 28 C6
Chelmarsh Shrops 34 G3
Chelmer Village Essex 30 H4
Chelmondiston Suff 31 E9
Chelmorton Derbys 44 F5
Chelmsford Essex 30 H4
Chelsea London 19 D9
Chelsfield London 19 E11
Chelsworth Suff 30 D6
Cheltenham Glos 26 F6
Chelveston Northants 28 B6
Chelvey N Som 15 E10
Chelwood Bath 16 E3
Chelwood Common E Sus 12 D3
Chelwood Gate E Sus 12 D3
Chelworth Wilts 16 B6
Chelworth Green Wilts 17 B7
Chemistry Shrops 33 A11
Chenies Bucks 19 B7
Cheny Longville Shrops 33 G10
Chepstow = Cas-gwent Mon 15 B11
Chequerfield W Yorks 51 G10
Cherhill Wilts 17 D7
Cherington Glos 16 B6
Cherington Warks 27 E9
Cheriton Devon 7 B6
Cheriton Hants 10 B4
Cheriton Kent 21 H8
Cheriton Swansea 23 G9
Cheriton Bishop Devon 7 G6
Cheriton Fitzpaine Devon 7 F7
Cheriton or Stackpole Elidor Pembs 22 G4
Cherrington Telford 34 C2
Cherry Burton E Yorks 52 E5
Cherry Hinton Cambs 29 C11
Cherry Orchard Worcs 26 C5
Cherry Willingham Lincs 46 E4
Cherrybank Perth 76 E4
Cherrytree Sur 19 E7
Cheselbourne Dorset 9 E6
Chesham Bucks 18 A6
Chesham Bois Bucks 18 B6
Cheshunt Herts 19 A10
Cheslyn Hay Staffs 34 E5
Chessington London 19 E8
Chester Ches W 43 F7
Chester-Le-Street Durham 58 A3
Chester Moor Durham 58 B3
Chesterblade Som 16 G3
Chesterfield Derbys 45 E7
Chesters Borders 62 A2
Chesters Borders 62 B2
Chesterton Cambs 29 B11
Chesterton Cambs 37 F7
Chesterton Glos 17 A7
Chesterton Oxon 28 F2
Chesterton Shrops 34 F3
Chesterton Staffs 44 H2
Chesterton Warks 27 C10
Chesterwood Northumb 62 G4
Chestfield Kent 21 E8
Cheston Devon 5 F7
Cheswardine Shrops 34 C3
Cheswick Northumb 71 F9
Chetnole Dorset 8 D5
Chettiscombe Devon 7 E8
Chettisham Cambs 37 G11
Chettle Dorset 9 C8
Chetton Shrops 34 F2
Chetwode Bucks 28 F3
Chetwynd Aston Telford 34 D3
Cheveley Cambs 30 B3
Chevening Kent 19 F11
Chevington Suff 30 C4
Chevithorne Devon 7 E8
Chew Magna Bath 16 E2
Chew Stoke Bath 16 E2
Chewton Keynsham Bath 16 E3
Chewton Mendip Som 16 F2
Chicheley M Keynes 28 D6
Chichester W Sus 11 D7
Chickerell Dorset 8 F5
Chicklade Wilts 9 A8
Chicksgrove Wilts 9 A8
Chidden Hants 10 C5
Chiddingfold Sur 18 H6
Chiddingly E Sus 12 E4
Chiddingstone Kent 19 G11
Chiddingstone Causeway Kent 20 G2
Chiddingstone Hoath Kent 12 B3
Chideock Dorset 8 E3
Chidham W Sus 11 D6
Chidswell W Yorks 51 G8
Chieveley W Berks 17 D11
Chignall St James Essex 30 H3
Chignall Smealy Essex 30 G3
Chigwell Essex 19 B11
Chigwell Row Essex 19 B11
Chilbolton Hants 17 H10
Chilcomb Hants 10 B4
Chilcombe Dorset 8 E4
Chilcompton Som 16 F3
Chilcote Leics 35 D8
Child Okeford Dorset 9 C7
Childer Thornton Ches W 42 E6
Childrey Oxon 17 C10
Child's Ercall Shrops 34 C2
Childswickham Worcs 27 E7
Childwall Mers 43 D7
Childwick Green Herts 29 G8
Chilfrome Dorset 8 E4
Chilgrove W Sus 11 C7
Chilham Kent 21 F7
Chilhampton Wilts 9 A9
Chilla Devon 6 F3
Chillaton Devon 4 C5
Chillenden Kent 21 F9
Chillerton IoW 10 F3
Chillesford Suff 31 C10
Chillingham Northumb 71 H9
Chillington Devon 5 G8
Chillington Som 8 C2
Chilmark Wilts 9 A8
Chilson Oxon 27 G10
Chilsworthy Corn 4 D5
Chilsworthy Devon 6 F2
Chilthorne Domer Som 8 C4
Chiltington E Sus 12 E2
Chilton Bucks 28 G3
Chilton Durham 58 D3
Chilton Oxon 17 C11
Chilton Cantelo Som 8 B4
Chilton Foliat Wilts 17 D10
Chilton Lane Durham 58 C4
Chilton Polden Som 15 H9
Chilton Street Suff 30 D4
Chilton Trinity Som 15 H8
Chilvers Coton Warks 35 F9
Chilwell Notts 35 B11
Chilworth Hants 10 C3
Chilworth Sur 19 G7
Chimney Oxon 17 A10
Chineham Hants 18 F3
Chingford London 19 B10
Chinley Derbys 44 D4
Chinley Head Derbys 44 D4
Chinnor Oxon 18 A4
Chipnall Shrops 34 B3
Chippenhall Green Suff 39 H8
Chippenham Cambs 30 A3
Chippenham Wilts 16 D6
Chipperfield Herts 19 A7
Chipping Herts 29 E10
Chipping Lancs 50 E2
Chipping Campden Glos 27 E8
Chipping Hill Essex 30 G5
Chipping Norton Oxon 27 F10
Chipping Ongar Essex 20 A2
Chipping Sodbury S Glos 16 C4
Chipping Warden Northants 27 D11
Chipstable Som 7 D9
Chipstead Kent 19 F11
Chipstead Sur 19 F9
Chirbury Shrops 33 F8
Chirk = Y Waun Wrex 33 B8
Chirk Bank Shrops 33 B8
Chirmorrie S Ayrs 54 B5
Chirnside Borders 71 E7
Chirnsidebridge Borders 71 E7
Chirton Wilts 17 F7
Chisbury Wilts 17 E9
Chiselborough Som 8 C3
Chiseldon Swindon 17 D8
Chiserley W Yorks 50 G6
Chislehampton Oxon 18 B2
Chislehurst London 19 D11
Chislet Kent 21 E9
Chiswell Green Herts 19 A8
Chiswick London 19 D9
Chiswick End Cambs 29 D10
Chisworth Derbys 44 C3
Chithurst W Sus 11 B7
Chittering Cambs 29 A11
Chitterne Wilts 16 G6
Chittlehamholt Devon 6 D5
Chittlehampton Devon 6 D5
Chittoe Wilts 16 E6
Chivenor Devon 6 C4
Chobham Sur 18 E6
Choicelee Borders 70 E6
Cholderton Wilts 17 G9
Cholesbury Bucks 28 H6
Chollerford Northumb 62 F5
Chollerton Northumb 62 F5
Cholmondeston Ches E 43 F9
Cholsey Oxon 18 C2
Cholstrey Hereford 25 C11
Chop Gate N Yorks 59 G6
Choppington Northumb 63 E8
Chopwell T&W 63 H7
Chorley Ches E 43 G8
Chorley Lancs 50 H1
Chorley Shrops 34 G2
Chorley Staffs 35 D6
Chorleywood Herts 19 B7
Chorlton cum Hardy Gtr Man 44 C2
Chorlton Lane Ches W 43 H7
Choulton Shrops 33 G9
Chowdene T&W 63 H8
Chowley Ches W 43 G7
Chrishall Essex 29 E11
Christchurch Cambs 37 F10
Christchurch Dorset 9 E10
Christchurch Glos 26 G2
Christchurch Newport 15 C9
Christian Malford Wilts 16 D6
Christleton Ches W 43 F7
Christmas Common Oxon 18 B4
Christon N Som 15 F9
Christon Bank Northumb 63 A8
Christow Devon 5 C9
Chryston N Lanark 68 C5
Chudleigh Devon 5 D9
Chudleigh Knighton Devon 5 D9
Chulmleigh Devon 6 E5
Chunal Derbys 44 C4
Church Lancs 50 G3
Church Aston Telford 34 D3
Church Brampton Northants 28 B4
Church Broughton Derbys 35 B8
Church Crookham Hants 18 F5
Church Eaton Staffs 34 D4
Church End C Beds 28 E6
Church End C Beds 28 F6
Church End C Beds 29 E8
Church End Cambs 37 E9
Church End Cambs 37 G8
Church End E Yorks 53 D6
Church End Essex 30 D2
Church End Essex 30 F4
Church End Hants 18 F3
Church End Lincs 37 B8
Church End Warks 35 F8
Church End Warks 35 F8
Church End Wilts 17 D7
Church Enstone Oxon 27 F10
Church Fenton N Yorks 51 F11
Church Green Devon 7 G10
Church Green Norf 39 F6
Church Gresley Derbys 35 D8
Church Hanborough Oxon 27 G11
Church Hill Ches W 43 F9
Church Houses N Yorks 59 G7
Church Knowle Dorset 9 F8
Church Laneham Notts 46 E2
Church Langton Leics 36 F3
Church Lawford Warks 35 H10
Church Lawton Ches E 44 G2
Church Leigh Staffs 34 B6
Church Lench Worcs 27 C7
Church Mayfield Staffs 35 A7
Church Minshull Ches E 43 F9
Church Norton W Sus 11 E7
Church Preen Shrops 33 F11
Church Pulverbatch Shrops 33 E10
Church Stoke Powys 33 F8
Church Stowe Northants 28 C3
Church Street Kent 20 D4
Church Stretton Shrops 33 F10
Church Town N Lincs 45 B11
Church Town Sur 19 F10
Church Village Rhondda 14 C6
Church Warsop Notts 45 F9
Churcham Glos 26 G4
Churchbank Shrops 33 H8
Churchbridge Staffs 34 E5
Churchdown Glos 26 G5
Churchend Essex 21 B7
Churchend Essex 30 F3
Churchend S Glos 16 B4
Churchfield W Mid 34 F6
Churchgate Street Essex 29 G11
Churchill Devon 6 B4
Churchill Devon 8 D2

Churchill N Som 15 F10
Churchill Oxon 27 F9
Churchill Worcs 26 C6
Churchill Worcs 34 H4
Churchinford Som 7 E11
Churchover Warks 35 G11
Churchstanton Som 7 E10
Churchstow Devon 5 G8
Churchtown Derbys 44 F6
Churchtown IoM 48 C4
Churchtown Lancs 49 E4
Churchtown Mers 49 H3
Churnsike Lodge Northumb 62 F2
Churston Ferrers Torbay 5 F10
Churt Sur 18 H5
Churton Ches W 43 G7
Churwell W Yorks 51 G8
Chute Standen Wilts 17 F10
Chwilog Gwyn 40 G6
Chyandour Corn 2 F3
Cilan Uchaf Gwyn 40 H4
Cilcain Flint 42 F4
Cilcennin Ceredig 24 B2
Cilfor Gwyn 41 G8
Cilfrew Neath 14 A3
Cilfynydd Rhondda 14 B6
Cilgerran Pembs 22 B6
Cilgwyn Carms 24 F4
Cilgwyn Gwyn 40 E6
Cilgwyn Pembs 22 C5
Ciliau Aeron Ceredig 23 A9
Cill Donnain W Isles 84 F2
Cille Bhrighde W Isles 84 G2
Cille Pheadair W Isles 84 G2
Cilmery Powys 25 C7
Cilsan Carms 23 D10
Ciltalgarth Gwyn 41 F10
Cilwendeg Pembs 23 C7
Cilybebyll Neath 14 A3
Cilycwm Carms 24 E4
Cimla Neath 14 B3
Cinderford Glos 26 G3
Cippyn Pembs 22 B6
Circebost W Isles 90 D6
Cirencester Glos 17 A7
Ciribhig W Isles 90 C6
City London 19 C10
City Powys 33 G8
City Dulas Anglesey 40 B6
Clachaig Argyll 73 E10
Clachan Argyll 72 B6
Clachan Argyll 72 H6
Clachan Argyll 74 F4
Clachan Argyll 79 G11
Clachan Highld 85 E10
Clachan W Isles 84 D2
Clachan na Luib W Isles 84 B3
Clachan of Campsie E Dunb 68 C5
Clachan of Glendaruel Argyll 73 E8
Clachan-Seil Argyll 72 B6
Clachan Strachur Argyll 73 C9
Clachaneasy Dumfries 54 B6
Clachanmore Dumfries 54 E3
Clachbreck Argyll 72 F6
Clachnabrain Angus 82 G5
Clachtoll Highld 92 G3
Clackmannan Clack 69 A8
Clacton-on-Sea Essex 31 G8
Cladach Chireboist W Isles 84 B2
Claddach-knockline W Isles 84 B2
Cladich Argyll 74 E3
Claggan Highld 79 G9
Claggan Highld 80 F3
Claigan Highld 84 C7
Claines Worcs 26 C5
Clandown Bath 16 F3
Clanfield Hants 10 C5
Clanfield Oxon 17 A9
Clanville Hants 17 G10
Claonaig Argyll 73 H7
Claonel Highld 93 J8
Clap Hill Kent 13 C9
Clapgate Dorset 9 D9
Clapgate Herts 29 F11
Clapham Bedford 29 C7
Clapham London 19 D9
Clapham N Yorks 50 C3
Clapham W Sus 11 D9
Clappers Borders 71 E8
Clappersgate Cumb 56 F5
Clapton Som 8 D3
Clapton-in-Gordano N Som 15 D10
Clapton-on-the-Hill Glos 27 G8
Clapworthy Devon 6 D5
Clara Vale T&W 63 G7
Clarach Ceredig 32 G2
Clarbeston Pembs 22 D5
Clarbeston Road Pembs 22 D5
Clarborough Notts 45 D11
Clardon Highld 94 D3
Clare Suff 30 D4
Clarebrand Dumfries 55 C10
Clarencefield Dumfries 60 G6
Clarilaw Borders 61 B11
Clark's Green Sur 19 H8
Clarkston E Renf 68 E4
Clashandorran Highld 87 G8
Clashcoig Highld 87 B9
Clashindarroch Aberds 88 E4
Clashmore Highld 87 C10
Clashmore Highld 92 F3
Clashnessie Highld 92 F3
Clashnoir Moray 82 A4
Clate Shetland 96 G7
Clathy Perth 76 F2
Clatt Aberds 83 A7
Clatter Powys 32 F5
Clatterford IoW 10 F3
Clatterin Bridge Aberds 83 F8
Clatworthy Som 7 C9
Claughton Lancs 49 E5
Claughton Lancs 50 C1
Claughton Mers 42 D6
Claverdon Warks 27 B8
Claverham N Som 15 E10
Clavering Essex 29 E11
Claverley Shrops 34 F3
Claverton Bath 16 E4
Clawdd-newydd Denb 42 G3
Clawthorpe Cumb 49 B5
Clawton Devon 6 G2
Claxby Lincs 46 C5
Claxby Lincs 47 E8
Claxton NYorks 52 C2
Claxton Norf 39 E9
Clay Common Suff 39 G10
Clay Coton Northants 36 H1
Clay Cross Derbys 45 F7
Clay Hill W Berks 18 D2
Clay Lake Lincs 37 C8
Claybokie Aberds 82 D2
Claybrooke Magna Leics 35 G10
Claybrooke Parva Leics 35 G10
Claydon Oxon 27 C11
Claydon Suff 31 C8
Claygate Dumfries 61 F9
Claygate Kent 12 B6
Claygate Sur 19 E8
Claygate Cross Kent 20 F3
Clayhanger Devon 7 D9
Clayhanger W Mid 34 E6
Clayhidon Devon 7 E10
Clayhill E Sus 13 D7
Clayhill Hants 10 D2
Clayock Highld 94 E3
Claypole Lincs 46 H2
Clayton S Yorks 45 B8
Clayton Staffs 34 A4
Clayton W Sus 12 E1
Clayton W Yorks 51 F7
Clayton Green Lancs 50 G1
Clayton-le-Moors Lancs 50 F3
Clayton-le-Woods Lancs 50 G1
Clayton West W Yorks 44 A6
Clayworth Notts 45 D11
Cleadale Highld 78 C7
Cleadon T&W 63 G9
Clearbrook Devon 4 E6
Clearwell Glos 26 H2
Cleasby N Yorks 58 E3
Cleat Orkney 95 K5
Cleatlam Durham 58 E2
Cleator Cumb 56 E2
Cleator Moor Cumb 56 E2
Clebrig Highld 93 F8
Cleckheaton W Yorks 51 G7
Clee St Margaret Shrops 34 G1
Cleedownton Shrops 34 G1
Cleehill Shrops 34 H1
Cleethorpes NE Lincs 47 B7
Cleeton St Mary Shrops 34 H2
Cleeve N Som 15 E10
Cleeve Hill Glos 26 F6
Cleeve Prior Worcs 27 D7
Clegyrnant Powys 32 E5
Clehonger Hereford 25 E11
Cleish Perth 76 H3
Cleland N Lanark 69 E7
Clench Common Wilts 17 E8
Clenchwarton Norf 38 C1
Clent Worcs 34 H5
Cleobury Mortimer Shrops 34 H2
Cleobury North Shrops 34 G2
Cleongart Argyll 65 E7
Clephanton Highld 87 F11
Clerklands Borders 61 A11
Clestrain Orkney 95 H4
Cleuch Head Borders 61 B11
Cleughbrae Dumfries 60 F6
Clevancy Wilts 17 D7
Clevedon N Som 15 D10
Cleveley Oxon 27 F10
Cleveleys Lancs 49 E3
Cleverton Wilts 16 C6
Clevis Bridgend 14 D4
Clewer Som 15 F10
Cley next the Sea Norf 38 A6
Cliaid W Isles 84 H1
Cliasmol W Isles 90 G5
Cliburn Cumb 57 D7
Click Mill Orkney 95 F4
Cliddesden Hants 18 G3
Cliff End E Sus 13 E7
Cliffburn Angus 77 C9
Cliffe Medway 20 D4
Cliffe N Yorks 52 F2
Cliffe Woods Medway 20 D4
Clifford Hereford 25 D9
Clifford W Yorks 51 E10
Clifford Chambers Warks 27 C8
Clifford's Mesne Glos 26 F4
Cliffsend Kent 21 E10
Clifton Bristol 16 D2
Clifton C Beds 29 E8
Clifton Cumb 57 D7
Clifton Derbys 35 A7
Clifton Lancs 49 F4
Clifton N Yorks 51 E7
Clifton Northumb 63 E8
Clifton Nottingham 36 B1
Clifton Oxon 27 E11
Clifton S Yorks 45 C9
Clifton Stirling 74 D6
Clifton Worcs 26 D5
Clifton York 52 D1
Clifton Campville Staffs 35 D8
Clifton Green Gtr Man 43 B10
Clifton Hampden Oxon 18 B2
Clifton Reynes M Keynes 28 C6
Clifton upon Dunsmore Warks 35 H11
Clifton upon Teme Worcs 26 B4
Cliftoncote Borders 62 A4
Cliftonville Kent 21 D10
Climaen gwyn Neath 24 H4
Climping W Sus 11 D9
Climpy S Lanark 69 E8
Clink Som 16 G4
Clint N Yorks 51 D8
Clint Green Norf 38 D6
Clintmains Borders 70 G5
Cliobh W Isles 90 D5
Clippesby Norf 39 D10
Clipsham Rutland 36 D5
Clipston Northants 36 G3
Clipstone Notts 45 F9
Clitheroe Lancs 50 E3
Cliuthar W Isles 90 H6
Clive Shrops 33 C11
Clivocast Shetland 96 C8
Clixby Lincs 46 B5
Clocaenog Denb 42 G3
Clochan Moray 88 B4
Clock Face Mers 43 C8
Clockmill Borders 70 E6
Cloddiau Powys 33 E8
Clodock Hereford 25 F10
Clola Aberds 89 D10
Clophill C Beds 29 E7
Clopton Northants 37 G6
Clopton Suff 31 C9
Clopton Corner Suff 31 C9
Clopton Green Suff 30 C4
Close Clark IoM 48 E2
Closeburn Dumfries 60 D4
Closworth Som 8 C4
Clothall Herts 29 E9
Clotton Ches W 43 F8
Clough Foot W Yorks 50 G5
Cloughton N Yorks 59 G11
Cloughton Newlands N Yorks 59 G11
Clousta Shetland 96 H5
Clouston Orkney 95 G3
Clova Aberds 82 A6
Clova Angus 82 F5
Clove Lodge Durham 57 E11
Clovelly Devon 6 D2
Clovenfords Borders 70 G3
Clovenstone Aberds 83 B9
Clovullin Highld 74 A3
Clow Bridge Lancs 50 G4
Clowne Derbys 45 E8
Clows Top Worcs 26 A4
Cloy Wrex 33 A9
Cluanie Inn Highld 80 B2
Cluanie Lodge Highld 80 B2
Clun Shrops 33 G9
Clunbury Shrops 33 G9
Clunderwen Carms 22 E6
Clune Highld 81 A9
Clunes Highld 80 E4
Clungunford Shrops 33 H9
Clunie Aberds 89 C6
Clunie Perth 76 C4
Clunton Shrops 33 G9
Cluny Fife 76 H5
Cluny Castle Highld 81 D8
Clutton Bath 16 F3
Clutton Ches W 43 G7
Clwt-grugoer Conwy 42 F2
Clwt-y-bont Gwyn 41 D7
Clydach Mon 25 G9
Clydach Swansea 14 A2
Clydach Vale Rhondda 14 B5
Clydebank W Dunb 68 C3
Clydey Pembs 23 C7
Clyffe Pypard Wilts 17 D7
Clynder Argyll 73 E11
Clyne Neath 14 A4
Clynelish Highld 93 J11
Clynnog-fawr Gwyn 40 E6
Clyro Powys 25 D9
Clyst Honiton Devon 7 G8
Clyst Hydon Devon 7 F9
Clyst St George Devon 5 C10
Clyst St Lawrence Devon 7 F9
Clyst St Mary Devon 7 G8
Cnoc Amhlaigh W Isles 91 D10
Cnwch-coch Ceredig 32 H2
Coachford Aberds 88 D4
Coad's Green Corn 4 D3
Coal Aston Derbys 45 E7
Coalbrookdale Telford 34 E2
Coalbrookvale Bl Gwent 25 H8
Coalburn S Lanark 69 G7
Coalburns T&W 63 G7
Coalcleugh Northumb 57 B10
Coaley Glos 16 A4
Coalhall E Ayrs 67 E7
Coalhill Essex 20 B4
Coalpit Heath S Glos 16 C3
Coalport Telford 34 E2
Coalsnaughton Clack 76 H2
Coaltown of Balgonie Fife 76 H5
Coaltown of Wemyss Fife 76 H6
Coalville Leics 35 D10
Coalway Glos 26 G2
Coat Som 8 B3
Coatbridge N Lanark 68 D6
Coatdyke N Lanark 68 D6
Coate Swindon 17 C8
Coate Wilts 17 E7
Coates Cambs 37 F9
Coates Glos 16 A6
Coates Lancs 50 E4
Coates Notts 46 D2
Coates W Sus 11 C8
Coatham Redcar 59 D6
Coatham Mundeville Darl 58 D3
Coatsgate Dumfries 60 C6
Cobbaton Devon 6 D5
Cobbler's Green Norf 39 F8
Coberley Glos 26 G6
Cobham Kent 20 E3
Cobham Sur 19 E8
Cobholm Island Norf 39 E11
Cobleland Stirling 75 H8
Cobnash Hereford 25 B11
Coburty Aberds 89 B9
Cock Bank Wrex 42 H6
Cock Bridge Aberds 82 C4
Cock Clarks Essex 20 A5
Cockayne N Yorks 59 G7
Cockayne Hatley Cambs 29 D9
Cockburnspath Borders 70 C6
Cockenzie and Port Seton E Loth 70 C3
Cockerham Lancs 49 D4
Cockermouth Cumb 56 C3
Cockernhoe Green Herts 29 F8
Cockfield Durham 58 D2
Cockfield Suff 30 C6
Cockfosters London 19 B9
Cocking W Sus 11 C7
Cockington Torbay 5 E9
Cocklake Som 15 G10
Cockley Beck Cumb 56 F4
Cockley Cley Norf 38 E3
Cockshutt Shrops 33 C10
Cockthorpe Norf 38 A5
Cockwood Devon 5 C10
Cockyard Hereford 25 E11
Codda Corn 4 D2
Coddenham Suff 31 C8
Coddington Ches W 43 G7
Coddington Hereford 26 D4
Coddington Notts 46 G2
Codford St Mary Wilts 16 H6
Codford St Peter Wilts 16 H6
Codicote Herts 29 G9
Codmore Hill W Sus 11 B9
Codnor Derbys 45 H8
Codrington S Glos 16 D4
Codsall Staffs 34 E4
Codsall Wood Staffs 34 E4
Coed Duon = Blackwood Caerph 15 B7
Coed Mawr Gwyn 41 C7
Coed Morgan Mon 25 G10
Coed-Talon Flint 42 G5
Coed-y-bryn Ceredig 23 B8
Coed-y-paen Mon 15 B9
Coed-yr-ynys Powys 25 F8
Coed Ystumgwern Gwyn 32 C1
Coedely Rhondda 14 C6
Coedkernew Newport 15 C8
Coedpoeth Wrex 42 G5
Coedway Powys 33 D9
Coelbren Powys 24 G5
Coffinswell Devon 5 E9
Cofton Hackett Worcs 34 H6
Cogan V Glam 15 D7
Cogenhoe Northants 28 B5
Cogges Oxon 27 H10
Coggeshall Essex 30 F5
Coggeshall Hamlet Essex 30 F5
Coggins Mill E Sus 12 D4
Coig Peighinnean W Isles 91 A10
Coig Peighinnean Bhuirgh W Isles 91 B9
Coignafearn Lodge Highld 81 B8
Coilacriech Aberds 82 D5
Coilantogle Stirling 75 G8
Coilleag W Isles 84 G2
Coillore Highld 85 E8
Coity Bridgend 14 C5
Col W Isles 91 C9
Col Uarach W Isles 91 D9
Colaboll Highld 93 H8
Colan Corn 3 C7
Colaton Raleigh Devon 7 H9
Colbost Highld 84 D7
Colburn N Yorks 58 G2
Colby Cumb 57 D8
Colby IoM 48 E2
Colby Norf 39 B8
Colchester Essex 31 F7
Colcot V Glam 15 E7
Cold Ash W Berks 18 E2
Cold Ashby Northants 36 H2
Cold Ashton S Glos 16 D4
Cold Aston Glos 27 G8
Cold Blow Pembs 22 E6
Cold Brayfield M Keynes 28 C6
Cold Hanworth Lincs 46 D4
Cold Harbour Lincs 36 B5
Cold Hatton Telford 34 C2
Cold Hesledon Durham 58 B5
Cold Higham Northants 28 C3
Cold Kirby N Yorks 51 A11
Cold Newton Leics 36 E3
Cold Northcott Corn 4 C3
Cold Norton Essex 20 A5
Cold Overton Leics 36 D4
Coldbackie Highld 93 D9
Coldbeck Cumb 57 F9
Coldblow London 20 D2
Coldean Brighton 12 F2
Coldeast Devon 5 D9
Colden W Yorks 50 G5
Colden Common Hants 10 B3
Coldfair Green Suff 31 B11
Coldham Cambs 37 E10
Coldharbour Glos 16 A2
Coldharbour Kent 20 F2
Coldharbour Sur 19 G8
Coldingham Borders 71 D8
Coldrain Perth 76 G3
Coldred Kent 21 G9
Coldridge Devon 6 F5
Coldstream Angus 76 D6
Coldstream Borders 71 G7
Coldwaltham W Sus 11 C9
Coldwells Aberds 89 D11
Coldwells Croft Aberds 83 A7
Coldyeld Shrops 33 F9
Cole Som 8 A5
Cole Green Herts 29 G9
Cole Henley Hants 17 F11
Colebatch Shrops 33 G9
Colebrook Devon 7 F9
Colebrooke Devon 7 G6
Coleby Lincs 46 F3
Coleby N Lincs 52 H4
Coleford Devon 7 F6
Coleford Glos 26 G2
Coleford Som 16 G3
Colehill Dorset 9 D9
Coleman's Hatch E Sus 12 C3
Colemere Shrops 33 B10
Colemore Hants 10 A6
Coleorton Leics 35 D10
Colerne Wilts 16 D5
Cole's Green Suff 31 B9
Coles Green Suff 31 D7
Colesbourne Glos 26 G6
Colesden Bedford 29 C8
Coleshill Bucks 18 B6
Coleshill Oxon 17 B9
Coleshill Warks 35 G8
Colestocks Devon 7 F9
Colgate W Sus 11 A11
Colgrain Argyll 68 B2
Colinsburgh Fife 77 G7
Colinton Edin 69 D11
Colintraive Argyll 73 F9
Colkirk Norf 38 C5
Collace Perth 76 D5
Collafirth Shetland 96 G6
Collaton St Mary Torbay 5 F9
College Milton S Lanark 68 E5
Collessie Fife 76 F5
Collier Row London 20 B2
Collier Street Kent 20 G4
Collier's End Herts 29 F10
Collier's Green Kent 13 C6
Colliery Row T&W 58 B4
Collieston Aberds 89 F10
Collin Dumfries 60 F6
Collingbourne Ducis Wilts 17 F9
Collingbourne Kingston Wilts 17 F9
Collingham Notts 46 F2
Collingham W Yorks 51 E9
Collington Hereford 26 B3
Collingtree Northants 28 C4
Collins Green Warr 43 C8
Colliston Angus 77 C9
Collycroft Warks 35 G9
Collynie Aberds 89 E8
Collyweston Northants 36 E5
Colmonell S Ayrs 66 H4
Colmworth Bedford 29 C8
Coln Rogers Glos 27 H7
Coln St Aldwyn's Glos 27 H8
Coln St Dennis Glos 27 G7
Colnabaichin Aberds 82 C4
Colnbrook Slough 19 D7
Colne Cambs 37 H9
Colne Lancs 50 E4
Colne Edge Lancs 50 E4
Colne Engaine Essex 30 E5
Colney Norf 39 E7
Colney Heath Herts 29 H9
Colney Street Herts 19 A8
Colpy Aberds 89 E6
Colquhar Borders 70 F2
Colsterdale N Yorks 51 A7
Colsterworth Lincs 36 C5
Colston Bassett Notts 36 B2
Coltfield Moray 87 E14
Colthouse Cumb 56 G5
Coltishall Norf 39 D8
Coltness N Lanark 69 E7
Colton Cumb 56 H5
Colton N Yorks 51 E11
Colton Norf 39 E7
Colton Staffs 35 C6
Colton W Yorks 51 F9
Colva Powys 25 C9
Colvend Dumfries 55 D11
Colvister Shetland 96 D7
Colwall Green Hereford 26 D4
Colwall Stone Hereford 26 D4
Colwell Northumb 62 F5
Colwich Staffs 34 C6
Colwick Notts 36 A2
Colwinston V Glam 14 D5
Colworth W Sus 11 D8
Colwyn Bay = Bae Colwyn Conwy 41 C10
Colyford Devon 8 E1
Colyton Devon 8 E1
Combe Hereford 25 B10
Combe Oxon 27 G11
Combe W Berks 17 E10
Combe Common Sur 18 H6
Combe Down Bath 16 E4
Combe Florey Som 7 C10
Combe Hay Bath 16 F4
Combe Martin Devon 6 B4
Combe Moor Hereford 25 B10
Combe Raleigh Devon 7 F10
Combe St Nicholas Som 8 C2
Combeinteignhead Devon 5 D10
Comberbach Ches W 43 E9
Comberton Cambs 29 C10
Comberton Hereford 25 B11
Combpyne Devon 8 E1
Combridge Staffs 35 B6
Combrook Warks 27 C10
Combs Derbys 44 E4
Combs Suff 31 C7
Combs Ford Suff 31 C7
Combwich Som 15 G8
Comers Aberds 83 C8
Comins Coch Ceredig 32 G2
Commercial End Cambs 30 B2
Commins Capel Betws Ceredig 24 C3
Commins Coch Powys 32 E4
Common Edge Blackpool 49 F3
Common Side Derbys 45 E7
Commondale N Yorks 59 E7
Commonmoor Corn 4 E3
Commonside Ches W 43 E8
Compstall Gtr Man 44 C3
Compton Devon 5 E9
Compton Hants 10 B3
Compton Sur 18 G5
Compton Sur 18 G6
Compton W Berks 18 D2
Compton W Sus 11 C6
Compton Wilts 17 F8
Compton Abbas Dorset 9 C7
Compton Abdale Glos 27 G7
Compton Bassett Wilts 17 D7
Compton Beauchamp Oxon 17 C9
Compton Bishop Som 15 F9
Compton Chamberlayne Wilts 9 B9
Compton Dando Bath 16 E3
Compton Dundon Som 8 A3
Compton Martin Bath 15 F11
Compton Pauncefoot Som 8 B5
Compton Valence Dorset 8 E4
Comrie Fife 69 B9
Comrie Perth 75 E10
Conaglen House Highld 80 G2
Conchra Argyll 73 E9
Concraigie Perth 76 C4
Conder Green Lancs 49 D4
Conderton Worcs 26 E6
Condicote Glos 27 F8
Condorrat N Lanark 68 C6
Condover Shrops 33 E10
Coney Weston Suff 38 H5
Coneyhurst W Sus 11 B10
Coneysthorpe N Yorks 52 B3
Coneythorpe N Yorks 51 D9
Conford Hants 11 A7
Congash Highld 82 A2
Congdon's Shop Corn 4 D3
Congerstone Leics 35 E9
Congham Norf 38 C3
Congl-y-wal Gwyn 41 F9
Congleton Ches E 44 F2
Congresbury N Som 15 E10
Congreve Staffs 34 D5
Conicavel Moray 87 F12
Coningsby Lincs 46 G6
Conington Cambs 29 B10
Conington Cambs 37 G7
Conisbrough S Yorks 45 C9
Conisby Argyll 64 B3
Conisholme Lincs 47 C8
Coniston Cumb 56 G5
Coniston E Yorks 53 F7
Coniston Cold N Yorks 50 D5
Conistone N Yorks 50 C5
Connah's Quay Flint 42 F5
Connel Argyll 74 D2
Connel Park E Ayrs 67 E9
Connor Downs Corn 2 F4
Conon Bridge Highld 87 F8
Conon House Highld 87 F8
Cononley N Yorks 50 E5
Conordan Highld 85 E10
Consall Staffs 44 H3
Consett Durham 58 A2
Constable Burton N Yorks 58 G2
Constantine Corn 2 G6
Constantine Bay Corn 3 B7
Contin Highld 86 F7
Contlaw Aberdeen 83 C10
Conwy Conwy 41 C9
Conyer Kent 20 E6
Conyers Green Suff 30 B5
Cooden E Sus 12 F6
Cooil IoM 48 E3
Cookbury Devon 6 F3
Cookham Windsor 18 C5
Cookham Dean Windsor 18 C5
Cookham Rise Windsor 18 C5
Cookhill Worcs 27 C7
Cookley Suff 39 H9
Cookley Worcs 34 G4
Cookley Green Oxon 18 B3
Cookney Aberds 83 D10
Cookridge W Yorks 51 E8
Cooksbridge E Sus 12 E3
Cooksmill Green Essex 30 H3
Coolham W Sus 11 B10
Cooling Medway 20 D4
Coombe Corn 3 D8
Coombe Corn 6 E1
Coombe Hants 10 B5
Coombe Wilts 17 F8
Coombe Bissett Wilts 9 B10
Coombe Hill Glos 26 F5
Coombe Keynes Dorset 9 F7
Coombes W Sus 11 D10
Coopersale Common Essex 19 A11
Cootham W Sus 11 C9
Copdock Suff 31 D8
Copford Green Essex 30 F6
Copgrove N Yorks 51 C9
Copister Shetland 96 F6
Cople Bedford 29 D8
Copley Durham 58 D1
Coplow Dale Derbys 44 E5
Copmanthorpe York 52 E1
Coppathorne Corn 4 A3
Coppenhall Staffs 34 D5
Coppenhall Moss Ches E 43 G10
Copperhouse Corn 2 F4
Coppingford Cambs 37 G7
Copplestone Devon 7 F6
Coppull Lancs 43 A8
Coppull Moor Lancs 43 A8
Copsale W Sus 11 B10
Copster Green Lancs 50 F2
Copston Magna Warks 35 G10
Copt Heath W Mid 35 H7
Copt Hewick N Yorks 51 B9
Copt Oak Leics 35 D10
Copthorne Shrops 33 D10
Copthorne Sur 12 C2
Copy's Green Norf 38 B5
Copythorne Hants 10 C2
Corbets Tey London 20 C2
Corbridge Northumb 62 G5
Corby Northants 36 G4
Corby Glen Lincs 36 C5
Cordon N Ayrs 66 C3
Coreley Shrops 26 A3
Cores End Bucks 18 C6
Corfe Som 7 E11
Corfe Castle Dorset 9 F8
Corfe Mullen Dorset 9 E8
Corfton Shrops 33 G10
Corgarff Aberds 82 C4
Corhampton Hants 10 B5
Corlae Dumfries 67 G9
Corley Warks 35 G9
Corley Ash Warks 35 G8
Corley Moor Warks 35 G8
Cornaa IoM 48 D4
Cornabus Argyll 64 D4
Cornel Conwy 41 D9
Corner Row Lancs 49 F4
Corney Cumb 56 G3
Cornforth Durham 58 C4
Cornhill Aberds 88 C5
Cornhill-on-Tweed Northumb 71 G7
Cornholme W Yorks 50 G5
Cornish Hall End Essex 30 E3
Cornquoy Orkney 95 J6
Cornsay Durham 58 B2
Cornsay Colliery Durham 58 B2
Corntown Highld 87 F8
Corntown V Glam 14 D5
Cornwell Oxon 27 F9
Cornwood Devon 5 F7
Cornworthy Devon 5 F9
Corpach Highld 80 F2
Corpusty Norf 39 B7
Corran Highld 74 A3
Corran Highld 85 H13
Corranbuie Argyll 73 G7
Corrany IoM 48 D4
Corrie N Ayrs 66 B3
Corrie Common Dumfries 61 E8
Corriecravie N Ayrs 66 D2
Corriemoillie Highld 86 E6
Corriemulzie Lodge Highld 86 B6
Corrievarkie Lodge Perth 81 F7
Corrievorrie Highld 81 A9
Corrimony Highld 86 H6
Corringham Lincs 46 C2
Corringham Thurrock 20 C4
Corris Gwyn 32 E3
Corris Uchaf Gwyn 32 E3
Corrour Shooting Lodge Highld 80 G6
Corrow Argyll 74 G4
Corry Highld 85 F11
Corry of Ardnagrask Highld 87 G8
Corrykinloch Highld 92 G6
Corrymuckloch Perth 75 D11
Corrynachenchy Argyll 79 G9
Cors-y-Gedol Gwyn 32 C1
Corsback Highld 94 C4
Corscombe Dorset 8 D4
Corse Aberds 88 D6
Corse Glos 26 F4
Corse Lawn Worcs 26 E5
Corse of Kinnoir Aberds 88 D5
Corsewall Dumfries 54 C3
Corsham Wilts 16 D5
Corsindae Aberds 83 C8
Corsley Wilts 16 G5
Corsley Heath Wilts 16 G5
Corsock Dumfries 60 F3
Corston Bath 16 E3
Corston Wilts 16 C6
Corstorphine Edin 69 C10
Cortachy Angus 76 B6
Corton Suff 39 F11
Corton Wilts 16 G6
Corton Denham Som 8 B5
Coruanan Lodge Highld 80 G2
Corunna W Isles 84 B3
Corwen Denb 33 A6
Coryton Devon 4 C5
Coryton Thurrock 20 C4
Cosby Leics 35 F11
Coseley W Mid 34 F5
Cosgrove Northants 28 D4
Cosham Ptsmth 10 D5
Cosheston Pembs 22 F5
Cossall Notts 35 A10
Cossington Leics 36 D2
Cossington Som 15 G9
Costa Orkney 95 F4
Costessey Norf 39 D7
Costock Notts 36 C1
Coston Leics 36 C4
Cote Oxon 17 A10
Cotebrook Ches W 43 F8
Cotehill Cumb 56 A6
Cotes Cumb 57 H6
Cotes Leics 36 C1
Cotes Staffs 34 B4
Cotesbach Leics 35 G11
Cotgrave Notts 36 B2
Cothall Aberds 83 B10
Cotham Notts 45 H11
Cothelstone Som 7 C10
Cotherstone Durham 58 E1
Cothill Oxon 17 B11
Cotleigh Devon 7 F11
Cotmanhay Derbys 35 A10
Cotmaton Devon 7 H10
Coton Cambs 29 C11
Coton Northants 28 A3
Coton Staffs 34 B5
Coton Staffs 34 C4
Coton Clanford Staffs 34 C4
Coton Hill Shrops 33 D10
Coton Hill Staffs 34 B5
Coton in the Elms Derbys 35 D8
Cott Devon 5 E8
Cottam E Yorks 52 C5
Cottam Lancs 49 F5
Cottam Notts 46 E2
Cottartown Highld 87 H13
Cottenham Cambs 29 B11
Cotterdale N Yorks 57 G10
Cottered Herts 29 F10
Cotteridge W Mid 34 H6
Cotterstock Northants 36 F6
Cottesbrooke Northants 28 A4
Cottesmore Rutland 36 D5
Cotteylands Devon 7 E8
Cottingham E Yorks 52 F6
Cottingham Northants 36 F4
Cottingley W Yorks 51 F7
Cottisford Oxon 28 E2
Cotton Staffs 44 H4
Cotton Suff 31 B7
Cotton End Bedford 29 D7
Cottown Aberds 83 A7
Cottown Aberds 83 B9
Cottown Aberds 89 D8
Cotwalton Staffs 34 B5
Couch's Mill Corn 4 F2
Coughton Hereford 26 F2
Coughton Warks 27 B7
Coulaghailtro Argyll 72 G6
Coulags Highld 86 G2
Coulby Newham Mbro 58 E6
Coulderton Cumb 56 F1
Coulin Highld 86 F3
Coull Aberds 83 C7
Coull Argyll 64 B3
Coulport Argyll 73 E11
Coulsdon London 19 F9
Coulston Wilts 16 F6
Coulter S Lanark 69 G9
Coulton N Yorks 52 B2
Cound Shrops 34 E1
Coundon Durham 58 D3
Coundon W Mid 35 G9
Coundon Grange Durham 58 D3
Countersett N Yorks 57 H11
Countess Wilts 17 G8
Countess Wear Devon 5 C10
Countesthorpe Leics 36 F1
Countisbury Devon 7 B6
County Oak W Sus 12 C1
Coup Green Lancs 50 G1
Coupar Angus Perth 76 C5
Coupland Northumb 71 G8
Cour Argyll 65 D9
Courance Dumfries 60 D6
Court-at-Street Kent 13 C9
Court Henry Carms 23 D10
Courteenhall Northants 28 C4
Courtsend Essex 21 B7
Courtway Som 7 C11
Cousland Midloth 70 D2
Cousley Wood E Sus 12 C5
Cove Argyll 73 E11
Cove Borders 70 C6
Cove Devon 7 E8
Cove Hants 18 F5
Cove Highld 91 H13
Cove Bay Aberdeen 83 C11
Cove Bottom Suff 39 H10
Covehithe Suff 39 G11
Coven Staffs 34 E5
Coveney Cambs 37 G10
Covenham St Bartholomew Lincs 47 C7
Covenham St Mary Lincs 47 C7
Coventry W Mid 35 H9
Coverack Corn 3 H6
Coverham N Yorks 58 H2
Covesea Moray 88 A1
Covington Cambs 29 A7
Covington S Lanark 69 G8
Cow Ark Lancs 50 E2
Cowan Bridge Lancs 50 B2
Cowbeech E Sus 12 E5
Cowbit Lincs 37 D8
Cowbridge Lincs 47 H7
Cowbridge Som 7 B8
Cowbridge = Y Bont-Faen V Glam 14 D5
Cowdale Derbys 44 E4
Cowden Kent 12 B3
Cowdenbeath Fife 69 A10
Cowdenburn Borders 69 E11
Cowers Lane Derbys 45 H7
Cowes IoW 10 E3
Cowesby N Yorks 58 H5
Cowfold W Sus 11 B11
Cowgill Cumb 57 H9
Cowie Aberds 83 E10
Cowie Stirling 69 B7
Cowley Devon 7 G8
Cowley Glos 26 G6
Cowley London 19 C7
Cowley Oxon 18 A2
Cowleymoor Devon 7 E8
Cowling Lancs 50 H1
Cowling N Yorks 50 E5
Cowling N Yorks 58 H3
Cowlinge Suff 30 C4
Cowpe Lancs 50 G4
Cowpen Northumb 63 E8
Cowpen Bewley Stockton 58 D5
Cowplain Hants 10 C5
Cowshill Durham 57 B10
Cowslip Green N Som 15 E10
Cowstrandburn Fife 69 A9
Cowthorpe N Yorks 51 D10
Cox Common Suff 39 G9
Cox Green Windsor 18 D5
Cox Moor Notts 45 G9
Coxbank Ches E 34 A2
Coxbench Derbys 35 A9
Coxford Norf 38 C4
Coxford Soton 10 C2
Coxheath Kent 20 F4
Coxhill Kent 21 G9
Coxhoe Durham 58 C4
Coxley Som 15 G11
Coxwold N Yorks 51 B11
Coychurch Bridgend 14 D5
Coylton S Ayrs 67 D7
Coylumbridge Highld 81 B11
Coynach Aberds 82 C6
Coynachie Aberds 88 E4
Coytrahen Bridgend 14 C4
Crabadon Devon 5 F8
Crabbs Cross Worcs 27 B7
Crabtree W Sus 11 B11
Crackenthorpe Cumb 57 D8
Crackington Haven Corn 4 B2
Crackley Warks 27 A9
Crackleybank Shrops 34 D3
Crackpot N Yorks 57 G11
Cracoe N Yorks 50 C5
Craddock Devon 7 E9
Cradhlastadh W Isles 90 D5
Cradley Hereford 26 D4
Cradley Heath W Mid 34 G5
Crafthole Corn 4 F4
Cragg Vale W Yorks 50 G6
Craggan Highld 82 A2
Craggie Highld 87 H10
Craggie Highld 93 H11
Craghead Durham 58 A3
Crai Powys 24 F5
Craibstone Moray 88 C4
Craichie Angus 77 C8
Craig Dumfries 55 B9
Craig Dumfries 55 C9
Craig Highld 86 G3
Craig Castle Aberds 82 A6
Craig-cefn-parc Swansea 14 A2
Craig Penllyn V Glam 14 D5
Craig-y-don Conwy 41 B9
Craig-y-nos Powys 24 G5
Craiganor Lodge Perth 75 B9
Craigdam Aberds 89 E8
Craigdarroch Dumfries 60 D3
Craigdarroch Highld 86 F7
Craigdhu Highld 86 G7
Craigearn Aberds 83 B9
Craigellachie Moray 88 D2
Craigencross Dumfries 54 C3
Craigend Perth 76 E4
Craigend Stirling 68 B6
Craigendive Argyll 73 E9
Craigendoran Argyll 68 B2
Craigends Renfs 68 D3
Craigens Argyll 64 B3
Craigens E Ayrs 67 E8
Craighat Stirling 68 B3
Craighead Fife 77 G9
Craighlaw Mains Dumfries 54 C6
Craighouse Argyll 72 G4
Craigie Aberds 83 B11
Craigie Dundee 77 D7
Craigie Perth 76 C4
Craigie Perth 76 E4
Craigie S Ayrs 67 C7
Craigiefield Orkney 95 G5
Craigielaw E Loth 70 C3
Craiglockhart Edin 69 C11
Craigmalloch E Ayrs 67 G7
Craigmaud Aberds 89 C8
Craigmillar Edin 69 C11
Craigmore Argyll 73 G10
Craignant Shrops 33 B8
Craigneuk N Lanark 68 D6
Craigneuk N Lanark 68 E6
Craignure Argyll 79 H10
Craigo Angus 77 A9
Craigow Perth 76 G3
Craigrothie Fife 76 F6
Craigroy Moray 87 F14
Craigruie Stirling 75 E7
Craigston Castle Aberds 89 C7
Craigton Aberdeen 83 C10
Craigton Angus 76 B6
Craigton Angus 77 D8
Craigton Highld 87 B9
Craigtown Highld 93 D11
Craik Borders 61 C9
Crail Fife 77 G9
Crailing Borders 62 A2
Crailinghall Borders 62 A2
Craiselound N Lincs 45 C11
Crakehill N Yorks 51 B10
Crakemarsh Staffs 35 B6
Crambe N Yorks 52 C3
Cramlington Northumb 63 F8
Cramond Edin 69 C10
Cramond Bridge Edin 69 C10
Cranage Ches E 43 F10
Cranberry Staffs 34 B4
Cranborne Dorset 9 C9
Cranbourne Brack 18 D6
Cranbrook Kent 13 C6
Cranbrook Common Kent 13 C6
Crane Moor S Yorks 45 B7
Crane's Corner Norf 38 D5
Cranfield C Beds 28 D
Cranford London 19 D
Cranford St Andrew Northants 36 H
Cranford St John Northants 36 H
Cranham Glos 26 G
Cranham London 20 C
Crank Mers 43 C
Crank Wood Gtr Man 43 B
Cranleigh Sur 19 H
Cranley Suff 31 A
Cranmer Green Suff 31 A
Cranmore IoW 10 F
Cranna Aberds 89 C
Crannich Argyll 79 G
Crannoch Moray 88 C
Cranoe Leics 36 F
Cransford Suff 31 B1
Cranshaws Borders 70 D
Cranstal IoM 48 B
Crantock Corn 3 C
Cranwell Lincs 46 H
Cranwich Norf 38 F
Cranworth Norf 38 E
Craobh Haven Argyll 72 C
Crapstone Devon 4 E
Crarae Argyll 73 D
Crask Inn Highld 93 G
Crask of Aigas Highld 86 G
Craskins Aberds 83 C
Craster Northumb 63 B
Craswall Hereford 25 E
Cratfield Suff 39 H
Crathes Aberds 83 D
Crathie Aberds 82 D
Crathie Highld 81 D
Crathorne N Yorks 58 F
Craven Arms Shrops 33 G
Crawcrook T&W 63 G
Crawford Lancs 43 B
Crawford S Lanark 60 A
Crawfordjohn S Lanark 60 A
Crawick Dumfries 60 B
Crawley Hants 10 A
Crawley Oxon 27 G
Crawley W Sus 12 C
Crawley Down W Sus 12 C
Crawleyside Durham 57 B
Crawshawbooth Lancs 50 G
Crawton Aberds 83 F1
Cray N Yorks 50 B
Cray Perth 76 A
Crayford London 20 D
Crayke N Yorks 52 B
Crays Hill Essex 20 B
Cray's Pond Oxon 18 C
Creacombe Devon 7 E
Creag Ghoraidh W Isles 84 D
Creagan Argyll 74 C
Creaguaineach Lodge Highld 80 G
Creaksea Essex 20 B
Creaton Northants 28 A
Creca Dumfries 61 F
Credenhill Hereford 25 D
Crediton Devon 7 F
Creebridge Dumfries 55 C
Creech Heathfield Som 8 B
Creech St Michael Som 8 B
Creed Corn 3 E
Creekmouth London 19 C1
Creeting Bottoms Suff 31 C
Creeting St Mary Suff 31 C
Creeton Lincs 36 C
Creetown Dumfries 55 D
Creg-ny-Baa IoM 48 D
Creggans Argyll 73 C
Cregneash IoM 48 F
Cregrina Powys 25 C
Creich Fife 76 E
Creigiau Cardiff 14 C
Cremyll Corn 4 F
Creslow Bucks 28 F
Cressage Shrops 34 E
Cressbrook Derbys 44 E
Cresselly Pembs 22 F
Cressing Essex 30 F
Cresswell Northumb 63 D
Cresswell Staffs 34 B
Cresswell Quay Pembs 22 F
Creswell Derbys 45 E
Cretingham Suff 31 B
Cretshengan Argyll 72 G
Crewe Ches E 43 G
Crewe Ches W 43 G
Crewgreen Powys 33 D
Crewkerne Som 8 D
Crianlarich Stirling 74 E
Cribyn Ceredig 23 A
Criccieth Gwyn 40 G
Crich Derbys 45 G
Crichie Aberds 89 D
Crichton Midloth 70 D
Crick Mon 15 B1
Crick Northants 28 A
Crickadarn Powys 25 D
Cricket Malherbie Som 8 C
Cricket St Thomas Som 8 D
Crickheath Shrops 33 C
Crickhowell Powys 25 G
Cricklade Wilts 17 B
Cricklewood London 19 C
Cridling Stubbs N Yorks 51 G1
Crieff Perth 75 E1
Criggion Powys 33 D
Crigglestone W Yorks 51 H
Crimond Aberds 89 C1
Crimonmogate Aberds 89 C1
Crimplesham Norf 38 E
Crinan Argyll 72 D
Cringleford Norf 39 E
Cringles W Yorks 50 E
Crinow Pembs 22 E
Cripplesease Corn 2 F
Cripplestyle Dorset 9 C
Cripp's Corner E Sus 13 D
Croasdale Cumb 56 E
Crock Street Som 8 C
Crockenhill Kent 20 E
Crockernwell Devon 7 C
Crockerton Wilts 16 G
Crocketford or Ninemile Bar Dumfries 60
Crockey Hill York 52
Crockham Hill Kent 19 F
Crockleford Heath Essex 31
Crockness Orkney 95
Croes-goch Pembs 22
Croes-lan Ceredig 23

D

Dundonnell Highld 86 C3
Dundonnell Hotel Highld 86 C3
Dundonnell House Highld 86 C4
Dundraw Cumb 56 B4
Dundreggan Highld 80 B5
Dundreggan Lodge Highld 80 B5
Dundrennan Dumfries 55 E10
Dundry N Som 16 E2
Dunecht Aberds 83 C9
Dunfermline Fife 69 B9
Dunfield Glos 17 B8
Dunford Bridge S Yorks 44 B5
Dungworth S Yorks 44 D6
Dunham Notts 46 E2
Dunham-on-the-Hill Ches W 43 E7
Dunham Town Gtr Man 43 D10
Dunhampton Worcs 26 B5
Dunholme Lincs 46 E4
Dunino Fife 77 F8
Dunipace Falk 69 B7
Dunira Perth 75 E10
Dunkeld Perth 76 C3
Dunkerton Bath 16 F4
Dunkeswell Devon 7 F10
Dunkeswick N Yorks 51 E9
Dunkirk Kent 21 F7
Dunkirk Norf 39 C8
Dunk's Green Kent 20 F3
Dunlappie Angus 83 G7
Dunley Hants 17 F11
Dunley Worcs 26 B4
Dunlichity Lodge Highld 87 H9
Dunlop E Ayrs 67 B7
Dunmaglass Lodge Highld 81 A7
Dunmore Argyll 72 G6
Dunmore Falk 69 B7
Dunnet Highld 94 C4
Dunnichen Angus 77 C8
Dunninald Angus 77 B10
Dunning Perth 76 F3
Dunnington E Yorks 53 D7
Dunnington Warks 27 C7
Dunnington York 52 D2
Dunnockshaw Lancs 50 G4
Dunollie Argyll 79 H11
Dunoon Argyll 73 F10
Dunragit Dumfries 54 D4
Dunrostan Argyll 72 E6
Duns Borders 70 E6
Duns Tew Oxon 27 F11
Dunsby Lincs 37 C7
Dunscore Dumfries 60 E4
Dunscroft S Yorks 45 B10
Dunsdale Redcar 59 E7
Dunsden Green Oxon 18 D4
Dunsfold Sur 19 H7
Dunsford Devon 5 C9
Dunshalt Fife 76 F5
Dunshillock Aberds 89 D9
Dunskey Ho. Dumfries 54 D3
Dunsley N Yorks 59 E9
Dunsmore Bucks 28 H5
Dunsop Bridge Lancs 50 D2
Dunstable C Beds 29 F7
Dunstall Staffs 35 C7
Dunstall Common Worcs 26 D5
Dunstall Green Suff 30 B4
Dunstan Northumb 63 B8
Dunstan Steads Northumb 63 A8
Dunster Som 7 B8
Dunston Lincs 46 F4
Dunston Norf 39 E8
Dunston Staffs 34 D5
Dunston T&W 63 G8
Dunsville S Yorks 45 B10
Dunswell E Yorks 53 F6
Dunsyre S Lanark 69 F9
Dunterton Devon 4 D4
Duntisbourne Abbots Glos 26 H6
Duntisbourne Leer Glos 26 H6
Duntisbourne Rouse Glos 26 H6
Duntish Dorset 8 D5
Duntocher W Dunb 68 C3
Dunton Bucks 28 F5
Dunton C Beds 29 D9
Dunton Norf 38 B4
Dunton Bassett Leics 35 F11
Dunton Green Kent 20 F2
Dunton Wayletts Essex 20 B3
Duntulm Highld 85 A9
Dunure S Ayrs 66 E5
Dunvant Swansea 23 G10
Dunvegan Highld 84 D7
Dunwich Suff 31 A11
Dunwood Staffs 44 G3
Dupplin Castle Perth 76 F3
Durdar Cumb 56 A6
Durgates E Sus 12 C5
Durham Durham 58 B3
Durisdeer Dumfries 60 C4
Durisdeermill Dumfries 60 C4
Durkar W Yorks 51 H9
Durleigh Som 15 H8
Durley Hants 10 C4
Durley Wilts 17 E9
Durnamuck Highld 86 B3
Durness Highld 92 C7
Durno Aberds 83 A9
Duror Highld 74 B2
Durran Argyll 73 C8
Durran Highld 94 D3
Durrington W Sus 11 D10
Durrington Wilts 17 G8
Dursley Glos 16 B4
Durston Som 8 B1
Durweston Dorset 9 D7
Dury Shetland 96 G6
Duston Northants 28 B4
Duthil Highld 81 A11
Dutlas Powys 33 H8
Duton Hill Essex 30 F3
Dutson Corn 4 C4
Dutton Ches W 43 E8
Duxford Cambs 29 D11
Duxford Oxon 17 B10
Dwygyfylchi Conwy 41 C9
Dwyran Anglesey 40 D6
Dyce Aberdeen 83 B10
Dye House Northumb 62 H5
Dyffryn Bridgend 14 B4
Dyffryn Carms 23 D8
Dyffryn Pembs 22 C4
Dyffryn Ardudwy Gwyn 32 C1
Dyffryn Castell Ceredig 32 G3
Dyffryn Ceidrych Carms 24 F4
Dyffryn Cellwen Neath 24 H5
Dyke Lincs 37 C7
Dyke Moray 87 F12
Dykehead Angus 76 A6
Dykehead N Lanark 69 E7
Dykehead Stirling 75 H8
Dykelands Aberds 83 G9
Dykends Angus 76 B5
Dykeside Aberds 89 D7
Dykesmains N Ayrs 66 B5
Dylife Powys 32 F4
Dymchurch Kent 13 D9
Dymock Glos 26 E4
Dyrham S Glos 16 D4
Dysart Fife 70 A2
Dyserth Denb 42 E3

E

Eachwick Northumb 63 F7
Eadar Dha Fhadhail W Isles 90 D5
Eagland Hill Lancs 49 E4
Eagle Lincs 46 F2
Eagle Barnsdale Lincs 46 F2
Eagle Moor Lincs 46 F2
Eaglescliffe Stockton 58 E5
Eaglesfield Cumb 56 D2
Eaglesfield Dumfries 61 F8
Eaglesham E Renf 68 E4
Eaglethorpe Northants 37 F6
Eairy IoM 48 E2
Eakley Lanes M Keynes 28 C5
Eakring Notts 45 F10
Ealand N Lincs 45 A11
Ealing London 19 C8
Eals Northumb 62 H2
Eamont Bridge Cumb 57 D7
Earby Lancs 50 E5
Earcroft Blackburn 50 G2
Eardington Shrops 34 F3
Eardisland Hereford 25 C11
Eardisley Hereford 25 D10
Eardiston Shrops 33 C9
Eardiston Worcs 26 B3
Earith Cambs 29 A10
Earl Shilton Leics 35 F10
Earl Soham Suff 31 B9
Earl Sterndale Derbys 44 F4
Earl Stonham Suff 31 C8
Earle Northumb 71 H8
Earley Wokingham 18 D4
Earlham Norf 39 E8
Earlish Highld 85 B8
Earls Barton Northants 28 B5
Earls Colne Essex 30 F5
Earl's Croome Worcs 26 D5
Earl's Green Suff 31 B7
Earlsdon W Mid 35 H9
Earlsferry Fife 77 H7
Earlsfield Lincs 36 B5
Earlsford Aberds 89 E8
Earlsheaton W Yorks 51 G8
Earlsmill Moray 87 F12
Earlston Borders 70 G4
Earlston E Ayrs 67 C7
Earlswood Mon 15 B10
Earlswood Sur 19 G9
Earlswood Warks 27 A8
Earnley W Sus 11 E7
Earsairidh W Isles 84 J2
Earsdon T&W 63 F9
Earsham Norf 39 G9
Earswick York 52 D2
Eartham W Sus 11 D8
Easby N Yorks 58 F2
Easby N Yorks 59 F6
Easdale Argyll 72 B6
Easebourne W Sus 11 B7
Easenhall Warks 35 H10
Eashing Sur 18 G6
Easington Bucks 28 G3
Easington Durham 58 B5
Easington E Yorks 53 H9
Easington Northumb 71 G10
Easington Oxon 18 B3
Easington Oxon 27 E11
Easington Redcar 59 E8
Easington Colliery Durham 58 B5
Easington Lane T&W 58 B4
Easingwold N Yorks 51 C11
Easole Street Kent 21 F9
Eassie Angus 76 C6
East Aberthaw V Glam 14 E6
East Adderbury Oxon 27 E11
East Allington Devon 5 G8
East Anstey Devon 7 D7
East Appleton N Yorks 58 G3
East Ardsley W Yorks 51 G9
East Ashling W Sus 11 D7
East Auchronie Aberds 83 C10
East Ayton N Yorks 59 H10
East Bank Bl Gwent 25 H9
East Barkwith Lincs 46 D5
East Barming Kent 20 F4
East Barnby N Yorks 59 E9
East Barnet London 19 B9
East Barns E Loth 70 C6
East Barsham Norf 38 B5
East Beckham Norf 39 B7
East Bedfont London 19 D7
East Bergholt Suff 31 E7
East Bilney Norf 38 D5
East Blatchington E Sus 12 F3
East Boldre Hants 10 D2
East Brent Som 15 F9
East Bridgford Notts 36 A2
East Buckland Devon 6 C5
East Budleigh Devon 7 H9
East Burrafirth Shetland 96 H5
East Burton Dorset 9 F7
East Butsfield Durham 58 B2
East Butterwick N Lincs 46 B2
East Cairnbeg Aberds 83 F9
East Calder W Loth 69 D9
East Carleton Norf 39 E7
East Carlton Northants 36 G4
East Carlton W Yorks 51 E8
East Chaldon Dorset 9 F6
East Challow Oxon 17 C10
East Chiltington E Sus 12 E2
East Chinnock Som 8 C3
East Chisenbury Wilts 17 F8
East Clandon Sur 19 F7
East Claydon Bucks 28 F4
East Clyne Highld 93 J12
East Coker Som 8 C4
East Combe Som 7 C10
East Common N Yorks 52 F2
East Compton Som 16 G3
East Cottingwith E Yorks 52 E3
East Cowes IoW 10 E4
East Cowick E Yorks 52 G2
East Cowton N Yorks 58 F4
East Cramlington Northumb 63 F8
East Cranmore Som 16 G3
East Creech Dorset 9 F8
East Croachy Highld 81 A8
East Croftmore Highld 81 B11
East Curthwaite Cumb 56 B5
East Dean E Sus 12 G4
East Dean Hants 10 B1
East Dean W Sus 11 C8
East Down Devon 6 B5
East Drayton Notts 45 E11
East Ella Hull 53 G6
East End Dorset 9 E8
East End E Yorks 53 G8
East End Hants 10 B5
East End Hants 10 E2
East End Hants 17 E11
East End Herts 29 F11
East End Kent 13 C7
East End N Som 15 D10
East End Oxon 27 G10
East Farleigh Kent 20 F4
East Farndon Northants 36 G3
East Ferry Lincs 46 C2
East Fortune E Loth 70 C4
East Garston W Berks 17 D10
East Ginge Oxon 17 C11
East Goscote Leics 36 D2
East Grafton Wilts 17 E9
East Grimstead Wilts 9 B11
East Grinstead W Sus 12 C2
East Guldeford E Sus 13 D8
East Haddon Northants 28 B3
East Hagbourne Oxon 18 C2
East Halton N Lincs 53 H7
East Ham London 19 C11
East Hanney Oxon 17 B11
East Hanningfield Essex 20 A4
East Hardwick W Yorks 51 H10
East Harling Norf 38 G5
East Harlsey N Yorks 58 G5
East Harnham Wilts 9 B10
East Harptree Bath 16 F2
East Hartford Northumb 63 F8
East Harting W Sus 11 C6
East Hatley Cambs 29 C9
East Hauxwell N Yorks 58 G2
East Haven Angus 77 D8
East Heckington Lincs 37 A7
East Hedleyhope Durham 58 B2
East Hendred Oxon 17 C11
East Herrington T&W 58 A4
East Heslerton N Yorks 52 B5
East Hoathly E Sus 12 E4
East Horrington Som 16 G2
East Horsley Sur 19 F7
East Horton Northumb 71 G9
East Huntspill Som 15 G9
East Hyde C Beds 29 G8
East Ilkerton Devon 6 B6
East Ilsley W Berks 17 C11
East Keal Lincs 47 F7
East Kennett Wilts 17 E8
East Keswick W Yorks 51 E9
East Kilbride S Lanark 68 E5
East Kirkby Lincs 47 F7
East Knapton N Yorks 52 B4
East Knighton Dorset 9 F7
East Knoyle Wilts 9 A7
East Kyloe Northumb 71 G9
East Lambrook Som 8 C3
East Lamington Highld 87 D10
East Langdon Kent 21 G10
East Langton Leics 36 F3
East Langwell Highld 93 J10
East Lavant W Sus 11 D7
East Lavington W Sus 11 C8
East Layton N Yorks 58 F2
East Leake Notts 36 C1
East Learmouth Northumb 71 G7
East Leigh Devon 6 F5
East Lexham Norf 38 D4
East Lilburn Northumb 62 A6
East Linton E Loth 70 C4
East Liss Hants 11 B6
East Looe Corn 4 F3
East Lound N Lincs 45 C11
East Lulworth Dorset 9 F7
East Lutton N Yorks 52 C5
East Lydford Som 8 A4
East Mains Aberds 83 D8
East Malling Kent 20 F4
East March Angus 77 D7
East Marden W Sus 11 C7
East Markham Notts 45 E11
East Marton N Yorks 50 D5
East Meon Hants 10 B5
East Mere Devon 7 E8
East Mersea Essex 31 G7
East Mey Highld 94 C5
East Molesey Sur 19 E8
East Morden Dorset 9 E8
East Morton W Yorks 51 E6
East Ness N Yorks 52 B2
East Newton E Yorks 53 F8
East Norton Leics 36 E3
East Nynehead Som 7 D10
East Oakley Hants 18 F2
East Ogwell Devon 5 D9
East Orchard Dorset 9 C7
East Ord Northumb 71 E8
East Panson Devon 6 G2
East Peckham Kent 20 G3
East Pennard Som 16 H2
East Perry Cambs 29 B8
East Portlemouth Devon 5 H8
East Prawle Devon 5 H8
East Preston W Sus 11 D9
East Putford Devon 6 E2
East Quantoxhead Som 7 B10
East Rainton T&W 58 B4
East Ravendale NE Lincs 46 C6
East Raynham Norf 38 C4
East Rhidorroch Lodge Highld 86 B5
East Rigton W Yorks 51 E9
East Rounton N Yorks 58 F5
East Row N Yorks 59 E9
East Rudham Norf 38 C4
East Runton Norf 39 A7
East Ruston Norf 39 C9
East Saltoun E Loth 70 D3
East Sleekburn Northumb 63 E8
East Somerton Norf 39 D10
East Stockwith Lincs 45 C11
East Stoke Dorset 9 F7
East Stoke Notts 45 H11
East Stour Dorset 9 B7
East Stourmouth Kent 21 E9
East Stowford Devon 6 D5
East Stratton Hants 18 H2
East Studdal Kent 21 G10
East Suisnish Highld 85 E10
East Taphouse Corn 4 E2
East-the-Water Devon 6 D3
East Thirston Northumb 63 D7
East Tilbury Thurrock 20 D3
East Tisted Hants 10 A6
East Torrington Lincs 46 D5
East Tuddenham Norf 39 D6
East Tytherley Hants 10 B1
East Tytherton Wilts 16 D6
East Village Devon 7 F7
East Wall Shrops 33 F11
East Walton Norf 38 D3
East Wellow Hants 10 B2
East Wemyss Fife 76 H6
East Whitburn W Loth 69 D8
East Williamston Pembs 22 F5
East Winch Norf 38 D2
East Winterslow Wilts 9 A11
East Wittering W Sus 11 E6
East Witton N Yorks 58 H2
East Woodburn Northumb 62 E5
East Woodhay Hants 17 E11
East Worldham Hants 18 H4
East Worlington Devon 7 E6
East Worthing W Sus 11 D10
Eastbourne E Sus 12 G5
Eastbridge Suff 31 B11
Eastburn W Yorks 50 E6
Eastbury London 19 B7
Eastbury W Berks 17 D10
Eastby N Yorks 50 D6
Eastchurch Kent 20 D6
Eastcombe Glos 16 A5
Eastcote London 19 C8
Eastcote Northants 28 C3
Eastcote W Mid 35 H7
Eastcott Corn 6 E1
Eastcott Wilts 17 F7
Eastcourt Wilts 16 B6
Eastcourt Wilts 17 E9
Easter Ardross Highld 87 D9
Easter Balmoral Aberds 82 D4
Easter Boleskine Highld 81 A7
Easter Compton S Glos 16 C2
Easter Cringate Stirling 68 B6
Easter Davoch Aberds 82 C6
Easter Earshaig Dumfries 60 C6
Easter Fearn Highld 87 C9
Easter Galcantray Highld 87 G11
Easter Howgate Midloth 69 D11
Easter Howlaws Borders 70 F6
Easter Kinkell Highld 87 F8
Easter Lednathie Angus 76 A6
Easter Milton Highld 87 F12
Easter Moniack Highld 87 G8
Easter Ord Aberdeen 83 C10
Easter Quarff Shetland 96 K6
Easter Rhynd Perth 76 F4
Easter Row Stirling 75 H10
Easter Silverford Aberds 89 B7
Easter Skeld Shetland 96 J5
Easter Whyntie Aberds 88 B6
Eastergate W Sus 11 D8
Easterhouse Glasgow 68 D5
Eastern Green W Mid 35 G8
Easterton Wilts 17 F7
Eastertown Som 15 F9
Eastertown of Auchleuchries Aberds 89 E10
Eastfield N Lanark 69 D7
Eastfield N Yorks 52 A6
Eastfield Hall Northumb 63 C8
Eastgate Durham 57 C11
Eastgate Norf 39 C7
Eastham Mers 42 D6
Eastham Ferry Mers 42 D6
Easthampstead Brack 18 E5
Eastheath Wokingham 18 E5
Easthope Shrops 34 F1
Easthorpe Essex 30 F6
Easthorpe Leics 36 B4
Easthorpe Notts 45 G11
Easthouses Midloth 70 D2
Eastington Devon 7 F6
Eastington Glos 26 H4
Eastington Glos 27 G8
Eastleach Martin Glos 27 H9
Eastleach Turville Glos 27 H8
Eastleigh Devon 6 D3
Eastleigh Hants 10 C3
Eastling Kent 20 F6
Eastmoor Derbys 45 E7
Eastmoor Norf 38 E3
Eastney Ptsmth 10 E5
Eastnor Hereford 26 E4
Eastoft N Lincs 52 H4
Eastoke Hants 10 E6
Easton Cambs 29 A8
Easton Cumb 61 F10
Easton Cumb 61 H8
Easton Devon 5 C8
Easton Dorset 8 G5
Easton Hants 10 A4
Easton Lincs 36 C5
Easton Norf 39 D7
Easton Som 15 G11
Easton Suff 31 C9
Easton Wilts 16 D5
Easton Grey Wilts 16 C5
Easton-in-Gordano N Som 15 D11
Easton Maudit Northants 28 C5
Easton on the Hill Northants 36 E6
Easton Royal Wilts 17 E9
Eastpark Dumfries 60 G6
Eastrea Cambs 37 F8
Eastriggs Dumfries 61 G8
Eastrington E Yorks 52 G3
Eastry Kent 21 F10
Eastville Bristol 16 D3
Eastville Lincs 47 G8
Eastwell Leics 36 C3
Eastwick Herts 29 G11
Eastwick Shetland 96 F5
Eastwood Notts 45 H8
Eastwood Southend 20 C5
Eastwood W Yorks 50 G5
Eathorpe Warks 27 B10
Eaton Ches E 44 F2
Eaton Ches W 43 F8
Eaton Leics 36 C3
Eaton Norf 39 E8
Eaton Notts 45 E11
Eaton Oxon 17 A11
Eaton Shrops 33 G9
Eaton Shrops 33 G11
Eaton Bishop Hereford 25 E11
Eaton Bray C Beds 28 F6
Eaton Constantine Shrops 34 E1
Eaton Green C Beds 28 F6
Eaton Hastings Oxon 17 B9
Eaton on Tern Shrops 34 C2
Eaton Socon Cambs 29 C8
Eavestone N Yorks 51 C8
Ebberston N Yorks 52 A4
Ebbesbourne Wake Wilts 9 B8
Ebbw Vale = Glyn Ebwy Bl Gwent 25 H8
Ebchester Durham 63 H7
Ebford Devon 5 C10
Ebley Glos 26 H5
Ebnal Ches W 43 H7
Ebrington Glos 27 D8
Ecchinswell Hants 17 F11
Ecclaw Borders 70 D6
Ecclefechan Dumfries 61 F7
Eccles Borders 70 F6
Eccles Gtr Man 43 C10
Eccles Kent 20 E4
Eccles on Sea Norf 39 C10
Eccles Road Norf 38 F6
Ecclesall S Yorks 45 D7
Ecclesfield S Yorks 45 C7
Ecclesgreig Aberds 83 G9
Eccleshall Staffs 34 C4
Eccleshill W Yorks 51 F7
Ecclesmachan W Loth 69 C9
Eccleston Ches W 43 F7
Eccleston Lancs 49 H5
Eccleston Mers 43 C7
Eccleston Park Mers 43 C7
Eccup W Yorks 51 E8
Echt Aberds 83 C9
Eckford Borders 70 H6
Eckington Derbys 45 E8
Eckington Worcs 26 D6
Ecton Northants 28 B5
Edale Derbys 44 D5
Edburton W Sus 11 C11
Edderside Cumb 56 B2
Edderton Highld 87 C10
Eddistone Devon 6 D1
Eddleston Borders 69 F11
Eden Park London 19 E10
Edenbridge Kent 19 G11
Edenfield Lancs 50 H3
Edenhall Cumb 57 C7
Edenham Lincs 37 C6
Edensor Derbys 44 F6
Edentaggart Argyll 68 A2
Edenthorpe S Yorks 45 B10
Edentown Cumb 61 H9
Ederline Argyll 73 C7
Edern Gwyn 40 G4
Edgarley Som 15 H11
Edgbaston W Mid 35 G6
Edgcott Bucks 28 F3
Edgcott Som 7 C7
Edge Shrops 33 E9
Edge End Glos 26 G2
Edge Green Ches W 43 G7
Edge Hill Mers 42 C6
Edgebolton Shrops 34 C1
Edgefield Norf 39 B6
Edgefield Street Norf 39 B6
Edgeside Lancs 50 G4
Edgeworth Glos 26 H6
Edgmond Telford 34 D3
Edgmond Marsh Telford 34 C3
Edgton Shrops 33 G9
Edgware London 19 B8
Edgworth Blackburn 50 H3
Edinample Stirling 75 E8
Edinbane Highld 85 C8
Edinburgh Edin 69 C11
Edingale Staffs 35 D8
Edingight Ho. Moray 88 C5
Edingley Notts 45 G10
Edingthorpe Norf 39 B9
Edingthorpe Green Norf 39 B9
Edington Som 15 H9
Edington Wilts 16 F6
Edintore Moray 88 D4
Edith Weston Rutland 36 E5
Edithmead Som 15 G9
Edlesborough Bucks 28 G6
Edlingham Northumb 63 C7
Edlington Lincs 46 E6
Edmondsham Dorset 9 C9
Edmondsley Durham 58 B3
Edmondthorpe Leics 36 D4
Edmonstone Orkney 95 F6
Edmonton London 19 B10
Edmundbyers Durham 58 A1
Ednam Borders 70 G6
Ednaston Derbys 35 A8
Edradynate Perth 75 B11
Edrom Borders 71 E7
Edstaston Shrops 33 B11
Edstone Warks 27 B8
Edvin Loach Hereford 26 C3
Edwalton Notts 36 B1
Edwardstone Suff 30 D6
Edwinsford Carms 24 E3
Edwinstowe Notts 45 F10
Edworth C Beds 29 D9
Edwyn Ralph Hereford 26 C3
Edzell Angus 83 G7
Efail Isaf Rhondda 14 C6
Efailnewydd Gwyn 40 G5
Efailwen Carms 22 D6
Efenechtyd Denb 42 G4
Effingham Sur 19 F8
Effirth Shetland 96 H5
Efford Devon 7 F7
Egdon Worcs 26 C6
Egerton Gtr Man 43 A10
Egerton Kent 20 G6
Egerton Forstal Kent 20 G5
Eggborough N Yorks 52 G1
Eggbuckland Plym 4 F6
Eggington C Beds 28 F6
Egginton Derbys 35 C8
Egglescliffe Stockton 58 E5
Eggleston Durham 57 D11
Egham Sur 19 D7
Egleton Rutland 36 E4
Eglingham Northumb 63 B7
Egloshayle Corn 3 B8
Egloskerry Corn 4 C3
Eglwys-Brewis V Glam 14 E6
Eglwys Cross Wrex 33 A10
Eglwys Fach Ceredig 32 F2
Eglwysbach Conwy 41 C10
Eglwyswen Pembs 22 C6
Eglwyswrw Pembs 22 C6
Egmanton Notts 45 F11
Egremont Cumb 56 E2
Egremont Mers 42 C6
Egton N Yorks 59 F9
Egton Bridge N Yorks 59 F9
Eight Ash Green Essex 30 F6
Eignaig Highld 79 G10
Eil Highld 81 B10
Eilanreach Highld 85 G13
Eilean Darach Highld 86 C4
Eileanach Lodge Highld 87 E8
Einacleite W Isles 90 E6
Eisgean W Isles 91 F8
Eisingrug Gwyn 41 G8
Elan Village Powys 24 B6
Elberton S Glos 16 C3
Elburton Plym 4 F6
Elcho Perth 76 E4
Elcombe Swindon 17 C8
Eldernell Cambs 37 F9
Eldersfield Worcs 26 E5
Elderslie Renfs 68 D3
Eldon Durham 58 D3
Eldrick S Ayrs 54 A5
Eldroth N Yorks 50 C3
Eldwick W Yorks 51 E7
Elfhowe Cumb 56 G6
Elford Northumb 71 G10
Elford Staffs 35 D7
Elgin Moray 88 B2
Elgol Highld 85 G10
Elham Kent 21 G8
Elie Fife 77 G7
Elim Anglesey 40 B5
Eling Hants 10 C2
Elishader Highld 85 B10
Elishaw Northumb 62 D4
Elkesley Notts 45 E10
Elkstone Glos 26 G6
Ellan Highld 81 A10
Elland W Yorks 51 G7
Ellary Argyll 72 F6
Ellastone Staffs 35 A7
Ellemford Borders 70 D6
Ellenbrook IoM 48 E3
Ellenhall Staffs 34 C4
Ellen's Green Sur 19 H7
Ellerbeck N Yorks 58 G5
Ellerburn N Yorks 52 A4
Ellerby N Yorks 59 E8
Ellerdine Heath Telford 34 C2
Ellerhayes Devon 7 F8
Elleric Argyll 74 C3
Ellerker E Yorks 52 G5
Ellerton E Yorks 52 F3
Ellerton Shrops 34 C3
Ellesborough Bucks 28 H5
Ellesmere Shrops 33 B10
Ellesmere Port Ches W 43 E7
Ellingham Norf 39 F9
Ellingham Northumb 71 H10
Ellingstring N Yorks 51 A7
Ellington Cambs 29 A8
Ellington Northumb 63 D8
Elliot Angus 77 D9
Ellisfield Hants 18 G3
Ellistown Leics 35 D10
Ellon Aberds 89 E9
Ellonby Cumb 56 C6
Ellough Suff 39 G10
Elloughton E Yorks 52 G5
Ellwood Glos 26 H2
Elm Cambs 37 E10
Elm Hill Dorset 9 B7
Elm Park London 20 C2
Elmbridge Worcs 26 B6
Elmdon Essex 29 E11
Elmdon W Mid 35 G7
Elmdon Heath W Mid 35 G7
Elmers End London 19 E10
Elmesthorpe Leics 35 F10
Elmfield IoW 10 E5
Elmhurst Staffs 35 D7
Elmley Castle Worcs 26 D6
Elmley Lovett Worcs 26 B5
Elmore Glos 26 G4
Elmore Back Glos 26 G4
Elmscott Devon 6 D1
Elmsett Suff 31 D7
Elmstead Market Essex 31 F7
Elmsted Kent 13 B10
Elmstone Kent 21 E9
Elmstone Hardwicke Glos 26 F6
Elmswell E Yorks 52 D5
Elmswell Suff 30 B6
Elmton Derbys 45 E9
Elphin Highld 92 H5
Elphinstone E Loth 70 C2
Elrick Aberds 83 C10
Elrig Dumfries 54 E6
Elsdon Northumb 62 D5
Elsecar S Yorks 45 C7
Elsenham Essex 30 F2
Elsfield Oxon 28 G2
Elsham N Lincs 46 A4
Elsing Norf 39 D6
Elslack N Yorks 50 E5
Elson Shrops 33 B9
Elsrickle S Lanark 69 F9
Elstead Sur 18 G6
Elsted W Sus 11 C7
Elsthorpe Lincs 37 C6
Elstob Durham 58 D4
Elston Notts 45 H11
Elston Wilts 17 G7
Elstone Devon 6 E5
Elstow Bedford 29 D7
Elstree Herts 19 B8
Elstronwick E Yorks 53 F8
Elswick Lancs 49 F4
Elsworth Cambs 29 B10
Elterwater Cumb 56 F5
Eltham London 19 D11
Eltisley Cambs 29 C9
Elton Cambs 37 F6
Elton Ches W 43 E7
Elton Derbys 44 F6
Elton Glos 26 G4
Elton Hereford 25 A11
Elton Notts 36 B3
Elton Stockton 58 E5
Elton Green Ches W 43 E7
Elvanfoot S Lanark 60 B5
Elvaston Derbys 35 B10
Elveden Suff 38 H4
Elvingston E Loth 70 C3
Elvington Kent 21 F9
Elvington York 52 E2
Elwick Hrtlpl 58 C5
Elwick Northumb 71 G10
Elworth Ches E 43 F10
Elworthy Som 7 C9
Ely Cambs 37 G11
Ely Cardiff 15 D7
Emberton M Keynes 28 D5
Embleton Cumb 56 C3
Embleton Northumb 63 A8
Embo Highld 87 B11
Embo Street Highld 87 B11
Emborough Som 16 F3
Embsay N Yorks 50 D6
Emery Down Hants 10 D1
Emley W Yorks 44 A6
Emmbrook Wokingham 18 E4
Emmer Green Reading 18 D4
Emmington Oxon 18 A4
Emneth Norf 37 E10
Emneth Hungate Norf 37 E11
Empingham Rutland 36 E5
Empshott Hants 11 A6
Emstrey Shrops 33 D11
Emsworth Hants 10 D6
Enborne W Berks 17 E11
Enchmarsh Shrops 33 F11
Enderby Leics 35 F11
Endmoor Cumb 49 A5
Endon Staffs 44 G3
Endon Bank Staffs 44 G3
Enfield London 19 B10
Enfield Wash London 19 B10
Enford Wilts 17 F8
Engamoor Shetland 96 H4
Engine Common S Glos 16 C3
Englefield W Berks 18 D3
Englefield Green Sur 18 D6
Englesea-brook Ches E 43 G10
English Bicknor Glos 26 G2
English Frankton Shrops 33 C10
Englishcombe Bath 16 E4
Enham Alamein Hants 17 G10
Enmore Som 8 A1
Ennerdale Bridge Cumb 56 E2
Enoch Dumfries 60 C4
Enochdhu Perth 76 A3
Ensay Argyll 78 G6
Ensbury Bmouth 9 E9
Ensdon Shrops 33 D10
Ensis Devon 6 D4
Enstone Oxon 27 F10
Enterkinfoot Dumfries 60 C4
Enterpen N Yorks 58 F5
Enville Staffs 34 G4
Eolaigearraidh W Isles 84 H2
Eorabus Argyll 78 J6
Eòropaidh W Isles 91 A10
Epperstone Notts 45 H10
Epping Essex 19 A11
Epping Green Essex 29 H11
Epping Green Herts 29 H9
Epping Upland Essex 19 A11
Eppleby N Yorks 58 E2
Eppleworth E Yorks 52 F6
Epsom Sur 19 E9
Epwell Oxon 27 D10
Epworth N Lincs 45 B11
Epworth Turbary N Lincs 45 B11
Erbistock Wrex 33 A9
Erbusaig Highld 85 F12
Erchless Castle Highld 86 G7
Erdington W Mid 35 F7
Eredine Argyll 73 C8
Eriboll Highld 92 D7
Ericstane Dumfries 60 B6
Eridge Green E Sus 12 C4
Erines Argyll 73 F7
Eriswell Suff 38 H3
Erith London 20 D2
Erlestoke Wilts 16 F6
Ermine Lincs 46 E3
Ermington Devon 5 F7
Erpingham Norf 39 B7
Errogie Highld 81 A7
Errol Perth 76 E5
Erskine Renfs 68 C3
Erskine Bridge Renfs 68 C3
Ervie Dumfries 54 C3
Erwarton Suff 31 E9
Erwood Powys 25 D7
Eryholme N Yorks 58 F4
Eryrys Denb 42 G5
Escomb Durham 58 D2
Escrick N Yorks 52 E2
Esgairdawe Carms 24 D3
Esgairgeiliog Powys 32 E3
Esh Durham 58 B2
Esh Winning Durham 58 B2
Esher Sur 19 E8
Esholt W Yorks 51 E7
Eshott Northumb 63 D8
Eshton N Yorks 50 D5
Esk Valley N Yorks 59 F9
Eskadale Highld 86 H7
Eskbank Midloth 70 D2
Eskdale Green Cumb 56 F3
Eskdalemuir Dumfries 61 D8
Eske E Yorks 53 E6
Eskham Lincs 47 C7
Esprick Lancs 49 F4
Essendine Rutland 36 D6
Essendon Herts 29 H9
Essich Highld 87 H9
Essington Staffs 34 E5
Esslemont Aberds 89 F9
Eston Redcar 59 E6
Eswick Shetland 96 H6
Etal Northumb 71 G8
Etchilhampton Wilts 17 E7
Etchingham E Sus 12 D6
Etchinghill Kent 21 H8
Etchinghill Staffs 34 D6
Ethie Castle Angus 77 C9
Ethie Mains Angus 77 C9
Etling Green Norf 38 D6
Eton Windsor 18 D6
Eton Wick Windsor 18 D6
Etteridge Highld 81 D8
Ettersgill Durham 57 D10
Ettingshall W Mid 34 F5
Ettington Warks 27 D9
Etton E Yorks 52 E5
Etton Pboro 37 E7
Ettrick Borders 61 B8
Ettrickbridge Borders 61 A9
Ettrickhill Borders 61 B8
Etwall Derbys 35 B8
Euston Suff 38 H4
Euximoor Drove Cambs 37 F10
Euxton Lancs 50 H1
Evanstown Bridgend 14 C5
Evanton Highld 87 E9
Evedon Lincs 46 H4
Evelix Highld 87 B10
Evenjobb Powys 25 B9
Evenley Northants 28 E2
Evenlode Glos 27 F9
Evenwood Durham 58 D2
Evenwood Gate Durham 58 D2
Everbay Orkney 95 F7
Evercreech Som 16 H3
Everdon Northants 28 C2
Everingham E Yorks 52 E4
Everleigh Wilts 17 F9
Everley N Yorks 59 H10
Eversholt C Beds 28 E6
Evershot Dorset 8 D4
Eversley Hants 18 E4
Eversley Cross Hants 18 E4
Everthorpe E Yorks 52 F5
Everton C Beds 29 C9
Everton Hants 10 E1
Everton Mers 42 C6
Everton Notts 45 C10
Evertown Dumfries 61 F9
Evesbatch Hereford 26 D3
Evesham Worcs 27 D7
Evington Leicester 36 E2
Ewden Village S Yorks 44 C6
Ewell Sur 19 E9
Ewell Minnis Kent 21 G9
Ewelme Oxon 18 B3
Ewen Glos 17 B7
Ewenny V Glam 14 D5
Ewerby Lincs 46 H5
Ewerby Thorpe Lincs 46 H5
Ewes Dumfries 61 D9
Ewesley Northumb 62 D6
Ewhurst Sur 19 G7
Ewhurst Green E Sus 13 D6
Ewhurst Green Sur 19 H7
Ewloe Flint 42 F6
Ewloe Green Flint 42 F5
Ewood Blackburn 50 G2
Eworthy Devon 6 G3
Ewshot Hants 18 G5
Ewyas Harold Hereford 25 F10
Exbourne Devon 6 F5
Exbury Hants 10 E3
Exebridge Devon 7 D8
Exelby N Yorks 58 H3
Exeter Devon 7 G8
Exford Som 7 C7
Exhall Warks 27 C8
Exley Head W Yorks 50 F6
Exminster Devon 5 C10
Exmouth Devon 5 C11
Exnaboe Shetland 96 M5
Exning Suff 30 B3
Exton Devon 5 C10
Exton Hants 10 B5
Exton Rutland 36 D5
Exton Som 7 C8
Exwick Devon 7 G8
Eyam Derbys 44 E6
Eydon Northants 28 C2
Eye Hereford 25 B11
Eye Pboro 37 E8
Eye Suff 31 A8
Eye Green Pboro 37 E8
Eyemouth Borders 71 D8
Eyeworth C Beds 29 D9
Eyhorne Street Kent 20 F5
Eyke Suff 31 C10
Eynesbury Cambs 29 C8
Eynort Highld 85 F8
Eynsford Kent 20 E2
Eynsham Oxon 27 H11
Eype Dorset 8 E3
Eyre Highld 85 C9
Eyre Highld 85 E10
Eythorne Kent 21 G9
Eyton Hereford 25 B11
Eyton Shrops 33 G9
Eyton Wrex 33 A9
Eyton upon the Weald Moors Telford 34 D2

F

Faccombe Hants 17 F10
Faceby N Yorks 58 F5
Facit Lancs 50 H4
Faddiley Ches E 43 G8
Fadmoor N Yorks 59 H7
Faerdre Swansea 14 A2
Failand N Som 15 D11
Failford S Ayrs 67 D7
Failsworth Gtr Man 44 B2
Fain Highld 86 D4
Fair Green Norf 38 D2
Fair Hill Cumb 57 C7
Fair Oak Hants 10 C3
Fair Oak Green Hants 18 E3
Fairbourne Gwyn 32 D2
Fairburn N Yorks 51 G10
Fairfield Derbys 44 E4
Fairfield Stockton 58 E5
Fairfield Worcs 27 D7
Fairfield Worcs 34 H5
Fairford Glos 17 A8
Fairhaven Lancs 49 G3
Fairlie N Ayrs 73 H11
Fairlight E Sus 13 E7
Fairlight Cove E Sus 13 E7
Fairmile Devon 7 G9
Fairmilehead Edin 69 D11
Fairoak Staffs 34 B3
Fairseat Kent 20 E3
Fairstead Essex 30 G4
Fairstead Norf 38 C2
Fairwarp E Sus 12 D3
Fairy Cottage IoM 48 D4
Fairy Cross Devon 6 D3
Fakenham Norf 38 C5
Fakenham Magna Suff 38 H5
Fala Midloth 70 D3
Fala Dam Midloth 70 D3
Falahill Borders 70 E2
Falcon Hereford 26 E3
Faldingworth Lincs 46 D4
Falfield S Glos 16 B3
Falkenham Suff 31 E9
Falkirk Falk 69 C7
Falkland Fife 76 G5
Falla Borders 62 B3
Fallgate Derbys 45 F7
Fallin Stirling 69 A7
Fallowfield Gtr Man 44 C2
Fallsidehill Borders 70 F5
Falmer E Sus 12 F2
Falmouth Corn 3 F7
Falsgrave N Yorks 59 H11
Falstone Northumb 62 E3
Fanagmore Highld 92 E4
Fangdale Beck N Yorks 59 G6
Fangfoss E Yorks 52 D3
Fankerton Falk 68 B6
Fanmore Argyll 78 G7
Fannich Lodge Highld 86 E5
Fans Borders 70 F5
Far Bank S Yorks 45 A10
Far Bletchley M Keynes 28 E5
Far Cotton Northants 28 C4
Far Forest Worcs 26 A4
Far Laund Derbys 45 H7
Far Sawrey Cumb 56 G5
Farcet Cambs 37 F8
Farden Shrops 34 H1
Fareham Hants 10 D4
Farewell Staffs 35 D6
Farforth Lincs 47 E7
Faringdon Oxon 17 B9
Farington Lancs 49 G5
Farlam Cumb 61 H11
Farlary Highld 93 J10
Farleigh N Som 15 E10
Farleigh Sur 19 E10
Farleigh Hungerford Som 16 F5
Farleigh Wallop Hants 18 G3
Farlesthorpe Lincs 47 E8
Farleton Cumb 49 A5
Farleton Lancs 50 C1
Farley Shrops 33 E9
Farley Staffs 35 A6
Farley Wilts 9 B11
Farley Green Sur 19 G7
Farley Hill Luton 29 F7
Farley Hill Wokingham 18 E4
Farleys End Glos 26 G4
Farlington N Yorks 52 C2
Farlow Shrops 34 G2
Farmborough Bath 16 E3
Farmcote Glos 27 F7
Farmcote Shrops 34 F3
Farmington Glos 27 G8
Farmoor Oxon 27 H11
Farmtown Moray 88 C5
Farnborough Hants 18 F5
Farnborough London 19 E11
Farnborough W Berks 17 C11
Farnborough Warks 27 D11
Farnborough Green Hants 18 F5
Farncombe Sur 18 G6
Farndish Bedford 28 B6
Farndon Ches W 43 G7
Farndon Notts 45 G11
Farnell Angus 77 B9
Farnham Dorset 9 C8
Farnham Essex 29 F11
Farnham N Yorks 51 C9
Farnham Suff 31 B10
Farnham Sur 18 G5
Farnham Common Bucks 18 C6
Farnham Green Essex 29 F11
Farnham Royal Bucks 18 C6
Farnhill N Yorks 50 E6
Farningham Kent 20 E2
Farnley N Yorks 51 E8
Farnley W Yorks 51 F8
Farnley Tyas W Yorks 44 A5
Farnsfield Notts 45 G10
Farnworth Gtr Man 43 B10
Farnworth Halton 43 D8
Farr Highld 81 C10
Farr Highld 87 H9
Farr Highld 93 C10
Farr House Highld 87 H9
Farringdon Devon 7 G9
Farrington Gurney Bath 16 F3
Farsley W Yorks 51 F8
Farthinghoe Northants 28 E2
Farthingloe Kent 21 G9
Farthingstone Northants 28 C3
Fartown W Yorks 51 H7
Farway Devon 7 G10
Fasag Highld 85 C13
Fascadale Highld 78 D8
Faslane Port Argyll 73 E11
Fasnacloich Argyll 74 C3
Fasnakyle Ho Highld 80 A5
Fassfern Highld 80 F2
Fatfield T&W 58 A4
Fattahead Aberds 89 C6
Faugh Cumb 57 A7
Fauldhouse W Loth 69 D8
Faulkbourne Essex 30 G4
Faulkland Som 16 F4

Fauls Shrops 34 B1
Faversham Kent 21 E7
Favillar Moray 88 E2
Fawdington N Yorks 51 B10
Fawfieldhead Staffs 44 F4
Fawkham Green Kent 20 E2
Fawler Oxon 27 G10
Fawley Bucks 18 C4
Fawley Hants 10 D3
Fawley W Berks 17 C10
Fawley Chapel Hereford 26 F2
Faxfleet E Yorks 52 G4
Faygate W Sus 11 A11
Fazakerley Mers 43 C6
Fazeley Staffs 35 E8
Fearby N Yorks 51 A7
Fearn Highld 87 D11
Fearn Lodge Highld 87 C9
Fearn Station Highld 87 D11
Fearnan Perth 75 C10
Fearnbeg Highld 85 C12
Fearnhead Warr 43 C9
Fearnmore Highld 85 B12
Featherstone Staffs 34 E5
Featherstone W Yorks 51 G10
Featherwood Northumb 62 C4
Feckenham Worcs 27 B7
Feering Essex 30 F5
Feetham N Yorks 57 G11
Feizor N Yorks 50 C3
Felbridge Sur 12 C2
Felbrigg Norf 39 B8
Felcourt Sur 12 B2
Felden Herts 19 A7
Felin-Crai Powys 24 F5
Felindre Carms 23 C8
Felindre Carms 23 D10
Felindre Carms 24 E3
Felindre Carms 24 F4
Felindre Ceredig 23 A10
Felindre Powys 33 G7
Felindre Swansea 14 A2
Felindre Farchog Pembs 22 C6
Felinfach Ceredig 23 A10
Felinfach Powys 25 E7
Felinfoel Carms 23 F10
Felingwm isaf Carms 23 D10
Felingwm uchaf Carms 23 D10
Felinwynt Ceredig 23 A7
Felixkirk N Yorks 51 A10
Felixstowe Suff 31 E9
Felixstowe Ferry Suff 31 E10
Felkington Northumb 71 F8
Felkirk W Yorks 45 A7
Fell Side Cumb 56 C5
Felling T&W 63 G8
Felmersham Bedford 28 C6
Felmingham Norf 39 C8
Felpham W Sus 11 E8
Felsham Suff 30 C6
Felsted Essex 30 F3
Feltham London 19 D8
Felthorpe Norf 39 D7
Felton Hereford 26 D2
Felton N Som 15 E11
Felton Northumb 63 C7
Felton Butler Shrops 33 D9
Feltwell Norf 38 F3
Fen Ditton Cambs 29 B11
Fen Drayton Cambs 29 B10
Fen End W Mid 35 H8
Fen Side Lincs 47 G7
Fenay Bridge W Yorks 51 H7
Fence Lancs 50 F4
Fence Houses T&W 58 A4
Fengate Norf 39 C7
Fengate Pboro 37 F8
Fenham Northumb 71 F9
Fenhouses Lincs 37 A8
Feniscliffe Blackburn 50 G2
Feniscowles Blackburn 50 G2
Feniton Devon 7 G10
Fenlake Bedford 29 D7
Fenny Bentley Derbys 44 G5
Fenny Bridges Devon 7 G10
Fenny Compton Warks 27 C11
Fenny Drayton Leics 35 F9
Fenny Stratford M Keynes 28 E5
Fenrother Northumb 63 D7
Fenstanton Cambs 29 B10
Fenton Cambs 37 H9
Fenton Lincs 46 E2
Fenton Lincs 46 G2
Fenton Stoke 34 A4
Fenton Barns E Loth 70 B4
Fenton Town Northumb 71 G8
Fenwick E Ayrs 67 B7
Fenwick Northumb 62 F6
Fenwick Northumb 71 F9
Fenwick S Yorks 52 H1
Feochaig Argyll 65 G8
Feock Corn 3 F7
Feolin Ferry Argyll 72 G3
Ferindonald Highld 85 H11
Feriniquarrie Highld 84 C6
Ferlochan Argyll 74 C2
Fern Angus 77 A7
Ferndale Rhondda 14 B6
Ferndown Dorset 9 D9
Ferness Highld 87 G12
Ferney Green Cumb 56 G6
Fernham Oxon 17 B9
Fernhill Heath Worcs 26 C5
Fernhurst W Sus 11 B7
Fernie Fife 76 F6
Ferniegair S Lanark 68 E6
Fernilea Highld 85 E8
Fernilee Derbys 44 E4
Ferrensby N Yorks 51 C9
Ferring W Sus 11 D9
Ferry Hill Cambs 37 G9
Ferry Point Highld 87 C10
Ferrybridge W Yorks 51 G10
Ferryden Angus 77 B10
Ferryhill Aberdeen 83 C11
Ferryhill Durham 58 C3
Ferryhill Station Durham 58 C4
Ferryside Carms 23 E8
Fersfield Norf 39 G6
Fersit Highld 80 F5
Ferwig Ceredig 22 B6
Feshiebridge Highld 81 C10
Fetcham Sur 19 F8
Fetterangus Aberds 89 C9
Fettercairn Aberds 83 F8
Fettes Highld 87 F8
Fewcott Oxon 28 F2
Fewston N Yorks 51 D7
Ffair-Rhos Ceredig 24 B4
Ffairfach Carms 24 F3
Ffaldybrenin Carms 24 D3
Ffarmers Carms 24 D3
Ffawyddog Powys 25 G9
Fforest Carms 23 F10
Fforest-fâch Swansea 14 B2
Ffos-y-ffin Ceredig 24 B1
Ffostrasol Ceredig 23 B8
Ffridd-Uchaf Gwyn 41 E7
Ffrith Wrex 42 G5
Ffrwd Gwyn 40 E6
Ffynnon ddrain Carms 23 D9
Ffynnon-oer Ceredig 23 A10
Ffynnongroyw Flint 42 D4
Fidden Argyll 78 J6
Fiddes Aberds 83 E10
Fiddington Glos 26 E6
Fiddington Som 7 B11
Fiddleford Dorset 9 C7
Fiddlers Hamlet Essex 19 A11
Field Staffs 34 B6
Field Broughton Cumb 49 A3
Field Dalling Norf 38 B6
Field Head Leics 35 E10
Fifehead Magdalen Dorset 9 B6
Fifehead Neville Dorset 9 C6
Fifield Oxon 27 G9
Fifield Wilts 17 F8
Fifield Windsor 18 D6
Fifield Bavant Wilts 9 B9
Figheldean Wilts 17 G8
Filands Wilts 16 C6
Filby Norf 39 D10
Filey N Yorks 53 A7
Filgrave M Keynes 28 D5
Filkins Oxon 17 A9
Filleigh Devon 6 D5
Filleigh Devon 7 E6
Fillingham Lincs 46 D3
Fillongley Warks 35 G8
Filton S Glos 16 D3
Fimber E Yorks 52 C4
Finavon Angus 77 B7
Finchairn Argyll 73 C8
Fincham Norf 38 E2
Finchampstead Wokingham 18 E4
Finchdean Hants 10 C6
Finchingfield Essex 30 E3
Finchley London 19 B9
Findern Derbys 35 B9
Findhorn Moray 87 E13
Findhorn Bridge Highld 81 A10
Findo Gask Perth 76 E3
Findochty Moray 88 B4
Findon Aberds 83 D11
Findon W Sus 11 D10
Findon Mains Highld 87 E9
Findrack Ho. Aberds 83 C8
Finedon Northants 28 A6
Fingal Street Suff 31 B9
Fingask Aberds 83 A9
Fingerpost Worcs 26 A4
Fingest Bucks 18 B4
Finghall N Yorks 58 H2
Fingland Cumb 61 H8
Fingland Dumfries 60 B3
Finglesham Kent 21 F10
Fingringhoe Essex 31 F7
Finlarig Stirling 75 D8
Finmere Oxon 28 E3
Finnart Perth 75 B8
Finningham Suff 31 B7
Finningley S Yorks 45 C10
Finnygaud Aberds 88 C5
Finsbury London 19 C10
Finstall Worcs 26 B6
Finsthwaite Cumb 56 H5
Finstock Oxon 27 G10
Finstown Orkney 95 G4
Fintry Aberds 89 C7
Fintry Dundee 77 D7
Fintry Stirling 68 B5
Finzean Aberds 83 D8
Fionnphort Argyll 78 J6
Fionnsbhagh W Isles 90 J5
Fir Tree Durham 58 C2
Firbeck S Yorks 45 D9
Firby N Yorks 52 C3
Firby N Yorks 58 H3
Firgrove Gtr Man 44 A3
Firsby Lincs 47 F8
Firsdown Wilts 9 A11
First Coast Highld 86 B2
Fishbourne IoW 10 E4
Fishbourne W Sus 11 D7
Fishburn Durham 58 C4
Fishcross Clack 75 H11
Fisher Place Cumb 56 E5
Fisherford Aberds 89 E6
Fisher's Pond Hants 10 B3
Fisherstreet W Sus 11 A8
Fisherton Highld 87 F10
Fisherton S Ayrs 66 E5
Fishguard = Abergwaun Pembs 22 C4
Fishlake S Yorks 45 A10
Fishleigh Barton Devon 6 D4
Fishponds Bristol 16 D3
Fishpool Glos 26 F3
Fishtoft Lincs 37 A9
Fishtoft Drove Lincs 47 H7
Fishtown of Usan Angus 77 B10
Fishwick Borders 71 E8
Fiskavaig Highld 85 E8
Fiskerton Lincs 46 E4
Fiskerton Notts 45 G11
Fitling E Yorks 53 F8
Fittleton Wilts 17 G8
Fittleworth W Sus 11 C9
Fitton End Cambs 37 D10
Fitz Shrops 33 D10
Fitzhead Som 7 D10
Fitzwilliam W Yorks 51 H10
Fiunary Highld 79 G9
Five Acres Glos 26 G2
Five Ashes E Sus 12 D4
Five Oak Green Kent 20 G3
Five Oaks Jersey 11
Five Oaks W Sus 11 B9
Five Roads Carms 23 F9
Fivecrosses Ches W 43 E8
Fivehead Som 8 B2
Flack's Green Essex 30 G4
Flackwell Heath Bucks 18 C5
Fladbury Worcs 26 D6
Fladdabister Shetland 96 K6
Flagg Derbys 44 F5
Flamborough E Yorks 53 B8
Flamstead Herts 29 G7
Flamstead End Herts 19 A10
Flansham W Sus 11 D8
Flanshaw W Yorks 51 G9
Flasby N Yorks 50 D5
Flash Staffs 44 F4
Flashader Highld 85 C8
Flask Inn N Yorks 59 F10
Flaunden Herts 19 A7
Flawborough Notts 36 A3
Flawith N Yorks 51 C10
Flax Bourton N Som 15 E11
Flaxby N Yorks 51 D9
Flaxholme Derbys 35 A9
Flaxley Glos 26 G3
Flaxpool Som 7 C10
Flaxton N Yorks 52 C2
Fleckney Leics 36 F2
Flecknoe Warks 28 B2
Fledborough Notts 46 E2
Fleet Hants 10 D6
Fleet Hants 18 F5
Fleet Lincs 37 C9
Fleet Hargate Lincs 37 C9
Fleetham Northumb 71 H10
Fleetlands Hants 10 D4
Fleetville Herts 29 H8
Fleetwood Lancs 49 E3
Flemingston V Glam 14 D6
Flemington S Lanark 68 E5
Flempton Suff 30 B5
Fleoideabhagh W Isles 90 J5
Fletchertown Cumb 56 B4
Fletching E Sus 12 D3
Flexbury Corn 6 F1
Flexford Sur 18 G6
Flimby Cumb 56 C2
Flimwell E Sus 12 C6
Flint = Y Fflint Flint 42 E5
Flint Mountain Flint 42 E5
Flintham Notts 45 H11
Flinton E Yorks 53 F8
Flintsham Hereford 25 C10
Flitcham Norf 38 C3
Flitton C Beds 29 E7
Flitwick C Beds 29 E7
Flixborough N Lincs 52 H4
Flixborough Stather N Lincs 46 A2
Flixton Gtr Man 43 C10
Flixton N Yorks 52 B6
Flixton Suff 39 G9
Flockton W Yorks 44 A6
Flodaigh W Isles 84 C3
Flodden Northumb 71 G8
Flodigarry Highld 85 A9
Flood's Ferry Cambs 37 F9
Flookburgh Cumb 49 B3
Florden Norf 39 F7
Flore Northants 28 B3
Flotterton Northumb 62 C5
Flowton Suff 31 D7
Flush House W Yorks 44 B5
Flushing Aberds 89 D10
Flushing Corn 3 F7
Flyford Flavell Worcs 26 C6
Foals Green Suff 31 A9
Fobbing Thurrock 20 C4
Fochabers Moray 88 C3
Fochriw Caerph 25 H8
Fockerby N Lincs 52 H4
Fodderletter Moray 82 A3
Fodderty Highld 87 F8
Foel Powys 32 D5
Foel-gastell Carms 23 E10
Foffarty Angus 77 C7
Foggathorpe E Yorks 52 F3
Fogo Borders 70 F6
Fogorig Borders 70 F6
Foindle Highld 92 E4
Folda Angus 76 A4
Fole Staffs 34 B6
Foleshill W Mid 35 G9
Folke Dorset 8 C5
Folkestone Kent 21 H10
Folkingham Lincs 37 B6
Folkington E Sus 12 F4
Folksworth Cambs 37 G7
Folkton N Yorks 53 B6
Folla Rule Aberds 89 E7
Follifoot N Yorks 51 D9
Folly Gate Devon 6 G4
Fonthill Bishop Wilts 9 A8
Fonthill Gifford Wilts 9 A8
Fontmell Magna Dorset 9 C7
Fontwell W Sus 11 D8
Foolow Derbys 44 E5
Foots Cray London 19 D11
Forbestown Aberds 82 B5
Force Mills Cumb 56 G5
Forcett N Yorks 58 E2
Ford Argyll 73 C7
Ford Bucks 28 H4
Ford Devon 6 D3
Ford Glos 27 F7
Ford Northumb 71 G8
Ford Shrops 33 D10
Ford Staffs 44 G4
Ford W Sus 11 D9
Ford Wilts 16 D5
Ford End Essex 30 G3
Ford Street Som 7 E10
Fordcombe Kent 12 B4
Fordell Fife 69 B10
Forden Powys 33 E8
Forder Green Devon 5 E8
Fordham Cambs 30 A3
Fordham Essex 30 F6
Fordham Norf 38 F2
Fordhouses W Mid 34 E5
Fordingbridge Hants 9 C10
Fordon E Yorks 52 B6
Fordoun Aberds 83 F9
Ford's Green Suff 31 B7
Fordstreet Essex 30 F6
Fordwells Oxon 27 G10
Fordwich Kent 21 F8
Fordyce Aberds 88 B5
Forebridge Staffs 34 C5
Forest Durham 57 C10
Forest Becks Lancs 50 D3
Forest Gate London 19 C11
Forest Green Sur 19 G8
Forest Hall Cumb 57 F7
Forest Head Cumb 61 H11
Forest Hill Oxon 28 H2
Forest Lane Head N Yorks 51 D9
Forest Lodge Argyll 74 C5
Forest Lodge Highld 82 B2
Forest Lodge Perth 81 F11
Forest Mill Clack 69 A8
Forest Row E Sus 12 C3
Forest Town Notts 45 F9
Forestburn Gate Northumb 62 D6
Foresterseat Moray 88 C1
Forestside W Sus 11 C6
Forfar Angus 77 B7
Forgandenny Perth 76 F3
Forge Powys 32 F3
Forge Side Torf 25 H9
Forgewood N Lanark 68 E6
Forgie Moray 88 C3
Forglen Ho. Aberds 89 C6
Formby Mers 42 B6
Forncett End Norf 39 F7
Forncett St Mary Norf 39 F7
Forncett St Peter Norf 39 F7
Forneth Perth 76 C3
Fornham All Saints Suff 30 B5
Fornham St Martin Suff 30 B5
Forres Moray 87 F13
Forrest Lodge Dumfries 67 H8
Forrestfield N Lanark 69 D7
Forsbrook Staffs 34 A5
Forse Highld 94 G4
Forse Ho. Highld 94 G4
Forsinain Highld 93 E12
Forsinard Highld 93 E11
Forsinard Station Highld 93 E11
Forston Dorset 8 E5
Fort Augustus Highld 80 C5
Fort George Guern 11
Fort George Highld 87 F10
Fort William Highld 80 F3
Forteviot Perth 76 F3
Forth S Lanark 69 E8
Forth Road Bridge Edin 69 C10
Forthampton Glos 26 E5
Fortingall Perth 75 C10
Forton Hants 17 G11
Forton Lancs 49 D4
Forton Shrops 33 D10
Forton Som 8 D2
Forton Staffs 34 C3
Forton Heath Shrops 33 D10
Fortrie Aberds 89 D6
Fortrose Highld 87 F10
Fortuneswell Dorset 8 G5
Forty Green Bucks 18 B6
Forty Hill London 19 B10
Forward Green Suff 31 C7
Fosbury Wilts 17 F10
Fosdyke Lincs 37 B9
Foss Perth 75 B10
Foss Cross Glos 27 H7
Fossebridge Glos 27 G7
Foster Street Essex 29 H11
Fosterhouses S Yorks 45 A10
Foston Derbys 35 B7
Foston Lincs 36 A4
Foston N Yorks 52 C2
Foston on the Wolds E Yorks 53 D7
Fotherby Lincs 47 C7
Fotheringhay Northants 37 F6
Foubister Orkney 95 H6
Foul Mile E Sus 12 E5
Foulby W Yorks 51 H9
Foulden Borders 71 E8
Foulden Norf 38 F3
Foulis Castle Highld 87 E8
Foulridge Lancs 50 E4
Foulsham Norf 38 C6
Fountainhall Borders 70 F3
Four Ashes Staffs 34 G4
Four Ashes Suff 31 A7
Four Crosses Powys 33 D8
Four Crosses Powys 33 E6
Four Crosses Wrex 42 G5
Four Elms Kent 19 G11
Four Forks Som 7 C11
Four Gotes Cambs 37 D10
Four Lane Ends Ches W 43 F8
Four Lanes Corn 2 F5
Four Marks Hants 10 A5
Four Mile Bridge Anglesey 40 C4
Four Oaks E Sus 13 D7
Four Oaks W Mid 35 F7
Four Oaks W Mid 35 G8
Four Roads Carms 23 F9
Four Roads IoM 48 F2
Four Throws Kent 13 D6
Fourlane Ends Derbys 45 G7
Fourlanes End Ches E 44 G2
Fourpenny Highld 87 B11
Fourstones Northumb 62 G4
Fovant Wilts 9 B9
Foveran Aberds 89 F9
Fowey Corn 4 F2
Fowley Common Warr 43 C9
Fowlis Angus 76 D6
Fowlis Wester Perth 76 E2
Fowlmere Cambs 29 D11
Fownhope Hereford 26 E2
Fox Corner Sur 18 F6
Fox Lane Hants 18 F5
Fox Street Essex 31 F7
Foxbar Renfs 68 D3
Foxcombe Hill Oxon 17 A11
Foxdale IoM 48 E2
Foxearth Essex 30 D5
Foxfield Cumb 56 H4
Foxham Wilts 16 D6
Foxhole Corn 3 D8
Foxhole Swansea 14 B2
Foxholes N Yorks 52 B6
Foxhunt Green E Sus 12 E4
Foxley Norf 38 C6
Foxley Wilts 16 C5
Foxt Staffs 44 H4
Foxton Cambs 29 D11
Foxton Durham 58 D4
Foxton Leics 36 F3
Foxup N Yorks 50 B4
Foxwist Green Ches W 43 F9
Foxwood Shrops 34 H2
Foy Hereford 26 F2
Foyers Highld 81 A6
Fraddam Corn 2 F4
Fraddon Corn 3 D8
Fradley Staffs 35 D7
Fradswell Staffs 34 B5
Fraisthorpe E Yorks 53 C7
Framfield E Sus 12 D3
Framingham Earl Norf 39 E8
Framingham Pigot Norf 39 E8
Framlingham Suff 31 B9
Frampton Dorset 8 E5
Frampton Lincs 37 B9
Frampton Cotterell S Glos 16 C3
Frampton Mansell Glos 16 A6
Frampton on Severn Glos 26 H4
Frampton West End Lincs 37 A8
Framsden Suff 31 C8
Framwellgate Moor Durham 58 B3
Franche Worcs 34 H4
Frankby Mers 42 D5
Frankley Worcs 34 G5
Frank's Bridge Powys 25 C8
Frankton Warks 27 A11
Frant E Sus 12 C4
Fraserburgh Aberds 89 B9
Frating Green Essex 31 F7
Fratton Ptsmth 10 E5
Freathy Corn 4 F4
Freckenham Suff 30 A3
Freckleton Lancs 49 G4
Freeby Leics 36 C4
Freehay Staffs 34 A6
Freeland Oxon 27 G11
Freester Shetland 96 H6
Freethorpe Norf 39 E10
Freiston Lincs 37 A9
Fremington Devon 6 C4
Fremington N Yorks 58 G1
Frenchay S Glos 16 D3
Frenchbeer Devon 5 C7
Frenich Stirling 75 G7
Frensham Sur 18 G5
Fresgoe Highld 93 C12
Freshfield Mers 42 B5
Freshford Bath 16 E4
Freshwater IoW 10 F2
Freshwater Bay IoW 10 F2
Freshwater East Pembs 22 G5
Fressingfield Suff 39 H8
Freston Suff 31 E8
Freswick Highld 94 D5
Fretherne Glos 26 H4
Frettenham Norf 39 D8
Freuchie Fife 76 G5
Freuchies Angus 76 A5
Freystrop Pembs 22 E4
Friar's Gate E Sus 12 C3
Friarton Perth 76 E4
Friday Bridge Cambs 37 E10
Friday Street E Sus 12 F5
Fridaythorpe E Yorks 52 D4
Friern Barnet London 19 B9
Friesland Argyll 78 F4
Friesthorpe Lincs 46 D4
Frieston Lincs 46 H3
Frieth Bucks 18 B4
Frilford Oxon 17 B11
Frilsham W Berks 18 D2
Frimley Sur 18 F5
Frimley Green Sur 18 F5
Frindsbury Medway 20 D4
Fring Norf 38 B3
Fringford Oxon 28 F3
Frinsted Kent 20 F5
Frinton-on-Sea Essex 31 F9
Friockheim Angus 77 C8
Friog Gwyn 32 D2
Frisby on the Wreake Leics 36 D2
Friskney Lincs 47 G8
Friskney Eaudike Lincs 47 G8
Friskney Tofts Lincs 47 G8
Friston E Sus 12 G4
Friston Suff 31 B11
Fritchley Derbys 45 G7
Frith Bank Lincs 47 H7
Frith Common Worcs 26 B3
Fritham Hants 9 C11
Frithelstock Devon 6 E3
Frithelstock Stone Devon 6 E3
Frithville Lincs 47 G7
Frittenden Kent 13 B7
Frittiscombe Devon 5 G9
Fritton Norf 39 E10
Fritton Norf 39 F8
Fritwell Oxon 28 F2
Frizinghall W Yorks 51 F7
Frizington Cumb 56 E2
Frocester Glos 16 A4
Frodesley Shrops 33 E11
Frodingham N Lincs 46 A2
Frodsham Ches W 43 E8
Frogden Borders 70 H6
Froggatt Derbys 44 E6
Froghall Staffs 44 H4
Frogmore Devon 5 G8
Frogmore Hants 18 F5
Frognall Lincs 37 D7
Frogshail Norf 39 B8
Frolesworth Leics 35 F11
Frome Som 16 G4
Frome St Quintin Dorset 8 D4
Fromes Hill Hereford 26 D3
Fron Denb 42 F3
Fron Gwyn 40 G5
Fron Gwyn 41 E7
Fron Powys 25 B7
Fron Powys 33 E8
Fron Powys 33 F7
Froncysyllte Wrex 33 A8
Frongoch Gwyn 32 B5
Frostenden Suff 39 G10
Frosterley Durham 58 C1
Frotoft Orkney 95 F5
Froxfield Wilts 17 E9
Froxfield Green Hants 10 B6
Froyle Hants 18 G4
Fryerning Essex 20 A3
Fryton N Yorks 52 B2
Fulbeck Lincs 46 G3
Fulbourn Cambs 30 C2
Fulbrook Oxon 27 G9
Fulford Som 7 D11
Fulford Staffs 34 B5
Fulford York 52 E2
Fulham London 19 D9
Fulking W Sus 11 C11
Full Sutton E Yorks 52 D3
Fullarton Glasgow 68 D5
Fullarton N Ayrs 66 C6
Fuller Street Essex 30 G4
Fuller's Moor Ches W 43 G7
Fullerton Hants 17 H10
Fulletby Lincs 46 E6
Fullwood E Ayrs 67 A7
Fulmer Bucks 18 C6
Fulmodestone Norf 38 B5
Fulnetby Lincs 46 E4
Fulstow Lincs 47 C7
Fulwell T&W 63 H9
Fulwood Lancs 49 F5
Fulwood S Yorks 45 D7
Fundenhall Norf 39 F7
Fundenhall Street Norf 39 F7
Funtington W Sus 11 D6
Funtley Hants 10 D4
Funtullich Perth 75 E10
Funzie Shetland 96 D8
Furley Devon 8 D1
Furnace Argyll 73 C9
Furnace Carms 23 F10
Furnace End Warks 35 F8
Furneaux Pelham Herts 29 F11
Furness Vale Derbys 44 D4
Furze Platt Windsor 18 C5
Furzehill Devon 7 B6
Fyfett Som 7 E11
Fyfield Essex 30 H2
Fyfield Glos 17 A9
Fyfield Hants 17 G9
Fyfield Oxon 17 B11
Fyfield Wilts 17 E8
Fylingthorpe N Yorks 59 F10
Fyvie Aberds 89 E7

G

Gabhsann bho Dheas W Isles 91 B9
Gabhsann bho Thuath W Isles 91 B9
Gablon Highld 87 B10
Gabroc Hill E Ayrs 67 A7
Gaddesby Leics 36 D2
Gadebridge Herts 29 H7
Gaer Powys 25 F8
Gaerllwyd Mon 15 B10
Gaerwen Anglesey 40 C6
Gagingwell Oxon 27 F11
Gaick Lodge Highld 81 E9
Gailey Staffs 34 D5
Gainford Durham 58 E2
Gainsborough Lincs 46 C2
Gainsborough Suff 31 D8
Gainsford End Essex 30 E4
Gairloch Highld 85 A13
Gairlochy Highld 80 E3
Gairney Bank Perth 76 H4
Gairnshiel Lodge Aberds 82 C4
Gaisgill Cumb 57 F8
Gaitsgill Cumb 56 B5
Galashiels Borders 70 G3
Galgate Lancs 49 D4
Galhampton Som 8 B5
Gallaberry Dumfries 60 E5
Gallachoille Argyll 72 E6
Gallanach Argyll 78 E5
Gallanach Argyll 79 J11
Gallantry Bank Ches E 43 G8
Gallatown Fife 69 A11
Galley Common Warks 35 F9
Galley Hill Cambs 29 B10
Galleyend Essex 20 A4
Galleywood Essex 20 A4
Gallin Perth 75 C8
Gallowfauld Angus 77 C7
Gallows Green Staffs 35 A6
Galltair Highld 85 F13
Galmisdale Highld 78 C7
Galmpton Devon 5 G7
Galmpton Torbay 5 F9
Galphay N Yorks 51 B8
Galston E Ayrs 67 C8
Galtrigill Highld 84 C6
Gamblesby Cumb 57 C8
Gamesley Derbys 44 C4
Gamlingay Cambs 29 C9
Gammersgill N Yorks 51 A6
Gamston Notts 45 E11
Ganarew Hereford 26 G2
Ganavan Argyll 79 H11
Gang Corn 4 E4
Ganllwyd Gwyn 32 C3
Gannochy Angus 83 F7
Gannochy Perth 76 E4
Gansclet Highld 94 F5
Ganstead E Yorks 53 F7
Ganthorpe N Yorks 52 B2
Ganton N Yorks 52 B5
Garbat Highld 86 E7
Garbhallt Argyll 73 D9
Garboldisham Norf 38 G6
Garden City Flint 42 F6
Garden Village W Yorks 51 F10
Garden Village Wrex 42 G6
Gardenstown Aberds 89 B7
Garderhouse Shetland 96 J5
Gardham E Yorks 52 E5
Gardin Shetland 96 G6
Gare Hill Som 16 G4
Garelochhead Argyll 73 D11
Garford Oxon 17 B11
Garforth W Yorks 51 F10
Gargrave N Yorks 50 D5
Gargunnock Stirling 68 A6
Garlic Street Norf 39 G8
Garlieston Dumfries 55 E7
Garlinge Green Kent 21 F8
Garlogie Aberds 83 C9
Garmond Aberds 89 C8
Garmony Argyll 79 G9
Garmouth Moray 88 B3
Garn-yr-erw Torf 25 G9
Garnant Carms 24 G3
Garndiffaith Torf 15 A8
Garndolbenmaen Gwyn 40 F6
Garnedd Conwy 41 E9
Garnett Bridge Cumb 57 G7
Garnfadryn Gwyn 40 G4
Garnkirk N Lanark 68 D5
Garnlydan Bl Gwent 25 G8
Garnswllt Swansea 24 H3
Garrabost W Isles 91 D10
Garraron Argyll 73 C7
Garras Corn 2 G6
Garreg Gwyn 41 F8
Garrick Perth 75 F11
Garrigill Cumb 57 B9
Garriston N Yorks 58 G2
Garroch Dumfries 55 A8
Garrogie Lodge Highld 81 B7
Garros Highld 85 B9
Garrow Perth 75 C11
Garryhorn Dumfries 67 G8
Garsdale Cumb 57 H9
Garsdale Head Cumb 57 G9
Garsdon Wilts 16 C6
Garshall Green Staffs 34 B5
Garsington Oxon 18 A2
Garstang Lancs 49 E4
Garston Mers 43 D7
Garswood Mers 43 C8
Gartcosh N Lanark 68 D5
Garth Bridgend 14 B4
Garth Gwyn 41 C7
Garth Powys 24 D6
Garth Shetland 96 H4
Garth Wrex 33 A8
Garth Row Cumb 57 G7
Garthamlock Glasgow 68 D5
Garthbrengy Powys 25 E7
Garthdee Aberdeen 83 C11
Gartheli Ceredig 23 A10
Garthmyl Powys 33 F7
Garthorpe Leics 36 C4
Garthorpe N Lincs 52 H4
Gartly Aberds 88 E5
Gartmore Stirling 75 H8
Gartnagrenach Argyll 72 H6
Gartness N Lanark 68 D6
Gartness Stirling 68 B4
Gartocharn W Dunb 68 B3
Garton E Yorks 53 F8
Garton-on-the-Wolds E Yorks 52 D5
Gartsherrie N Lanark 68 D6
Gartymore Highld 93 H13
Garvald E Loth 70 C4
Garvamore Highld 81 D7
Garvard Argyll 72 D2
Garvault Hotel Highld 93 F10
Garve Highld 86 E6
Garvestone Norf 38 E6
Garvock Aberds 83 F9
Garvock Invclyd 73 F11
Garway Hereford 25 F11
Garway Hill Hereford 25 F11
Gaskan Highld 79 D10
Gastard Wilts 16 E5
Gasthorpe Norf 38 G5
Gatcombe IoW 10 F3
Gate Burton Lincs 46 D2
Gate Helmsley N Yorks 52 D2
Gateacre Mers 43 D7
Gatebeck Cumb 57 H7
Gateford Notts 45 D9
Gateforth N Yorks 52 G1
Gatehead E Ayrs 67 C6
Gatehouse Northumb 62 E3
Gatehouse of Fleet Dumfries 55 D9
Gatelawbridge Dumfries 60 D5
Gateley Norf 38 C5
Gatenby N Yorks 58 H4
Gateshead T&W 63 G8
Gatesheath Ches W 43 F7
Gateside Aberds 83 B8
Gateside Angus 77 C7
Gateside E Renf 68 E3
Gateside Fife 76 G4
Gateside N Ayrs 67 A6
Gathurst Gtr Man 43 B8
Gatley Gtr Man 44 D2
Gattonside Borders 70 G4
Gatwick Airport W Sus 12 B1
Gaufron Powys 24 B6
Gaulby Leics 36 E2
Gauldry Fife 76 E6
Gaunt's Common Dorset 9 D9
Gautby Lincs 46 E5
Gavinton Borders 70 E6
Gawber S Yorks 45 B7
Gawcott Bucks 28 E3
Gawsworth Ches E 44 F2
Gawthorpe W Yorks 51 G8
Gawthrop Cumb 57 H8
Gawthwaite Cumb 49 A2
Gay Street W Sus 11 B9
Gaydon Warks 27 C10
Gayfield Orkney 95 C5
Gayhurst M Keynes 28 D5
Gayle N Yorks 57 H10
Gayles N Yorks 58 F2
Gayton Mers 42 D5
Gayton Norf 38 D3
Gayton Northants 28 C4
Gayton Staffs 34 C5
Gayton le Marsh Lincs 47 D8
Gayton le Wold Lincs 46 D6
Gayton Thorpe Norf 38 D3
Gaywood Norf 38 C2
Gazeley Suff 30 B4
Geanies House Highld 87 D11
Gearraidh Bhailteas W Isles 84 F2
Gearraidh Bhaird W Isles 91 E8
Gearraidh na h-Aibhne W Isles 90 D7
Gearraidh na Monadh W Isles 84 G2
Geary Highld 84 B7
Geddes House Highld 87 F11
Gedding Suff 30 C6
Geddington Northants 36 G4
Gedintailor Highld 85 E10
Gedling Notts 36 A2
Gedney Lincs 37 C10
Gedney Broadgate Lincs 37 C10
Gedney Drove End Lincs 37 C10
Gedney Dyke Lincs 37 C10
Gedney Hill Lincs 37 D9
Gee Cross Gtr Man 44 C3
Geilston Argyll 68 C2
Geirinis W Isles 84 D2
Geise Highld 94 D3
Geisiadar W Isles 90 D6
Geldeston Norf 39 F9
Gell Conwy 41 D10
Gelli Pembs 22 E5
Gelli Rhondda 14 B5
Gellideg M Tydf 25 H7
Gellifor Denb 42 F4
Gelligaer Caerph 15 B7
Gellilydan Gwyn 41 G8
Gellinudd Neath 14 A3
Gellyburn Perth 76 D3
Gellywen Carms 23 D7
Gelston Dumfries 55 D10
Gelston Lincs 36 A5
Gembling E Yorks 53 D7
Gentleshaw Staffs 35 D6
Geocrab W Isles 90 H6
George Green Bucks 19 C7
George Nympton Devon 6 D6
Georgefield Dumfries 61 D8
Georgeham Devon 6 C3
Georgetown Bl Gwent 25 H8
Gerlan Gwyn 41 D8
Germansweek Devon 6 G3
Germoe Corn 2 G4
Gerrans Corn 3 F7
Gerrards Cross Bucks 19 C7
Gestingthorpe Essex 30 E5
Geuffordd Powys 33 D8
Gib Hill Ches W 43 E9
Gibbet Hill Warks 35 G11
Gibbshill Dumfries 60 F3
Gidea Park London 20 C2
Gidleigh Devon 5 C7
Giffnock E Renf 68 E4
Gifford E Loth 70 D4
Giffordland N Ayrs 66 B5
Giffordtown Fife 76 F5
Giggleswick N Yorks 50 C4
Gilberdyke E Yorks 52 G4
Gilchriston E Loth 70 D3
Gilcrux Cumb 56 C3
Gildersome W Yorks 51 G8
Gildingwells S Yorks 45 D9
Gileston V Glam 14 E6
Gilfach Caerph 15 B7
Gilfach Goch Rhondda 14 C5
Gilfachrheda Ceredig 23 A9
Gillamoor N Yorks 59 H7
Gillar's Green Mers 43 C7
Gillen Highld 84 C7
Gilling East N Yorks 52 B2
Gilling West N Yorks 58 F2
Gillingham Dorset 9 B7
Gillingham Medway 20 E4
Gillingham Norf 39 F10
Gillock Highld 94 E4
Gillow Heath Staffs 44 G2
Gills Highld 94 C5
Gill's Green Kent 13 C6
Gilmanscleuch Borders 61 A9
Gilmerton Edin 69 D11
Gilmerton Perth 75 E11
Gilmonby Durham 57 E11
Gilmorton Leics 36 G1
Gilmourton S Lanark 68 F5
Gilsland Northumb 62 G2
Gilsland Spa Cumb 62 G2
Gilston Borders 70 E3
Gilston Herts 29 G11
Gilwern Mon 25 G9
Gimingham Norf 39 B8
Giosla W Isles 90 E6
Gipping Suff 31 B7
Gipsey Bridge Lincs 46 H6
Girdle Toll N Ayrs 66 B6
Girlsta Shetland 96 H6
Girsby N Yorks 58 F4
Girtford C Beds 29 C8
Girthon Dumfries 55 D9
Girton Cambs 29 B11
Girton Notts 46 F2
Girvan S Ayrs 66 G4
Gisburn Lancs 50 E4
Gisleham Suff 39 G11
Gislingham Suff 31 A7
Gissing Norf 39 G7
Gittisham Devon 7 G10
Gladestry Powys 25 C9
Gladsmuir E Loth 70 C3
Glais Swansea 14 A3
Glaisdale N Yorks 59 F8
Glame Highld 85 D10
Glamis Angus 76 C6
Glan Adda Gwyn 41 C7
Glan Conwy Conwy 41 C10
Glan-Conwy Conwy 41 E10
Glan-Duar Carms 23 B10
Glan-Dwyfach Gwyn 40 F6
Glan Gors Anglesey 40 C6
Glan-rhyd Gwyn 40 E6
Glan-traeth Anglesey 40 C4
Glan-y-don Flint 42 E4
Glan-y-nant Powys 32 G5
Glan-y-wern Gwyn 41 G8
Glan-yr-afon Anglesey 41 B8
Glan-yr-afon Gwyn 32 A5
Glan-yr-afon Gwyn 32 A6
Glanaman Carms 24 G3
Glandford Norf 38 A6
Glandwr Pembs 22 D6
Glandy Cross Carms 22 D6
Glandyfi Ceredig 32 F2
Glangrwyney Powys 25 G9
Glanmule Powys 33 F7
Glanrafon Ceredig 32 G2
Glanrhyd Gwyn 40 G4
Glanrhyd Pembs 22 B6
Glanton Northumb 62 B6
Glanton Pike Northumb 62 B6
Glanvilles Wootton Dorset 8 D5
Glapthorn Northants 36 F6
Glapwell Derbys 45 F8
Glas-allt Shiel Aberds 82 E4
Glasbury Powys 25 E8
Glaschoil Highld 87 H13
Glascoed Denb 42 E2
Glascoed Mon 15 A9
Glascoed Powys 33 D7
Glascorrie Aberds 82 D5
Glascote Staffs 35 E8
Glascwm Powys 25 C8
Glasdrum Argyll 74 C3
Glasfryn Conwy 42 G2
Glasgow Glasgow 68 D4
Glashvin Highld 85 B9
Glasinfryn Gwyn 41 D7
Glasnacardoch Highld 79 B9
Glasnakille Highld 85 G10
Glasphein Highld 84 D6
Glaspwll Powys 32 F3
Glassburn Highld 86 H6
Glasserton Dumfries 55 F7
Glassford S Lanark 68 F6
Glasshouse Hill Glos 26 F4
Glasshouses N Yorks 51 C7
Glasslie Fife 76 G5
Glasson Cumb 61 G8
Glasson Lancs 49 D4
Glassonby Cumb 57 C7
Glasterlaw Angus 77 B8
Glaston Rutland 36 E4
Glastonbury Som 15 H11
Glatton Cambs 37 G7
Glazebrook Warr 43 C9
Glazebury Warr 43 C9
Glazeley Shrops 34 G3
Gleadless S Yorks 45 D7
Gleadsmoss Ches E 44 F2
Gleann Tholàstaidh W Isles 91 C10
Gleaston Cumb 49 B2
Gleiniant Powys 32 F5
Glemsford Suff 30 D5
Glen Dumfries 55 D8
Glen Dumfries 60 F4
Glen Auldyn IoM 48 C4
Glen Bernisdale Highld 85 D9
Glen Ho Borders 69 G11
Glen Mona IoM 48 D4
Glen Nevis House Highld 80 F3
Glen Parva Leics 36 F1
Glen Sluain Argyll 73 D9
Glen Tanar House Aberds 82 D6
Glen Trool Lodge Dumfries 55 A7
Glen Village Falk 69 C7
Glen Vine IoM 48 E3
Glenamachrie Argyll 74 E2
Glenbarr Argyll 65 E7
Glenbeg Highld 79 E8
Glenbeg Highld 82 A2
Glenbervie Aberds 83 E9
Glenboig N Lanark 68 D6
Glenborrodale Highld 79 E9
Glenbranter Argyll 73 D10
Glenbreck Borders 60 A6
Glenbrein Lodge Highld 81 B6
Glenbrittle House Highld 85 F9
Glenbuchat Lodge Aberds 82 B5
Glenbuck E Ayrs 68 H6
Glenburn Renfs 68 D3
Glencalvie Lodge Highld 86 C7
Glencanisp Lodge Highld 92 G4
Glencaple Dumfries 60 G5
Glencarron Lodge Highld 86 F3
Glencarse Perth 76 E4
Glencassley Castle Highld 92 J7
Glenceitlein Highld 74 C4
Glencoe Highld 74 B3
Glencraig Fife 76 H4
Glencripesdale Highld 79 F9
Glencrosh Dumfries 60 E3
Glendavan Ho. Aberds 82 C6
Glendevon Perth 76 G2
Glendoe Lodge Highld 80 C6
Glendoebeg Highld 80 C6
Glendoick Perth 76 E5
Glendoll Lodge Angus 82 F4
Glendoune S Ayrs 66 G4
Glenduckie Fife 76 F5
Glendye Lodge Aberds 83 E8
Gleneagles Hotel Perth 76 F2
Gleneagles House Perth 76 G2
Glenegedale Argyll 64 C4
Glenelg Highld 85 G13
Glenernie Moray 87 G13
Glenfarg Perth 76 F4
Glenfarquhar Lodge Aberds 83 E9
Glenferness House Highld 87 G12
Glenfeshie Lodge Highld 81 D10
Glenfield Leics 35 E11
Glenfinnan Highld 79 C11
Glenfoot Perth 76 F4
Glenfyne Lodge Argyll 74 F5
Glengap Dumfries 55 D9
Glengarnock N Ayrs 66 A6
Glengorm Castle Argyll 78 F7
Glengrasco Highld 85 D9
Glenhead Farm Angus 76 A5
Glenhoul Dumfries 67 H9
Glenhurich Highld 79 E11
Glenkerry Borders 61 B8
Glenkiln Dumfries 60 F4
Glenkindie Aberds 82 B6
Glenlatterach Moray 88 C1
Glenlee Dumfries 55 A9
Glenlichorn Perth 75 F10
Glenlivet Moray 82 A3
Glenlochsie Perth 82 F2
Glenloig N Ayrs 66 C2
Glenluce Dumfries 54 D5
Glenmallan Argyll 74 H5
Glenmarksie Highld 86 F6
Glenmassan Argyll 73 E10
Glenmavis N Lanark 68 D6
Glenmaye IoM 48 E2
Glenmidge Dumfries 60 E4
Glenmore Argyll 73 B7
Glenmore Highld 85 D9
Glenmore Lodge Highld 82 C1
Glenmoy Angus 77 A7
Glenogil Angus 77 A7
Glenprosen Lodge Angus 82 G4
Glenprosen Village Angus 82 G5
Glenquiech Angus 77 A7
Glenreasdell Mains Argyll 73 H7
Glenree N Ayrs 66 D2
Glenridding Cumb 56 E5
Glenrossal Highld 92 J7
Glenrothes Fife 76 G5
Glensanda Highld 79 G11
Glensaugh Aberds 83 F8
Glenshero Lodge Highld 81 D7
Glenstockadale Dumfries 54 C3
Glenstriven Argyll 73 F9
Glentaggart S Lanark 69 H7
Glentham Lincs 46 C4
Glentirranmuir Stirling 68 A5
Glenton Aberds 83 A8
Glentress Borders 69 G11
Glentromie Lodge Highld 81 D9
Glentrool Village Dumfries 54 B6
Glentruan IoM 48 B4
Glentruim House Highld 81 D8
Glentworth Lincs 46 D3
Glenuig Highld 79 D9
Glenurquhart Highld 87 E10
Glespin S Lanark 69 H7
Gletness Shetland 96 H6
Glewstone Hereford 26 F2
Glinton Pboro 37 E7
Glooston Leics 36 F3
Glororum Northumb 71 G10
Glossop Derbys 44 C4
Gloster Hill Northumb 63 C8
Gloucester Glos 26 G5
Gloup Shetland 96 C7
Glusburn N Yorks 50 E6
Glutt Lodge Highld 93 F12
Glutton Bridge Staffs 44 F4
Glympton Oxon 27 F11
Glyn-Ceiriog Wrex 33 B8
Glyn-cywarch Gwyn 41 G8
Glyn Ebwy = Ebbw Vale Bl Gwent 25 H8
Glyn-neath = Glynedd Neath 24 H5
Glynarthen Ceredig 23 B8
Glynbrochan Powys 32 G5
Glyncoch Rhondda 14 B6
Glyncorrwg Neath 14 B4
Glynde E Sus 12 F3

Glyndebourne E Sus 12 E3
Glyndyfrdwy Denb 33 A7
Glynedd = Glyn-neath Neath 24 H5
Glynogwr Bridgend 14 C5
Glyntaff Rhondda 14 C6
Glyntawe Powys 24 G5
Gnosall Staffs 34 C4
Gnosall Heath Staffs 34 C4
Goadby Leics 36 F3
Goadby Marwood Leics 36 C3
Goat Lees Kent 21 G7
Goatacre Wilts 17 D7
Goathill Dorset 8 C5
Goathland N Yorks 59 F9
Goathurst Som 8 A1
Gobernuisgach Lodge Highld 92 E7
Gobhaig W Isles 90 G5
Gobowen Shrops 33 B9
Godalming Sur 18 G6
Godley Gtr Man 44 C3
Godmanchester Cambs 29 A9
Godmanstone Dorset 8 E5
Godmersham Kent 21 F7
Godney Som 15 G10
Godolphin Cross Corn 2 F5
Godre'r-graig Neath 24 H4
Godshill Hants 9 C10
Godshill IoW 10 F4
Godstone Sur 19 F10
Godwinscroft Hants 9 E10
Goetre Mon 25 H10
Goferydd Anglesey 40 B4
Goff's Oak Herts 19 A10
Gogar Edin 69 C10
Goginan Ceredig 32 G2
Golan Gwyn 41 F7
Golant Corn 4 F2
Golberdon Corn 4 D4
Golborne Gtr Man 43 C9
Golcar W Yorks 51 H7
Gold Hill Norf 37 F11
Goldcliff Newport 15 C9
Golden Cross E Sus 12 E4
Golden Green Kent 20 G3
Golden Grove Carms 23 E10
Golden Hill Hants 10 E1
Golden Pot Hants 18 G4
Golden Valley Glos 26 F6
Goldenhill Stoke 44 G2
Golders Green London 19 C9
Goldhanger Essex 30 H6
Golding Shrops 33 E11
Goldington Bedford 29 C7
Goldsborough N Yorks 51 D9
Goldsborough N Yorks 59 E9
Goldsithney Corn 2 F4
Goldsworthy Devon 6 D2
Goldthorpe S Yorks 45 B8
Gollanfield Highld 87 F11
Golspie Highld 93 J11
Golval Highld 93 C11
Gomeldon Wilts 17 H8
Gomersal W Yorks 51 G8
Gomshall Sur 19 G7
Gonalston Notts 45 H10
Gonfirth Shetland 96 G5
Good Easter Essex 30 G3
Gooderstone Norf 38 E3
Goodleigh Devon 6 C5
Goodmanham E Yorks 52 E4
Goodnestone Kent 21 E7
Goodnestone Kent 21 F9
Goodrich Hereford 26 G2
Goodrington Torbay 5 F9
Goodshaw Lancs 50 G4
Goodwick = Wdig Pembs 22 C4
Goodworth Clatford Hants 17 G10
Goole E Yorks 52 G3
Goonbell Corn 2 E6
Goonhavern Corn 3 D6
Goose Eye W Yorks 50 E6
Goose Green Gtr Man 43 B8
Goose Green Norf 39 G7
Goose Green W Sus 11 C10
Gooseham Corn 6 E1
Goosey Oxon 17 B10
Goosnargh Lancs 50 F1
Goostrey Ches E 43 E10
Gorcott Hill Warks 27 B7
Gord Shetland 96 L6
Gordon Borders 70 F5
Gordonbush Highld 93 J11
Gordonsburgh Moray 88 B4
Gordonstoun Moray 88 B1
Gordonstown Aberds 88 C5
Gordonstown Aberds 89 E7
Gore Kent 21 F10
Gore Cross Wilts 17 F7
Gore Pit Essex 30 G5
Gorebridge Midloth 70 D2
Gorefield Cambs 37 D10
Gorey Jersey 11
Gorgie Edin 69 C11
Goring Oxon 18 C3
Goring-by-Sea W Sus 11 D10
Goring Heath Oxon 18 D3
Gorleston-on-Sea Norf 39 E11
Gornalwood W Mid 34 F5
Gorrachie Aberds 89 C7
Gorran Churchtown Corn 3 E8
Gorran Haven Corn 3 E9
Gorrenberry Borders 61 D10
Gors Ceredig 32 H2
Gorse Hill Swindon 17 C8
Gorsedd Flint 42 E4
Gorseinon Swansea 23 G10
Gorseness Orkney 95 G5
Gorsgoch Ceredig 23 A9
Gorslas Carms 23 E10
Gorsley Glos 26 F3
Gorstan Highld 86 E6
Gorstanvorran Highld 79 D11
Gorsteyhill Staffs 43 G10
Gorsty Hill Staffs 35 C7
Gortantaoid Argyll 64 A4
Gorton Gtr Man 44 C2
Gosbeck Suff 31 C8
Gosberton Lincs 37 B8
Gosberton Clough Lincs 37 C7
Gosfield Essex 30 F4
Gosford Hereford 26 B2
Gosforth Cumb 56 F2
Gosforth T&W 63 G8
Gosmore Herts 29 F8
Gosport Hants 10 E5
Gossabrough Shetland 96 E7
Gossington Glos 16 A4
Goswick Northumb 71 F9
Gotham Notts 35 B11
Gotherington Glos 26 F6
Gott Shetland 96 J6
Goudhurst Kent 12 C6
Goulceby Lincs 46 E6
Gourdas Aberds 89 D7
Gourdon Aberds 83 F10
Gourock Invclyd 73 F11
Govan Glasgow 68 D4
Govanhill Glasgow 68 D4
Goveton Devon 5 G8
Govilon Mon 25 G9
Gowanhill Aberds 89 B10
Gowdall E Yorks 52 G2
Gowerton Swansea 23 G10
Gowkhall Fife 69 B9
Gowthorpe E Yorks 52 D3
Goxhill E Yorks 53 E7
Goxhill N Lincs 53 G7
Goxhill Haven N Lincs 53 G7
Goybre Neath 14 C3
Grabhair W Isles 91 F8
Graby Lincs 37 C6
Grade Corn 2 H6
Graffham W Sus 11 C8
Grafham Cambs 29 B8
Grafham Sur 19 G7
Grafton Hereford 25 E11
Grafton N Yorks 51 C10
Grafton Oxon 17 A9
Grafton Shrops 33 D10
Grafton Worcs 26 B2
Grafton Flyford Worcs 26 C6
Grafton Regis Northants 28 D4
Grafton Underwood Northants 36 G5
Grafty Green Kent 20 G5
Graianrhyd Denb 42 G5
Graig Conwy 41 C10
Graig Denb 42 E3
Graig-fechan Denb 42 G4
Grain Medway 20 D5
Grainsby Lincs 46 C6
Grainthorpe Lincs 47 C7
Grampound Corn 3 E8
Grampound Road Corn 3 D8
Gramsdal W Isles 84 C3
Granborough Bucks 28 F4
Granby Notts 36 B3
Grandborough Warks 27 B11
Grandtully Perth 76 B2
Grange Cumb 56 E4
Grange E Ayrs 67 C7
Grange Medway 20 E4
Grange Mers 42 D5
Grange Perth 76 E5
Grange Crossroads Moray 88 C4
Grange Hall Moray 87 E13
Grange Hill Essex 19 B11
Grange Moor W Yorks 51 H8
Grange of Lindores Fife 76 F5
Grange-over-Sands Cumb 49 B4
Grange Villa Durham 58 A3
Grangemill Derbys 44 G6
Grangemouth Falk 69 B8
Grangepans Falk 69 B9
Grangetown Cardiff 15 D7
Grangetown Redcar 59 D6
Granish Highld 81 B11
Gransmoor E Yorks 53 D7
Granston Pembs 22 C3
Grantchester Cambs 29 C11
Grantham Lincs 36 B5
Grantley N Yorks 51 C8
Grantlodge Aberds 83 B9
Granton Dumfries 60 C6
Granton Edin 69 C11
Grantown-on-Spey Highld 82 A2
Grantshouse Borders 71 D7
Grappenhall Warr 43 D9
Grasby Lincs 46 B4
Grasmere Cumb 56 F5
Grasscroft Gtr Man 44 B3
Grassendale Mers 43 D6
Grassholme Durham 57 D11
Grassington N Yorks 50 C6
Grassmoor Derbys 45 F8
Grassthorpe Notts 45 F11
Grateley Hants 17 G9
Gratwich Staffs 34 B6
Graveley Cambs 29 B9
Graveley Herts 29 F9
Gravelly Hill W Mid 35 F7
Gravels Shrops 33 E9
Graven Shetland 96 F6
Graveney Kent 21 E7
Gravesend Herts 29 F11
Gravesend Kent 20 D3
Grayingham Lincs 46 C3
Grayrigg Cumb 57 G7
Grays Thurrock 20 D3
Grayshott Hants 18 H5
Grayswood Sur 11 A8
Graythorp Hrtlpl 58 D6
Grazeley Wokingham 18 E3
Greasbrough S Yorks 45 C8
Greasby Mers 42 D5
Great Abington Cambs 30 D2
Great Addington Northants 28 A6
Great Alne Warks 27 C8
Great Altcar Lancs 42 B6
Great Amwell Herts 29 G10
Great Asby Cumb 57 E8
Great Ashfield Suff 30 B6
Great Ayton N Yorks 59 E6
Great Baddow Essex 20 A4
Great Bardfield Essex 30 E3
Great Barford Bedford 29 C8
Great Barr W Mid 34 F6
Great Barrington Glos 27 G9
Great Barrow Ches W 43 F7
Great Barton Suff 30 B5
Great Barugh N Yorks 52 B3
Great Bavington Northumb 62 E5
Great Bealings Suff 31 D9
Great Bedwyn Wilts 17 E9
Great Bentley Essex 31 F8
Great Billing Northants 28 B5
Great Bircham Norf 38 B3
Great Blakenham Suff 31 C8
Great Blencow Cumb 56 C6
Great Bolas Telford 34 C2
Great Bookham Sur 19 F8
Great Bourton Oxon 27 D11
Great Bowden Leics 36 G3
Great Bradley Suff 30 C3
Great Braxted Essex 30 G5
Great Bricett Suff 31 C7
Great Brickhill Bucks 28 E6
Great Bridge W Mid 34 F5
Great Bridgeford Staffs 34 C4
Great Brington Northants 28 B3
Great Bromley Essex 31 F7
Great Broughton Cumb 56 C2
Great Broughton N Yorks 59 F6
Great Budworth Ches W 43 E9
Great Burdon Darl 58 E4
Great Burgh Sur 19 F9
Great Burstead Essex 20 B3
Great Busby N Yorks 58 F6
Great Canfield Essex 30 G2
Great Carlton Lincs 47 D8
Great Casterton Rutland 36 E6
Great Chart Kent 13 B8
Great Chatwell Staffs 34 D3
Great Chesterford Essex 30 D2
Great Cheverell Wilts 16 F6
Great Chishill Cambs 29 E11
Great Clacton Essex 31 G8
Great Cliff W Yorks 51 H9
Great Clifton Cumb 56 D2
Great Coates NE Lincs 46 B6
Great Comberton Worcs 26 D6
Great Corby Cumb 56 A6
Great Cornard Suff 30 D5
Great Cowden E Yorks 53 E8
Great Coxwell Oxon 17 B9
Great Crakehall N Yorks 58 G3
Great Cransley Northants 36 H4
Great Cressingham Norf 38 E4
Great Crosby Mers 42 C6
Great Cubley Derbys 35 B7
Great Dalby Leics 36 D3
Great Denham Bedford 29 D7
Great Doddington Northants 28 B5
Great Dunham Norf 38 D4
Great Dunmow Essex 30 F3
Great Durnford Wilts 17 H8
Great Easton Essex 30 F3
Great Easton Leics 36 F4
Great Eccleston Lancs 49 E4
Great Edstone N Yorks 52 A3
Great Ellingham Norf 38 F6
Great Elm Som 16 G4
Great Eversden Cambs 29 C10
Great Fencote N Yorks 58 G3
Great Finborough Suff 31 C7
Great Fransham Norf 38 D4
Great Gaddesden Herts 29 G7
Great Gidding Cambs 37 G7
Great Givendale E Yorks 52 D4
Great Glemham Suff 31 B10
Great Glen Leics 36 F2
Great Gonerby Lincs 36 B4
Great Gransden Cambs 29 C9
Great Green Norf 39 G8
Great Green Suff 30 C6
Great Habton N Yorks 52 B3
Great Hale Lincs 37 A7
Great Hallingbury Essex 30 G2
Great Hampden Bucks 18 A5
Great Harrowden Northants 28 A5
Great Harwood Lancs 50 F3
Great Haseley Oxon 18 A3
Great Hatfield E Yorks 53 E7
Great Haywood Staffs 34 C6
Great Heath W Mid 35 G9
Great Heck N Yorks 52 G1
Great Henny Essex 30 E5
Great Hinton Wilts 16 F6
Great Hockham Norf 38 F5
Great Holland Essex 31 G9
Great Horkesley Essex 30 E6
Great Hormead Herts 29 F10
Great Horton W Yorks 51 F7
Great Horwood Bucks 28 E4
Great Houghton Northants 28 C4
Great Houghton S Yorks 45 B8
Great Hucklow Derbys 44 E5
Great Kelk E Yorks 53 D7
Great Kimble Bucks 28 H5
Great Kingshill Bucks 18 B5
Great Langton N Yorks 58 G3
Great Leighs Essex 30 G4
Great Lever Gtr Man 43 B10
Great Limber Lincs 46 B5
Great Linford M Keynes 28 D5
Great Livermere Suff 30 A5
Great Longstone Derbys 44 E6
Great Lumley Durham 58 B3
Great Lyth Shrops 33 E10
Great Malvern Worcs 26 D4
Great Maplestead Essex 30 E5
Great Marton Blackpool 49 F3
Great Massingham Norf 38 C3
Great Melton Norf 39 E7
Great Milton Oxon 18 A3
Great Missenden Bucks 18 A5
Great Mitton Lancs 50 F3
Great Mongeham Kent 21 F10
Great Moulton Norf 39 F7
Great Munden Herts 29 F10
Great Musgrave Cumb 57 E9
Great Ness Shrops 33 D9
Great Notley Essex 30 F4
Great Oakley Essex 31 F8
Great Oakley Northants 36 G4
Great Offley Herts 29 F8
Great Ormside Cumb 57 E9
Great Orton Cumb 56 A5
Great Ouseburn N Yorks 51 C10
Great Oxendon Northants 36 G3
Great Oxney Green Essex 30 H3
Great Palgrave Norf 38 D4
Great Parndon Essex 29 H11
Great Paxton Cambs 29 B9
Great Plumpton Lancs 49 F3
Great Plumstead Norf 39 D9
Great Ponton Lincs 36 B5
Great Preston W Yorks 51 G10
Great Raveley Cambs 37 G8
Great Rissington Glos 27 G8
Great Rollright Oxon 27 E10
Great Ryburgh Norf 38 C5
Great Ryle Northumb 62 B6
Great Ryton Shrops 33 E10
Great Saling Essex 30 F4
Great Salkeld Cumb 57 C7
Great Sampford Essex 30 E3
Great Sankey Warr 43 D8
Great Saxham Suff 30 B4
Great Shefford W Berks 17 D10
Great Shelford Cambs 29 C11
Great Smeaton N Yorks 58 F4
Great Snoring Norf 38 B5
Great Somerford Wilts 16 C6
Great Stainton Darl 58 D4
Great Stambridge Essex 20 B5
Great Staughton Cambs 29 B8
Great Steeping Lincs 47 F8
Great Stonar Kent 21 F10
Great Strickland Cumb 57 D7
Great Stukeley Cambs 29 A9
Great Sturton Lincs 46 E6
Great Sutton Ches W 43 E6
Great Sutton Shrops 33 G11
Great Swinburne Northumb 62 F5
Great Tew Oxon 27 F10
Great Tey Essex 30 F5
Great Thurkleby N Yorks 51 B10
Great Thurlow Suff 30 C3
Great Torrington Devon 6 E3
Great Tosson Northumb 62 C6
Great Totham Essex 30 G5
Great Totham Essex 30 G5
Great Tows Lincs 46 C6
Great Urswick Cumb 49 B2
Great Wakering Essex 20 C6
Great Waldingfield Suff 30 D6
Great Walsingham Norf 38 B5
Great Waltham Essex 30 G3
Great Warley Essex 20 B2
Great Washbourne Glos 26 E6
Great Weldon Northants 36 G5
Great Welnetham Suff 30 C5
Great Wenham Suff 31 E7
Great Whittington Northumb 62 F6
Great Wigborough Essex 30 G6
Great Wilbraham Cambs 30 C2
Great Wishford Wilts 17 H7
Great Witcombe Glos 26 G6
Great Witley Worcs 26 B4
Great Wolford Warks 27 E9
Great Wratting Suff 30 D3
Great Wymondley Herts 29 F9
Great Wyrley Staffs 34 E5
Great Wytheford Shrops 34 D1
Great Yarmouth Norf 39 E11
Great Yeldham Essex 30 E4
Greater Doward Hereford 26 G2
Greatford Lincs 37 D6
Greatgate Staffs 35 A6
Greatham Hants 11 A6
Greatham Hrtlpl 58 D5
Greatham W Sus 11 C9
Greatstone on Sea Kent 13 D9
Greatworth Northants 28 D2
Greave Lancs 50 G4
Greeba IoM 48 D3
Green Denb 42 F3
Green End Bedford 29 C8
Green Hammerton N Yorks 51 D10
Green Lane Powys 33 F7
Green Ore Som 16 F2
Green St Green London 19 E11
Green Street Herts 19 B8
Greenbank Shetland 96 C7
Greenburn W Loth 69 D8
Greendikes Northumb 71 H9
Greenfield C Beds 29 E7
Greenfield Flint 42 E4
Greenfield Gtr Man 44 B3
Greenfield Highld 80 C4
Greenfield Oxon 18 B4
Greenford London 19 C8
Greengairs N Lanark 68 C6
Greenham W Berks 17 E11
Greenhaugh Northumb 62 E3
Greenhead Northumb 62 G2
Greenhill Falk 69 C7
Greenhill Kent 21 E8
Greenhill Leics 35 D10
Greenhill London 19 C8
Greenhills N Ayrs 67 A6
Greenhithe Kent 20 D2
Greenholm E Ayrs 67 C8
Greenholme Cumb 57 F7
Greenhouse Borders 61 A11
Greenhow Hill N Yorks 51 C7
Greenigoe Orkney 95 H5
Greenland Highld 94 D4
Greenlands Bucks 18 C4
Greenlaw Aberds 89 C6
Greenlaw Borders 70 F6
Greenlea Dumfries 60 F6
Greenloaning Perth 75 G11
Greenmount Gtr Man 43 A10
Greenmow Shetland 96 L6
Greenock Invclyd 73 F11
Greenock West Invclyd 73 F11
Greenodd Cumb 49 A3
Greenrow Cumb 56 A3
Greens Norton Northants 28 D3
Greenside T&W 63 G7
Greensidehill Northumb 62 B5
Greenstead Green Essex 30 F5
Greensted Essex 20 A2
Greenwich London 19 D10
Greet Glos 27 E7
Greete Shrops 26 A2
Greetham Lincs 47 E7
Greetham Rutland 36 D5
Greetland W Yorks 51 G6
Gregg Hall Cumb 56 G6
Gregson Lane Lancs 50 G1
Greinetobht W Isles 84 A3
Greinton Som 15 H10
Gremista Shetland 96 J6
Grenaby IoM 48 E2
Grendon Northants 28 B5
Grendon Warks 35 E8
Grendon Common Warks 35 F8
Grendon Green Hereford 26 C2
Grendon Underwood Bucks 28 F3
Grenofen Devon 4 D5
Grenoside S Yorks 45 C7
Greosabhagh W Isles 90 H6
Gresford Wrex 42 G6
Gresham Norf 39 B7
Greshornish Highld 85 C8
Gressenhall Norf 38 D5
Gressingham Lancs 50 C1
Gresty Green Ches E 43 G10
Greta Bridge Durham 58 E1
Gretna Dumfries 61 G9
Gretna Green Dumfries 61 G9
Gretton Glos 27 E7
Gretton Northants 36 F4
Gretton Shrops 33 F11
Grewelthorpe N Yorks 51 B8
Grey Green N Lincs 45 B11
Greygarth N Yorks 51 B7
Greynor Carms 23 F10
Greysouthen Cumb 56 D2
Greystoke Cumb 56 C6
Greystone Angus 77 C8
Greystone Dumfries 60 F5
Greywell Hants 18 F4
Griais W Isles 91 C9
Grianan W Isles 91 D9
Gribthorpe E Yorks 52 F3
Gridley Corner Devon 6 G2
Griff Warks 35 G9
Griffithstown Torf 15 B8
Grimbister Orkney 95 G4
Grimblethorpe Lincs 46 D6
Grimeford Village Lancs 43 A9
Grimethorpe S Yorks 45 B8
Griminis W Isles 84 C2
Grimister Shetland 96 D6
Grimley Worcs 26 B5
Grimness Orkney 95 J5
Grimoldby Lincs 47 D7
Grimpo Shrops 33 C9
Grimsargh Lancs 50 F1
Grimsbury Oxon 27 D11
Grimsby NE Lincs 46 A6
Grimscote Northants 28 C3
Grimscott Corn 4 A3
Grimsthorpe Lincs 36 C6
Grimston E Yorks 53 F8
Grimston Leics 36 C2
Grimston Norf 38 C3
Grimston York 52 D2
Grimstone Dorset 8 E5
Grinacombe Moor Devon 6 G3
Grindale E Yorks 53 B7
Grindigar Orkney 95 H6
Grindiscol Shetland 96 K6
Grindle Shrops 34 E3
Grindleford Derbys 44 E6
Grindleton Lancs 50 E3
Grindley Staffs 34 C6
Grindley Brook Shrops 33 A11
Grindlow Derbys 44 E5
Grindon Northumb 71 F8
Grindon Staffs 44 G4
Grindonmoor Gate Staffs 44 G4
Gringley on the Hill Notts 45 C11
Grinsdale Cumb 61 H9
Grinshill Shrops 33 C11
Grinton N Yorks 58 G1
Griomsidar W Isles 91 E8
Grishipoll Argyll 78 F4
Grisling Common E Sus 12 D3
Gristhorpe N Yorks 53 A6
Griston Norf 38 F5
Gritley Orkney 95 H6
Grittenham Wilts 17 C7
Grittleton Wilts 16 C5
Grizebeck Cumb 49 A2
Grizedale Cumb 56 G5
Grobister Orkney 95 F7
Groby Leics 35 E11
Groes Conwy 42 F3
Groes Neath 14 C3
Groes-faen Rhondda 14 C6
Groes-lwyd Powys 33 D8
Groesffordd Marli Denb 42 E3
Groeslon Gwyn 41 D7
Groeslon Gwyn 40 E6
Grogport Argyll 65 D9
Gromford Suff 31 C10
Gronant Flint 42 D3
Groombridge E Sus 12 C4
Grosmont Mon 25 F11
Grosmont N Yorks 59 F9
Groton Suff 30 D6
Grougfoot Falk 69 C9
Grouville Jersey 11
Grove Dorset 8 G6
Grove Kent 21 E9
Grove Notts 45 E11
Grove Oxon 17 B11
Grove Park London 19 D11
Grove Vale W Mid 34 F6
Grovesend Swansea 23 F10
Grudie Highld 86 E6
Gruids Highld 93 J8
Gruinard House Highld 86 B2
Grula Highld 85 F8
Gruline Argyll 79 G8
Grunasound Shetland 96 K5
Grundisburgh Suff 31 C9
Grunsagill Lancs 50 D3
Gruting Shetland 96 J4
Grutness Shetland 96 N6
Gualachulain Highld 74 C4
Gualin Ho. Highld 92 D6
Guardbridge Fife 77 F7
Guarlford Worcs 26 D5
Guay Perth 76 C3
Guestling Green E Sus 13 E7
Guestling Thorn E Sus 13 E7
Guestwick Norf 39 C6
Guestwick Green Norf 39 C6
Guide Blackburn 50 G3
Guide Post Northumb 63 E8
Guilden Morden Cambs 29 D9
Guilden Sutton Ches W 43 F7
Guildford Sur 18 G6
Guildtown Perth 76 D4
Guilsborough Northants 28 A3
Guilsfield Powys 33 D8
Guilton Kent 21 F9
Guineaford Devon 6 C4
Guisborough Redcar 59 E7
Guiseley W Yorks 51 E7
Guist Norf 38 C5
Guith Orkney 95 E6
Guiting Power Glos 27 F7
Gulberwick Shetland 96 K6
Gullane E Loth 70 B3
Gulval Corn 2 F3
Gulworthy Devon 4 D5
Gumfreston Pembs 22 F6
Gumley Leics 36 F2
Gummow's Shop Corn 3 D7
Gun Hill E Sus 12 E4
Gunby E Yorks 52 F3
Gunby Lincs 36 C5
Gundleton Hants 10 A5
Gunn Devon 6 C5
Gunnerside N Yorks 57 G11
Gunnerton Northumb 62 F5
Gunness N Lincs 46 A2
Gunnislake Corn 4 D5
Gunnista Shetland 96 J7
Gunthorpe Norf 38 B6
Gunthorpe Notts 36 A2
Gunthorpe Pboro 37 E7
Gunville IoW 10 F3
Gunwalloe Corn 2 G5
Gurnard IoW 10 E3
Gurnett Ches E 44 E3
Gurney Slade Som 16 G3
Gurnos Powys 24 H4
Gussage All Saints Dorset 9 C9
Gussage St Michael Dorset 9 C8
Guston Kent 21 G10
Gutcher Shetland 96 D7
Guthrie Angus 77 B8
Guyhirn Cambs 37 E9
Guyhirn Gull Cambs 37 E9
Guy's Head Lincs 37 C10
Guy's Marsh Dorset 9 B7
Guyzance Northumb 63 C8
Gwaenysgor Flint 42 D3
Gwalchmai Anglesey 40 C5
Gwaun-Cae-Gurwen Neath 24 G4
Gwaun-Leision Neath 24 G4
Gwbert Ceredig 22 B6
Gweek Corn 2 G6
Gwehelog Mon 15 A9
Gwenddwr Powys 25 D7
Gwennap Corn 2 F6
Gwenter Corn 2 H6
Gwernaffield Flint 42 F5
Gwernesney Mon 15 A10
Gwernogle Carms 23 C10
Gwernymynydd Flint 42 F5
Gwersyllt Wrex 42 G6
Gwespyr Flint 42 D4
Gwithian Corn 2 E4
Gwredog Anglesey 40 B6
Gwyddelwern Denb 42 H3
Gwyddgrug Carms 23 C9
Gwydyr Uchaf Conwy 41 D9
Gwynfryn Wrex 42 G5
Gwystre Powys 25 B7
Gwytherin Conwy 41 D10
Gyfelia Wrex 42 H6
Gyffin Conwy 41 C9
Gyre Orkney 95 H4
Gyrn-goch Gwyn 40 F6

H

Habberley Shrops 33 E9
Habergham Lancs 50 F4
Habrough NE Lincs 46 A5
Haceby Lincs 36 B6
Hacheston Suff 31 C10
Hackbridge London 19 E9
Hackenthorpe S Yorks 45 D8
Hackford Norf 39 E6
Hackforth N Yorks 58 G3
Hackland Orkney 95 F4
Hackleton Northants 28 C5
Hackness N Yorks 59 G10
Hackness Orkney 95 J4
Hackney London 19 C10
Hackthorn Lincs 46 D3
Hackthorpe Cumb 57 D7
Haconby Lincs 37 C7
Hacton London 20 C2
Hadden Borders 70 G6
Haddenham Bucks 28 H4
Haddenham Cambs 37 H10
Haddington E Loth 70 C4
Haddington Lincs 46 F3
Haddiscoe Norf 39 F10
Haddon Cambs 37 F7
Haddon Ches E 44 F3
Hade Edge W Yorks 44 B5
Hademore Staffs 35 E7
Hadfield Derbys 44 C4
Hadham Cross Herts 29 G11
Hadham Ford Herts 29 F11
Hadleigh Essex 20 C5
Hadleigh Suff 31 D7
Hadley Telford 34 D2
Hadley End Staffs 35 C7
Hadlow Kent 20 G3
Hadlow Down E Sus 12 D4
Hadnall Shrops 33 D11
Hadstock Essex 30 D2
Hady Derbys 45 E7
Hadzor Worcs 26 B6
Haffenden Quarter Kent 13 B7
Hafod-Dinbych Conwy 41 E10
Hafod-Iom Conwy 41 C10
Haggate Lancs 50 F4
Haggbeck Cumb 61 F10
Haggerston Northumb 71 F9
Haggrister Shetland 96 F5
Hagley Hereford 26 D2
Hagley Worcs 34 G5
Hagworthingham Lincs 47 F7
Haigh Gtr Man 43 B9
Haigh S Yorks 44 A6
Haigh Moor W Yorks 51 G8
Haighton Green Lancs 50 F1
Hail Weston Cambs 29 B8
Haile Cumb 56 F2
Hailes Glos 27 E7
Hailey Herts 29 G10
Hailey Oxon 27 G10
Hailsham E Sus 12 F4
Haimer Highld 94 D3
Hainault London 19 B11
Hainford Norf 39 D8
Hainton Lincs 46 D5
Hairmyres S Lanark 68 E5
Haisthorpe E Yorks 53 C7
Hakin Pembs 22 F3
Halam Notts 45 G10
Halbeath Fife 69 B10
Halberton Devon 7 E9
Halcro Highld 94 D4
Hale Gtr Man 43 D10
Hale Halton 43 D7
Hale Hants 9 C10
Hale Bank Halton 43 D7
Hale Street Kent 20 G3
Halebarns Gtr Man 43 D10
Hales Norf 39 F9
Hales Staffs 34 B3
Hales Place Kent 21 F8
Halesfield Telford 34 E3
Halesgate Lincs 37 C9
Halesowen W Mid 34 G5
Halesworth Suff 39 H9
Halewood Mers 43 D7
Halford Shrops 33 G10
Halford Warks 27 D9
Halfpenny Furze Carms 23 E7
Halfpenny Green Staffs 34 F4
Halfway Carms 24 E3
Halfway Carms 24 E5
Halfway W Berks 17 E11
Halfway Bridge W Sus 11 B8
Halfway House Shrops 33 D9
Halfway Houses Kent 20 D6
Halifax W Yorks 51 G6
Halket E Ayrs 67 A7
Halkirk Highld 94 E3
Halkyn Flint 42 E5
Hall Dunnerdale Cumb 56 G4
Hall Green W Mid 35 G7
Hall Green W Yorks 51 H9
Hall Grove Herts 29 G9
Hall of Tankerness Orkney 95 H6
Hall of the Forest Shrops 33 G8
Halland E Sus 12 E3
Hallaton Leics 36 F3
Hallatrow Bath 16 F3
Hallbankgate Cumb 61 H11
Hallen S Glos 15 C11
Halliburton Borders 70 F5
Hallin Highld 84 C7
Halling Medway 20 E4
Hallington Lincs 47 D7
Hallington Northumb 62 F5
Halliwell Gtr Man 43 A10
Halloughton Notts 45 G10
Hallow Worcs 26 C5
Hallrule Borders 61 B11
Halls E Loth 70 C5
Hall's Green Herts 29 F9
Hallsands Devon 5 H9
Hallthwaites Cumb 56 H3
Hallworthy Corn 4 C2
Hallyburton House Perth 76 D5
Hallyne Borders 69 F10
Halmer End Staffs 43 H10
Halmore Glos 16 A3
Halmyre Mains Borders 69 F10
Halnaker W Sus 11 D8
Halsall Lancs 42 A6
Halse Northants 28 D2
Halse Som 7 D10
Halsetown Corn 2 F4
Halsham E Yorks 53 G8
Halsinger Devon 6 C4
Halstead Essex 30 E5
Halstead Kent 19 E11
Halstead Leics 36 E3
Halstock Dorset 8 D4
Haltham Lincs 46 F6
Haltoft End Lincs 47 H7
Halton Bucks 28 G5
Halton Halton 43 D8
Halton Lancs 49 C5
Halton Northumb 62 G5
Halton W Yorks 51 F9
Halton Wrex 33 B9
Halton East N Yorks 50 D6
Halton Gill N Yorks 50 B4
Halton Holegate Lincs 47 F8
Halton Lea Gate Northumb 62 H2
Halton West N Yorks 50 D4
Haltwhistle Northumb 62 G3
Halvergate Norf 39 E10
Halwell Devon 5 F8
Halwill Devon 6 G3
Halwill Junction Devon 6 F3
Ham Devon 7 F11
Ham Glos 16 B3
Ham Highld 94 C4
Ham Kent 21 F10
Ham London 19 D8
Ham Shetland 96 K1
Ham Wilts 17 E10
Ham Common Dorset 9 B7
Ham Green Hereford 26 D4
Ham Green Kent 13 D7
Ham Green Kent 20 E5
Ham Green N Som 15 D11
Ham Green Worcs 27 B7
Ham Street Som 8 A4
Hamble-le-Rice Hants 10 D3
Hambleden Bucks 18 C4
Hambledon Hants 10 C5
Hambledon Sur 18 H6
Hambleton Lancs 49 E3
Hambleton N Yorks 52 F1
Hambridge Som 8 B2
Hambrook S Glos 16 D3
Hambrook W Sus 11 D6
Hameringham Lincs 47 F7
Hamerton Cambs 37 H7
Hametoun Shetland 96 K1
Hamilton S Lanark 68 E6
Hammer W Sus 11 A7
Hammerpot W Sus 11 D9
Hammersmith London 19 D9
Hammerwich Staffs 35 E6
Hammerwood E Sus 12 C3
Hammond Street Herts 19 A10
Hammoon Dorset 9 C7
Hamnavoe Shetland 96 E4
Hamnavoe Shetland 96 E6
Hamnavoe Shetland 96 F6
Hamnavoe Shetland 96 K5
Hampden Park E Sus 12 F5
Hamperden End Essex 30 E2
Hampnett Glos 27 G7
Hampole S Yorks 45 A9
Hampreston Dorset 9 E9
Hampstead London 19 C9
Hampstead Norreys W Berks 18 D2
Hampsthwaite N Yorks 51 D8
Hampton London 19 E8
Hampton Shrops 34 G3
Hampton Worcs 27 D7
Hampton Bishop Hereford 26 E2
Hampton Heath Ches W 43 H7
Hampton in Arden W Mid 35 G8
Hampton Loade Shrops 34 G3
Hampton Lovett Worcs 26 B5
Hampton Lucy Warks 27 C9
Hampton on the Hill Warks 27 B9
Hampton Poyle Oxon 28 G2
Hamrow Norf 38 C5
Hamsey E Sus 12 E3
Hamsey Green London 19 F10
Hamstall Ridware Staffs 35 D7
Hamstead IoW 10 E3
Hamstead W Mid 34 F6
Hamstead Marshall W Berks 17 E11
Hamsterley Durham 58 C2
Hamsterley Durham 63 H7
Hamstreet Kent 13 C9
Hamworthy Poole 9 E8
Hanbury Staffs 35 C7
Hanbury Worcs 26 B6
Hanbury Woodend Staffs 35 C7
Hanby Lincs 36 B6
Hanchurch Staffs 34 A4
Handbridge Ches W 43 F7
Handcross W Sus 12 D1
Handforth Ches E 44 D2
Handley Ches W 43 G7
Handsacre Staffs 35 D6
Handsworth S Yorks 45 D8
Handsworth W Mid 34 F6
Handy Cross Devon 6 D3
Hanford Stoke 34 A4
Hanging Langford Wilts 17 H7
Hangleton W Sus 11 D9
Hanham S Glos 16 D3
Hankelow Ches E 43 H9
Hankerton Wilts 16 B6
Hankham E Sus 12 F5
Hanley Stoke 44 H2
Hanley Castle Worcs 26 D5
Hanley Child Worcs 26 B3
Hanley Swan Worcs 26 D5
Hanley William Worcs 26 B3
Hanlith N Yorks 50 C5
Hanmer Wrex 33 B10
Hannah Lincs 47 E9
Hannington Hants 18 F2
Hannington Northants 28 A5
Hannington Swindon 17 B8
Hannington Wick Swindon 17 B8
Hansel Village S Ayrs 67 C6
Hanslope M Keynes 28 D5
Hanthorpe Lincs 37 C6
Hanwell London 19 C8
Hanwell Oxon 27 D11
Hanwood Shrops 33 E10
Hanworth London 19 D8
Hanworth Norf 39 B7
Happendon S Lanark 69 G7
Happisburgh Norf 39 B9
Happisburgh Common Norf 39 C9
Hapsford Ches W 43 E7
Hapton Lancs 50 F3
Hapton Norf 39 F7
Harberton Devon 5 F8
Harbertonford Devon 5 F8
Harbledown Kent 21 F8
Harborne W Mid 34 G6
Harborough Magna Warks 35 H10
Harbottle Northumb 62 C5
Harbury Warks 27 C10
Harby Leics 36 B3
Harby Notts 46 E2
Harcombe Devon 7 G10
Harden W Mid 34 E6
Harden W Yorks 51 F6
Hardenhuish Wilts 16 D6
Hardgate Aberds 83 C9
Hardham W Sus 11 C9
Hardingham Norf 38 E6
Hardingstone Northants 28 C4
Hardington Som 16 F4
Hardington Mandeville Som 8 C4
Hardington Marsh Som 8 D4
Hardley Hants 10 D3
Hardley Street Norf 39 E9
Hardmead M Keynes 28 D6
Hardrow N Yorks 57 G10
Hardstoft Derbys 45 F8
Hardway Hants 10 D5
Hardway Som 8 A6
Hardwick Bucks 28 G5
Hardwick Cambs 29 C10
Hardwick Norf 38 D2
Hardwick Norf 39 G8
Hardwick Northants 28 B5
Hardwick Notts 45 E10
Hardwick Oxon 27 H10
Hardwick Oxon 28 F2
Hardwick W Mid 35 F6
Hardwicke Glos 26 F6
Hardwicke Glos 26 G4
Hardwicke Hereford 25 D9
Hardy's Green Essex 30 F6
Hare Green Essex 31 F7
Hare Hatch Wokingham 18 D5
Hare Street Herts 29 F10
Hareby Lincs 47 F7
Hareden Lancs 50 D2
Harefield London 19 B7
Harehills W Yorks 51 F9
Harehope Northumb 62 A6
Haresceugh Cumb 57 B8
Harescombe Glos 26 G5
Haresfield Glos 26 G5
Hareshaw N Lanark 69 D7
Hareshaw Head Northumb 62 E4
Harewood W Yorks 51 E9
Harewood End Hereford 26 F2
Harford Carms 24 D3
Harford Devon 5 F7
Hargate Norf 39 F7
Hargatewall Derbys 44 E5
Hargrave Ches W 43 F7
Hargrave Northants 29 A7
Hargrave Suff 30 C4
Harker Cumb 61 G9
Harkland Shetland 96 E6
Harkstead Suff 31 E8
Harlaston Staffs 35 D8
Harlaw Ho. Aberds 83 A9
Harlaxton Lincs 36 B4
Harle Syke Lancs 50 F4
Harlech Gwyn 41 G7
Harlequin Notts 36 B2
Harlescott Shrops 33 D11
Harlesden London 19 C9
Harleston Devon 5 G8
Harleston Norf 39 G8
Harleston Suff 31 C7
Harlestone Northants 28 B4
Harley S Yorks 45 C7
Harley Shrops 34 E1
Harleyholm S Lanark 69 G8
Harlington C Beds 29 E7
Harlington London 19 D7
Harlington S Yorks 45 B8
Harlosh Highld 85 D7
Harlow Essex 29 G11
Harlow Hill N Yorks 51 D8
Harlow Hill Northumb 62 G6
Harlthorpe E Yorks 52 F3
Harlton Cambs 29 C10
Harman's Cross Dorset 9 F8
Harmby N Yorks 58 H2
Harmer Green Herts 29 G9
Harmer Hill Shrops 33 C10
Harmondsworth London 19 D7
Harmston Lincs 46 F3
Harnham Northumb 62 F6
Harnhill Glos 17 A7
Harold Hill London 20 B2
Harold Wood London 20 B2
Haroldston West Pembs 22 E3
Haroldswick Shetland 96 B8
Harome N Yorks 52 A2
Harpenden Herts 29 G8
Harpford Devon 7 G9
Harpham E Yorks 53 C6
Harpley Norf 38 C
Harpley Worcs 26 B
Harpole Northants 28 B
Harpsdale Highld 94 E
Harpsden Oxon 18 C
Harpswell Lincs 46 D
Harpur Hill Derbys 44 E
Harpurhey Gtr Man 44 B
Harraby Cumb 56 A
Harrapool Highld 85 F1
Harrier Shetland 96
Harrietfield Perth 76 E
Harrietsham Kent 20 F
Harrington Cumb 56 D
Harrington Lincs 47 E
Harrington Northants 36 G
Harringworth Northants 36
Harris Highld 78
Harrogate N Yorks 51 D
Harrold Bedford 28
Harrow London 19
Harrow on the Hill London 19
Harrow Street Suff 30
Harrow Weald London 19
Harrowbarrow Corn 4
Harrowden Bedford 29
Harrowgate Hill Darl 58
Harston Cambs 29 C
Harston Leics 36
Harswell E Yorks 52

Hart Hrtlpl 58 C5
Hart Common Gtr Man 43 B9
Hart Hill Luton 29 F8
Hart Station Hrtlpl 58 C5
Hartburn Northumb 62 E6
Hartburn Stockton 58 E5
Hartest Suff 30 C5
Hartfield E Sus 12 C3
Hartford Cambs 29 A9
Hartford Ches W 43 E9
Hartford End Essex 30 G3
Hartfordbridge Hants 18 F4
Hartforth N Yorks 58 F2
Harthill Ches W 43 G8
Harthill N Lanark 69 D8
Harthill S Yorks 45 D8
Hartington Derbys 44 F5
Hartland Devon 6 D1
Hartlebury Worcs 26 A5
Hartlepool Hrtlpl 58 C6
Hartley Cumb 57 F9
Hartley Kent 13 C6
Hartley Kent 20 E3
Hartley Northumb 63 F9
Hartley Westpall Hants 18 F3
Hartley Wintney Hants 18 F4
Hartlip Kent 20 E5
Hartoft End N Yorks 59 G8
Harton N Yorks 52 C3
Harton Shrops 33 G10
Harton T&W 63 G9
Hartpury Glos 26 F4
Hartshead W Yorks 51 G7
Hartshill Warks 35 F9
Hartshorne Derbys 35 C9
Hartsop Cumb 56 E6
Hartwell Northants 28 C4
Hartwood N Lanark 69 E7
Harvieston Stirling 68 B4
Harvington Worcs 27 D7
Harvington Cross Worcs 27 D7
Harwell Oxon 17 C11
Harwich Essex 31 E9
Harwood Durham 57 C10
Harwood Gtr Man 43 A10
Harwood Dale N Yorks 59 G10
Harworth Notts 45 C10
Hasbury W Mid 34 G5
Hascombe Sur 18 G6
Haselbech Northants 36 H3
Haselbury Plucknett Som 8 C3
Haseley Warks 27 B9
Haselor Warks 27 C8
Hasfield Glos 26 F5
Hasguard Pembs 22 F3
Haskayne Lancs 42 B6
Hasketon Suff 31 C9
Hasland Derbys 45 F7
Haslemere Sur 11 A8
Haslingden Lancs 50 G3
Haslingfield Cambs 29 C11
Haslington Ches E 43 G10
Hassall Ches E 43 G10
Hassall Green Ches E 43 G10
Hassell Street Kent 21 G7
Hassendean Borders 61 A11
Hassingham Norf 39 E9
Hassocks W Sus 12 E1
Hassop Derbys 44 E6
Hastigrow Highld 94 D4
Hastingleigh Kent 13 B9
Hastings E Sus 13 F7
Hastingwood Essex 29 H11
Hastoe Herts 28 H6
Haswell Durham 58 B4
Haswell Plough Durham 58 B4
Hatch C Beds 29 D8
Hatch Hants 18 F3
Hatch Wilts 9 B8
Hatch Beauchamp Som 8 B2
Hatch End London 19 B8
Hatch Green Som 8 C2
Hatchet Gate Hants 10 D2
Hatching Green Herts 29 G8
Hatchmere Ches W 43 E8
Hatcliffe NE Lincs 46 B6
Hatfield Hereford 26 C2
Hatfield Herts 29 H9
Hatfield S Yorks 45 B10
Hatfield Worcs 26 C5
Hatfield Broad Oak Essex 30 G2
Hatfield Garden Village Herts 29 H9
Hatfield Heath Essex 30 G2
Hatfield Hyde Herts 29 G9
Hatfield Peverel Essex 30 G4
Hatfield Woodhouse S Yorks 45 B10
Hatford Oxon 17 B10
Hatherden Hants 17 F10
Hatherleigh Devon 6 F4
Hathern Leics 35 C10
Hatherop Glos 27 H8
Hathersage Derbys 44 D6
Hathershaw Gtr Man 44 B3
Hatherton Ches E 43 H9
Hatherton Staffs 34 D5
Hatley St George Cambs 29 C9
Hatt Corn 4 E4
Hattingley Hants 18 H3
Hatton Aberds 89 E10
Hatton Derbys 35 C8
Hatton Lincs 46 E5
Hatton Shrops 33 F10
Hatton Warks 27 B9
Hatton Warr 43 D8
Hatton Castle Aberds 89 D7
Hatton Heath Ches W 43 F7
Hatton of Fintray Aberds 83 B10
Hattoncrook Aberds 89 F8
Haugh E Ayrs 67 D7
Haugh Gtr Man 44 A3
Haugh Lincs 47 E8
Haugh Head Northumb 71 H9
Haugh of Glass Moray 88 E4
Haugh of Urr Dumfries 55 C11
Haugham Lincs 47 D7
Haughley Suff 31 B7
Haughley Green Suff 31 B7
Haughs of Clinterty Aberdeen 83 B10
Haughton Notts 45 E10
Haughton Shrops 33 C9
Haughton Shrops 34 D1
Haughton Shrops 34 E3
Haughton Shrops 34 F2
Haughton Staffs 34 C4
Haughton Castle Northumb 62 F5
Haughton Green Gtr Man 44 C3
Haughton Moss Ches E 43 G8
Haultwick Herts 29 F10
Haunn Argyll 78 G6
Haunn W Isles 84 G2
Haunton Staffs 35 D8
Hauxley Northumb 63 C8
Hauxton Cambs 29 C11
Havant Hants 10 D6
Haven Hereford 25 C11
Haven Bank Lincs 46 G6
Haven Side E Yorks 53 G7
Havenstreet IoW 10 E4
Havercroft W Yorks 45 A7
Haverfordwest = Hwlffordd Pembs 22 E4
Haverhill Suff 30 D3
Haverigg Cumb 49 B1
Havering-atte-Bower London 20 B2
Haveringland Norf 39 C7
Haversham M Keynes 28 D5
Haverthwaite Cumb 49 A3
Haverton Hill Stockton 58 D5
Hawarden = Penarlâg Flint 42 F6
Hawcoat Cumb 49 B2
Hawen Ceredig 23 B8
Hawes N Yorks 57 H10
Hawes' Green Norf 39 F8
Hawes Side Blackpool 49 F3
Hawford Worcs 26 B5
Hawick Borders 61 B11
Hawk Green Gtr Man 44 D3
Hawkchurch Devon 8 D2
Hawkedon Suff 30 C4
Hawkenbury Kent 12 C4
Hawkenbury Kent 13 B7
Hawkeridge Wilts 16 F5
Hawkerland Devon 7 H9
Hawkes End W Mid 35 G9
Hawkesbury S Glos 16 C4
Hawkesbury Warks 35 G9
Hawkesbury Upton S Glos 16 C4
Hawkhill Northumb 63 B8
Hawkhurst Kent 13 C6
Hawkinge Kent 21 H9
Hawkley Hants 10 B6
Hawkridge Som 7 C7
Hawkshead Cumb 56 G5
Hawkshead Hill Cumb 56 G5
Hawksland S Lanark 69 G7
Hawkswick N Yorks 50 B5
Hawksworth Notts 36 A3
Hawksworth W Yorks 51 E7
Hawksworth W Yorks 51 F8
Hawkwell Essex 20 B5
Hawley Hants 18 F5
Hawley Kent 20 D2
Hawling Glos 27 F7
Hawnby N Yorks 59 H6
Haworth W Yorks 50 F6
Hawstead Suff 30 C5
Hawthorn Durham 58 B5
Hawthorn Rhondda 15 C7
Hawthorn Wilts 16 E5
Hawthorn Hill Brack 18 D5
Hawthorn Hill Lincs 46 G6
Hawthorpe Lincs 36 C6
Hawton Notts 45 G11
Haxby York 52 D2
Haxey N Lincs 45 C11
Hay Green Norf 37 D11
Hay-on-Wye = Y Gelli Gandryll Powys 25 D9
Hay Street Herts 29 F10
Haydock Mers 43 C8
Haydon Dorset 8 C5
Haydon Bridge Northumb 62 G4
Haydon Wick Swindon 17 C8
Haye Corn 4 E4
Hayes London 19 C8
Hayes London 19 E11
Hayfield Derbys 44 D4
Hayfield Fife 69 A11
Hayhill E Ayrs 67 E7
Hayhillock Angus 77 C8
Hayle Corn 2 F4
Haynes C Beds 29 D7
Haynes Church End C Beds 29 D7
Hayscastle Pembs 22 D3
Hayscastle Cross Pembs 22 D4
Hayshead Angus 77 C9
Hayton Aberdeen 83 C11
Hayton Cumb 56 B3
Hayton Cumb 61 H11
Hayton E Yorks 52 E4
Hayton Notts 45 D11
Hayton's Bent Shrops 33 G11
Haytor Vale Devon 5 D8
Haywards Heath W Sus 12 D2
Haywood S Yorks 45 A9
Haywood Oaks Notts 45 G10
Hazel Grove Gtr Man 44 D3
Hazel Street Kent 12 C5
Hazelbank S Lanark 69 F7
Hazelbury Bryan Dorset 8 D6
Hazeley Hants 18 F4
Hazelhurst Gtr Man 44 B3
Hazelslade Staffs 34 D6
Hazelton Glos 27 G7
Hazelton Walls Fife 76 E6
Hazelwood Derbys 45 H7
Hazlemere Bucks 18 B5
Hazlerigg T&W 63 F8
Hazlewood N Yorks 51 D6
Hazon Northumb 63 C7
Heacham Norf 38 B2
Head of Muir Falk 69 B7
Headbourne Worthy Hants 10 A3
Headbrook Hereford 25 C10
Headcorn Kent 13 B7
Headingley W Yorks 51 F8
Headington Oxon 28 H2
Headlam Durham 58 E2
Headless Cross Worcs 27 B7
Headley Hants 18 E2
Headley Hants 18 H5
Headley Sur 19 F9
Headon Notts 45 E11
Heads S Lanark 68 F6
Heads Nook Cumb 61 H10
Heage Derbys 45 G7
Healaugh N Yorks 51 E10
Healaugh N Yorks 58 G1
Heald Green Gtr Man 44 D2
Heale Devon 6 B5
Heale Som 16 G3
Healey Gtr Man 50 H4
Healey N Yorks 51 A7
Healey Northumb 62 H6
Healing NE Lincs 46 A6
Heamoor Corn 2 F3
Heanish Argyll 78 G3
Heanor Derbys 45 H8
Heanton Punchardon Devon 6 C4
Heapham Lincs 46 D2
Hearthstane Borders 69 H10
Heasley Mill Devon 7 C6
Heast Highld 85 G11
Heath Cardiff 15 D7
Heath Derbys 45 F8
Heath and Reach C Beds 28 F6
Heath End Hants 18 E2
Heath End Sur 18 G5
Heath End Warks 27 B9
Heath Hayes Staffs 34 D6
Heath Hill Shrops 34 D3
Heath House Som 15 G10
Heath Town W Mid 34 F5
Heathcote Derbys 44 F5
Heather Leics 35 D9
Heatherfield Highld 85 D9
Heathfield Devon 5 D9
Heathfield E Sus 12 D4
Heathfield Som 7 D10
Heathhall Dumfries 60 F5
Heathrow Airport London 19 D7
Heathstock Devon 8 D1
Heathton Shrops 34 F4
Heatley Warr 43 D10
Heaton Lancs 49 C4
Heaton Staffs 44 F3
Heaton T&W 63 G8
Heaton W Yorks 51 F7
Heaton Moor Gtr Man 44 C2
Heaverham Kent 20 F2
Heaviley Gtr Man 44 D3
Heavitree Devon 7 G8
Hebburn T&W 63 G9
Hebden N Yorks 50 C6
Hebden Bridge W Yorks 50 G5
Hebron Anglesey 40 B6
Hebron Carms 22 D6
Hebron Northumb 63 E7
Heck Dumfries 60 E6
Heckfield Hants 18 E4
Heckfield Green Suff 39 H7
Heckfordbridge Essex 30 F6
Heckington Lincs 37 A7
Heckmondwike W Yorks 51 G8
Heddington Wilts 16 E6
Heddle Orkney 95 G4
Heddon-on-the-Wall Northumb 63 G7
Hedenham Norf 39 F9
Hedge End Hants 10 C3
Hedgerley Bucks 18 C6
Hedging Som 8 B2
Hedley on the Hill Northumb 62 H6
Hednesford Staffs 34 D6
Hedon E Yorks 53 G7
Hedsor Bucks 18 C6
Hedworth T&W 63 G9
Hegdon Hill Hereford 26 C2
Heggerscales Cumb 57 E10
Heglibister Shetland 96 H5
Heighington Darl 58 D3
Heighington Lincs 46 F4
Heights of Brae Highld 87 E8
Heights of Kinlochewe Highld 86 E3
Heilam Highld 92 C7
Heiton Borders 70 G6
Hele Devon 6 B4
Hele Devon 7 F8
Helensburgh Argyll 73 E11
Helford Corn 3 G6
Helford Passage Corn 3 G6
Helhoughton Norf 38 C4
Helions Bumpstead Essex 30 D3
Hellaby S Yorks 45 C9
Helland Corn 4 D1
Hellesdon Norf 39 D8
Hellidon Northants 28 C2
Hellifield N Yorks 50 D4
Hellingly E Sus 12 E4
Hellington Norf 39 E9
Hellister Shetland 96 J5
Helm Northumb 63 D7
Helmdon Northants 28 D2
Helmingham Suff 31 C8
Helmington Row Durham 58 C2
Helmsdale Highld 93 H13
Helmshore Lancs 50 G3
Helmsley N Yorks 52 A2
Helperby N Yorks 51 C10
Helperthorpe N Yorks 52 B5
Helpringham Lincs 37 A7
Helpston Pboro 37 E7
Helsby Ches W 43 E7
Helsey Lincs 47 E9
Helston Corn 2 G5
Helstone Corn 4 C1
Helton Cumb 57 D7
Helwith Bridge N Yorks 50 C4
Hemblington Norf 39 D9
Hemel Hempstead Herts 29 H7
Hemingbrough N Yorks 52 F2
Hemingby Lincs 46 E6
Hemingford Abbots Cambs 29 A9
Hemingford Grey Cambs 29 A9
Hemingstone Suff 31 C8
Hemington Leics 35 C10
Hemington Northants 37 G6
Hemington Som 16 F4
Hemley Suff 31 D9
Hemlington Mbro 58 E6
Hemp Green Suff 31 B10
Hempholme E Yorks 53 D6
Hempnall Norf 39 F8
Hempnall Green Norf 39 F8
Hempriggs House Highld 94 F5
Hempstead Essex 30 E3
Hempstead Medway 20 E4
Hempstead Norf 39 B7
Hempstead Norf 39 C10
Hempsted Glos 26 G5
Hempton Norf 38 C5
Hempton Oxon 27 E11
Hemsby Norf 39 D10
Hemswell Lincs 46 C3
Hemswell Cliff Lincs 46 D3
Hemsworth W Yorks 45 A8
Hemyock Devon 7 E10
Hen-feddau fawr Pembs 23 C7
Henbury Bristol 16 D2
Henbury Ches E 44 E2
Hendon London 19 C9
Hendon T&W 63 H10
Hendre Flint 42 F4
Hendre-ddu Conwy 41 D10
Hendreforgan Rhondda 14 C5
Hendy Carms 23 F10
Heneglwys Anglesey 40 C6
Henfield W Sus 11 C11
Henford Devon 6 G2
Henghurst Kent 13 C8
Hengoed Caerph 15 B7
Hengoed Powys 25 C9
Hengoed Shrops 33 B8
Hengrave Suff 30 B5
Henham Essex 30 F2
Heniarth Powys 33 E7
Henlade Som 8 B1
Henley Shrops 33 H11
Henley Som 8 A3
Henley Suff 31 C8
Henley W Sus 11 B7
Henley-in-Arden Warks 27 B8
Henley-on-Thames Oxon 18 C4
Henley's Down E Sus 12 E6
Henllan Ceredig 23 B8
Henllan Denb 42 F3
Henllan Amgoed Carms 22 D6
Henllys Torf 15 B8
Henlow C Beds 29 E8
Hennock Devon 5 C9
Henny Street Essex 30 E5
Henryd Conwy 41 C9
Henry's Moat Pembs 22 D5
Hensall N Yorks 52 G1
Henshaw Northumb 62 G3
Hensingham Cumb 56 E1
Henstead Suff 39 G10
Henstridge Som 8 C6
Henstridge Ash Som 8 B6
Henstridge Marsh Som 8 B6
Henton Oxon 18 A4
Henton Som 15 G10
Henwood Corn 4 D3
Heogan Shetland 96 J6
Heol-las Swansea 14 B2
Heol Senni Powys 24 F6
Heol-y-Cyw Bridgend 14 C5
Hepburn Northumb 62 A6
Hepple Northumb 62 C5
Hepscott Northumb 63 E8
Heptonstall W Yorks 50 G5
Hepworth Suff 30 A6
Hepworth W Yorks 44 B5
Herbrandston Pembs 22 F3
Hereford Hereford 26 D2
Heriot Borders 70 E2
Hermiston Edin 69 C10
Hermitage Borders 61 D11
Hermitage Dorset 8 D5
Hermitage W Berks 18 D2
Hermitage W Sus 11 D6
Hermon Anglesey 40 D5
Hermon Carms 23 C8
Hermon Carms 24 F3
Hermon Pembs 23 C7
Herne Kent 21 E8
Herne Bay Kent 21 E8
Herner Devon 6 D4
Hernhill Kent 21 E7
Herodsfoot Corn 4 E3
Herongate Essex 20 B3
Heronsford S Ayrs 54 A4
Herriard Hants 18 G3
Herringfleet Suff 39 F10
Herringswell Suff 30 A4
Hersden Kent 21 E9
Hersham Corn 6 F1
Hersham Sur 19 E8
Herstmonceux E Sus 12 E5
Herston Orkney 95 J5
Hertford Herts 29 G10
Hertford Heath Herts 29 G10
Hertingfordbury Herts 29 G10
Hesket Newmarket Cumb 56 C5
Hesketh Bank Lancs 49 G4
Hesketh Lane Lancs 50 E2
Heskin Green Lancs 49 H5
Hesleden Durham 58 C5
Hesleyside Northumb 62 E4
Heslington York 52 D2
Hessay York 51 D11
Hessenford Corn 4 F4
Hessett Suff 30 B6
Hessle E Yorks 52 G6
Hest Bank Lancs 49 C4
Heston London 19 D8
Hestwall Orkney 95 G3
Heswall Mers 42 D5
Hethe Oxon 28 F2
Hethersett Norf 39 E7
Hethersgill Cumb 61 G10
Hethpool Northumb 71 H7
Hett Durham 58 C3
Hetton N Yorks 50 D5
Hetton-le-Hole T&W 58 B4
Hetton Steads Northumb 71 G9
Heugh Northumb 62 F6
Heugh-head Aberds 82 B5
Heveningham Suff 31 A10
Hever Kent 12 B3
Heversham Cumb 49 A4
Hevingham Norf 39 C7
Hewas Water Corn 3 E8
Hewelsfield Glos 16 A2
Hewish N Som 15 E10
Hewish Som 8 D3
Heworth York 52 D2
Hexham Northumb 62 G5
Hextable Kent 20 D2
Hexton Herts 29 E8
Hexworthy Devon 5 D7
Hey Lancs 50 E4
Heybridge Essex 20 B3
Heybridge Essex 30 H5
Heybridge Basin Essex 30 H5
Heybrook Bay Devon 4 G6
Heydon Cambs 29 D11
Heydon Norf 39 C7
Heydour Lincs 36 B6
Heylipol Argyll 78 G2
Heylor Shetland 96 E4
Heysham Lancs 49 C4
Heyshott W Sus 11 C7
Heyside Gtr Man 44 B3
Heytesbury Wilts 16 G6
Heythrop Oxon 27 F10
Heywood Gtr Man 44 A2
Heywood Wilts 16 F5
Hibaldstow N Lincs 46 B3
Hickleton S Yorks 45 B8
Hickling Norf 39 C10
Hickling Notts 36 C2
Hickling Green Norf 39 C10
Hickling Heath Norf 39 C10
Hickstead W Sus 12 D1
Hidcote Boyce Glos 27 D8
High Ackworth W Yorks 51 H10
High Angerton Northumb 62 E6
High Bankhill Cumb 57 B7
High Barnes T&W 63 H9
High Beach Essex 19 B11
High Bentham N Yorks 50 C2
High Bickington Devon 6 D5
High Birkwith N Yorks 50 B3
High Blantyre S Lanark 68 E5
High Bonnybridge Falk 69 C7
High Bradfield S Yorks 44 C6
High Bray Devon 6 C5
High Brooms Kent 12 B4
High Bullen Devon 6 D4
High Buston Northumb 63 C8
High Callerton Northumb 63 F7
High Catton E Yorks 52 D3
High Cogges Oxon 27 H10
High Coniscliffe Darl 58 E3
High Cross Hants 10 B6
High Cross Herts 29 G10
High Easter Essex 30 G3
High Eggborough N Yorks 52 G1
High Ellington N Yorks 51 A7
High Ercall Telford 34 D1
High Etherley Durham 58 D2
High Garrett Essex 30 F4
High Grange Durham 58 C2
High Green Norf 39 E7
High Green S Yorks 45 C7
High Green Worcs 26 D5
High Halden Kent 13 C7
High Halstow Medway 20 D4
High Ham Som 8 A3
High Harrington Cumb 56 D2
High Hatton Shrops 34 C2
High Hawsker N Yorks 59 F10
High Hesket Cumb 57 B6
High Hesleden Durham 58 C5
High Hoyland S Yorks 44 A6
High Hunsley E Yorks 52 F5
High Hurstwood E Sus 12 D3
High Hutton N Yorks 52 C3
High Ireby Cumb 56 C4
High Kelling Norf 39 A7
High Kilburn N Yorks 51 B11
High Lands Durham 58 D2
High Lane Gtr Man 44 D3
High Lane Worcs 26 B3
High Laver Essex 30 H2
High Legh Ches E 43 D10
High Leven Stockton 58 E5
High Littleton Bath 16 F3
High Lorton Cumb 56 D3
High Marishes N Yorks 52 B4
High Marnham Notts 46 E2
High Melton S Yorks 45 B9
High Mickley Northumb 62 G6
High Mindork Dumfries 54 D6
High Newton Cumb 49 A4
High Newton-by-the-Sea Northumb 71 H11
High Nibthwaite Cumb 56 H4
High Offley Staffs 34 C3
High Ongar Essex 20 A2
High Onn Staffs 34 D4
High Roding Essex 30 G3
High Row Cumb 56 C5
High Salvington W Sus 11 D10
High Sellafield Cumb 56 F2
High Shaw N Yorks 57 G10
High Spen T&W 63 H7
High Stoop Durham 58 B2
High Street Corn 3 D8
High Street Kent 12 C6
High Street Suff 30 D5
High Street Suff 31 A11
High Street Suff 31 C11
High Street Green Suff 31 C7
High Throston Hrtlpl 58 C5
High Toynton Lincs 46 F6
High Trewhitt Northumb 62 C6
High Valleyfield Fife 69 B9
High Westwood Durham 63 H7
High Wray Cumb 56 F5
High Wych Herts 29 G11
High Wycombe Bucks 18 B5
Higham Derbys 45 G7
Higham Kent 20 D4
Higham Lancs 50 F4
Higham Suff 30 B4
Higham Suff 31 E7
Higham Dykes Northumb 63 F7
Higham Ferrers Northants 28 B6
Higham Gobion C Beds 29 E8
Higham on the Hill Leics 35 F9
Higham Wood Kent 20 G2
Highampton Devon 6 F3
Highbridge Highld 80 E3
Highbridge Som 15 G9
Highbrook W Sus 12 C2
Highburton W Yorks 44 A5
Highbury Som 16 G3
Highclere Hants 17 E11
Highcliffe Dorset 9 E11
Higher Ansty Dorset 9 D6
Higher Ashton Devon 5 C9
Higher Ballam Lancs 49 F3
Higher Bartle Lancs 49 F5
Higher Boscaswell Corn 2 F2
Higher Burwardsley Ches W 43 G8
Higher Clovelly Devon 6 D2
Higher End Gtr Man 43 B8
Higher Kinnerton Flint 42 F6
Higher Penwortham Lancs 49 G5
Higher Town Scilly 2 C3
Higher Walreddon Devon 4 D5
Higher Walton Lancs 50 G1
Higher Walton Warr 43 D8
Higher Wheelton Lancs 50 G2
Higher Whitley Ches W 43 D9
Higher Wincham Ches W 43 E9
Higher Wych Ches W 33 A10
Highfield E Yorks 52 F3
Highfield Gtr Man 43 B10
Highfield N Ayrs 66 A6
Highfield Oxon 28 F2
Highfield S Yorks 45 D7
Highfield T&W 63 H7
Highfields Cambs 29 C10
Highfields Northumb 71 E8
Highgate London 19 C9
Highlane Ches E 44 F2
Highlane Derbys 45 D8
Highlaws Cumb 56 B3
Highleadon Glos 26 F4
Highleigh W Sus 11 E7
Highley Shrops 34 G3
Highmoor Cross Oxon 18 C4
Highmoor Hill Mon 15 C10
Highnam Glos 26 G4
Highnam Green Glos 26 F4
Highsted Kent 20 E6
Highstreet Green Essex 30 E4
Hightae Dumfries 60 F6
Hightown Ches E 44 F2
Hightown Mers 42 B6
Hightown Green Suff 30 C6
Highway Wilts 17 D7
Highweek Devon 5 D9
Highworth Swindon 17 B9
Hilborough Norf 38 E4
Hilcote Derbys 45 G8
Hilcott Wilts 17 F8
Hilden Park Kent 20 G2
Hildenborough Kent 20 G2
Hildersham Cambs 30 D2
Hilderstone Staffs 34 B5
Hilderthorpe E Yorks 53 C7
Hilfield Dorset 8 D5
Hilgay Norf 38 F2
Hill Pembs 22 F6
Hill S Glos 16 B3
Hill W Mid 35 F7
Hill Brow W Sus 11 B6
Hill Dale Lancs 43 A7
Hill Dyke Lincs 47 H7
Hill End Durham 58 C1
Hill End Fife 76 H3
Hill End N Yorks 51 D6
Hill Head Hants 10 D4
Hill Head Northumb 62 G5
Hill Mountain Pembs 22 F4
Hill of Beath Fife 69 A10
Hill of Fearn Highld 87 D11
Hill of Mountblairy Aberds 89 C6
Hill Ridware Staffs 35 D6
Hill Top Durham 57 D11
Hill Top Hants 10 D3
Hill Top W Mid 34 F5
Hill Top W Yorks 51 H9
Hill View Dorset 9 E8
Hillam N Yorks 51 G11
Hillbeck Cumb 57 E9
Hillborough Kent 21 E9
Hillbrae Aberds 83 A9
Hillbrae Aberds 88 D6
Hillbutts Dorset 9 D8
Hillclifflane Derbys 44 H6
Hillcommon Som 7 D10
Hillend Fife 69 B10
Hillerton Devon 7 G6
Hillesden Bucks 28 F3
Hillesley Glos 16 C4
Hillfarance Som 7 D10
Hillhead Aberds 88 E5
Hillhead Devon 5 F10
Hillhead S Ayrs 67 E7
Hillhead of Auchentumb Aberds 89 C9
Hillhead of Cocklaw Aberds 89 D10
Hillhouse Borders 70 E4
Hilliclay Highld 94 D3
Hillingdon London 19 C7
Hillington Glasgow 68 D4
Hillington Norf 38 C3
Hillmorton Warks 28 A2
Hillockhead Aberds 82 B6
Hillockhead Aberds 82 C5
Hillside Aberds 83 D11
Hillside Angus 77 A10
Hillside Mers 42 A6
Hillside Orkney 95 J5
Hillside Shetland 96 G6
Hillswick Shetland 96 F4
Hillway IoW 10 F5
Hillwell Shetland 96 M5
Hilmarton Wilts 17 D7
Hilperton Wilts 16 F5
Hilsea Ptsmth 10 D5
Hilston E Yorks 53 F8
Hilton Aberds 89 E9
Hilton Cambs 29 B9
Hilton Cumb 57 D9
Hilton Derbys 35 B8
Hilton Dorset 9 D6
Hilton Durham 58 D2
Hilton Highld 87 C10
Hilton Shrops 34 F3
Hilton Stockton 58 E5
Hilton of Cadboll Highld 87 D11
Himbleton Worcs 26 C6
Himley Staffs 34 F4
Hincaster Cumb 49 A5
Hinckley Leics 35 F10
Hinderclay Suff 38 H6
Hinderton Ches W 42 E6
Hinderwell N Yorks 59 E8
Hindford Shrops 33 B9
Hindhead Sur 18 H5
Hindley Gtr Man 43 B9
Hindley Green Gtr Man 43 B9
Hindlip Worcs 26 C5
Hindolveston Norf 38 C6
Hindon Wilts 9 A8
Hindringham Norf 38 B5
Hingham Norf 38 E6
Hinstock Shrops 34 C2
Hintlesham Suff 31 D7
Hinton Hants 9 E11
Hinton Hereford 25 E10
Hinton Northants 28 C2
Hinton S Glos 16 D4
Hinton Shrops 33 E10
Hinton Ampner Hants 10 B4
Hinton Blewett Bath 16 F2
Hinton Charterhouse Bath 16 F4
Hinton-in-the-Hedges Northants 28 E2
Hinton Martell Dorset 9 D9
Hinton on the Green Worcs 27 D7
Hinton Parva Swindon 17 C9
Hinton St George Som 8 C3
Hinton St Mary Dorset 9 C6
Hinton Waldrist Oxon 17 B10
Hints Shrops 26 A3
Hints Staffs 35 E7
Hinwick Bedford 28 B6
Hinxhill Kent 13 B9
Hinxton Cambs 29 D11
Hinxworth Herts 29 D9
Hipperholme W Yorks 51 G7
Hipswell N Yorks 58 G2
Hirael Gwyn 41 C7
Hiraeth Carms 22 D6
Hirn Aberds 83 C9
Hirnant Powys 33 C6
Hirst N Lanark 69 D7
Hirst Northumb 63 E8
Hirst Courtney N Yorks 52 G2
Hirwaen Denb 42 F4
Hirwaun Rhondda 24 H6
Hiscott Devon 6 D4
Histon Cambs 29 B11
Hitcham Suff 30 C6
Hitchin Herts 29 F8
Hither Green London 19 D10
Hittisleigh Devon 7 G6
Hive E Yorks 52 F4
Hixon Staffs 34 C6
Hoaden Kent 21 F9
Hoaldalbert Mon 25 F10
Hoar Cross Staffs 35 C7
Hoarwithy Hereford 26 F2
Hoath Kent 21 E9
Hobarris Shrops 33 H9
Hobbister Orkney 95 H4
Hobkirk Borders 61 B11
Hobson Durham 63 H7
Hoby Leics 36 D2
Hockering Norf 39 D6
Hockerton Notts 45 G11
Hockley Essex 20 B5
Hockley Heath W Mid 27 A8
Hockliffe C Beds 28 F6
Hockwold cum Wilton Norf 38 G3
Hockworthy Devon 7 E9
Hoddesdon Herts 29 H10
Hoddlesden Blackburn 50 G3
Hoddom Mains Dumfries 61 F7
Hoddomcross Dumfries 61 F7
Hodgeston Pembs 22 G5
Hodley Powys 33 F7
Hodnet Shrops 34 C2
Hodthorpe Derbys 45 E9
Hoe Hants 10 C4
Hoe Norf 38 D5
Hoe Gate Hants 10 C5
Hoff Cumb 57 E8
Hog Patch Sur 18 G5
Hoggard's Green Suff 30 C5
Hoggeston Bucks 28 F5
Hogha Gearraidh W Isles 84 A2
Hoghton Lancs 50 G2
Hognaston Derbys 44 G6
Hogsthorpe Lincs 47 E9
Holbeach Lincs 37 C9
Holbeach Bank Lincs 37 C9
Holbeach Clough Lincs 37 C9
Holbeach Drove Lincs 37 D9
Holbeach Hurn Lincs 37 C9
Holbeach St Johns Lincs 37 D9
Holbeach St Marks Lincs 37 B9
Holbeach St Matthew Lincs 37 B10
Holbeck Notts 45 E9
Holbeck W Yorks 51 F8
Holbeck Woodhouse Notts 45 E9
Holberrow Green Worcs 27 C7
Holbeton Devon 5 F7
Holborn London 19 C10
Holbrook Derbys 35 A9
Holbrook S Yorks 45 D8
Holbrook Suff 31 E8
Holburn Northumb 71 G9
Holbury Hants 10 D3
Holcombe Devon 5 D10
Holcombe Som 16 G3
Holcombe Rogus Devon 7 E9
Holcot Northants 28 B4
Holden Lancs 50 E3
Holdenby Northants 28 B3
Holdenhurst Bmouth 9 E10
Holdgate Shrops 34 G1
Holdingham Lincs 46 H4
Holditch Dorset 8 D2
Hole-in-the-Wall Hereford 26 F3
Holefield Borders 71 G7
Holehouses Ches E 43 E10
Holemoor Devon 6 F3
Holestane Dumfries 60 D4
Holford Som 7 B10
Holgate York 52 D1
Holker Cumb 49 B3
Holkham Norf 38 A4
Hollacombe Devon 6 F2
Holland Orkney 95 C5
Holland Orkney 95 F7
Holland Fen Lincs 46 H6
Holland-on-Sea Essex 31 G9
Hollandstoun Orkney 95 C8
Hollee Dumfries 61 G8
Hollesley Suff 31 D10
Hollicombe Torbay 5 E9
Hollingbourne Kent 20 F5
Hollington Derbys 35 B8
Hollington E Sus 13 E6
Hollington Staffs 35 B6
Hollington Grove Derbys 35 B8
Hollingworth Gtr Man 44 C4
Hollins Gtr Man 44 B2
Hollins Green Warr 43 C9
Hollins Lane Lancs 49 D4
Hollinsclough Staffs 44 F4
Hollinwood Gtr Man 44 B3
Hollinwood Shrops 33 B11
Hollocombe Devon 6 E5
Hollow Meadows S Yorks 44 D6
Holloway Derbys 45 G7
Hollowell Northants 28 A3
Holly End Norf 37 E10
Holly Green Worcs 26 D5
Hollybush Caerph 15 A7
Hollybush E Ayrs 67 E6
Hollybush Worcs 26 E4
Hollym E Yorks 53 G9
Hollywood Worcs 35 H6
Holmbridge W Yorks 44 B5
Holmbury St Mary Sur 19 G8
Holmbush Corn 3 D9
Holmcroft Staffs 34 C5
Holme Cambs 37 G7
Holme Cumb 49 B5
Holme N Yorks 51 A9
Holme Notts 46 G2
Holme W Yorks 44 B5
Holme Chapel Lancs 50 G4
Holme Green N Yorks 52 E1
Holme Hale Norf 38 E4
Holme Lacy Hereford 26 E2
Holme Marsh Hereford 25 C10
Holme next the Sea Norf 38 A3
Holme-on-Spalding-Moor E Yorks 52 F4
Holme on the Wolds E Yorks 52 E5
Holme Pierrepont Notts 36 B2
Holme St Cuthbert Cumb 56 B3
Holme Wood W Yorks 51 F7
Holmer Hereford 26 D2
Holmer Green Bucks 18 B6
Holmes Chapel Ches E 43 F10
Holmesfield Derbys 45 E7
Holmeswood Lancs 49 H4
Holmewood Derbys 45 F8
Holmfirth W Yorks 44 B5
Holmhead Dumfries 60 E3
Holmhead E Ayrs 67 D8
Holmisdale Highld 84 D6
Holmrook Cumb 56 G2
Holmsgarth Shetland 96 J6
Holmwrangle Cumb 57 B7
Holne Devon 5 E8
Holnest Dorset 8 D5
Holsworthy Devon 6 F2
Holsworthy Beacon Devon 6 F2
Holt Dorset 9 D9
Holt Norf 39 B6
Holt Wilts 16 E5
Holt Worcs 26 B5
Holt Wrex 43 G7
Holt End Hants 18 H3
Holt End Worcs 27 B7
Holt Fleet Worcs 26 B5
Holt Heath Worcs 26 B5
Holt Park W Yorks 51 E8
Holtby York 52 D2
Holton Oxon 28 H3
Holton Som 8 B5
Holton Suff 39 H9
Holton cum Beckering Lincs 46 D5
Holton Heath Dorset 9 E8
Holton le Clay Lincs 46 B6
Holton le Moor Lincs 46 C4
Holton St Mary Suff 31 E7
Holwell Dorset 8 C6
Holwell Herts 29 E8
Holwell Leics 36 C3
Holwell Oxon 27 H9
Holwick Durham 57 D11
Holworth Dorset 9 F6
Holy Cross Worcs 34 H5
Holy Island Northumb 71 F10
Holybourne Hants 18 G4
Holyhead = Caergybi Anglesey 40 B4
Holymoorside Derbys 45 F7
Holyport Windsor 18 D5
Holystone Northumb 62 C5
Holytown N Lanark 68 D6
Holywell Cambs 29 A10
Holywell Corn 3 D6
Holywell Dorset 8 D4
Holywell E Sus 12 G4
Holywell = Treffynnon Flint 42 E4
Holywell Northumb 63 F9
Holywell Green W Yorks 51 H6
Holywell Lake Som 7 D10
Holywell Row Suff 38 H3
Holywood Dumfries 60 E5
Hom Green Hereford 26 F2
Homer Shrops 34 E2
Homersfield Suff 39 G8
Homington Wilts 9 B10
Honey Hill Kent 21 E8
Honey Street Wilts 17 E8
Honey Tye Suff 30 E6
Honeyborough Pembs 22 F4
Honeybourne Worcs 27 D8
Honeychurch Devon 6 F5
Honiley Warks 27 A9
Honing Norf 39 C9
Honingham Norf 39 D7
Honington Lincs 36 A5
Honington Suff 30 A6
Honington Warks 27 D9
Honiton Devon 7 F10
Honley W Yorks 44 A5
Hoo Green Ches E 43 D10
Hoo St Werburgh Medway 20 D4
Hood Green S Yorks 45 B7
Hooe E Sus 12 F5
Hooe Plym 4 F6
Hooe Common E Sus 12 E5
Hook E Yorks 52 G3
Hook Hants 18 F4
Hook London 19 E8
Hook Pembs 22 E4
Hook Wilts 17 C7
Hook Green Kent 12 C5
Hook Green Kent 20 E3
Hook Norton Oxon 27 E10
Hooke Dorset 8 E4
Hookgate Staffs 34 B3
Hookway Devon 7 G7
Hookwood Sur 12 B1
Hoole Ches W 43 F7
Hooley Sur 19 F9
Hoop Mon 26 H2
Hooton Ches W 42 E6
Hooton Levitt S Yorks 45 C9
Hooton Pagnell S Yorks 45 B8
Hooton Roberts S Yorks 45 C8
Hop Pole Lincs 37 D7
Hope Derbys 44 D5
Hope Devon 5 H7
Hope = Yr Hôb Flint 42 G6
Hope Highld 92 C7
Hope Powys 33 E8
Hope Shrops 33 E9
Hope Staffs 44 G5
Hope Bagot Shrops 26 A2
Hope Bowdler Shrops 33 F10
Hope End Green Essex 30 F2
Hope Green Ches E 44 D3
Hope Mansell Hereford 26 G3
Hope under Dinmore Hereford 26 C2
Hopeman Moray 88 B1
Hope's Green Essex 20 C4
Hopesay Shrops 33 G9
Hopley's Green Hereford 25 C10
Hopperton N Yorks 51 D10
Hopstone Shrops 34 F3
Hopton Shrops 33 C9
Hopton Shrops 34 C1
Hopton Staffs 34 C5
Hopton Suff 38 H5
Hopton Cangeford Shrops 33 G11
Hopton Castle Shrops 33 H9
Hopton on Sea Norf 39 E11
Hopton Wafers Shrops 34 H2
Hoptonheath Shrops 33 H9
Hopwas Staffs 35 E7
Hopwood Gtr Man 44 B2
Hopwood Worcs 34 H6
Horam E Sus 12 E4
Horbling Lincs 37 B7
Horbury W Yorks 51 H8
Horcott Glos 17 A8
Horden Durham 58 B5
Horderley Shrops 33 G10
Hordle Hants 10 E1
Hordley Shrops 33 B9
Horeb Carms 23 D10
Horeb Carms 23 F9
Horeb Ceredig 23 B8
Horfield Bristol 16 D3
Horham Suff 31 A9
Horkesley Heath Essex 30 F6
Horkstow N Lincs 52 H5
Horley Oxon 27 D11
Horley Sur 12 B1
Hornblotton Green Som 8 A4
Hornby Lancs 50 C1
Hornby N Yorks 58 F4
Hornby N Yorks 58 G3
Horncastle Lincs 46 F6
Hornchurch London 20 C2
Horncliffe Northumb 71 F8
Horndean Borders 71 F7
Horndean Hants 10 C6
Horndon Devon 4 D6
Horndon on the Hill Thurrock 20 C3
Horne Sur 12 B2
Horniehaugh Angus 77 A7
Horning Norf 39 D9
Horninghold Leics 36 F4
Horninglow Staffs 35 C8
Horningsea Cambs 29 B11
Horningsham Wilts 16 G5
Horningtoft Norf 38 C5
Horns Corner Kent 12 D6
Horns Cross Devon 6 D2
Horns Cross E Sus 13 D7
Hornsby Cumb 57 A7
Hornsea E Yorks 53 E8
Hornsea Bridge E Yorks 53 E8
Hornsey London 19 C10
Hornton Oxon 27 D10
Horrabridge Devon 4 E6
Horringer Suff 30 B5
Horringford IoW 10 F4
Horse Bridge Staffs 44 G3
Horsebridge Devon 4 D5
Horsebridge Hants 10 A2
Horsebrook Staffs 34 D4
Horsehay Telford 34 E2
Horseheath Cambs 30 D3
Horsehouse N Yorks 50 A6
Horsell Sur 18 F6
Horseman's Green Wrex 33 A10
Horseway Cambs 37 G10
Horsey Norf 39 C10
Horsford Norf 39 D7
Horsforth W Yorks 51 F8
Horsham W Sus 11 A10
Horsham Worcs 26 C4
Horsham St Faith Norf 39 D8
Horsington Lincs 46 F5
Horsington Som 8 B6
Horsley Derbys 35 A9
Horsley Glos 16 B5
Horsley Northumb 62 D4
Horsley Northumb 62 G6
Horsley Cross Essex 31 F8
Horsley Woodhouse Derbys 35 A9
Horsleycross Street Essex 31 F8
Horsleyhill Borders 61 B11
Horsleyhope Durham 58 B1
Horsmonden Kent 12 B5
Horspath Oxon 18 A2
Horstead Norf 39 D8
Horsted Keynes W Sus 12 D2
Horton Bucks 28 G6
Horton Dorset 9 D9
Horton Lancs 50 D4
Horton Northants 28 C5
Horton S Glos 16 C4
Horton Shrops 33 C10
Horton Som 8 C2
Horton Staffs 44 G3
Horton Swansea 23 H9

rby Underdale E Yorks 52 D4
irby Wiske N Yorks 51 A9
irdford W Sus 11 B9
irk Highld 94 E4
irk Bramwith S Yorks 45 A10
irk Deighton N Yorks 51 D9
irk Ella E Yorks 52 G6
irk Hallam Derbys 35 A10
irk Hammerton N Yorks 51 D10
irk Ireton Derbys 44 G6
irk Langley Derbys 35 B8
irk Merrington Durham 58 C3
irk Michael IoM 48 C3
irk of Shotts N Lanark 69 D7
irk Sandall S Yorks 45 B10
irk Smeaton N Yorks 51 H11
rk Yetholm Borders 71 H7
irkabister Shetland 96 K6
irkandrews Dumfries 55 E9
irkandrews upon Eden Cumb 61 H9
irkbampton Cumb 61 H9
irkbean Dumfries 60 H5
irkbride Cumb 61 H8
irkbuddo Angus 77 C8
irkburn Borders 69 G11
irkburn E Yorks 52 D5
irkburton W Yorks 44 A5
irkby Lincs 46 C4
irkby Mers 43 C7
irkby N Yorks 59 F6
irkby Fleetham N Yorks 58 G3
irkby Green Lincs 46 G4
irkby In Ashfield Notts 45 G9
irkby-in-Furness Cumb 49 A2
irkby la Thorpe Lincs 46 H5
irkby Lonsdale Cumb 50 B2
irkby Malham N Yorks 50 C4
irkby Mallory Leics 35 E10
irkby Malzeard N Yorks 51 B8
irkby Mills N Yorks 59 H8
irkby on Bain Lincs 46 F6
irkby Overflow N Yorks 51 E9
irkby Stephen Cumb 57 F9
irkby Thore Cumb 57 D8
irkby Underwood Lincs 37 C6
irkby Wharfe N Yorks 51 E11
irkbymoorside N Yorks 59 H7
irkcaldy Fife 69 A11
irkcambeck Cumb 61 G11
irkcarswell Dumfries 55 E10
irkcolm Dumfries 54 C3
irkconnel Dumfries 60 B3
irkconnell Dumfries 60 G5
irkcowan Dumfries 54 C6
irkcudbright Dumfries 55 D9
irkdale Mers 42 C6
irkfieldbank S Lanark 69 F7
irkgunzeon Dumfries 55 C11
irkham Lancs 49 F4
irkham N Yorks 52 C3
irkhamgate W Yorks 51 G8
irkharle Northumb 62 E6
irkheaton Northumb 62 F6
irkheaton W Yorks 51 H7
irkhill Angus 77 A9
irkhill Highld 87 G8
irkhill Midloth 69 D11
irkhill Moray 88 E2
irkhope Borders 61 A9
irkhouse Borders 70 G2
irkiboll Highld 93 D8
irkibost Highld 85 G10
irkinch Angus 76 C6
irkinner Dumfries 55 D7
irkintilloch E Dunb 68 C5
irkland Cumb 56 E2
irkland Cumb 57 C8
irkland Dumfries 60 B3
irkland Dumfries 60 D4
irkleatham Redcar 59 D6
irklevington Stockton 58 F5
irkley Suff 39 F11
irklington N Yorks 51 A9
irklington Notts 45 G10
irklinton Cumb 61 G10
irkliston Edin 69 C10
irkmaiden Dumfries 54 F4
irkmichael Perth 76 B3
irkmichael S Ayrs 66 F6
irkmuirhill S Lanark 68 F6
irknewton Northumb 71 G8
irknewton W Loth 69 D10
irkney Aberds 88 E5
irkoswald Cumb 57 B7
irkoswald S Ayrs 66 F5
irkpatrick Durham Dumfries 60 F3
irkpatrick-Fleming Dumfries 61 F8
irksanton Cumb 49 A1
irkstall W Yorks 51 F8
irkstead Lincs 46 F5
irkstile Aberds 88 E5
irkstyle Highld 94 C5
irkton Aberds 83 A8
irkton Aberds 89 D6
irkton Angus 77 C7
irkton Angus 77 D7
irkton Borders 61 B11
irkton Dumfries 60 E5
irkton Fife 76 E6
irkton Highld 85 F13
irkton Highld 86 G2
irkton Highld 87 B10
irkton Highld 87 F10
irkton Perth 76 F2
irkton S Lanark 60 A5
irkton Stirling 75 G8
irkton Manor Borders 69 G11
irkton of Airlie Angus 76 B6
irkton of Auchterhouse Angus 76 D6
irkton of Auchterless Aberds 89 D7
Kirkton of Barevan Highld 87 G11
Kirkton of Bourtie Aberds 89 F8
Kirkton of Collace Perth 76 D4
Kirkton of Craig Angus 77 B10
Kirkton of Culsalmond Aberds 89 E6
Kirkton of Durris Aberds 83 D9
Kirkton of Glenbuchat Aberds 82 B5
Kirkton of Glenisla Angus 76 A5
Kirkton of Kingoldrum Angus 76 B6
Kirkton of Largo Fife 77 G7
Kirkton of Lethendy Perth 76 C4
Kirkton of Logie Buchan Aberds 89 F9
Kirkton of Maryculter Aberds 83 D10
Kirkton of Menmuir Angus 77 A8
Kirkton of Monikie Angus 77 D8
Kirkton of Oyne Aberds 83 A8
Kirkton of Rayne Aberds 83 A8
Kirkton of Skene Aberds 83 C10
Kirkton of Tough Aberds 83 B8
Kirktonhill Borders 70 E3
Kirktown Aberds 89 C10
Kirktown of Alvah Aberds 89 B6
Kirktown of Deskford Moray 88 B5
Kirktown of Fetteresso Aberds 83 E10
Kirktown of Mortlach Moray 88 E3
Kirktown of Slains Aberds 89 F10
Kirkurd Borders 69 F10
Kirkwall Orkney 95 G5
Kirkwhelpington Northumb 62 E5
Kirmington N Lincs 46 A5
Kirmond le Mire Lincs 46 C5
Kirn Argyll 73 F10
Kirriemuir Angus 76 B6
Kirstead Green Norf 39 F8
Kirtlebridge Dumfries 61 F8
Kirtleton Dumfries 61 E8
Kirtling Cambs 30 C3
Kirtling Green Cambs 30 C3
Kirtlington Oxon 27 G11
Kirtomy Highld 93 C10
Kirton Lincs 37 B9
Kirton Notts 45 F10
Kirton Suff 31 E9
Kirton End Lincs 37 A8
Kirton Holme Lincs 37 A8
Kirton in Lindsey N Lincs 46 C3
Kislingbury Northants 28 C3
Kites Hardwick Warks 27 B11
Kittisford Som 7 D9
Kittle Swansea 23 H10
Kitt's Green W Mid 35 G7
Kitt's Moss Gtr Man 44 D2
Kittybrewster Aberdeen 83 C11
Kitwood Hants 10 A5
Kivernoll Hereford 25 E11
Kiveton Park S Yorks 45 D8
Knaith Lincs 46 D2
Knaith Park Lincs 46 D2
Knap Corner Dorset 9 B7
Knaphill Sur 18 F6
Knapp Perth 76 D5
Knapp Som 8 B2
Knapthorpe Notts 45 G11
Knapton Norf 39 B9
Knapton York 52 D1
Knapton Green Hereford 25 C11
Knapwell Cambs 29 B10
Knaresborough N Yorks 51 D9
Knarsdale Northumb 57 A8
Knauchland Moray 88 C5
Knaven Aberds 89 D8
Knayton N Yorks 58 H5
Knebworth Herts 29 F9
Knedlington E Yorks 52 G3
Kneesall Notts 45 F11
Kneesworth Cambs 29 D10
Kneeton Notts 45 H11
Knelston Swansea 23 H9
Knenhall Staffs 34 B5
Knettishall Suff 38 G5
Knightacott Devon 6 C5
Knightcote Warks 27 C10
Knightley Dale Staffs 34 C4
Knighton Devon 4 G6
Knighton Leicester 36 E1
Knighton = Tref-y-Clawdd Powys 25 A9
Knighton Staffs 34 A3
Knighton Staffs 34 C3
Knightswood Glasgow 68 D4
Knightwick Worcs 26 C4
Knill Hereford 25 B9
Knipton Leics 36 B4
Knitsley Durham 58 B2
Kniveton Derbys 44 G6
Knock Argyll 79 H8
Knock Cumb 57 D8
Knock Moray 88 C5
Knockally Highld 94 H3
Knockan Highld 92 H5
Knockandhu Moray 82 A4
Knockando Moray 88 D1
Knockando Ho. Moray 88 D2
Knockbain Highld 87 F9
Knockbreck Highld 84 B7
Knockbrex Dumfries 55 E8
Knockdee Highld 94 D3
Knockdolian S Ayrs 66 H4
Knockenkelly N Ayrs 66 D3
Knockentiber E Ayrs 67 C6
Knockespock Ho. Aberds 83 A7
Knockfarrel Highld 87 F8
Knockglass Dumfries 54 D3
Knockholt Kent 19 F11
Knockholt Pound Kent 19 F11
Knockie Lodge Highld 80 B6
Knockin Shrops 33 C9
Knockinlaw E Ayrs 67 C7
Knocklearn Dumfries 60 F3
Knocknaha Argyll 65 G7
Knocknain Dumfries 54 C2
Knockrome Argyll 72 F4
Knocksharry IoM 48 D2
Knodishall Suff 31 B11
Knolls Green Ches E 44 E2
Knolton Wrex 33 B9
Knolton Bryn Wrex 33 B9
Knook Wilts 16 G6
Knossington Leics 36 E4
Knott End-on-Sea Lancs 49 E3
Knotting Bedford 29 B7
Knotting Green Bedford 29 B7
Knottingley W Yorks 51 G11
Knotts Cumb 56 D6
Knotts Lancs 50 D3
Knotty Ash Mers 43 C7
Knotty Green Bucks 18 B6
Knowbury Shrops 26 A2
Knowe Dumfries 54 B6
Knowehead Dumfries 67 G9
Knowes of Elrick Aberds 88 C6
Knowesgate Northumb 62 E5
Knoweton N Lanark 68 E6
Knowhead Aberds 89 C9
Knowl Hill Windsor 18 D5
Knowle Bristol 16 D3
Knowle Devon 6 C3
Knowle Devon 7 F6
Knowle Devon 7 H9
Knowle Shrops 26 A2
Knowle W Mid 35 H7
Knowle Green Lancs 50 F2
Knowle Park W Yorks 51 E6
Knowlton Dorset 9 C9
Knowlton Kent 21 F9
Knowsley Mers 43 C7
Knowstone Devon 7 D7
Knox Bridge Kent 13 B6
Knucklas Powys 25 A9
Knuston Northants 28 B6
Knutsford Ches E 43 E10
Knutton Staffs 44 H2
Knypersley Staffs 44 G2
Kuggar Corn 2 H6
Kyle of Lochalsh Highld 85 F12
Kyleakin Highld 85 F12
Kylerhea Highld 85 F12
Kylesknoydart Highld 79 B11
Kylesku Highld 92 F5
Kylesmorar Highld 79 B11
Kylestrome Highld 92 F5
Kyllachy House Highld 81 A9
Kynaston Shrops 33 C9
Kynnersley Telford 34 D2
Kyre Magna Worcs 26 B3

L

La Fontenelle Guern 11
La Planque Guern 11
Labost W Isles 91 C7
Lacasaidh W Isles 91 E8
Lacasdal W Isles 91 D9
Laceby NE Lincs 46 B6
Lacey Green Bucks 18 B5
Lach Dennis Ches W 43 E10
Lackford Suff 30 A4
Lacock Wilts 16 E6
Ladbroke Warks 27 C11
Laddingford Kent 20 G3
Lade Bank Lincs 47 G7
Ladock Corn 3 D7
Lady Orkney 95 D7
Ladybank Fife 76 F6
Ladykirk Borders 71 F7
Ladysford Aberds 89 B9
Laga Highld 79 E9
Lagalochan Argyll 73 B7
Lagavulin Argyll 64 D5
Lagg Argyll 72 F4
Lagg N Ayrs 66 D2
Laggan Argyll 64 C3
Laggan Highld 79 D10
Laggan Highld 80 D4
Laggan Highld 81 D8
Laggan S Ayrs 54 A5
Lagganulva Argyll 78 G7
Laide Highld 91 H13
Laigh Fenwick E Ayrs 67 B7
Laigh Glengall S Ayrs 66 E6
Laighmuir E Ayrs 67 B7
Laindon Essex 20 C3
Lair Highld 86 G3
Lairg Highld 93 J8
Lairg Lodge Highld 93 J8
Lairg Muir Highld 93 J8
Lairgmore Highld 87 H8
Laisterdyke W Yorks 51 F7
Laithes Cumb 56 C6
Lake IoW 10 F4
Lake Wilts 17 H8
Lakenham Norf 39 E8
Lakenheath Suff 38 G3
Lakesend Norf 37 F11
Lakeside Cumb 56 H5
Laleham Sur 19 E7
Laleston Bridgend 14 D4
Lamarsh Essex 30 E5
Lamas Norf 39 C8
Lambden Borders 70 F6
Lamberhurst Kent 12 C5
Lamberhurst Quarter Kent 12 C5
Lamberton Borders 71 E8
Lambeth London 19 D10
Lambhill Glasgow 68 D4
Lambley Northumb 62 H2
Lambley Notts 45 H10
Lamborough Hill Oxon 17 A11
Lambourn W Berks 17 D10
Lambourne End Essex 19 B11
Lambs Green W Sus 19 H9
Lambston Pembs 22 E4
Lambton T&W 58 A3
Lamerton Devon 4 D5
Lamesley T&W 63 H8
Laminess Orkney 95 E7
Lamington Highld 87 D10
Lamington S Lanark 69 G8
Lamlash N Ayrs 66 C3
Lamloch Dumfries 67 G8
Lamonby Cumb 56 C6
Lamorna Corn 2 G3
Lamorran Corn 3 E7
Lampardbrook Suff 31 B9
Lampeter = Llanbedr Pont Steffan Ceredig 23 B10
Lampeter Velfrey Pembs 22 E6
Lamphey Pembs 22 F5
Lamplugh Cumb 56 D2
Lamport Northants 28 A4
Lamyatt Som 16 H3
Lana Devon 6 G2
Lanark S Lanark 69 F7
Lancaster Lancs 49 C4
Lanchester Durham 58 B2
Lancing W Sus 11 D10
Landbeach Cambs 29 B11
Landcross Devon 6 D3
Landerberry Aberds 83 C9
Landford Wilts 10 C1
Landford Manor Wilts 10 B1
Landimore Swansea 23 G9
Landkey Devon 6 C4
Landore Swansea 14 B2
Landrake Corn 4 E4
Landscove Devon 5 E8
Landshipping Pembs 22 E5
Landshipping Quay Pembs 22 E5
Landulph Corn 4 E5
Landwade Suff 30 B3
Lane Corn 3 C7
Lane End Bucks 18 B5
Lane End Cumb 56 G3
Lane End Dorset 9 E7
Lane End Hants 10 B4
Lane End IoW 10 F5
Lane End Lancs 50 E4
Lane Ends Lancs 50 D3
Lane Ends Lancs 50 F3
Lane Ends N Yorks 50 E5
Lane Head Derbys 44 E5
Lane Head Durham 58 E2
Lane Head Gtr Man 43 C9
Lane Head W Yorks 44 B5
Lane Side Lancs 50 G3
Laneast Corn 4 C3
Laneham Notts 46 E2
Lanehead Durham 57 B10
Lanehead Northumb 62 E3
Lanercost Cumb 61 G11
Laneshaw Bridge Lancs 50 E5
Lanfach Caerph 15 B8
Langar Notts 36 B3
Langbank Renfs 68 C2
Langbar N Yorks 51 D6
Langburnshiels Borders 61 C11
Langcliffe N Yorks 50 C4
Langdale Highld 93 E9
Langdale End N Yorks 59 G10
Langdon Corn 4 C4
Langdon Beck Durham 57 C10
Langdon Hills Essex 20 C3
Langdyke Fife 76 G6
Langenhoe Essex 31 G7
Langford C Beds 29 D8
Langford Devon 7 F9
Langford Essex 30 H5
Langford Notts 46 G2
Langford Oxon 17 A9
Langford Budville Som 7 D10
Langham Essex 31 E7
Langham Norf 38 A6
Langham Rutland 36 D4
Langham Suff 30 B6
Langhaugh Borders 69 G11
Langho Lancs 50 F3
Langholm Dumfries 61 E9
Langleeford Northumb 62 A5
Langley Ches E 44 E3
Langley Hants 10 D3
Langley Herts 29 F9
Langley Kent 20 F5
Langley Northumb 62 G4
Langley Slough 19 D7
Langley W Sus 11 B7
Langley Warks 27 B8
Langley Burrell Wilts 16 D6
Langley Common Derbys 35 B8
Langley Heath Kent 20 F5
Langley Lower Green Essex 29 E11
Langley Marsh Som 7 D9
Langley Park Durham 58 B3
Langley Street Norf 39 E9
Langley Upper Green Essex 29 E11
Langney E Sus 12 F5
Langold Notts 45 D9
Langore Corn 4 C4
Langport Som 8 B3
Langrick Lincs 46 H6
Langridge Bath 16 E4
Langridge Ford Devon 6 D4
Langrigg Cumb 56 B3
Langrish Hants 10 B6
Langsett S Yorks 44 B6
Langshaw Borders 70 G4
Langside Perth 75 F10
Langskaill Orkney 95 D5
Langstone Hants 10 D6
Langstone Newport 15 B9
Langthorne N Yorks 58 G3
Langthorpe N Yorks 51 C9
Langthwaite N Yorks 58 F1
Langtoft E Yorks 52 C6
Langtoft Lincs 37 D7
Langton Durham 58 E2
Langton Lincs 46 F6
Langton Lincs 47 E7
Langton N Yorks 52 C3
Langton by Wragby Lincs 46 E5
Langton Green Kent 12 C4
Langton Green Suff 31 A8
Langton Herring Dorset 8 F5
Langton Matravers Dorset 9 G9
Langtree Devon 6 E3
Langwathby Cumb 57 C7
Langwell Ho. Highld 94 H3
Langwell Lodge Highld 92 J4
Langwith Derbys 45 F9
Langwith Junction Derbys 45 F9
Langworth Lincs 46 E4
Lanivet Corn 3 C8
Lanlivery Corn 4 F1
Lanner Corn 2 F6
Lanreath Corn 4 F2
Lansallos Corn 4 F2
Lansdown Glos 26 F6
Lanteglos Highway Corn 4 F2
Lanton Borders 62 A2
Lanton Northumb 71 G8
Lapford Devon 7 F6
Laphroaig Argyll 64 D4
Lapley Staffs 34 D4
Lapworth Warks 27 A8
Larachbeg Highld 79 G9
Larbert Falk 69 B7
Larden Green Ches E 43 G8
Largie Aberds 88 E6
Largiemore Argyll 73 E8
Largoward Fife 77 G7
Largs N Ayrs 73 H11
Largybeg N Ayrs 66 D3
Largymore N Ayrs 66 D3
Larkfield Invclyd 73 F11
Larkhall S Lanark 68 E6
Larkhill Wilts 17 G8
Larling Norf 38 G5
Larriston Borders 61 D11
Lartington Durham 58 E1
Lary Aberds 82 C5
Lasham Hants 18 G3
Lashenden Kent 13 B7
Lassington Glos 26 F4
Lassodie Fife 69 A10
Lastingham N Yorks 59 G8
Latcham Som 15 G10
Latchford Herts 29 F10
Latchford Warr 43 D9
Latchingdon Essex 20 A5
Latchley Corn 4 D5
Lately Common Warr 43 C9
Lathbury M Keynes 28 D5
Latheron Highld 94 G3
Latheronwheel Highld 94 G3
Latheronwheel Ho. Highld 94 G3
Lathones Fife 77 G7
Latimer Bucks 19 B7
Latteridge S Glos 16 C3
Lattiford Som 8 B5
Latton Wilts 17 B7
Latton Bush Essex 29 H11
Lauchintilly Aberds 83 B9
Lauder Borders 70 F4
Laugharne Carms 23 E8
Laughterton Lincs 46 E2
Laughton E Sus 12 E4
Laughton Leics 36 G2
Laughton Lincs 37 B6
Laughton Lincs 46 C2
Laughton Common S Yorks 45 D9
Laughton en le Morthen S Yorks 45 D9
Launcells Corn 6 F1
Launceston Corn 4 C4
Launton Oxon 28 F3
Laurencekirk Aberds 83 F9
Laurieston Dumfries 55 C9
Laurieston Falk 69 C8
Lavendon M Keynes 28 C6
Lavenham Suff 30 D6
Laverhay Dumfries 61 D7
Laversdale Cumb 61 G10
Laverstock Wilts 9 A10
Laverstoke Hants 17 G11
Laverton Glos 27 E7
Laverton N Yorks 51 B8
Laverton Som 16 F4
Lavister Wrex 42 G6
Law S Lanark 69 E7
Lawers Perth 75 D9
Lawers Perth 75 E10
Lawford Essex 31 E7
Lawhitton Corn 4 C4
Lawkland N Yorks 50 C3
Lawley Telford 34 E2
Lawnhead Staffs 34 C4
Lawrenny Pembs 22 F5
Lawshall Suff 30 C5
Lawton Hereford 25 C11
Laxey IoM 48 D4
Laxfield Suff 31 A9
Laxfirth Shetland 96 H6
Laxfirth Shetland 96 J6
Laxford Bridge Highld 92 E5
Laxo Shetland 96 G6
Laxobigging Shetland 96 F6
Laxton E Yorks 52 G3
Laxton Northants 36 F5
Laxton Notts 45 F11
Laycock W Yorks 50 E6
Layer Breton Essex 30 G6
Layer de la Haye Essex 30 F6
Layer Marney Essex 30 G6
Layham Suff 31 D7
Laylands Green W Berks 17 E10
Laytham E Yorks 52 F3
Layton Blackpool 49 F3
Lazenby Redcar 59 E6
Lazonby Cumb 57 C7
Le Planel Guern 11
Le Skerne Haughton Darl 58 E4
Le Villocq Guern 11
Lea Derbys 45 G7
Lea Hereford 26 F3
Lea Lincs 46 D2
Lea Shrops 33 E10
Lea Shrops 33 G9
Lea Wilts 16 C6
Lea Marston Warks 35 F8
Lea Town Lancs 49 F4
Leabrooks Derbys 45 G8
Leac a Li W Isles 90 H6
Leachkin Highld 87 G9
Leadburn Midloth 69 E11
Leaden Roding Essex 30 G2
Leadenham Lincs 46 G3
Leadgate Cumb 57 B9
Leadgate Durham 58 A2
Leadgate T&W 63 H7
Leadhills S Lanark 60 B4
Leafield Oxon 27 G10
Leagrave Luton 29 F7
Leake N Yorks 58 G5
Leake Commonside Lincs 47 G7
Lealholm N Yorks 59 F8
Lealt Argyll 72 D5
Lealt Highld 85 B10
Leamington Hastings Warks 27 B11
Leamonsley Staffs 35 E7
Leamside Durham 58 B4
Leanaig Highld 87 F8
Leargybreck Argyll 72 F4
Leasgill Cumb 49 A4
Leasingham Lincs 46 H4
Leasingthorne Durham 58 D3
Leasowe Mers 42 C5
Leatherhead Sur 19 F8
Leatherhead Common Sur 19 F8
Leathley N Yorks 51 E8
Leaton Shrops 33 D10
Leaveland Kent 21 F7
Leavening N Yorks 52 C3
Leaves Green London 19 E11
Leazes Durham 63 H7
Lebberston N Yorks 53 A6
Lechlade-on-Thames Glos 17 B9
Leck Lancs 50 B2
Leckford Hants 17 H10
Leckfurin Highld 93 D10
Leckgruinart Argyll 64 B3
Leckhampstead Bucks 28 E4
Leckhampstead W Berks 17 D11
Leckhampstead Thicket W Berks 17 D11
Leckhampton Glos 26 G6
Leckie Highld 86 E3
Leckmelm Highld 86 B4
Leckwith V Glam 15 D7
Leconfield E Yorks 52 E6
Ledaig Argyll 74 D2
Ledburn Bucks 28 F6
Ledbury Hereford 26 E4
Ledcharrie Stirling 75 E8
Ledgemoor Hereford 25 C11
Ledicot Hereford 25 B11
Ledmore Highld 92 H5
Lednagullin Highld 93 C10
Ledsham Ches W 42 E6
Ledsham W Yorks 51 G10
Ledston W Yorks 51 G10
Ledston Luck W Yorks 51 F10
Ledwell Oxon 27 F11
Lee Argyll 78 J7
Lee Devon 6 B3
Lee Hants 10 C2
Lee Lancs 50 D1
Lee Shrops 33 B10
Lee Brockhurst Shrops 33 C11
Lee Clump Bucks 18 A6
Lee Mill Devon 5 F7
Lee Moor Devon 5 E6
Lee-on-the-Solent Hants 10 D4
Leeans Shetland 96 J5
Leebotten Shetland 96 L6
Leebotwood Shrops 33 F10
Leece Cumb 49 C2
Leechpool Pembs 22 E4
Leeds Kent 20 F5
Leeds W Yorks 51 F8
Leedstown Corn 2 F5
Leek Staffs 44 G3
Leek Wootton Warks 27 B9
Leekbrook Staffs 44 G3
Leeming N Yorks 58 H3
Leeming Bar N Yorks 58 G3
Lees Derbys 35 B8
Lees Gtr Man 44 B3
Lees W Yorks 50 F6
Leeswood Flint 42 F5
Legbourne Lincs 47 D7
Legerwood Borders 70 F4
Legsby Lincs 46 D5
Leicester Leicester 36 E1
Leicester Forest East Leics 35 E11
Leigh Dorset 8 D5
Leigh Glos 26 F5
Leigh Gtr Man 43 B9
Leigh Kent 20 G2
Leigh Shrops 33 E9
Leigh Sur 19 G9
Leigh Wilts 17 B7
Leigh Worcs 26 C4
Leigh Beck Essex 20 C5
Leigh Common Som 8 B6
Leigh Delamere Wilts 16 D5
Leigh Green Kent 13 C8
Leigh on Sea Southend 20 C5
Leigh Park Hants 10 D6
Leigh Sinton Worcs 26 C4
Leigh upon Mendip Som 16 G3
Leigh Woods N Som 16 D2
Leighswood W Mid 35 E6
Leighterton Glos 16 B5
Leighton N Yorks 51 B7
Leighton Powys 33 E8
Leighton Shrops 34 E2
Leighton Som 16 G4
Leighton Bromswold Cambs 37 H7
Leighton Buzzard C Beds 28 F6
Leinthall Earls Hereford 25 B11
Leinthall Starkes Hereford 25 B11
Leintwardine Hereford 25 A11
Leire Leics 35 F11
Leirinmore Highld 92 C7
Leiston Suff 31 B11
Leitfie Perth 76 C5
Leith Edin 69 C11
Leitholm Borders 70 F6
Lelant Corn 2 F4
Lelley E Yorks 53 F8
Lem Hill Worcs 26 A4
Lemmington Hall Northumb 63 B7
Lempitlaw Borders 70 G6
Lenchwick Worcs 27 D7
Lendalfoot S Ayrs 66 H4
Lendrick Lodge Stirling 75 G8
Lenham Kent 20 F5
Lenham Heath Kent 20 G6
Lennel Borders 71 F7
Lennoxtown E Dunb 68 C5
Lenton Lincs 36 B6
Lenton Nottingham 36 B1
Lentran Highld 87 G8
Lenwade Norf 39 D6
Leny Ho. Stirling 75 G9
Lenzie E Dunb 68 C5
Leoch Angus 76 D6
Leochel-Cushnie Aberds 83 B7
Leominster Hereford 25 C11
Leonard Stanley Glos 16 A5
Leorin Argyll 64 D4
Lepe Hants 10 E3
Lephin Highld 84 D6
Lephinchapel Argyll 73 D8
Lephinmore Argyll 73 D8
Leppington N Yorks 52 C3
Lepton W Yorks 51 H8
Lerryn Corn 4 F2
Lerwick Shetland 96 J6
Lesbury Northumb 63 B8
Leslie Aberds 83 A7
Leslie Fife 76 G5
Lesmahagow S Lanark 69 G7
Lesnewth Corn 4 B2
Lessendrum Aberds 88 D5
Lessingham Norf 39 C9
Lessonhall Cumb 56 A4
Leswalt Dumfries 54 C3
Letchmore Heath Herts 19 B8
Letchworth Herts 29 E9
Letcombe Bassett Oxon 17 C10
Letcombe Regis Oxon 17 C10
Letham Angus 77 C8
Letham Falk 69 B7
Letham Fife 76 F6
Letham Perth 76 E3
Letham Grange Angus 77 C9
Lethenty Aberds 89 D8
Letheringham Suff 31 C9
Letheringsett Norf 39 B6
Lettaford Devon 5 C8
Lettan Orkney 95 D8
Letterewe Highld 86 D2
Letterfearn Highld 85 F13
Letterfinlay Highld 80 D4
Lettermorar Highld 79 C10
Lettermore Argyll 78 G7
Letters Highld 86 C4
Letterston Pembs 22 D4
Lettoch Highld 82 B2
Lettoch Highld 87 H13
Letton Hereford 25 A10
Letton Hereford 25 D10
Letton Green Norf 38 E5
Letty Green Herts 29 G9
Letwell S Yorks 45 D9
Leuchars Fife 77 E7
Leuchars Ho. Moray 88 B2
Leumrabhagh W Isles 91 F8
Levan Invclyd 73 F11
Levaneap Shetland 96 G6
Levedale Staffs 34 D4
Leven E Yorks 53 E7
Leven Fife 76 G6
Levencorroch N Ayrs 66 D3
Levens Cumb 57 H6
Levens Green Herts 29 F10
Levenshulme Gtr Man 44 C2
Levenwick Shetland 96 L6
Leverburgh = An t-Ob W Isles 90 J5
Leverington Cambs 37 D10
Leverton Lincs 47 H8
Leverton Highgate Lincs 47 H8
Leverton Lucasgate Lincs 47 H8
Leverton Outgate Lincs 47 H8
Levington Suff 31 E9
Levisham N Yorks 59 G9
Levishie Highld 80 B6
Lew Oxon 27 H10
Lewannick Corn 4 C3
Lewdown Devon 4 C5
Lewes E Sus 12 E3
Leweston Pembs 22 D4
Lewisham London 19 D10
Lewiston Highld 81 A7
Lewistown Bridgend 14 C5
Lewknor Oxon 18 B4
Leworthy Devon 6 C5
Leworthy Devon 6 F2
Lewtrenchard Devon 4 C5
Lexden Essex 30 F6
Ley Aberds 83 B7
Ley Corn 4 E2
Leybourne Kent 20 F3
Leyburn N Yorks 58 G2
Leyfields Staffs 35 E8
Leyhill Bucks 18 A6
Leyland Lancs 49 G5
Leylodge Aberds 83 B9
Leymoor W Yorks 51 H7
Leys Aberds 89 C10
Leys Perth 76 D5
Leys Castle Highld 87 G9
Leys of Cossans Angus 76 C6
Leysdown-on-Sea Kent 21 D7
Leysmill Angus 77 C9
Leysters Pole Hereford 26 B2
Leyton London 19 C10
Leytonstone London 19 C10
Lezant Corn 4 D4
Leziate Norf 38 D2
Lhanbryde Moray 88 B2
Liatrie Highld 86 H5
Libanus Powys 24 F6
Libberton S Lanark 69 F8
Liberton Edin 69 D11
Liceasto W Isles 90 H6
Lichfield Staffs 35 E7
Lickey Worcs 34 H5
Lickey End Worcs 26 A6
Lickfold W Sus 11 B8
Liddel Orkney 95 K5
Liddesdale Highld 79 F10
Liddington Swindon 17 C9
Lidgate Suff 30 C4
Lidget S Yorks 45 B10
Lidget Green W Yorks 51 F7
Lidgett Notts 45 F10
Lidlington C Beds 28 E6
Lidstone Oxon 27 F10
Lieurary Highld 94 D2
Liff Angus 76 D6
Lifton Devon 4 C4
Liftondown Devon 4 C4
Lighthorne Warks 27 C10
Lightwater Sur 18 E6
Lightwood Stoke 34 A5
Lightwood Green Ches E 34 A2
Lightwood Green Wrex 33 A9
Lilbourne Northants 36 H1
Lilburn Tower Northumb 62 A6
Lilleshall Telford 34 D3
Lilley Herts 29 F8
Lilley W Berks 17 D11
Lilliesleaf Borders 61 A11
Lillingstone Dayrell Bucks 28 E4
Lillingstone Lovell Bucks 28 D4
Lillington Dorset 8 C5
Lillington Warks 27 B10
Lilliput Poole 9 E9
Lilstock Som 7 B10
Lilyhurst Shrops 34 D3
Limbury Luton 29 F7
Limebrook Hereford 25 B10
Limefield Gtr Man 44 A2
Limekilnburn S Lanark 68 E6
Limekilns Fife 69 B9
Limerigg Falk 69 C7
Limerstone IoW 10 F3
Limington Som 8 B4
Limpenhoe Norf 39 E9
Limpley Stoke Wilts 16 E4
Limpsfield Sur 19 F11
Limpsfield Chart Sur 19 F11
Linby Notts 45 G9
Linchmere W Sus 11 A7
Lincluden Dumfries 60 F5
Lincoln Lincs 46 E3
Lincomb Worcs 26 B5
Lincombe Devon 5 F8
Lindal in Furness Cumb 49 B2
Lindale Cumb 49 A4
Lindean Borders 70 G3
Lindfield W Sus 12 D2
Lindford Hants 18 H5
Lindifferon Fife 76 F6
Lindley W Yorks 51 H7
Lindley Green N Yorks 51 E8
Lindores Fife 76 F5
Lindridge Worcs 26 B3
Lindsell Essex 30 F3
Lindsey Suff 30 D6
Linford Hants 9 D10
Linford Thurrock 20 D3
Lingague IoM 48 E2
Lingards Wood W Yorks 44 A4
Lingbob W Yorks 51 F6
Lingdale Redcar 59 E7
Lingen Hereford 25 B10
Lingfield Sur 12 B2
Lingreabhagh W Isles 90 J5
Lingwood Norf 39 E9
Linicro Highld 85 B8
Linkenholt Hants 17 F10
Linkhill Kent 13 D7
Linkinhorne Corn 4 D4
Linklater Orkney 95 K5
Linksness Orkney 95 H3
Linktown Fife 69 A11
Linley Shrops 33 F9
Linley Green Hereford 26 C3
Linlithgow W Loth 69 C9
Linlithgow Bridge W Loth 69 C8
Linshiels Northumb 62 C4
Linsiadar W Isles 90 D7
Linsidemore Highld 87 B8
Linslade C Beds 28 F6
Linstead Parva Suff 39 H9
Linstock Cumb 61 H10
Linthwaite W Yorks 44 A5
Lintlaw Borders 71 E7
Lintmill Moray 88 B5
Linton Borders 70 H6
Linton Cambs 30 D2
Linton Derbys 35 D8
Linton Hereford 26 F3
Linton Kent 20 G4
Linton N Yorks 50 C5
Linton Northumb 63 D8
Linton W Yorks 51 E9
Linton-on-Ouse N Yorks 51 C10
Linwood Hants 9 D10
Linwood Lincs 46 D5
Linwood Renfs 68 D3
Lionacleit W Isles 84 D2
Lional W Isles 91 A10
Liphook Hants 11 A7
Liscard Mers 42 C6
Liscombe Som 7 C7
Liskeard Corn 4 E3
L'Islet Guern 11
Liss Hants 11 B6
Liss Forest Hants 11 B6
Lissett E Yorks 53 D7
Lissington Lincs 46 D5
Lisvane Cardiff 15 C7
Liswerry Newport 15 C9
Litcham Norf 38 D4
Litchborough Northants 28 C3
Litchfield Hants 17 F11
Litherland Mers 42 C6
Litlington Cambs 29 D10
Litlington E Sus 12 F4
Little Abington Cambs 30 D2
Little Addington Northants 28 A6
Little Alne Warks 27 B8
Little Altcar Mers 42 B6
Little Asby Cumb 57 F8
Little Assynt Highld 92 G4
Little Aston Staffs 35 E6
Little Atherfield IoW 10 F3
Little Ayre Orkney 95 J4
Little-ayre Shetland 96 G5
Little Ayton N Yorks 59 E6
Little Baddow Essex 30 H4
Little Badminton S Glos 16 C5
Little Ballinluig Perth 76 B2
Little Bampton Cumb 61 H8
Little Bardfield Essex 30 E3
Little Barford Bedford 29 C8
Little Barningham Norf 39 B7
Little Barrington Glos 27 G9
Little Barrow Ches W 43 F7
Little Barugh N Yorks 52 B3
Little Bavington Northumb 62 F5
Little Bealings Suff 31 D9
Little Bedwyn Wilts 17 E9
Little Bentley Essex 31 F8
Little Berkhamsted Herts 29 H9
Little Billing Northants 28 B5
Little Birch Hereford 26 E2
Little Blakenham Suff 31 D8
Little Blencow Cumb 56 C6
Little Bollington Ches E 43 D10
Little Bookham Sur 19 F8
Little Bowden Leics 36 G3
Little Bradley Suff 30 C3
Little Brampton Shrops 33 G9
Little Brechin Angus 77 A8
Little Brickhill M Keynes 28 E6
Little Brington Northants 28 B3
Little Bromley Essex 31 F7
Little Broughton Cumb 56 C2
Little Budworth Ches W 43 F8
Little Burstead Essex 20 B3
Little Bytham Lincs 36 D6
Little Carlton Lincs 47 D7
Little Carlton Notts 45 G11
Little Casterton Rutland 36 E6
Little Cawthorpe Lincs 47 D7
Little Chalfont Bucks 18 B6
Little Chart Kent 20 G6
Little Chesterford Essex 30 D2
Little Cheverell Wilts 16 F6
Little Chishill Cambs 29 E11
Little Clacton Essex 31 G8
Little Clifton Cumb 56 D2
Little Colp Aberds 89 D7
Little Comberton Worcs 26 D6
Little Common E Sus 12 F6
Little Compton Warks 27 E9
Little Cornard Suff 30 E5
Little Cowarne Hereford 26 C3
Little Coxwell Oxon 17 B9
Little Crakehall N Yorks 58 G3
Little Cressingham Norf 38 F4
Little Crosby Mers 42 B6
Little Dalby Leics 36 D3
Little Dawley Telford 34 E2
Little Dens Aberds 89 D10
Little Dewchurch Hereford 26 E2
Little Downham Cambs 37 G11
Little Driffield E Yorks 52 D6
Little Dunham Norf 38 D4
Little Dunkeld Perth 76 C3
Little Dunmow Essex 30 F3
Little Easton Essex 30 F3
Little Eaton Derbys 35 A9
Little Eccleston Lancs 49 E4
Little Ellingham Norf 38 F6
Little End Essex 20 A2
Little Eversden Cambs 29 C10
Little Faringdon Oxon 17 A9
Little Fencote N Yorks 58 G3
Little Fenton N Yorks 51 F11
Little Finborough Suff 31 C7
Little Fransham Norf 38 D5
Little Gaddesden Herts 28 G6
Little Gidding Cambs 37 G7
Little Glemham Suff 31 C10
Little Glenshee Perth 76 D2
Little Gransden Cambs 29 C9
Little Green Som 16 G4
Little Grimsby Lincs 47 C7
Little Gruinard Highld 86 C2
Little Habton N Yorks 52 B3
Little Hadham Herts 29 F11
Little Hale Lincs 37 A7
Little Hallingbury Essex 29 G11
Little Hampden Bucks 18 A5
Little Harrowden Northants 28 A5
Little Haseley Oxon 18 A3
Little Hatfield E Yorks 53 E7
Little Hautbois Norf 39 C8
Little Haven Pembs 22 E3
Little Hay Staffs 35 E7
Little Hayfield Derbys 44 D4
Little Haywood Staffs 34 C6
Little Heath W Mid 35 G9
Little Hereford Hereford 26 B2
Little Horkesley Essex 30 E6
Little Horsted E Sus 12 E3
Little Horton W Yorks 51 F7
Little Horwood Bucks 28 E4
Little Houghton Northants 28 C5
Little Houghton S Yorks 45 B8
Little Hucklow Derbys 44 E5
Little Hulton Gtr Man 43 B10
Little Humber E Yorks 53 G7
Little Hungerford W Berks 18 D2
Little Irchester Northants 28 B6
Little Kimble Bucks 28 H5
Little Kineton Warks 27 C10
Little Kingshill Bucks 18 B5
Little Langdale Cumb 56 F5
Little Langford Wilts 17 H7
Little Laver Essex 30 H2
Little Leigh Ches W 43 E9
Little Leighs Essex 30 G4
Little Lever Gtr Man 43 B10
Little London Bucks 28 G3
Little London E Sus 12 E4
Little London Hants 17 G10
Little London Hants 18 F3
Little London Lincs 37 C10
Little London Lincs 37 C8
Little London Norf 39 C7
Little London Powys 32 G6
Little Longstone Derbys 44 E5
Little Lynturk Aberds 83 B7
Little Malvern Worcs 26 D4
Little Maplestead Essex 30 E5
Little Marcle Hereford 26 E3
Little Marlow Bucks 18 C5
Little Marsden Lancs 50 F4
Little Massingham Norf 38 C3
Little Melton Norf 39 E7
Little Mill Mon 15 A9
Little Milton Oxon 18 A3
Little Missenden Bucks 18 B6
Little Musgrave Cumb 57 E9
Little Ness Shrops 33 D10
Little Neston Ches W 42 E5
Little Newcastle Pembs 22 D4
Little Newsham Durham 58 E2
Little Oakley Essex 31 F9
Little Oakley Northants 36 G4
Little Orton Cumb 61 H9

Little Ouseburn N Yorks 51 C10
Little Paxton Cambs 29 B8
Little Petherick Corn 3 B8
Little Pitlurg Moray 88 D4
Little Plumpton Lancs 49 F3
Little Plumstead Norf 39 D9
Little Ponton Lincs 36 B5
Little Raveley Cambs 37 H8
Little Reedness E Yorks 52 G4
Little Ribston N Yorks 51 D9
Little Rissington Glos 27 G8
Little Ryburgh Norf 38 C5
Little Ryle Northumb 62 B6
Little Salkeld Cumb 57 C7
Little Sampford Essex 30 E3
Little Sandhurst Brack 18 E5
Little Saxham Suff 30 B4
Little Scatwell Highld 86 F6
Little Sessay N Yorks 51 B10
Little Shelford Cambs 29 C11
Little Singleton Lancs 49 F3
Little Skillymarno Aberds 89 C9
Little Smeaton N Yorks 51 H11
Little Snoring Norf 38 B5
Little Sodbury S Glos 16 C4
Little Somborne Hants 10 A2
Little Somerford Wilts 16 C6
Little Stainforth N Yorks 50 C4
Little Stainton Darl 58 D4
Little Stanney Ches W 43 E7
Little Staughton Bedford 29 B8
Little Steeping Lincs 47 F8
Little Stoke Staffs 34 B5
Little Stonham Suff 31 B8
Little Stretton Leics 36 E2
Little Stretton Shrops 33 F10
Little Strickland Cumb 57 E7
Little Stukeley Cambs 37 H8
Little Sutton Ches W 42 E6
Little Tew Oxon 27 F10
Little Thetford Cambs 37 H11
Little Thirkleby N Yorks 51 B10
Little Thurlow Suff 30 C3
Little Thurrock Thurrock 20 D3
Little Torboll Highld 87 B10
Little Torrington Devon 6 E3
Little Totham Essex 30 G5
Little Toux Aberds 88 C5
Little Town Cumb 56 E4
Little Town Lancs 50 F2
Little Urswick Cumb 49 B2
Little Wakering Essex 20 C6
Little Walden Essex 30 D2
Little Waldingfield Suff 30 D6
Little Walsingham Norf 38 B5
Little Waltham Essex 30 G4
Little Warley Essex 20 B3
Little Weighton E Yorks 52 F5
Little Weldon Northants 36 G5
Little Welnetham Suff 30 B5
Little Wenlock Telford 34 E2
Little Whittingham Green Suff 39 H8
Little Wilbraham Cambs 30 C2
Little Wishford Wilts 17 H7
Little Witley Worcs 26 B4
Little Wittenham Oxon 18 B2
Little Wolford Warks 27 E9
Little Wratting Suff 30 D3
Little Wymington Bedford 28 B6
Little Wymondley Herts 29 F9
Little Wyrley Staffs 34 E6
Little Yeldham Essex 30 E4
Littlebeck N Yorks 59 F9
Littleborough Gtr Man 50 H5
Littleborough Notts 46 D2
Littlebourne Kent 21 F9
Littlebredy Dorset 8 F4
Littlebury Essex 30 E2
Littlebury Green Essex 29 E11
Littledean Glos 26 G3
Littleferry Highld 87 B11
Littleham Devon 5 C11
Littleham Devon 6 D3
Littlehampton W Sus 11 D9
Littlehempston Devon 5 E9
Littlehoughton Northumb 63 B8
Littlemill Aberds 82 D5
Littlemill E Ayrs 67 E7
Littlemill Highld 87 F12
Littlemill Northumb 63 B8
Littlemoor Dorset 8 F5
Littlemore Oxon 18 A2
Littleover Derby 35 B9
Littleport Cambs 38 G1
Littlestone on Sea Kent 13 D9
Littlethorpe Leics 35 F11
Littlethorpe N Yorks 51 C9
Littleton Ches W 43 F7
Littleton Hants 10 A3
Littleton Perth 76 D5
Littleton Som 8 A3
Littleton Sur 18 G6
Littleton Sur 19 E7
Littleton Drew Wilts 16 C5
Littleton-on-Severn S Glos 16 C2
Littleton Pannell Wilts 17 F7
Littletown Durham 58 B4
Littlewick Green Windsor 18 D5
Littleworth Bedford 29 D7
Littleworth Glos 16 A5
Littleworth Oxon 17 B10
Littleworth Staffs 34 D6
Littleworth Worcs 26 C5
Litton Derbys 44 E5
Litton N Yorks 50 B5
Litton Som 16 F2
Litton Cheney Dorset 8 E4
Liurbost W Isles 91 E8
Liverpool Mers 42 C6
Liverpool Airport Mers 43 D7
Liversedge W Yorks 51 G8
Liverton Devon 5 D9
Liverton Redcar 59 E8
Livingston W Loth 69 D9
Livingston Village W Loth 69 D9
Lixwm Flint 42 E4
Lizard Corn 2 H6
Llaingoch Anglesey 40 B4
Llaithddu Powys 33 G6
Llan Powys 32 E4
Llan Ffestiniog Gwyn 41 F9
Llan-y-pwll Wrex 42 G6
Llanaber Gwyn 32 D2
Llanaelhaearn Gwyn 40 F5
Llanafan Ceredig 24 A3
Llanafan-fawr Powys 24 C6
Llanallgo Anglesey 40 B6
Llanandras = Presteigne Powys 25 B10
Llanarmon Gwyn 40 G6
Llanarmon Dyffryn Ceiriog Wrex 33 B7
Llanarmon-yn-Ial Denb 42 G4
Llanarth Ceredig 23 A9
Llanarth Mon 25 G10
Llanarthne Carms 23 D10
Llanasa Flint 42 D4
Llanbabo Anglesey 40 B5
Llanbadarn Fawr Ceredig 32 G2
Llanbadarn Fynydd Powys 33 H7
Llanbadarn-y-Garreg Powys 25 D8
Llanbadoc Mon 15 B9
Llanbadrig Anglesey 40 A5
Llanbeder Newport 15 B9
Llanbedr Gwyn 32 C1
Llanbedr Powys 25 D8
Llanbedr Powys 25 F9
Llanbedr-Dyffryn-Clwyd Denb 42 G4
Llanbedr Pont Steffan = Lampeter Ceredig 23 B10
Llanbedr-y-cennin Conwy 41 D9
Llanbedrgoch Anglesey 41 B7
Llanbedrog Gwyn 40 G5
Llanberis Gwyn 41 D7
Llanbethêry V Glam 14 E6
Llanbister Powys 25 A8
Llanblethian V Glam 14 D5
Llanboidy Carms 23 D7
Llanbradach Caerph 15 B7
Llanbrynmair Powys 32 E4
Llancarfan V Glam 14 D6
Llancayo Mon 15 A9
Llancloudy Hereford 25 F11
Llancynfelyn Ceredig 32 F2
Llandaff Cardiff 15 D7
Llandanwg Gwyn 32 C1
Llandarcy Neath 14 B3
Llandawke Carms 23 E7
Llanddaniel Fab Anglesey 40 C6
Llanddarog Carms 23 E10
Llanddeiniol Ceredig 24 A2
Llanddeiniolen Gwyn 41 D7
Llandderfel Gwyn 32 B5
Llanddeusant Anglesey 40 B5
Llanddeusant Carms 24 F4
Llanddew Powys 25 E7
Llanddewi Swansea 23 H9
Llanddewi-Brefi Ceredig 24 C3
Llanddewi Rhydderch Mon 25 G10
Llanddewi Velfrey Pembs 22 E6
Llanddewi'r Cwm Powys 25 D7
Llanddoged Conwy 41 D10
Llanddona Anglesey 41 C7
Llanddowror Carms 23 E7
Llanddulas Conwy 42 E2
Llanddwywe Gwyn 32 C1
Llanddyfynan Anglesey 41 C7
Llandefaelog Fach Powys 25 E7
Llandefaelog-tre'r-graig Powys 25 F8
Llandefalle Powys 25 E8
Llandegai Gwyn 41 C7
Llandegfan Anglesey 41 C7
Llandegla Denb 42 G4
Llandegley Powys 25 B8
Llandegveth Mon 15 B9
Llandegwning Gwyn 40 G4
Llandeilo Carms 24 F3
Llandeilo Graban Powys 25 D7
Llandeilo'r Fan Powys 24 E5
Llandeloy Pembs 22 D3
Llandenny Mon 15 A10
Llandevenny Mon 15 C10
Llandewednock Corn 2 H6
Llandewi Ystradenny Powys 25 B8
Llandinabo Hereford 26 F2
Llandinam Powys 32 G6
Llandissilio Pembs 22 D6
Llandogo Mon 15 A11
Llandough V Glam 14 D5
Llandough V Glam 15 D7
Llandovery = Llanymddyfri Carms 24 E4
Llandow V Glam 14 D5
Llandre Carms 24 D3
Llandre Ceredig 32 G2
Llandrillo Denb 32 B6
Llandrillo-yn-Rhos Conwy 41 B10
Llandrindod = Llandrindod Wells Powys 25 B7
Llandrindod Wells = Llandrindod Powys 25 B7
Llandrinio Powys 33 D8
Llandudno Conwy 41 B9
Llandudno Junction = Cyffordd Llandudno Conwy 41 C9
Llandwrog Gwyn 40 E6
Llandybie Carms 24 G3
Llandyfaelog Carms 23 E9
Llandyfan Carms 24 G3
Llandyfriog Ceredig 23 B8
Llandyfrydog Anglesey 40 B6
Llandygwydd Ceredig 23 B7
Llandynan Denb 42 H4
Llandyrnog Denb 42 F4
Llandysilio Powys 33 D8
Llandyssil Powys 33 F7
Llandysul Ceredig 23 B9
Llanedeyrn Cardiff 15 C8
Llanedi Carms 23 F10
Llaneglwys Powys 25 E7
Llanegryn Gwyn 32 E1
Llanegwad Carms 23 D10
Llaneilian Anglesey 40 A6
Llanelian-yn-Rhos Conwy 41 C10
Llanelidan Denb 42 G4
Llanelieu Powys 25 E8
Llanellen Mon 25 G10
Llanelli Carms 23 G10
Llanelltyd Gwyn 32 D3
Llanelly Mon 25 G9
Llanelly Hill Mon 25 G9
Llanelwedd Powys 25 C7
Llanelwy = St Asaph Denb 42 E3
Llanenddwyn Gwyn 32 C1
Llanengan Gwyn 40 H4
Llanerchymedd Anglesey 40 B6
Llanerfyl Powys 32 E6
Llanfachraeth Anglesey 40 B5
Llanfachreth Gwyn 32 C3
Llanfaelog Anglesey 40 C5
Llanfaelrhys Gwyn 40 H4
Llanfaenor Mon 25 G11
Llanfaes Anglesey 41 C8
Llanfaes Powys 25 F7
Llanfaethlu Anglesey 40 B5
Llanfaglan Gwyn 40 D6
Llanfair Gwyn 32 C1
Llanfair-ar-y-bryn Carms 24 E5
Llanfair Caereinion Powys 33 E7
Llanfair Clydogau Ceredig 24 C3
Llanfair-Dyffryn-Clwyd Denb 42 G4
Llanfair Kilgheddin Mon 25 H10
Llanfair-Nant-Gwyn Pembs 22 C6
Llanfair Talhaiarn Conwy 42 E2
Llanfair Waterdine Shrops 33 H8
Llanfair-ym-Muallt = Builth Wells Powys 25 C7
Llanfairfechan Conwy 41 C8
Llanfairpwll-gwyngyll Anglesey 41 C7
Llanfairyneubwll Anglesey 40 C5
Llanfairynghornwy Anglesey 40 A5
Llanfallteg Carms 22 E6
Llanfaredd Powys 25 C7
Llanfarian Ceredig 32 H1
Llanfechain Powys 33 C7
Llanfechan Powys 24 C6
Llanfechell Anglesey 40 A5
Llanfendigaid Gwyn 32 E1
Llanferres Denb 42 F4
Llanfflewyn Anglesey 40 B5
Llanfihangel-ar-arth Carms 23 C9
Llanfihangel-Crucorney Mon 25 F10
Llanfihangel Glyn Myfyr Conwy 42 H2
Llanfihangel Nant Bran Powys 24 E6
Llanfihangel-nant-Melan Powys 25 C8
Llanfihangel Rhydithon Powys 25 B8
Llanfihangel Rogiet Mon 15 C10
Llanfihangel Tal-y-llyn Powys 25 F8
Llanfihangel-uwch-Gwili Carms 23 D9
Llanfihangel-y-Creuddyn Ceredig 32 H2
Llanfihangel-y-pennant Gwyn 32 E2
Llanfihangel-y-pennant Gwyn 41 F7
Llanfihangel-y-traethau Gwyn 41 G7
Llanfihangel-yn-Ngwynfa Powys 33 D6
Llanfihangel yn Nhowyn Anglesey 40 C5
Llanfilo Powys 25 E8
Llanfoist Mon 25 G9
Llanfor Gwyn 32 B5
Llanfrechfa Torf 15 B9
Llanfrothen Gwyn 41 F8
Llanfrynach Powys 25 F7
Llanfwrog Anglesey 40 B5
Llanfwrog Denb 42 G4
Llanfyllin Powys 33 D7
Llanfynydd Carms 23 D10
Llanfynydd Flint 42 G5
Llanfyrnach Pembs 23 C7
Llangadfan Powys 32 D6
Llangadog Carms 24 F4
Llangadwaladr Anglesey 40 D5
Llangadwaladr Powys 33 B7
Llangaffo Anglesey 40 D6
Llangain Carms 23 E8
Llangammarch Wells Powys 24 D6
Llangan V Glam 14 D5
Llangarron Hereford 26 F2
Llangasty Talyllyn Powys 25 F8
Llangathen Carms 23 D10
Llangattock Powys 25 G9
Llangattock Lingoed Mon 25 F10
Llangattock nigh Usk Mon 25 H10
Llangattock-Vibon-Avel Mon 25 G11
Llangedwyn Powys 33 C7
Llangefni Anglesey 40 C6
Llangeinor Bridgend 14 C5
Llangeitho Ceredig 24 C3
Llangeler Carms 23 C8
Llangelynin Gwyn 32 E1
Llangendeirne Carms 23 E9
Llangennech Carms 23 F10
Llangennith Swansea 23 G9
Llangenny Powys 25 G9
Llangernyw Conwy 41 D10
Llangian Gwyn 40 H4
Llanglydwen Carms 22 D6
Llangoed Anglesey 41 C8
Llangoedmor Ceredig 22 B6
Llangollen Denb 33 A8
Llangolman Pembs 22 D6
Llangors Powys 25 F8
Llangovan Mon 25 H11
Llangower Gwyn 32 B5
Llangrannog Ceredig 23 A8
Llangristiolus Anglesey 40 C6
Llangrove Hereford 26 G2
Llangua Mon 25 F10
Llangunllo Powys 25 A9
Llangunnor Carms 23 E9
Llangurig Powys 32 H5
Llangwm Conwy 32 A5
Llangwm Mon 15 A10
Llangwm Pembs 22 F4
Llangwnnadl Gwyn 40 G4
Llangwyfan Denb 42 F4
Llangwyfan-isaf Anglesey 40 D5
Llangwyllog Anglesey 40 C6
Llangwyryfon Ceredig 24 A2
Llangybi Ceredig 24 C3
Llangybi Gwyn 40 F6
Llangybi Mon 15 B9
Llangyfelach Swansea 14 B2
Llangynhafal Denb 42 F4
Llangynidr Powys 25 G8
Llangynin Carms 23 E7
Llangynog Carms 23 E8
Llangynog Powys 33 C6
Llangynwyd Bridgend 14 C4
Llanhamlach Powys 25 F7
Llanharan Rhondda 14 C6
Llanharry Rhondda 14 C6
Llanhennock Mon 15 B9
Llanhiledd = Llanhilleth Bl Gwent 15 A8
Llanhilleth = Llanhiledd Bl Gwent 15 A8
Llanidloes Powys 32 G5
Llaniestyn Gwyn 40 G4
Llanifyny Powys 32 G4
Llanigon Powys 25 E9
Llanilar Ceredig 24 A3
Llanilid Rhondda 14 C5
Llanilltud Fawr = Llantwit Major V Glam 14 E5
Llanishen Cardiff 15 C7
Llanishen Mon 15 A10
Llanllawddog Carms 23 D9
Llanllechid Gwyn 41 D8
Llanllowell Mon 15 B9
Llanllugan Powys 33 E6
Llanllwch Carms 23 E8
Llanllwchaiarn Powys 33 F7
Llanllwni Carms 23 C9
Llanllyfni Gwyn 40 E6
Llanmadoc Swansea 23 G9
Llanmaes V Glam 14 E5
Llanmartin Newport 15 C9
Llanmihangel V Glam 14 D5
Llanmorlais Swansea 23 G10
Llannefydd Conwy 42 E2
Llannon Carms 23 F10
Llannor Gwyn 40 G5
Llanon Ceredig 24 B2
Llanover Mon 25 H10
Llanpumsaint Carms 23 D9
Llanreithan Pembs 22 D3
Llanrhaeadr Denb 42 F3
Llanrhaeadr-ym-Mochnant Powys 33 C7
Llanrhian Pembs 22 C3
Llanrhidian Swansea 23 G9
Llanrhos Conwy 41 B9
Llanrhyddlad Anglesey 40 B5
Llanrhystud Ceredig 24 B2
Llanrosser Hereford 25 E9
Llanrothal Hereford 25 G11
Llanrug Gwyn 41 D7
Llanrumney Cardiff 15 C8
Llanrwst Conwy 41 D10
Llansadurnen Carms 23 E7
Llansadwrn Anglesey 41 C7
Llansadwrn Carms 24 E3
Llansaint Carms 23 F8
Llansamlet Swansea 14 B2
Llansannan Conwy 42 F2
Llansannor V Glam 14 D5
Llansantffraed Ceredig 24 B2
Llansantffraed Powys 25 F8
Llansantffraed Cwmdeuddwr Powys 24 B6
Llansantffraed-in-Elvel Powys 25 C7
Llansantffraid-ym-Mechain Powys 33 C8
Llansawel Carms 24 E3
Llansilin Powys 33 C8
Llansoy Mon 15 A10
Llanspyddid Powys 25 F7
Llanstadwell Pembs 22 F4
Llansteffan Carms 23 E8
Llanstephan Powys 25 D8
Llantarnam Torf 15 B9
Llanteg Pembs 22 E6
Llanthony Mon 25 F9
Llantilio Crossenny Mon 25 G10
Llantilio Pertholey Mon 25 G10
Llantood Pembs 22 B6
Llantrisant Anglesey 40 B5
Llantrisant Mon 15 B9
Llantrisant Rhondda 14 C6
Llantrithyd V Glam 14 D6
Llantwit Fardre Rhondda 14 C6
Llantwit Major = Llanilltud Fawr V Glam 14 E5
Llanuwchllyn Gwyn 41 G10
Llanvaches Newport 15 B10
Llanvair Discoed Mon 15 B10
Llanvapley Mon 25 G10
Llanvetherine Mon 25 G10
Llanveynoe Hereford 25 E10
Llanvihangel Gobion Mon 25 H10
Llanvihangel-Ystern-Llewern Mon 25 G11
Llanwarne Hereford 26 F2
Llanwddyn Powys 32 D6
Llanwenog Ceredig 23 B9
Llanwern Newport 15 C9
Llanwinio Carms 23 D7
Llanwnda Gwyn 40 E6
Llanwnda Pembs 22 C4
Llanwnnen Ceredig 23 B10
Llanwnog Powys 32 F6
Llanwrda Carms 24 E4
Llanwrin Powys 32 E3
Llanwrthwl Powys 24 B6
Llanwrtud = Llanwrtyd Wells Powys 24 D5
Llanwrtyd Powys 24 D5
Llanwrtyd Wells = Llanwrtud Powys 24 D5
Llanwyddelan Powys 33 E6
Llanyblodwel Shrops 33 C8
Llanybri Carms 23 E8
Llanybydder Carms 23 B10
Llanycefn Pembs 22 D5
Llanychaer Pembs 22 C4
Llanycil Gwyn 32 B5
Llanycrwys Carms 24 D3
Llanymawddwy Gwyn 32 D5
Llanymddyfri = Llandovery Carms 24 E4
Llanymynech Powys 33 C8
Llanynghenedl Anglesey 40 B5
Llanynys Denb 42 F4
Llanyre Powys 25 B7
Llanystumdwy Gwyn 40 G6
Llanywern Powys 25 F8
Llawhaden Pembs 22 E5
Llawnt Shrops 33 B8
Llawr Dref Gwyn 40 H4
Llawryglyn Powys 32 F5
Llay Wrex 42 G6
Llechcynfarwy Anglesey 40 B5
Llecheiddior Gwyn 40 F6
Llechfaen Powys 25 F7
Llechryd Caerph 25 H8
Llechryd Ceredig 23 B7
Llechrydau Powys 33 B8
Lledrod Ceredig 24 A3
Llenmerewig Powys 33 F7
Llethrid Swansea 23 G10
Llidiad Nenog Carms 23 C10
Llidiardau Gwyn 41 G10
Llidiart-y-parc Denb 33 A7
Llithfaen Gwyn 40 F5
Llong Flint 42 F5
Llowes Powys 25 D8
Llundain-fach Ceredig 23 A10
Llwydcoed Rhondda 14 A5
Llwyn Shrops 33 G8
Llwyn-du Mon 25 G9
Llwyn-hendy Carms 23 G10
Llwyn-têg Carms 23 F10
Llwyn-y-brain Carms 22 E6
Llwyn-y-groes Ceredig 23 A10
Llwyncelyn Ceredig 23 A9
Llwyndafydd Ceredig 23 A8
Llwynderw Powys 33 E8
Llwyndyrys Gwyn 40 F5
Llwyngwril Gwyn 32 E1
Llwynmawr Wrex 33 B8
Llwynypia Rhondda 14 B5
Llynclys Shrops 33 C8
Llynfaes Anglesey 40 C6
Llys-y-frân Pembs 22 D5
Llysfaen Conwy 41 C10
Llyswen Powys 25 E8
Llysworney V Glam 14 D5
Llywel Powys 24 E5
Loan Falk 69 C8
Loanend Northumb 71 E8
Loanhead Midloth 69 D11
Loans S Ayrs 66 C6
Loans of Tullich Highld 87 D11
Lobb Devon 6 C3
Loch a Charnain W Isles 84 D3
Loch a' Ghainmhich W Isles 91 E7
Loch Baghasdail = Lochboisdale W Isles 84 G2
Loch Choire Lodge Highld 93 F9
Loch Euphoirt W Isles 84 B3
Loch Head Dumfries 54 E6
Loch Loyal Lodge Highld 93 E9
Loch nam Madadh = Lochmaddy W Isles 84 B4
Loch Sgioport W Isles 84 E3
Lochailort Highld 79 C10
Lochaline Highld 79 G9
Lochanhully Highld 81 A11
Lochans Dumfries 54 D3
Locharbriggs Dumfries 60 E5
Lochassynt Lodge Highld 92 G4
Lochavich Ho Argyll 73 B8
Lochawe Argyll 74 E4
Lochboisdale = Loch Baghasdail W Isles 84 G2
Lochbuie Argyll 79 J9
Lochcarron Highld 85 E13
Lochdhu Highld 93 E13
Lochdochart House Stirling 75 E7
Lochdon Argyll 79 H10
Lochdrum Highld 86 D5
Lochead Argyll 72 F6
Lochearnhead Stirling 75 E8
Lochee Dundee 76 D6
Lochend Highld 87 H8
Lochend Highld 94 D4
Locherben Dumfries 60 D5
Lochfoot Dumfries 60 F4
Lochgair Argyll 73 D8
Lochgarthside Highld 81 B7
Lochgelly Fife 69 A10
Lochgilphead Argyll 73 E7
Lochgoilhead Argyll 74 G5
Lochhill Moray 88 B2
Lochindorb Lodge Highld 87 H12
Lochinver Highld 92 G3
Lochlane Perth 75 E11
Lochluichart Highld 86 E6
Lochmaben Dumfries 60 E6
Lochmaddy = Loch nam Madadh W Isles 84 B4
Lochmore Cottage Highld 94 F2
Lochmore Lodge Highld 92 F5
Lochore Fife 76 H4
Lochportain W Isles 84 A4
Lochranza N Ayrs 66 A2
Lochs Crofts Moray 88 B3
Lochside Aberds 77 A10
Lochside Highld 87 F11
Lochside Highld 92 D7
Lochside Highld 93 F11
Lochslin Highld 87 C11
Lochstack Lodge Highld 92 E5
Lochton Aberds 83 D9
Lochty Angus 77 A8
Lochty Fife 77 G8
Lochty Perth 76 E3
Lochuisge Highld 79 F10
Lochurr Dumfries 60 E3
Lochwinnoch Renfs 68 E2
Lochwood Dumfries 60 D6
Lochyside Highld 80 F3
Lockengate Corn 3 C9
Lockerbie Dumfries 61 E7
Lockeridge Wilts 17 E8
Lockerley Hants 10 B1
Locking N Som 15 F9
Lockinge Oxon 17 C11
Lockington E Yorks 52 E5
Lockington Leics 35 C10
Lockleywood Shrops 34 C2
Locks Heath Hants 10 D4
Lockton N Yorks 59 G9
Lockwood W Yorks 51 H7
Loddington Leics 36 E3
Loddington Northants 36 H4
Loddiswell Devon 5 G8
Loddon Norf 39 F9
Lode Cambs 30 B2
Loders Dorset 8 E3
Lodsworth W Sus 11 B8
Lofthouse N Yorks 51 B7
Lofthouse W Yorks 51 G9
Loftus Redcar 59 E8
Logan E Ayrs 67 D8
Logan Mains Dumfries 54 E3
Loganlea W Loth 69 D8
Loggerheads Staffs 34 B3
Logie Angus 77 A9
Logie Fife 77 E7
Logie Moray 87 F13
Logie Coldstone Aberds 82 C6
Logie Hill Highld 87 D10
Logie Newton Aberds 89 E6
Logie Pert Angus 77 A9
Logiealmond Lodge Perth 76 D2
Logierait Perth 76 B2
Login Carms 22 D6
Lolworth Cambs 29 B10
Lonbain Highld 85 C11
Londesborough E Yorks 52 E4
London Colney Herts 19 A8
Londonderry N Yorks 58 H4
Londonthorpe Lincs 36 B5
Londubh Highld 91 J13
Lonemore Highld 87 C10
Long Ashton N Som 15 D11
Long Bennington Lincs 36 A4
Long Bredy Dorset 8 E4
Long Buckby Northants 28 B3
Long Clawson Leics 36 C3
Long Common Hants 10 C4
Long Compton Staffs 34 C4
Long Compton Warks 27 E9
Long Crendon Bucks 28 H3
Long Crichel Dorset 9 C8
Long Ditton Sur 19 E8
Long Drax N Yorks 52 G2
Long Duckmanton Derbys 45 E8
Long Eaton Derbys 35 B10
Long Green Worcs 26 E5
Long Hanborough Oxon 27 G11
Long Itchington Warks 27 B11
Long Lawford Warks 35 H10
Long Load Som 8 B3
Long Marston Herts 28 G5
Long Marston N Yorks 51 D11
Long Marston Warks 27 D8
Long Marton Cumb 57 D8
Long Melford Suff 30 D5
Long Newnton Glos 16 B6
Long Newton E Loth 70 D4
Long Preston N Yorks 50 D4
Long Riston E Yorks 53 E7
Long Sight Gtr Man 44 B3
Long Stratton Norf 39 F7
Long Street M Keynes 28 D4
Long Sutton Hants 18 G4
Long Sutton Lincs 37 C10
Long Sutton Som 8 B3
Long Thurlow Suff 31 B7
Long Whatton Leics 35 C10
Long Wittenham Oxon 18 B2
Longbar N Ayrs 66 A6
Longbenton T&W 63 G8
Longborough Glos 27 F8
Longbridge W Mid 34 H6
Longbridge Warks 27 B9
Longbridge Deverill Wilts 16 G5
Longburton Dorset 8 C5
Longcliffe Derbys 44 G6
Longcot Oxon 17 B9
Longcroft Falk 68 C6
Longden Shrops 33 E10
Longdon Staffs 35 D6
Longdon Worcs 26 E5
Longdon Green Staffs 35 D6
Longdon on Tern Telford 34 D2
Longdown Devon 7 G7
Longdowns Corn 2 F6
Longfield Kent 20 E3
Longfield Shetland 96 M5
Longford Derbys 35 B8
Longford Glos 26 F5
Longford London 19 D7
Longford Shrops 34 B2
Longford Telford 34 D3
Longford W Mid 35 G9
Longfordlane Derbys 35 B8
Longforgan Perth 76 E6
Longformacus Borders 70 E5
Longframlington Northumb 63 C7
Longham Dorset 9 E9
Longham Norf 38 D5
Longhaven Aberds 89 E11
Longhill Aberds 89 C9
Longhirst Northumb 63 E8
Longhope Glos 26 G3
Longhope Orkney 95 J4
Longhorsley Northumb 63 D7
Longhoughton Northumb 63 B8
Longlane Derbys 35 B8
Longlane W Berks 17 D11
Longlevens Glos 26 F5
Longley W Yorks 44 B5
Longley Green Worcs 26 C4
Longmanhill Aberds 89 B7
Longmoor Camp Hants 11 A6
Longmorn Moray 88 C2
Longnewton Borders 70 H4
Longnewton Stockton 58 E4
Longney Glos 26 G4
Longniddry E Loth 70 C3
Longnor Shrops 33 E10
Longnor Staffs 44 F4
Longparish Hants 17 G11
Longport Stoke 44 H2
Longridge Lancs 50 F2
Longridge Staffs 34 D5
Longridge W Loth 69 D8
Longriggend N Lanark 69 C7
Longsdon Staffs 44 G3
Longshaw Gtr Man 43 B8
Longside Aberds 89 D10
Longstanton Cambs 29 B10
Longstock Hants 17 H10
Longstone Pembs 22 F6
Longstowe Cambs 29 C10
Longthorpe Pboro 37 F7
Longthwaite Cumb 56 D6
Longton Lancs 49 G4
Longton Stoke 34 A5
Longtown Cumb 61 G9
Longtown Hereford 25 F10
Longview Mers 43 C7
Longville in the Dale Shrops 33 F11
Longwick Bucks 28 H4
Longwitton Northumb 62 E6
Longwood Shrops 34 E2
Longworth Oxon 17 B10
Longyester E Loth 70 D4
Lonmay Aberds 89 C10
Lonmore Highld 84 D7
Looe Corn 4 F3
Loose Kent 20 F4
Loosley Row Bucks 18 A5
Lopcombe Corner Wilts 17 H9
Lopen Som 8 C3
Loppington Shrops 33 C10
Lopwell Devon 4 E5
Lorbottle Northumb 62 C6
Lorbottle Hall Northumb 62 C6
Lornty Perth 76 C4
Loscoe Derbys 45 H8
Losgaintir W Isles 90 H5
Lossiemouth Moray 88 A2
Lossit Argyll 64 C2
Lostford Shrops 34 B2
Lostock Gralam Ches W 43 E9
Lostock Green Ches W 43 E9
Lostock Hall Lancs 49 G5
Lostock Junction Gtr Man 43 B9
Lostwithiel Corn 4 F2
Loth Orkney 95 E7
Lothbeg Highld 93 H12
Lothersdale N Yorks 50 E5
Lothmore Highld 93 H12
Loudwater Bucks 18 B6
Loughborough Leics 35 D11
Loughor Swansea 23 G10
Loughton Essex 19 B11
Loughton M Keynes 28 E5
Loughton Shrops 34 G2
Lound Lincs 37 D6
Lound Notts 45 D10
Lound Suff 39 F11
Lount Leics 35 D9
Louth Lincs 47 D7
Love Clough Lancs 50 G4
Lovedean Hants 10 C5
Lover Wilts 9 B11
Loversall S Yorks 45 C9
Loves Green Essex 20 A3
Lovesome Hill N Yorks 58 G4
Loveston Pembs 22 F5
Lovington Som 8 A4
Low Ackworth W Yorks 51 H10
Low Barlings Lincs 46 E4
Low Bentham N Yorks 50 C2
Low Bradfield S Yorks 44 C6
Low Bradley N Yorks 50 E6
Low Braithwaite Cumb 56 B6
Low Brunton Northumb 62 F5
Low Burnham N Lincs 45 B11
Low Burton N Yorks 51 A8
Low Buston Northumb 63 C8
Low Catton E Yorks 52 D3
Low Clanyard Dumfries 54 F4
Low Coniscliffe Darl 58 E3
Low Crosby Cumb 61 H10
Low Dalby N Yorks 59 H9
Low Dinsdale Darl 58 E4
Low Ellington N Yorks 51 A8
Low Etherley Durham 58 D2
Low Fell T&W 63 H8
Low Fulney Lincs 37 C8
Low Garth N Yorks 59 F8
Low Gate Northumb 62 G5
Low Grantley N Yorks 51 B8
Low Habberley Worcs 34 H4
Low Ham Som 8 B3
Low Hesket Cumb 56 B6
Low Hesleyhurst Northumb 62 D6
Low Hutton N Yorks 52 C3
Low Laithe N Yorks 51 C7
Low Leighton Derbys 44 D4
Low Lorton Cumb 56 D3
Low Marishes N Yorks 52 B4
Low Marnham Notts 46 F2
Low Mill N Yorks 59 G7
Low Moor Lancs 50 E3
Low Moor W Yorks 51 G7
Low Moorsley T&W 58 B4
Low Newton Cumb 49 A4
Low Newton-by-the-Sea Northumb 63 A8
Low Row Cumb 56 C5
Low Row Cumb 61 G11
Low Row N Yorks 57 G11
Low Salchrie Dumfries 54 C3
Low Smerby Argyll 65 F8
Low Torry Fife 69 B9
Low Worsall N Yorks 58 F4
Low Wray Cumb 56 F5
Lowbridge House Cumb 57 F7
Lowca Cumb 56 D1
Lowdham Notts 45 H10
Lowe Shrops 33 B11
Lowe Hill Staffs 44 G3
Lower Aisholt Som 7 C11
Lower Arncott Oxon 28 G3
Lower Ashton Devon 5 C9
Lower Assendon Oxon 18 C4
Lower Badcall Highld 92 E4
Lower Bartle Lancs 49 F4
Lower Basildon W Berks 18 D3
Lower Beeding W Sus 11 B11
Lower Benefield Northants 36 G5
Lower Boddington Northants 27 C11
Lower Brailes Warks 27 E10
Lower Breakish Highld 85 F11
Lower Broadheath Worcs 26 C5
Lower Bullingham Hereford 26 E2
Lower Cam Glos 16 A4
Lower Chapel Powys 25 E7
Lower Chute Wilts 17 F10
Lower Cragabus Argyll 64 D4
Lower Crossings Derbys 44 D4
Lower Cumberworth W Yorks 44 B6
Lower Cwm-twrch Powys 24 G4
Lower Darwen Blackburn 50 G2
Lower Dean Bedford 29 B7
Lower Diabaig Highld 85 B12
Lower Dicker E Sus 12 E4
Lower Dinchope Shrops 33 G10
Lower Down Shrops 33 G9
Lower Drift Corn 2 G3
Lower Dunsforth N Yorks 51 C10
Lower Egleton Hereford 26 D3
Lower Elkstone Staffs 44 G4
Lower End C Beds 28 F6
Lower Everleigh Wilts 17 F8
Lower Farringdon Hants 18 H4
Lower Foxdale IoM 48 E2
Lower Frankton Shrops 33 B9
Lower Froyle Hants 18 G4
Lower Gledfield Highld 87 B8
Lower Green Norf 38 B5
Lower Hacheston Suff 31 C10
Lower Halistra Highld 84 C7
Lower Halstow Kent 20 E5
Lower Hardres Kent 21 F8
Lower Hawthwaite Cumb 56 H4
Lower Heath Ches E 44 F2
Lower Hempriggs Moray 87 E14
Lower Hergest Hereford 25 C9
Lower Heyford Oxon 27 F11
Lower Higham Kent 20 D4
Lower Holbrook Suff 31 E8
Lower Hordley Shrops 33 C9
Lower Horsebridge E Sus 12 E4
Lower Killeyan Argyll 64 D3
Lower Kingswood Sur 19 F9
Lower Kinnerton Ches W 42 F6
Lower Langford N Som 15 E10
Lower Largo Fife 77 G7
Lower Leigh Staffs 34 B6
Lower Lemington Glos 27 E9
Lower Lenie Highld 81 A7
Lower Lydbrook Glos 26 G2
Lower Lye Hereford 25 B11
Lower Machen Newport 15 C8
Lower Maes-coed Hereford 25 E10
Lower Mayland Essex 20 A6
Lower Midway Derbys 35 C9
Lower Milovaig Highld 84 C6
Lower Moor Worcs 26 D6
Lower Nazeing Essex 29 H10
Lower Netchwood Shrops 34 F2
Lower Ollach Highld 85 E10
Lower Penarth V Glam 15 D7
Lower Penn Staffs 34 F4
Lower Pennington Hants 10 E2
Lower Peover Ches W 43 E10
Lower Pexhill Ches E 44 E2
Lower Place Gtr Man 44 A3
Lower Quinton Warks 27 D8
Lower Rochford Worcs 26 B3
Lower Seagry Wilts 16 C6
Lower Shelton C Beds 28 D6
Lower Shiplake Oxon 18 D4
Lower Shuckburgh Warks 27 B11
Lower Slaughter Glos 27 F8
Lower Stanton St Quintin Wilts 16 C6
Lower Stoke Medway 20 D5
Lower Stondon C Beds 29 E8
Lower Stow Bedon Norf 38 F5
Lower Street Norf 39 B8
Lower Street Norf 39 D9
Lower Strensham Worcs 26 D6
Lower Stretton Warr 43 D9
Lower Sundon C Beds 29 F7
Lower Swanwick Hants 10 D3
Lower Swell Glos 27 F8
Lower Tean Staffs 34 B6
Lower Thurlton Norf 39 F10
Lower Tote Highld 85 B10
Lower Town Pembs 22 C4
Lower Tysoe Warks 27 D10
Lower Upham Hants 10 C4
Lower Vexford Som 7 C10
Lower Weare Som 15 F10
Lower Welson Hereford 25 C9
Lower Whitley Ches W 43 E9
Lower Wield Hants 18 G3
Lower Winchendon Bucks 28 G4
Lower Withington Ches E 44 F2
Lower Woodend Bucks 18 C5
Lower Woodford Wilts 9 A10
Lower Wyche Worcs 26 D4
Lowesby Leics 36 E3
Lowestoft Suff 39 F11
Loweswater Cumb 56 D3
Lowford Hants 10 C3
Lowgill Cumb 57 G8
Lowgill Lancs 50 C2
Lowick Northants 36 G5
Lowick Northumb 71 G9
Lowick Bridge Cumb 56 H4
Lowick Green Cumb 56 H4
Lowlands Torf 15 B8
Lowmoor Row Cumb 57 D8
Lownie Moor Angus 77 C7
Lowsonford Warks 27 B8
Lowther Cumb 57 D7
Lowthorpe E Yorks 53 C6
Lowton Gtr Man 43 C9
Lowton Common Gtr Man 43 C9
Loxbeare Devon 7 E8
Loxhill Sur 19 H7
Loxhore Devon 6 C5
Loxley Warks 27 C9
Loxton N Som 15 F9
Loxwood W Sus 11 A9
Lubcroy Highld 92 J6
Lubenham Leics 36 G3
Luccombe Som 7 B8
Luccombe Village IoW 10 G4
Lucker Northumb 71 G10
Luckett Corn 4 D4
Luckington Wilts 16 C5
Lucklawhill Fife 77 E7
Luckwell Bridge Som 7 C8
Lucton Hereford 25 B11
Ludag W Isles 84 G2
Ludborough Lincs 46 C6
Ludchurch Pembs 22 E6
Luddenden W Yorks 50 G6
Luddenden Foot W Yorks 50 G6
Luddesdown Kent 20 E3
Luddington N Lincs 52 H4
Luddington Warks 27 C8
Luddington in the Brook Northants 37 G7
Lude House Perth 81 G10
Ludford Lincs 46 D6
Ludford Shrops 26 A2
Ludgershall Bucks 28 G3
Ludgershall Wilts 17 F9
Ludgvan Corn 2 F4
Ludham Norf 39 D9
Ludlow Shrops 26 A2
Ludwell Wilts 9 B8
Ludworth Durham 58 B4
Luffincott Devon 6 G2
Lugar E Ayrs 67 D8
Lugg Green Hereford 25 B11
Luggate Burn E Loth 70 C5
Luggiebank N Lanark 68 C6
Lugton E Ayrs 67 A7
Lugwardine Hereford 26 D2
Luib Highld 85 F10
Lulham Hereford 25 D11
Lullenden Sur 12 B3
Lullington Derbys 35 D8
Lullington Som 16 F4
Lulsgate Bottom N Som 15 E11
Lulsley Worcs 26 C4
Lumb W Yorks 50 G6
Lumby N Yorks 51 F10
Lumloch E Dunb 68 D5
Lumphanan Aberds 83 C7
Lumphinnans Fife 69 A10
Lumsdaine Borders 71 D7
Lumsden Aberds 82 A6
Lunan Angus 77 B9
Lunanhead Angus 77 B7
Luncarty Perth 76 E3
Lund E Yorks 52 E5
Lund N Yorks 52 F2
Lund Shetland 96 C7
Lunderton Aberds 89 D11
Lundie Angus 76 D5
Lundie Highld 80 B3
Lundin Links Fife 77 G7
Lunga Argyll 72 C6
Lunna Shetland 96 G6
Lunning Shetland 96 G7
Lunnon Swansea 23 H10
Lunsford's Cross E Sus 12 E6
Lunt Mers 42 B6
Luntley Hereford 25 C10
Luppitt Devon 7 F10
Lupset W Yorks 51 H9
Lupton Cumb 50 A1
Lurgashall W Sus 11 B8
Lusby Lincs 47 F
Luson Devon 5 G
Luss Argyll 68 A
Lussagiven Argyll 72 E
Lusta Highld 85 C
Lustleigh Devon 5 C
Luston Hereford 25 B1
Luthermuir Aberds 83 G
Luthrie Fife 76 F
Luton Devon 5 D1
Luton Luton 29 F
Luton Medway 20

Monmouth Cap Mon 25 F10
Monnington on Wye Hereford 25 D10
Monreith Dumfries 54 E6
Monreith Mains Dumfries 54 E6
Mont Saint Guern 11
Montacute Som 8 C3
Montcoffer Ho. Aberds 89 B6
Montford Argyll 73 G10
Montford Shrops 33 D10
Montford Bridge Shrops 33 D10
Montgarrie Aberds 83 B7
Montgomery = Trefaldwyn Powys 33 F8
Montrave Fife 76 G6
Montrose Angus 77 B10
Montsale Essex 21 B7
Monxton Hants 17 G10
Monyash Derbys 44 F5
Monymusk Aberds 83 B8
Monzie Perth 75 E11
Monzie Castle Perth 75 E11
Moodiesburn N Lanark 68 C5
Moonzie Fife 76 F6
Moor Allerton W Yorks 51 F8
Moor Crichel Dorset 9 D8
Moor End E Yorks 52 F4
Moor End York 52 D2
Moor Monkton N Yorks 51 D11
Moor of Granary Moray 87 F13
Moor of Ravenstone Dumfries 54 E6
Moor Row Cumb 56 E2
Moor Street Kent 20 E5
Moorby Lincs 46 F6
Moordown Bmouth 9 E9
Moore Halton 43 D8
Moorend Glos 16 A4
Moorends S Yorks 52 H2
Moorgate S Yorks 45 C8
Moorgreen Notts 45 H8
Moorhall Derbys 45 E7
Moorhampton Hereford 25 D10
Moorhead W Yorks 51 F7
Moorhouse Cumb 61 H9
Moorhouse Notts 45 F11
Moorlinch Som 15 H9
Moorsholm Redcar 59 E7
Moorside Gtr Man 44 B3
Moorthorpe W Yorks 45 A8
Moortown Hants 9 D10
Moortown IoW 10 F3
Moortown Lincs 46 C4
Morangie Highld 87 C10
Morar Highld 79 B9
Morborne Cambs 37 F7
Morchard Bishop Devon 7 F6
Morcombelake Dorset 8 E3
Morcott Rutland 36 E5
Morda Shrops 33 C8
Morden Dorset 9 E8
Morden London 19 E9
Mordiford Hereford 26 E2
Mordon Durham 58 D4
More Shrops 33 F9
Morebath Devon 7 D8
Morebattle Borders 62 A3
Morecambe Lancs 49 C4
Morefield Highld 86 B4
Moreleigh Devon 5 F8
Morenish Perth 75 D8
Moresby Cumb 56 D1
Moresby Parks Cumb 56 E1
Morestead Hants 10 B4
Moreton Dorset 9 F7
Moreton Essex 30 H2
Moreton Mers 42 C5
Moreton Oxon 18 A3
Moreton Staffs 34 D3
Moreton Corbet Shrops 34 C1
Moreton-in-Marsh Glos 27 E9
Moreton Jeffries Hereford 26 D3
Moreton Morrell Warks 27 C10
Moreton on Lugg Hereford 26 D2
Moreton Pinkney Northants 28 D2
Moreton Say Shrops 34 B2
Moreton Valence Glos 26 H4
Moretonhampstead Devon 5 C8
Morfa Carms 23 E10
Morfa Carms 23 G10
Morfa Bach Carms 23 E8
Morfa Bychan Gwyn 41 G7
Morfa Dinlle Gwyn 40 E6
Morfa Glas Neath 24 H5
Morfa Nefyn Gwyn 40 F4
Morfydd Denb 42 H4
Morgan's Vale Wilts 9 B10
Moriah Ceredig 32 H2
Morland Cumb 57 D7
Morley Derbys 35 A9
Morley Durham 58 D2
Morley W Yorks 51 G8
Morley Green Ches E 44 D2
Morley St Botolph Norf 39 F6
Morningside Edin 69 C11
Morningside N Lanark 69 E7
Morningthorpe Norf 39 F8
Morpeth Northumb 63 E8
Morphie Aberds 77 A10
Morrey Staffs 35 D7
Morris Green Essex 30 E4
Morriston Swansea 14 B2
Morston Norf 38 A6
Mortehoe Devon 6 B3
Mortimer W Berks 18 E3
Mortimer West End Hants 18 E3
Mortimer's Cross Hereford 25 B11
Mortlake London 19 D9
Morton Cumb 56 A5
Morton Derbys 45 F8
Morton Lincs 37 C6
Morton Lincs 46 C2
Morton Lincs 46 F2
Morton Norf 39 D7
Morton Notts 45 G11
Morton S Glos 16 B3
Morton Shrops 33 C8
Morton Bagot Warks 27 B8
Morton-on-Swale N Yorks 58 G4
Morvah Corn 2 F3
Morval Corn 4 F3
Morvich Highld 80 A1
Morvich Highld 93 J10
Morville Shrops 34 F2
Morville Heath Shrops 34 F2
Morwenstow Corn 6 E1
Mosborough S Yorks 45 D8
Moscow E Ayrs 67 B7
Mosedale Cumb 56 C5
Moseley W Mid 34 F5
Moseley W Mid 35 G6
Moseley Worcs 26 C5
Moss Argyll 78 G2
Moss Highld 79 E9
Moss S Yorks 45 A9
Moss Wrex 42 G6
Moss Bank Mers 43 C8
Moss Edge Lancs 49 E4
Moss End Brack 18 D5
Moss of Barmuckity Moray 88 B2
Moss Pit Staffs 34 C5
Moss-side Highld 87 F11
Moss Side Lancs 49 F3
Mossat Aberds 82 B6
Mossbank Shetland 96 F6
Mossbay Cumb 56 D1
Mossblown S Ayrs 67 D7
Mossbrow Gtr Man 43 D10
Mossburnford Borders 62 B2
Mossdale Dumfries 55 B9
Mossend N Lanark 68 D6
Mosser Cumb 56 D3
Mossfield Highld 87 D9
Mossgiel E Ayrs 67 D7
Mossie Angus 77 B7
Mossley Ches E 44 F2
Mossley Gtr Man 44 B3
Mossley Hill Mers 43 D6
Mosstodloch Moray 88 C3
Mosston Angus 77 C8
Mossy Lea Lancs 43 A8
Mosterton Dorset 8 D3
Moston Gtr Man 44 B2
Moston Shrops 34 C1
Moston Green Ches E 43 F10
Mostyn Flint 42 D4
Mostyn Quay Flint 42 D4
Motcombe Dorset 9 B7
Mothecombe Devon 5 G7
Motherby Cumb 56 D6
Motherwell N Lanark 68 E6
Mottingham London 19 D11
Mottisfont Hants 10 B2
Mottistone IoW 10 F3
Mottram in Longdendale Gtr Man 44 C3
Mottram St Andrew Ches E 44 E2
Mouilpied Guern 11
Mouldsworth Ches W 43 E8
Moulin Perth 76 B2
Moulsecoomb Brighton 12 F2
Moulsford Oxon 18 C2
Moulsoe M Keynes 28 D6
Moulton Ches W 43 F9
Moulton Lincs 37 C9
Moulton N Yorks 58 F3
Moulton Northants 28 B4
Moulton Suff 30 B3
Moulton V Glam 14 D6
Moulton Chapel Lincs 37 D8
Moulton Eaugate Lincs 37 D9
Moulton St Mary Norf 39 E9
Moulton Seas End Lincs 37 C9
Mounie Castle Aberds 83 A9
Mount Corn 3 D6
Mount Corn 4 E2
Mount Highld 87 G12
Mount Bures Essex 30 E6
Mount Canisp Highld 87 D10
Mount Hawke Corn 2 E6
Mount Pleasant Ches E 44 G2
Mount Pleasant Derbys 35 D8
Mount Pleasant Derbys 45 H7
Mount Pleasant Flint 42 E5
Mount Pleasant Hants 10 E1
Mount Pleasant W Yorks 51 G8
Mount Sorrel Wilts 9 B9
Mount Tabor W Yorks 51 G6
Mountain W Yorks 51 F6
Mountain Ash = Aberpennar Rhondda 14 B6
Mountain Cross Borders 69 F10
Mountain Water Pembs 22 D4
Mountbenger Borders 70 H2
Mountfield E Sus 12 D6
Mountgerald Highld 87 E8
Mountjoy Corn 3 C7
Mountnessing Essex 20 B3
Mounton Mon 15 B11
Mountsorrel Leics 36 D1
Mousehole Corn 2 G3
Mousen Northumb 71 G10
Mouswald Dumfries 60 F6
Mow Cop Ches E 44 G2
Mowhaugh Borders 62 A4
Mowsley Leics 36 G2
Moxley W Mid 34 F5
Moy Highld 80 E6
Moy Highld 87 H10
Moy Hall Highld 87 H10
Moy Ho. Moray 87 E13
Moy Lodge Highld 80 E6
Moyles Court Hants 9 D10
Moylgrove Pembs 22 B6
Musadale Argyll 65 D7
Much Birch Hereford 26 E2
Much Cowarne Hereford 26 D3
Much Dewchurch Hereford 25 E11
Much Hadham Herts 29 G11
Much Hoole Lancs 49 G4
Much Marcle Hereford 26 E3
Much Wenlock Shrops 34 E2
Muchalls Aberds 83 D11
Muchelney Som 8 B3
Muchlarnick Corn 4 F3
Muchrachd Highld 86 H5
Muckernich Highld 87 F8
Mucking Thurrock 20 C3
Muckleford Dorset 8 E5
Mucklestone Staffs 34 B3
Muckleton Shrops 34 C1
Muckletown Aberds 83 A7
Muckley Corner Staffs 35 E6
Muckton Lincs 47 D7
Mudale Highld 93 F8
Muddiford Devon 6 C4
Mudeford Dorset 9 E10
Mudford Som 8 C4
Mudgley Som 15 G10
Mugdock Stirling 68 C4
Mugeary Highld 85 E9
Mugginton Derbys 35 A8
Muggleswick Durham 58 B1
Muie Highld 93 J9
Muir Aberds 82 E2
Muir of Fairburn Highld 86 F7
Muir of Fowlis Aberds 83 B7
Muir of Ord Highld 87 F8
Muir of Pert Angus 77 D7
Muirden Aberds 89 C7
Muirdrum Angus 77 D8
Muirhead Angus 76 D6
Muirhead Fife 76 G5
Muirhead N Lanark 68 D5
Muirhead S Ayrs 66 C6
Muirhouselaw Borders 70 H5
Muirhouses Falk 69 B9
Muirkirk E Ayrs 68 H5
Muirmill Stirling 68 B6
Muirshearlich Highld 80 E3
Muirskie Aberds 83 D10
Muirtack Aberds 89 E9
Muirton Highld 87 E10
Muirton Perth 76 E4
Muirton Perth 76 F2
Muirton Mains Highld 86 F7
Muirton of Ardblair Perth 76 C4
Muirton of Ballochy Angus 77 A9
Muiryfold Aberds 89 C7
Muker N Yorks 57 G11
Mulbarton Norf 39 E7
Mulben Moray 88 C3
Mulindry Argyll 64 C4
Mullardoch House Highld 86 H5
Mullion Corn 2 H5
Mullion Cove Corn 2 H5
Mumby Lincs 47 E9
Munderfield Row Hereford 26 C3
Munderfield Stocks Hereford 26 C3
Mundesley Norf 39 B9
Mundford Norf 38 F4
Mundham Norf 39 F9
Mundon Essex 20 A5
Mundurno Aberdeen 83 B11
Munerigie Highld 80 C4
Muness Shetland 96 C8
Mungasdale Highld 86 B2
Mungrisdale Cumb 56 C5
Munlochy Highld 87 F9
Munsley Hereford 26 D3
Munslow Shrops 33 G11
Murchington Devon 5 C7
Murcott Oxon 28 G2
Murkle Highld 94 D3
Murlaggan Highld 80 D2
Murlaggan Highld 80 E5
Murra Orkney 95 H3
Murrayfield Edin 69 C11
Murrow Cambs 37 E9
Mursley Bucks 28 F5
Murthill Angus 77 B7
Murthly Perth 76 D3
Murton Cumb 57 D9
Murton Durham 58 B4
Murton Northumb 71 F8
Murton York 52 D2
Musbury Devon 8 E1
Muscoates N Yorks 52 A2
Musdale Argyll 74 E2
Musselburgh E Loth 70 C2
Muston Leics 36 B4
Muston N Yorks 53 B6
Mustow Green Worcs 26 A5
Mutehill Dumfries 55 E9
Mutford Suff 39 G10
Muthill Perth 75 F11
Mutterton Devon 7 F9
Muxton Telford 34 D3
Mybster Highld 94 E3
Myddfai Carms 24 F4
Myddle Shrops 33 C10
Mydroilyn Ceredig 23 A9
Myerscough Lancs 49 F4
Mylor Bridge Corn 3 F7
Mynachlog-ddu Pembs 22 C6
Myndtown Shrops 33 G9
Mynydd Bach Ceredig 32 H3
Mynydd-bach Mon 15 B10
Mynydd Bodafon Anglesey 40 B6
Mynydd-isa Flint 42 F5
Mynyddygarreg Carms 23 F9
Mynytho Gwyn 40 G5
Myrebird Aberds 83 D9
Myrelandhorn Highld 94 E4
Myreside Perth 76 E5
Myrtle Hill Carms 24 E4
Mytchett Sur 18 F5
Mytholm W Yorks 50 G5
Mytholmroyd W Yorks 50 G6
Myton-on-Swale N Yorks 51 C10
Mytton Shrops 33 D10

N

Na Gearrannan W Isles 90 C6
Naast Highld 91 J13
Naburn York 52 E1
Nackington Kent 21 F8
Nacton Suff 31 D9
Nafferton E Yorks 53 D6
Nailbridge Glos 26 G3
Nailsbourne Som 7 D11
Nailsea N Som 15 D10
Nailstone Leics 35 E10
Nailsworth Glos 16 B5
Nairn Highld 87 F11
Nalderswood Sur 19 G9
Nancegollan Corn 2 F5
Nancledra Corn 2 F3
Nanhoron Gwyn 40 G4
Nannau Gwyn 32 C3
Nannerch Flint 42 F4
Nanpantan Leics 35 D11
Nanpean Corn 3 D8
Nanstallon Corn 3 C9
Nant-ddu Powys 25 G7
Nant-glas Powys 24 B6
Nant Peris Gwyn 41 E8
Nant Uchaf Denb 42 G3
Nant-y-Bai Carms 24 D4
Nant-y-cafn Neath 24 H5
Nant-y-derry Mon 25 H10
Nant-y-ffin Carms 23 C10
Nant-y-moel Bridgend 14 B5
Nant-y-pandy Conwy 41 C8
Nanternis Ceredig 23 A8
Nantgaredig Carms 23 D9
Nantgarw Rhondda 15 C7
Nantglyn Denb 42 F3
Nantgwyn Powys 32 H5
Nantlle Gwyn 41 E7
Nantmawr Shrops 33 C8
Nantmel Powys 25 B7
Nantmor Gwyn 41 F8
Nantwich Ches E 43 G9
Nantycaws Carms 23 E9
Nantyffyllon Bridgend 14 B4
Nantyglo Bl Gwent 25 G8
Naphill Bucks 18 B5
Nappa N Yorks 50 D4
Napton on the Hill Warks 27 B11
Narberth = Arberth Pembs 22 E6
Narborough Leics 35 F11
Narborough Norf 38 D3
Nasareth Gwyn 40 E6
Naseby Northants 36 H2
Nash Bucks 28 E4
Nash Hereford 25 B10
Nash Newport 15 C9
Nash Shrops 26 A3
Nash Lee Bucks 28 H5
Nassington Northants 37 F6
Nasty Herts 29 F10
Nateby Cumb 57 F9
Nateby Lancs 49 E4
Natland Cumb 57 H7
Naughton Suff 31 D7
Naunton Glos 27 F8
Naunton Worcs 26 E5
Naunton Beauchamp Worcs 26 C6
Navenby Lincs 46 G3
Navestock Heath Essex 20 B2
Navestock Side Essex 20 B2
Navidale Highld 93 H13
Nawton N Yorks 52 A2
Nayland Suff 30 E6
Nazeing Essex 29 H11
Neacroft Hants 9 E10
Neal's Green Warks 35 G9
Neap Shetland 96 H7
Near Sawrey Cumb 56 G5
Neasham Darl 58 E4
Neath = Castell-Nedd Neath 14 B3
Neath Abbey Neath 14 B3
Neatishead Norf 39 C9
Nebo Anglesey 40 A6
Nebo Ceredig 24 B2
Nebo Conwy 41 E10
Nebo Gwyn 40 E6
Necton Norf 38 E4
Nedd Highld 92 F4
Nedderton Northumb 63 E8
Nedging Tye Suff 31 D7
Needham Norf 39 G8
Needham Market Suff 31 C7
Needingworth Cambs 29 A10
Needwood Staffs 35 C7
Neen Savage Shrops 34 H2
Neen Sollars Shrops 26 A3
Neenton Shrops 34 G2
Nefyn Gwyn 40 F5
Neilston E Renf 68 E3
Neinthirion Powys 32 E5
Neithrop Oxon 27 D11
Nelly Andrews Green Powys 33 E8
Nelson Caerph 15 B7
Nelson Lancs 50 F4
Nelson Village Northumb 63 F8
Nemphlar S Lanark 69 F7
Nempnett Thrubwell N Som 15 E11
Nene Terrace Lincs 37 E8
Nenthall Cumb 57 B9
Nenthead Cumb 57 B9
Nenthorn Borders 70 G5
Nerabus Argyll 64 C3
Nercwys Flint 42 F5
Nerston S Lanark 68 E5
Nesbit Northumb 71 G8
Ness Ches W 42 E6
Nesscliffe Shrops 33 D9
Neston Ches W 42 E5
Neston Wilts 16 E5
Nether Alderley Ches E 44 E2
Nether Blainslie Borders 70 F4
Nether Booth Derbys 44 D5
Nether Broughton Leics 36 C2
Nether Burrow Lancs 50 B2
Nether Cerne Dorset 8 E5
Nether Compton Dorset 8 C4
Nether Crimond Aberds 89 F8
Nether Dalgliesh Borders 61 C8
Nether Dallachy Moray 88 B3
Nether Exe Devon 7 F8
Nether Glasslaw Aberds 89 C8
Nether Handwick Angus 76 C6
Nether Haugh S Yorks 45 C8
Nether Heage Derbys 45 G7
Nether Heyford Northants 28 C3
Nether Hindhope Borders 62 B3
Nether Howecleuch S Lanark 60 B6
Nether Kellet Lancs 49 C5
Nether Kinmundy Aberds 89 D10
Nether Langwith Notts 45 E9
Nether Leask Aberds 89 E10
Nether Lenshie Aberds 89 D6
Nether Monynut Borders 70 D6
Nether Padley Derbys 44 E6
Nether Park Aberds 89 C10
Nether Poppleton York 52 D1
Nether Silton N Yorks 58 G5
Nether Stowey Som 7 C10
Nether Urquhart Fife 76 G4
Nether Wallop Hants 17 H10
Nether Wasdale Cumb 56 F3
Nether Whitacre Warks 35 F8
Nether Worton Oxon 27 E11
Netheravon Wilts 17 G8
Netherbrae Aberds 89 C7
Netherbrough Orkney 95 G4
Netherburn S Lanark 69 F7
Netherbury Dorset 8 E3
Netherby Cumb 61 F9
Netherby N Yorks 51 E9
Nethercote Warks 28 B2
Nethercott Devon 6 C3
Netherend Glos 16 A2
Netherfield E Sus 12 E6
Netherhampton Wilts 9 B10
Netherlaw Dumfries 55 E10
Netherley Aberds 83 D10
Netherley Mers 43 D7
Nethermill Dumfries 60 E6
Nethermuir Aberds 89 D9
Netherplace E Renf 68 E4
Netherseal Derbys 35 D8
Netherthird E Ayrs 67 E8
Netherthong W Yorks 44 B5
Netherthorpe S Yorks 45 D9
Netherton Angus 77 B8
Netherton Devon 5 D9
Netherton Hants 17 F10
Netherton Mers 42 B6
Netherton Northumb 62 C5
Netherton Oxon 17 B11
Netherton Perth 76 B4
Netherton Stirling 68 C4
Netherton W Mid 34 G5
Netherton W Yorks 44 A5
Netherton W Yorks 51 H8
Netherton Worcs 26 D6
Nethertown Cumb 56 F1
Nethertown Highld 94 C5
Netherwitton Northumb 63 D7
Netherwood E Ayrs 68 H5
Nethy Bridge Highld 82 A2
Netley Hants 10 D3
Netley Marsh Hants 10 C2
Netteswell Essex 29 G11
Nettlebed Oxon 18 C4
Nettlebridge Som 16 G3
Nettlecombe Dorset 8 E4
Nettleden Herts 29 G7
Nettleham Lincs 46 E4
Nettlestead Kent 20 F3
Nettlestead Green Kent 20 F3
Nettlestone IoW 10 E5
Nettlesworth Durham 58 B3
Nettleton Lincs 46 B5
Nettleton Wilts 16 D5
Neuadd Carms 24 F3
Nevendon Essex 20 B4
Nevern Pembs 22 B5
New Abbey Dumfries 60 G5
New Aberdour Aberds 89 B8
New Addington London 19 E10
New Alresford Hants 10 A4
New Alyth Perth 76 C5
New Arley Warks 35 G8
New Ash Green Kent 20 E3
New Barn Kent 20 E3
New Barnetby N Lincs 46 A4
New Barton Northants 28 B5
New Bewick Northumb 62 A6
New-bigging Angus 76 C5
New Bilton Warks 35 H10
New Bolingbroke Lincs 47 G7
New Boultham Lincs 46 E3
New Bradwell M Keynes 28 D5
New Brancepeth Durham 58 B3
New Bridge Wrex 33 A8
New Brighton Flint 42 F5
New Brighton Mers 42 C6
New Brinsley Notts 45 G8
New Broughton Wrex 42 G6
New Buckenham Norf 39 F6
New Byth Aberds 89 C8
New Catton Norf 39 D8
New Cheriton Hants 10 B4
New Costessey Norf 39 D7
New Cowper Cumb 56 B3
New Cross Ceredig 32 H2
New Cross London 19 D10
New Cumnock E Ayrs 67 E9
New Deer Aberds 89 D8
New Delaval Northumb 63 F8
New Duston Northants 28 B4
New Earswick York 52 D2
New Edlington S Yorks 45 C9
New Elgin Moray 88 B2
New Ellerby E Yorks 53 F7
New Eltham London 19 D11
New End Worcs 27 C7
New Farnley W Yorks 51 F8
New Ferry Mers 42 D6
New Fryston W Yorks 51 G10
New Galloway Dumfries 55 B9
New Gilston Fife 77 G7
New Grimsby Scilly 2 C2
New Hainford Norf 39 D8
New Hartley Northumb 63 F9
New Haw Sur 19 E7
New Hedges Pembs 22 F6
New Herrington T&W 58 A4
New Hinksey Oxon 18 A2
New Holkham Norf 38 B4
New Holland N Lincs 53 G6
New Houghton Derbys 45 F8
New Houghton Norf 38 C3
New Houses N Yorks 50 B4
New Humberstone Leicester 36 E2
New Hutton Cumb 57 G7
New Hythe Kent 20 F4
New Inn Carms 23 C9
New Inn Mon 15 A10
New Inn Pembs 22 C5
New Inn Torf 15 B9
New Invention Shrops 33 H8
New Invention W Mid 34 E5
New Kelso Highld 86 G2
New Kingston Notts 35 C11
New Lanark S Lanark 69 F7
New Lane Lancs 43 A7
New Lane End Warr 43 C9
New Leake Lincs 47 G8
New Leeds Aberds 89 C9
New Longton Lancs 49 G5
New Luce Dumfries 54 C4
New Malden London 19 E9
New Marske Redcar 59 D7
New Marton Shrops 33 B9
New Micklefield W Yorks 51 F10
New Mill Aberds 83 E9
New Mill Herts 28 G6
New Mill W Yorks 44 B5
New Mill Wilts 17 E8
New Mills Ches E 43 D10
New Mills Corn 3 D7
New Mills Derbys 44 D3
New Mills Powys 33 E6
New Milton Hants 9 E11
New Moat Pembs 22 D5
New Ollerton Notts 45 F10
New Oscott W Mid 35 F6
New Park N Yorks 51 D8
New Pitsligo Aberds 89 C8
New Polzeath Corn 3 B8
New Quay = Ceinewydd Ceredig 23 A8
New Rackheath Norf 39 D8
New Radnor Powys 25 B9
New Rent Cumb 56 C6
New Ridley Northumb 62 H6
New Road Side N Yorks 50 E5
New Romney Kent 13 D9
New Rossington S Yorks 45 C10
New Row Ceredig 24 A4
New Row Lancs 50 F2
New Row N Yorks 59 E7
New Sarum Wilts 9 A10
New Silksworth T&W 58 A4
New Stevenston N Lanark 68 E6
New Street Staffs 44 G4
New Street Lane Shrops 34 B2
New Swanage Dorset 9 F9
New Totley S Yorks 45 E7
New Town E Loth 70 C3
New Tredegar = Tredegar Newydd Caerph 15 A7
New Trows S Lanark 69 G7
New Ulva Argyll 72 E6
New Walsoken Cambs 37 E10
New Waltham NE Lincs 46 B6
New Whittington Derbys 45 E7
New Wimpole Cambs 29 D10
New Winton E Loth 70 C3
New Yatt Oxon 27 G10
New York Lincs 46 G6
New York N Yorks 51 C7
Newall W Yorks 51 E7
Newark Orkney 95 D8
Newark Phoro 37 E8
Newark-on-Trent Notts 45 G11
Newarthill N Lanark 68 E6
Newbarns Cumb 49 B2
Newbattle Midloth 70 D2
Newbiggin Cumb 49 C2
Newbiggin Cumb 56 D6
Newbiggin Cumb 56 G2
Newbiggin Cumb 57 B7
Newbiggin Cumb 57 D8
Newbiggin Durham 57 D11
Newbiggin N Yorks 57 G11
Newbiggin N Yorks 57 H11
Newbiggin-by-the-Sea Northumb 63 E9
Newbiggin-on-Lune Cumb 57 F9
Newbigging Angus 77 D7
Newbigging Angus 77 D8
Newbigging S Lanark 69 F9
Newbold Derbys 45 E7
Newbold Leics 35 D10
Newbold on Avon Warks 35 H10
Newbold on Stour Warks 27 D9
Newbold Pacey Warks 27 C9
Newbold Verdon Leics 35 E10
Newborough Anglesey 40 D6
Newborough Phoro 37 E8
Newborough Staffs 35 C7
Newbottle Northants 28 E2
Newbottle T&W 58 A4
Newbourne Suff 31 D9
Newbridge Caerph 15 B8
Newbridge Ceredig 23 A10
Newbridge Corn 2 F3
Newbridge Corn 4 E4
Newbridge Dumfries 60 F5
Newbridge Edin 69 C10
Newbridge Hants 10 C1
Newbridge IoW 10 F3
Newbridge Pembs 22 C4
Newbridge Green Worcs 26 E5
Newbridge-on-Usk Mon 15 B9
Newbridge on Wye Powys 25 C7
Newbrough Northumb 62 G4
Newbuildings Devon 7 F6
Newburgh Aberds 89 C9
Newburgh Aberds 89 F9
Newburgh Borders 61 B9
Newburgh Fife 76 F5
Newburgh Lancs 43 A7
Newburn T&W 63 G7
Newbury W Berks 17 E11
Newbury Park London 19 C11
Newby Cumb 57 D7
Newby Lancs 50 E4
Newby N Yorks 50 B3
Newby N Yorks 58 E6
Newby N Yorks 59 G11
Newby Bridge Cumb 56 H5
Newby East Cumb 61 H10
Newby West Cumb 56 A5
Newby Wiske N Yorks 58 H4
Newcastle Mon 25 G11
Newcastle Shrops 33 G8
Newcastle Emlyn = Castell Newydd Emlyn Carms 23 B8
Newcastle-under-Lyme Staffs 44 H2
Newcastle Upon Tyne T&W 63 G8
Newcastleton or Copshaw Holm Borders 61 E10
Newchapel Pembs 23 C7
Newchapel Powys 32 G5
Newchapel Staffs 44 G2
Newchapel Sur 12 B2
Newchurch Carms 23 D8
Newchurch IoW 10 F4
Newchurch Kent 13 C9
Newchurch Lancs 50 F4
Newchurch Mon 15 B10
Newchurch Powys 25 C9
Newchurch Staffs 35 C7
Newcott Devon 7 F11
Newcraighall Edin 70 C2
Newdigate Sur 19 G8
Newell Green Brack 18 D5
Newenden Kent 13 D7
Newent Glos 26 F4
Newerne Glos 16 A3
Newfield Durham 58 C3
Newfield Highld 87 D10
Newford Scilly 2 C3
Newfound Hants 18 F2
Newgale Pembs 22 D3
Newgate Norf 39 A6
Newgate Street Herts 19 A10
Newhall Ches E 43 H9
Newhall Derbys 35 C8
Newhall House Highld 87 E9
Newhall Point Highld 87 E10
Newham Northumb 71 H10
Newham Hall Northumb 71 H10
Newhaven Derbys 44 G5
Newhaven E Sus 12 F3
Newhaven Edin 69 C11
Newhey Gtr Man 44 A3
Newholm N Yorks 59 E9
Newhouse N Lanark 68 D6
Newick E Sus 12 D3
Newingreen Kent 13 C10
Newington Kent 20 E5
Newington Kent 21 E10
Newington Kent 21 H8
Newington Notts 45 C10
Newington Oxon 18 B3
Newington Shrops 33 G10
Newland Glos 26 H2
Newland Hull 53 F6
Newland N Yorks 52 G2
Newland Worcs 26 D4
Newlandrig Midloth 70 D2
Newlands Borders 61 D11
Newlands Highld 87 G10
Newlands Moray 88 C3
Newlands Northumb 62 H6
Newland's Corner Sur 19 G7
Newlands of Geise Highld 94 D2
Newlands of Tynet Moray 88 B3
Newlands Park Anglesey 40 B4
Newlandsmuir S Lanark 68 E5
Newlot Orkney 95 G6
Newlyn Corn 2 G3
Newmachar Aberds 83 B10
Newmains N Lanark 69 E7
Newmarket Suff 30 B3
Newmarket W Isles 91 D9
Newmill Borders 61 B10
Newmill Corn 2 F3
Newmill Moray 88 C4
Newmill of Inshewan Angus 77 A7
Newmills of Boyne Aberds 88 C5
Newmiln Perth 76 D4
Newmilns E Ayrs 67 C8
Newnham Cambs 29 C11
Newnham Glos 26 G3
Newnham Hants 18 F4
Newnham Herts 29 E9
Newnham Kent 20 F6
Newnham Northants 28 C2
Newnham Bridge Worcs 26 B3
Newpark Fife 77 F7
Newport Devon 6 C4
Newport E Yorks 52 F4
Newport Essex 30 E2
Newport Highld 94 H3
Newport IoW 10 F4
Newport = Casnewydd Newport 15 C9
Newport Norf 39 D11
Newport = Trefdraeth Pembs 22 C5
Newport Telford 34 D3
Newport-on-Tay Fife 77 E7
Newport Pagnell M Keynes 28 D5
Newpound Common W Sus 11 B9
Newquay Corn 3 C7
Newsbank Ches E 44 F2
Newseat Aberds 89 D10
Newseat Aberds 89 E7
Newsham N Yorks 51 A9
Newsham N Yorks 58 E2
Newsham Northumb 63 F9
Newsholme E Yorks 52 G3
Newsholme Lancs 50 D4
Newsome W Yorks 44 A5
Newstead Borders 70 G4
Newstead Northumb 71 H10
Newstead Notts 45 G9
Newthorpe N Yorks 51 F10
Newton Argyll 73 D9
Newton Borders 62 A1
Newton Bridgend 14 D4
Newton Cambs 29 D11
Newton Cambs 37 D10
Newton Cardiff 15 D8
Newton Ches W 43 E8
Newton Ches W 43 F7
Newton Ches W 43 G8
Newton Cumb 49 B2
Newton Derbys 45 G8
Newton Dorset 9 C6
Newton Dumfries 61 D7
Newton Dumfries 61 F8
Newton Gtr Man 44 C3
Newton Hereford 25 E10
Newton Hereford 26 C2
Newton Highld 87 E10
Newton Highld 87 G10
Newton Highld 92 F5
Newton Highld 94 F5
Newton Lancs 49 F4
Newton Lancs 50 B1
Newton Lancs 50 D2
Newton Lincs 36 B6
Newton Moray 88 B1
Newton Norf 38 D4
Newton Northants 36 G4
Newton Northumb 62 G6
Newton Notts 36 A2
Newton Perth 75 D11
Newton S Lanark 68 D5
Newton S Lanark 69 G8
Newton S Yorks 45 B9
Newton Staffs 34 C6
Newton Suff 30 D6
Newton Swansea 14 C2
Newton W Loth 69 C9
Newton Warks 35 H11
Newton Wilts 9 B11
Newton Abbot Devon 5 D9
Newton Arlosh Cumb 61 H7
Newton Aycliffe Durham 58 D3
Newton Bewley Hrtlpl 58 D5
Newton Blossomville M Keynes 28 C6
Newton Bromswold Northants 28 B6
Newton Burgoland Leics 35 E9
Newton by Toft Lincs 46 D4
Newton Ferrers Devon 4 G6
Newton Flotman Norf 39 F8
Newton Hall Northumb 62 G6
Newton Harcourt Leics 36 F2
Newton Heath Gtr Man 44 B2
Newton Ho. Aberds 83 A8
Newton Kyme N Yorks 51 E10
Newton-le-Willows Mers 43 C8
Newton-le-Willows N Yorks 58 H3
Newton Longville Bucks 28 E5
Newton Mearns E Renf 68 E4
Newton Morrell N Yorks 58 F3
Newton Mulgrave N Yorks 59 E8
Newton of Ardtoe Highld 79 D9
Newton of Balcanquhal Perth 76 F4
Newton of Falkland Fife 76 G5
Newton on Ayr S Ayrs 66 D6
Newton on Ouse N Yorks 51 D11
Newton-on-Rawcliffe N Yorks 59 G9
Newton-on-the-Moor Northumb 63 C7
Newton on Trent Lincs 46 E2
Newton Park Argyll 73 G10
Newton Poppleford Devon 7 H9
Newton Purcell Oxon 28 E3
Newton Regis Warks 35 E8
Newton Reigny Cumb 57 C6
Newton St Cyres Devon 7 G7
Newton St Faith Norf 39 D8
Newton St Loe Bath 16 E4
Newton St Petrock Devon 6 E3
Newton Solney Derbys 35 C8
Newton Stacey Hants 17 G11
Newton Stewart Dumfries 55 C7
Newton Tony Wilts 17 G9
Newton Tracey Devon 6 D4
Newton under Roseberry Redcar 59 E6
Newton upon Derwent E Yorks 52 E3
Newton Valence Hants 10 A6
Newtonairds Dumfries 60 E4
Newtongrange Midloth 70 D2
Newtonhill Aberds 83 D11
Newtonhill Highld 87 G8
Newtonmill Angus 77 A9
Newtonmore Highld 81 D9
Newtown Argyll 73 C9
Newtown Ches W 43 E8
Newtown Corn 2 G6
Newtown Cumb 56 B2
Newtown Cumb 61 G11
Newtown Derbys 44 D3
Newtown Devon 7 D6
Newtown Glos 16 A3
Newtown Glos 26 E6
Newtown Hants 10 B2
Newtown Hants 10 C4
Newtown Hants 10 C1
Newtown Hants 10 C5
Newtown Hants 10 D3
Newtown Hants 17 E11
Newtown Hereford 26 D3
Newtown Highld 80 C5
Newtown IoM 48 E3
Newtown IoW 10 E3
Newtown Northumb 62 C6
Newtown Northumb 71 G8
Newtown Northumb 71 H9
Newtown Poole 9 E9
Newtown = Y Drenewydd Powys 33 F7
Newtown Shrops 33 B10
Newtown Staffs 44 F4
Newtown Staffs 44 F3
Newtown Wilts 9 B8
Newtown Linford Leics 35 E11
Newtown St Boswells Borders 70 G4
Newtown Unthank Leics 35 E10
Newtyle Angus 76 C5
Neyland Pembs 22 F4
Niarbyl IoM 48 E2
Nibley S Glos 16 C3
Nibley Green Glos 16 B4
Nibon Shetland 96 F5
Nicholashayne Devon 7 E10
Nicholaston Swansea 23 H1
Nidd N Yorks 51 C
Nigg Aberdeen 83 C1
Nigg Highld 87 D1
Nigg Ferry Highld 87 E1
Nightcott Som 7 D
Nilig Denb 42 G
Nine Ashes Essex 20 A
Nine Mile Burn Midloth 69 E1
Nine Wells Pembs 22 D
Ninebanks Northumb 57 A
Ninfield E Sus 12 E
Ningwood IoW 10 F
Nisbet Borders 70 H
Nisthouse Orkney 95 G
Nisthouse Shetland 96 G
Niton IoW 10 G
Nitshill Glasgow 68 D
No Man's Heath Ches W 43 H
No Man's Heath Warks 35 E
Noak Hill London 20 B
Noblethorpe S Yorks 44 B
Nobottle Northants 28 B
Nocton Lincs 46 F
Noke Oxon 28 G
Nolton Pembs 22 E
Nolton Haven Pembs 22 E
Nomansland Devon 7 E
Nomansland Wilts 10 C
Noneley Shrops 33 C1
Nonikiln Highld 87 D
Nonington Kent 21 F
Noonsbrough Shetland 96 H
Norbreck Blackpool 49 E
Norbridge Hereford 26 D
Norbury Ches E 43 H
Norbury Derbys 35 A
Norbury Shrops 33 F
Norbury Staffs 34 C
Nordelph Norf 38 E
Norden Gtr Man 44 A
Norden Heath Dorset 9 F
Nordley Shrops 34 F
Norham Northumb 71 F
Norley Ches W 43 E
Norleywood Hants 10 E
Norman Cross Cambs 37 F
Normanby N Lincs 52 H
Normanby N Yorks 52 A
Normanby Redcar 59 E
Normanby-by-Spital Lincs 46 D
Normanby by Stow Lincs 46 D
Normanby le Wold Lincs 46 C
Norman's Bay E Sus 12 F
Norman's Green Devon 7 F
Normanstone Suff 39 F1
Normanton Derby 35 B
Normanton Leics 36 A
Normanton Lincs 46 H
Normanton Notts 45 G1
Normanton Rutland 36 E
Normanton W Yorks 51 G
Normanton le Heath Leics 35 D
Normanton on Soar Notts 35 C1
Normanton-on-the-Wolds Notts 36 B
Normanton on Trent Notts 45 F1
Normoss Lancs 49 F
Norney Sur 18 G
Norrington Common Wilts 16 E
Norris Green Mers 43 C
Norris Hill Leics 35 D
North Anston S Yorks 45 D
North Aston Oxon 27 F1
North Baddesley Hants 10 C
North Ballachulish Highld 74 A
North Barrow Som 8 B
North Barsham Norf 38 B
North Benfleet Essex 20 C
North Bersted W Sus 11 D
North Berwick E Loth 70 B
North Boarhunt Hants 10 C
North Bovey Devon 5 C
North Bradley Wilts 16 F
North Brentor Devon 4 C
North Brewham Som 16 H
North Buckland Devon 6 B
North Burlingham Norf 39 D
North Cadbury Som 8 B
North Cairn Dumfries 54 B
North Carlton Lincs 46 E
North Carrine Argyll 65 H
North Cave E Yorks 52 F
North Cerney Glos 27 H
North Charford Wilts 9 C
North Charlton Northumb 63 A
North Cheriton Som 8 B
North Cliff E Yorks 53 E
North Cliffe E Yorks 52 F
North Clifton Notts 46 E
North Cockerington Lincs 47 C
North Coker Som 8 C
North Collafirth Shetland 96 E
North Common E Sus 12 D
North Connel Argyll 74 D
North Cornelly Bridgend 14 C
North Cotes Lincs 47 B
North Cove Suff 39 G1
North Cowton N Yorks 58 F
North Crawley M Keynes 28 D
North Cray London 19 D1
North Creake Norf 38 B
North Curry Som 8 B
North Dalton E Yorks 52 D
North Dawn Orkney 95 H
North Deighton N Yorks 51 D
North Duffield N Yorks 52 F
North Elkington Lincs 46 C
North Elmham Norf 38 C

North Elmshall W Yorks 45 A8
North End Bucks 28 F5
North End E Yorks 53 F8
North End Essex 30 G3
North End Hants 17 E11
North End Lincs 37 A8
North End N Som 15 E10
North End Ptsmth 10 D5
North End Som 8 B1
North End W Sus 11 D10
North Erradale Highld 91 J12
North Fambridge Essex 20 B5
North Fearns Highld 85 E10
North Featherstone W Yorks 51 G10
North Ferriby E Yorks 52 G5
North Frodingham E Yorks 53 D7
North Gluss Shetland 96 F5
North Gorley Hants 9 C10
North Green Norf 39 G8
North Green Suff 31 B10
North Greetwell Lincs 46 E4
North Grimston N Yorks 52 C4
North Halley Orkney 95 H6
North Halling Medway 20 E4
North Hayling Hants 10 D6
North Hazelrigg Northumb 71 G9
North Heasley Devon 7 C6
North Heath W Sus 11 B9
North Hill Cambs 37 H10
North Hill Corn 4 D3
North Hinksey Oxon 27 H11
North Holmwood Sur 19 G8
North Howden E Yorks 52 F3
North Huish Devon 5 F8
North Hykeham Lincs 46 F3
North Johnston Pembs 22 E4
North Kelsey Lincs 46 B4
North Kelsey Moor Lincs 46 B4
North Kessock Highld 87 G9
North Killingholme N Lincs 53 H7
North Kilvington N Yorks 58 H5
North Kilworth Leics 36 G2
North Kirkton Aberds 89 C11
North Kiscadale N Ayrs 66 D3
North Kyme Lincs 46 G5
North Lancing W Sus 11 D10
North Lee Bucks 28 H5
North Leigh Oxon 27 G10
North Leverton with Habblesthorpe Notts 45 D11
North Littleton Worcs 27 D7
North Lopham Norf 38 G6
North Luffenham Rutland 36 E5
North Marden W Sus 11 C7
North Marston Bucks 28 F4
North Middleton Midloth 70 E2
North Middleton Northumb 62 A6
North Molton Devon 7 D6
North Moreton Oxon 18 C2
North Mundham W Sus 11 D7
North Muskham Notts 45 G11
North Newbald E Yorks 52 F5
North Newington Oxon 27 E11
North Newnton Wilts 17 F8
North Newton Som 8 A1
North Nibley Glos 16 B4
North Oakley Hants 18 F2
North Ockendon London 20 C2
North Ormesby Mbro 58 D6
North Ormsby Lincs 46 C6
North Otterington N Yorks 58 H4
North Owersby Lincs 46 C4
North Perrott Som 8 D3
North Petherton Som 8 A1
North Petherwin Corn 4 C3
North Pickenham Norf 38 E4
North Piddle Worcs 26 C6
North Poorton Dorset 8 E4
North Port Argyll 74 E3
North Queensferry Fife 69 B10
North Radworthy Devon 7 C6
North Rauceby Lincs 46 H4
North Reston Lincs 47 D7
North Rigton N Yorks 51 E8
North Rode Ches E 44 F2
North Roe Shetland 96 E5
North Runcton Norf 38 D2
North Sandwick Shetland 96 D7
North Scale Cumb 49 C1
North Scarle Lincs 46 F2
North Seaton Northumb 63 E8
North Shian Argyll 74 C2
North Shields T&W 63 G9
North Shoebury Southend 20 C6
North Shore Blackpool 49 F3
North Side Cumb 56 D2
North Side Pboro 37 F8
North Skelton Redcar 59 E7
North Somercotes Lincs 47 C8
North Stainley N Yorks 51 B8
North Stainmore Cumb 57 E10
North Stifford Thurrock 20 C3
North Stoke Bath 16 E4
North Stoke Oxon 18 C3
North Stoke W Sus 11 C9
North Street Hants 10 A5
North Street Kent 21 F7
North Street Medway 20 D5
North Street W Berks 18 D3
North Sunderland Northumb 71 G11
North Tamerton Corn 6 G2
North Tawton Devon 6 F5
North Thoresby Lincs 46 C6
North Tidworth Wilts 17 G9
North Togston Northumb 63 C8
North Tuddenham Norf 38 D6
North Walbottle T&W 63 G7
North Walsham Norf 39 B8
North Waltham Hants 18 G2
North Warnborough Hants 18 F4
North Water Bridge Angus 83 G8
North Watten Highld 94 E4
North Weald Bassett Essex 19 A11
North Wheatley Notts 45 D11
North Whilborough Devon 5 E9
North Wick Bath 16 E2
North Willingham Lincs 46 D5
North Wingfield Derbys 45 F8
North Witham Lincs 36 C5
North Woolwich London 19 D11
North Wootton Dorset 8 C5
North Wootton Norf 38 C2
North Wootton Som 16 G2
North Wraxall Wilts 16 D5
North Wroughton Swindon 17 C8
Northacre Norf 38 F5
Northallerton N Yorks 58 G4
Northam Devon 6 D3
Northam Soton 10 C3
Northampton Northants 28 B4
Northaw Herts 19 A9
Northbeck Lincs 37 A6
Northborough Pboro 37 E7
Northbourne Kent 21 F10
Northbridge Street E Sus 12 D6
Northchapel W Sus 11 B8
Northchurch Herts 28 H6
Northcott Devon 6 G2
Northdown Kent 21 D10
Northdyke Orkney 95 F3
Northend Bath 16 E4
Northend Bucks 18 B4
Northend Warks 27 C10
Northenden Gtr Man 44 C2
Northfield Aberdeen 83 C11
Northfield Borders 71 D8
Northfield E Yorks 52 G6
Northfield W Mid 34 H6
Northfields Lincs 36 E6
Northfleet Kent 20 D3
Northgate Lincs 37 C7
Northhouse Borders 61 C10
Northiam E Sus 13 D7
Northill C Beds 29 D8
Northington Hants 18 H2
Northlands Lincs 47 G7
Northlea Durham 58 A5
Northleach Glos 27 G8
Northleigh Devon 7 G10
Northlew Devon 6 G4
Northmoor Oxon 17 A11
Northmoor Green or Moorland Som 8 A2
Northmuir Angus 76 B6
Northney Hants 10 D6
Northolt London 19 C8
Northop Flint 42 F5
Northop Hall Flint 42 F5
Northorpe Lincs 37 B8
Northorpe Lincs 37 D6
Northorpe Lincs 46 C2
Northover Som 8 B4
Northover Som 15 H10
Northowram W Yorks 51 G7
Northport Dorset 9 F8
Northpunds Shetland 96 L6
Northrepps Norf 39 B8
Northtown Orkney 95 J5
Northway Glos 26 E6
Northwich Ches W 43 E9
Northwick S Glos 16 C2
Northwold Norf 38 F3
Northwood Derbys 44 F6
Northwood IoW 10 E3
Northwood Kent 21 E10
Northwood London 19 B7
Northwood Shrops 33 B10
Northwood Green Glos 26 G4
Norton E Sus 12 F3
Norton Glos 26 F5
Norton Halton 43 D8
Norton Herts 29 E9
Norton IoW 10 F2
Norton Mon 25 G11
Norton Northants 28 B3
Norton Notts 45 E9
Norton Powys 25 B10
Norton S Yorks 51 H11
Norton Shrops 33 G10
Norton Shrops 34 E1
Norton Shrops 34 E3
Norton Stockton 58 D5
Norton Suff 30 B6
Norton W Sus 11 D8
Norton W Sus 11 E7
Norton Wilts 16 C5
Norton Worcs 26 C5
Norton Worcs 27 D7
Norton Bavant Wilts 16 G6
Norton Bridge Staffs 34 B4
Norton Canes Staffs 34 E6
Norton Canon Hereford 25 D10
Norton Corner Norf 39 C6
Norton Disney Lincs 46 G2
Norton East Staffs 34 E6
Norton Ferris Wilts 16 H4
Norton Fitzwarren Som 7 D10
Norton Green IoW 10 F2
Norton Hawkfield Bath 16 E2
Norton Heath Essex 20 A3
Norton in Hales Shrops 34 B3
Norton-in-the-Moors Stoke 44 G2
Norton-Juxta-Twycross Leics 35 E9
Norton-le-Clay N Yorks 51 B10
Norton Lindsey Warks 27 B9
Norton Malreward Bath 16 E3
Norton Mandeville Essex 20 A2
Norton-on-Derwent N Yorks 52 B3
Norton St Philip Som 16 F4
Norton sub Hamdon Som 8 C3
Norton Woodseats S Yorks 45 D7
Norwell Notts 45 F11
Norwell Woodhouse Notts 45 F11
Norwich Norf 39 E8
Norwick Shetland 96 B8
Norwood Derbys 45 D8
Norwood Hill Sur 19 G9
Norwoodside Cambs 37 F10
Noseley Leics 36 F3
Noss Shetland 96 M5
Noss Mayo Devon 4 G6
Nosterfield N Yorks 51 A8
Nostie Highld 85 F13
Notgrove Glos 27 F8
Nottage Bridgend 14 D4
Nottingham Nottingham 36 B1
Nottington Dorset 8 F5
Notton W Yorks 45 A7
Notton Wilts 16 E6
Nounsley Essex 30 G4
Noutard's Green Worcs 26 B4
Novar House Highld 87 E9
Nox Shrops 33 D10
Nuffield Oxon 18 C3
Nun Hills Lancs 50 G4
Nun Monkton N Yorks 51 D11
Nunburnholme E Yorks 52 E4
Nuncargate Notts 45 G9
Nuneaton Warks 35 F9
Nuneham Courtenay Oxon 18 B2
Nunney Som 16 G4
Nunnington N Yorks 52 B2
Nunnykirk Northumb 62 D6
Nunsthorpe NE Lincs 46 B6
Nunthorpe Mbro 59 E6
Nunthorpe York 52 D2
Nunton Wilts 9 B10
Nunwick N Yorks 51 B9
Nupend Glos 26 H4
Nursling Hants 10 C2
Nursted Hants 11 B6
Nutbourne W Sus 11 C9
Nutbourne W Sus 11 D6
Nutfield Sur 19 F10
Nuthall Notts 35 A11
Nuthampstead Herts 29 E11
Nuthurst W Sus 11 B10
Nutley E Sus 12 D3
Nutley Hants 18 G3
Nutwell S Yorks 45 B10
Nybster Highld 94 D5
Nyetimber W Sus 11 E7
Nyewood W Sus 11 B7
Nymet Rowland Devon 6 F6
Nymet Tracey Devon 7 F6
Nympsfield Glos 16 A5
Nynehead Som 7 D10
Nyton W Sus 11 D8

O

Oad Street Kent 20 E5
Oadby Leics 36 E2
Oak Cross Devon 6 G4
Oakamoor Staffs 35 A6
Oakbank W Loth 69 D9
Oakdale Caerph 15 B7
Oake Som 7 D10
Oaken Staffs 34 E4
Oakenclough Lancs 49 E5
Oakengates Telford 34 D3
Oakenholt Flint 42 E5
Oakenshaw Durham 58 C3
Oakenshaw W Yorks 51 G7
Oakerthorpe Derbys 45 G7
Oakes W Yorks 51 H7
Oakfield Torf 15 B9
Oakford Ceredig 23 A9
Oakford Devon 7 D8
Oakfordbridge Devon 7 D8
Oakgrove Ches E 44 F3
Oakham Rutland 36 E4
Oakhanger Hants 18 H4
Oakhill Som 16 G3
Oakhurst Kent 20 F2
Oakington Cambs 29 B11
Oaklands Herts 29 G9
Oaklands Powys 25 C7
Oakle Street Glos 26 G4
Oakley Bedford 29 C7
Oakley Bucks 28 G3
Oakley Fife 69 B9
Oakley Hants 18 F2
Oakley Oxon 18 A4
Oakley Poole 9 E9
Oakley Suff 39 H7
Oakley Green Windsor 18 D6
Oakley Park Powys 32 G5
Oakmere Ches W 43 F8
Oakridge Glos 16 A6
Oakridge Hants 18 F3
Oaks Shrops 33 E10
Oaks Green Derbys 35 B7
Oaksey Wilts 16 B6
Oakthorpe Leics 35 D9
Oakwoodhill Sur 19 H8
Oakworth W Yorks 50 F6
Oape Highld 92 J7
Oare Kent 21 E7
Oare Som 7 B7
Oare W Berks 18 D2
Oare Wilts 17 E8
Oasby Lincs 36 B6
Oathlaw Angus 77 B7
Oatlands N Yorks 51 D9
Oban Argyll 79 J11
Oban Highld 79 C11
Oborne Dorset 8 C5
Obthorpe Lincs 37 D6
Occlestone Green Ches W 43 F9
Occold Suff 31 A8
Ochiltree E Ayrs 67 D8
Ochtermuthill Perth 75 F11
Ochtertyre Perth 75 E11
Ockbrook Derbys 35 B10
Ockham Sur 19 F7
Ockle Highld 79 D8
Ockley Sur 19 H8
Ocle Pychard Hereford 26 D2
Octon E Yorks 52 C6
Octon Cross Roads E Yorks 52 C6
Odcombe Som 8 C4
Odd Down Bath 16 E4
Oddendale Cumb 57 E7
Odder Lincs 46 E3
Oddingley Worcs 26 C6
Oddington Glos 27 F9
Oddington Oxon 28 G2
Odell Bedford 28 C6
Odie Orkney 95 F7
Odiham Hants 18 F4
Odstock Wilts 9 B10
Odstone Leics 35 E9
Offchurch Warks 27 B10
Offenham Worcs 27 D7
Offham E Sus 12 E2
Offham Kent 20 F3
Offham W Sus 11 D9
Offord Cluny Cambs 29 B9
Offord Darcy Cambs 29 B9
Offton Suff 31 D7
Offwell Devon 7 G10
Ogbourne Maizey Wilts 17 D8
Ogbourne St Andrew Wilts 17 D8
Ogbourne St George Wilts 17 D9
Ogil Angus 77 A7
Ogle Northumb 63 F7
Ogmore V Glam 14 D4
Ogmore-by-Sea V Glam 14 D4
Ogmore Vale Bridgend 14 B5
Okeford Fitzpaine Dorset 9 C7
Okehampton Devon 6 G4
Okehampton Camp Devon 6 G4
Okraquoy Shetland 96 K6
Old Northants 28 A4
Old Aberdeen Aberdeen 83 C11
Old Alresford Hants 10 A4
Old Arley Warks 35 F8
Old Basford Nottingham 35 A11
Old Basing Hants 18 F3
Old Bewick Northumb 62 A6
Old Bolingbroke Lincs 47 F7
Old Bramhope W Yorks 51 E8
Old Brampton Derbys 45 E7
Old Bridge of Tilt Perth 81 G10
Old Bridge of Urr Dumfries 55 C10
Old Buckenham Norf 39 F6
Old Burghclere Hants 17 F11
Old Byland N Yorks 59 H6
Old Cassop Durham 58 C4
Old Castleton Borders 61 D11
Old Catton Norf 39 D8
Old Clee NE Lincs 46 B6
Old Cleeve Som 7 B9
Old Clipstone Notts 45 F10
Old Colwyn Conwy 41 C10
Old Coulsdon London 19 F10
Old Crombie Aberds 88 C5
Old Dailly S Ayrs 66 G5
Old Dalby Leics 36 C2
Old Deer Aberds 89 D9
Old Denaby S Yorks 45 C8
Old Edlington S Yorks 45 C9
Old Eldon Durham 58 D3
Old Ellerby E Yorks 53 F7
Old Felixstowe Suff 31 E10
Old Fletton Pboro 37 F7
Old Glossop Derbys 44 C4
Old Goole E Yorks 52 G3
Old Hall Powys 32 G5
Old Heath Essex 31 F7
Old Heathfield E Sus 12 D4
Old Hill W Mid 34 G5
Old Hunstanton Norf 38 A2
Old Hurst Cambs 37 H8
Old Hutton Cumb 57 H7
Old Kea Corn 3 E7
Old Kilpatrick W Dunb 68 C3
Old Kinnernie Aberds 83 C9
Old Knebworth Herts 29 F9
Old Langho Lancs 50 F3
Old Laxey IoM 48 D4
Old Leake Lincs 47 G8
Old Malton N Yorks 52 B3
Old Micklefield W Yorks 51 F10
Old Milton Hants 9 E11
Old Milverton Warks 27 B9
Old Monkland N Lanark 68 D6
Old Netley Hants 10 D3
Old Philpstoun W Loth 69 C9
Old Quarrington Durham 58 C4
Old Radnor Powys 25 C9
Old Rattray Aberds 89 C10
Old Rayne Aberds 83 A8
Old Romney Kent 13 D9
Old Sodbury S Glos 16 C4
Old Somerby Lincs 36 B5
Old Stratford Northants 28 D4
Old Thirsk N Yorks 51 A10
Old Town Cumb 50 A1
Old Town Cumb 57 B6
Old Town Northumb 62 D4
Old Town Scilly 2 C3
Old Trafford Gtr Man 44 C2
Old Tupton Derbys 45 F7
Old Warden C Beds 29 D8
Old Weston Cambs 37 H6
Old Whittington Derbys 45 E7
Old Wick Highld 94 E5
Old Windsor Windsor 18 D6
Old Wives Lees Kent 21 F7
Old Woking Sur 19 F7
Old Woodhall Lincs 46 F6
Oldany Highld 92 F4
Oldberrow Warks 27 B8
Oldborough Devon 7 F6
Oldbury Shrops 34 F3
Oldbury W Mid 34 G5
Oldbury Warks 35 F9
Oldbury-on-Severn S Glos 16 B3
Oldbury on the Hill Glos 16 C5
Oldcastle Bridgend 14 D5
Oldcastle Mon 25 F10
Oldcotes Notts 45 D9
Oldfallow Staffs 34 D5
Oldfield Worcs 26 B5
Oldford Som 16 F4
Oldham Gtr Man 44 B3
Oldhamstocks E Loth 70 C6
Oldland S Glos 16 D3
Oldmeldrum Aberds 89 F8
Oldshore Beg Highld 92 D4
Oldshoremore Highld 92 D5
Oldstead N Yorks 51 A11
Oldtown Aberds 83 A7
Oldtown of Ord Aberds 88 C6
Oldway Swansea 23 H10
Oldways End Devon 7 D7
Oldwhat Aberds 89 C8
Olgrinmore Highld 94 E2
Oliver's Battery Hants 10 B3
Ollaberry Shetland 96 E5
Ollerton Ches E 43 E10
Ollerton Notts 45 F10
Ollerton Shrops 34 C2
Olmarch Ceredig 24 C3
Olney M Keynes 28 C5
Olrig Ho. Highld 94 D3
Olton W Mid 35 G7
Olveston S Glos 16 C3
Olwen Ceredig 23 B10
Ombersley Worcs 26 B5
Ompton Notts 45 F10
Onchan IoM 48 E3
Onecote Staffs 44 G4
Onen Mon 25 G11
Ongar Hill Norf 38 C1
Ongar Street Hereford 25 B10
Onibury Shrops 33 H10
Onich Highld 74 A3
Onllwyn Neath 24 G5
Onneley Staffs 34 A3
Onslow Village Sur 18 G6
Onthank E Ayrs 67 B7
Openwoodgate Derbys 45 H7
Opinan Highld 85 A12
Opinan Highld 91 H13
Orange Lane Borders 70 F6
Orange Row Norf 37 C11
Orasaigh W Isles 91 F8
Orbliston Moray 88 C3
Orbost Highld 84 D7
Orby Lincs 47 F8
Orchard Hill Devon 6 D3
Orchard Portman Som 8 B1
Orcheston Wilts 17 G7
Orcop Hereford 25 F11
Orcop Hill Hereford 25 F11
Ord Highld 85 G11
Ordhead Aberds 83 B8
Ordie Aberds 82 C6
Ordiequish Moray 88 C3
Ordsall Notts 45 D10
Ore E Sus 13 E7
Oreton Shrops 34 G2
Orford Suff 31 D11
Orford Warr 43 C9
Orgreave Staffs 35 D7
Orlestone Kent 13 C8
Orleton Hereford 25 B11
Orleton Worcs 26 B3
Orlingbury Northants 28 A5
Ormesby Redcar 59 E6
Ormesby St Margaret Norf 39 D10
Ormesby St Michael Norf 39 D10
Ormiclate Castle W Isles 84 E2
Ormiscaig Highld 91 H13
Ormiston E Loth 70 D3
Ormsaigbeg Highld 78 E7
Ormsaigmore Highld 78 E7
Ormsary Argyll 72 F6
Ormsgill Cumb 49 B1
Ormskirk Lancs 43 B7
Orpington London 19 E11
Orrell Gtr Man 43 B8
Orrell Mers 42 C6
Orrisdale IoM 48 C3
Orroland Dumfries 55 E10
Orsett Thurrock 20 C3
Orslow Staffs 34 D4
Orston Notts 36 A3
Orthwaite Cumb 56 C4
Ortner Lancs 49 D5
Orton Cumb 57 F8
Orton Northants 36 H4
Orton Longueville Pboro 37 F7
Orton-on-the-Hill Leics 35 E9
Orton Waterville Pboro 37 F7
Orwell Cambs 29 C10
Osbaldeston Lancs 50 F2
Osbaldwick York 52 D2
Osbaston Shrops 33 C9
Osbournby Lincs 37 B6
Oscroft Ches W 43 F8
Ose Highld 85 D8
Osgathorpe Leics 35 D10
Osgodby Lincs 46 C4
Osgodby N Yorks 52 F2
Osgodby N Yorks 53 A6
Oskaig Highld 85 E10
Oskamull Argyll 78 G7
Osmaston Derby 35 B9
Osmaston Derbys 35 A8
Osmington Dorset 8 F6
Osmington Mills Dorset 8 F6
Osmotherley N Yorks 58 G5
Ospisdale Highld 87 C10
Ospringe Kent 21 E7
Ossett W Yorks 51 G8
Ossington Notts 45 F11
Ostend Essex 20 B6
Oswaldkirk N Yorks 52 B2
Oswaldtwistle Lancs 50 G3
Oswestry Shrops 33 C8
Otford Kent 20 F2
Otham Kent 20 F4
Othery Som 8 A2
Otley Suff 31 C9
Otley W Yorks 51 E8
Otter Ferry Argyll 73 E8
Otterbourne Hants 10 B3
Otterburn N Yorks 50 D4
Otterburn Northumb 62 D4
Otterburn Camp Northumb 62 D4
Otterham Corn 4 B2
Otterhampton Som 15 G8
Ottershaw Sur 19 E7
Otterswick Shetland 96 E7
Otterton Devon 7 H9
Ottery St Mary Devon 7 G10
Ottinge Kent 21 G8
Ottringham E Yorks 53 G8
Oughterby Cumb 61 H8
Oughtershaw N Yorks 50 A4
Oughterside Cumb 56 B3
Oughtibridge S Yorks 45 C7
Oughtrington Warr 43 D9
Oulston N Yorks 51 B11
Oulton Cumb 56 A4
Oulton Norf 39 C7
Oulton Staffs 34 B5
Oulton Suff 39 F11
Oulton W Yorks 51 G9
Oulton Broad Suff 39 F11
Oulton Street Norf 39 C7
Oundle Northants 36 G6
Ousby Cumb 57 C8
Ousdale Highld 94 H2
Ousden Suff 30 C4
Ousefleet E Yorks 52 G4
Ouston Durham 58 A3
Ouston Northumb 62 F6
Out Newton E Yorks 53 G9
Out Rawcliffe Lancs 49 E4
Outertown Orkney 95 G3
Outgate Cumb 56 G5
Outhgill Cumb 57 F9
Outlane W Yorks 51 H6
Outwell Norf 37 E11
Outwick Hants 9 C10
Outwood Sur 19 G10
Outwood W Yorks 51 G9
Outwoods Staffs 34 D3
Ovenden W Yorks 51 G6
Ovenscloss Borders 70 G3
Over Cambs 29 A10
Over Ches W 43 F9
Over S Glos 16 C2
Over Compton Dorset 8 C4
Over Green W Mid 35 F7
Over Haddon Derbys 44 F6
Over Hulton Gtr Man 43 B9
Over Kellet Lancs 49 B5
Over Kiddington Oxon 27 F11
Over Knutsford Ches E 43 E10
Over Monnow Mon 26 G2
Over Norton Oxon 27 F10
Over Peover Ches E 43 E10
Over Silton N Yorks 58 G5
Over Stowey Som 7 C10
Over Stratton Som 8 C3
Over Tabley Ches E 43 D10
Over Wallop Hants 17 H9
Over Whitacre Warks 35 F8
Over Worton Oxon 27 F11
Overbister Orkney 95 D7
Overbury Worcs 26 E6
Overcombe Dorset 8 F5
Overgreen Derbys 45 E7
Overleigh Som 15 H10
Overley Green Warks 27 C7
Overpool Ches W 43 E6
Overscaig Hotel Highld 92 G7
Overseal Derbys 35 D8
Oversland Kent 21 F7
Overstone Northants 28 B5
Overstrand Norf 39 A8
Overthorpe Northants 27 D11
Overton Aberdeen 83 B10
Overton Ches W 43 E8
Overton Dumfries 60 G5
Overton Hants 18 G2
Overton Lancs 49 D4
Overton N Yorks 52 D1
Overton Shrops 26 A2
Overton Swansea 23 H9
Overton W Yorks 51 H8
Overton = Owrtyn Wrex 33 A9
Overton Bridge Wrex 33 A9
Overtown N Lanark 69 E7
Oving Bucks 28 F4
Oving W Sus 11 D8
Ovingdean Brighton 12 F2
Ovingham Northumb 62 G6
Ovington Durham 58 E2
Ovington Essex 30 D4
Ovington Hants 10 A4
Ovington Norf 38 E5
Ovington Northumb 62 G6
Ower Hants 10 C2
Owermoigne Dorset 9 F6
Owlbury Shrops 33 F9
Owler Bar Derbys 44 E6
Owlerton S Yorks 45 D7
Owl's Green Suff 31 B9
Owlswick Bucks 28 H4
Owmby Lincs 46 B4
Owmby-by-Spital Lincs 46 D4
Owrtyn = Overton Wrex 33 A9
Owslebury Hants 10 B4
Owston Leics 36 E3
Owston S Yorks 45 A9
Owston Ferry N Lincs 46 B2
Owstwick E Yorks 53 F8
Owthorne E Yorks 53 G9
Owthorpe Notts 36 B2
Oxborough Norf 38 E3
Oxcombe Lincs 47 E7
Oxen Park Cumb 56 H5
Oxenholme Cumb 57 H7
Oxenhope W Yorks 50 F6
Oxenton Glos 26 E6
Oxenwood Wilts 17 F10
Oxford Oxon 28 H2
Oxhey Herts 19 B8
Oxhill Warks 27 D10
Oxley W Mid 34 E5
Oxley Green Essex 30 G6
Oxley's Green E Sus 12 D5
Oxnam Borders 62 B3
Oxshott Sur 19 E8
Oxspring S Yorks 44 B6
Oxted Sur 19 F10
Oxton Borders 70 E3
Oxton Notts 45 G10
Oxwich Swansea 23 H9
Oxwick Norf 38 C5
Oykel Bridge Highld 92 J6
Oyne Aberds 83 A8

P

Pabail Iarach W Isles 91 D10
Pabail Uarach W Isles 91 D10
Pace Gate N Yorks 51 D7
Packington Leics 35 D9
Padanaram Angus 77 B7
Padbury Bucks 28 E4
Paddington London 19 C9
Paddlesworth Kent 21 H8
Paddock Wood Kent 12 B5
Paddockhaugh Moray 88 C2
Paddockhole Dumfries 61 E8
Padfield Derbys 44 C4
Padiham Lancs 50 F3
Padog Conwy 41 E10
Padside N Yorks 51 D7
Padstow Corn 3 B8
Padworth W Berks 18 E3
Page Bank Durham 58 C3
Pagelsham Eastend Essex 20 B6
Pagham W Sus 11 E7
Paglesham Churchend Essex 20 B6
Paibeil W Isles 84 B2
Paible W Isles 90 H5
Paignton Torbay 5 E9
Pailton Warks 35 G10
Painscastle Powys 25 D8
Painshawfield Northumb 62 G6
Painsthorpe E Yorks 52 D4
Painswick Glos 26 H5
Pairc Shiaboist W Isles 90 C7
Paisley Renfs 68 D3
Pakefield Suff 39 F11
Pakenham Suff 30 B6
Pale Gwyn 32 B5
Palestine Hants 17 G9
Paley Street Windsor 18 D5
Palfrey W Mid 34 F6
Palgowan Dumfries 54 A6
Palgrave Suff 39 H7
Pallion T&W 63 H9
Palmarsh Kent 13 C10
Palnackie Dumfries 55 D11
Palnure Dumfries 55 C7
Palterton Derbys 45 F8
Pamber End Hants 18 F3
Pamber Green Hants 18 F3
Pamber Heath Hants 18 E3
Pamphill Dorset 9 D8
Pampisford Cambs 29 D11
Pan Orkney 95 J4
Panbride Angus 77 D8
Pancrasweek Devon 6 F1
Pandy Gwyn 32 E2
Pandy Mon 25 F10
Pandy Powys 32 E5
Pandy Wrex 33 B7
Pandy Tudur Conwy 41 D10
Panfield Essex 30 F4
Pangbourne W Berks 18 D3
Pannal N Yorks 51 D9
Panshanger Herts 29 G9
Pant Shrops 33 C8
Pant-glâs Powys 32 F3
Pant-glas Carms 23 D10
Pant-glas Gwyn 40 F6
Pant-glas Shrops 33 B8
Pant-lasau Swansea 14 B2
Pant Mawr Powys 32 G4
Pant-teg Carms 23 D9
Pant-y-Caws Carms 22 D6
Pant-y-dwr Powys 32 H5
Pant-y-ffridd Powys 33 E7
Pant-y-Wacco Flint 42 E4
Pant-yr-awel Bridgend 14 C5
Pantgwyn Carms 23 D10
Pantgwyn Ceredig 23 B7
Panton Lincs 46 E5
Pantperthog Gwyn 32 E3
Pantyffynnon Carms 24 G3
Pantymwyn Flint 42 F4
Panxworth Norf 39 D9
Papcastle Cumb 56 C3
Papigoe Highld 94 E5
Papil Shetland 96 K5
Papley Orkney 95 J5
Papple E Loth 70 C4
Papplewick Notts 45 G9
Papworth Everard Cambs 29 B9
Papworth St Agnes Cambs 29 B9
Par Corn 4 F1
Parbold Lancs 43 A7
Parbrook Som 16 H2
Parbrook W Sus 11 B9
Parc Gwyn 41 G10
Parc-Seymour Newport 15 B10
Parc-y-rhôs Carms 23 B10
Parcllyn Ceredig 23 A7
Pardshaw Cumb 56 D2
Parham Suff 31 B10
Park Dumfries 60 D5
Park Corner Oxon 18 C3
Park Corner Windsor 18 C5
Park End Mbro 58 E6
Park End Northumb 62 F4
Park Gate Hants 10 D4
Park Hill N Yorks 51 C9
Park Hill Notts 45 G10
Park Street W Sus 11 A10
Parkend Glos 26 H3
Parkeston Essex 31 E9
Parkgate Ches W 42 E5
Parkgate Dumfries 60 E6
Parkgate Kent 13 C7
Parkgate Sur 19 G9
Parkham Devon 6 D2
Parkham Ash Devon 6 D2
Parkhill Ho. Aberds 83 B10
Parkhouse Mon 15 A10
Parkhouse Green Derbys 45 F8
Parkhurst IoW 10 E3
Parkmill Swansea 23 H10
Parkneuk Aberds 83 F9
Parkstone Poole 9 E9
Parley Cross Dorset 9 E9
Parracombe Devon 6 B5
Parrog Pembs 22 C5
Parsley Hay Derbys 44 F5
Parson Cross S Yorks 45 C7
Parson Drove Cambs 37 E9
Parsonage Green Essex 30 H4
Parsonby Cumb 56 C3
Parson's Heath Essex 31 F7
Partick Glasgow 68 D4
Partington Gtr Man 43 C10
Partney Lincs 47 F8
Parton Cumb 56 D1
Parton Dumfries 55 B9
Parton Glos 26 F5
Partridge Green W Sus 11 C10
Parwich Derbys 44 G5
Passenham Northants 28 E4
Paston Norf 39 B9
Patchacott Devon 6 G3
Patcham Brighton 12 F2
Patching W Sus 11 D9
Patchole Devon 6 B5
Pateley Bridge N Yorks 51 C7
Paternoster Heath Essex 30 G6
Path of Condie Perth 76 F3
Pathe Som 8 A2
Pathhead Aberds 77 A10
Pathhead E Ayrs 67 E9
Pathhead Fife 69 A11
Pathhead Midloth 70 D2
Pathstruie Perth 76 F3
Patna E Ayrs 67 E7
Patney Wilts 17 F7
Patrick IoM 48 D2
Patrick Brompton N Yorks 58 G3
Patrington E Yorks 53 G9
Patrixbourne Kent 21 F8
Patterdale Cumb 56 E5
Pattingham Staffs 34 F4
Pattishall Northants 28 C3
Pattiswick Green Essex 30 F5
Patton Bridge Cumb 57 G7
Paul Corn 2 G3
Paulerspury Northants 28 D4
Paull E Yorks 53 G7
Paulton Bath 16 F3
Pavenham Bedford 28 C6
Pawlett Som 15 G9
Pawston Northumb 71 G7
Paxford Glos 27 E8
Paxton Borders 71 E8
Payhembury Devon 7 F9
Paythorne Lancs 50 D4
Peacehaven E Sus 12 F3
Peak Dale Derbys 44 E4
Peak Forest Derbys 44 E5
Peakirk Pboro 37 E7
Pearsie Angus 76 B6
Pease Pottage W Sus 12 C1
Peasedown St John Bath 16 F4
Peasemore W Berks 17 D11
Peasenhall Suff 31 B10
Peaslake Sur 19 G7
Peasley Cross Mers 43 C8
Peasmarsh E Sus 13 D7
Peaston E Loth 70 D3
Peastonbank E Loth 70 D3
Peat Inn Fife 77 G7
Peathill Aberds 89 B9
Peatling Magna Leics 36 F1
Peatling Parva Leics 36 G1
Peaton Shrops 33 G11
Peats Corner Suff 31 B8
Pebmarsh Essex 30 E5
Pebworth Worcs 27 D8
Pecket Well W Yorks 50 G5
Peckforton Ches E 43 G8
Peckham London 19 D10
Peckleton Leics 35 E10
Pedlinge Kent 13 C10
Pedmore W Mid 34 G5
Pedwell Som 15 H10
Peebles Borders 69 F11
Peel IoM 48 D2
Peel Common Hants 10 D4
Peel Park S Lanark 68 E5
Peening Quarter Kent 13 D7
Pegsdon C Beds 29 E8
Pegswood Northumb 63 E8
Pegwell Kent 21 E10
Peinchorran Highld 85 E10
Peinlich Highld 85 C9
Pelaw T&W 63 G8
Pelcomb Bridge Pembs 22 E4
Pelcomb Cross Pembs 22 E4
Peldon Essex 30 G6
Pellon W Yorks 51 G6
Pelsall W Mid 34 E6
Pelton Durham 58 A3
Pelutho Cumb 56 B3
Pelynt Corn 4 F3
Pemberton Gtr Man 43 B8
Pembrey Carms 23 F9
Pembridge Hereford 25 C10
Pembroke = Penfro Pembs 22 F4
Pembroke Dock = Doc Penfro Pembs 22 F4
Pembury Kent 12 B5
Pen-bont Rhydybeddau Ceredig 32 G2
Pen-clawdd Swansea 23 G10
Pen-ffordd Pembs 22 D5
Pen-groes-oped Mon 25 H10
Pen-llyn Anglesey 40 B5
Pen-lon Anglesey 40 D6
Pen-sarn Gwyn 32 C1
Pen-sarn Gwyn 40 F6
Pen-twyn Mon 26 H2
Pen-y-banc Carms 24 F3
Pen-y-bont Carms 23 D8
Pen-y-bont Gwyn 32 C2
Pen-y-bont Gwyn 32 E3
Pen-y-bont Powys 33 C8
Pen-y-bont ar Ogwr = Bridgend Bridgend 14 D5
Pen-y-bryn Gwyn 32 D2
Pen-y-bryn Pembs 22 B6
Pen-y-cae Powys 24 G5
Pen-y-cae-mawr Mon 15 B10
Pen-y-cefn Flint 42 E4
Pen-y-clawdd Mon 25 H11
Pen-y-coedcae Rhondda 14 C6
Pen-y-fai Bridgend 14 C4
Pen-y-garn Carms 23 C10
Pen-y-garn Ceredig 32 G2
Pen-y-garnedd Anglesey 41 C7
Pen-y-gop Conwy 32 A5
Pen-y-graig Gwyn 40 G3
Pen-y-groes Carms 23 E10
Pen-y-groeslon Gwyn 40 G4
Pen-y-Gwryd Hotel Gwyn 41 E8
Pen-y-stryt Denb 42 G4
Pen-yr-heol Mon 25 G11
Pen-yr-Heolgerrig M Tydf 25 H7
Penallt Mon 26 G2
Penally Pembs 22 G6
Penalt Hereford 26 F2
Penare Corn 3 E8
Penarlâg = Hawarden Flint 42 F6
Penarth V Glam 15 D7
Penbryn Ceredig 23 A7
Pencader Carms 23 C9
Pencaenewydd Gwyn 40 F6
Pencaitland E Loth 70 D3
Pencarnisiog Anglesey 40 C5
Pencarreg Carms 23 B10
Pencelli Powys 25 F7
Pencoed Bridgend 14 C5
Pencombe Hereford 26 C2
Pencoyd Hereford 26 F2
Pencraig Hereford 26 F2
Pencraig Powys 32 C6
Pendeen Corn 2 F2
Penderyn Rhondda 24 H6
Pendine Carms 23 F7
Pendlebury Gtr Man 43 B10
Pendleton Lancs 43 F3
Pendock Worcs 26 E4
Pendoggett Corn 3 B9
Pendomer Som 8 C4
Pendoylan V Glam 14 D6
Pendre Bridgend 14 C5
Penegoes Powys 32 E3
Penfro = Pembroke Pembs 22 F4
Pengam Caerph 15 B7
Penge London 19 D10
Pengenffordd Powys 25 E8
Pengorffwysfa Anglesey 40 A6
Pengover Green Corn 4 E3
Penhale Corn 2 H5
Penhale Corn 3 D8
Penhalvaen Corn 2 F6
Penhill Swindon 17 C8
Penhow Newport 15 B10
Penhurst E Sus 12 E5
Peniarth Gwyn 32 E2
Penicuik Midloth 69 D11
Peniel Carms 23 D9
Peniel Denb 42 F3
Penifiler Highld 85 D9
Peninver Argyll 65 F8
Penisarwaun Gwyn 41 D7
Penistone S Yorks 44 B6
Penjerrick Corn 3 F6
Penketh Warr 43 D8
Penkill S Ayrs 66 G5
Penkridge Staffs 34 D5
Penley Wrex 33 B10
Penllergaer Swansea 14 B2
Penllyn V Glam 14 D5
Penmachno Conwy 41 E9
Penmaen Swansea 23 H10
Penmaenan Conwy 41 C9
Penmaenmawr Conwy 41 C9
Penmaenpool Gwyn 32 D2
Penmark V Glam 14 E6
Penmarth Corn 2 F6
Penmon Anglesey 41 B8
Penmore Mill Argyll 78 F7
Penmorfa Ceredig 23 A8
Penmorfa Gwyn 41 F7
Penmynydd Anglesey 41 C7
Penn Bucks 18 B6
Penn W Mid 34 F4
Penn Street Bucks 18 B6
Pennal Gwyn 32 E3
Pennan Aberds 89 B8
Pennant Ceredig 24 B2
Pennant Denb 32 B6
Pennant Denb 42 G3
Pennant Powys 32 F4
Pennant Melangell Powys 32 C6
Pennar Pembs 22 F4
Pennard Swansea 23 H10
Pennerley Shrops 33 F9
Pennington Cumb 49 B2
Pennington Gtr Man 43 C9
Pennington Hants 10 E2
Penny Bridge Cumb 49 A3
Pennycross Argyll 79 J8
Pennygate Norf 39 C9
Pennygown Argyll 79 G8
Pennymoor Devon 7 E7
Pennywell T&W 63 H9
Penparc Ceredig 23 B7
Penparc Pembs 22 C3
Penparcau Ceredig 32 G1
Penperlleni Mon 15 A9
Penpillick Corn 4 F1
Penpol Corn 3 F7
Penpoll Corn 4 F2
Penpont Dumfries 60 D4
Penpont Powys 24 F6
Penrhôs Mon 25 G11
Penrherber Carms 23 C7
Penrhiw goch Carms 23 E10
Penrhiw-llan Ceredig 23 B8
Penrhiw-pâl Ceredig 23 B8
Penrhiwceiber Rhondda 14 B6
Penrhos Gwyn 40 G5
Penrhos Powys 24 G4
Penrhosfeilw Anglesey 40 B4
Penrhyn Bay Conwy 41 B10
Penrhyn-coch Ceredig 32 G2
Penrhyndeudraeth Gwyn 41 G8
Penrhynside Conwy 41 B10
Penrice Swansea 23 H9
Penrith Cumb 57 C7
Penrose Corn 3 B7
Penruddock Cumb 56 D6
Penryn Corn 3 F6
Pensarn Carms 23 E9
Pensarn Conwy 42 E2
Pensax Worcs 26 B4
Pensby Mers 42 D5
Penselwood Som 9 A6
Pensford Bath 16 E3
Penshaw T&W 58 A4
Penshurst Kent 12 B4
Pensilva Corn 4 E3
Penston E Loth 70 C3
Pentewan Corn 3 E9
Pentir Gwyn 41 D7
Pentire Corn 3 C6
Pentlow Essex 30 D5
Pentney Norf 38 D3
Penton Mewsey Hants 17 G10
Pentraeth Anglesey 41 C7
Pentre Carms 23 E10
Pentre Powys 33 F8
Pentre Powys 33 G6
Pentre Rhondda 14 B5
Pentre Shrops 33 D9
Pentre Wrex 33 A8
Pentre Wrex 33 B7
Pentre-bâch Ceredig 23 B10
Pentre-bach Powys 24 E6
Pentre Berw Anglesey 40 C6
Pentre-bont Conwy 41 E9
Pentre-celyn Denb 42 G4
Pentre-Celyn Powys 32 E4
Pentre-chwyth Swansea 14 B2
Pentre-cwrt Carms 23 C8
Pentre Dolau-Honddu Powys 24 D6
Pentre-dwr Swansea 14 B2
Pentre-galar Pembs 22 C6
Pentre-Gwenlais Carms 24 G3
Pentre Gwynfryn Gwyn 32 C1
Pentre Halkyn Flint 42 E5
Pentre-Isaf Conwy 41 D10
Pentre Llanrhaeadr Denb 42 F3
Pentre-llwyn-llŵyd Powys 24 C6
Pentre-llyn Ceredig 24 A3

Pentre-llyn cymmer Conwy 42 G2
Pentre Meyrick V Glam 14 D5
Pentre-poeth Newport 15 C8
Pentre-rhew Ceredig 24 C3
Pentre-tafarn-y-fedw Conwy 41 D10
Pentre-ty-gwyn Carms 24 E5
Pentrebach M Tydf 14 A6
Pentrebach Swansea 24 H3
Pentrebeirdd Powys 33 D7
Pentrecagal Carms 23 B8
Pentredwr Denb 42 H4
Pentrefelin Carms 23 D10
Pentrefelin Ceredig 24 D3
Pentrefelin Conwy 41 C10
Pentrefelin Gwyn 41 G7
Pentrefoelas Conwy 41 E10
Pentregat Ceredig 23 A8
Pentreheyling Shrops 33 F8
Pentre'r Felin Conwy 41 D10
Pentre'r-felin Powys 24 E6
Pentrich Derbys 45 G7
Pentridge Dorset 9 C9
Pentyrch Cardiff 15 C7
Penuchadre V Glam 14 D4
Penuwch Ceredig 24 B2
Penwithick Corn 3 D9
Penwyllt Powys 24 G5
Penybanc Carms 24 G3
Penybont Powys 25 B8
Penybontfawr Powys 33 C6
Penycae Wrex 42 H5
Penycwm Pembs 22 D3
Penyffordd Flint 42 F6
Penyffridd Gwyn 41 E7
Penygarnedd Powys 33 C7
Penygraig Rhondda 14 B5
Penygroes Gwyn 40 E6
Penygroes Pembs 22 C6
Penyrheol Caerph 15 C7
Penysarn Anglesey 40 A6
Penywaun Rhondda 14 A5
Penzance Corn 2 F3
Peopleton Worcs 26 C6
Peover Heath Ches E 43 E10
Peper Harow Sur 18 G6
Perceton N Ayrs 67 B6
Percie Aberds 83 D7
Percyhorner Aberds 89 B9
Periton Som 7 B8
Perivale London 19 C8
Perkinsville Durham 58 A3
Perlethorpe Notts 45 E10
Perranarworthal Corn 3 F6
Perranporth Corn 3 D6
Perranuthnoe Corn 2 G4
Perranzabuloe Corn 3 D6
Perry Barr W Mid 35 F6
Perry Green Herts 29 G11
Perry Green Wilts 16 C6
Perry Street Kent 20 D3
Perryfoot Derbys 44 D5
Pershall Staffs 34 B4
Pershore Worcs 26 D6
Pert Angus 83 G8
Pertenhall Bedford 29 B7
Perth Perth 76 E4
Perthy Shrops 33 B9
Perton Staffs 34 F4
Pertwood Wilts 16 H5
Peter Tavy Devon 4 D6
Peterborough Pboro 37 F7
Peterburn Highld 91 J12
Peterchurch Hereford 25 E10
Peterculter Aberdeen 83 C10
Peterhead Aberds 89 D11
Peterlee Durham 58 B5
Peter's Green Herts 29 G8
Peters Marland Devon 6 E3
Petersfield Hants 10 B6
Peterston super-Ely V Glam 14 D6
Peterstone Wentlooge Newport 15 C8
Peterstow Hereford 26 F2
Petertown Orkney 95 H4
Petham Kent 21 F8
Petrockstow Devon 6 F4
Pett E Sus 13 E7
Pettaugh Suff 31 C8
Petteridge Kent 12 B5
Pettinain S Lanark 69 F8
Pettistree Suff 31 C9
Petton Devon 7 D9
Petton Shrops 33 C10
Petts Wood London 19 E11
Petty Aberds 89 E7
Pettycur Fife 69 B11
Pettymuick Aberds 89 F9
Petworth W Sus 11 B8
Pevensey E Sus 12 F5
Pevensey Bay E Sus 12 F5
Pewsey Wilts 17 E8
Philham Devon 6 D1
Philiphaugh Borders 70 H3
Phillack Corn 2 F4
Philleigh Corn 3 F7
Philpstoun W Loth 69 C9
Phocle Green Hereford 26 F3
Phoenix Green Hants 18 F4
Pica Cumb 56 D2
Piccotts End Herts 29 H7
Pickering N Yorks 52 A3
Picket Piece Hants 17 G10
Picket Post Hants 9 D10
Pickhill N Yorks 51 A9
Picklescott Shrops 33 F10
Pickletillem Fife 77 E7
Pickmere Ches E 43 E9
Pickney Som 7 D10
Pickstock Telford 34 C3
Pickwell Devon 6 B3
Pickwell Leics 36 D3
Pickworth Lincs 36 B6
Pickworth Rutland 36 D5
Picton Ches W 43 E7
Picton Flint 42 D4
Picton N Yorks 58 F5
Piddinghoe E Sus 12 F3
Piddington Northants 28 C5
Piddington Oxon 28 G3
Piddlehinton Dorset 8 E6
Piddletrenthide Dorset 8 E6
Pidley Cambs 37 H9
Piercebridge Darl 58 E3
Pierowall Orkney 95 D5
Pigdon Northumb 63 E7
Pikehall Derbys 44 G5
Pilgrims Hatch Essex 20 B2
Pilham Lincs 46 C2
Pill N Som 15 D11
Pillaton Corn 4 E4
Pillerton Hersey Warks 27 D10
Pillerton Priors Warks 27 D9
Pilleth Powys 25 B9
Pilley Hants 10 E2
Pilley S Yorks 45 B7
Pilling Lancs 49 E4
Pilling Lane Lancs 49 E3
Pillowell Glos 26 H3
Pillwell Dorset 9 C6
Pilning S Glos 16 C2
Pilsbury Derbys 44 F5
Pilsdon Dorset 8 E3
Pilsgate Pboro 37 E6
Pilsley Derbys 44 E6
Pilsley Derbys 45 F8
Pilton Devon 6 C4
Pilton Northants 36 G6
Pilton Rutland 36 E5
Pilton Som 16 G2
Pilton Green Swansea 23 H9
Pimperne Dorset 9 D8
Pin Mill Suff 31 E9
Pinchbeck Lincs 37 C8
Pinchbeck Bars Lincs 37 C7
Pinchbeck West Lincs 37 C8
Pincheon Green S Yorks 52 H2
Pinehurst Swindon 17 C8
Pinfold Lancs 43 A6
Pinged Carms 23 F9
Pinhoe Devon 7 G8
Pinkneys Green Windsor 18 C5
Pinley W Mid 35 H9
Pinminnoch S Ayrs 66 G4
Pinmore S Ayrs 66 G5
Pinmore Mains S Ayrs 66 G5
Pinner London 19 C8
Pinvin Worcs 26 D6
Pinwherry S Ayrs 66 H4
Pinxton Derbys 45 G8
Pipe and Lyde Hereford 26 D2
Pipe Gate Shrops 34 A3
Piperhill Highld 87 F11
Piper's Pool Corn 4 C3
Pipewell Northants 36 G4
Pippacott Devon 6 C4
Pipton Powys 25 E8
Pirbright Sur 18 F6
Pirnmill N Ayrs 66 B1
Pirton Herts 29 E8
Pirton Worcs 26 D5
Pisgah Ceredig 32 H2
Pisgah Stirling 75 G10
Pishill Oxon 18 C4
Pistyll Gwyn 40 F5
Pitagowan Perth 81 G10
Pitblae Aberds 89 B9
Pitcairngreen Perth 76 E3
Pitcalnie Highld 87 D11
Pitcaple Aberds 83 A9
Pitch Green Bucks 18 A4
Pitch Place Sur 18 F6
Pitchcombe Glos 26 H5
Pitchcott Bucks 28 F4
Pitchford Shrops 33 E11
Pitcombe Som 8 A5
Pitcorthie Fife 77 G8
Pitcox E Loth 70 C5
Pitcur Perth 76 D5
Pitfichie Aberds 83 B8
Pitforthie Aberds 83 F10
Pitgrudy Highld 87 B10
Pitkennedy Angus 77 B8
Pitkevy Fife 76 G5
Pitkierie Fife 77 G8
Pitlessie Fife 76 G6
Pitlochry Perth 76 B2
Pitmachie Aberds 83 A8
Pitmain Highld 81 C9
Pitmedden Aberds 89 F8
Pitminster Som 7 E11
Pitmuies Angus 77 C8
Pitmunie Aberds 83 B8
Pitney Som 8 B3
Pitscottie Fife 77 F7
Pitsea Essex 20 C4
Pitsford Northants 28 B4
Pitsmoor S Yorks 45 D7
Pitstone Bucks 28 G6
Pitstone Green Bucks 28 G6
Pittendreich Moray 88 B1
Pittentrail Highld 93 J10
Pittenweem Fife 77 G8
Pittington Durham 58 B4
Pittodrie Aberds 83 A8
Pitton Wilts 9 A11
Pittswood Kent 20 G3
Pittulie Aberds 89 B9
Pity Me Durham 58 B3
Pityme Corn 3 B8
Pityoulish Highld 81 B11
Pixey Green Suff 39 H8
Pixham Sur 19 F8
Pixley Hereford 26 E3
Place Newton N Yorks 52 B4
Plaidy Aberds 89 C7
Plains N Lanark 68 D6
Plaish Shrops 33 F11
Plaistow W Sus 11 A9
Plaitford Wilts 10 C1
Plank Lane Gtr Man 43 C9
Plas-canol Gwyn 32 D1
Plas Gogerddan Ceredig 32 G2
Plas Llwyngwern Powys 32 E3
Plas Nantyr Wrex 33 B7
Plas-yn-Cefn Denb 42 E3
Plastow Green Hants 18 E2
Platt Kent 20 F3
Platt Bridge Gtr Man 43 B9
Platts Common S Yorks 45 B7
Plawsworth Durham 58 B3
Plaxtol Kent 20 F3
Play Hatch Oxon 18 D4
Playden E Sus 13 D8
Playford Suff 31 D9
Playing Place Corn 3 E7
Playley Green Glos 26 E4
Plealey Shrops 33 E10
Plean Stirling 69 B7
Pleasington Blackburn 50 G2
Pleasley Derbys 45 F9
Pleckgate Blackburn 50 F2
Plenmeller Northumb 62 G3
Pleshey Essex 30 G3
Plockton Highld 85 E13
Plocrapol W Isles 90 H6
Ploughfield Hereford 25 D10
Plowden Shrops 33 G9
Ploxgreen Shrops 33 E9
Pluckley Kent 20 G6
Pluckley Thorne Kent 13 B8
Plumbland Cumb 56 C3
Plumley Ches E 43 E10
Plumpton Cumb 57 C6
Plumpton E Sus 12 E2
Plumpton Green E Sus 12 E2
Plumpton Head Cumb 57 C7
Plumstead London 19 D11
Plumstead Norf 39 B7
Plumtree Notts 36 B2
Plungar Leics 36 B3
Plush Dorset 8 D6
Plwmp Ceredig 23 A8
Plymouth Plym 4 F5
Plympton Plym 4 F6
Plymstock Plym 4 F6
Plymtree Devon 7 F9
Pockley N Yorks 59 H7
Pocklington E Yorks 52 E4
Pode Hole Lincs 37 C8
Podimore Som 8 B4
Podington Bedford 28 B6
Podmore Staffs 34 B3
Point Clear Essex 31 G7
Pointon Lincs 37 B7
Pokesdown Bmouth 9 E10
Pol a Charra W Isles 84 G2
Polbae Dumfries 54 B5
Polbain Highld 92 H2
Polbathic Corn 4 F4
Polbeth W Loth 69 D9
Polchar Highld 81 C10
Pole Elm Worcs 26 D5
Polebrook Northants 37 G6
Polegate E Sus 12 F4
Poles Highld 87 B10
Polesworth Warks 35 E8
Polgigga Corn 2 G2
Polglass Highld 92 J3
Polgooth Corn 3 D8
Poling W Sus 11 D9
Polkerris Corn 4 F1
Polla Highld 92 D6
Pollington E Yorks 52 H2
Polloch Highld 79 E10
Pollok Glasgow 68 D4
Pollokshields Glasgow 68 D4
Polmassick Corn 3 E8
Polmont Falk 69 C8
Polnessan E Ayrs 67 E7
Polnish Highld 79 C10
Polperro Corn 4 F3
Polruan Corn 4 F2
Polsham Som 15 G11
Polstead Suff 30 E6
Poltalloch Argyll 73 D7
Poltimore Devon 7 G8
Polton Midloth 69 D11
Polwarth Borders 70 E6
Polyphant Corn 4 C3
Polzeath Corn 3 B8
Ponders End London 19 B10
Pondersbridge Cambs 37 F8
Pondtail Hants 18 F5
Ponsanooth Corn 3 F6
Ponsworthy Devon 5 D8
Pont Aber Carms 24 F4
Pont Aber-Geirw Gwyn 32 C3
Pont-ar-gothi Carms 23 D10
Pont ar Hydfer Powys 24 F5
Pont-ar-llechau Carms 24 F4
Pont Cwm Pydew Denb 32 B6
Pont Cyfyng Conwy 41 E9
Pont Cysyllte Wrex 33 A8
Pont Dolydd Prysor Gwyn 41 G9
Pont-faen Powys 24 E6
Pont Fronwydd Gwyn 32 C4
Pont-gareg Pembs 22 B6
Pont-Henri Carms 23 F9
Pont-Llogel Powys 32 D6
Pont Pen-y-benglog Gwyn 41 D8
Pont Rhyd-goch Conwy 41 D8
Pont-Rhyd-sarn Gwyn 32 C4
Pont Rhyd-y-cyff Bridgend 14 C4
Pont-rhyd-y-groes Ceredig 24 A4
Pont-rug Gwyn 41 D7
Pont Senni = Sennybridge Powys 24 F6
Pont-siân Ceredig 23 B9
Pont-y-gwaith Rhondda 14 B6
Pont-y-Pŵl = Pontypool Torf 15 A8
Pont-y-pant Conwy 41 E9
Pont y Pennant Gwyn 32 C5
Pont yr Afon-Gam Gwyn 41 F9
Pont-yr-hafod Pembs 22 D4
Pontamman Carms 24 G3
Pontantwn Carms 23 E9
Pontardawe Neath 14 A3
Pontarddulais Swansea 23 F10
Pontarsais Carms 23 D9
Pontblyddyn Flint 42 F5
Pontbren Araeth Carms 24 F3
Pontbren Llwyd Rhondda 24 H6
Pontefract W Yorks 51 G10
Ponteland Northumb 63 F7
Ponterwyd Ceredig 32 G3
Pontesbury Shrops 33 E9
Pontfadog Wrex 33 B8
Pontfaen Pembs 22 C5
Pontgarreg Ceredig 23 A8
Ponthir Torf 15 B9
Ponthirwaun Ceredig 23 B7
Pontllanfraith Caerph 15 B7
Pontlliw Swansea 14 A2
Pontllyfni Gwyn 40 E6
Pontlottyn Caerph 25 H8
Pontneddfechan Powys 24 H6
Pontnewydd Torf 15 B8
Pontrhydfendigaid Ceredig 24 B4
Pontrhydyfen Neath 14 B3
Pontrilas Hereford 25 F10
Pontrobert Powys 33 D7
Ponts Green E Sus 12 E5
Pontshill Hereford 26 F3
Pontsticill M Tydf 25 G7
Pontwgan Conwy 41 C9
Pontyates Carms 23 F9
Pontyberem Carms 23 E10
Pontyclun Rhondda 14 C6
Pontycymer Bridgend 14 B5
Pontyglasier Pembs 22 C6
Pontypool = Pont-y-Pŵl Torf 15 A8
Pontypridd Rhondda 14 C6
Pontywaun Caerph 15 B8
Pooksgreen Hants 10 C2
Pool Corn 2 E5
Pool W Yorks 51 E8
Pool o' Muckhart Clack 76 G3
Pool Quay Powys 33 D8
Poole Poole 9 E9
Poole Keynes Glos 16 B6
Poolend Staffs 44 G3
Poolewe Highld 91 J13
Pooley Bridge Cumb 56 D6
Poolfold Staffs 44 G2
Poolhill Glos 26 F4
Poolsbrook Derbys 45 E8
Pootings Kent 19 G11
Pope Hill Pembs 22 E4
Popeswood Brack 18 E5
Popham Hants 18 G2
Poplar London 19 C10
Popley Hants 18 F3
Porchester Nottingham 36 A1
Porchfield IoW 10 E3
Porin Highld 86 F6
Poringland Norf 39 E8
Porkellis Corn 2 F5
Porlock Som 7 B7
Porlock Weir Som 7 B7
Port Ann Argyll 73 E8
Port Appin Argyll 74 C2
Port Arthur Shetland 96 K5
Port Askaig Argyll 64 B5
Port Bannatyne Argyll 73 G9
Port Carlisle Cumb 61 G8
Port Charlotte Argyll 64 C3
Port Clarence Stockton 58 D5
Port Driseach Argyll 73 F8
Port e Vullen IoM 48 C4
Port Ellen Argyll 64 D4
Port Elphinstone Aberds 83 B9
Port Erin IoM 48 F1
Port Erroll Aberds 89 E10
Port-Eynon Swansea 23 H9
Port Gaverne Corn 3 A9
Port Glasgow Invclyd 68 C2
Port Henderson Highld 85 A12
Port Isaac Corn 3 A8
Port Lamont Argyll 73 F9
Port Lion Pembs 22 F4
Port Logan Dumfries 54 E3
Port Mholair W Isles 91 D10
Port Mor Highld 78 D7
Port Mulgrave N Yorks 59 E8
Port Nan Giùran W Isles 91 D10
Port nan Long W Isles 84 A3
Port Nis W Isles 91 A10
Port of Menteith Stirling 75 G8
Port Quin Corn 3 A8
Port Ramsay Argyll 79 G11
Port St Mary IoM 48 F2
Port Sunlight Mers 42 D6
Port Talbot Neath 14 B3
Port Tennant Swansea 14 B2
Port Wemyss Argyll 64 C2
Port William Dumfries 54 E6
Portachoillan Argyll 72 H6
Portavadie Argyll 73 G8
Portbury N Som 15 D11
Portchester Hants 10 D5
Portclair Highld 80 B6
Portencalzie Dumfries 54 B3
Portencross N Ayrs 66 B4
Portesham Dorset 8 F5
Portessie Moray 88 B4
Portfield Gate Pembs 22 E4
Portgate Devon 4 C5
Portgordon Moray 88 B3
Portgower Highld 93 H13
Porth Corn 3 C7
Porth Rhondda 14 B6
Porth Navas Corn 3 G6
Porth Tywyn = Burry Port Carms 23 F9
Porth-y-waen Shrops 33 C8
Porthaethwy = Menai Bridge Anglesey 41 C7
Porthallow Corn 3 G6
Porthallow Corn 4 F3
Porthcawl Bridgend 14 D4
Porthcothan Corn 3 B7
Porthcurno Corn 2 G2
Porthgain Pembs 22 C3
Porthill Shrops 33 D10
Porthkerry V Glam 14 E6
Porthleven Corn 2 G5
Porthllechog Anglesey 40 A6
Porthmadog Gwyn 41 G7
Porthmeor Corn 2 F3
Portholland Corn 3 E8
Porthoustock Corn 3 G7
Porthpean Corn 3 D9
Porthtowan Corn 2 E5
Porthyrhyd Carms 23 E10
Porthyrhyd Carms 24 E4
Portincaple Argyll 73 D11
Portington E Yorks 52 F3
Portinnisherrich Argyll 73 B8
Portinscale Cumb 56 D4
Portishead N Som 15 D10
Portkil Argyll 73 E11
Portknockie Moray 88 B4
Portlethen Aberds 83 D11
Portling Dumfries 55 D11
Portloe Corn 3 F8
Portmahomack Highld 87 C12
Portmeirion Gwyn 41 G7
Portmellon Corn 3 E9
Portmore Hants 10 E2
Portnacroish Argyll 74 C2
Portnahaven Argyll 64 C2
Portnalong Highld 85 E8
Portnaluchaig Highld 79 C9
Portnancon Highld 92 C7
Portnellan Stirling 75 E7
Portobello Edin 70 C2
Porton Wilts 17 H8
Portpatrick Dumfries 54 D3
Portreath Corn 2 E5
Portree Highld 85 D9
Portscatho Corn 3 F7
Portsea Ptsmth 10 D5
Portskerra Highld 93 C11
Portskewett Mon 15 C11
Portslade Brighton 12 F1
Portslade-by-Sea Brighton 12 F1
Portsmouth Ptsmth 10 D5
Portsmouth W Yorks 50 G5
Portsonachan Argyll 74 E3
Portsoy Aberds 88 B5
Portswood Soton 10 C3
Porttanachy Moray 88 B3
Portuairk Highld 78 E7
Portway Hereford 25 E11
Portway Worcs 27 A7
Portwrinkle Corn 4 F4
Poslingford Suff 30 D4
Postbridge Devon 5 D7
Postcombe Oxon 18 B4
Postling Kent 13 C10
Postwick Norf 39 E8
Potholm Dumfries 61 E9
Potsgrove C Beds 28 F6
Pott Row Norf 38 C3
Pott Shrigley Ches E 44 E3
Potten End Herts 29 H7
Potter Brompton N Yorks 52 B5
Potter Heigham Norf 39 D10
Potter Street Essex 29 H11
Potterhanworth Lincs 46 F4
Potterhanworth Booths Lincs 46 F4
Potterne Wilts 16 F6
Potterne Wick Wilts 17 F7
Potternewton W Yorks 51 F9
Potters Bar Herts 19 A9
Potter's Cross Staffs 34 G4
Potterspury Northants 28 D4
Potterton Aberds 83 B11
Potterton W Yorks 51 F10
Potto N Yorks 58 F5
Potton C Beds 29 D9
Poughill Corn 6 F1
Poughill Devon 7 F7
Poulshot Wilts 16 F6
Poulton Glos 17 A8
Poulton Mers 42 C6
Poulton-le-Fylde Lancs 49 F3
Pound Bank Worcs 26 A4
Pound Green E Sus 12 D4
Pound Green IoW 10 F2
Pound Green Worcs 34 H3
Pound Hill W Sus 12 C1
Poundfield E Sus 12 C4
Poundland S Ayrs 66 H4
Poundon Bucks 28 F3
Poundsgate Devon 5 D8
Poundstock Corn 4 B3
Powburn Northumb 62 B6
Powderham Devon 5 C10
Powerstock Dorset 8 E4
Powfoot Dumfries 61 G7
Powick Worcs 26 C5
Powmill Perth 76 H3
Poxwell Dorset 8 F6
Poyle Slough 19 D7
Poynings W Sus 12 E1
Poyntington Dorset 8 C5
Poynton Ches E 44 D3
Poynton Green Telford 34 D1
Poystreet Green Suff 30 C6
Praa Sands Corn 2 G4
Pratt's Bottom London 19 E11
Praze Corn 2 F4
Praze-an-Beeble Corn 2 F5
Predannack Wollas Corn 2 H5
Prees Shrops 34 B1
Prees Green Shrops 34 B1
Prees Heath Shrops 34 B1
Prees Higher Heath Shrops 34 B1
Prees Lower Heath Shrops 34 B1
Preesall Lancs 49 E3
Preesgweene Shrops 33 B8
Prenderguest Borders 71 E8
Prendwick Northumb 62 B6
Prengwyn Ceredig 23 B9
Prenteg Gwyn 41 F7
Prenton Mers 42 D6
Prescot Mers 43 C7
Prescott Shrops 33 C10
Pressen Northumb 71 G7
Prestatyn Denb 42 D3
Prestbury Ches E 44 E3
Prestbury Glos 26 F6
Presteigne = Llanandras Powys 25 B10
Presthope Shrops 34 F1
Prestleigh Som 16 G3
Preston Borders 70 E6
Preston Brighton 12 F2
Preston Devon 5 D9
Preston Dorset 8 F6
Preston E Loth 70 C4
Preston E Yorks 53 F7
Preston Glos 17 A7
Preston Glos 26 E3
Preston Herts 29 F8
Preston Kent 21 E9
Preston Kent 21 E7
Preston Lancs 49 G5
Preston Northumb 71 H10
Preston Rutland 36 E4
Preston Shrops 33 D11
Preston Wilts 17 D7
Preston Wilts 17 D9
Preston Bagot Warks 27 B8
Preston Bissett Bucks 28 F3
Preston Bowyer Som 7 D10
Preston Brockhurst Shrops 33 C11
Preston Brook Halton 43 D8
Preston Candover Hants 18 G3
Preston Capes Northants 28 C2
Preston Crowmarsh Oxon 18 B3
Preston Gubbals Shrops 33 D10
Preston on Stour Warks 27 C9
Preston on the Hill Halton 43 D8
Preston on Wye Hereford 25 D10
Preston Plucknett Som 8 C4
Preston St Mary Suff 30 C6
Preston-under-Scar N Yorks 58 G1
Preston upon the Weald Moors Telford 34 D2
Preston Wynne Hereford 26 D2
Prestonmill Dumfries 60 H5
Prestonpans E Loth 70 C2
Prestwich Gtr Man 44 B2
Prestwick Northumb 63 F7
Prestwick S Ayrs 67 D6
Prestwood Bucks 18 A5
Price Town Bridgend 14 B5
Prickwillow Cambs 38 G1
Priddy Som 15 F11
Priest Hutton Lancs 49 B5
Priest Weston Shrops 33 F8
Priesthaugh Borders 61 C10
Primethorpe Leics 35 F11
Primrose Green Norf 39 D6
Primrose Valley N Yorks 53 B7
Primrosehill Herts 19 A7
Princes Gate Pembs 22 E6
Princes Risborough Bucks 18 A5
Princethorpe Warks 27 A11
Princetown Caerph 25 G8
Princetown Devon 5 D6
Prion Denb 42 F3
Prior Muir Fife 77 F8
Prior Park Northumb 71 E8
Priors Frome Hereford 26 E2
Priors Hardwick Warks 27 C11
Priors Marston Warks 27 C11
Priorslee Telford 34 D3
Priory Wood Hereford 25 D9
Priston Bath 16 E3
Pristow Green Norf 39 G7
Prittlewell Southend 20 C5
Privett Hants 10 B5
Prixford Devon 6 C4
Probus Corn 3 E7
Proncy Highld 87 B10
Prospect Cumb 56 B3
Prudhoe Northumb 62 G6
Ptarmigan Lodge Stirling 74 G6
Pubil Perth 75 C7
Puckeridge Herts 29 F10
Puckington Som 8 C2
Pucklechurch S Glos 16 D3
Pucknall Hants 10 B2
Puckrup Glos 26 E5
Puddinglake Ches W 43 F10
Puddington Ches W 42 E6
Puddington Devon 7 E7
Puddledock Norf 39 F6
Puddletown Dorset 9 E6
Pudleston Hereford 26 C2
Pudsey W Yorks 51 F8
Pulborough W Sus 11 C9
Puleston Telford 34 C3
Pulford Ches W 43 G6
Pulham Dorset 8 D6
Pulham Market Norf 39 G7
Pulham St Mary Norf 39 G8
Pulloxhill C Beds 29 E7
Pumpherston W Loth 69 D9
Pumsaint Carms 24 D3
Puncheston Pembs 22 D5
Puncknowle Dorset 8 F4
Punnett's Town E Sus 12 D5
Purbrook Hants 10 D5
Purewell Dorset 9 E10
Purfleet Thurrock 20 D2
Puriton Som 15 G9
Purleigh Essex 20 A5
Purley London 19 E10
Purley W Berks 18 D3
Purlogue Shrops 33 H8
Purls Bridge Cambs 37 G10
Purse Caundle Dorset 8 C5
Purslow Shrops 33 G9
Purston Jaglin W Yorks 51 H10
Purton Glos 16 A3
Purton Glos 16 A3
Purton Wilts 17 C7
Purton Stoke Wilts 17 B7
Pury End Northants 28 D4
Pusey Oxon 17 B10
Putley Hereford 26 E3
Putney London 19 D9
Putsborough Devon 6 B3
Puttenham Herts 28 G5
Puttenham Sur 18 G6
Puxton N Som 15 E10
Pwll Carms 23 F9
Pwll-glas Denb 42 G4
Pwll-trap Carms 23 E7
Pwll-y-glaw Neath 14 B3
Pwllcrochan Pembs 22 F4
Pwllgloyw Powys 25 E7
Pwllheli Gwyn 40 G5
Pwllmeyric Mon 15 B11
Pye Corner Newport 15 C9
Pye Green Staffs 34 D5
Pyecombe W Sus 12 E1
Pyewipe NE Lincs 46 A6
Pyle = Y Pîl Bridgend 14 C4
Pyle IoW 10 G3
Pylle Som 16 H3
Pymoor Cambs 37 G10
Pyrford Sur 19 F7
Pyrton Oxon 18 B3
Pytchley Northants 28 A5
Pyworthy Devon 6 F2

Q

Quabbs Shrops 33 G8
Quadring Lincs 37 B8
Quainton Bucks 28 G4
Quarley Hants 17 G9
Quarndon Derbys 35 A9
Quarrier's Homes Invclyd 68 D2
Quarrington Lincs 37 A6
Quarrington Hill Durham 58 C4
Quarry Bank W Mid 34 G5
Quarryford E Loth 70 D4
Quarryhill Highld 87 C10
Quarrywood Moray 88 B1
Quarter S Lanark 68 E6
Quatford Shrops 34 F3
Quatt Shrops 34 G3
Quebec Durham 58 B2
Quedgeley Glos 26 G5
Queen Adelaide Cambs 38 G1
Queen Camel Som 8 B4
Queen Charlton Bath 16 E3
Queen Dart Devon 7 E7
Queen Oak Dorset 9 A6
Queen Street Kent 20 G3
Queen Street Wilts 17 C7
Queenborough Kent 20 D6
Queenhill Worcs 26 E5
Queen's Head Shrops 33 C9
Queen's Park Bedford 29 D7
Queen's Park Northants 28 B4
Queensbury W Yorks 51 F7
Queensferry Edin 69 C10
Queensferry Flint 42 F6
Queenstown Blackpool 49 F3
Queenzieburn N Lanark 68 C5
Quemerford Wilts 17 E7
Quendale Shetland 96 M5
Quendon Essex 30 E2
Queniborough Leics 36 D2
Quenington Glos 17 A8
Quernmore Lancs 49 D5
Quethiock Corn 4 E4
Quholm Orkney 95 G3
Quicks Green W Berks 18 D2
Quidenham Norf 38 G6
Quidhampton Hants 18 F2
Quidhampton Wilts 9 A10
Quilquox Aberds 89 E9
Quina Brook Shrops 33 B11
Quindry Orkney 95 J5
Quinton Northants 28 C4
Quinton W Mid 34 G5
Quintrell Downs Corn 3 C7
Quixhill Staffs 35 A7
Quoditch Devon 6 G3
Quoig Perth 75 E11
Quorndon Leics 36 D1
Quothquan S Lanark 69 G8
Quoyloo Orkney 95 F3
Quoyness Orkney 95 H3
Quoys Shetland 96 B8
Quoys Shetland 96 G6

R

Raasay Ho. Highld 85 E10
Rabbit's Cross Kent 20 G4
Raby Mers 42 E6
Rachan Mill Borders 69 G10
Rachub Gwyn 41 D8
Rackenford Devon 7 E7
Rackham W Sus 11 C9
Rackheath Norf 39 D8
Racks Dumfries 60 F6
Rackwick Orkney 95 D5
Rackwick Orkney 95 J3
Radbourne Derbys 35 B8
Radcliffe Gtr Man 43 B10
Radcliffe Northumb 63 C8
Radcliffe on Trent Notts 36 B2
Radclive Bucks 28 E3
Radcot Oxon 17 B9
Raddery Highld 87 F10
Radernie Fife 77 G7
Radford Semele Warks 27 B10
Radipole Dorset 8 F5
Radlett Herts 19 B8
Radley Oxon 18 B2
Radmanthwaite Notts 45 F9
Radmoor Shrops 34 C2
Radmore Green Ches E 43 G8
Radnage Bucks 18 B4
Radstock Bath 16 F3
Radstone Northants 28 D2
Radway Warks 27 D10
Radway Green Ches E 43 G10
Radwell Bedford 29 C7
Radwell Herts 29 E9
Radwinter Essex 30 E3
Radyr Cardiff 15 C7
Rafford Moray 87 F13
Ragdale Leics 36 D2
Raglan Mon 25 H11
Ragnall Notts 46 E2
Rahane Argyll 73 E11
Rainford Mers 43 B7
Rainford Junction Mers 43 B7
Rainham London 20 C2
Rainham Medway 20 E5
Rainhill Mers 43 C7
Rainhill Stoops Mers 43 C8
Rainow Ches E 44 E3
Rainton N Yorks 51 B9
Rainworth Notts 45 G9
Raisbeck Cumb 57 F8
Raise Cumb 57 B9
Rait Perth 76 E5
Raithby Lincs 47 D7
Raithby Lincs 47 F7
Rake W Sus 11 B7
Rakewood Gtr Man 44 A3
Ram Carms 23 B10
Ram Lane Kent 20 G6
Ramasaig Highld 84 D6
Rame Corn 2 F6
Rame Corn 4 G5
Rameldry Mill Bank Fife 76 G6
Ramnageo Shetland 96 C8
Rampisham Dorset 8 D4
Rampside Cumb 49 C2
Rampton Cambs 29 B11
Rampton Notts 45 E11
Ramsbottom Gtr Man 50 H3
Ramsbury Wilts 17 D9
Ramscraigs Highld 94 H3
Ramsdean Hants 10 B6
Ramsdell Hants 18 F2
Ramsden Oxon 27 G10
Ramsden Bellhouse Essex 20 B4
Ramsden Heath Essex 20 B4
Ramsey Cambs 37 G8
Ramsey Essex 31 E9
Ramsey IoM 48 C4
Ramsey Forty Foot Cambs 37 G9
Ramsey Heights Cambs 37 G8
Ramsey Island Essex 30 H6
Ramsey Mereside Cambs 37 G8
Ramsey St Mary's Cambs 37 G8
Ramseycleuch Borders 61 B8
Ramsgate Kent 21 E10
Ramsgill N Yorks 51 B7
Ramshorn Staffs 44 H4
Ramsnest Common Sur 11 A8
Ranais W Isles 91 E9
Ranby Lincs 46 E6
Ranby Notts 45 D10
Rand Lincs 46 E5
Randwick Glos 26 H5
Ranfurly Renfs 68 D2
Rangag Highld 94 F3
Rangemore Staffs 35 C7
Rangeworthy S Glos 16 C3
Rankinston E Ayrs 67 E7
Ranmoor S Yorks 45 D7
Ranmore Common Sur 19 F8
Rannerdale Cumb 56 E3
Rannoch Station Perth 75 B7
Ranochan Highld 79 C11
Ranskill Notts 45 D10
Ranton Staffs 34 C4
Ranworth Norf 39 D9
Raploch Stirling 68 A6
Rapness Orkney 95 D6
Rascal Moor E Yorks 52 F4
Rascarrel Dumfries 55 E10
Rashiereive Aberds 89 F9
Raskelf N Yorks 51 B10
Rassau Bl Gwent 25 G8
Rastrick W Yorks 51 G7
Ratagan Highld 85 G14
Ratby Leics 35 E11
Ratcliffe Culey Leics 35 F9
Ratcliffe on Soar Leics 35 C10
Ratcliffe on the Wreake Leics 36 D2
Rathen Aberds 89 B10
Rathillet Fife 76 E6
Rathmell N Yorks 50 D4
Ratho Edin 69 C10
Ratho Station Edin 69 C10
Rathven Moray 88 B4
Ratley Warks 27 D10
Ratlinghope Shrops 33 F10
Rattar Highld 94 C4
Ratten Row Lancs 49 E4
Rattery Devon 5 E8
Rattlesden Suff 30 C6
Rattray Perth 76 C4
Raughton Head Cumb 56 B5
Raunds Northants 28 A6
Ravenfield S Yorks 45 C8
Ravenglass Cumb 56 G2
Raveningham Norf 39 F9
Ravenscar N Yorks 59 F10
Ravenscraig Invclyd 73 F11
Ravensdale IoM 48 C3
Ravensden Bedford 29 C7
Ravenseat N Yorks 57 F10
Ravenshead Notts 45 G9
Ravensmoor Ches E 43 G9
Ravensthorpe Northants 28 A3
Ravensthorpe W Yorks 51 G8
Ravenstone Leics 35 D10
Ravenstone M Keynes 28 C5
Ravenstonedale Cumb 57 F9
Ravenstown Cumb 49 B3
Ravenstruther S Lanark 69 F8
Ravensworth N Yorks 58 F2
Raw N Yorks 59 F10
Rawcliffe E Yorks 52 G2
Rawcliffe York 52 D1
Rawcliffe Bridge E Yorks 52 G2
Rawdon W Yorks 51 F8
Rawmarsh S Yorks 45 C8
Rawreth Essex 20 B4
Rawridge Devon 7 F11
Rawtenstall Lancs 50 G4
Raxton Aberds 89 E8
Raydon Suff 31 E7
Raylees Northumb 62 D5
Rayleigh Essex 20 B5
Rayne Essex 30 F4
Rayners Lane London 19 C8
Raynes Park London 19 E9
Reach Cambs 30 B2
Read Lancs 50 F3
Reading Reading 18 D4
Reading Street Kent 13 C8
Reagill Cumb 57 E8
Rearquhar Highld 87 B10
Rearsby Leics 36 D2
Reaster Highld 94 D4
Reawick Shetland 96 J5
Reay Highld 93 C12
Rechullin Highld 85 C13
Reculver Kent 21 E9
Red Dial Cumb 56 B4
Red Hill Worcs 26 C5
Red Houses Jersey 11
Red Lodge Suff 30 A3
Red Rail Hereford 26 F2
Red Rock Gtr Man 43 B8
Red Roses Carms 23 E7
Red Row Northumb 63 D8
Red Street Staffs 44 G2
Red Wharf Bay Anglesey 41 B7
Redberth Pembs 22 F5
Redbourn Herts 29 G8
Redbourne N Lincs 46 C3
Redbrook Mon 26 G2
Redbrook Wrex 33 A11
Redburn Highld 87 E8
Redburn Highld 87 G12
Redburn Northumb 62 G3
Redcar Redcar 59 D7
Redcastle Angus 77 B9
Redcastle Highld 87 G8
Redcliff Bay N Som 15 D10
Redding Falk 69 C8
Reddingmuirhead Falk 69 C8
Reddish Gtr Man 44 C2
Redditch Worcs 27 B7
Rede Suff 30 C5
Redenhall Norf 39 G8
Redesdale Camp Northumb 62 D4
Redesmouth Northumb 62 E4
Redford Aberds 83 F9
Redford Angus 77 C8
Redford Durham 58 C1
Redfordgreen Borders 61 B9
Redgorton Perth 76 E3
Redgrave Suff 38 H6
Redhill Aberds 83 C9
Redhill Aberds 89 E6
Redhill N Som 15 E11
Redhill Sur 19 F9
Redhouse Argyll 73 G7
Redhouses Argyll 64 B4
Redisham Suff 39 G10
Redland Bristol 16 D2
Redland Orkney 95 F4
Redlingfield Suff 31 A8
Redlynch Som 8 A6
Redlynch Wilts 9 B11
Redmarley D'Abitot Glos 26 E4
Redmarshall Stockton 58 D4
Redmile Leics 36 B3
Redmire N Yorks 58 G1
Redmoor Corn 4 E1
Rednal Shrops 33 C9
Redpath Borders 70 G4
Redpoint Highld 85 B12
Redruth Corn 2 E
Redvales Gtr Man 44 B
Redwick Newport 15 C1
Redwick S Glos 15 C1
Redworth Darl 58 D
Reed Herts 29 E1
Reedham Norf 39 E1
Reedness E Yorks 52 G
Reeds Beck Lincs 46 F
Reepham Lincs 46 E
Reepham Norf 39 C
Reeth N Yorks 58 G
Regaby IoM 48 C
Regoul Highld 87 F1
Reiff Highld 92 H
Reigate Sur 19 F
Reighton N Yorks 53 B
Reighton Gap N Yorks 53 B
Reinigeadal W Isles 90 G
Reiss Highld 94 E
Rejerrah Corn 3 D
Releath Corn 2 F
Relubbus Corn 2 F
Relugas Moray 87 G1
Remenham Wokingham 18 C
Remenham Hill Wokingham 18 C
Remony Perth 75 C1
Rempstone Notts 36 C
Rendcomb Glos 27 H
Rendham Suff 31 B1
Rendlesham Suff 31 C1
Renfrew Renfs 68 D
Renhold Bedford 29 C
Renishaw Derbys 45 E
Rennington Northumb 63 B
Renton W Dunb 68 C
Renwick Cumb 57 B
Repps Norf 39 D1
Repton Derbys 35 C
Reraig Highld 85 F1
Rescobie Angus 77 B
Resipole Highld 79 E1
Resolis Highld 87 E
Resolven Neath 14 A
Reston Borders 71 D
Reswallie Angus 77 B
Retew Corn 3 D
Retford Notts 45 D1
Rettendon Essex 20 B
Rettendon Place Essex 20 B
Revesby Lincs 46 F
Revesby Bridge Lincs 47 F
Rew Street IoW 10 E
Rewe Devon 7 G
Reydon Suff 39 H1
Reydon Smear Suff 39 H1
Reymerston Norf 38 E
Reynalton Pembs 22 F
Reynoldston Swansea 23 G
Rezare Corn 4 D
Rhôs Carms 23 C
Rhôs Neath 14 A
Rhŷd-y-foel Conwy 42 E
Rhaeadr Gwy = Rhayader Powys 24 B
Rhandirmwyn Carms 24 D
Rhayader = Rhaeadr Gwy Powys 24 B
Rhedyn Gwyn 40 G
Rhemore Highld 79 F
Rhencullen IoM 48 C
Rhes-y-cae Flint 42 E
Rhewl Denb 42 F
Rhewl Denb 42 H
Rhian Highld 93 H
Rhicarn Highld 92 G
Rhiconich Highld 92 D
Rhicullen Highld 87 D
Rhidorroch Ho. Highld 86 B
Rhifail Highld 93 E1
Rhigos Rhondda 24 H
Rhilochan Highld 93 J1
Rhiroy Highld 86 C
Rhisga = Risca Caerph 15 B
Rhiw Gwyn 40 H
Rhiwabon = Ruabon Wrex 33 A
Rhiwbina Cardiff 15 C
Rhiwbryfdir Gwyn 41 F
Rhiwderin Newport 15 C
Rhiwlas Gwyn 32 B
Rhiwlas Gwyn 41 D
Rhiwlas Powys 33 B
Rhodes Gtr Man 44 B
Rhodes Minnis Kent 21 G
Rhodesia Notts 45 E
Rhodiad Pembs 22 D
Rhondda Rhondda 14 B
Rhonehouse or Kelton Hill Dumfries 55 D1
Rhoose = Y Rhws V Glam 14 E
Rhos-fawr Gwyn 40 G
Rhos-goch Powys 25 D
Rhos-hill Pembs 22 B
Rhos-on-Sea Conwy 41 B1
Rhos-y-brithdir Powys 33 C
Rhos-y-garth Ceredig 24 A
Rhos-y-gwaliau Gwyn 32 B
Rhos-y-llan Gwyn 40 G
Rhos-y-Madoc Wrex 33 A
Rhos-y-meirch Powys 25 B
Rhosaman Carms 24 G
Rhosbeirio Anglesey 40 A
Rhoscefnhir Anglesey 41 C
Rhoscolyn Anglesey 40 C
Rhoscrowther Pembs 22 F
Rhosesmor Flint 42 F
Rhosgadfan Gwyn 41 E
Rhosgoch Anglesey 40 B
Rhoshirwaun Gwyn 40 H
Rhoslan Gwyn 40 F
Rhoslefain Gwyn 32 E
Rhosllanerchrugog Wrex 42 H
Rhosmaen Carms 24 F
Rhosmeirch Anglesey 40 C
Rhosneigr Anglesey 40 C
Rhosnesni Wrex 42 G
Rhosrobin Wrex 42 G
Rhossili Swansea 23 H
Rhosson Pembs 22 D
Rhostryfan Gwyn 40 E
Rhostyllen Wrex 42 H
Rhosybol Anglesey 40 B
Rhu Argyll 73 E1
Rhu Argyll 73 G
Rhuallt Denb 42 E

uddall Heath
les W 43 F8
uddlan Ceredig 23 B9
uddlan Den 42 E3
ue Highld 86 B3
ulen Powys 25 D8
unahaorine
rgyll 65 D8
uthun = Ruthin
enb 42 G4
yd Gwyn 41 F8
yd Powys 32 E5
yd-Ddu Gwyn 41 E7
yd-moel-ddu
owys 33 H6
yd-Rosser Ceredig 24 B2
yd-uchaf Gwyn 32 B5
yd-wen Gwyn 32 D3
yd-y-clafdy
wyn 40 G5
yd-y-fro Neath 24 H4
yd-y-gwin
wansea 14 A2
yd-y-meirch
on 25 H10
yd-y-meudwy
enb 42 G4
yd-y-pandy
wansea 14 A2
yd-y-sarn Gwyn 41 F8
yd-yr-onen Gwyn 32 E2
ydaman =
mmanford Carms 24 G3
ydargaeau Carms 23 D9
ydcymerau
arms 23 C10
ydd Worcs 26 D5
ydding Neath 14 B3
ydfudr Ceredig 24 B2
ydlewis Ceredig 23 B8
ydlios Gwyn 40 G3
ydlydan Conwy 41 E10
ydness Powys 25 D8
ydowen Ceredig 23 B9
ydspence
ereford 25 D9
ydtalog Flint 42 G5
ydwyn Anglesey 40 B5
ydycroesau
owys 33 B8
ydyfelin Ceredig 32 H1
ydyfelin Rhondda 14 C6
ydymain Gwyn 32 C4
ydymwyn Flint 42 F5
yl = Y Rhyl Denb 42 D3
ymney =
hymni Caerph 25 H8
ymni =
hymney Caerph 25 H8
ynd Fife 77 E7
ynd Perth 76 E4
ynie Aberds 82 A6
ynie Highld 87 D11
bbesford Worcs 26 A4
bblehead N Yorks 50 B3
bbleton Lancs 50 F1
bchester Lancs 50 F2
bigill Highld 93 D8
by Lincs 46 B5
by Cross Roads
ncs 46 B5
ccall N Yorks 52 F2
ccarton E Ayrs 67 C7
chards Castle
ereford 25 B11
chings Park Bucks 19 D7
chmond London 19 D8
chmond N Yorks 58 F2
ckarton Aberds 83 E10
ckinghall Suff 38 H6
ckleton T&W 58 A3
ckling Essex 29 E11
ckmansworth
erts 19 B7
ddings Cumb 61 F10
ddings Derbys 45 G8
ddlecombe Devon 6 E5
ddlesden W Yorks 51 E6
ddrie Glasgow 68 D5
dge Dorset 9 F8
dge Hants 10 C2
dge Wilts 9 A8
dge Green Sur 19 G10
dge Lane Warks 35 F8
dgebourne Powys 25 B7
dgehill N Som 15 E11
dgeway Cross
ereford 26 D4
dgewell Essex 30 D4
dgewood E Sus 12 E3
dgmont C Beds 28 E6
ding Mill Northumb 62 G6
dleywood Wrex 43 G7
dlington Norf 39 B9
dlington Rutland 36 E4
dsdale Northumb 62 E5
echip Perth 76 C3
emore Perth 76 C3
enachait Highld 92 F3
evaulx N Yorks 59 H6
ft House Hrtlpl 58 C5
gg Dumfries 61 G8
ggend N Lanark 68 C6
gsby Lincs 47 E8
gside S Lanark 69 G7
ley Green Lancs 50 G2
leyhill Staffs 35 D7
lla Mill Corn 4 D3
llington N Yorks 52 B4
mington Lancs 50 E4
mpton Som 8 B5
mswell E Yorks 53 G9
naston Pembs 22 D4
ngasta Shetland 96 M5
ngford Dumfries 55 D9
nginglow S Yorks 44 D6
ngland Norf 39 D7
ngles Cross E Sus 12 D3
ngmer E Sus 12 E3
ngmore Devon 5 G7
ngorm Moray 88 D2
ng's End Cambs 37 F9
ngsfield Suff 39 G10
ngsfield Corner
uff 39 G10
ngshall Herts 28 G6
ngshall Suff 31 C7
ngshall Stocks
uff 31 C7
ngstead Norf 38 A3
ngstead Northants 36 H5
ngwood Hants 9 D10
ngwould Kent 21 G10
nmore Aberds 82 B6
nnigill Orkney 95 J4
nsey Corn 2 G4
of W Isles 90 D6
pe E Sus 12 E4
pley Derbys 45 G7
pley Hants 9 E10
pley N Yorks 51 C8
pley Sur 19 F7
plingham E Yorks 52 F5
pon N Yorks 51 B9
ppingale Lincs 37 C6
pple Kent 21 G10
pple Worcs 26 E5
pponden W Yorks 50 H6
reavach Highld 86 B3
sabus Argyll 64 D4
Risbury Hereford 26 C2
Risby Suff 30 B4
Risca = Rhisga
Caerph 15 B8
Rise E Yorks 53 E7
Riseden E Sus 12 C5
Risegate Lincs 37 C8
Riseholme Lincs 46 E3
Riseley Bedford 29 B7
Riseley Wokingham 18 E4
Rishangles Suff 31 B8
Rishton Lancs 50 F3
Rishworth W Yorks 50 H6
Rising Bridge Lancs 50 G3
Risley Derbys 35 B10
Risley Warr 43 C9
Risplith N Yorks 51 C8
Rispond Highld 92 C7
Rivar Wilts 17 E10
Rivenhall End Essex 30 G5
River Bank Cambs 30 B2
Riverhead Kent 20 F2
Rivington Lancs 43 A9
Roa Island Cumb 49 C2
Roachill Devon 7 D7
Road Green Norf 39 F8
Roade Northants 28 C4
Roadhead Cumb 61 F11
Roadmeetings
S Lanark 69 F7
Roadside Highld 94 D3
Roadside of
Catterline Aberds 83 F10
Roadside of
Kinneff Aberds 83 F10
Roadwater Som 7 C9
Roag Highld 85 D7
Roath Cardiff 15 D7
Roberton Borders 61 B10
Roberton S Lanark 69 H8
Robertsbridge E Sus 12 D6
Roberttown W Yorks 51 G7
Robeston Cross
Pembs 22 F3
Robeston Wathen
Pembs 22 E5
Robin Hood W Yorks 51 G9
Robin Hood's Bay
N Yorks 59 F10
Roborough Devon 4 E6
Roborough Devon 6 E4
Roby Mers 43 C7
Roby Mill Lancs 43 B8
Rocester Staffs 35 B7
Roch Pembs 22 D3
Roch Gate Pembs 22 D3
Rochdale Gtr Man 44 A2
Roche Corn 3 C8
Rochester Medway 20 E4
Rochester Northumb 62 D4
Rochford Essex 20 B5
Rock Corn 3 B8
Rock Northumb 63 A8
Rock W Sus 11 C10
Rock Worcs 26 A4
Rock Ferry Mers 42 D6
Rockbeare Devon 7 G9
Rockbourne Hants 9 C10
Rockcliffe Cumb 61 G9
Rockcliffe Dumfries 55 D11
Rockfield Highld 87 C12
Rockfield Mon 25 G11
Rockford Hants 9 D10
Rockhampton S Glos 16 B3
Rockingham
Northants 36 F4
Rockland All
Saints Norf 38 F5
Rockland St Mary
Norf 39 E9
Rockland St Peter
Norf 38 F5
Rockley Wilts 17 D8
Rockwell End Bucks 18 C4
Rockwell Green
Som 7 D10
Rodborough Glos 16 A5
Rodbourne Swindon 17 C8
Rodbourne Wilts 16 C6
Rodbourne
Cheney Swindon 17 C8
Rodd Hereford 25 B10
Roddam Northumb 62 A6
Rodden Dorset 8 F5
Rode Som 16 F5
Rode Heath Ches E 44 G2
Rodeheath Ches E 44 F2
Roden Telford 34 D1
Rodhuish Som 7 C9
Rodington Telford 34 D1
Rodley Glos 26 G4
Rodley W Yorks 51 F8
Rodmarton Glos 16 B6
Rodmell E Sus 12 F3
Rodmersham Kent 20 E6
Rodney Stoke Som 15 F10
Rodsley Derbys 35 A8
Rodway Som 15 H8
Rodwell Dorset 8 G5
Roe Green Herts 29 E10
Roecliffe N Yorks 51 C9
Roehampton London 19 D9
Roesound Shetland 96 G5
Roffey W Sus 11 A10
Rogart Highld 93 J10
Rogart Station
Highld 93 J10
Rogate W Sus 11 B7
Rogerstone Newport 15 C8
Roghadal W Isles 90 J5
Rogiet Mon 15 C10
Rogue's Alley Cambs 37 E9
Roke Oxon 18 B3
Roker T&W 63 H10
Rollesby Norf 39 D10
Rolleston Leics 36 E3
Rolleston Notts 45 G11
Rolleston-on-
Dove Staffs 35 C8
Rolston E Yorks 53 E8
Rolvenden Kent 13 C7
Rolvenden Layne
Kent 13 C7
Romaldkirk Durham 57 D11
Romanby N Yorks 58 G4
Romannobridge
Borders 69 F10
Romansleigh Devon 7 D6
Romford London 20 C2
Romiley Gtr Man 44 C3
Romsey Hants 10 B2
Romsey Town
Cambs 29 C11
Romsley Shrops 34 G3
Romsley Worcs 34 H5
Ronague IoM 48 E2
Rookhope Durham 57 B11
Rookley IoW 10 F4
Rooks Bridge Som 15 F9
Roos E Yorks 53 F8
Roosebeck Cumb 49 C2
Rootham's Green
Bedford 29 C8
Rootpark S Lanark 69 E8
Ropley Hants 10 A5
Ropley Dean Hants 10 A5
Ropsley Lincs 36 B5
Rora Aberds 89 C10
Rorandle Aberds 83 B8
Rorrington Shrops 33 E9
Roscroggan Corn 2 E5
Rose Corn 3 D6
Rose Ash Devon 7 D6
Rose Green W Sus 11 E8
Rose Grove Lancs 50 F4
Rose Hill E Sus 12 E3
Rose Hill Lancs 50 F4
Rose Hill Suff 31 D8
Roseacre Kent 20 F4
Roseacre Lancs 49 F4
Rosebank S Lanark 69 F7
Rosebrough
Northumb 71 H10
Rosebush Pembs 22 D5
Rosecare Corn 4 B2
Rosedale Abbey
N Yorks 59 G8
Roseden Northumb 62 A6
Rosefield Highld 87 F11
Rosehall Highld 92 J7
Rosehaugh Mains
Highld 87 F9
Rosehearty Aberds 89 B9
Rosehill Shrops 34 B2
Roseisle Moray 88 B1
Roselands E Sus 12 F5
Rosemarket Pembs 22 F4
Rosemarkie Highld 87 F10
Rosemary Lane
Devon 7 E10
Rosemount Perth 76 C4
Rosenannon Corn 3 C8
Rosewell Midloth 69 D11
Roseworth Stockton 58 D5
Roseworthy Corn 2 F5
Rosgill Cumb 57 E7
Roshven Highld 79 D10
Roskhill Highld 85 D7
Roskill House Highld 87 F9
Rosley Cumb 56 B5
Roslin Midloth 69 D11
Rosliston Derbys 35 D8
Rosneath Argyll 73 E11
Ross Dumfries 55 E9
Ross Northumb 71 G10
Ross Perth 75 E10
Ross-on-Wye
Hereford 26 F3
Rossett Wrex 42 G6
Rossett Green
N Yorks 51 D9
Rossie Ochill Perth 76 F3
Rossie Priory
Perth 76 D5
Rossington S Yorks 45 C10
Rosskeen Highld 87 E9
Rossland Renfs 68 C3
Roster Highld 94 G4
Rostherne Ches E 43 D10
Rosthwaite Cumb 56 E4
Roston Derbys 35 A7
Rosyth Fife 69 B10
Rothbury Northumb 62 C6
Rotherby Leics 36 D2
Rotherfield E Sus 12 D4
Rotherfield Greys
Oxon 18 C4
Rotherfield
Peppard Oxon 18 C4
Rotherham S Yorks 45 C8
Rothersthorpe
Northants 28 C4
Rotherwick Hants 18 F4
Rothes Moray 88 D2
Rothesay Argyll 73 G9
Rothiebrisbane
Aberds 89 E7
Rothienorman
Aberds 89 E7
Rothiesholm Orkney 95 F7
Rothley Leics 36 D1
Rothley Northumb 62 E6
Rothley Shield
East Northumb 62 D6
Rothmaise Aberds 89 E6
Rothwell Lincs 46 C5
Rothwell Northants 36 G4
Rothwell W Yorks 51 G9
Rothwell Haigh
W Yorks 51 G9
Rotsea E Yorks 53 D6
Rottal Angus 82 G5
Rotten End Suff 31 B10
Rottingdean
Brighton 12 F2
Rottington Cumb 56 E1
Roud IoW 10 F4
Rough Close Staffs 34 B5
Rough Common
Kent 21 F8
Rougham Norf 38 C4
Rougham Suff 30 B6
Rougham Green
Suff 30 B6
Roughburn Highld 80 E5
Roughlee Lancs 50 E4
Roughley W Mid 35 F7
Roughsike Cumb 61 F11
Roughton Lincs 46 F6
Roughton Norf 39 B8
Roughton Shrops 34 F3
Roughton Moor
Lincs 46 F6
Roundhay W Yorks 51 F9
Roundstonefoot
Dumfries 61 C7
Roundstreet
Common W Sus 11 B9
Roundway Wilts 17 E7
Rous Lench Worcs 27 C7
Rousdon Devon 8 E1
Routenburn N Ayrs 73 G10
Routh E Yorks 53 E6
Row Corn 4 D1
Row Cumb 56 H6
Row Heath Essex 31 G8
Rowanburn
Dumfries 61 F10
Rowardennan
Stirling 74 H6
Rowde Wilts 16 E6
Rowen Conwy 41 C9
Rowfoot Northumb 62 G2
Rowhedge Essex 31 F7
Rowhook W Sus 11 A10
Rowington Warks 27 B9
Rowland Derbys 44 E6
Rowlands Castle
Hants 10 C6
Rowlands Gill T&W 63 H7
Rowledge Sur 18 G5
Rowlestone
Hereford 25 F10
Rowley E Yorks 52 F5
Rowley Shrops 33 E9
Rowley Hill W Yorks 44 A5
Rowley Regis W Mid 34 G5
Rowly Sur 19 G7
Rowney Green
Worcs 27 A7
Rownhams Hants 10 C2
Rowrah Cumb 56 E2
Rowsham Bucks 28 G5
Rowsley Derbys 44 F6
Rowstock Oxon 17 C11
Rowston Lincs 46 G4
Rowton Ches W 43 F7
Rowton Shrops 33 D9
Rowton Telford 34 D2
Roxburgh Borders 70 G6
Roxby N Lincs 52 H5
Roxby N Yorks 59 E8
Roxton Bedford 29 C8
Roxwell Essex 30 H3
Royal Leamington
Spa Warks 27 B10
Royal Oak Darl 58 D3
Royal Oak Lancs 43 B7
Royal Tunbridge
Wells Kent 12 C4
Roybridge Highld 80 E4
Roydhouse
W Yorks 44 A6
Roydon Essex 29 H11
Roydon Norf 38 C3
Roydon Norf 39 G6
Roydon Hamlet
Essex 29 H11
Royston Herts 29 D10
Royston S Yorks 45 A7
Royton Gtr Man 44 B3
Rozel Jersey 11
Ruabon =
Rhiwabon Wrex 33 A9
Ruaig Argyll 78 G3
Ruan Lanihorne
Corn 3 E7
Ruan Minor Corn 2 H6
Ruarach Highld 80 A1
Ruardean Glos 26 G3
Ruardean
Woodside Glos 26 G3
Rubery Worcs 34 H5
Ruckcroft Cumb 57 B7
Ruckhall Hereford 25 E11
Ruckinge Kent 13 C9
Ruckland Lincs 47 E7
Ruckley Shrops 33 E11
Rudbaxton Pembs 22 D4
Rudby N Yorks 58 F5
Ruddington Notts 36 B1
Rudford Glos 26 F4
Rudge Shrops 34 F4
Rudge Som 16 F5
Rudgeway S Glos 16 C3
Rudgwick W Sus 11 A9
Rudhall Hereford 26 F3
Rudheath Ches W 43 E9
Rudley Green Essex 20 A5
Rudry Caerph 15 C7
Rudston E Yorks 53 C6
Rudyard Staffs 44 G3
Rufford Lancs 49 H4
Rufforth York 51 D11
Rugby Warks 35 H11
Rugeley Staffs 34 D6
Ruglen S Ayrs 66 F5
Ruilick Highld 87 G8
Ruishton Som 8 B1
Ruisigearraidh
W Isles 90 J4
Ruislip London 19 C7
Ruislip Common
London 19 C7
Rumbling Bridge
Perth 76 H3
Rumburgh Suff 39 G9
Rumford Corn 3 B7
Rumney Cardiff 15 D8
Runcorn Halton 43 D8
Runcton W Sus 11 D7
Runcton Holme
Norf 38 E2
Rundlestone Devon 5 D6
Runfold Sur 18 G5
Runhall Norf 39 E6
Runham Norf 39 D10
Runham Norf 39 E11
Runnington Som 7 D10
Russell Green
Essex 30 H4
Runswick Bay
N Yorks 59 E9
Runwell Essex 20 B4
Ruscombe
Wokingham 18 D4
Rush Green London 20 C2
Rush-head Aberds 89 D8
Rushall Hereford 26 E3
Rushall Norf 39 G7
Rushall W Mid 34 E6
Rushall Wilts 17 F8
Rushbrooke Suff 30 B5
Rushbury Shrops 33 F11
Rushden Herts 29 E10
Rushden Northants 28 B6
Rushenden Kent 20 D6
Rushford Norf 38 G5
Rushlake Green
E Sus 12 E5
Rushmere Suff 39 G10
Rushmere
St Andrew Suff 31 D9
Rushmoor Sur 18 G5
Rushock Worcs 26 A5
Rusholme Gtr Man 44 C2
Rushton Ches W 43 F8
Rushton Northants 36 G4
Rushton Shrops 34 E2
Rushton Spencer
Staffs 44 F3
Rushwick Worcs 26 C5
Rushyford Durham 58 D3
Ruskie Stirling 75 G9
Ruskington Lincs 46 G4
Rusland Cumb 56 H5
Rusper W Sus 19 H9
Ruspidge Glos 26 G3
Russell's Water
Oxon 18 C4
Russel's Green Suff 31 A9
Rusthall Kent 12 C4
Rustington W Sus 11 D9
Ruston N Yorks 52 A5
Ruston Parva E Yorks 53 C6
Ruswarp N Yorks 59 F9
Rutherford Borders 70 G5
Rutherglen S Lanark 68 D5
Ruthernbridge Corn 3 C9
Ruthin = Rhuthun
Denb 42 G4
Ruthrieston
Aberdeen 83 C11
Ruthven Aberds 88 D5
Ruthven Angus 76 C5
Ruthven Highld 81 D9
Ruthven Highld 87 H11
Ruthven House
Angus 76 C6
Ruthvoes Corn 3 C8
Ruthwell Dumfries 60 G6
Ruyton-XI-Towns
Shrops 33 C9
Ryal Northumb 62 F6
Ryal Fold Blackburn 50 G2
Ryall Dorset 8 E3
Ryarsh Kent 20 F3
Rydal Cumb 56 F5
Ryde IoW 10 E4
Rye E Sus 13 D8
Rye Foreign E Sus 13 D7
Rye Harbour E Sus 13 E8
Rye Park Herts 29 G10
Rye Street Worcs 26 E4
Ryecroft Gate Staffs 44 F3
Ryehill E Yorks 53 G8
Ryhall Rutland 36 D6
Ryhill W Yorks 45 A7
Ryhope T&W 58 A5
Rylstone N Yorks 50 D5
Ryme Intrinseca
Dorset 8 C4
Ryther N Yorks 52 F1
Ryton Glos 26 E4
Ryton N Yorks 52 B3
Ryton Shrops 34 E3
Ryton T&W 63 G7
Ryton-on-
Dunsmore Warks 27 A10

S

Sabden Lancs 50 F3
Sacombe Herts 29 G10
Sacriston Durham 58 B3
Sadberge Darl 58 E4
Saddell Argyll 65 E8
Saddington Leics 36 F2
Saddle Bow Norf 38 D2
Saddlescombe
W Sus 12 E1
Sadgill Cumb 57 F6
Saffron Walden
Essex 30 E2
Sageston Pembs 22 F5
Saham Hills Norf 38 E5
Saham Toney Norf 38 E5
Saighdinis W Isles 84 B3
Saighton Ches W 43 F7
St Abbs Borders 71 D8
St Abb's Haven
Borders 71 D8
St Agnes Corn 2 D6
St Agnes Scilly 2 D2
St Albans Herts 29 H8
St Allen Corn 3 D7
St Andrews Fife 77 F8
St Andrew's Major
V Glam 15 D7
St Anne Ald 11
St Annes Lancs 49 G3
St Ann's Dumfries 60 D6
St Ann's Chapel
Corn 4 D5
St Ann's Chapel
Devon 5 G7
St Anthony-in-
Meneage Corn 3 G6
St Anthony's Hill
E Sus 12 F5
St Arvans Mon 15 B11
St Asaph =
Llanelwy Denb 42 E3
St Athan V Glam 14 E6
St Aubin Jersey 11
St Austell Corn 3 D9
St Bees Cumb 56 E1
St Blazey Corn 4 F1
St. Boswells Borders 70 G4
St Brelade Jersey 11
St Breock Corn 3 B8
St Breward Corn 4 D1
St Briavels Glos 16 A2
St Bride's Pembs 22 E3
St Brides Major
V Glam 14 D4
St Bride's
Netherwent Mon 15 C10
St Brides super
Ely V Glam 14 D6
St Brides Wentlooge
Newport 15 C8
St Budeaux Plym 4 F5
St Buryan Corn 2 G3
St Catherine Bath 16 D4
St Catherine's
Argyll 73 C10
St Clears =
Sanclêr Carms 23 E7
St Cleer Corn 4 E3
St Clement Corn 3 E7
St Clements Jersey 11
St Clether Corn 4 C3
St Colmac Argyll 73 G9
St Columb Major
Corn 3 C8
St Columb Minor
Corn 3 C7
St Columb Road
Corn 3 D8
St Combs Aberds 89 B10
St Cross South
Elmham Suff 39 G8
St Cyrus Aberds 77 A10
St David's Perth 76 E2
St David's =
Tyddewi Pembs 22 D2
St Day Corn 2 E6
St Dennis Corn 3 D8
St Devereux
Hereford 25 E11
St Dogmaels Pembs 22 B6
St Dogwells Pembs 22 D4
St Dominick Corn 4 E5
St Donat's V Glam 14 E5
St Edith's Wilts 16 E6
St Endellion Corn 3 B8
St Enoder Corn 3 D7
St Erme Corn 3 D7
St Erney Corn 4 F4
St Erth Corn 2 F4
St Ervan Corn 3 B7
St Eval Corn 3 C7
St Ewe Corn 3 E8
St Fagans Cardiff 15 D7
St Fergus Aberds 89 C10
St Fillans Perth 75 E9
St Florence Pembs 22 F5
St Genny's Corn 4 B2
St George Conwy 42 E2
St George's V Glam 14 D6
St Germans Corn 4 F4
St Giles Lincs 46 E3
St Giles in the
Wood Devon 6 E4
St Giles on the
Heath Devon 6 G2
St Harmon Powys 24 A6
St Helen Auckland
Durham 58 D2
St Helena Warks 35 E8
St Helen's E Sus 13 E7
St Helens IoW 10 F5
St Helens Mers 43 C8
St Helier Jersey 11
St Helier London 19 E9
St Hilary Corn 2 F4
St Hilary V Glam 14 D6
Saint Hill W Sus 12 C2
St Illtyd Bl Gwent 15 A8
St Ippollytts Herts 29 F8
St Ishmael's Pembs 22 F3
St Issey Corn 3 B8
St Ive Corn 4 E4
St Ives Cambs 29 A10
St Ives Corn 2 E4
St Ives Dorset 9 D10
St James South
Elmham Suff 39 G9
St Jidgey Corn 3 C8
St John Corn 4 F5
St John's IoM 48 D2
St John's Jersey 11
St John's Sur 18 F6
St John's Worcs 26 C5
St John's Chapel
Durham 57 C10
St John's Fen End
Norf 37 D11
St John's Highway
Norf 37 D11
St John's Town
of Dalry Dumfries 55 A9
St Judes IoM 48 C3
St Just Corn 2 F2
St Just in
Roseland Corn 3 F7
St Katherine's
Aberds 89 E7
St Keverne Corn 3 G6
St Kew Corn 3 B9
St Kew Highway Corn 3 B9
St Keyne Corn 4 E3
St Lawrence Corn 3 C9
St Lawrence Essex 20 A6
St Lawrence IoW 10 G4
St Leonard's Bucks 28 H6
St Leonards Dorset 9 D10
St Leonards E Sus 13 F6
Saint Leonards
S Lanark 68 E5
St Levan Corn 2 G2
St Lythans V Glam 15 D7
St Mabyn Corn 3 B9
St Madoes Perth 76 E4
St Margaret South
Elmham Suff 39 G9
St Margaret's
Hereford 25 E10
St Margarets Herts 29 G10
St Margaret's at
Cliffe Kent 21 G10
St Margaret's
Hope Orkney 95 J5
St Mark's IoM 48 E2
St Martin Corn 4 F3
St Martins Corn 2 G6
St Martin's Jersey 11
St Martins Perth 76 D4
St Martin's Shrops 33 B9
St Mary Bourne
Hants 17 F11
St Mary Church
V Glam 14 D6
St Mary Cray London 19 E11
St Mary Hill V Glam 14 D5
St Mary Hoo
Medway 20 D5
St Mary in the
Marsh Kent 13 D9
St Mary's Jersey 11
St Mary's Orkney 95 H5
St Mary's Bay Kent 13 D9
St Maughans Mon 25 G11
St Mawes Corn 3 F7
St Mawgan Corn 3 C7
St Mellion Corn 4 E4
St Mellons Cardiff 15 C8
St Merryn Corn 3 B7
St Mewan Corn 3 D8
St Michael
Caerhays Corn 3 E8
St Michael
Penkevil Corn 3 E7
St Michael South
Elmham Suff 39 G9
St Michael's Kent 13 C7
St Michaels Worcs 26 B2
St Michael's on
Wyre Lancs 49 E4
St Minver Corn 3 B8
St Monans Fife 77 G8
St Neot Corn 4 E2
St Neots Cambs 29 B8
St Newlyn East Corn 3 D7
St Nicholas Pembs 22 C3
St Nicholas V Glam 14 D6
St Nicholas at
Wade Kent 21 E9
St Ninians Stirling 68 A6
St Osyth Essex 31 G8
St Osyth Heath
Essex 31 G8
St Ouens Jersey 11
St Owens Cross
Hereford 26 F2
St Paul's Cray
London 19 E11
St Paul's Walden
Herts 29 F8
St Peter Port Guern 11
St Peter's Jersey 11
St Peter's Kent 21 E10
St Petrox Pembs 22 G4
St Pinnock Corn 4 E3
St Quivox S Ayrs 67 D6
St Ruan Corn 2 H6
St Sampson Guern 11
St Stephen Corn 3 D8
St Stephen's Corn 4 C4
St Stephens Corn 4 F5
St Stephens Herts 29 H8
St Teath Corn 4 C1
St Thomas Devon 7 G8
St Tudy Corn 4 D1
St Twynnells Pembs 22 G4
St Veep Corn 4 F2
St Vigeans Angus 77 C9
St Wenn Corn 3 C8
St Weonards
Hereford 25 F11
Saintbury Glos 27 E8
Salcombe Devon 5 H8
Salcombe Regis
Devon 7 H10
Salcott Essex 30 G6
Sale Gtr Man 43 C10
Sale Green Worcs 26 C6
Saleby Lincs 47 E8
Salehurst E Sus 12 D6
Salem Carms 24 F3
Salem Ceredig 32 G2
Salen Argyll 79 G8
Salen Highld 79 E9
Salesbury Lancs 50 F2
Salford C Beds 28 E6
Salford Gtr Man 44 C2
Salford Oxon 27 F9
Salford Priors
Warks 27 C7
Salfords Sur 19 G9
Salhouse Norf 39 D9
Saline Fife 69 A9
Salisbury Wilts 9 B10
Sallachan Highld 74 A2
Sallachy Highld 86 H2
Sallachy Highld 93 J8
Salle Norf 39 C7
Salmonby Lincs 47 E7
Salmond's Muir
Angus 77 D8
Salperton Glos 27 F7
Salph End Bedford 29 C7
Salsburgh N Lanark 69 D7
Salt Staffs 34 C5
Salt End E Yorks 53 G7
Saltaire W Yorks 51 F7
Saltash Corn 4 F5
Saltburn Highld 87 E10
Saltburn-by-the-
Sea Redcar 59 D7
Saltby Leics 36 C4
Saltcoats Cumb 56 G2
Saltcoats N Ayrs 66 B5
Saltdean Brighton 12 F2
Salter Lancs 50 C2
Salterforth Lancs 50 E4
Salterswall Ches W 43 F9
Saltfleet Lincs 47 C8
Saltfleetby All
Saints Lincs 47 C8
Saltfleetby
St Clements Lincs 47 C8
Saltfleetby
St Peter Lincs 47 D8
Saltford Bath 16 E3
Salthouse Norf 39 A6
Saltmarshe E Yorks 52 G3
Saltney Flint 43 F6
Salton N Yorks 52 B3
Saltwick Northumb 63 F7
Saltwood Kent 21 H8
Salum Argyll 78 G3
Salvington W Sus 11 D10
Salwarpe Worcs 26 B5
Salwayash Dorset 8 E3
Sambourne Warks 27 B7
Sambrook Telford 34 C3
Samhla W Isles 84 B2
Samlesbury Lancs 50 F1
Samlesbury
Bottoms Lancs 50 G2
Sampford Arundel
Som 7 E10
Sampford Brett Som 7 B9
Sampford
Courtenay Devon 6 F5
Sampford Peverell
Devon 7 E9
Sampford Spiney
Devon 4 D6
Sampool Bridge
Cumb 56 H6
Samuelston E Loth 70 C3
Sanachan Highld 85 D13
Sanaigmore Argyll 64 A3
Sanclêr =
St Clears Carms 23 E7
Sancreed Corn 2 G3
Sancton E Yorks 52 F5
Sand Highld 86 B2
Sand Shetland 96 J5
Sand Hole E Yorks 52 F4
Sand Hutton N Yorks 52 D2
Sandaig Highld 85 H12
Sandal Magna
W Yorks 51 H9
Sandale Cumb 56 B4
Sandbach Ches E 43 F10
Sandbank Argyll 73 E10
Sandbanks Poole 9 F9
Sandend Aberds 88 B5
Sanderstead London 19 E10
Sandfields Glos 26 F6
Sandford Cumb 57 E9
Sandford Devon 7 F7
Sandford Dorset 9 F8
Sandford IoW 10 F4
Sandford N Som 15 F10
Sandford S Lanark 68 F6
Sandford Shrops 34 B1
Sandford on
Thames Oxon 18 A2
Sandford Orcas
Dorset 8 B5
Sandford
St Martin Oxon 27 F11
Sandfordhill
Aberds 89 D11
Sandgate Kent 21 H8
Sandgreen Dumfries 55 D8
Sandhaven Aberds 89 B9
Sandhead Dumfries 54 E3
Sandhills Sur 18 G6
Sandhoe Northumb 62 G5
Sandholme E Yorks 52 F4
Sandholme Lincs 37 B9
Sandhurst Brack 18 E5
Sandhurst Glos 26 F5
Sandhurst Kent 13 D6
Sandhurst Cross
Kent 13 D6
Sandhutton N Yorks 51 A9
Sandiacre Derbys 35 B10
Sandilands Lincs 47 D9
Sandilands S Lanark 69 G7
Sandiway Ches W 43 E9
Sandleheath Hants 9 C10
Sandling Kent 20 F4
Sandlow Green
Ches E 43 F10
Sandness Shetland 96 H3
Sandon Essex 20 A4
Sandon Herts 29 E10
Sandon Staffs 34 B5
Sandown IoW 10 F4
Sandplace Corn 4 F3
Sandridge Herts 29 G8
Sandridge Wilts 16 E6
Sandringham Norf 38 C2
Sandsend N Yorks 59 E9
Sandside Ho. Highld 93 C12
Sandsound Shetland 96 J5
Sandtoft N Lincs 45 B11
Sandway Kent 20 F5
Sandwell W Mid 34 G6
Sandwich Kent 21 F10
Sandwick Cumb 56 E6
Sandwick Orkney 95 K5
Sandwick Shetland 96 L6
Sandwith Cumb 56 E1
Sandy C Beds 29 D8
Sandy Carms 23 F9
Sandy Bank Lincs 46 G6
Sandy Haven Pembs 22 F3
Sandy Lane Wilts 16 E6
Sandy Lane Wrex 33 A9
Sandycroft Flint 42 F6
Sandyford Dumfries 61 D8
Sandyford Stoke 44 G2
Sandygate IoM 48 C3
Sandyhills Dumfries 55 D11
Sandylands Lancs 49 C4
Sandypark Devon 5 C8
Sandysike Cumb 61 G9
Sangobeg Highld 92 C7
Sangomore Highld 92 C7
Sanna Highld 78 E7
Sannadabhaig
W Isles 84 D3
Sanndabhaig
W Isles 91 D9
Sannox N Ayrs 66 B3
Sanquhar Dumfries 60 C3
Santon N Lincs 46 A3
Santon Bridge Cumb 56 F3
Santon Downham
Suff 38 G4
Sapcote Leics 35 F10
Sapey Common
Hereford 26 B4
Sapiston Suff 38 H5
Sapley Cambs 29 A9
Sapperton Glos 16 A6
Sapperton Lincs 36 B6
Saracen's Head
Lincs 37 C9
Sarclet Highld 94 F5
Sardis Carms 23 F10
Sarn Bridgend 14 C5
Sarn Powys 33 F8
Sarn Bach Gwyn 40 H5
Sarn Meyllteyrn
Gwyn 40 G4
Sarnau Carms 23 E8
Sarnau Ceredig 23 A8
Sarnau Gwyn 32 B5
Sarnau Powys 25 E7
Sarnau Powys 33 D8
Sarnesfield
Hereford 25 C10
Saron Carms 23 C8
Saron Carms 24 G3
Saron Denb 42 F3
Saron Gwyn 40 E6
Saron Gwyn 41 D7
Sarratt Herts 19 B7
Sarre Kent 21 E9
Sarsden Oxon 27 F9
Sarsgrum Highld 92 C6
Satley Durham 58 B2
Satron N Yorks 57 G11
Satterleigh Devon 6 D5
Satterthwaite Cumb 56 G5
Satwell Oxon 18 C4
Sauchen Aberds 83 B8
Saucher Perth 76 D4
Sauchie Clack 69 A7
Sauchieburn Aberds 83 G8
Saughall Ches W 42 E6
Saughtree Borders 61 D11
Saul Glos 26 H4
Saundby Notts 45 D11
Saundersfoot
Pembs 22 F6
Saunderton Bucks 18 A4
Saunton Devon 6 C3
Sausthorpe Lincs 47 F7
Saval Highld 93 J8
Savary Highld 79 G9
Savile Park W Yorks 51 G6
Sawbridge Warks 28 B2
Sawbridgeworth
Herts 29 G11
Sawdon N Yorks 59 H10
Sawley Derbys 35 B10
Sawley Lancs 50 E3
Sawley N Yorks 51 C8
Sawston Cambs 29 D11
Sawtry Cambs 37 G7
Saxby Leics 36 D4
Saxby Lincs 46 D4
Saxby All Saints
N Lincs 52 H5
Saxelbye Leics 36 C3
Saxham Street Suff 31 B7
Saxilby Lincs 46 E2
Saxlingham Norf 38 B6
Saxlingham
Green Norf 39 F8
Saxlingham
Nethergate Norf 39 F8
Saxlingham
Thorpe Norf 39 F8
Saxmundham Suff 31 B10
Saxon Street Cambs 30 C3
Saxondale Notts 36 B2
Saxtead Suff 31 B9
Saxtead Green Suff 31 B9
Saxthorpe Norf 39 B7
Saxton N Yorks 51 F10
Sayers Common
W Sus 12 E1
Scackleton N Yorks 52 B2
Scadabhagh W Isles 90 H6
Scaftworth Notts 45 C10
Scagglethorpe
N Yorks 52 B4
Scaitcliffe Lancs 50 G3
Scalasaig Argyll 72 D2
Scalby E Yorks 52 G4
Scalby N Yorks 59 G11
Scaldwell Northants 28 A4
Scale Houses Cumb 57 B7
Scaleby Cumb 61 G10
Scaleby Hill Cumb 61 G10
Scales Cumb 49 B2
Scales Cumb 56 D5
Scales Lancs 49 F4
Scalford Leics 36 C3
Scaling Redcar 59 E8
Scallastle Argyll 79 H9
Scalloway Shetland 96 K6
Scalpay W Isles 90 H7
Scalpay Ho. Highld 85 F11
Scalpsie Argyll 73 H9
Scamadale Highld 79 B10
Scamblesby Lincs 46 E6
Scamodale Highld 79 D11
Scampston N Yorks 52 B4
Scampton Lincs 46 E3
Scapa Orkney 95 H5
Scapegoat Hill
W Yorks 51 H6
Scar Orkney 95 D7
Scarborough
N Yorks 59 H11
Scarcliffe Derbys 45 F8
Scarcroft W Yorks 51 E9
Scarcroft Hill
W Yorks 51 E9
Scardroy Highld 86 F5
Scarff Shetland 96 E4
Scarfskerry Highld 94 C4
Scargill Durham 58 E1
Scarinish Argyll 78 G3
Scarisbrick Lancs 43 A6
Scarning Norf 38 D5
Scarrington Notts 36 A3
Scartho NE Lincs 46 B6
Scarwell Orkney 95 F3
Scatness Shetland 96 M5
Scatraig Highld 87 H10
Scawby N Lincs 46 B3
Scawsby S Yorks 45 B9
Scawton N Yorks 51 A11
Scayne's Hill W Sus 12 D2
Scethrog Powys 25 F8
Scholar Green
Ches E 44 G2
Scholes W Yorks 44 B5
Scholes W Yorks 51 F9
Scholes W Yorks 51 G7
School Green
Ches W 43 F9
Scleddau Pembs 22 C4
Sco Ruston Norf 39 C8
Scofton Notts 45 D10
Scole Norf 39 H7
Scolpaig W Isles 84 A2
Scone Perth 76 E4
Sconser Highld 85 E10
Scoonie Fife 76 G6
Scoor Argyll 78 K7
Scopwick Lincs 46 G4
Scoraig Highld 86 B3
Scorborough
E Yorks 52 E6
Scorrier Corn 2 E6
Scorton Lancs 49 E5
Scorton N Yorks 58 F3
Scotbheinn W Isles 84 C3
Scotby Cumb 61 H10
Scotch Corner
N Yorks 58 F3
Scotforth Lancs 49 D4
Scothern Lincs 46 E4
Scotland Gate
Northumb 63 E8
Scotlandwell Perth 76 G4
Scots' Gap Northumb 62 E6
Scotsburn Highld 87 D10
Scotscalder
Station Highld 94 E2
Scotscraig Fife 77 E7
Scotston Aberds 83 F9
Scotston Perth 76 C2
Scotstoun Glasgow 68 D4
Scotstown Highld 79 E11
Scotswood T&W 63 G7
Scottas Highld 85 H12
Scotter Lincs 46 B2
Scotterthorpe Lincs 46 B2
Scottlethorpe Lincs 37 C6
Scotton Lincs 46 C2
Scotton N Yorks 51 D9
Scotton N Yorks 58 G2
Scottow Norf 39 C8
Scoughall E Loth 70 B5
Scoulag Argyll 73 H10
Scoulton Norf 38 E5
Scourie Highld 92 E4
Scourie More Highld 92 E4
Scousburgh
Shetland 96 M5
Scrabster Highld 94 C2
Scrafield Lincs 47 F7
Scrainwood
Northumb 62 C5
Scrane End Lincs 37 A9
Scraptoft Leics 36 E2
Scratby Norf 39 D11
Scrayingham
N Yorks 52 C3
Scredington Lincs 37 A6
Scremby Lincs 47 F8
Scremerston
Northumb 71 F9
Screveton Notts 36 A3
Scrivelsby Lincs 46 F6
Scriven N Yorks 51 D9
Scrooby Notts 45 C10
Scropton Derbys 35 B7
Scrub Hill Lincs 46 G6
Scruton N Yorks 58 G3
Sculcoates Hull 53 F6
Sculthorpe Norf 38 B4
Scunthorpe N Lincs 46 A2
Scurlage Swansea 23 H9
Sea Palling Norf 39 C10
Seaborough Dorset 8 D3
Seacombe Mers 42 C6
Seacroft Lincs 47 F9
Seacroft W Yorks 51 F9
Seadyke Lincs 37 B9
Seafield S Ayrs 66 D6
Seafield W Loth 69 D9
Seaford E Sus 12 G3
Seaforth Mers 42 C6
Seagrave Leics 36 D2
Seaham Durham 58 B5
Seahouses
Northumb 71 G11
Seal Kent 20 F2
Sealand Flint 42 F6
Seale Sur 18 G5
Seamer N Yorks 52 A6
Seamer N Yorks 58 E5
Seamill N Ayrs 66 B5
Searby Lincs 46 B4
Seasalter Kent 21 E7
Seascale Cumb 56 F2
Seathorne Lincs 47 F9
Seathwaite Cumb 56 E4
Seathwaite Cumb 56 G4
Seatoller Cumb 56 E4
Seaton Corn 4 F4
Seaton Cumb 56 C2
Seaton Devon 8 F1
Seaton Durham 58 A4
Seaton E Yorks 53 E7
Seaton Northumb 63 F9
Seaton Rutland 36 F5
Seaton Burn T&W 63 F8
Seaton Carew
Hrtlpl 58 D6
Seaton Delaval
Northumb 63 F9
Seaton Ross E Yorks 52 E3
Seaton Sluice
Northumb 63 F9
Seatown Aberds 88 B5
Seatown Dorset 8 E3
Seave Green N Yorks 59 F6
Seaview IoW 10 E5
Seaville Cumb 56 A3
Seavington
St Mary Som 8 C3
Seavington
St Michael Som 8 C3
Sebergham Cumb 56 B5
Seckington Warks 35 E8
Second Coast
Highld 86 B2
Sedbergh Cumb 57 G8
Sedbury Glos 15 B11
Sedbusk N Yorks 57 G10
Sedgeberrow Worcs 27 E7
Sedgebrook Lincs 36 B4
Sedgefield Durham 58 D4
Sedgeford Norf 38 B3
Sedgehill Wilts 9 B7
Sedgley W Mid 34 F5
Sedgwick Cumb 57 H7
Sedlescombe E Sus 13 E6
Sedlescombe
Street E Sus 13 E6
Seend Wilts 16 E6
Seend Cleeve Wilts 16 E6
Seer Green Bucks 18 B6
Seething Norf 39 F9
Sefton Mers 42 B6
Seghill Northumb 63 F8
Seifton Shrops 33 G10
Seighford Staffs 34 C4
Seilebost W Isles 90 H5
Seion Gwyn 41 D7
Seisdon Staffs 34 F4
Seisiadar W Isles 91 D10
Selattyn Shrops 33 B8
Selborne Hants 10 A6
Selby N Yorks 52 F2
Selham W Sus 11 B8
Selhurst London 19 E10
Selkirk Borders 70 H3
Sellack Hereford 26 F2
Sellafirth Shetland 96 D7
Sellibister Orkney 95 D8
Sellindge Kent 13 C9
Sellindge Lees
Kent 13 C10
Selling Kent 21 F7
Sells Green Wilts 16 E6
Selly Oak W Mid 34 G6
Selmeston E Sus 12 F4
Selsdon London 19 E10
Selsey W Sus 11 E7
Selsfield Common
W Sus 12 C2
Selsted Kent 21 G9
Selston Notts 45 G8
Selworthy Som 7 B8
Semblister Shetland 96 H5
Semer Suff 30 D6
Semington Wilts 16 E5
Semley Wilts 9 B7
Send Sur 19 F7
Send Marsh Sur 19 F7
Senghenydd Caerph 15 B7
Sennen Corn 2 G2
Sennen Cove Corn 2 G2
Sennybridge =
Pont Senni Powys 24 F6
Serlby Notts 45 D10
Sessay N Yorks 51 B10
Setchey Norf 38 D2

Setley Hants 10 D2
Setter Shetland 96 E6
Setter Shetland 96 H5
Setter Shetland 96 J7
Settiscarth Orkney 95 G4
Settle N Yorks 50 C4
Settrington N Yorks 52 B4
Seven Kings London 19 C11
Seven Sisters Neath 24 H5
Sevenhampton Glos 27 F7
Sevenoaks Kent 20 F2
Sevenoaks Weald Kent 20 F2
Severn Beach S Glos 15 C11
Severn Stoke Worcs 26 D5
Severnhampton Swindon 17 B9
Sevington Kent 13 B9
Sewards End Essex 30 E2
Sewardstone Essex 19 B10
Sewardstonebury Essex 19 B10
Sewerby E Yorks 53 C7
Seworgan Corn 2 F6
Sewstern Leics 36 C4
Sezincote Glos 27 E8
Sgarasta Mhor W Isles 90 H5
Sgiogarstaigh W Isles 91 A10
Shabbington Bucks 28 H3
Shackerstone Leics 35 E9
Shackleford Sur 18 G6
Shade W Yorks 50 G5
Shadforth Durham 58 B4
Shadingfield Suff 39 G10
Shadoxhurst Kent 13 C8
Shadsworth Blackburn 50 G3
Shadwell Norf 38 G5
Shadwell W Yorks 51 F9
Shaftesbury Dorset 9 B7
Shafton S Yorks 45 A7
Shalbourne Wilts 17 E10
Shalcombe IoW 10 F2
Shalden Hants 18 G3
Shaldon Devon 5 D10
Shalfleet IoW 10 F3
Shalford Essex 30 F4
Shalford Sur 19 G7
Shalford Green Essex 30 F4
Shallowford Devon 6 B6
Shalmsford Street Kent 21 F7
Shalstone Bucks 28 E3
Shamley Green Sur 19 G7
Shandon Argyll 73 E11
Shandwick Highld 87 D11
Shangton Leics 36 F3
Shankhouse Northumb 63 F8
Shanklin IoW 10 F4
Shanquhar Aberds 88 E5
Shanzie Perth 76 B5
Shap Cumb 57 E7
Shapwick Dorset 9 D8
Shapwick Som 15 H10
Shardlow Derbys 35 B10
Shareshill Staffs 34 E5
Sharlston W Yorks 51 H9
Sharlston Common W Yorks 51 H9
Sharnbrook Bedford 28 C6
Sharnford Leics 35 F10
Sharoe Green Lancs 49 F5
Sharow N Yorks 51 B9
Sharp Street Norf 39 C9
Sharpenhoe C Beds 29 E7
Sharperton Northumb 62 C5
Sharpness Glos 16 A3
Sharpthorne W Sus 12 C2
Sharrington Norf 38 B6
Shatterford Worcs 34 G3
Shaugh Prior Devon 4 E6
Shavington Ches E 43 G10
Shaw Gtr Man 44 B3
Shaw W Berks 17 E11
Shaw Wilts 16 E5
Shaw Green Lancs 49 H5
Shaw Mills N Yorks 51 C8
Shawbury Shrops 34 C1
Shawdon Hall Northumb 62 B6
Shawell Leics 35 G11
Shawford Hants 10 B3
Shawforth Lancs 50 G4
Shawhead Dumfries 60 F4
Shawhill Dumfries 61 G8
Shawton S Lanark 68 F5
Shawtonhill S Lanark 68 F5
Shear Cross Wilts 16 G5
Shearington Dumfries 60 G6
Shearsby Leics 36 F2
Shebbear Devon 6 F3
Shebdon Staffs 34 C3
Shebster Highld 93 C13
Sheddens E Renf 68 E4
Shedfield Hants 10 C4
Sheen Staffs 44 F5
Sheepscar W Yorks 51 F9
Sheepscombe Glos 26 G5
Sheepstor Devon 5 E6
Sheepwash Devon 6 F3
Sheepway N Som 15 D10
Sheepy Magna Leics 35 E9
Sheepy Parva Leics 35 E9
Sheering Essex 30 G2
Sheerness Kent 20 D6
Sheet Hants 11 B6
Sheffield S Yorks 45 D7
Sheffield Bottom W Berks 18 E3
Sheffield Green E Sus 12 D3
Shefford C Beds 29 E8
Shefford Woodlands W Berks 17 D10
Sheigra Highld 92 C4
Sheinton Shrops 34 E2
Shelderton Shrops 33 H10
Sheldon Derbys 44 F5
Sheldon Devon 7 F10
Sheldon W Mid 35 G7
Sheldwich Kent 21 F7
Shelf W Yorks 51 G7
Shelfanger Norf 39 G7
Shelfield W Mid 34 E6
Shelfield Warks 27 B8
Shelford Notts 36 A2
Shellacres Northumb 71 F7
Shelley Essex 20 A2
Shelley Suff 31 E7
Shelley W Yorks 44 A6
Shellingford Oxon 17 B10
Shellow Bowells Essex 30 H3
Shelsley Beauchamp Worcs 26 B4
Shelsley Walsh Worcs 26 B4
Shelthorpe Leics 35 D11
Shelton Bedford 29 B7
Shelton Norf 39 F8
Shelton Notts 36 A3
Shelton Shrops 33 D10
Shelton Green Norf 39 F8
Shelve Shrops 33 F9
Shelwick Hereford 26 D2
Shenfield Essex 20 B3
Shenington Oxon 27 D10
Shenley Herts 19 A8
Shenley Brook End M Keynes 28 E5
Shenley Church End M Keynes 28 E5
Shenleybury Herts 19 A8
Shenmore Hereford 25 E10
Shennanton Dumfries 54 C6
Shenstone Staffs 35 E7
Shenstone Worcs 26 A5
Shenton Leics 35 E9
Shenval Highld 80 A6
Shenval Moray 82 A4
Shepeau Stow Lincs 37 D9
Shephall Herts 29 F9
Shepherd's Green Oxon 18 C4
Shepherd's Port Norf 38 B2
Shepherdswell Kent 21 G9
Shepley W Yorks 44 B5
Shepperdine S Glos 16 B3
Shepperton Sur 19 E7
Shepreth Cambs 29 D10
Shepshed Leics 35 D10
Shepton Beauchamp Som 8 C3
Shepton Mallet Som 16 G3
Shepton Montague Som 8 A5
Shepway Kent 20 F4
Sheraton Durham 58 C5
Sherborne Dorset 8 C5
Sherborne Glos 27 G8
Sherborne St John Hants 18 F3
Sherbourne Warks 27 B9
Sherburn Durham 58 B4
Sherburn N Yorks 52 B5
Sherburn Hill Durham 58 B4
Sherburn in Elmet N Yorks 51 F10
Shere Sur 19 G7
Shereford Norf 38 C4
Sherfield English Hants 10 B1
Sherfield on Loddon Hants 18 F3
Sherford Devon 5 G8
Sheriff Hutton N Yorks 52 C2
Sheriffhales Shrops 34 D3
Sheringham Norf 39 A7
Sherington M Keynes 28 D5
Shernal Green Worcs 26 B6
Shernborne Norf 38 B3
Sherrington Wilts 16 H6
Sherston Wilts 16 C5
Sherwood Green Devon 6 D4
Shettleston Glasgow 68 D5
Shevington Gtr Man 43 B8
Shevington Moor Gtr Man 43 A8
Shevington Vale Gtr Man 43 B8
Sheviock Corn 4 F4
Shide IoW 10 F3
Shiel Bridge Highld 80 B1
Shieldaig Highld 85 A13
Shieldaig Highld 85 C13
Shieldhill Dumfries 60 E6
Shieldhill Falk 69 C7
Shieldhill S Lanark 69 F9
Shielfoot Highld 79 E9
Shielhill Angus 77 B7
Shielhill Invclyd 73 F11
Shifford Oxon 17 A10
Shifnal Shrops 34 E3
Shilbottle Northumb 63 C7
Shildon Durham 58 D3
Shillingford Devon 7 D9
Shillingford Oxon 18 B2
Shillingford St George Devon 5 C10
Shillingstone Dorset 9 C7
Shillington C Beds 29 E8
Shillmoor Northumb 62 C4
Shilton Oxon 27 H9
Shilton Warks 35 G10
Shilvington Northumb 63 E7
Shimpling Norf 39 G7
Shimpling Suff 30 C5
Shimpling Street Suff 30 C5
Shincliffe Durham 58 B3
Shiney Row T&W 58 A4
Shinfield Wokingham 18 E4
Shingham Norf 38 E3
Shingle Street Suff 31 D10
Shinner's Bridge Devon 5 E8
Shinness Highld 93 H8
Shipbourne Kent 20 F2
Shipdham Norf 38 E5
Shipham Som 15 F10
Shiphay Torbay 5 E9
Shiplake Oxon 18 D4
Shipley Derbys 35 A10
Shipley Northumb 63 B7
Shipley Shrops 34 F4
Shipley W Sus 11 B10
Shipley W Yorks 51 F7
Shipley Shiels Northumb 62 D3
Shipmeadow Suff 39 G9
Shippea Hill Sta. Cambs 38 G2
Shippon Oxon 17 B11
Shipston-on-Stour Warks 27 D9
Shipton Glos 27 G7
Shipton N Yorks 52 D1
Shipton Shrops 34 F1
Shipton Bellinger Hants 17 G9
Shipton Gorge Dorset 8 E3
Shipton Green W Sus 11 D7
Shipton Moyne Glos 16 C5
Shipton on Cherwell Oxon 27 G11
Shipton Solers Glos 27 G7
Shipton-under-Wychwood Oxon 27 G9
Shiptonthorpe E Yorks 52 E4
Shirburn Oxon 18 B3
Shirdley Hill Lancs 42 A6
Shirebrook Derbys 45 F9
Shiregreen S Yorks 45 C7
Shirehampton Bristol 15 D11
Shiremoor T&W 63 F9
Shirenewton Mon 15 B10
Shireoaks Notts 45 D9
Shirkoak Kent 13 C8
Shirl Heath Hereford 25 C11
Shirland Derbys 45 G7
Shirley Derbys 35 A8
Shirley London 19 E10
Shirley Soton 10 C3
Shirley W Mid 35 H7
Shirrell Heath Hants 10 C4
Shirwell Devon 6 C4
Shirwell Cross Devon 6 C4
Shiskine N Ayrs 66 D2
Shobdon Hereford 25 B11
Shobnall Staffs 35 C8
Shobrooke Devon 7 F7
Shoby Leics 36 D2
Shocklach Ches W 43 H7
Shoeburyness Southend 20 C6
Sholden Kent 21 F10
Sholing Soton 10 C3
Shoot Hill Shrops 33 D10
Shop Corn 3 B7
Shop Corn 6 E1
Shop Corner Suff 31 E9
Shore Mill Highld 87 E10
Shoreditch London 19 C10
Shoreham Kent 20 E2
Shoreham-By-Sea W Sus 11 D11
Shoresdean Northumb 71 F8
Shoreswood Northumb 71 F8
Shoreton Highld 87 E9
Shorncote Glos 17 B7
Shorne Kent 20 D3
Short Heath W Mid 34 E5
Shortacombe Devon 4 C6
Shortgate E Sus 12 E3
Shortlanesend Corn 3 E7
Shortlees E Ayrs 67 C7
Shortstown Bedford 29 D7
Shorwell IoW 10 F3
Shoscombe Bath 16 F4
Shotatton Shrops 33 C9
Shotesham Norf 39 F8
Shotgate Essex 20 B4
Shotley Suff 31 E9
Shotley Bridge Durham 58 A1
Shotley Gate Suff 31 E9
Shotleyfield Northumb 58 A1
Shottenden Kent 21 F7
Shottermill Sur 11 A7
Shottery Warks 27 C8
Shotteswell Warks 27 D11
Shottisham Suff 31 D10
Shottle Derbys 45 H7
Shottlegate Derbys 45 H7
Shotton Durham 58 C5
Shotton Flint 42 F6
Shotton Northumb 71 G7
Shotton Colliery Durham 58 B4
Shotts N Lanark 69 D7
Shotwick Ches W 42 E6
Shouldham Norf 38 E2
Shouldham Thorpe Norf 38 E2
Shoulton Worcs 26 C5
Shover's Green E Sus 12 C5
Shrawardine Shrops 33 D10
Shrawley Worcs 26 B5
Shrewley Common Warks 27 B9
Shrewsbury Shrops 33 D10
Shrewton Wilts 17 G7
Shripney W Sus 11 D8
Shrivenham Oxon 17 C9
Shropham Norf 38 F5
Shrub End Essex 30 F6
Shucknall Hereford 26 D2
Shudy Camps Cambs 30 D3
Shulishadermor Highld 85 D9
Shurdington Glos 26 G6
Shurlock Row Windsor 18 D5
Shurrery Highld 93 D13
Shurrery Lodge Highld 93 D13
Shurton Som 7 B11
Shustoke Warks 35 F8
Shute Devon 7 F7
Shute Devon 8 E1
Shutford Oxon 27 D10
Shuthonger Glos 26 E5
Shutlanger Northants 28 C4
Shuttington Warks 35 E8
Shuttlewood Derbys 45 E8
Siabost bho Dheas W Isles 90 C7
Siabost bho Thuath W Isles 90 C7
Siadar W Isles 91 B8
Siadar Iarach W Isles 91 B8
Siadar Uarach W Isles 91 B8
Sibbaldbie Dumfries 61 E7
Sibbertoft Northants 36 G2
Sibdon Carwood Shrops 33 G10
Sibford Ferris Oxon 27 E10
Sibford Gower Oxon 27 E10
Sible Hedingham Essex 30 E4
Sibsey Lincs 47 G7
Sibson Cambs 37 F6
Sibson Leics 35 E9
Sibthorpe Notts 45 H11
Sibton Suff 31 B10
Sibton Green Suff 31 A10
Sicklesmere Suff 30 B5
Sicklinghall N Yorks 51 E9
Sid Devon 7 H10
Sidbury Devon 7 G10
Sidbury Shrops 34 G2
Sidcot N Som 15 F10
Sidcup London 19 D11
Siddick Cumb 56 C2
Siddington Ches E 44 E2
Siddington Glos 17 B7
Sidemoor Worcs 26 A6
Sidestrand Norf 39 B8
Sidford Devon 7 G10
Sidlesham W Sus 11 E7
Sidley E Sus 12 F6
Sidlow Sur 19 G9
Sidmouth Devon 7 H10
Sigford Devon 5 D8
Sigglesthorne E Yorks 53 E7
Sighthill Edin 69 C10
Sigingstone V Glam 14 D5
Signet Oxon 27 G9
Silchester Hants 18 E3
Sildinis W Isles 91 F7
Sileby Leics 36 D1
Silecroft Cumb 49 A1
Silfield Norf 39 F7
Silian Ceredig 23 A10
Silk Willoughby Lincs 37 A6
Silkstone S Yorks 44 B6
Silkstone Common S Yorks 44 B6
Silloth Cumb 56 A3
Sills Northumb 62 C4
Sillyearn Moray 88 C5
Siloh Carms 24 E4
Silpho N Yorks 59 G10
Silsden W Yorks 50 E6
Silsoe C Beds 29 E7
Silver End Essex 30 G5
Silverburn Midloth 69 D11
Silverdale Lancs 49 B4
Silverdale Staffs 44 H2
Silvergate Norf 39 C7
Silverhill E Sus 13 E6
Silverley's Green Suff 39 H8
Silverstone Northants 28 D3
Silverton Devon 7 F8
Silvington Shrops 34 H2
Silwick Shetland 96 J4
Simmondley Derbys 44 C4
Simonburn Northumb 62 F4
Simonsbath Som 7 C6
Simonstone Lancs 50 F3
Simprim Borders 71 F7
Simpson M Keynes 28 E5
Simpson Cross Pembs 22 E3
Sinclair's Hill Borders 71 E7
Sinclairston E Ayrs 67 E7
Sinderby N Yorks 51 A9
Sinderhope Northumb 57 A10
Sindlesham Wokingham 18 E4
Singdean Borders 61 C11
Singleborough Bucks 28 E4
Singleton Lancs 49 F3
Singleton W Sus 11 C7
Singlewell Kent 20 D3
Sinkhurst Green Kent 13 B7
Sinnahard Aberds 82 B6
Sinnington N Yorks 59 H8
Sinton Green Worcs 26 B5
Sipson London 19 D7
Sirhowy Bl Gwent 25 G8
Sisland Norf 39 F9
Sissinghurst Kent 13 C6
Sisterpath Borders 70 F6
Siston S Glos 16 D3
Sithney Corn 2 G5
Sittingbourne Kent 20 E6
Six Ashes Staffs 34 G3
Six Hills Leics 36 C2
Six Mile Bottom Cambs 30 C2
Sixhills Lincs 46 D5
Sixpenny Handley Dorset 9 C8
Sizewell Suff 31 B11
Skail Highld 93 E10
Skaill Orkney 95 E5
Skaill Orkney 95 G3
Skaill Orkney 95 H6
Skares E Ayrs 67 E8
Skateraw E Loth 70 C6
Skaw Shetland 96 G7
Skeabost Highld 85 D9
Skeabrae Orkney 95 F3
Skeeby N Yorks 58 F3
Skeffington Leics 36 E3
Skeffling E Yorks 53 H9
Skegby Notts 45 F8
Skegness Lincs 47 F9
Skelberry Shetland 96 M5
Skelbo Highld 87 B10
Skelbrooke S Yorks 45 A9
Skeldyke Lincs 37 B9
Skellingthorpe Lincs 46 E3
Skellister Shetland 96 H6
Skellow S Yorks 45 A9
Skelmanthorpe W Yorks 44 A6
Skelmersdale Lancs 43 B7
Skelmonae Aberds 89 E8
Skelmorlie N Ayrs 73 G10
Skelmuir Aberds 89 D9
Skelpick Highld 93 D10
Skelton Cumb 56 C6
Skelton E Yorks 52 G3
Skelton N Yorks 58 F1
Skelton Redcar 59 E7
Skelton York 52 D1
Skelton-on-Ure N Yorks 51 C9
Skelwick Orkney 95 D5
Skelwith Bridge Cumb 56 F5
Skendleby Lincs 47 F8
Skene Ho. Aberds 83 C9
Skenfrith Mon 25 F11
Skerne E Yorks 52 D6
Skeroblingarry Argyll 65 F8
Skerray Highld 93 C9
Skerton Lancs 49 C4
Sketchley Leics 35 F10
Sketty Swansea 14 B2
Skewen Neath 14 B3
Skewsby N Yorks 52 B2
Skeyton Norf 39 C8
Skiag Bridge Highld 92 G5
Skibo Castle Highld 87 C10
Skidbrooke Lincs 47 C8
Skidbrooke North End Lincs 47 C8
Skidby E Yorks 52 F6
Skilgate Som 7 D8
Skillington Lincs 36 C4
Skinburness Cumb 61 H7
Skinflats Falk 69 B8
Skinidin Highld 84 D7
Skinnet Highld 93 C8
Skinningrove Redcar 59 D8
Skipness Argyll 73 H7
Skippool Lancs 49 E3
Skipsea E Yorks 53 D7
Skipsea Brough E Yorks 53 D7
Skipton N Yorks 50 D5
Skipton-on-Swale N Yorks 51 B9
Skipwith N Yorks 52 F2
Skirbeck Lincs 37 A9
Skirbeck Quarter Lincs 37 A9
Skirlaugh E Yorks 53 F7
Skirling Borders 69 G9
Skirmett Bucks 18 C4
Skirpenbeck E Yorks 52 D3
Skirwith Cumb 57 C8
Skirza Highld 94 D5
Skulamus Highld 85 F11
Skullomie Highld 93 C9
Skyborry Green Shrops 25 A9
Skye of Curr Highld 81 A10
Skyreholme N Yorks 51 C6
Slackhall Derbys 44 D4
Slackhead Moray 88 B4
Slad Glos 26 H5
Slade Devon 6 B4
Slade Pembs 22 E4
Slade Green London 20 D2
Slaggyford Northumb 57 A8
Slaidburn Lancs 50 D3
Slaithwaite W Yorks 44 A4
Slaley Northumb 62 H5
Slamannan Falk 69 C7
Slapton Bucks 28 F6
Slapton Devon 5 G9
Slapton Northants 28 D3
Slatepit Dale Derbys 45 F7
Slattocks Gtr Man 44 B2
Slaugham W Sus 12 D1
Slaughterford Wilts 16 D5
Slawston Leics 36 F3
Sleaford Hants 18 H5
Sleaford Lincs 46 H4
Sleagill Cumb 57 E7
Sleapford Telford 34 D2
Sledge Green Worcs 26 E5
Sledmere E Yorks 52 C5
Sleightholme Durham 57 E11
Sleights N Yorks 59 F9
Slepe Dorset 9 E8
Slickly Highld 94 D4
Sliddery N Ayrs 66 D2
Sligachan Hotel Highld 85 F9
Slimbridge Glos 16 A4
Slindon Staffs 34 B4
Slindon W Sus 11 D8
Slinfold W Sus 11 A10
Sling Gwyn 41 D8
Slingsby N Yorks 52 B2
Slioch Aberds 88 E5
Slip End C Beds 29 G7
Slip End Herts 29 E9
Slipton Northants 36 H5
Slitting Mill Staffs 34 D6
Slochd Highld 81 A10
Slockavullin Argyll 73 D7
Sloley Norf 39 C8
Sloothby Lincs 47 E8
Slough Slough 18 D6
Slough Green W Sus 12 D1
Sluggan Highld 81 A10
Slumbay Highld 85 E13
Slyfield Sur 18 F6
Slyne Lancs 49 C4
Smailholm Borders 70 G5
Small Dole W Sus 11 C11
Small Hythe Kent 13 C7
Smallbridge Gtr Man 50 H5
Smallburgh Norf 39 C9
Smallburn Aberds 89 D10
Smallburn E Ayrs 68 H5
Smalley Derbys 35 A10
Smallfield Sur 12 B2
Smallridge Devon 8 D2
Smannell Hants 17 G10
Smardale Cumb 57 F9
Smarden Kent 13 B7
Smarden Bell Kent 13 B7
Smeatharpe Devon 7 E10
Smeeth Kent 13 C9
Smeeton Westerby Leics 36 F2
Smercleit W Isles 84 G2
Smerral Highld 94 G3
Smethwick W Mid 34 G6
Smirisary Highld 79 D9
Smisby Derbys 35 D9
Smith Green Lancs 49 D4
Smithfield Cumb 61 G10
Smithincott Devon 7 E9
Smith's Green Essex 30 F2
Smithstown Highld 85 A12
Smithton Highld 87 G10
Smithy Green Ches E 43 E10
Smockington Leics 35 G10
Smoogro Orkney 95 H4
Smythe's Green Essex 30 G6
Snaigow House Perth 76 C3
Snailbeach Shrops 33 E9
Snailwell Cambs 30 B3
Snainton N Yorks 52 A5
Snaith E Yorks 52 G2
Snape N Yorks 51 A8
Snape Suff 31 C10
Snape Green Lancs 43 A6
Snarestone Leics 35 E9
Snarford Lincs 46 D4
Snargate Kent 13 D8
Snave Kent 13 D9
Snead Powys 33 F9
Sneath Common Norf 39 G7
Sneaton N Yorks 59 F9
Sneatonthorpe N Yorks 59 F10
Snelland Lincs 46 D4
Snelston Derbys 35 A7
Snettisham Norf 38 B2
Sniseabhal W Isles 84 E2
Snitter Northumb 62 C6
Snitterby Lincs 46 C3
Snitterfield Warks 27 C9
Snitton Shrops 34 H1
Snodhill Hereford 25 D10
Snodland Kent 20 E3
Snowden Hill S Yorks 44 B6
Snowdown Kent 21 F9
Snowshill Glos 27 E7
Snydale W Yorks 51 H10
Soar Anglesey 40 C5
Soar Carms 24 F3
Soar Devon 5 H8
Soar-y-Mynydd Ceredig 24 C4
Soberton Hants 10 C5
Soberton Heath Hants 10 C5
Sockbridge Cumb 57 D7
Sockburn Darl 58 F4
Soham Cambs 30 A2
Soham Cotes Cambs 38 H1
Solas W Isles 84 A3
Soldon Cross Devon 6 E2
Soldridge Hants 10 A5
Sole Street Kent 20 E3
Sole Street Kent 21 G7
Solihull W Mid 35 H7
Sollers Dilwyn Hereford 25 C11
Sollers Hope Hereford 26 E3
Sollom Lancs 49 H4
Solva Pembs 22 D2
Somerby Leics 36 D3
Somerby Lincs 46 B4
Somercotes Derbys 45 G8
Somerford Dorset 9 E10
Somerford Keynes Glos 17 B7
Somerley W Sus 11 E7
Somerleyton Suff 39 F10
Somersal Herbert Derbys 35 B7
Somersby Lincs 47 E7
Somersham Cambs 37 H9
Somersham Suff 31 D7
Somerton Oxon 27 F11
Somerton Som 8 B3
Sompting W Sus 11 D10
Sonning Wokingham 18 D4
Sonning Common Oxon 18 C4
Sonning Eye Oxon 18 D4
Sontley Wrex 42 H6
Sopley Hants 9 E10
Sopwell Herts 29 H8
Sopworth Wilts 16 C5
Sorbie Dumfries 55 E7
Sordale Highld 94 D3
Sorisdale Argyll 78 E5
Sorn E Ayrs 68 H4
Sornhill E Ayrs 67 C8
Sortat Highld 94 D4
Sotby Lincs 46 E6
Sots Hole Lincs 46 F5
Sotterley Suff 39 G10
Soudley Shrops 34 C3
Soughton Flint 42 F5
Soulbury Bucks 28 F5
Soulby Cumb 57 E9
Souldern Oxon 28 E2
Souldrop Bedford 28 B6
Sound Ches E 43 H9
Sound Shetland 96 H5
Sound Shetland 96 J6
Sound Heath Ches E 43 H9
Soundwell S Glos 16 D3
Sourhope Borders 62 A4
Sourin Orkney 95 E5
Sourton Devon 6 G4
Soutergate Cumb 49 A2
South Acre Norf 38 D4
South Allington Devon 5 H8
South Alloa Falk 69 A7
South Ambersham W Sus 11 B8
South Anston S Yorks 45 D9
South Ascot Windsor 18 E6
South Ballachulish Highld 74 B3
South Balloch S Ayrs 66 G6
South Bank Redcar 59 D6
South Barrow Som 8 B5
South Beach Gwyn 40 G5
South Benfleet Essex 20 C4
South Bersted W Sus 11 D8
South Brent Devon 5 E7
South Brewham Som 16 H4
South Broomhill Northumb 63 D8
South Burlingham Norf 39 E9
South Cadbury Som 8 B5
South Cairn Dumfries 54 C2
South Carlton Lincs 46 E3
South Cave E Yorks 52 F5
South Cerney Glos 17 B7
South Chard Som 8 D2
South Charlton Northumb 63 A7
South Cheriton Som 8 B5
South Cliffe E Yorks 52 F4
South Clifton Notts 46 E2
South Cockerington Lincs 47 D7
South Cornelly Bridgend 14 C4
South Cove Suff 39 G10
South Creagan Argyll 74 C2
South Creake Norf 38 B4
South Croxton Leics 36 D2
South Croydon London 19 E10
South Dalton E Yorks 52 E5
South Darenth Kent 20 E2
South Duffield N Yorks 52 F2
South Elkington Lincs 46 D6
South Elmsall W Yorks 45 A8
South End Bucks 28 F5
South End Cumb 49 C2
South End N Lincs 53 G7
South Erradale Highld 85 A12
South Fambridge Essex 20 B5
South Fawley W Berks 17 C10
South Ferriby N Lincs 52 G5
South Garth Shetland 96 D7
South Garvan Highld 80 F1
South Glendale W Isles 84 G2
South Godstone Sur 19 G10
South Gorley Hants 9 C10
South Green Essex 20 B3
South Green Kent 20 E5
South-haa Shetland 96 E5
South Ham Hants 18 F3
South Hanningfield Essex 20 B4
South Harting W Sus 11 C6
South Hatfield Herts 29 H9
South Hayling Hants 10 E6
South Hazelrigg Northumb 71 G9
South Heath Bucks 18 A6
South Heighton E Sus 12 F3
South Hetton Durham 58 B4
South Hiendley W Yorks 45 A7
South Hill Corn 4 D4
South Hinksey Oxon 18 A2
South Hole Devon 6 D1
South Holme N Yorks 52 B2
South Holmwood Sur 19 G8
South Hornchurch London 20 C2
South Hykeham Lincs 46 F3
South Hylton T&W 63 H9
South Kelsey Lincs 46 C4
South Kessock Highld 87 G9
South Killingholme N Lincs 53 H7
South Kilvington N Yorks 51 A10
South Kilworth Leics 36 G2
South Kirkby W Yorks 45 A8
South Kirkton Aberds 83 C9
South Kiscadale N Ayrs 66 D3
South Kyme Lincs 46 H5
South Lancing W Sus 11 D10
South Leigh Oxon 27 H10
South Leverton Notts 45 D11
South Littleton Worcs 27 D7
South Lopham Norf 38 G6
South Luffenham Rutland 36 E5
South Malling E Sus 12 E3
South Marston Swindon 17 C8
South Middleton Northumb 62 A5
South Milford N Yorks 51 F10
South Millbrex Aberds 89 D8
South Milton Devon 5 G8
South Mimms Herts 19 A9
South Molton Devon 6 D6
South Moreton Oxon 18 C2
South Mundham W Sus 11 D7
South Muskham Notts 45 G11
South Newbald E Yorks 52 F5
South Newington Oxon 27 E11
South Newton Wilts 9 A9
South Normanton Derbys 45 G8
South Norwood London 19 E10
South Nutfield Sur 19 G10
South Ockendon Thurrock 20 C2
South Ormsby Lincs 47 E7
South Otterington N Yorks 58 H4
South Owersby Lincs 46 C4
South Oxhey Herts 19 B8
South Perrott Dorset 8 D3
South Petherton Som 8 C3
South Petherwin Corn 4 C4
South Pickenham Norf 38 E4
South Pool Devon 5 G8
South Port Argyll 74 E3
South Radworthy Devon 7 C6
South Rauceby Lincs 46 H4
South Raynham Norf 38 C4
South Reston Lincs 47 D8
South Runcton Norf 38 E2
South Scarle Notts 46 F2
South Shian Argyll 74 C2
South Shields T&W 63 G9
South Shore Blackpool 49 F3
South Somercotes Lincs 47 C8
South Stainley N Yorks 51 C9
South Stainmore Cumb 57 E10
South Stifford Thurrock 20 D3
South Stoke Oxon 18 C2
South Stoke W Sus 11 D9
South Street E Sus 12 E2
South Street Kent 21 E8
South Street Kent 21 F7
South Street London 19 F11
South Tawton Devon 6 G5
South Thoresby Lincs 47 E8
South Tidworth Wilts 17 G9
South Town Hants 18 H3
South View Hants 18 F3
South Walsham Norf 39 D9
South Warnborough Hants 18 G4
South Weald Essex 20 B2
South Weston Oxon 18 B4
South Wheatley Corn 4 B3
South Wheatley Notts 45 D11
South Whiteness Shetland 96 J5
South Widcombe Bath 16 F2
South Wigston Leics 36 F1
South Willingham Lincs 46 D5
South Wingfield Derbys 45 G7
South Witham Lincs 36 D5
South Wonston Hants 17 H11
South Woodham Ferrers Essex 20 B5
South Wootton Norf 38 C2
South Wraxall Wilts 16 E5
South Zeal Devon 6 G5
Southall London 19 C8
Southam Glos 26 F6
Southam Warks 27 B11
Southampton Soton 10 C3
Southborough Kent 12 B4
Southbourne Bmouth 9 E10
Southbourne W Sus 11 D6
Southburgh Norf 38 E5
Southburn E Yorks 52 D5
Southchurch Southend 20 C6
Southcott Wilts 17 F8
Southcourt Bucks 28 G5
Southdean Borders 62 C2
Southdene Mers 43 C7
Southease E Sus 12 F3
Southend Argyll 65 H7
Southend W Berks 18 D2
Southend Wilts 17 D8
Southend-on-Sea Southend 20 C5
Southernden Kent 20 G5
Southerndown V Glam 14 D4
Southerness Dumfries 60 H5
Southery Norf 38 F2
Southfield Northumb 63 F8
Southfleet Kent 20 D3
Southgate Ceredig 32 H1
Southgate London 19 B9
Southgate Norf 39 C7
Southgate Swansea 23 H10
Southill C Beds 29 D8
Southleigh Devon 7 G11
Southminster Essex 20 B6
Southmoor Oxon 17 B10
Southoe Cambs 29 B8
Southolt Suff 31 B8
Southorpe Pboro 37 E6
Southowram W Yorks 51 G7
Southport Mers 49 H3
Southpunds Shetland 96 L6
Southrepps Norf 39 B8
Southrey Lincs 46 F5
Southrop Glos 17 A8
Southrope Hants 18 G3
Southsea Ptsmth 10 E5
Southstoke Bath 16 E4
Southtown Norf 39 E11
Southtown Orkney 95 J5
Southwaite Cumb 56 B6
Southwark London 19 D10
Southwater W Sus 11 B10
Southwater Street W Sus 11 B10
Southway Som 15 G11
Southwell Dorset 8 G5
Southwell Notts 45 G10
Southwick Hants 10 D5
Southwick Northants 36 F6
Southwick T&W 63 H9
Southwick W Sus 11 D11
Southwick Wilts 16 F5
Southwold Suff 39 H11
Southwood Norf 39 E9
Southwood Som 8 A4
Soval Lodge W Isles 91 E8
Sowber Gate N Yorks 58 H4
Sowerby N Yorks 51 A10
Sowerby W Yorks 50 G6
Sowerby Bridge W Yorks 51 G6
Sowerby Row Cumb 56 C5
Sowood W Yorks 51 H6
Sowton Devon 7 G8
Soyal Highld 87 B8
Spa Common Norf 39 B8
Spacey Houses N Yorks 51 D9
Spadeadam Farm Cumb 61 F11
Spalding Lincs 37 C8
Spaldington E Yorks 52 F3
Spaldwick Cambs 29 A8
Spalford Notts 46 F2
Spanby Lincs 37 B6
Sparham Norf 39 D6
Spark Bridge Cumb 49 A3
Sparkford Som 8 B5
Sparkhill W Mid 35 G6
Sparkwell Devon 5 F6
Sparrow Green Norf 38 D5
Sparrowpit Derbys 44 D4
Sparsholt Hants 10 A3
Sparsholt Oxon 17 C10
Spartylea Northumb 57 B10
Spaunton N Yorks 59 H8
Spaxton Som 7 C11
Spean Bridge Highld 80 E4
Spear Hill W Sus 11 C10
Speen Bucks 18 B5
Speen W Berks 17 E11
Speeton N Yorks 53 B7
Speke Mers 43 D7
Speldhurst Kent 12 B4
Spellbrook Herts 29 G11
Spelsbury Oxon 27 F10
Spelter Bridgend 14 B4
Spencers Wood Wokingham 18 E4
Spennithorne N Yorks 58 H2
Spennymoor Durham 58 C3
Spetchley Worcs 26 C5
Spetisbury Dorset 9 D8
Spexhall Suff 39 G9
Spey Bay Moray 88 B3
Speybridge Highld 82 A2
Speyview Moray 88 D2
Spilsby Lincs 47 F8
Spindlestone Northumb 71 G10
Spinkhill Derbys 45 E8
Spinningdale Highld 87 C9
Spirthill Wilts 16 D6
Spital Hill S Yorks 45 C10
Spital in the Street Lincs 46 D3
Spithurst E Sus 12 E3
Spittal Dumfries 54 D6
Spittal E Loth 70 C3
Spittal Highld 94 E3
Spittal Northumb 71 E9
Spittal Pembs 22 D4
Spittal Stirling 68 B4
Spittal of Glenmuick Aberds 82 E5
Spittal of Glenshee Perth 82 F3
Spittalfield Perth 76 C4
Spixworth Norf 39 D8
Splayne's Green E Sus 12 D3
Spofforth N Yorks 51 D9
Spon End W Mid 35 H9
Spon Green Flint 42 F5
Spondon Derby 35 B10
Spooner Row Norf 39 F6
Sporle Norf 38 D4
Spott E Loth 70 C5
Spratton Northants 28 A4
Spreakley Sur 18 G5
Spreyton Devon 6 G5
Spridlington Lincs 46 D4
Spring Vale S Yorks 44 B6
Spring Valley IoM 48 E3
Springburn Glasgow 68 D5
Springfield Dumfries 61 G9
Springfield Essex 30 H4
Springfield Fife 76 F6
Springfield Moray 87 F13
Springfield W Mid 35 G6
Springhill Staffs 34 E5
Springholm Dumfries 55 C11
Springkell Dumfries 61 F8
Springside N Ayrs 67 C6
Springthorpe Lincs 46 D2
Springwell T&W 63 H8
Sproatley E Yorks 53 F7
Sproston Green Ches W 43 F10
Sprotbrough S Yorks 45 B9
Sproughton Suff 31 D8
Sprouston Borders 70 G6
Sprowston Norf 39 D8
Sproxton Leics 36 C4
Sproxton N Yorks 52 A2
Spurstow Ches E 43 G8
Spynie Moray 88 B2
Squires Gate Blackpool 49 F3
Srannda W Isles 90 J5
Sronphadruig Lodge Perth 81 F9
Stableford Shrops 34 F3
Stableford Staffs 34 B4
Stacey Bank S Yorks 44 C6
Stackhouse N Yorks 50 C4
Stackpole Pembs 22 G4
Staddiscombe Plym 4 F6
Staddlethorpe E Yorks 52 G4
Stadhampton Oxon 18 B3
Stadhlaigearraidh W Isles 84 E2
Staffield Cumb 57 B7
Staffin Highld 85 B9
Stafford Staffs 34 C5
Stagsden Bedford 28 D6
Stainburn Cumb 56 D2
Stainburn N Yorks 51 E8
Stainby Lincs 36 C5
Staincross S Yorks 45 A7
Staindrop Durham 58 D2
Staines Sur 19 D7
Stainfield Lincs 37 C6
Stainfield Lincs 46 E5
Stainforth N Yorks 50 C4
Stainforth S Yorks 45 A10
Staining Lancs 49 F3
Stainland W Yorks 51 H6
Stainsacre N Yorks 59 F10
Stainsby Derbys 45 F8
Stainton Cumb 57 D6
Stainton Cumb 57 H7
Stainton Durham 58 E1
Stainton Mbro 58 E5
Stainton N Yorks 58 G2
Stainton S Yorks 45 C9
Stainton by Langworth Lincs 46 E4
Stainton le Vale Lincs 46 C5
Stainton with Adgarley Cumb 49 B2
Staintondale N Yorks 59 G10
Stair Cumb 56 D4
Stair E Ayrs 67 D7
Stairhaven Dumfries 54 D5
Staithes N Yorks 59 E8
Stake Pool Lancs 49 E4
Stakeford Northumb 63 E8
Stalbridge Dorset 8 C6
Stalbridge Weston Dorset 8 C6
Stalham Norf 39 C9
Stalham Green Norf 39 C9
Stalisfield Green Kent 20 F6
Stalling Busk N Yorks 57 H11
Stallingborough NE Lincs 46 A5
Stalmine Lancs 49 E3
Stalybridge Gtr Man 44 C3
Stambourne Essex 30 E4
Stambourne Green Essex 30 E4
Stamford Lincs 36 E6
Stamford Bridge Ches W 43 F7
Stamford Bridge E Yorks 52 D3
Stamfordham Northumb 62 F6
Stanah Cumb 56 E5
Stanborough Herts 29 G9
Stanbridge C Beds 28 F6
Stanbridge Dorset 9 D9
Stanbrook Worcs 26 D5
Stanbury W Yorks 50 F6
Stand Gtr Man 43 B10
Stand N Lanark 68 D6
Standburn Falk 69 C8
Standeford Staffs 34 E5
Standen Kent 13 B7
Standford Hants 11 A7
Standingstone Cumb 56 C2
Standish Gtr Man 43 A8
Standlake Oxon 17 A10
Standon Hants 10 B3
Standon Herts 29 F10
Standon Staffs 34 B4
Stane N Lanark 69 E7
Stanfield Norf 38 C5
Stanford C Beds 29 D8
Stanford Kent 13 C10
Stanford Bishop Hereford 26 C3
Stanford Bridge Worcs 26 B4
Stanford Dingley W Berks 18 D2
Stanford in the Vale Oxon 17 B10
Stanford-le-Hope Thurrock 20 C3
Stanford on Avon Northants 36 H1
Stanford on Soar Notts 35 C11
Stanford on Teme Worcs 26 B4
Stanford Rivers Essex 20 A2
Stanfree Derbys 45 E8
Stanghow Redcar 59 E7
Stanground Pboro 37 F8
Stanhoe Norf 38 B4
Stanhope Borders 69 H10
Stanhope Durham 57 C11
Stanion Northants 36 G5
Stanley Derbys 35 A10
Stanley Durham 58 A2
Stanley Lancs 43 B7
Stanley Perth 76 D4
Stanley Staffs 44 G3
Stanley W Yorks 51 G9
Stanley Common Derbys 35 A10
Stanley Gate Lancs 43 B7
Stanley Hill Hereford 26 D3
Stanlow Ches W 43 E7
Stanmer Brighton 12 F2
Stanmore Hants 10 B3
Stanmore London 19 B8
Stanmore W Berks 17 D11
Stannergate Dundee 77 D7
Stanningley W Yorks 51 F8
Stannington Northumb 63 F8
Stannington S Yorks 45 D7
Stansbatch Hereford 25 B10
Stansfield Suff 30 C4
Stanstead Suff 30 D5
Stanstead Abbotts Herts 29 G10
Stansted Kent 20 E3
Stansted Airport Essex 30 F2
Stansted Mountfitchet Essex 30 F2
Stanton Glos 27 E7
Stanton Mon 25 F10
Stanton Northumb 63 E7
Stanton Staffs 44 H5
Stanton Suff 30 A6
Stanton by Bridge Derbys 35 C9
Stanton-by-Dale Derbys 35 B10
Stanton Drew Bath 16 E2
Stanton Fitzwarren Swindon 17 B8

Thixendale N Yorks 52 C4
Thockrington Northumb 62 F5
Tholomas Drove Cambs 37 E9
Tholthorpe N Yorks 51 C10
Thomas Chapel Pembs 22 F6
Thomas Close Cumb 56 B6
Thomastown Aberds 88 E5
Thompson Norf 38 F5
Thomshill Moray 88 C2
Thong Kent 20 D3
Thongsbridge W Yorks 44 B5
Thoralby N Yorks 58 H1
Thoresway Lincs 46 C5
Thorganby Lincs 46 C6
Thorganby N Yorks 52 E2
Thorgill N Yorks 59 G8
Thorington Suff 31 A11
Thorington Street Suff 31 E7
Thorlby N Yorks 50 D5
Thorley Herts 29 G11
Thorley Street Herts 29 G11
Thorley Street IoW 10 F2
Thormanby N Yorks 51 B10
Thornaby-on-Tees Stockton 58 E5
Thornage Norf 38 B6
Thornborough Bucks 28 E4
Thornborough N Yorks 51 B8
Thornbury Devon 6 F3
Thornbury Hereford 26 C3
Thornbury S Glos 16 B3
Thornbury W Yorks 51 F7
Thornby Northants 36 H2
Thorncliffe Staffs 44 G4
Thorncombe Dorset 8 D2
Thorncombe Dorset 9 D7
Thorncombe Street Sur 19 G7
Thorncote Green C Beds 29 D8
Thorncross IoW 10 F3
Thorndon Suff 31 B8
Thorndon Cross Devon 6 G4
Thorne S Yorks 45 A10
Thorne St Margaret Som 7 D9
Thorner W Yorks 51 E9
Thorney Notts 46 E2
Thorney Pboro 37 E8
Thorney Crofts E Yorks 53 G8
Thorney Green Suff 31 B7
Thorney Hill Hants 9 E10
Thorney Toll Pboro 37 E9
Thornfalcon Som 8 B1
Thornford Dorset 8 C5
Thorngumbald E Yorks 53 G8
Thornham Norf 38 A3
Thornham Magna Suff 31 A8
Thornham Parva Suff 31 A8
Thornhaugh Pboro 37 E6
Thornhill Cardiff 15 C7
Thornhill Cumb 56 F2
Thornhill Derbys 44 D5
Thornhill Dumfries 60 D4
Thornhill Soton 10 C3
Thornhill Stirling 75 H9
Thornhill W Yorks 51 H8
Thornhill Edge W Yorks 51 H8
Thornhill Lees W Yorks 51 H8
Thornholme E Yorks 53 C7
Thornley Durham 58 C4
Thornley Durham 58 C2
Thornliebank E Renf 68 E4
Thorns Suff 30 C4
Thorns Green Ches E 43 D10
Thornsett Derbys 44 D4
Thornthwaite Cumb 56 D4
Thornthwaite N Yorks 51 D7
Thornton Angus 76 C6
Thornton Bucks 28 E4
Thornton E Yorks 52 E3
Thornton Fife 76 H5
Thornton Lancs 49 E3
Thornton Leics 35 E10
Thornton Lincs 46 F6
Thornton Mbro 58 E5
Thornton Mers 42 B6
Thornton Northumb 71 F8
Thornton Pembs 22 F4
Thornton W Yorks 51 F7
Thornton Curtis N Lincs 53 H6
Thornton Heath London 19 E10
Thornton Hough Mers 42 D6
Thornton in Craven N Yorks 50 E5
Thornton-le-Beans N Yorks 58 G4
Thornton-le-Clay N Yorks 52 C2
Thornton-le-Dale N Yorks 52 A4
Thornton le Moor Lincs 46 C4
Thornton-le-Moor N Yorks 58 H4
Thornton-le-Moors Ches W 43 E7
Thornton-le-Street N Yorks 58 H5
Thornton Rust N Yorks 57 H11
Thornton Steward N Yorks 58 H2
Thornton Watlass N Yorks 58 H3
Thorntonhall S Lanark 68 E4
Thorntonloch E Loth 70 C6
Thorntonpark Northumb 71 F8
Thornwood Common Essex 19 A11
Thornydykes Borders 70 F5
Thoroton Notts 36 A3
Thorp Arch W Yorks 51 E10
Thorpe Derbys 44 G5
Thorpe E Yorks 52 E5
Thorpe Lincs 47 D8
Thorpe N Yorks 50 C6
Thorpe Norf 39 F10
Thorpe Notts 45 H11
Thorpe Sur 19 E7
Thorpe Abbotts Norf 39 H7
Thorpe Acre Leics 35 C11
Thorpe Arnold Leics 36 C3
Thorpe Audlin W Yorks 51 H10
Thorpe Bassett N Yorks 52 B4
Thorpe Bay Southend 20 C6
Thorpe by Water Rutland 36 F4
Thorpe Common Suff 31 E9
Thorpe Constantine Staffs 35 E8
Thorpe Culvert Lincs 47 F8
Thorpe End Norf 39 D8
Thorpe Fendykes Lincs 47 F8
Thorpe Green Essex 31 F8
Thorpe Green Suff 30 C6
Thorpe Hesley S Yorks 45 C7
Thorpe in Balne S Yorks 45 A9
Thorpe in the Fallows Lincs 46 D3
Thorpe Langton Leics 36 F3
Thorpe Larches Durham 58 D4
Thorpe-le-Soken Essex 31 F8
Thorpe le Street E Yorks 52 E4
Thorpe Malsor Northants 36 H4
Thorpe Mandeville Northants 28 D2
Thorpe Market Norf 39 B8
Thorpe Marriot Norf 39 D7
Thorpe Morieux Suff 30 C6
Thorpe on the Hill Lincs 46 F3
Thorpe St Andrew Norf 39 E8
Thorpe St Peter Lincs 47 F8
Thorpe Salvin S Yorks 45 D9
Thorpe Satchville Leics 36 D3
Thorpe Thewles Stockton 58 D5
Thorpe Tilney Lincs 46 G5
Thorpe Underwood N Yorks 51 D10
Thorpe Waterville Northants 36 G6
Thorpe Willoughby N Yorks 52 F1
Thorpeness Suff 31 C11
Thorrington Essex 31 F7
Thorverton Devon 7 F8
Thrandeston Suff 39 H7
Thrapston Northants 36 H5
Thrashbush N Lanark 68 D6
Threapland Cumb 56 C3
Threapland N Yorks 50 C5
Threapwood Ches W 43 H7
Threapwood Staffs 34 A6
Three Ashes Hereford 26 F2
Three Bridges W Sus 12 C1
Three Burrows Corn 2 E6
Three Chimneys Kent 13 C7
Three Cocks Powys 25 E8
Three Crosses Swansea 23 G10
Three Cups Corner E Sus 12 D5
Three Holes Norf 37 E11
Three Leg Cross E Sus 12 C5
Three Legged Cross Dorset 9 D9
Three Oaks E Sus 13 E7
Threehammer Common Norf 39 D9
Threekingham Lincs 37 B6
Threemile Cross Wokingham 18 E4
Threemilestone Corn 3 E6
Threemiletown W Loth 69 C9
Threlkeld Cumb 56 D5
Threshfield N Yorks 50 C5
Thrigby Norf 39 D10
Thringarth Durham 57 D11
Thringstone Leics 35 D10
Thrintoft N Yorks 58 G4
Thriplow Cambs 29 D11
Throckenholt Lincs 37 E9
Throcking Herts 29 E10
Throckley T&W 63 G7
Throckmorton Worcs 26 D6
Throphill Northumb 63 E7
Thropton Northumb 62 C6
Throsk Stirling 69 A7
Throwleigh Devon 6 G5
Throwley Kent 20 F6
Thrumpton Notts 35 B11
Thrumster Highld 94 F5
Thrunton Northumb 62 B6
Thrupp Glos 16 A5
Thrupp Oxon 27 G11
Thrushelton Devon 4 C5
Thrussington Leics 36 D2
Thruxton Hants 17 G9
Thruxton Hereford 25 E11
Thrybergh S Yorks 45 C8
Thulston Derbys 35 B10
Thundergay N Ayrs 66 B1
Thundersley Essex 20 C4
Thundridge Herts 29 G10
Thurcaston Leics 36 D1
Thurcroft S Yorks 45 D8
Thurgarton Norf 39 B7
Thurgarton Notts 45 H10
Thurgoland S Yorks 44 B6
Thurlaston Leics 35 F11
Thurlaston Warks 27 A11
Thurlbear Som 8 B1
Thurlby Lincs 37 D7
Thurlby Lincs 46 F3
Thurleigh Bedford 29 C7
Thurlestone Devon 5 G7
Thurloxton Som 8 A1
Thurlstone S Yorks 44 B6
Thurlton Norf 39 F10
Thurlwood Ches E 44 G2
Thurmaston Leics 36 E2
Thurnby Leics 36 E2
Thurne Norf 39 D10
Thurnham Kent 20 F5
Thurnham Lancs 49 D4
Thurning Norf 39 C6
Thurning Northants 37 G6
Thurnscoe S Yorks 45 B8
Thurnscoe East S Yorks 45 B8
Thursby Cumb 56 A5
Thursford Norf 38 B5
Thursley Sur 18 H6
Thurso Highld 94 D3
Thurso East Highld 94 D3
Thurstaston Mers 42 D5
Thurston Suff 30 B6
Thurstonfield Cumb 61 H9
Thurstonland W Yorks 44 A5
Thurton Norf 39 E9
Thurvaston Derbys 35 B8
Thuxton Norf 38 E6
Thwaite N Yorks 57 G10
Thwaite Suff 31 B8
Thwaite St Mary Norf 39 F9
Thwaites W Yorks 51 E6
Thwaites Brow W Yorks 51 E6
Thwing E Yorks 53 B6
Tibbermore Perth 76 E3
Tibberton Glos 26 F4
Tibberton Telford 34 C2
Tibberton Worcs 26 C6
Tibenham Norf 39 G7
Tibshelf Derbys 45 F8
Tibthorpe E Yorks 52 D5
Ticehurst E Sus 12 C5
Tichborne Hants 10 A4
Tickencote Rutland 36 E5
Tickenham N Som 15 D10
Tickhill S Yorks 45 C9
Ticklerton Shrops 33 F10
Ticknall Derbys 35 C9
Tickton E Yorks 53 E6
Tidcombe Wilts 17 F9
Tiddington Oxon 18 A3
Tiddington Warks 27 C9
Tidebrook E Sus 12 D5
Tideford Corn 4 F4
Tideford Cross Corn 4 E4
Tidenham Glos 16 B2
Tideswell Derbys 44 E5
Tidmarsh W Berks 18 D3
Tidmington Warks 27 E9
Tidpit Hants 9 C9
Tidworth Wilts 17 G9
Tiers Cross Pembs 22 E4
Tiffield Northants 28 C3
Tifty Aberds 89 D7
Tigerton Angus 77 A8
Tigh-na-Blair Perth 75 F10
Tighnabruaich Argyll 73 F8
Tighnafiline Highld 91 J13
Tigley Devon 5 E8
Tilbrook Cambs 29 B7
Tilbury Thurrock 20 D3
Tilbury Juxta Clare Essex 30 D4
Tile Cross W Mid 35 G7
Tile Hill W Mid 35 H8
Tilehurst Reading 18 D3
Tilford Sur 18 G5
Tilgate W Sus 12 C1
Tilgate Forest Row W Sus 12 C1
Tillathrowie Aberds 88 E4
Tilley Shrops 33 C11
Tillicoultry Clack 76 H2
Tillingham Essex 20 A6
Tillington Hereford 25 D11
Tillington W Sus 11 B8
Tillington Common Hereford 25 D11
Tillyarblet Angus 83 G7
Tillybirloch Aberds 83 C8
Tillycorthie Aberds 89 F9
Tillydrine Aberds 83 D8
Tillyfour Aberds 83 B7
Tillyfourie Aberds 83 B8
Tillygarmond Aberds 83 D8
Tillygreig Aberds 89 F8
Tillykerrie Aberds 89 F8
Tilmanstone Kent 21 F10
Tilney All Saints Norf 38 D1
Tilney High End Norf 38 D1
Tilney St Lawrence Norf 37 D11
Tilshead Wilts 17 G7
Tilstock Shrops 33 B11
Tilston Ches W 43 G7
Tilstone Fearnall Ches W 43 F8
Tilsworth C Beds 28 F6
Tilton on the Hill Leics 36 E3
Timberland Lincs 46 G5
Timbersbrook Ches E 44 F2
Timberscombe Som 7 B8
Timble N Yorks 51 D7
Timperley Gtr Man 43 D10
Timsbury Bath 16 F3
Timsbury Hants 10 B2
Timsgearraidh W Isles 90 D5
Timworth Green Suff 30 B5
Tincleton Dorset 9 E6
Tindale Cumb 62 H2
Tingewick Bucks 28 E3
Tingley W Yorks 51 G8
Tingrith C Beds 29 E7
Tingwall Orkney 95 F4
Tinhay Devon 4 C4
Tinshill W Yorks 51 F8
Tinsley S Yorks 45 C8
Tintagel Corn 4 C1
Tintern Parva Mon 15 A11
Tintinhull Som 8 C4
Tintwistle Derbys 44 C4
Tinwald Dumfries 60 E6
Tinwell Rutland 36 E6
Tipperty Aberds 89 F9
Tipsend Norf 37 F11
Tipton W Mid 34 F5
Tipton St John Devon 7 G9
Tiptree Essex 30 G5
Tir-y-dail Carms 24 G3
Tirabad Powys 24 D5
Tiraghoil Argyll 78 J6
Tirley Glos 26 F5
Tirphil Caerph 15 A7
Tirril Cumb 57 D7
Tisbury Wilts 9 B8
Tisman's Common W Sus 11 A9
Tissington Derbys 44 G5
Titchberry Devon 6 D1
Titchfield Hants 10 D4
Titchmarsh Northants 36 H6
Titchwell Norf 38 A3
Tithby Notts 36 B2
Titley Hereford 25 B10
Titlington Northumb 63 B7
Titsey Sur 19 F11
Tittensor Staffs 34 B4
Tittleshall Norf 38 C4
Tiverton Ches W 43 F8
Tiverton Devon 7 E8
Tivetshall St Margaret Norf 39 G7
Tivetshall St Mary Norf 39 G7
Tividale W Mid 34 F5
Tivy Dale S Yorks 44 B6
Tixall Staffs 34 C5
Tixover Rutland 36 E5
Toab Orkney 95 H6
Toab Shetland 96 M5
Toadmoor Derbys 45 G7
Tobermory Argyll 79 F8
Toberonochy Argyll 72 C6
Tobha Mor W Isles 84 E2
Tobhtarol W Isles 90 D6
Tobson W Isles 90 D6
Tocher Aberds 89 E6
Tockenham Wilts 17 D7
Tockenham Wick Wilts 17 C7
Tockholes Blackburn 50 G2
Tockington S Glos 16 C3
Tockwith N Yorks 51 D10
Todber Dorset 9 B7
Todding Hereford 33 H10
Toddington C Beds 29 F7
Toddington Glos 27 E7
Todenham Glos 27 E9
Todhills Cumb 61 G9
Todlachie Aberds 83 B8
Todmorden W Yorks 50 G5
Todrig Borders 61 B10
Todwick S Yorks 45 D8
Toft Cambs 29 C10
Toft Lincs 37 D6
Toft Hill Durham 58 D2
Toft Hill Lincs 46 F6
Toft Monks Norf 39 F10
Toft next Newton Lincs 46 D4
Toftrees Norf 38 C4
Tofts Highld 94 D5
Toftwood Norf 38 D5
Togston Northumb 63 C8
Tokavaig Highld 85 G11
Tokers Green Oxon 18 D4
Tolastadh a Chaolais W Isles 90 D6
Tolastadh bho Thuath W Isles 91 C10
Toll Bar S Yorks 45 B9
Toll End W Mid 34 F5
Toll of Birness Aberds 89 E10
Tolland Som 7 C10
Tollard Royal Wilts 9 C8
Tollbar End W Mid 35 H9
Toller Fratrum Dorset 8 E4
Toller Porcorum Dorset 8 E4
Tollerton N Yorks 51 C11
Tollerton Notts 36 B2
Tollesbury Essex 30 G6
Tolleshunt D'Arcy Essex 30 G6
Tolleshunt Major Essex 30 G6
Tolm W Isles 91 D9
Tolpuddle Dorset 9 E6
Tolvah Highld 81 D10
Tolworth London 19 E8
Tomatin Highld 81 A10
Tombreck Highld 87 H9
Tomchrasky Highld 80 B4
Tomdoun Highld 80 C3
Tomich Highld 80 A5
Tomich Highld 87 D9
Tomich House Highld 87 G8
Tomintoul Aberds 82 D3
Tomintoul Moray 82 B3
Tomnaven Moray 88 E4
Tomnavoulin Moray 82 A4
Ton-Pentre Rhondda 14 B5
Tonbridge Kent 20 G2
Tondu Bridgend 14 C4
Tonfanau Gwyn 32 E1
Tong Shrops 34 E3
Tong W Yorks 51 F8
Tong Norton Shrops 34 E3
Tonge Leics 35 C10
Tongham Sur 18 G5
Tongland Dumfries 55 D9
Tongue Highld 93 D8
Tongue End Lincs 37 D7
Tongwynlais Cardiff 15 C7
Tonna Neath 14 B3
Tonwell Herts 29 G10
Tonypandy Rhondda 14 B5
Tonyrefail Rhondda 14 C6
Toot Baldon Oxon 18 A2
Toot Hill Essex 20 A2
Toothill Hants 10 C2
Top of Hebers Gtr Man 44 B2
Topcliffe N Yorks 51 B10
Topcroft Norf 39 F8
Topcroft Street Norf 39 F8
Toppesfield Essex 30 E4
Toppings Gtr Man 43 A10
Topsham Devon 5 C10
Torbay Torbay 5 F10
Torbeg N Ayrs 66 D2
Torboll Farm Highld 87 B10
Torbrex Stirling 68 A6
Torbryan Devon 5 E9
Torcross Devon 5 G9
Tore Highld 87 F9
Torinturk Argyll 73 G7
Torksey Lincs 46 E2
Torlum W Isles 84 C2
Torlundy Highld 80 F3
Tormarton S Glos 16 D4
Tormisdale Argyll 64 C2
Tormitchell S Ayrs 66 G5
Tormore N Ayrs 66 C1
Tornagrain Highld 87 G10
Tornahaish Aberds 82 C4
Tornaveen Aberds 83 C8
Torness Highld 81 A7
Toronto Durham 58 C2
Torpenhow Cumb 56 C4
Torphichen W Loth 69 C8
Torphins Aberds 83 C8
Torpoint Corn 4 F5
Torquay Torbay 5 E10
Torquhan Borders 70 F3
Torran Argyll 73 C7
Torran Highld 85 D10
Torran Highld 87 D10
Torrance E Dunb 68 C5
Torrans Argyll 78 J7
Torranyard N Ayrs 67 B6
Torre Torbay 5 E10
Torridon Highld 86 F2
Torridon Ho. Highld 85 C13
Torrin Highld 85 F10
Torrisdale Highld 93 C9
Torrisdale-Square Argyll 65 E8
Torrish Highld 93 H12
Torrisholme Lancs 49 C4
Torroble Highld 93 J8
Torry Aberdeen 83 C11
Torry Aberds 88 E4
Torryburn Fife 69 B9
Torterston Aberds 89 D10
Torthorwald Dumfries 60 F6
Tortington W Sus 11 D9
Tortworth S Glos 16 B4
Torvaig Highld 85 D9
Torver Cumb 56 G4
Torwood Falk 69 B7
Torworth Notts 45 D10
Tosberry Devon 6 D1
Toscaig Highld 85 E12
Toseland Cambs 29 B9
Tosside N Yorks 50 D3
Tostock Suff 30 B6
Totaig Highld 84 C7
Totaig Highld 85 F13
Tote Highld 85 D9
Totegan Highld 93 C11
Tothill Lincs 47 D8
Totland IoW 10 F2
Totnes Devon 5 E9
Toton Notts 35 B11
Totronald Argyll 78 F4
Totscore Highld 85 B8
Tottenham London 19 B10
Tottenhill Norf 38 D2
Tottenhill Row Norf 38 D2
Totteridge London 19 B9
Totternhoe C Beds 28 F6
Tottington Gtr Man 43 A10
Totton Hants 10 C2
Touchen End Windsor 18 D5
Tournaig Highld 91 J13
Toux Aberds 89 C9
Tovil Kent 20 F4
Tow Law Durham 58 C2
Toward Argyll 73 G10
Towcester Northants 28 D3
Towednack Corn 2 F3
Tower End Norf 38 D2
Towersey Oxon 28 H4
Towie Aberds 82 B6
Towie Aberds 89 B8
Towiemore Moray 88 D3
Town End Cambs 37 F10
Town End Cumb 49 A4
Town Row E Sus 12 C4
Town Yetholm Borders 71 H7
Townend W Dunb 68 C3
Towngate Lincs 37 D7
Townhead Cumb 57 C7
Townhead Dumfries 55 E9
Townhead S Ayrs 66 F5
Townhead S Yorks 44 B5
Townhead of Greenlaw Dumfries 55 C10
Townhill Fife 69 B10
Townsend Bucks 28 H4
Townsend Herts 29 H8
Townshend Corn 2 F4
Towthorpe York 52 D2
Towton N Yorks 51 F10
Towyn Conwy 42 E2
Toxteth Mers 42 D6
Toynton All Saints Lincs 47 F7
Toynton Fen Side Lincs 47 F7
Toynton St Peter Lincs 47 F8
Toy's Hill Kent 19 F11
Trabboch E Ayrs 67 D7
Traboe Corn 2 G6
Tradespark Highld 87 F11
Tradespark Orkney 95 H5
Trafford Park Gtr Man 43 C10
Trallong Powys 24 F6
Tranent E Loth 70 C3
Tranmere Mers 42 D6
Trantlebeg Highld 93 D11
Trantlemore Highld 93 D11
Tranwell Northumb 63 E7
Trapp Carms 24 G3
Traprain E Loth 70 C4
Traquair Borders 70 G2
Trawden Lancs 50 F5
Trawsfynydd Gwyn 41 G9
Tre-Gibbon Rhondda 24 H6
Tre-Taliesin Ceredig 32 F2
Tre-vaughan Carms 23 D8
Tre-wyn Mon 25 F10
Trealaw Rhondda 14 B6
Treales Lancs 49 F4
Trearddur Anglesey 40 C4
Treaslane Highld 85 C8
Trebanog Rhondda 14 B6
Trebanos Neath 14 A3
Trebartha Corn 4 D3
Trebarwith Corn 4 C1
Trebetherick Corn 3 B8
Treborough Som 7 C9
Trebudannon Corn 3 C7
Trebullett Corn 4 D4
Treburley Corn 4 D4
Trebyan Corn 4 E1
Trecastle Powys 24 F5
Trecenydd Caerph 15 C7
Trecwn Pembs 22 C4
Trecynon Rhondda 14 A5
Tredavoe Corn 2 G3
Treddiog Pembs 22 D3
Tredegar Bl Gwent 25 H8
Tredegar Newydd = New Tredegar Caerph 15 A7
Tredington Glos 26 F6
Tredington Warks 27 D9
Tredinnick Corn 3 B8
Tredomen Powys 25 E8
Tredunnock Mon 15 B9
Tredustan Powys 25 E8
Treen Corn 2 G2
Treeton S Yorks 45 D8
Tref-y-Clawdd = Knighton Powys 25 A9
Trefaldwyn = Montgomery Powys 33 F8
Trefasser Pembs 22 C3
Trefdraeth Anglesey 40 C6
Trefdraeth = Newport Pembs 22 C5
Trefecca Powys 25 E8
Trefechan Ceredig 32 G1
Trefeglwys Powys 32 F5
Trefenter Ceredig 24 B3
Treffgarne Pembs 22 D4
Treffynnon = Holywell Flint 42 E4
Treffynnon Pembs 22 D3
Trefgarn Owen Pembs 22 D3
Trefil Bl Gwent 25 G8
Trefilan Ceredig 23 A10
Trefin Pembs 22 C3
Treflach Shrops 33 C8
Trefnanney Powys 33 D8
Trefnant Denb 42 E3
Trefonen Shrops 33 C8
Trefor Anglesey 40 B5
Trefor Gwyn 40 F5
Treforest Rhondda 14 C6
Trefriw Conwy 41 D9
Trefynwy = Monmouth Mon 26 G2
Tregadillett Corn 4 C3
Tregaian Anglesey 40 C6
Tregare Mon 25 G11
Tregaron Ceredig 24 C3
Tregarth Gwyn 41 D8
Tregeare Corn 4 C3
Tregeiriog Wrex 33 B7
Tregele Anglesey 40 A5
Tregidden Corn 3 G6
Treglemais Pembs 22 D3
Tregole Corn 4 B2
Tregonetha Corn 3 C8
Tregony Corn 3 E8
Tregoss Corn 3 C8
Tregoyd Powys 25 E9
Tregroes Ceredig 23 B9
Tregurrian Corn 3 C7
Tregynon Powys 33 F6
Trehafod Rhondda 14 B6
Treharris M Tydf 14 B6
Treherbert Rhondda 14 B5
Trekenner Corn 4 D4
Treknow Corn 4 C1
Trelan Corn 2 H6
Trelash Corn 4 B2
Trelassick Corn 3 D7
Trelawnyd Flint 42 E3
Trelech Carms 23 C7
Treleddyd-fawr Pembs 22 D2
Trelewis M Tydf 15 B7
Treligga Corn 4 C1
Trelights Corn 3 B8
Trelill Corn 3 B9
Trelissick Corn 3 F7
Trellech Mon 26 H2
Trelleck Grange Mon 15 A10
Trelogan Flint 42 D4
Trelystan Powys 33 E8
Tremadog Gwyn 41 F7
Tremail Corn 4 C2
Tremain Ceredig 23 B7
Tremaine Corn 4 C3
Tremar Corn 4 E3
Trematon Corn 4 F4
Tremeirchion Denb 42 E3
Trenance Corn 3 C7
Trenarren Corn 3 E9
Trench Telford 34 D2
Treneglos Corn 4 C3
Trenewan Corn 4 F2
Trent Dorset 8 C4
Trent Vale Stoke 34 A4
Trentham Stoke 34 A4
Trentishoe Devon 6 B5
Treoes V Glam 14 D5
Treorchy = Treorci Rhondda 14 B5
Treorci = Treorchy Rhondda 14 B5
Tre'r-ddôl Ceredig 32 F2
Trerule Foot Corn 4 F4
Tresaith Ceredig 23 A7
Tresawle Corn 3 E7
Trescott Staffs 34 F4
Trescowe Corn 2 F4
Tresham Glos 16 B4
Tresillian Corn 3 E7
Tresinwen Pembs 22 B4
Treskinnick Cross Corn 4 B3
Tresmeer Corn 4 C3
Tresparrett Corn 4 B2
Tresparrett Posts Corn 4 B2
Tressait Perth 75 A11
Tresta Shetland 96 D8
Tresta Shetland 96 H5
Treswell Notts 45 E11
Trethosa Corn 3 D8
Trethurgy Corn 3 D9
Tretio Pembs 22 D2
Tretire Hereford 26 F2
Tretower Powys 25 F8
Treuddyn Flint 42 G5
Trevalga Corn 4 C1
Trevalyn Wrex 43 G6
Trevanson Corn 3 B8
Trevarren Corn 3 C8
Trevarrian Corn 3 C7
Trevarrick Corn 3 E8
Trevaughan Carms 22 E6
Treveighan Corn 4 D1
Trevellas Corn 2 D6
Treverva Corn 3 F6
Trevethin Torf 15 A8
Trevigro Corn 4 E4
Treviscoe Corn 3 D8
Trevone Corn 3 B7
Trewarmett Corn 4 C1
Trewassa Corn 4 C2
Trewellard Corn 2 F2
Trewen Corn 4 C3
Trewennack Corn 2 G5
Trewern Powys 33 D8
Trewethern Corn 3 B9
Trewidland Corn 4 F3
Trewint Corn 4 B2
Trewint Corn 4 C3
Trewithian Corn 3 F7
Trewoofe Corn 2 G3
Trewoon Corn 3 D8
Treworga Corn 3 E7
Treworlas Corn 3 F7
Treyarnon Corn 3 B7
Treyford W Sus 11 C7
Trezaise Corn 3 D8
Triangle W Yorks 50 G6
Triffleton Pembs 22 D4
Trimdon Durham 58 C4
Trimdon Colliery Durham 58 C4
Trimdon Grange Durham 58 C4
Trimingham Norf 39 B8
Trimley Lower Street Suff 31 E9
Trimley St Martin Suff 31 E9
Trimley St Mary Suff 31 E9
Trimpley Worcs 34 H3
Trimsaran Carms 23 F9
Trimstone Devon 6 B3
Trinafour Perth 75 A10
Trinant Caerph 15 A8
Tring Herts 28 G6
Tring Wharf Herts 28 G6
Trinity Angus 77 A9
Trinity Jersey 11
Trisant Ceredig 32 H3
Trislaig Highld 80 F2
Trispen Corn 3 D7
Tritlington Northumb 63 D8
Trochry Perth 76 C2
Trodigal Argyll 65 F7
Troed-rhiwdalar Powys 24 C6
Troedyraur Ceredig 23 B8
Troedyrhiw M Tydf 14 A6
Tromode IoM 48 E3
Trondavoe Shetland 96 F5
Troon Corn 2 F5
Troon S Ayrs 66 C6
Trosaraidh W Isles 84 G2
Trossachs Hotel Stirling 75 G8
Troston Suff 30 A5
Trottiscliffe Kent 20 E3
Trotton W Sus 11 B7
Troutbeck Cumb 56 D5
Troutbeck Cumb 56 F6
Troutbeck Bridge Cumb 56 F6
Trow Green Glos 26 H2
Trowbridge Wilts 16 F5
Trowell Notts 35 B10
Trowle Common Wilts 16 F5
Trowley Bottom Herts 29 G7
Trows Borders 70 G5
Trowse Newton Norf 39 E8
Trudoxhill Som 16 G4
Trull Som 7 D11
Trumaisgearraidh W Isles 84 A3
Trumpan Highld 84 B7
Trumpet Hereford 26 E3
Trumpington Cambs 29 C11
Trunch Norf 39 B8
Trunnah Lancs 49 E3
Truro Corn 3 E7
Trusham Devon 5 C9
Trusley Derbys 35 B8
Trusthorpe Lincs 47 D9
Trysull Staffs 34 F4
Tubney Oxon 17 B11
Tuckenhay Devon 5 F9
Tuckhill Shrops 34 G3
Tuckingmill Corn 2 E5
Tuddenham Suff 30 A4
Tuddenham St Martin Suff 31 D8
Tudeley Kent 20 G3
Tudhoe Durham 58 C3
Tudorville Hereford 26 F2
Tudweiliog Gwyn 40 G4
Tuesley Sur 18 G6
Tuffley Glos 26 G5
Tufton Hants 17 G11
Tufton Pembs 22 D5
Tugby Leics 36 E3
Tugford Shrops 34 G1
Tullibardine Perth 76 F2
Tullibody Clack 75 H11
Tullich Argyll 73 B9
Tullich Highld 81 A8
Tullich Muir Highld 87 D10
Tulliemet Perth 76 B2
Tulloch Aberds 83 F9
Tulloch Aberds 89 E8
Tulloch Perth 76 E3
Tulloch Castle Highld 87 E8
Tullochgorm Argyll 73 D8
Tulloes Angus 77 C8
Tullybannocher Perth 75 E10
Tullybelton Perth 76 D3
Tullyfergus Perth 76 C5
Tullymurdoch Perth 76 B4
Tullynessle Aberds 83 B7
Tumble Carms 23 E10
Tumby Woodside Lincs 46 G6
Tummel Bridge Perth 75 B10
Tunga W Isles 91 D9
Tunstall E Yorks 53 F9
Tunstall Kent 20 E5
Tunstall Lancs 50 B2
Tunstall N Yorks 58 G3
Tunstall Norf 39 E10
Tunstall Stoke 44 G2
Tunstall Suff 31 C10
Tunstall T&W 58 A4
Tunstead Derbys 44 E5
Tunstead Gtr Man 44 B4
Tunstead Norf 39 C8
Tunworth Hants 18 G3
Tupsley Hereford 26 D2
Tupton Derbys 45 F7
Tur Langton Leics 36 F3
Turgis Green Hants 18 F3
Turin Angus 77 B8
Turkdean Glos 27 G8
Turleigh Wilts 16 E5
Turn Lancs 50 H4
Turnastone Hereford 25 E10
Turnberry S Ayrs 66 F5
Turnditch Derbys 44 H6
Turners Hill W Sus 12 C2
Turners Puddle Dorset 9 E7
Turnford Herts 19 A10
Turnhouse Edin 69 C10
Turnworth Dorset 9 D7
Turriff Aberds 89 C7
Turton Bottoms Blackburn 50 H3
Turves Cambs 37 F9
Turvey Bedford 28 C6
Turville Bucks 18 B4
Turville Heath Bucks 18 B4
Turweston Bucks 28 E3
Tushielaw Borders 61 B9
Tutbury Staffs 35 C8
Tutnall Worcs 26 A6
Tutshill Glos 15 B11
Tuttington Norf 39 C8
Tutts Clump W Berks 18 D2
Tuxford Notts 45 E11
Twatt Orkney 95 F3
Twatt Shetland 96 H5
Twechar E Dunb 68 C6
Tweedmouth Northumb 71 E8
Tweedsmuir Borders 60 A6
Twelve Heads Corn 3 E6
Twemlow Green Ches E 43 F10
Twenty Lincs 37 C7
Twerton Bath 16 E4
Twickenham London 19 D8
Twigworth Glos 26 F5
Twineham W Sus 12 E1
Twinhoe Bath 16 F4
Twinstead Essex 30 E5
Twinstead Green Essex 30 E5
Twiss Green Warr 43 C9
Twiston Lancs 50 E4
Twitchen Devon 7 C6
Twitchen Shrops 33 H9
Two Bridges Devon 5 D7
Two Dales Derbys 44 F6
Two Mills Ches W 42 E6
Twycross Leics 35 E9
Twyford Bucks 28 F3
Twyford Derbys 35 C9
Twyford Hants 10 B3
Twyford Leics 36 D3
Twyford Lincs 36 C5
Twyford Norf 38 C6
Twyford Wokingham 18 D4
Twyford Common Hereford 26 E2
Twyn-y-Sheriff Mon 25 H11
Twynholm Dumfries 55 D9
Twyning Glos 26 E5
Twyning Green Glos 26 E6
Twynllanan Carms 24 F4
Twynmynydd Carms 24 G3
Twywell Northants 36 H5
Ty-draw Conwy 41 E10
Ty-hen Carms 23 D8
Ty-hen Gwyn 40 G3
Ty-mawr Anglesey 40 B6
Ty Mawr Carms 23 B10
Ty Mawr Cwm Conwy 42 H2
Ty-nant Conwy 32 A5
Ty-nant Gwyn 32 C5
Ty-uchaf Powys 32 C5
Tyberton Hereford 25 E10
Tyburn W Mid 35 F7
Tycroes Carms 24 G3
Tycrwyn Powys 33 D7
Tydd Gote Lincs 37 D10
Tydd St Giles Cambs 37 D10
Tydd St Mary Lincs 37 D10
Tyddewi = St David's Pembs 22 D2
Tyddyn-mawr Gwyn 41 F7
Tye Green Essex 29 H11
Tye Green Essex 30 E2
Tye Green Essex 30 F4
Tyldesley Gtr Man 43 B9
Tyler Hill Kent 21 E8
Tylers Green Bucks 18 B6
Tylorstown Rhondda 14 B6
Tylwch Powys 32 G5
Tyn-y-celyn Wrex 33 B7
Tyn-y-coed Shrops 33 C8
Tyn-y-fedwen Powys 33 B7
Tyn-y-ffridd Powys 33 B7
Tyn-y-graig Powys 25 C7
Ty'n-y-groes Conwy 41 C9
Ty'n-y-maes Gwyn 41 D8
Tyn-y-pwll Anglesey 40 B6
Ty'n-yr-eithin Ceredig 24 B3
Tyncelyn Ceredig 24 B3
Tyndrum Stirling 74 D6
Tyne Tunnel T&W 63 G9
Tyneham Dorset 9 F7
Tynehead Midloth 70 E2
Tynemouth T&W 63 G9
Tynewydd Rhondda 14 B5
Tyninghame E Loth 70 C5
Tynron Dumfries 60 D4
Tynygongl Anglesey 41 B7
Tynygraig Ceredig 24 B3
Tŷ'r-felin-isaf Conwy 41 D10
Tyrie Aberds 89 B9
Tyringham M Keynes 28 D5
Tythecott Devon 6 E3
Tythegston Bridgend 14 D4
Tytherington Ches E 44 E3
Tytherington S Glos 16 C3
Tytherington Som 16 G4
Tytherington Wilts 16 G6
Tytherleigh Devon 8 D2
Tywardreath Corn 4 F1
Tywyn Conwy 41 C9
Tywyn Gwyn 32 E1

U

Uachdar W Isles 84 C2
Uags Highld 85 E12
Ubbeston Green Suff 31 A10
Ubley Bath 15 F11
Uckerby N Yorks 58 F3
Uckfield E Sus 12 D3
Uckington Glos 26 F6
Uddingston S Lanark 68 D5
Uddington S Lanark 69 G7
Udimore E Sus 13 E7
Udny Green Aberds 89 F8
Udny Station Aberds 89 F9
Udston S Lanark 68 E5
Udstonhead S Lanark 68 F6
Uffcott Wilts 17 D8
Uffculme Devon 7 E9
Uffington Lincs 37 E6
Uffington Oxon 17 C10
Uffington Shrops 33 D11
Ufford Pboro 37 E6
Ufford Suff 31 C9
Ufton Warks 27 B10
Ufton Nervet W Berks 18 E3
Ugadale Argyll 65 F8
Ugborough Devon 5 F7
Uggeshall Suff 39 G10
Ugglebarnby N Yorks 59 F9
Ughill S Yorks 44 C6
Ugley Essex 30 F2
Ugley Green Essex 30 F2
Ugthorpe N Yorks 59 E8
Uidh W Isles 84 J1
Uig Argyll 73 E10
Uig Highld 84 C6
Uig Highld 85 B8
Uigen W Isles 90 D5
Uigshader Highld 85 D9
Uisken Argyll 78 K6
Ulbster Highld 94 F5
Ulceby Lincs 47 E8
Ulceby N Lincs 46 A5
Ulceby Skitter N Lincs 46 A5
Ulcombe Kent 20 G5
Uldale Cumb 56 C4
Uley Glos 16 B4
Ulgham Northumb 63 D8
Ullapool Highld 86 B4
Ullenhall Warks 27 B8
Ullenwood Glos 26 G6
Ulleskelf N Yorks 51 E11
Ullesthorpe Leics 35 G11
Ulley S Yorks 45 D8
Ullingswick Hereford 26 D2
Ullinish Highld 85 E8
Ullock Cumb 56 D2
Ulnes Walton Lancs 49 H5
Ulpha Cumb 56 G3
Ulrome E Yorks 53 D7
Ulsta Shetland 96 E6
Ulva House Argyll 78 H7
Ulverston Cumb 49 B2
Ulwell Dorset 9 F9
Umberleigh Devon 6 D5
Unapool Highld 92 F5
Unasary W Isles 84 F2
Underbarrow Cumb 56 G6
Undercliffe W Yorks 51 F7
Underhoull Shetland 96 C7
Underriver Kent 20 F2
Underwood Notts 45 G8
Undy Mon 15 C10
Unifirth Shetland 96 H4
Union Cottage Aberds 83 D10
Union Mills IoM 48 E3
Union Street E Sus 12 C6
Unstone Derbys 45 E7
Unstone Green Derbys 45 E7
Unthank Cumb 56 C6
Unthank Cumb 57 B8
Unthank End Cumb 56 C6
Up Cerne Dorset 8 D5
Up Exe Devon 7 F8
Up Hatherley Glos 26 F6
Up Holland Lancs 43 B8
Up Marden W Sus 11 C6
Up Nately Hants 18 F3
Up Somborne Hants 10 A2
Up Sydling Dorset 8 D5
Upavon Wilts 17 F8
Upchurch Kent 20 E5
Upcott Hereford 25 C10
Upend Cambs 30 C3
Upgate Norf 39 D7
Uphall W Loth 69 C9
Uphall Station W Loth 69 C9
Upham Devon 7 F7
Upham Hants 10 B4
Uphampton Worcs 26 B5
Uphill N Som 15 F9
Uplawmoor E Renf 68 E3
Upleadon Glos 26 F4
Upleatham Redcar 59 E7
Uplees Kent 20 E6
Uploders Dorset 8 E4
Uplowman Devon 7 E9
Uplyme Devon 8 E2
Upminster London 20 C2
Upnor Medway 20 D4
Upottery Devon 7 F
Upper Affcot Shrops 33 G
Upper Ardchronie Highld 87
Upper Arley Worcs 34
Upper Arncott Oxon 28
Upper Astrop Northants 28
Upper Badcall Highld 92
Upper Basildon W Berks 18
Upper Beeding W Sus 11 C
Upper Benefield Northants 36
Upper Bighouse Highld 93
Upper Boddington Northants 27
Upper Borth Ceredig 32
Upper Boyndlie Aberds 89
Upper Brailes Warks 27
Upper Breakish Highld 85
Upper Breinton Hereford 25
Upper Broadheath Worcs 26
Upper Broughton Notts 36
Upper Bucklebury W Berks 18
Upper Burnhaugh Aberds 83
Upper Caldecote C Beds 29
Upper Catesby Northants 28
Upper Chapel Powys 25
Upper Church Village Rhondda 14
Upper Chute Wilts 17
Upper Clatford Hants 17
Upper Clynnog Gwyn 40
Upper Cumberworth W Yorks 44
Upper Cwm-twrch Powys 24
Upper Cwmbran Torf 15
Upper Dallachy Moray 88
Upper Dean Bedford 29
Upper Denby W Yorks 44
Upper Denton Cumb 62
Upper Derraid Highld 87 H
Upper Dicker E Sus 12
Upper Dovercourt Essex 31
Upper Druimfin Argyll 79
Upper Dunsforth N Yorks 51
Upper Eathie Highld 87
Upper Elkstone Staffs 44
Upper End Derbys 44
Upper Farringdon Hants 18
Upper Framilode Glos 26
Upper Glenfintaig Highld 80
Upper Gornal W Mid 34
Upper Gravenhurst C Beds 29
Upper Green Mon 25
Upper Green W Berks 17
Upper Grove Common Hereford 26
Upper Hackney Derbys 44
Upper Hale Sur 18
Upper Halistra Highld 84
Upper Halling Medway 20
Upper Hambleton Rutland 36
Upper Hardres Court Kent 21
Upper Hartfield E Sus 12
Upper Haugh S Yorks 45
Upper Heath Shrops 34
Upper Hellesdon Norf 39
Upper Helmsley N Yorks 52
Upper Hergest Hereford 25
Upper Heyford Northants 28
Upper Heyford Oxon 27 F
Upper Hill Hereford 25 C
Upper Hopton W Yorks 51
Upper Horsebridge E Sus 12
Upper Hulme Staffs 44
Upper Inglesham Swindon 17
Upper Inverbrough Highld 87 H
Upper Killay Swansea 23 G
Upper Knockando Moray 88
Upper Lambourn W Berks 17 C
Upper Leigh Staffs 34
Upper Lenie Highld 81
Upper Lochton Aberds 83
Upper Longdon Staffs 35
Upper Lybster Highld 94
Upper Lydbrook Glos 26
Upper Maes-coed Hereford 25 E
Upper Midway Derbys 35
Upper Milovaig Highld 84
Upper Minety Wilts 17
Upper Mitton Worcs 26
Upper North Dean Bucks 18
Upper Obney Perth 76
Upper Ollach Highld 85 E
Upper Padley Derbys 44
Upper Pollicott Bucks 28
Upper Poppleton York 52

pper Quinton Warks 27 D8
pper Ratley Hants 10 B2
pper Rissington Glos 27 G9
pper Rochford Worcs 26 B3
pper Sandaig Highld 85 G12
pper Sanday Orkney 95 H6
pper Sapey Hereford 26 B3
pper Saxondale Notts 36 B2
pper Seagry Wilts 16 C6
pper Shelton C Beds 28 D6
pper Sheringham Norf 39 A7
pper Skelmorlie N Ayrs 73 G11
pper Slaughter Glos 27 F8
pper Soudley Glos 26 G3
pper Stondon C Beds 29 E8
pper Stowe Northants 28 C3
pper Stratton Swindon 17 C8
pper Street Hants 9 C10
pper Street Norf 39 D9
pper Street Norf 39 D9
pper Street Suff 31 E8
pper Strensham Worcs 26 E6
pper Sundon C Beds 29 F7
pper Swell Glos 27 F8
pper Tean Staffs 34 B6
pper Tillyrie Perth 76 G4
pper Tooting London 19 D9
pper Tote Highld 85 C10
pper Town N Som 15 E11
pper Treverward Shrops 33 H8
pper Tysoe Warks 27 D10
pper Upham Wilts 17 D9
pper Wardington Oxon 27 D11
pper Weald M Keynes 28 E4
pper Weedon Northants 28 C3
pper Wield Hants 18 H3
pper Winchendon Bucks 28 G4
pper Witton W Mid 35 F6
pper Woodend Aberds 83 B8
pper Woodford Wilts 17 H8
pper Wootton Hants 18 F2
pper Wyche Hereford 26 D4
pperby Cumb 56 A6
ppermill Gtr Man 44 B3
ppersound Shetland 96 J6
pperthong W Yorks 44 B5
pperthorpe N Lincs 45 B11
pperton W Sus 11 B8
ppertown Derbys 45 F7
ppertown Highld 94 C5
ppertown Orkney 95 J5
ppingham Rutland 36 F4
ppington Shrops 34 E2
psall N Yorks 58 H5
pshire Essex 19 A11
pstreet Kent 21 E9
pthorpe Suff 30 A6
pton Cambs 37 H7
pton Ches W 43 F7
pton Corn 6 F1
pton Dorset 8 F6
pton Dorset 9 E8
pton Hants 10 C2
pton Hants 17 F10
pton Leics 35 F9
pton Lincs 46 D2
pton Mers 42 D5
pton Norf 39 D9
pton Northants 28 B4
pton Notts 45 E11
pton Notts 45 G11
pton Oxon 18 C2
pton Pboro 37 E7
pton Slough 18 D6
pton Som 7 D8
pton W Yorks 45 A8
pton Bishop Hereford 26 F3
pton Cheyney S Glos 16 E3
pton Cressett Shrops 34 F2
pton Cross Corn 4 D3
pton Grey Hants 18 G3
pton Hellions Devon 7 F7
pton Lovell Wilts 16 G6
pton Magna Shrops 34 D1
pton Noble Som 16 H4
pton Pyne Devon 7 G8
pton St Leonard's Glos 26 G5
pton Scudamore Wilts 16 G5
pton Snodsbury Worcs 26 C6
pton upon Severn Worcs 26 D5
pton Warren Worcs 26 B6
pwaltham W Sus 11 C8
pware Cambs 30 A2
pwell Norf 37 E10
pwey Dorset 8 F5
pwood Cambs 37 G8
radale Shetland 96 K6
rafirth Shetland 96 F5
rchfont Wilts 17 F7
rdimarsh Hereford 26 D2
re Shetland 96 F4
re Bank N Yorks 51 B9
rgha W Isles 90 H6
rishay Common Hereford 25 E10
rlay Nook Stockton 58 E4
rmston Gtr Man 43 C10
rpeth Durham 58 A3
rquhart Highld 87 F8
rquhart Moray 88 B2
rra N Yorks 59 F6
rray Highld 87 F8
shaw Moor Durham 58 B3
sk = Brynbuga Mon 15 A9
sselby Lincs 46 C4
sworth T&W 63 H9
tkinton Ches W 43 F8
tley W Yorks 50 E6
ton Devon 7 G7
tterby Lincs 47 C7
Uttoxeter Staffs 35 B6
Uwchmynydd Gwyn 40 H3
Uxbridge London 19 C7
Uyeasound Shetland 96 C7
Uzmaston Pembs 22 E4

V

Valley Anglesey 40 C4
Valley Truckle Corn 4 C1
Valleyfield Dumfries 55 D9
Valsgarth Shetland 96 B8
Valtos Highld 85 B10
Van Powys 32 G5
Vange Essex 20 C4
Varteg Torf 25 H9
Vatten Highld 85 D7
Vaul Argyll 78 G3
Vaynor M Tydf 25 G7
Veensgarth Shetland 96 J6
Velindre Powys 25 E8
Vellow Som 7 C9
Veness Orkney 95 F6
Venn Green Devon 6 E2
Venn Ottery Devon 7 G9
Vennington Shrops 33 E9
Venny Tedburn Devon 7 G7
Ventnor IoW 10 G4
Vernham Dean Hants 17 F10
Vernham Street Hants 17 F10
Vernolds Common Shrops 33 G10
Verwood Dorset 9 D9
Veryan Corn 3 F8
Vicarage Devon 7 H11
Vickerstown Cumb 49 C1
Victoria Corn 3 C8
Victoria S Yorks 44 B5
Vidlin Shetland 96 G6
Viewpark N Lanark 68 D6
Vigo Village Kent 20 E3
Vinehall Street E Sus 13 D6
Vine's Cross E Sus 12 E4
Viney Hill Glos 26 H3
Virginia Water Sur 18 E6
Virginstow Devon 6 G2
Vobster Som 16 G4
Voe Shetland 96 E5
Voe Shetland 96 G6
Vowchurch Hereford 25 E10
Voxter Shetland 96 F5
Voy Orkney 95 G3

W

Wackerfield Durham 58 D2
Wacton Norf 39 F7
Wadbister Shetland 96 J6
Wadborough Worcs 26 D6
Waddesdon Bucks 28 G4
Waddingham Lincs 46 C3
Waddington Lancs 50 E3
Waddington Lincs 46 F3
Wadebridge Corn 3 B8
Wadeford Som 8 C2
Wadenhoe Northants 36 G6
Wadesmill Herts 29 G10
Wadhurst E Sus 12 C5
Wadshelf Derbys 45 E7
Wadsley S Yorks 45 C7
Wadsley Bridge S Yorks 45 C7
Wadworth S Yorks 45 C9
Waen Denb 42 F4
Waen Denb 42 F2
Waen Fach Powys 33 D8
Waen Goleugoed Denb 42 E3
Wag Highld 93 G13
Wainfleet All Saints Lincs 47 G8
Wainfleet Bank Lincs 47 G8
Wainfleet St Mary Lincs 47 G9
Wainfleet Tofts Lincs 47 G8
Wainhouse Corner Corn 4 B2
Wainscott Medway 20 D4
Wainstalls W Yorks 50 G6
Waitby Cumb 57 F9
Waithe Lincs 46 B6
Wake Lady Green N Yorks 59 G7
Wakefield W Yorks 51 G9
Wakerley Northants 36 F5
Wakes Colne Essex 30 F5
Walberswick Suff 31 A11
Walberton W Sus 11 D8
Walbottle T&W 63 G7
Walcot Lincs 37 B6
Walcot N Lincs 52 G4
Walcot Shrops 33 G9
Walcot Swindon 17 C8
Walcot Telford 34 D1
Walcot Green Norf 39 G7
Walcote Leics 36 G1
Walcote Warks 27 C8
Walcott Lincs 46 G5
Walcott Norf 39 B9
Walden N Yorks 50 A6
Walden Head N Yorks 50 A5
Walden Stubbs N Yorks 52 H1
Waldersey Cambs 37 E10
Walderslade Medway 20 E4
Walderton W Sus 11 C6
Walditch Dorset 8 E3
Waldley Derbys 35 B7
Waldridge Durham 58 A3
Waldringfield Suff 31 D9
Waldringfield Heath Suff 31 D9
Waldron E Sus 12 E4
Wales S Yorks 45 D8
Walesby Lincs 46 C5
Walesby Notts 45 E10
Walford Hereford 25 A10
Walford Hereford 26 F2
Walford Shrops 33 C10
Walford Heath Shrops 33 D10
Walgherton Ches E 43 H9
Walgrave Northants 28 A5
Walhampton Hants 10 E2
Walk Mill Lancs 50 F4
Walkden Gtr Man 43 B10
Walker T&W 63 G8
Walker Barn Ches E 44 E3
Walker Fold Lancs 50 E2
Walkerburn Borders 70 G2
Walkeringham Notts 45 C11
Walkerith Lincs 45 C11
Walkern Herts 29 F9
Walker's Green Hereford 26 D2
Walkerville N Yorks 58 G3
Walkford Dorset 9 E11
Walkhampton Devon 4 E6
Walkington E Yorks 52 F5
Walkley S Yorks 45 D7
Wall Northumb 62 G5
Wall Staffs 35 E7
Wall Bank Shrops 33 F11
Wall Heath W Mid 34 G4
Wall under Heywood Shrops 33 F11
Wallaceton Dumfries 60 E4
Wallacetown S Ayrs 66 D6
Wallacetown S Ayrs 66 F5
Wallands Park E Sus 12 E3
Wallasey Mers 42 C6
Wallcrouch E Sus 12 C5
Wallingford Oxon 18 C3
Wallington Hants 10 D4
Wallington Herts 29 E9
Wallington London 19 E9
Wallis Pembs 22 D5
Walliswood Sur 19 H8
Walls Shetland 96 J4
Wallsend T&W 63 G8
Wallston V Glam 15 D7
Wallyford E Loth 70 C2
Walmer Kent 21 F10
Walmer Bridge Lancs 49 G4
Walmersley Gtr Man 44 A2
Walmley W Mid 35 F7
Walpole Suff 31 A10
Walpole Cross Keys Norf 37 D11
Walpole Highway Norf 37 D11
Walpole Marsh Norf 37 D10
Walpole St Andrew Norf 37 D11
Walpole St Peter Norf 37 D11
Walsall W Mid 34 F6
Walsall Wood W Mid 34 E6
Walsden W Yorks 50 G5
Walsgrave on Sowe W Mid 35 G9
Walsham le Willows Suff 30 A6
Walshaw Gtr Man 43 A10
Walshford N Yorks 51 D10
Walsoken Cambs 37 D10
Walston S Lanark 69 F9
Walsworth Herts 29 E9
Walters Ash Bucks 18 B5
Walterston V Glam 14 D6
Walterstone Hereford 25 F10
Waltham Kent 21 G8
Waltham NE Lincs 46 B6
Waltham Abbey Essex 19 A10
Waltham Chase Hants 10 C4
Waltham Cross Herts 19 A10
Waltham on the Wolds Leics 36 C4
Waltham St Lawrence Windsor 18 D5
Walthamstow London 19 C10
Walton Cumb 61 G11
Walton Derbys 45 F7
Walton Leics 36 G1
Walton M Keynes 28 E5
Walton Mers 42 C6
Walton Pboro 37 E7
Walton Powys 25 C9
Walton Som 15 H10
Walton Staffs 34 B4
Walton Suff 31 E9
Walton Telford 34 D1
Walton W Yorks 51 E10
Walton W Yorks 51 H9
Walton Warks 27 C9
Walton Cardiff Glos 26 E6
Walton East Pembs 22 D5
Walton-in-Gordano N Som 15 D10
Walton-le-Dale Lancs 50 G1
Walton-on-Thames Sur 19 E8
Walton on the Hill Staffs 34 C5
Walton on the Hill Sur 19 F9
Walton-on-the-Naze Essex 31 F9
Walton on the Wolds Leics 36 D1
Walton-on-Trent Derbys 35 D8
Walton West Pembs 22 E3
Walwen Flint 42 E5
Walwick Northumb 62 F5
Walworth Darl 58 E3
Walworth Gate Darl 58 D3
Walwyn's Castle Pembs 22 E3
Wambrook Som 8 D1
Wanborough Sur 18 G6
Wanborough Swindon 17 C9
Wandsworth London 19 D9
Wangford Suff 39 H10
Wanlockhead Dumfries 60 B4
Wansford E Yorks 53 D6
Wansford Pboro 37 F6
Wanstead London 19 C11
Wanstrow Som 16 G4
Wanswell Glos 16 A3
Wantage Oxon 17 C10
Wapley S Glos 16 D4
Wappenbury Warks 27 B10
Wappenham Northants 28 D3
Warbleton E Sus 12 E5
Warblington Hants 10 D6
Warborough Oxon 18 B2
Warboys Cambs 37 G9
Warbreck Blackpool 49 F3
Warbstow Corn 4 B3
Warburton Gtr Man 43 D10
Warcop Cumb 57 E9
Ward End W Mid 35 G7
Ward Green Suff 31 B7
Warden Kent 21 D7
Warden Northumb 62 G5
Wardhill Orkney 95 F7
Wardington Oxon 27 D11
Wardlaw Borders 61 B8
Wardle Ches E 43 G9
Wardle Gtr Man 50 H5
Wardley Rutland 36 E4
Wardlow Derbys 44 E5
Wardy Hill Cambs 37 G10
Ware Herts 29 G10
Ware Kent 21 E9
Wareham Dorset 9 F8
Warehorne Kent 13 C8
Waren Mill Northumb 71 G10
Warenford Northumb 71 H10
Warenton Northumb 71 G10
Wareside Herts 29 G10
Waresley Cambs 29 C9
Waresley Worcs 26 A5
Warfield Brack 18 D5
Warfleet Devon 5 F9
Wargrave Wokingham 18 D4
Warham Norf 38 A5
Warhill Gtr Man 44 C3
Wark Northumb 62 F4
Wark Northumb 71 G7
Warkleigh Devon 6 D5
Warkton Northants 36 H4
Warkworth Northants 27 D11
Warkworth Northumb 63 C8
Warlaby N Yorks 58 G4
Warland W Yorks 50 G5
Warleggan Corn 4 E2
Warlingham Sur 19 F10
Warmfield W Yorks 51 G9
Warmingham Ches E 43 F10
Warmington Northants 37 F6
Warmington Warks 27 D11
Warminster Wilts 16 G5
Warmlake Kent 20 F5
Warmley S Glos 16 D3
Warmley Tower S Glos 16 D3
Warmonds Hill Northants 28 B6
Warmsworth S Yorks 45 B9
Warmwell Dorset 9 F6
Warndon Worcs 26 C5
Warnford Hants 10 B5
Warnham W Sus 11 A10
Warninglid W Sus 11 B11
Warren Ches E 44 E2
Warren Pembs 22 G4
Warren Heath Suff 31 D9
Warren Row Windsor 18 C5
Warren Street Kent 20 F6
Warrington M Keynes 28 C5
Warrington Warr 43 D9
Warsash Hants 10 D3
Warslow Staffs 44 G4
Warter E Yorks 52 D4
Warthermarske N Yorks 51 B8
Warthill N Yorks 52 D2
Wartling E Sus 12 F5
Wartnaby Leics 36 C3
Warton Lancs 49 B4
Warton Lancs 49 G4
Warton Northumb 62 C6
Warton Warks 35 E8
Warwick Warks 27 B9
Warwick Bridge Cumb 61 H10
Warwick on Eden Cumb 61 H10
Wasbister Orkney 95 E4
Wasdale Head Cumb 56 F3
Wash Common W Berks 17 E11
Washaway Corn 3 C9
Washbourne Devon 5 F8
Washfield Devon 7 E8
Washfold N Yorks 58 F1
Washford Som 7 B9
Washford Pyne Devon 7 E7
Washingborough Lincs 46 E4
Washington T&W 63 H9
Washington W Sus 11 C10
Wasing W Berks 18 E2
Waskerley Durham 58 B1
Wasperton Warks 27 C9
Wasps Nest Lincs 46 F4
Wass N Yorks 52 B1
Watchet Som 7 B9
Watchfield Oxon 17 B9
Watchfield Som 15 G9
Watchgate Cumb 57 G7
Watchhill Cumb 56 B3
Watcombe Torbay 5 E10
Watendlath Cumb 56 E4
Water Devon 5 C8
Water Lancs 50 G4
Water End E Yorks 52 F3
Water End Herts 19 A9
Water End Herts 29 G7
Water Newton Cambs 37 F7
Water Orton Warks 35 F7
Water Stratford Bucks 28 E3
Water Yeat Cumb 56 H4
Waterbeach Cambs 29 B11
Waterbeck Dumfries 61 F8
Waterden Norf 38 B4
Waterfall Staffs 44 G4
Waterfoot E Renf 68 E4
Waterfoot Lancs 50 G4
Waterford Hants 10 E2
Waterford Herts 29 G10
Waterhead Cumb 56 F5
Waterhead Dumfries 61 D7
Waterheads Borders 69 E11
Waterhouses Durham 58 B2
Waterhouses Staffs 44 G4
Wateringbury Kent 20 F3
Waterloo Gtr Man 44 B3
Waterloo Highld 85 F11
Waterloo Mers 42 C6
Waterloo N Lanark 69 E7
Waterloo Norf 39 D8
Waterloo Perth 76 D3
Waterloo Poole 9 E9
Waterloo Shrops 33 B11
Waterloo Port Gwyn 40 D6
Waterlooville Hants 10 D5
Watermeetings S Lanark 60 B5
Watermillock Cumb 56 D6
Waterperry Oxon 28 H3
Waterrow Som 7 D9
Water's Nook Gtr Man 43 B9
Waters Upton Telford 34 D2
Watersfield W Sus 11 C9
Waterside Aberds 89 F10
Waterside Blackburn 50 G3
Waterside Cumb 56 B4
Waterside E Ayrs 67 B7
Waterside E Ayrs 67 F7
Waterside E Dunb 68 C5
Waterside E Renf 68 E4
Waterstock Oxon 28 H3
Waterston Pembs 22 F4
Watford Herts 19 B8
Watford Northants 28 B3
Watford Gap Staffs 35 E7
Wath N Yorks 51 B9
Wath N Yorks 51 C7
Wath N Yorks 52 B2
Wath Brow Cumb 56 E2
Wath upon Dearne S Yorks 45 B8
Watley's End S Glos 16 C3
Watlington Norf 38 D2
Watlington Oxon 18 B3
Watnall Notts 45 H9
Watten Highld 94 E4
Wattisfield Suff 31 A7
Wattisham Suff 31 C7
Wattlesborough Heath Shrops 33 D9
Watton E Yorks 52 D6
Watton Norf 38 E5
Watton at Stone Herts 29 G10
Wattston N Lanark 68 C6
Wattstown Rhondda 14 B6
Wauchan Highld 80 E1
Waulkmill Lodge Orkney 95 H4
Waun Powys 32 E4
Waun-y-clyn Carms 23 F9
Waunarlwydd Swansea 14 B2
Wauncluda Carms 24 E3
Waunfawr Gwyn 41 E7
Waungron Swansea 23 F10
Waunlwyd Bl Gwent 25 H8
Wavendon M Keynes 28 E6
Waverbridge Cumb 56 B4
Waverton Ches W 43 F7
Waverton Cumb 56 B4
Wavertree Mers 43 D6
Wawne E Yorks 53 F6
Waxham Norf 39 C10
Waxholme E Yorks 53 G9
Way Kent 21 E10
Way Village Devon 7 E7
Wayfield Medway 20 E4
Wayford Som 8 D3
Waymills Shrops 34 A1
Wayne Green Mon 25 G11
Wdig = Goodwick Pembs 22 C4
Weachyburn Aberds 89 C6
Weald Oxon 17 A10
Wealdstone London 19 C8
Weardley W Yorks 51 E8
Weare Som 15 F10
Weare Giffard Devon 6 D3
Wearhead Durham 57 C10
Weasdale Cumb 57 F8
Weasenham All Saints Norf 38 C4
Weasenham St Peter Norf 38 C4
Weatherhill Sur 12 B2
Weaverham Ches W 43 E9
Weaverthorpe N Yorks 52 B5
Webheath Worcs 27 B7
Wedderlairs Aberds 89 E8
Wedderlie Borders 70 E5
Weddington Warks 35 F9
Wedhampton Wilts 17 F7
Wedmore Som 15 G10
Wednesbury W Mid 34 F5
Wednesfield W Mid 34 E5
Weedon Bucks 28 G5
Weedon Bec Northants 28 C3
Weedon Lois Northants 28 D3
Weeford Staffs 35 E7
Week Devon 7 E6
Week St Mary Corn 4 B3
Weeke Hants 10 A3
Weekley Northants 36 G4
Weel E Yorks 53 F6
Weeley Essex 31 F8
Weeley Heath Essex 31 F8
Weem Perth 75 C11
Weeping Cross Staffs 34 C5
Weethley Gate Warks 27 C7
Weeting Norf 38 G3
Weeton E Yorks 53 G9
Weeton Lancs 49 F3
Weeton N Yorks 51 E8
Weetwood Hall Northumb 71 H9
Weir Lancs 50 G4
Weir Quay Devon 4 E5
Welborne Norf 39 E6
Welbourn Lincs 46 G3
Welburn N Yorks 52 A2
Welburn N Yorks 52 C3
Welbury N Yorks 58 F4
Welby Lincs 36 B5
Welches Dam Cambs 37 G10
Welcombe Devon 6 E1
Weld Bank Lancs 50 H1
Weldon Northumb 63 D7
Welford Northants 36 G2
Welford W Berks 17 D11
Welford-on-Avon Warks 27 C8
Welham Leics 36 F3
Welham Notts 45 D11
Welham Green Herts 29 H9
Well Hants 18 G4
Well Lincs 47 E8
Well N Yorks 51 A8
Well End Bucks 18 C5
Well Heads W Yorks 51 F6
Well Hill Kent 19 E11
Well Town Devon 7 F8
Welland Worcs 26 D4
Wellbank Angus 77 D7
Welldale Dumfries 61 G7
Wellesbourne Warks 27 C9
Welling London 19 D11
Wellingborough Northants 28 B5
Wellingham Norf 38 C4
Wellingore Lincs 46 G3
Wellington Cumb 56 F2
Wellington Hereford 25 D11
Wellington Som 7 D10
Wellington Telford 34 D2
Wellington Heath Hereford 26 D4
Wellington Hill W Yorks 51 F9
Wellow Bath 16 F4
Wellow IoW 10 F2
Wellow Notts 45 F10
Wellpond Green Herts 29 F11
Wells Som 15 G11
Wells Green Ches E 43 G9
Wells-Next-The-Sea Norf 38 A5
Wellsborough Leics 35 E9
Wellswood Torbay 5 E10
Wellwood Fife 69 B9
Welney Norf 37 F11
Welsh Bicknor Hereford 26 G2
Welsh End Shrops 33 B11
Welsh Frankton Shrops 33 B9
Welsh Hook Pembs 22 D4
Welsh Newton Hereford 25 G11
Welsh St Donats V Glam 14 D6
Welshampton Shrops 33 B10
Welshpool = Y Trallwng Powys 33 E8
Welton Cumb 56 B5
Welton E Yorks 52 G5
Welton Lincs 46 E4
Welton Northants 28 B2
Welton Hill Lincs 46 D4
Welton le Marsh Lincs 47 F8
Welton le Wold Lincs 46 D6
Welwick E Yorks 53 G9
Welwyn Herts 29 G9
Welwyn Garden City Herts 29 G9
Wem Shrops 33 C11
Wembdon Som 15 H8
Wembley London 19 C8
Wembury Devon 4 G6
Wembworthy Devon 6 F5
Wemyss Bay Invclyd 73 G10
Wenallt Ceredig 24 A3
Wenallt Gwyn 32 A5
Wendens Ambo Essex 30 E2
Wendlebury Oxon 28 G2
Wendling Norf 38 D5
Wendover Bucks 28 H5
Wendron Corn 2 F5
Wendy Cambs 29 D10
Wenfordbridge Corn 4 D1
Wenhaston Suff 39 H10
Wennington Cambs 37 H8
Wennington Lancs 50 B2
Wennington London 20 C2
Wensley Derbys 44 F6
Wensley N Yorks 58 H1
Wentbridge W Yorks 51 H10
Wentnor Shrops 33 F9
Wentworth Cambs 37 H10
Wentworth S Yorks 45 C7
Wenvoe V Glam 15 D7
Weobley Hereford 25 C11
Weobley Marsh Hereford 25 C11
Wereham Norf 38 E2
Wergs W Mid 34 E4
Wern Powys 32 D5
Wern Powys 33 D8
Wernffrwd Swansea 23 G10
Wernyrheolydd Mon 25 G10
Werrington Corn 4 C4
Werrington Pboro 37 E7
Werrington Staffs 44 H3
Wervin Ches W 43 E7
Wesham Lancs 49 F4
Wessington Derbys 45 G7
West Acre Norf 38 D3
West Adderbury Oxon 27 E11
West Allerdean Northumb 71 F8
West Alvington Devon 5 G8
West Amesbury Wilts 17 G8
West Anstey Devon 7 D7
West Ashby Lincs 46 E6
West Ashling W Sus 11 D7
West Ashton Wilts 16 F5
West Auckland Durham 58 D2
West Ayton N Yorks 52 A5
West Bagborough Som 7 C10
West Barkwith Lincs 46 D5
West Barnby N Yorks 59 E9
West Barns E Loth 70 C5
West Barsham Norf 38 B5
West Bay Dorset 8 E3
West Beckham Norf 39 B7
West Bedfont Sur 19 D7
West Benhar N Lanark 69 D7
West Bergholt Essex 30 F6
West Bexington Dorset 8 F4
West Bilney Norf 38 D3
West Blatchington Brighton 12 F1
West Bowling W Yorks 51 F7
West Bradford Lancs 50 E3
West Bradley Som 16 H2
West Bretton W Yorks 44 A6
West Bridgford Notts 36 B1
West Bromwich W Mid 34 F6
West Buckland Devon 6 C5
West Buckland Som 7 D10
West Burrafirth Shetland 96 H4
West Burton N Yorks 58 H1
West Burton W Sus 11 C8
West Butterwick N Lincs 46 B2
West Byfleet Sur 19 E7
West Caister Norf 39 D11
West Calder W Loth 69 D9
West Camel Som 8 B4
West Challow Oxon 17 C10
West Chelborough Dorset 8 D4
West Chevington Northumb 63 D8
West Chiltington W Sus 11 C9
West Chiltington Common W Sus 11 C9
West Chinnock Som 8 C3
West Chisenbury Wilts 17 F8
West Clandon Sur 19 F7
West Cliffe Kent 21 G10
West Clyne Highld 93 J11
West Clyth Highld 94 G4
West Coker Som 8 C4
West Compton Dorset 8 E4
West Compton Som 16 G2
West Cowick E Yorks 52 G2
West Cranmore Som 16 G3
West Cross Swansea 14 C2
West Cullery Aberds 83 C9
West Curry Corn 6 G1
West Curthwaite Cumb 56 B5
West Darlochan Argyll 65 F7
West Dean W Sus 11 C7
West Dean Wilts 10 B1
West Deeping Lincs 37 E7
West Derby Mers 43 C6
West Dereham Norf 38 E2
West Didsbury Gtr Man 44 C2
West Ditchburn Northumb 63 A7
West Down Devon 6 B4
West Drayton London 19 D7
West Drayton Notts 45 E11
West Ella E Yorks 52 G6
West End Bedford 28 C6
West End E Yorks 52 F5
West End E Yorks 53 F7
West End Hants 10 C3
West End Lancs 50 G3
West End N Som 15 E10
West End N Yorks 51 D7
West End Norf 38 E5
West End Norf 39 D11
West End Oxon 17 A11
West End S Lanark 69 F8
West End S Yorks 45 B10
West End Suff 39 G10
West End Sur 18 E6
West End W Sus 11 C11
West End Wilts 9 B8
West End Wilts 16 D6
West End Green Hants 18 E3
West Farleigh Kent 20 F4
West Felton Shrops 33 C9
West Fenton E Loth 70 B3
West Ferry Dundee 77 D7
West Firle E Sus 12 F3
West Ginge Oxon 17 C11
West Grafton Wilts 17 E9
West Green Hants 18 F4
West Greenskares Aberds 89 B7
West Grimstead Wilts 9 B11
West Grinstead W Sus 11 B10
West Haddlesey N Yorks 52 G1
West Haddon Northants 28 A3
West Hagbourne Oxon 18 C2
West Hagley Worcs 34 G5
West Hall Cumb 61 G11
West Hallam Derbys 35 A10
West Halton N Lincs 52 G5
West Ham London 19 C11
West Handley Derbys 45 E7
West Hanney Oxon 17 B11
West Hanningfield Essex 20 B4
West Hardwick W Yorks 51 H10
West Harnham Wilts 9 B10
West Harptree Bath 16 F2
West Hatch Som 8 B1
West Head Norf 38 E1
West Heath Ches E 44 F2
West Heath Hants 18 F2
West Heath Hants 18 F5
West Helmsdale Highld 93 H13
West Hendred Oxon 17 C11
West Heslerton N Yorks 52 B5
West Hill Devon 7 G9
West Hill E Yorks 53 C7
West Hill N Som 15 D10
West Hoathly W Sus 12 C2
West Holme Dorset 9 F7
West Horndon Essex 20 C3
West Horrington Som 16 G2
West Horsley Sur 19 F7
West Horton Northumb 71 G9
West Hougham Kent 21 G9
West Houlland Shetland 96 H4
West-houses Derbys 45 G8
West Huntington York 52 D2
West Hythe Kent 13 C10
West Ilsley W Berks 17 C11
West Itchenor W Sus 11 D6
West Keal Lincs 47 F7
West Kennett Wilts 17 E8
West Kilbride N Ayrs 66 B5
West Kingsdown Kent 20 E2
West Kington Wilts 16 D5
West Kinharrachie Aberds 89 E9
West Kirby Mers 42 D5
West Knapton N Yorks 52 B4
West Knighton Dorset 8 F6
West Knoyle Wilts 9 A7
West Kyloe Northumb 71 F9
West Lambrook Som 8 C3
West Langdon Kent 21 G10
West Langwell Highld 93 J9
West Lavington W Sus 11 B7
West Lavington Wilts 17 F7
West Layton N Yorks 58 F2
West Lea Durham 58 B5
West Leake Notts 35 C11
West Learmouth Northumb 71 G7
West Leigh Devon 6 F5
West Lexham Norf 38 D4
West Lilling N Yorks 52 C2
West Linton Borders 69 E10
West Liss Hants 11 B6
West Littleton S Glos 16 D4
West Looe Corn 4 F3
West Luccombe Som 7 B7
West Lulworth Dorset 9 F7
West Lutton N Yorks 52 C5
West Lydford Som 8 A4
West Lyng Som 8 B2
West Lynn Norf 38 C2
West Malling Kent 20 F3
West Malvern Worcs 26 D4
West Marden W Sus 11 C6
West Marina E Sus 13 F6
West Markham Notts 45 E11
West Marsh NE Lincs 46 A6
West Marton N Yorks 50 D4
West Meon Hants 10 B5
West Mersea Essex 31 G7
West Milton Dorset 8 E4
West Minster Kent 20 D6
West Molesey Sur 19 E8
West Monkton Som 8 B1
West Moors Dorset 9 D9
West Morriston Borders 70 F5
West Muir Angus 77 A8
West Ness N Yorks 52 B2
West Newham Northumb 62 F6
West Newton E Yorks 53 F7
West Newton Norf 38 C2
West Norwood London 19 D10
West Ogwell Devon 5 D9
West Orchard Dorset 9 C7
West Overton Wilts 17 E8
West Park Hrtlpl 58 C5
West Parley Dorset 9 E9
West Peckham Kent 20 F3
West Pelton Durham 58 A3
West Pennard Som 15 H11
West Pentire Corn 3 C6
West Perry Cambs 29 B8
West Putford Devon 6 E2
West Quantoxhead Som 7 B10
West Rainton Durham 58 B4
West Rasen Lincs 46 D4
West Raynham Norf 38 C4
West Retford Notts 45 D10
West Rounton N Yorks 58 F5
West Row Suff 38 H2
West Rudham Norf 38 C4
West Runton Norf 39 A7
West Saltoun E Loth 70 D3
West Sandwick Shetland 96 E6
West Scrafton N Yorks 51 A6
West Sleekburn Northumb 63 E8
West Somerton Norf 39 D10
West Stafford Dorset 8 F6
West Stockwith Notts 45 C11
West Stoke W Sus 11 D7
West Stonesdale N Yorks 57 F10
West Stoughton Som 15 G10
West Stour Dorset 9 B6
West Stourmouth Kent 21 E9
West Stow Suff 30 A5
West Stowell Wilts 17 E8
West Strathan Highld 93 C8
West Stratton Hants 18 G2
West Street Kent 20 F6
West Tanfield N Yorks 51 B8
West Taphouse Corn 4 E2
West Tarbert Argyll 73 G7
West Thirston Northumb 63 D7
West Thorney W Sus 11 D6
West Thurrock Thurrock 20 D2
West Tilbury Thurrock 20 D3
West Tisted Hants 10 B5
West Tofts Norf 38 F4
West Tofts Perth 76 D4
West Torrington Lincs 46 D5
West Town Hants 10 E6
West Town N Som 15 E10
West Tytherley Hants 10 B1
West Tytherton Wilts 16 D6
West Walton Norf 37 D10
West Walton Highway Norf 37 D10
West Wellow Hants 10 C1
West Wemyss Fife 70 A2
West Wick N Som 15 E9
West Wickham Cambs 30 D3
West Wickham London 19 E10
West Williamston Pembs 22 F5
West Willoughby Lincs 36 A5
West Winch Norf 38 D2
West Winterslow Wilts 9 A11
West Wittering W Sus 11 E6
West Witton N Yorks 58 H1
West Woodburn Northumb 62 E4
West Woodhay W Berks 17 E10
West Woodlands Som 16 G4
West Worldham Hants 18 H4
West Worlington Devon 7 E6
West Worthing W Sus 11 D10
West Wratting Cambs 30 C3
West Wycombe Bucks 18 B5
West Wylam Northumb 63 G7
West Yell Shetland 96 E6
Westacott Devon 6 C4
Westbere Kent 21 E8
Westborough Lincs 36 A4
Westbourne Bmouth 9 E9
Westbourne Suff 31 D8
Westbourne W Sus 11 D6
Westbrook W Berks 17 D11
Westbury Bucks 28 E3
Westbury Shrops 33 E9
Westbury Wilts 16 F5
Westbury Leigh Wilts 16 F5
Westbury-on-Severn Glos 26 G4
Westbury on Trym Bristol 16 D2
Westbury-sub-Mendip Som 15 G11
Westby Lancs 49 F3
Westcliff-on-Sea Southend 20 C5
Westcombe Som 16 H3
Westcote Glos 27 F9
Westcott Bucks 28 G4
Westcott Devon 7 F9
Westcott Sur 19 G8
Westcott Barton Oxon 27 F11
Westdean E Sus 12 G4
Westdene Brighton 12 F1
Wester Aberchalder Highld 81 A7
Wester Balgedie Perth 76 G4
Wester Culbeuchly Aberds 89 B6
Wester Dechmont W Loth 69 D9
Wester Denoon Angus 76 C6
Wester Fintray Aberds 83 B10
Wester Gruinards Highld 87 B8
Wester Lealty Highld 87 D9
Wester Milton Highld 87 F12
Wester Newburn Fife 77 G7
Wester Quarff Shetland 96 K6
Wester Skeld Shetland 96 J4
Westerdale Highld 94 E3
Westerdale N Yorks 59 F7
Westerfield Shetland 96 H5
Westerfield Suff 31 D8
Westergate W Sus 11 D8
Westerham Kent 19 F11
Westerhope T&W 63 G7
Westerleigh S Glos 16 D4
Westerton Angus 77 B9
Westerton Durham 58 C3
Westerton W Sus 11 D7
Westerwick Shetland 96 J4
Westfield Cumb 56 D1
Westfield E Sus 13 E7
Westfield Hereford 26 D4
Westfield Highld 94 D2
Westfield N Lanark 68 C6
Westfield Norf 38 E5
Westfield W Loth 69 C8
Westfields Dorset 8 D6
Westfields of Rattray Perth 76 C4
Westgate Durham 57 C11
Westgate N Lincs 45 B11
Westgate Norf 38 A4
Westgate Norf 38 A5
Westgate on Sea Kent 21 D10
Westhall Aberds 83 A8
Westhall Suff 39 G10
Westham Dorset 8 G5
Westham E Sus 12 F5
Westham Som 15 G10
Westhampnett W Sus 11 D7
Westhay Som 15 G10
Westhead Lancs 43 B7
Westhide Hereford 26 D2
Westhill Aberds 83 C10
Westhill Highld 87 G10
Westhope Hereford 25 C11
Westhope Shrops 33 G10
Westhorpe Lincs 37 B8
Westhorpe Suff 31 B7
Westhoughton Gtr Man 43 B9
Westhouse N Yorks 50 B2
Westhumble Sur 19 F8
Westing Shetland 96 C7
Westlake Devon 5 F7
Westleigh Devon 6 D3
Westleigh Devon 7 E9
Westleigh Gtr Man 43 B9
Westleton Suff 31 B11
Westley Shrops 33 E9
Westley Suff 30 B5
Westley Waterless Cambs 30 C3
Westlington Bucks 28 G4
Westlinton Cumb 61 G9
Westmarsh Kent 21 E9
Westmeston E Sus 12 E2
Westmill Herts 29 F10
Westminster London 19 D10
Westmuir Angus 76 B6
Westness Orkney 95 F4
Westnewton Cumb 56 B3
Westnewton Northumb 71 G8
Westoe T&W 63 G9
Weston Bath 16 E4
Weston Ches E 43 G10
Weston Devon 7 H10
Weston Dorset 8 G5
Weston Halton 43 D8
Weston Hants 10 B6
Weston Herts 29 E9
Weston Lincs 37 C8
Weston N Yorks 51 E7
Weston Northants 28 D2
Weston Notts 45 F11
Weston Shrops 34 C1
Weston Shrops 34 F1
Weston Staffs 34 C5
Weston W Berks 17 D10
Weston Beggard Hereford 26 D2
Weston by Welland Northants 36 F3
Weston Colville Cambs 30 C3
Weston Coyney Stoke 34 A5
Weston Favell Northants 28 B4
Weston Green Cambs 30 C3
Weston Green Norf 39 D7
Weston Heath Shrops 34 D3
Weston Hills Lincs 37 C8
Weston-in-Gordano N Som 15 D10
Weston Jones Staffs 34 C3
Weston Longville Norf 39 D7
Weston Lullingfields Shrops 33 C10
Weston-on-the-Green Oxon 28 G2
Weston-on-Trent Derbys 35 C10
Weston Patrick Hants 18 G3
Weston Rhyn Shrops 33 B8
Weston-Sub-Edge Glos 27 D8
Weston-super-Mare N Som 15 E9
Weston Turville Bucks 28 G5
Weston under Lizard Staffs 34 D4
Weston under Penyard Hereford 26 F3
Weston under Wetherley Warks 27 B10
Weston Underwood Derbys 35 A8
Weston Underwood M Keynes 28 C5
Westonbirt Glos 16 C5
Westoncommon Shrops 33 C10
Westoning C Beds 29 E7
Westonzoyland Som 8 A2
Westow N Yorks 52 C3
Westport Argyll 65 F7
Westport Som 8 C2
Westrigg W Loth 69 D8
Westruther Borders 70 F5
Westry Cambs 37 F9
Westville Notts 45 H9
Westward Cumb 56 B4
Westward Ho! Devon 6 D3
Westwell Kent 20 G6
Westwell Oxon 27 H9
Westwell Leacon Kent 20 G6
Westwick Cambs 29 B11
Westwick Durham 58 E1
Westwick Norf 39 C8
Westwood Devon 7 G9
Westwood Wilts 16 F5
Westwoodside N Lincs 45 C11
Wetheral Cumb 56 A6
Wetherby W Yorks 51 E10
Wetherden Suff 31 B7
Wetheringsett Suff 31 B8
Wethersfield Essex 30 E4
Wethersta Shetland 96 G5

Wetherup Street Suff 31 B8
Wetley Rocks Staffs 44 H3
Wettenhall Ches E 43 F9
Wetton Staffs 44 G5
Wetwang E Yorks 52 D5
Wetwood Staffs 34 B3
Wexcombe Wilts 17 F9
Wexham Street Bucks 18 C6
Weybourne Norf 39 A7
Weybread Suff 39 G8
Weybridge Sur 19 E7
Weycroft Devon 8 E2
Weydale Highld 94 D3
Weyhill Hants 17 G10
Weymouth Dorset 8 G5
Whaddon Bucks 28 E5
Whaddon Cambs 29 D10
Whaddon Glos 26 G5
Whaddon Wilts 9 B10
Whale Cumb 57 D7
Whaley Derbys 45 E9
Whaley Bridge Derbys 44 D4
Whaley Thorns Derbys 45 E9
Whaligoe Highld 94 F5
Whalley Lancs 50 F3
Whalton Northumb 63 E7
Wham N Yorks 50 C3
Whaplode Lincs 37 C9
Whaplode Drove Lincs 37 D9
Whaplode St Catherine Lincs 37 C9
Wharfe N Yorks 50 C3
Wharles Lancs 49 F4
Wharncliffe Side S Yorks 44 C6
Wharram le Street N Yorks 52 C4
Wharton Ches W 43 F9
Wharton Green Ches W 43 F9
Whashton N Yorks 58 F2
Whatcombe Dorset 9 D7
Whatcote Warks 27 D10
Whatfield Suff 31 D7
Whatley Som 8 D2
Whatley Som 16 G4
Whatlington E Sus 13 E6
Whatstandwell Derbys 45 G7
Whatton Notts 36 B3
Whauphill Dumfries 55 E7
Whaw N Yorks 57 F11
Wheatacre Norf 39 F10
Wheatcroft Derbys 45 G7
Wheathampstead Herts 29 G8
Wheathill Shrops 34 G2
Wheatley Devon 7 G8
Wheatley Hants 18 G4
Wheatley Oxon 28 H2
Wheatley S Yorks 45 B9
Wheatley W Yorks 51 G6
Wheatley Hill Durham 58 C4
Wheaton Aston Staffs 34 D4
Wheddon Cross Som 7 C8
Wheedlemont Aberds 82 A6
Wheelerstreet Sur 18 G6
Wheelock Ches E 43 G10
Wheelock Heath Ches E 43 G10
Wheelton Lancs 50 G2
Wheen Angus 82 F5
Wheldrake York 52 E2
Whelford Glos 17 B8
Whelpley Hill Herts 18 A6
Whempstead Herts 29 F10
Whenby N Yorks 52 C2
Whepstead Suff 30 C5
Wherstead Suff 31 D8
Wherwell Hants 17 G10
Wheston Derbys 44 E5
Whetsted Kent 20 G3
Whetstone Leics 36 F1
Whicham Cumb 49 A1
Whichford Warks 27 E10
Whickham T&W 63 G8
Whiddon Down Devon 6 G5
Whigstreet Angus 77 C7
Whilton Northants 28 B3
Whim Farm Borders 69 E11
Whimble Devon 6 F2
Whimple Devon 7 G9
Whimpwell Green Norf 39 C9
Whinburgh Norf 38 E6
Whinnieliggate Dumfries 55 D10
Whinnyfold Aberds 89 E10
Whippingham IoW 10 E4
Whipsnade C Beds 29 G7
Whipton Devon 7 G8
Whirlow S Yorks 45 D7
Whisby Lincs 46 F3
Whissendine Rutland 36 D4
Whissonsett Norf 38 C5
Whistlefield Argyll 73 D10
Whistlefield Argyll 73 D11
Whistley Green Wokingham 18 D4
Whiston Mers 43 C7
Whiston Northants 28 B5
Whiston S Yorks 45 D8
Whiston Staffs 34 D4
Whiston Staffs 44 H4
Whitbeck Cumb 49 A1
Whitbourne Hereford 26 C4
Whitburn T&W 63 G10
Whitburn W Loth 69 D8
Whitburn Colliery T&W 63 G10
Whitby Ches W 43 E6
Whitby N Yorks 59 E9
Whitbyheath Ches W 43 E6
Whitchurch Bath 16 E3
Whitchurch Bucks 28 F4
Whitchurch Cardiff 15 C7
Whitchurch Devon 4 D5
Whitchurch Hants 17 G11
Whitchurch Hereford 26 G2
Whitchurch Oxon 18 D3
Whitchurch Pembs 22 D2
Whitchurch Shrops 33 A11
Whitchurch Canonicorum Dorset 8 E2
Whitchurch Hill Oxon 18 D3
Whitcombe Dorset 8 F6
Whitcott Keysett Shrops 33 G8
White Coppice Lancs 50 H2
White Lackington Dorset 8 E6
White Ladies Aston Worcs 26 C6
White Lund Lancs 49 C4
White Mill Carms 23 D9
White Ness Shetland 96 J5
White Notley Essex 30 G4
White Pit Lincs 47 E7
White Post Notts 45 G10
White Rocks Hereford 25 F11
White Roding Essex 30 G2
White Waltham Windsor 18 D5
Whiteacen Moray 88 D2
Whiteacre Heath Warks 35 F8
Whitebridge Highld 81 B6
Whitebrook Mon 26 H2
Whiteburn Borders 70 F4
Whitecairn Dumfries 54 D5
Whitecairns Aberds 83 B11
Whitecastle S Lanark 69 F9
Whitechapel Lancs 50 E1
Whitecleat Orkney 95 H6
Whitecraig E Loth 70 C2
Whitecroft Glos 26 H3
Whitecross Corn 3 B8
Whitecross Falk 69 C8
Whitecross Staffs 34 C4
Whiteface Highld 87 C10
Whitefarland N Ayrs 66 B1
Whitefaulds S Ayrs 66 F5
Whitefield Gtr Man 44 B2
Whitefield Perth 76 D4
Whiteford Aberds 83 A9
Whitegate Ches W 43 F9
Whitehall Blackburn 50 G2
Whitehall W Sus 11 B10
Whitehall Village Orkney 95 F7
Whitehaven Cumb 56 E1
Whitehill Hants 11 A6
Whitehills Aberds 89 B6
Whitehills S Lanark 68 E5
Whitehough Derbys 44 D4
Whitehouse Aberds 83 B8
Whitehouse Argyll 73 G7
Whiteinch Glasgow 68 D4
Whitekirk E Loth 70 B4
Whitelaw S Lanark 68 F5
Whiteleas T&W 63 G9
Whiteley Bank IoW 10 F4
Whiteley Green Ches E 44 E3
Whiteley Village Sur 19 E7
Whitemans Green W Sus 12 D2
Whitemire Moray 87 F12
Whitemoor Corn 3 D8
Whitemore Staffs 44 F2
Whitenap Hants 10 B2
Whiteoak Green Oxon 27 G10
Whiteparish Wilts 9 B11
Whiterashes Aberds 89 F8
Whiterow Highld 94 F5
Whiteshill Glos 26 H5
Whiteside Northumb 62 G3
Whiteside W Loth 69 D8
Whitesmith E Sus 12 E4
Whitestaunton Som 8 C1
Whitestone Devon 6 B3
Whitestone Devon 7 G7
Whitestone Warks 35 G9
Whitestones Aberds 89 C8
Whitestreet Green Suff 30 E6
Whitewall Corner N Yorks 52 B3
Whiteway Glos 16 B5
Whiteway Glos 26 G6
Whitewell Aberds 89 B9
Whitewell Lancs 50 E2
Whitewell Bottom Lancs 50 G4
Whiteworks Devon 5 D7
Whitfield Kent 21 G10
Whitfield Northants 28 E3
Whitfield Northumb 62 H3
Whitfield S Glos 16 B3
Whitford Devon 8 E1
Whitford Flint 42 E4
Whitgift E Yorks 52 G4
Whitgreave Staffs 34 C4
Whithorn Dumfries 55 E7
Whiting Bay N Ayrs 66 D3
Whitkirk W Yorks 51 F9
Whitland Carms 22 E6
Whitletts S Ayrs 67 D6
Whitley N Yorks 52 G1
Whitley Reading 18 D4
Whitley Wilts 16 E5
Whitley Bay T&W 63 F9
Whitley Chapel Northumb 62 H5
Whitley Lower W Yorks 51 H8
Whitley Row Kent 19 F11
Whitlock's End W Mid 35 H7
Whitminster Glos 26 H4
Whitmore Staffs 34 A4
Whitnage Devon 7 E9
Whitnash Warks 27 B10
Whitney-on-Wye Hereford 25 D9
Whitrigg Cumb 56 C4
Whitrigg Cumb 61 H8
Whitsbury Hants 9 C10
Whitsome Borders 71 E7
Whitson Newport 15 C9
Whitstable Kent 21 E8
Whitstone Corn 6 G1
Whittingham Northumb 62 B6
Whittingslow Shrops 33 G10
Whittington Glos 27 F7
Whittington Lancs 50 B2
Whittington Norf 38 F3
Whittington Shrops 33 B9
Whittington Staffs 34 G4
Whittington Staffs 35 E7
Whittington Worcs 26 C5
Whittle-le-Woods Lancs 50 G1
Whittlebury Northants 28 D3
Whittlesey Cambs 37 F8
Whittlesford Cambs 29 D11
Whittlestone Head Blackburn 50 H3
Whitton Borders 62 A3
Whitton N Lincs 52 G5
Whitton Northumb 62 C6
Whitton Powys 25 B9
Whitton Shrops 26 A2
Whitton Stockton 58 D4
Whitton Suff 31 D8
Whittonditch Wilts 17 D9
Whittonstall Northumb 62 H6
Whitway Hants 17 F11
Whitwell Derbys 45 E9
Whitwell Herts 29 F8
Whitwell IoW 10 G4
Whitwell N Yorks 58 G3
Whitwell Rutland 36 E5
Whitwell-on-the-Hill N Yorks 52 C3
Whitwell Street Norf 39 C7
Whitwick Leics 35 D10
Whitwood W Yorks 51 G10
Whitworth Lancs 50 H4
Whixall Shrops 33 B11
Whixley N Yorks 51 D10
Whoberley W Mid 35 H9
Whorlton Durham 58 E2
Whorlton N Yorks 58 F5
Whygate Northumb 62 F3
Whyle Hereford 26 B2
Whyteleafe Sur 19 F10
Wibdon Glos 16 B2
Wibsey W Yorks 51 F7
Wibtoft Leics 35 G10
Wichenford Worcs 26 B4
Wichling Kent 20 F6
Wick Bmouth 9 E10
Wick Devon 7 F10
Wick Highld 94 E5
Wick S Glos 16 D4
Wick Shetland 96 K6
Wick V Glam 14 D5
Wick W Sus 11 D9
Wick Wilts 9 B10
Wick Worcs 26 D6
Wick Hill Wokingham 18 E4
Wick St Lawrence N Som 15 E9
Wicken Cambs 30 A2
Wicken Northants 28 E4
Wicken Bonhunt Essex 29 E11
Wicken Green Village Norf 38 B4
Wickenby Lincs 46 D4
Wickersley S Yorks 45 C8
Wickford Essex 20 B4
Wickham Hants 10 C4
Wickham W Berks 17 D10
Wickham Bishops Essex 30 G5
Wickham Market Suff 31 C10
Wickham Skeith Suff 31 B7
Wickham St Paul Essex 30 E5
Wickham Street Suff 30 C4
Wickham Street Suff 31 B7
Wickhambreux Kent 21 F9
Wickhambrook Suff 30 C4
Wickhamford Worcs 27 D7
Wickhampton Norf 39 E10
Wicklewood Norf 39 E6
Wickmere Norf 39 B7
Wickwar S Glos 16 C4
Widdington Essex 30 E2
Widdrington Northumb 63 D8
Widdrington Station Northumb 63 D8
Wide Open T&W 63 F8
Widecombe in the Moor Devon 5 D8
Widegates Corn 4 F3
Widemouth Bay Corn 4 A3
Widewall Orkney 95 J5
Widford Essex 30 H3
Widford Herts 29 G11
Widham Wilts 17 C7
Widmer End Bucks 18 B5
Widmerpool Notts 36 C2
Widnes Halton 43 D8
Wigan Gtr Man 43 B8
Wiggaton Devon 7 G10
Wiggenhall St Germans Norf 38 D1
Wiggenhall St Mary Magdalen Norf 38 D1
Wiggenhall St Mary the Virgin Norf 38 D1
Wigginton Herts 28 G6
Wigginton Oxon 27 E10
Wigginton Staffs 35 E8
Wigginton York 52 D1
Wigglesworth N Yorks 50 D4
Wiggonby Cumb 56 A4
Wiggonholt W Sus 11 C9
Wighill N Yorks 51 E10
Wighton Norf 38 B5
Wigley Hants 10 C2
Wigmore Hereford 25 B11
Wigmore Medway 20 E5
Wigsley Notts 46 E2
Wigsthorpe Northants 36 G6
Wigston Leics 36 F2
Wigthorpe Notts 45 D9
Wigtoft Lincs 37 B8
Wigton Cumb 56 B4
Wigtown Dumfries 55 D7
Wigtwizzle S Yorks 44 C6
Wike W Yorks 51 E9
Wike Well End S Yorks 45 A10
Wilbarston Northants 36 G4
Wilberfoss E Yorks 52 D3
Wilberlee W Yorks 44 A4
Wilburton Cambs 29 A11
Wilby Norf 38 G6
Wilby Northants 28 B5
Wilby Suff 31 A9
Wilcot Wilts 17 E8
Wilcott Shrops 33 D9
Wilcrick Newport 15 C10
Wilday Green Derbys 45 E7
Wildboarclough Ches E 44 F3
Wilden Bedford 29 C7
Wilden Worcs 26 A5
Wildhern Hants 17 F10
Wildhill Herts 29 H9
Wildmoor Worcs 34 H5
Wildsworth Lincs 46 C2
Wilford Nottingham 36 B1
Wilkesley Ches E 34 A2
Wilkhaven Highld 87 C12
Wilkieston W Loth 69 D10
Willand Devon 7 E9
Willaston Ches E 43 G9
Willaston Ches W 42 E6
Willen M Keynes 28 D5
Willenhall W Mid 34 F5
Willenhall W Mid 35 H9
Willerby E Yorks 52 F6
Willerby N Yorks 52 B6
Willersey Glos 27 E8
Willersley Hereford 25 D10
Willesborough Kent 13 B9
Willesborough Lees Kent 13 B9
Willesden London 19 C9
Willett Som 7 C10
Willey Shrops 34 F2
Willey Warks 35 G10
Willey Green Sur 18 F6
Williamscott Oxon 27 D11
Willian Herts 29 E9
Willingale Essex 30 H2
Willingdon E Sus 12 F4
Willingham Cambs 29 A11
Willingham by Stow Lincs 46 D2
Willington Bedford 29 D8
Willington Derbys 35 C8
Willington Durham 58 C2
Willington T&W 63 G9
Willington Warks 27 E9
Willington Corner Ches W 43 F8
Willisham Tye Suff 31 C7
Willitoft E Yorks 52 F3
Williton Som 7 B9
Willoughbridge Staffs 34 A3
Willoughby Lincs 47 E8
Willoughby Warks 28 B2
Willoughby-on-the-Wolds Notts 36 C2
Willoughby Waterleys Leics 36 F1
Willoughton Lincs 46 C3
Willows Green Essex 30 G4
Willsbridge S Glos 16 D3
Willsworthy Devon 4 C6
Wilmcote Warks 27 C8
Wilmington Devon 7 G11
Wilmington E Sus 12 F4
Wilmington Kent 20 D2
Wilminstone Devon 4 D5
Wilmslow Ches E 44 D2
Wilnecote Staffs 35 E8
Wilpshire Lancs 50 F2
Wilsden W Yorks 51 F6
Wilsford Lincs 36 A6
Wilsford Wilts 17 F8
Wilsford Wilts 17 H8
Wilsill N Yorks 51 C7
Wilsley Pound Kent 13 C6
Wilsom Hants 18 H4
Wilson Leics 35 C10
Wilsontown S Lanark 69 E8
Wilstead Bedford 29 D7
Wilsthorpe Lincs 37 D6
Wilstone Herts 28 G6
Wilton Borders 61 B10
Wilton Cumb 56 E2
Wilton N Yorks 52 A4
Wilton Redcar 59 E6
Wilton Wilts 9 A9
Wilton Wilts 17 E9
Wimbish Essex 30 E2
Wimbish Green Essex 30 E3
Wimblebury Staffs 34 D6
Wimbledon London 19 D9
Wimblington Cambs 37 F10
Wimborne Minster Dorset 9 E9
Wimborne St Giles Dorset 9 C9
Wimbotsham Norf 38 E2
Wimpson Soton 10 C2
Wimpstone Warks 27 D9
Wincanton Som 8 B6
Wincham Ches W 43 E9
Winchburgh W Loth 69 C9
Winchcombe Glos 27 F7
Winchelsea E Sus 13 E8
Winchelsea Beach E Sus 13 E8
Winchester Hants 10 B3
Winchet Hill Kent 12 B6
Winchfield Hants 18 F4
Winchmore Hill Bucks 18 B6
Winchmore Hill London 19 B10
Wincle Ches E 44 F3
Wincobank S Yorks 45 C7
Windermere Cumb 56 G6
Winderton Warks 27 D10
Windhill Highld 87 G8
Windhouse Shetland 96 D6
Windlehurst Gtr Man 44 D3
Windlesham Sur 18 E6
Windley Derbys 35 A9
Windmill Hill E Sus 12 E5
Windmill Hill Som 8 C2
Windrush Glos 27 G8
Windsor N Lincs 45 A11
Windsor Windsor 18 D6
Windsoredge Glos 16 A5
Windygates Fife 76 G6
Windyknowe W Loth 69 D8
Windywalls Borders 70 G6
Wineham W Sus 11 B11
Winestead E Yorks 53 G8
Winewall Lancs 50 E5
Winfarthing Norf 39 G7
Winford IoW 10 F4
Winford N Som 15 E11
Winforton Hereford 25 D9
Winfrith Newburgh Dorset 9 F7
Wing Bucks 28 F5
Wing Rutland 36 E4
Wingate Durham 58 C5
Wingates Gtr Man 43 B9
Wingates Northumb 63 D7
Wingerworth Derbys 45 F7
Wingfield C Beds 29 F7
Wingfield Suff 39 H8
Wingfield Wilts 16 F5
Wingham Kent 21 F9
Wingmore Kent 21 G8
Wingrave Bucks 28 G5
Winkburn Notts 45 G11
Winkfield Brack 18 D6
Winkfield Row Brack 18 D5
Winkhill Staffs 44 G4
Winklebury Hants 18 F3
Winkleigh Devon 6 F5
Winksley N Yorks 51 B8
Winkton Dorset 9 E10
Winlaton T&W 63 G7
Winless Highld 94 E5
Winmarleigh Lancs 49 E4
Winnal Hereford 25 E11
Winnall Hants 10 B3
Winnersh Wokingham 18 D4
Winscales Cumb 56 D2
Winscombe N Som 15 F10
Winsford Ches W 43 F9
Winsford Som 7 C8
Winsham Som 8 D2
Winshill Staffs 35 C8
Winskill Cumb 57 C7
Winslade Hants 18 G3
Winsley Wilts 16 E5
Winslow Bucks 28 F4
Winson Glos 27 H7
Winson Green W Mid 34 G6
Winsor Hants 10 C2
Winster Cumb 56 G6
Winster Derbys 44 F6
Winston Durham 58 E2
Winston Suff 31 B8
Winston Green Suff 31 B8
Winstone Glos 26 H6
Winswell Devon 6 E3
Winter Gardens Essex 20 C4
Winterborne Bassett Wilts 17 D8
Winterborne Clenston Dorset 9 D7
Winterborne Herringston Dorset 8 F5
Winterborne Houghton Dorset 9 D7
Winterborne Kingston Dorset 9 E7
Winterborne Monkton Dorset 8 F5
Winterborne Monkton Wilts 17 D8
Winterborne Stickland Dorset 9 D7
Winterborne Whitechurch Dorset 9 D7
Winterborne Zelston Dorset 9 E7
Winterbourne S Glos 16 C3
Winterbourne W Berks 17 D11
Winterbourne Abbas Dorset 8 E5
Winterbourne Dauntsey Wilts 9 A10
Winterbourne Down S Glos 16 D3
Winterbourne Earls Wilts 9 A10
Winterbourne Gunner Wilts 17 H8
Winterbourne Steepleton Dorset 8 F5
Winterbourne Stoke Wilts 17 G7
Winterburn N Yorks 50 D5
Winteringham N Lincs 52 G5
Winterley Ches E 43 G10
Wintersett W Yorks 51 H9
Wintershill Hants 10 C4
Winterton N Lincs 52 H5
Winterton-on-Sea Norf 39 D10
Winthorpe Lincs 47 F9
Winthorpe Notts 46 G2
Winton Bmouth 9 E9
Winton Cumb 57 E9
Winton N Yorks 58 G5
Wintringham N Yorks 52 B4
Winwick Cambs 37 G7
Winwick Northants 28 A3
Winwick Warr 43 C9
Wirksworth Derbys 44 G6
Wirksworth Moor Derbys 45 G7
Wirswall Ches E 33 A11
Wisbech Cambs 37 E10
Wisbech St Mary Cambs 37 E10
Wisborough Green W Sus 11 B9
Wiseton Notts 45 D11
Wishaw N Lanark 68 E6
Wishaw Warks 35 F7
Wisley Sur 19 F7
Wispington Lincs 46 E6
Wissenden Kent 13 B8
Wissett Suff 39 H9
Wistanstow Shrops 33 G10
Wistanswick Shrops 34 C2
Wistaston Ches E 43 G9
Wistaston Green Ches E 43 G9
Wiston Pembs 22 E5
Wiston S Lanark 69 G8
Wiston W Sus 11 C10
Wistow Cambs 37 G8
Wistow N Yorks 52 F1
Wiswell Lancs 50 F3
Witcham Cambs 37 G10
Witchampton Dorset 9 D8
Witchford Cambs 37 H11
Witham Essex 30 G5
Witham Friary Som 16 G4
Witham on the Hill Lincs 37 D6
Withcall Lincs 46 D6
Withdean Brighton 12 F2
Witherenden Hill E Sus 12 D5
Witheridge Devon 7 E7
Witherley Leics 35 F9
Withern Lincs 47 D8
Withernsea E Yorks 53 G9
Withernwick E Yorks 53 E7
Withersdale Street Suff 39 G8
Withersfield Suff 30 D3
Witherslack Cumb 49 A4
Withiel Corn 3 C8
Withiel Florey Som 7 C8
Withington Glos 27 G7
Withington Gtr Man 44 C2
Withington Hereford 26 D2
Withington Shrops 34 D1
Withington Staffs 34 B6
Withington Green Ches E 44 E2
Withleigh Devon 7 E8
Withnell Lancs 50 G2
Withybrook Warks 35 G10
Withycombe Som 7 B9
Withycombe Raleigh Devon 5 C11
Withyham E Sus 12 C3
Withypool Som 7 C7
Witley Sur 18 H6
Witnesham Suff 31 C8
Witney Oxon 27 G10
Wittering Pboro 37 E6
Wittersham Kent 13 D7
Witton Angus 83 F7
Witton Worcs 26 B5
Witton Bridge Norf 39 B9
Witton Gilbert Durham 58 B3
Witton-le-Wear Durham 58 C2
Witton Park Durham 58 C2
Wiveliscombe Som 7 D9
Wivelrod Hants 18 H3
Wivelsfield E Sus 12 D2
Wivelsfield Green E Sus 12 D2
Wivenhoe Essex 31 F7
Wivenhoe Cross Essex 31 F7
Wiveton Norf 38 A6
Wix Essex 31 F8
Wixford Warks 27 C7
Wixhill Shrops 34 C1
Wixoe Suff 30 D4
Woburn C Beds 28 E6
Woburn Sands M Keynes 28 E6
Wokefield Park W Berks 18 E3
Woking Sur 19 F7
Wokingham Wokingham 18 E5
Wolborough Devon 5 D9
Wold Newton E Yorks 52 B6
Wold Newton NE Lincs 46 C6
Woldingham Sur 19 F10
Wolfclyde S Lanark 69 G9
Wolferton Norf 38 C2
Wolfhill Perth 76 D4
Wolf's Castle Pembs 22 D4
Wolfsdale Pembs 22 D4
Woll Borders 61 A10
Wollaston Northants 28 B6
Wollaston Shrops 33 D9
Wollaton Nottingham 35 B11
Wollerton Shrops 34 B2
Wollescote W Mid 34 G5
Wolsingham Durham 58 C1
Wolstanton Staffs 44 H2
Wolston Warks 35 H10
Wolvercote Oxon 27 H11
Wolverhampton W Mid 34 F5
Wolverley Shrops 33 B10
Wolverley Worcs 34 H4
Wolverton Hants 18 F2
Wolverton M Keynes 28 D5
Wolverton Warks 27 B9
Wolverton Common Hants 18 F2
Wolvesnewton Mon 15 B10
Wolvey Warks 35 G10
Wolviston Stockton 58 D5
Wombleton N Yorks 52 A2
Wombourne Staffs 34 F4
Wombwell S Yorks 45 B7
Womenswold Kent 21 F9
Womersley N Yorks 51 H11
Wonastow Mon 25 G11
Wonersh Sur 19 G7
Wonson Devon 5 C7
Wonston Hants 17 H11
Wooburn Bucks 18 C6
Wooburn Green Bucks 18 C6
Wood Dalling Norf 39 C6
Wood End Herts 29 F10
Wood End Warks 27 A8
Wood End Warks 35 F8
Wood Enderby Lincs 46 F6
Wood Field Sur 19 F8
Wood Green London 19 B10
Wood Hayes W Mid 34 E5
Wood Lanes Ches E 44 D3
Wood Norton Norf 38 C6
Wood Street Norf 39 C9
Wood Street Sur 18 F6
Wood Walton Cambs 37 G8
Woodacott Devon 6 F2
Woodale N Yorks 50 B6
Woodbank Argyll 65 G7
Woodbastwick Norf 39 D9
Woodbeck Notts 45 E11
Woodborough Notts 45 H10
Woodborough Wilts 17 F8
Woodbridge Dorset 8 C6
Woodbridge Suff 31 D9
Woodbury Devon 5 C11
Woodbury Salterton Devon 5 C11
Woodchester Glos 16 A5
Woodchurch Kent 13 C8
Woodchurch Mers 42 D5
Woodcombe Som 7 B8
Woodcote Oxon 18 C3
Woodcott Hants 17 F11
Woodcroft Glos 15 B11
Woodcutts Dorset 9 C8
Woodditton Cambs 30 C3
Woodeaton Oxon 28 G2
Woodend Cumb 56 G3
Woodend Northants 28 D3
Woodend W Sus 11 D7
Woodend Green Northants 28 D3
Woodfalls Wilts 9 B10
Woodfield Oxon 28 F2
Woodfield S Ayrs 66 D6
Woodford Corn 6 E1
Woodford Devon 5 F8
Woodford Glos 16 B3
Woodford Gtr Man 44 D2
Woodford London 19 B11
Woodford Northants 36 H5
Woodford Bridge London 19 B11
Woodford Halse Northants 28 C2
Woodgate Norf 38 D6
Woodgate W Mid 34 G5
Woodgate W Sus 11 D8
Woodgate Worcs 26 B6
Woodgreen Hants 9 C10
Woodhall Herts 29 G9
Woodhall Invclyd 68 C2
Woodhall N Yorks 57 G11
Woodhall Spa Lincs 46 F5
Woodham Sur 19 E7
Woodham Ferrers Essex 20 B4
Woodham Mortimer Essex 20 A5
Woodham Walter Essex 30 H5
Woodhaven Fife 77 E7
Woodhead Aberds 89 E7
Woodhey Gtr Man 50 H3
Woodhill Shrops 34 G3
Woodhorn Northumb 63 E8
Woodhouse Leics 35 D11
Woodhouse N Lincs 45 B11
Woodhouse S Yorks 45 D8
Woodhouse W Yorks 51 F8
Woodhouse W Yorks 51 G9
Woodhouse Eaves Leics 35 D11
Woodhouse Park Gtr Man 44 D2
Woodhouselee Midloth 69 D11
Woodhouselees Dumfries 61 F9
Woodhouses Staffs 35 D7
Woodhurst Cambs 37 H9
Woodingdean Brighton 12 F2
Woodkirk W Yorks 51 G8
Woodland Devon 5 E8
Woodland Durham 58 D1
Woodlands Aberds 83 D9
Woodlands Dorset 9 D9
Woodlands Hants 10 C2
Woodlands Highld 87 E8
Woodlands N Yorks 51 D9
Woodlands S Yorks 45 B9
Woodlands Park Windsor 18 D5
Woodlands St Mary W Berks 17 D10
Woodlane Staffs 35 C7
Woodleigh Devon 5 G8
Woodlesford W Yorks 51 G9
Woodley Gtr Man 44 C3
Woodley Wokingham 18 D4
Woodmancote Glos 16 B4
Woodmancote Glos 26 F6
Woodmancote Glos 27 H7
Woodmancote W Sus 11 C11
Woodmancote W Sus 11 D6
Woodmancott Hants 18 G2
Woodmansey E Yorks 53 F6
Woodmansterne Sur 19 F9
Woodminton Wilts 9 B9
Woodnesborough Kent 21 F10
Woodnewton Northants 36 F6
Woodplumpton Lancs 49 F5
Woodrising Norf 38 E5
Wood's Green E Sus 12 C5
Woodseaves Shrops 34 B2
Woodseaves Staffs 34 C3
Woodsend Wilts 17 D9
Woodsetts S Yorks 45 D9
Woodsford Dorset 9 E6
Woodside Aberdeen 83 C11
Woodside Aberds 89 D10
Woodside Brack 18 D6
Woodside Fife 77 G7
Woodside Hants 10 E2
Woodside Herts 29 H9
Woodside Perth 76 D5
Woodside of Arbeadie Aberds 83 D9
Woodstock Oxon 27 G11
Woodstock Pembs 22 D5
Woodthorpe Derbys 45 E8
Woodthorpe Leics 35 D11
Woodthorpe Lincs 47 D8
Woodthorpe York 52 E1
Woodton Norf 39 F8
Woodtown Devon 6 D3
Woodtown Devon 6 D3
Woodvale Mers 42 A6
Woodville Derbys 35 D9
Woodyates Dorset 9 C9
Woofferton Shrops 26 B2
Wookey Som 15 G11
Wookey Hole Som 15 G11
Wool Dorset 9 F7
Woolacombe Devon 6 B3
Woolage Green Kent 21 G9
Woolaston Glos 16 B2
Woolavington Som 15 G9
Woolbeding W Sus 11 B7
Wooldale W Yorks 44 B5
Wooler Northumb 71 H8
Woolfardisworthy Devon 6 D2
Woolfardisworthy Devon 7 F7
Woolfords Cottages S Lanark 69 E9
Woolhampton W Berks 18 E2
Woolhope Hereford 26 E3
Woolhope Cockshoot Hereford 26 E3
Woolland Dorset 9 D6
Woollaton Devon 6 E3
Woolley Bath 16 E4
Woolley Cambs 29 A8
Woolley Corn 6 E1
Woolley Derbys 45 F7
Woolley W Yorks 45 A7
Woolmer Green Herts 29 G9
Woolmere Green Worcs 26 B6
Woolpit Suff 30 B6
Woolscott Warks 27 B11
Woolsington T&W 63 G7
Woolstanwood Ches E 43 G9
Woolstaston Shrops 33 F10
Woolsthorpe Lincs 36 B4
Woolsthorpe Lincs 36 C5
Woolston Devon 5 G8
Woolston Shrops 33 C9
Woolston Shrops 33 G10
Woolston Soton 10 C3
Woolston Warr 43 D9
Woolstone M Keynes 28 E5
Woolstone Oxon 17 C9
Woolton Mers 43 D7
Woolton Hill Hants 17 E11
Woolverstone Suff 31 E8
Woolverton Som 16 F4
Woolwich London 19 D11
Woolwich Ferry London 19 D11
Woonton Hereford 25 C10
Wooperton Northumb 62 A6
Woore Shrops 34 A3
Wootten Green Suff 31 A9
Wootton Bedford 29 D7
Wootton Hants 9 E11
Wootton Hereford 25 C10
Wootton Kent 21 G9
Wootton N Lincs 53 H6
Wootton Northants 28 C4
Wootton Oxon 17 A11
Wootton Oxon 27 G11
Wootton Shrops 33 C9
Wootton Shrops 33 H10
Wootton Staffs 34 C4
Wootton Staffs 44 H5
Wootton Bassett Wilts 17 C7
Wootton Bridge IoW 10 E4
Wootton Common IoW 10 E4
Wootton Courtenay Som 7 B8
Wootton Fitzpaine Dorset 8 E2
Wootton Rivers Wilts 17 E8
Wootton St Lawrence Hants 18 F2
Wootton Wawen Warks 27 B8
Worcester Worcs 26 C5
Worcester Park London 19 E9
Wordsley W Mid 34 G4
Worfield Shrops 34 F3
Work Orkney 95 G5
Workington Cumb 56 D1
Worksop Notts 45 E9
Worlaby N Lincs 46 A4
World's End W Berks 17 D11
Worle N Som 15 E9
Worleston Ches E 43 G9
Worlingham Suff 39 G10
Worlington Suff 30 A3
Worlingworth Suff 31 B9
Wormald Green N Yorks 51 C9
Wormbridge Hereford 25 E11
Wormegay Norf 38 D2
Wormelow Tump Hereford 25 E11
Wormhill Derbys 44 E5
Wormingford Essex 30 E6
Worminghall Bucks 28 H3
Wormington Glos 27 E7
Worminster Som 16 G2
Wormit Fife 76 E6
Wormleighton Warks 27 C11
Wormley Herts 29 H10
Wormley Sur 18 H6
Wormley West End Herts 29 H10
Wormshill Kent 20 F5
Wormsley Hereford 25 D11
Worplesdon Sur 18 F6
Worrall S Yorks 45 C7
Worsbrough S Yorks 45 B7
Worsbrough Common S Yorks 45 B7
Worsley Gtr Man 43 B10
Worstead Norf 39 C9
Worsthorne Lancs 50 F4
Worston Lancs 50 E3
Worswell Devon 4 G6
Worth Kent 21 F10
Worth W Sus 12 C2
Worth Matravers Dorset 9 G8
Wortham Suff 39 H6
Worthen Shrops 33 E9
Worthenbury Wrex 43 H7
Worthing Norf 38 D5
Worthing W Sus 11 D10
Worthington Leics 35 C10
Worting Hants 18 F3
Wortley S Yorks 45 C7
Wortley W Yorks 51 F8
Worton N Yorks 57 G11
Worton Wilts 16 F6
Wortwell Norf 39 G8
Wotherton Shrops 33 E8
Wotter Devon 5 E6
Wotton Sur 19 G8
Wotton-under-Edge Glos 16 B4
Wotton Underwood Bucks 28 G3
Woughton on the Green M Keynes 28 E5
Wouldham Kent 20 E4
Wrabness Essex 31 E8
Wrafton Devon 6 C3
Wragby Lincs 46 E5
Wragby W Yorks 51 H10
Wragholme Lincs 47 C7
Wramplingham Norf 39 E7
Wrangbrook W Yorks 45 A8
Wrangham Aberds 89 E6
Wrangle Lincs 47 G8
Wrangle Bank Lincs 47 G8
Wrangle Lowgate Lincs 47 G8
Wrangway Som 7 E10
Wrantage Som 8 B2
Wrawby N Lincs 46 B4
Wraxall Dorset 8 D4
Wraxall N Som 15 D10
Wraxall Som 16 H3
Wray Lancs 50 C2
Wraysbury Windsor 19 D7
Wrayton Lancs 50 B2
Wrea Green Lancs 49 F3
Wreay Cumb 56 B6
Wreay Cumb 56 D6
Wrecclesham Sur 18 G5
Wrecsam = Wrexham Wrex 42 G6
Wrekenton T&W 63 H8
Wrelton N Yorks 59 H8
Wrenbury Ches E 43 H8
Wrench Green N Yorks 59 H10
Wreningham Norf 39 F7
Wrentham Suff 39 G10
Wrenthorpe W Yorks 51 G9
Wrentnall Shrops 33 E10
Wressle E Yorks 52 F3
Wressle N Lincs 46 B3
Wrestlingworth C Beds 29 D9
Wretham Norf 38 G5
Wretton Norf 38 F2
Wrexham = Wrecsam Wrex 42 G6
Wrexham Industrial Estate Wrex 43 H6
Wribbenhall Worcs 34 H3
Wrightington Bar Lancs 43 A8
Wrinehill Staffs 43 H10
Wrington N Som 15 E10
Writhlington Bath 16 F4
Writtle Essex 30 H3
Wrockwardine Telford 34 D2
Wroot N Lincs 45 B11
Wrotham Kent 20 F3
Wrotham Heath Kent 20 F3
Wroughton Swindon 17 C8
Wroxall IoW 10 G4
Wroxall Warks 27 A9
Wroxeter Shrops 34 E1
Wroxham Norf 39 D9
Wroxton Oxon 27 D11
Wyaston Derbys 35 A7
Wyberton Lincs 37 A9
Wyboston Bedford 29 C8
Wybunbury Ches E 43 H10
Wych Cross E Sus 12 C3
Wychbold Worcs 26 B6
Wyck Hants 18 H4
Wyck Rissington Glos 27 F8
Wycoller Lancs 50 F5
Wycomb Leics 36 C3
Wycombe Marsh Bucks 18 B5
Wyddial Herts 29 E10
Wye Kent 21 G7
Wyesham Mon 26 G2
Wyfordby Leics 36 D3
Wyke Dorset 9 B6
Wyke Shrops 34 E2
Wyke Sur 18 F6
Wyke W Yorks 51 G7
Wyke Regis Dorset 8 G5
Wykeham N Yorks 52 A5
Wykeham N Yorks 52 B4
Wyken W Mid 35 G9
Wykey Shrops 33 C9
Wylam Northumb 63 G7
Wylde Green W Mid 35 F7
Wyllie Caerph 15 B7
Wylye Wilts 17 H7
Wymering Ptsmth 10 D5
Wymeswold Leics 36 C2
Wymington Bedford 28 B6
Wymondham Leics 36 D4
Wymondham Norf 39 E7
Wyndham Bridgend 14 B5
Wynford Eagle Dorset 8 E4
Wyng Orkney 95 J4
Wynyard Village Stockton 58 D5
Wyre Piddle Worcs 26 D6
Wysall Notts 36 C2
Wythall Worcs 35 H6
Wytham Oxon 27 H11
Wythburn Cumb 56 E5
Wythenshawe Gtr Man 44 D2
Wythop Mill Cumb 56 D3
Wyton Cambs 29 A9
Wyverstone Suff 31 B7
Wyverstone Street Suff 31 B7
Wyville Lincs 36 C4
Wyvis Lodge Highld 86 D7

Y

Y Bala = Bala Gwyn 32 B5
Y Barri = Barry V Glam 15 E7
Y Bont-Faen = Cowbridge V Glam 14 D5
Y Drenewydd = Newtown Powys 33 F7
Y Felinheli Gwyn 41 D7
Y Fenni = Abergavenny Mon 25 G9
Y Ffôr Gwyn 40 G5
Y Fflint = Flint Flint 42 E5
Y-Ffrith Denb 42 D3
Y Gelli Gandryll = Hay-on-Wye Powys 25 D9
Y Mwmbwls = The Mumbles Swansea 14
Y Pîl = Pyle Bridgend 14
Y Rhws = Rhoose V Glam 14
Y Rhyl = Rhyl Denb 42
Y Trallwng = Welshpool Powys 33
Y Waun = Chirk Wrex 33
Yaddlethorpe N Lincs 46
Yafford IoW 10
Yafforth N Yorks 58
Yalding Kent 20
Yanworth Glos 27
Yapham E Yorks 52
Yapton W Sus 11
Yarburgh Lincs 47
Yarcombe Devon 8
Yard Som 7
Yardley W Mid 35
Yardley Gobion Northants 28
Yardley Hastings Northants 28
Yardro Powys 25
Yarkhill Hereford 26
Yarlet Staffs 34
Yarlington Som 8
Yarlside Cumb 49
Yarm Stockton 58
Yarmouth IoW 10
Yarnbrook Wilts 16
Yarnfield Staffs 34
Yarnscombe Devon 6
Yarnton Oxon 27
Yarpole Hereford 25
Yarrow Borders 70
Yarrow Feus Borders 70
Yarsop Hereford 25
Yarwell Northants 37
Yate S Glos 16
Yateley Hants 18
Yatesbury Wilts 17
Yattendon W Berks 18
Yatton Hereford 25
Yatton N Som 15
Yatton Keynell Wilts 16
Yaverland IoW 10
Yaxham Norf 38
Yaxley Cambs 37
Yaxley Suff 31
Yazor Hereford 25
Yeading London 19
Yeadon W Yorks 51
Yealand Conyers Lancs 49
Yealand Redmayne Lancs 49
Yealmpton Devon 5
Yearby Redcar 59
Yearsley N Yorks 52
Yeaton Shrops 33
Yeaveley Derbys 35
Yedingham N Yorks 52
Yeldon Bedford 29
Yelford Oxon 17
Yelland Devon 6
Yelling Cambs 29
Yelvertoft Northants 36
Yelverton Devon 4
Yelverton Norf 39
Yenston Som 8
Yeo Mill Devon 7
Yeoford Devon 7
Yeolmbridge Corn 4
Yeovil Som 8
Yeovil Marsh Som 8
Yeovilton Som 8
Yerbeston Pembs 22
Yesnaby Orkney 95
Yetlington Northumb 62
Yetminster Dorset 8
Yettington Devon 7
Yetts o' Muckhart Clack 76
Yieldshields S Lanark 69
Yiewsley London 19
Ynys-meudwy Neath 24
Ynysboeth Rhondda 14
Ynysddu Caerph 15
Ynysgyfflog Gwyn 32
Ynyshir Rhondda 14
Ynyslas Ceredig 32
Ynystawe Swansea 14
Ynysybwl Rhondda 14
Yockenthwaite N Yorks 50
Yockleton Shrops 33
Yokefleet E Yorks 52
Yoker W Dunb 68
Yonder Bognie Aberds 88
York York 52
York Town Sur 18
Yorkletts Kent 21
Yorkley Glos 26
Yorton Shrops 33
Youlgreave Derbys 44
Youlstone Devon 6
Youlthorpe E Yorks 52
Youlton N Yorks 51
Young Wood Lincs 46
Young's End Essex 30
Yoxall Staffs 35
Yoxford Suff 31
Yr Hôb = Hope Flint 42
Yr Wyddgrug = Mold Flint 42
Ysbyty-Cynfyn Ceredig 32
Ysbyty Ifan Conwy 41
Ysbyty Ystwyth Ceredig 24
Ysceifiog Flint 42
Yspitty Carms 23
Ystalyfera Neath 24
Ystrad Rhondda 14
Ystrad Aeron Ceredig 23
Ystrad-mynach Caerph 15
Ystradfellte Powys 24
Ystradffin Carms 24
Ystradgynlais Powys 24
Ystradmeurig Ceredig 24
Ystradowen Carms 24
Ystradowen V Glam 14
Ystumtuen Ceredig 32
Ythanbank Aberds 89
Ythanwells Aberds 89
Ythsie Aberds 89

Z

Zeal Monachorum Devon 6
Zeals Wilts 9
Zelah Corn 3
Zennor Corn 2